BREAKING CONVENTIONS

Breaking Conventions

Five Couples in Search of Marriage-Career Balance at the Turn of the Nineteenth Century

Patricia Auspos

OpenBook Publishers

ISBN Paperback: 978–1-80064–835–7
ISBN Hardback: 978–1-80064–836–4
ISBN Digital (PDF): 978–1-80064–837–1
ISBN Digital ebook (EPUB): 978–1-80064–838–8
ISBN XML: 978–1-80064–840–1
ISBN HTML: 978–1-80064–841–8
DOI: 10.11647/OBP.0318

Cover images: background image by Annie Spratt. Vintage page sheet background, July 21, 2018, https://unsplash.com/photos/_dAnK9GJvdY. Silhouettes based on a digitised image from page 388 of "A Romance of N'Shabé," December 4, 2013, https://www.flickr.com/photos/britishlibrary/11209860083/in/album-72157640584771663/. Cover design: Jeevanjot Kaur Nagpal.

To Jim, Elena, and Matthew — with love.
You made my balancing act possible.

List of Illustrations

List of Abbreviations

Abbreviations of Names

AF	Alice Freeman
AFP	Alice Freeman Palmer
BP	Beatrice Potter
BW	Beatrice Webb
EC	Elsie Clews
ECP	Elsie Clews Parsons
GC	Grace Chisholm
GCY	Grace Chisholm Young
GHP	George Herbert Palmer
HP	Herbert Parsons
LS	Lucy Sprague
LSM	Lucy Sprague Mitchell
RH	Robert Herrick
SW	Sidney Webb
WCM	Wesley Clair Mitchell
WHY	William Henry Young

Abbreviations of Archival Sources

AFP Papers	Wellesley College Archives, Alice Freeman Palmer Papers
APS	American Philosophical Society Library, Elsie Clews Parsons Papers
BSCA	Bank Street College Archives, Records of the Bureau of Educational Experiments
GHP Papers	Harvard University, Houghton Library, George Herbert Palmer Correspondence
LSM Papers	Columbia University, Rare Book and Manuscript Library, Lucy Sprague Mitchell Papers
Passfield Papers	London School of Economics and Political Science, British Library of Political and Economic Science, Passfield Papers
RH Papers	University of Chicago, Hannah Holborn Gray Special Collections Research Center, Robert Herrick Papers
RHS	Rye Historical Society, Parsons Family Papers
Tanner Papers	University of Liverpool Library, Special Collections and Archives, Papers of Dr. R. C. H. Tanner
UC, OPHJB	University of Chicago, Hannah Holborn Gray Special Collections Research Center, University of Chicago, Office of the President, Harper, Judson, and Burton Administrations
WCM Papers	Columbia University, Rare Book and Manuscript Library, Wesley Clair Mitchell Papers
Young Papers	University of Liverpool Library, Special Collections and Archives, Papers of W. H. Young and Grace Chisholm Young

Acknowledgements

Like raising a child, it seems to take a village to produce a book. Many friends, colleagues, and relatives have contributed support, insights, and encouragement.

I am greatly indebted to the members of the Narrative Writing Group – Betty Caroli, Ruth Franklin, Barbara Fisher, Dorothy O. Helly, and Melissa Nathanson – for their close readings of multiple drafts of Breaking Conventions, probing questions and observations, sage advice, and unfailing encouragement. I have also benefitted from the guidance, knowledge, and inspiration of multiple members of the Women Writing Women's Lives Seminar in New York.

Thanks to Susan Blank, Marion Kaplan, Barbara Monteiro, Patricia Palmieri, Fredda Rosen, and Miriam Slater for reading chapters and giving very helpful feedback. Special thanks goes to Constance Brown, who accompanied me on a research trip to the University of Liverpool Archive, borrowed library books for me, critiqued draft chapters, and provided apartment space so I could have "a room of my own" to work in at a critical point. She has always been eager to deliberate about the lives and work of the five women.

A Travel Fellowship from The National Endowment for the Humanities helped finance my research in the University of Liverpool Archive. Archivists at the American Philosophical Society Library, Bank Street College of Education, Columbia University, Houghton Library at Harvard University, London School of Economics and Political Science, Rye Historical Society, University of Chicago, University of Liverpool, and Wellesley College helped guide me through manuscript collections, answered my questions, provided copies, and gave permissions to quote material and reproduce photographs. Staff at the archives of Göttingen University and the Université de Genève took the time to answer my email queries and identify sources that shed light on Grace Chisholm

Young's time at these schools. Although the individuals I write about have been long dead, I have made good faith efforts to contact family members who might have knowledge of copyright restrictions on their archival collections. Any oversight is unintentional.

I was fortunate to interview Patrick Young, the youngest child of Grace and Will Young, when I began this project. I have also benefitted from talking with Sylvia Wiegand and Dorothy Sampson, two of the Youngs' grandchildren; Beverly Corbett, a granddaughter of Lucy and Wesley Mitchell; David M. Parsons, a grandson of Elsie and Herbert Parsons; and two great-great-nieces of George Herbert Palmer – Sarah Lord Corson and Pat Bartlett. I thank them all for sharing their recollections and information about their families with me.

Staff at Open Book Publishers have been a pleasure to work with, from start to finish. Two anonymous peer reviewers also offered cogent suggestions on the manuscript.

Thanks to my late father, Lawrence Auspos, and my late mother-in-law, Dora Riccio, who each spent several days taking care of my young daughter so I was free to spend time in the archives at an early stage of this project.

I am indebted to my children, Elena and Matthew Riccio, now adults, for their loving patience and encouragement. Most of all, I am grateful to my husband, James Riccio, who has been unfailingly supportive, ever ready to read drafts and discuss the couples, and more than willing to share childrearing and household responsibilities. He continued to believe in the book whenever I became doubtful. A model of a supportive and engaged husband, he has met the challenges of a dual career marriage with good humor and creative problem-solving.

Contents

Introduction: Love, Power, and Profession in Early Dual Career Marriages

In September 1900, Elsie Clews, a twenty-four-year-old lecturer at Barnard College with a PhD in sociology, married Herbert Parsons, a lawyer and politician, despite serious doubts about how marriage would alter her professional life. The pioneering British social investigator Beatrice Webb was having equally unsettling thoughts about her own marriage of eight years, and could not stop daydreaming about the prominent politician she had hoped to spend her life with. Grace Chisholm Young, a British woman with a PhD in mathematics and two young children, was struggling to fit medical studies into her already overcrowded schedule assisting her husband, an ambitious but unknown mathematician, with his work in pure mathematics. Any of the three women might have benefited from a talk with the longer-married, more prominent Alice Freeman Palmer, a doyen of women's higher education in America, who had made major concessions in her career to accommodate her marriage. In the summer of 1900, she was watching her protégé, Lucy Sprague, a newly minted graduate of Radcliffe College, confront the same questions of family versus career that Alice had wrestled with for years.

These five accomplished women, all of whom married between 1887 and 1912, constructed marriages that are commonplace today, but were deeply shocking in their own time, when well-to-do white women in America and Britain were not supposed to have careers, and career women were not supposed to marry. They defied conventions to overcome what one contemporary described as the "marriage-career dilemma" — the agonizing choice between marrying for love or

    https://doi.org/10.11647/OBP.0318.08

remaining single to pursue a career. Discussions about the marriage-career dilemma reverberated in professional journals, popular fiction, and the courts from the 1840s on, as more women became doctors, lawyers, and college professors.[1] The emotional cost of making this choice could be devastating, and many accomplished women spent years of frustrated courtship deciding whether to marry the men they loved and give up their work, or give up the men and continue the work they loved. Few questioned that the choice had to be made. Medical expertise, professional and institutional practice, legal fiat, and social custom all conspired to keep married women out of the workplace and in the home. Only a small minority of highly educated, highly trained middle-class white women took the bold step of marrying and working outside the home.[2]

Breaking Conventions tells the stories of five prominent women who did and the equally prominent men they married—the power couples

---

1   For examples, see Lorna Duffin, "The Conspicuous Consumptive: Woman as an Invalid" in *The Nineteenth-century Woman: Her Cultural and Physical World*, ed. by Sara Delamont and Lorna Duffin (New York: Harper and Row, 1978), pp. 26–56 (p. 50); Regina M. Morantz-Sanchez, "The Many Faces of Intimacy" in *Uneasy Careers and Intimate Lives, Women in Science, 1789–1979*, ed. by Pnina G. Abir-am and Dorinda Outram (New Brunswick, NJ: Rutgers University Press, 1987), pp. 47–51; and Elizabeth Stuart Phelps, *Doctor Zay* and the "Afterward" by Michael Sartisky (New York: The Feminist Press, 1993; originally published in 1882).

2   About 12 percent of female professionals in the US who worked were married with a husband present in 1910, when fewer than 4 percent of married white women were combining marriage and career. See Nancy F. Cott, *The Grounding of Modern Feminism* (New Haven: Yale University Press, 1987), pp. 182–83, and Lois Scharf, *To Work and to Wed: Female Employment and the Great Depression* (Westport, CN: Greenwood Press, 1985), p. 16. Marriage rates among actively working women professionals varied by occupation: in 1900, 32 percent of female physicians in the United States were married, compared to just 5 percent of female teachers, including college professors. See Regina Markell Morantz-Sanchez, *Sympathy and Science: Women Physicians in American Medicine* (New York: Oxford University Press, 1985), Table 5–1, p. 137. In 1901, 13 percent of all women who worked full-time in Britain were married or widowed, while 21 percent of the more than 200 actively practicing female doctors were married or widowed. About 12 percent of female teachers in England before 1914 were married. See Carol Dyhouse, *Girls Growing Up in Late Victorian and Edwardian England* (London: Routledge and Kegan Paul, 1981), pp. 5–6; David Rubinstein, *Before the Suffragettes: Women's Emancipation in the 1890s* (New York: St. Martin's, 1986), p. 81; Mary Ann C. Elston, "Women Doctors in the British Health Services: A Sociological Study of their Careers and Opportunities" (unpublished PhD dissertation, University of Leeds, 1986), pp. 199–205, https://etheses.whiterose.ac.uk/247/1/uk_bl_ethos_375527.pdf; and Linda L. Clark, *Women and Achievement in Nineteenth-Century Europe* (Cambridge, UK: Cambridge University Press, 2008), p. 178.

of their day. Despite the wives' talents and determination, and the husbands' desire to support their careers, the couples faced daunting obstacles in their efforts to create more egalitarian and fulfilling marriages. Some succeeded; some failed; all struggled.

Alice Freeman Palmer was one of the most influential forces in women's education in late nineteenth-century America. She reluctantly gave up the Presidency of Wellesley College in 1887 when she married George Herbert Palmer, a member of Harvard University's Philosophy Department, and a translator of the Greek classics. After launching a new career as a paid public speaker on women's education, Alice became the first Dean of Women at the University of Chicago in 1892. She spent at least three months a year on the Chicago campus, leaving George in charge of running their Cambridge household.

The first woman to defend a thesis and earn a PhD in mathematics in Germany,[3] Grace Chisholm Young solidified her status as a mathematician and helped launch her husband's career as a mathematical researcher and professor by becoming his research partner in 1902. While working her way through a rigorous medical school curriculum, she helped him with his research and writing and raised their six children. Their partnership — which never fully acknowledged her contribution — established William Henry Young's reputation as "one of the most profound and original of the English mathematicians" during the early decades of the 1900s.[4] Though Grace completed all the course work required to become a doctor, she did not undertake a hospital residency and never practiced.

Elsie Clews was already an atheist, a feminist, and a social rebel when she married the more staid Herbert Parsons. He made his living as a lawyer, but his passion was progressive politics and municipal reform. The controversial views Elsie espoused in her first book set off a public furor just days after Herbert was elected to a second term in the US House of Representatives in 1906. After he left Congress in 1911, Elsie moved from sociology and college teaching to writing

---

3   The Russian Sonia Kovalevsky was awarded a PhD in mathematics from Göttingen University in 1874 but without making the thesis defense or taking the oral examinations required in Grace's day.

4   G. H. Hardy, "William Henry Young, 1863–1942", Royal Society of London, *Obituary Notices of Fellows*, 4:12 (November 1943), 307–23, https://royalsocietypublishing. org/doi/10.1098/rsbm.1943.0005.

what she described as "social propaganda" for the *New Republic, The Masses,* and other journals. Leaving Herbert and their four children for several months a year in order to conduct anthropological field work — sometimes in the company of a lover — Elsie won professional acclaim as a serious anthropologist studying the indigenous peoples of the American Southwest and Central and South America.

The extraordinary partnership that Beatrice Potter and Sidney Webb embarked on when they married in 1892 spanned almost fifty years and left a lasting mark on British sociology, social welfare policy, and public administration. Instead of having children, they wrote books together. They investigated social and economic issues, campaigned for sweeping changes in education and social policy, sat on government commissions, and founded the London School of Economics. Sidney was elected to Parliament and held two Cabinet posts. They are buried together in Westminster Abbey, the only non-royal couple to be so honored. But their seemingly perfect union was marred for many years by Beatrice's sublimated yearning for a more passionate relationship with a more compelling romantic partner.

A generation younger, Lucy Sprague lived with Alice and George Palmer while she attended Radcliffe College and was with them in Paris when Alice died in 1902. A brilliant teacher and gifted administrator, Lucy became a pioneering force in progressive education for young children after serving as Dean of Women at the University of California at Berkeley. After she and Wesley Clair Mitchell married in 1912 and moved to New York City, she developed an innovative approach to writing children's literature, and founded and led the organization that became the celebrated Bank Street College of Education. Wesley, one of the foremost economists of his generation, helped to develop the science of national statistics and launched and directed the National Bureau of Economic Research. They had four children, two of whom were adopted.

These five marriages inevitably undermined the system of male power, privilege, and prestige that was the cornerstone of nineteenth-century marriage and domestic life among the white middle classes in America and Britain.[5] Flaunting these conventions was both daunting and thrilling. Beatrice Potter felt "grave and anxious" about embarking

5   For how these themes played out in more traditional marriages, see Phyllis Rose, *Parallel Lives: Five Victorian Marriages* (New York: Vintage, 1984).

on "a true marriage of fellowworkers," but Sidney Webb was exuberant about the challenge. "Be it ours to prove to ourselves at any rate, that we are human beings of equivalent freedom and joint lives. What a chance we have!" he exulted.[6] Elsie Clews was even more apprehensive than Beatrice. "I have not changed my aversion to matrimony; indeed, it is stronger than ever, or rather I am more convinced than ever I shall never marry. For, although I love you better than I love or can conceive of loving anybody else, — moreover, if I had to choose between you on one side and all my family and friends on the other I would choose you — yet I should let you go entirely out of my life rather than marry you," Elsie wrote despairingly to Herbert Parsons in 1899, after five years of courtship.[7] Seven months later she finally capitulated and agreed to marry him.

More than a century later, dual career couples still wrestle with the same challenges these couples faced: balancing the demands of home, family, and work; justifying unconventional behavior that defies traditional gender norms; combining intimacy with autonomy. These five marriages remind us how far women have come and how much still needs to change if women and men are to be more equal in the home as well as in the workplace. Their experiences help us to understand why efforts to attain gender equality in the home have been so long in coming even when spouses are motivated to change. Personal ties and loyalties as well as societal norms and institutional barriers held these women back.

* * * * *

These five couples were very much the products of white middle-class culture, and their expectations and approaches to marriage were shaped by that world. Apart from the servants they and their families employed, they had limited exposure to people of other races and ethnicities, and to working-class women and men, in their upbringings and private

---

6   Beatrice Webb, Diary, 7 July 1891, London School of Economics Digital Library, https://digital.library.lse.ac.uk/objects/lse:bin716wef. Sidney Webb to Beatrice Potter, 5 December 1891. London School of Economics and Political Science, British Library of Political and Economic Science, Passfield Papers.

7   Elsie Clews to Herbert Parsons, April 29, 1899, American Philosophical Society Library, Elsie Clews Parsons Papers (APS).

lives. The wives had more encounters and interactions with members of other ethnic groups, races, and classes in their professional lives and volunteer activities, as researchers, settlement house workers, activists, and teachers. As highly privileged, highly educated white women, they benefitted from resources and supports that less well-off, less well-educated, less well-connected women workers lacked in their efforts to earn a living and support a family.[8]

Nevertheless, these five women were greatly constrained by the expectations and responsibilities imposed by their white middle-class world.[9] White middle-class culture in nineteenth-century America and Britain gave the sexes different functions and expected them to live in largely separate worlds. A woman's "destiny and fate" was to marry and have children; men were supposed to attend to business and public affairs. Women exercised moral influence in the home, but men set the rules and did not expect to have their judgments questioned. While girls were socialized from an early age for a life of domestic subordination and service, boys were brought up to be leaders and masters. Girls were instructed not to be self-willed or ambitious, taught to defer to men's opinions and whims, and trained to regard their fathers and brothers as superior intellects.[10] "Scientific" evidence, assembled by male scientists, showed that women were inferior to men in intelligence, reasoning ability, and judgment, and confirmed that it was their nature to be emotional, impulsive, and weak-willed.[11] Such beliefs made it clear why women required male protection and

---

8   For the history of working-class women's struggles to combine marriage and work in Britain, see Helen McCarthy, *Double Lives, A History of Working Motherhood* (London: Bloomsbury, 2020).

9   In contrast, Bart Landry, *Black Working Lives: Pioneers of the American Family Revolution* (Berkeley: University of California Press, 2000) shows that black middle-class couples were much more likely than whites to form two-earner families in the nineteenth century. Committed to family, community, and careers, wives in the black middle class developed "an egalitarian ideology of family that contrasted sharply with the cult of domesticity so prominent among whites", Landry argues (pp. 5, 30–31).

10   See Dyhouse, *Girls Growing Up*; Deborah Gorham, *The Victorian Girl and Feminine Ideal* (Bloomington: Indiana University Press, 1982); Pat Jalland, *Women, Marriage and Politics, 1860–1914* (Oxford: Oxford University Press, 1986).

11   Cynthia Eagle Russett, *Sexual Science: The Victorian Construction of Womanhood* (Cambridge, MA: Harvard University Press, 1991); Lorna Duffin, "Prisoners of Progress: Women and Evolution" in *The Nineteenth-century Woman*, ed. by Delamont and Duffin, 57–91.

guidance: it was for their own good. Women who sought professional or intellectual accomplishment were considered unnatural, even masculine in their tastes and temperament.

Throughout the nineteenth- and early twentieth-centuries, white middle-class women in both America and Britain had three models for what it meant to be a "good" wife: they were expected to be domestic angels, helpmate wives, or companionate spouses — or some combination of the three. The English poet Coventry Patmore immortalized the sentimentalized ideal of the domestic angel in the 1850s in his book-length poem, *The Angel in the House*. The poem, which went through numerous editions and thrilled several generations of nineteenth-century readers (including Alice and George Palmer), celebrated "the gentle wife [...] whose wishes wait upon her Lord,/who finds her own in his delight [...her] will's indomitably bent/On mere submissiveness to him."[12]

A domestic angel was supposed to create a home that was a haven of tranquility and order, a source of contentment and cheer, a sanctuary of virtue and modesty. Her grace, sweetness, and innocence epitomized the virtues associated with "true womanhood." She was expected to be docile and self-effacing, and offer her husband uncritical support and devotion. Marriage manuals, sermons, and public lectures gave similar advice and inspiration. Late in the century, women were still being told, "it is a man's place to rule, and a woman's place to yield. He must be held up as the head of the house, and it is her duty to bend unmurmuringly to his wishes."[13]

A second model of wifehood was the helpmate wife who worked as part of a team with her husband and gave him more substantive assistance than a domestic angel. Well-educated wives in middle-class and upper middle-class professional households in both America and Britain served as accountants, secretaries, research assistants, editors, proofreaders, sounding boards, and critics to their hard-working

---

12 Coventry Patmore, *The Angel in the House*, Canto II, "The Course of True Love, Prelude I, The Changed Allegiance" (London: Cassell, 1891), https://www.gutenberg.org/files/4099/4099-h/4099-h.htm

13 Mrs. S. A. Sewell, *Women and the Times We Live In*, 2nd edn. (Manchester: Tubbs and Brook, 1869), pp. 28–29.

husbands.[14] Wives of religious ministers, civic officials, and (by the end of the century) politicians carried out semi-official duties that helped advance the men's careers.[15] Helpmate marriages provided opportunities for wives to exercise their intellectual and managerial talents and develop companionate marriages, but they reinforced the man's dominant position and the woman's subordinate one. The wife worked for the husband, on behalf of his career, and rarely received public recognition for what she did.[16]

Late in the nineteenth century, as a new ideal of companionate marriage emerged, couples were encouraged to share more parts of their lives. Wives were expected to join husbands in leisure activities; husbands were expected to become more involved in the household and spend more time with their wives and children. In theory, companionate marriage strengthened the woman's position within the home and helped promote greater equality in marriage. However, in practice, companionate marriage could provide new opportunities and new areas for men to impose their tastes and interests on their wives. Some historians have argued that men's new interest in domestic life was an effort to reclaim male authority that was threatened by women's entry into the public sphere and professional life.[17]

---

14   M. Jeanne Peterson, *Family, Love, and Work in the Lives of Victorian Gentlewomen* (Bloomington: Indiana University Press, 1989); Barbara Miller Solomon, *In the Company of Educated Women: A History of Women and Higher Education in America* (New Haven: Yale University Press, 1986), pp. 37–39.

15   Leonore Davidoff and Catherine Hall, *Family Fortunes: Men and Women of the English Middle Class, 1780–1850* (Chicago: University of Chicago Press, 1987), p. 305; Jalland, pp. 221–49.

16   In contrast, Peterson, pp. 86, 162–91, sees such marriages as examples of "admirable mutuality", parity, and companionate partnership.

17   For women's power within the home, see E. Anthony Rotundo, "Patriarchs and Participants: A Historical Perspective on Fatherhood" in *Beyond Patriarchy: Essays by Men on Pleasure, Power, and Change*, ed. by Michael Kaufman (Toronto: Oxford University Press, 1987), pp. 64–80 (p. 69); Carl Degler, *At Odds: Women and the Family in America from the Revolution to the Present* (New York: Oxford University Press, 1981), p. 43; Mary P. Ryan, *Cradle of the Middle Class: The Family in Oneida County, New York, 1790–1865* (New York: Cambridge University Press, 1981), p. 232; Joan Perkin, *Women and Marriage in Nineteenth-Century England* (Chicago: Lyceum Books, 1989), pp. 248, 258–64; A. James Hammerton, *Cruelty and Companionship: Conflict in Nineteenth Century Married Life* (London: Routledge, 1992), pp. 76–79. On the persistence of male power, see David Roberts, "The Pater Familias of the Victorian Governing Class" in *The Victorian Family: Structure and Stresses*, ed. by Anthony S. Wohl (London: Croom Helm, 1978), pp. 59–81 (pp. 59–60); John Demos, *The Past, Present, and Personal: The Family and the Life Course in American History* (New

All three of these marital ideals — the domestic angel, the helpmate wife, and the companionate spouse — legitimized and supported male privilege, male authority, and male dominance in the workplace as well as in the home. A married man could invest long hours and single-minded concentration on his work because other people — his wife and the servants she employed — were attending to his needs by taking care of the house, the meals, the laundry, the shopping, and the children. Household spaces and routines were organized around men's work. If nineteenth-century husbands worked at home, they were isolated in well-appointed studies and libraries. Wives, children, and servants were trained not to interrupt them. If husbands worked in offices, their stay-at-homes wives dropped whatever they were doing to attend to their men when they returned home, and children were kept out of the way.[18]

This domestic support system was justified because the husband's work was seen as centrally important to the household. A man's potential earning power was a key consideration in a middle-class woman's choice of a marriage partner.[19] The whole family benefited from, and shared in, the reflected glory of the worker-husband-father. His work provided them with status, prestige, and social standing as well as economic security.

Over the course of the nineteenth century, the position of women improved in America and Britain, both within the home and within society at large. Opportunities for single women to receive higher education and professional training expanded, although only a tiny fraction of the female population went to college or received professional

York: Oxford, 1986), pp. 52–60; Nancy F. Cott, "On Men's History and Women's History" in *Meanings for Manhood: Constructions of Masculinity in Victorian America*, ed. by Mark C. Carnes and Clyde Griffen (Chicago: University of Chicago Press, 1990), pp. 206–08; and E. Anthony Rotundo, *American Manhood: Transformations in Masculinity from the Revolution to the Modern Era* (New York: Basic Books, 1993), pp. 26–27. On the transition from patriarchal father figures to companionate dads, see Robert L. Griswold, *Fatherhood in America: A History* (New York: Basic Books, 1993).

18 Margaret Marsh, *Suburban Lives* (New Brunswick, NJ: Rutgers University Press, 1990); Carol Dyhouse, "Mothers and Daughters in the Middle-class Home, c.1870–1914" in *Love and Labour: Women's Experience of Home and Family, 1850–1940*, ed. by Jane Lewis (Oxford: Blackwell, 1986), pp. 27–47 (pp. 30–32); Roberts, pp. 62–63; Margaret Mead, *Blackberry Winter: My Earlier Years* (New York: Washington Square Press, 1972).

19 Karen Lystra, *Searching the Heart: Women, Men, and Romantic Love in Nineteenth-Century America* (New York: Oxford University Press, 1989).

training.[20] By the end of the nineteenth century, an increasing number of female college graduates worked before marriage, and they had a greater array of employment options to choose from. Wives won more legal rights, including the right to own property, make contracts, and have ownership over the money they earned.[21] The angel in the house ideology was giving way to a more companionate ideal, and men devoted more time to domestic life and family activities. Greater numbers of middle-class wives were better educated and more likely to be involved in charitable and volunteer activities outside the home.[22] But marriage still reflected male power, interests, and economic dominance, and wives were still expected to focus their attention and energies on their husbands and children. A woman's desire to pursue a career while married remained a bold challenge to conventional standards of white middle-class behavior.

Challenging Marital Stereotypes

Scrambling to manage their households, keep their husbands happy, care for their children, and do their own work, wives who pursued careers found it difficult to be domestic angels, helpmate wives, or companionate spouses. With packed schedules and hectic days, the women were often — by their own admission — stressed, irritable, and

---

20 Less than 3 percent of the American female population aged 18 and 21 years was enrolled in college in 1900 — a total of 85,000 women. (See Solomon, *Educated Women*, Table 2, p. 63 and Table 3, p. 64.) The number of female physicians in the US rose steadily, from 525 in 1870 to over 9,000 in 1910 (ibid., pp. 45, 132). In 1880, there were 75 women lawyers in the US; in 1900 there were just over 1,000; by 1920, there were 1,738. See Virginia G. Drachman, *Sisters in Law: Women Lawyers in Modern American History* (Cambridge, MA: Harvard University Press, 1998), Table 2, p. 253. There were 29 active women doctors in Great Britain in 1881; by 1901, there were 277. Women lawyers were not admitted to the British Bar until 1922. See Elston, "Women Doctors", p. 57; Philippa Levine, *Victorian Feminism, 1850–1900* (Tallahassee: Florida State University Press, 1987), p. 96; Rubinstein, p. 81.

21 Mary Lyndon Shanley, *Feminism, Marriage, and the Law in Victorian England* (Princeton: Princeton University Press, 1989), pp. 102, 131. For the US, see Norma Basch, *In the Eyes of the Law: Women, Marriage and Property in Nineteenth-Century New York* (Ithaca, NY: Cornell University Press, 1982); Albie Sachs and Joan Hoff Wilson, *Sexism and the Law: A Study of Male Beliefs and Legal Bias in Britain and the United States* (New York: Free Press, 1979).

22 Karen Blair, *The Clubwoman as Feminist: True Womanhood Redefined, 1868–1914* (New York: Holmes and Meier, 1980) and F. K. Prochaska, *Women and Philanthropy in Nineteenth-Century England* (New York: Clarendon Press, 1980).

"unamiable." Sometimes, they were even angry. Inevitably, at some point, it became impossible for them to put their husbands' needs ahead of their own.

These pioneering couples wrestled with three major challenges in their marriages. Implicitly or explicitly, they were undoing the power dynamic that made men dominant and women subordinate in conventional marriages; replacing traditional notions of love and romance with new ways for couples to show support and create connection; and redrawing the accepted boundaries between domestic life and professional life. With few models or guidelines to follow, these couples had to make up their own rules as they went along. They illustrate three emblematic approaches for forging a new balance of power, intimacy, and work in a marriage. The Palmers and the Youngs were reluctant rebels who struggled to accommodate the wife's independent career within the framework of very traditional ideas of marriage, womanhood, and masculinity. Elsie Clews Parsons and her husband became increasingly contentious companions, unhappily divided by conflicting views about marriage, work, and companionship. The Webbs and the Mitchells were proud pioneers committed to creating more egalitarian relationships in society and in the workplace as well as in the home.

Challenging Stereotypes of Gender and Romantic Love

These five women and their husbands would have given very complicated answers to Freud's question, "What do women want?" Because they wanted to work, the women looked for different things in a husband and a marriage than the typical middle-class woman of their era did. They wanted freedom, independence, and challenges, not protection and a life of ease. The key thing the wives cared about was not whether a potential husband would be a good provider, but whether he would support her work. But they also wanted passion and romance. Discovering these were often conflicting rather than complementary desires, the women spent months, and in some cases, years in an agony of indecision about whether to marry and whether a particular suitor would be sufficiently supportive of her work. (Grace was unusual in quickly opting to marry.)

As women like Ruth Bader Ginsburg, Sheryl Sandberg, and Kamala Harris have discovered more recently, these wives also knew that marrying a sympathetic spouse was essential to the success of a dual career marriage. Finding a supportive mate was more problematic for these earlier women because the qualities that enabled a man to be a supportive husband clashed with nineteenth-century notions of masculinity. Their keen awareness of their own sexuality complicated the choice for many of these women. Several were deeply troubled about the prospect of marrying a man who seemed too weak or lacking in leadership and mastery. Just as they had been socialized to believe that their intellectual gifts and interests, administrative abilities, and ambition were unappealing "masculine" traits in a woman, they questioned the masculinity of a man who was too accommodating and too eager to follow a woman's lead.

Their concerns were fueled not only by the gender stereotypes of their day, but also by nineteenth-century concepts of romantic love that were predicated on the notion of female surrender to a masterful, heroic male. Women and men were taught that a loving couple fused their separate personalities into a single being. Studies of nineteenth-century courtship show how thoroughly both women and men internalized this ideal and sought "oneness" with the beloved.[23] Nevertheless, women and men experienced being in love and becoming one with the beloved quite differently. For a man, love involved feelings of power and conquest, and was equated with possessing and shaping the beloved. For a woman, it meant being possessed and shaped by, and surrendering to, a dominant male. The very language of courtship suggested a power struggle in which the man emerged victorious: he conquered and won; she surrendered and yielded. Female lovers were overcome, not just by the powerful emotions unlocked by love, but also by the force of the male personality. Women experienced romantic love as a loss of self, while men expected their women to become extensions of themselves. As a result, the "oneness" the couple experienced was more likely to reflect the man's tastes and interests rather than the woman's.

---

23 Lystra, pp. 9, 42–43, 54; Ellen K. Rothman, *Hands and Hearts: A History of Courtship in America* (New York: Basic Books, 1984), p. 247; Rotundo, *American Manhood*, pp. 110–11; Stephen Mintz, *A Prison of Expectations: The Family in Victorian Culture* (New York: New York University Press, 1983), p. 13; Jalland, p. 34.

The expectation that a man would mold his beloved to fit his concept of womanhood and to reflect his tastes and opinions was a key component of nineteenth-century white middle-class gender identity in America and Britain.[24] Without a woman to be dependent, subordinate, and malleable, a traditional man couldn't control, guide, and protect — and therefore, couldn't feel like a man. Conversely, submission to a powerful man enabled a nineteenth-century woman to feel feminine — all the more so if she were a strong woman in her own right, as all these wives were.

Such self-abnegation could be burdensome for women, but it could also be psychologically and sexually thrilling. No matter how independent and ambitious they were, none of these five women was immune to the appeal of submission to a powerful, dominating man. At times each of them yearned for such a relationship. In poems that celebrated her engagement in 1887, Alice Freeman, then President of Wellesley College, wrote about joyfully relinquishing herself to her "lord" and "king", and marveled, "Upon his face I saw such power/ As I had never known till now."[25] After months of courtship, Lucy Sprague candidly confessed to Wesley Clair Mitchell in 1911, "Character you have and I honor you; intellect you have & I admire you; Sweetness of nature you have and I love you: but leadership, mastery, personality you have not & you do not compel me."[26]

Years before she met Sidney, Beatrice Potter had been passionately in love with the powerful, dominating politician Joseph Chamberlain. She was attracted to him because he was "a great man" who exuded mastery. And yet she knew that, if he did propose, she should not marry him because he would crush her independent spirit and make it impossible for her to have a life separate from his. Although she was painfully aware she was not making the "good" marriage for which she had been groomed, she married Sidney Webb several years later because

---

24 John Tosh, *A Man's Place: Masculinity and the Middle-Class Home in Victorian England* (New Haven and London: Yale University Press, 1999), pp. 1–11; Leonore Davidoff, "Class and Gender in Victorian England" in *Sex and Class in Women's History: Essays from Feminist Studies*, ed. by Judith L. Newton, Mary P. Ryan, and Judith R. Walkowitz (London: Routledge, 1983), pp. 16–71 (p. 46).

25 Alice Freeman Palmer, "The Surrender" and "The Birthday" in Alice Freeman Palmer, *A Marriage Cycle* (Boston: Houghton Mifflin, 1915), pp. 3, 9.

26 Lucy Sprague to Wesley Clair Mitchell, December 10, 1911. Columbia University, Rare Book and Manuscript Library, MS#0884, Lucy Sprague Mitchell Papers.

she believed he would be the ideal partner for her work. "The world will wonder," she wrote after they became engaged. "On the face of it, it seems like an extraordinary end to the once brilliant Beatrice Potter [...] to marry an ugly little man with no social ambition and less means, whose only recommendation, some will say, is a certain pushing ability."[27] She was not alone: in order to find a husband who would support her work, both Lucy Sprague and Grace Chisholm also "married down", choosing men who were outside their social or economic class. This lowered the woman's status in her family and the world, but it boosted her position in the marriage.

Upending Traditional Power Dynamics

Tensions around masculine dominance and feminine subordination did not dissipate with the decision to marry; after the wedding, they only intensified. In the typical nineteenth-century household, the husband's superiority and authority were bolstered by the fact that he was older, more experienced, better educated, and more worldly than his wife. But these five working wives were not docile, sheltered women who had little experience outside the home. Accustomed to traveling and living on their own, they had overcome familial opposition, institutional barriers, and male hostility to obtain professional training and employment. Marrying in their early or mid-thirties, many were several years older than the typical brides of their day.[28] Several had been in love with another man before they married. All had distinguished themselves in a male-dominated scholarly or professional world. Some held a higher degree or a more prestigious position than their husbands did. Intellectually and professionally as well as socio-economically, several of these women married men who were less accomplished. That raised another potential stress on the marriage: professional jealousy or rivalry. Few men wanted to be eclipsed by a brilliant or talented wife.

Nor did these women want to be the dominant spouse in the relationship. Even the thought that they might be perceived to be dominant was troubling. This was especially true when the woman

---

27   BW, Diary, 20 June 1891, https://digital.library.lse.ac.uk/objects/lse:wip502kaf
28   The median age of first-time brides in the US was 22 in 1890 (Solomon, *Educated Women*, p. 121).

herself feared — as Beatrice Webb, Grace Chisholm Young, and Lucy Sprague Mitchell each did at the start of her marriage — that her husband was too weak or insufficiently successful. To the nineteenth-century mind, ideas of gender equality and marital equality were problematic concepts to grasp, let alone to put into practice. Having few models of shared decision-making in the home, men and women of the late nineteenth- and early twentieth- centuries assumed that one partner had to be dominant.[29] If it were not the man, then it had to be the woman, a troubling inversion of the natural order. "If two ride a horse, one must ride ahead and one must ride behind" was an often-quoted proverb that made the point clear.[30]

While the specialized knowledge and expertise acquired by male professionals increased their superiority in the home, women who worked outside the home — and the men who married them — encountered troubling inconsistencies between their professional and private lives. As a professional, a woman was trained to exercise independent judgment, decisiveness, and authority; as a wife, she was supposed to defer to her husband. The contradictions between these two positions created many tensions for dual career couples. As a college president and a university dean, Alice Freeman Palmer was a strong and effective administrator who wielded power with assurance. But in their home, George expected her to be a domestic angel, "sweet to the core [...] unselfish and responsive."[31] He treated her as a "little girl" who needed his protection and guidance and had trouble making up her mind. Reflecting on the difficulty of being "both sweet & gentle & loving & modest & also successful with a brilliant career of your own,"

---

29 Some early feminist/abolitionist leaders embarked on more egalitarian, companionate marriages in America in the 1830s and 1840s. See Blanche Glassman Hersh, "A Partnership of Equals: Feminist Marriages in Nineteenth-Century America" in *The American Man*, ed. by Elizabeth Pleck and Joseph Pleck (Englewood Cliffs, NJ: Prentice Hall, 1980), pp. 183–214. The marriages of late nineteenth and early twentieth century feminists in Britain offer other examples of husbands who supported their wives and sometimes shared in the wife's activities for the cause. See Olive Banks, *Becoming a Feminist: The Social Origins of "First Wave" Feminism* (Athens, GA: University of Georgia Press, 1987), pp. 39–40; and Philippa Levine, "'So Few Prizes and So Many Blanks': Marriage and Feminism in Later Nineteenth-Century England", *Journal of British Studies* 28 (April 1989), 150–74 (pp. 154–56).

30 Quoted in Shanley, p. 48.

31 George Herbert Palmer to Alice Freeman Palmer, June 1, 1890, Wellesley College Archives, Alice Freeman Palmer Papers.

Grace Chisholm Young warned her adult daughter "that is a very large order, it means *having* & *acting on* your own judgment & yet *distrusting* it & *giving way* to male opinions & desires."[32]

Forging a New Emotional Dynamic

These wives wanted more than a husband's tolerance or permission to work: they wanted his active involvement in and sympathetic understanding of what she did. Loving, supportive husbands encouraged their wives to talk about their work, discussed their triumphs and difficulties, and acted as sounding boards and cheerleaders for them. Some became helpmate husbands, serving as editors, managers, coaches, or advisors, doing for their wives what a helpmate wife traditionally did for a husband.

This shifted both the power balance and the emotional center of the typical nineteenth-century marriage. These husbands were often playing subordinate parts to their wives' leading roles. They were enabling and facilitating, not directing and commanding. It was no longer the wife's responsibility alone to ensure the happiness of the marriage: the husband had to meet her expectations and take responsibility for making her happy.

The three American husbands also showed support by taking on limited childcare and household responsibilities. In contrast, the two British husbands did not take on domestic tasks or childcare responsibilities, and their wives did not ask them to do so. The American husbands did more than most men of their time, but not nearly as much as the wives did. Much of their help was given when the wife was away, not while she was at home. There was little expectation that husbands would — or should — take over routine domestic tasks on a regular basis and no sense that there should be an equal division of household labor.

Whatever household help, emotional support, and substantive assistance a husband gave his wife was highly appreciated and greatly added to the happiness of the marriage, for husbands as well as wives,

---

32   Grace Chisholm Young to Cecily Young, November 9, 1937, University of Liverpool Library, Special Collections and Archives, D.140, Papers of Professor W H Young and his wife Grace Chisholm Young. Emphasis in the original.

just as it does today.[33] When Alice first set off for the University of Chicago, George happily noted, "You sometimes run a college and I a kitchen, and again I appear as the director of youth and you of servants. It makes our partnership a rich one that we each can comprehend and even perform the other's tasks."[34] Spousal support bolstered the wife's confidence, eased her guilt about not being a conventionally "good" wife, and provided couples with common concerns and shared experiences that were centered, significantly, around her interests as well as his.

Providing assistance and encouragement was not always easy for husbands, however. Both Sidney Webb and Wesley Clair Mitchell gave their wives heartfelt, ungrudging support and helped to advance their careers in multiple ways. Wesley was exceptional in forgoing a professional opportunity in order to accommodate Lucy's career. But in other marriages, enthusiasm and good intentions soon gave way to irritation and resentment, and husbands issued troubling mixed messages which undermined their expressions of support. Although George Herbert Palmer enthusiastically announced his willingness to keep house while Alice was in Chicago, he repeatedly instructed her to finish her work quickly and return home sooner than planned so she could deal with domestic crises or allay his loneliness. William Henry Young encouraged Grace to pursue a medical career, but his incessant demands for her help with his work in pure mathematics repeatedly interrupted her training.

Efforts to create intimacy and connection around the woman's work were especially difficult for couples who worked in different fields. The Mitchells found common ground by "talking all the time" about each other's work, giving Wesley a leadership position in the educational research organization that Lucy founded, and creating a shared social life with her colleagues. In contrast, Herbert Parsons's refusal to read Elsie's books and discuss the controversial themes she expounded wounded her deeply and damaged their relationship. They remained

---

33 Alyson Byrne and Julian Barling, "Does a Woman's High Status Career Hurt Her Marriage? Not If Her Husband Does the Laundry", *Harvard Business Review* (May 2, 2017), https://hbr.org/2017/05/does-a-womans-high-status-career-hurt-her-marriage-not-if-her-husband-does-the-laundry.

34 George Herbert Palmer to Alice Freeman Palmer, 23 September 1892. AFP Papers.

married, but she had affairs with men who took a very active interest in her work.

A woman who surrendered to the sweeping emotions associated with romance and passion and felt "one" with the man she loved found it especially hard to balance intimacy with autonomy. Alice was not alone in experiencing "oneness" as deeply fulfilling, but also suffocating and constraining. Dearly as she loved George, she lamented the marital "us" that eroded the "me," and sometimes longed to "escape" from him so she could be "alone and free!"[35] During a crisis in her marriage, Elsie agonized, "How are women to live *with* men, not *without* men like the ruthless fighters for institutional freedom, and not in the old way *through* men?"[36] Recognizing that many women had a "marked impulse to subjection", she promoted jobs for women as a safeguard against their emotional dependence on men. "It is only through work one can be quite sure one is taking life at first hand, and it is only by taking life at first hand, by being the spiritual equal of her lover that a woman may preserve a free and passionate life with him, a life of mutual joys and satisfactions, a life aglow through their imagination," she asserted.[37]

Redrawing the Balance between Work and Family Life

The volume and quality of work these women produced during their marriages is remarkable. Understanding the circumstances in which they worked and the obstacles they overcame makes their achievements all the more impressive.

Where to draw the line between work life and domestic life was a pressing issue for all five couples, and for husbands as well as wives. The wives were caught in a double bind that is all too familiar to working wives today. At a time when gender stereotyping and social taboos were much stronger than they are now, they had to live up to the exacting demands placed on professional workers as well as the exacting demands placed on wives and mothers. All five of the wives

---

35 AFP, "Myself," in Palmer, *Marriage Cycle*, p. 37.
36 ECP, "The Journal of a Feminist" mss., p. 53, APS. Also in ECP, *The Journal of a Feminist* with a New Introduction and Notes by Margaret C. Jones (Bristol: Thoemmes Press, 1994), p. 46. Emphasis in the original.
37 ECP, "Journal of a Feminist" mss., p. 54, APS (ECP, *Journal*, p. 47).

became multitaskers and labored late into the night or in the early hours of the day to complete their work.

Emerging standards of both professional work and childrearing at the end of the nineteenth century and start of the twentieth century increased the difficulty of their balancing act. To be taken seriously as professionals, women needed to show they could work the same long days worked by male professionals and by unmarried female professionals who adopted the standards set by men. Throughout the nineteenth century, the ability to work long and hard at their jobs was a mark of manhood in middle-class America and Britain.[38] As new professions and academic disciplines emerged in the late nineteenth and early twentieth centuries, and older ones developed more rigorous standards of training and practice, work demands became more intense. Male professionals and academics were expected to work increasingly long hours, devote more of their leisure time to work-related activities, and become increasingly specialized.[39] (Paradoxically, this was occurring just when men were being told to spend more time in companionate activities with their wives.) Associated with self-discipline and intellectual rigor, specialization was another mark of masculine character. Scholars and practitioners who crossed disciplines or spread themselves too thinly were looked down upon as mere dilettantes or amateurs.[40] Both trends — longer hours of work and greater specialization — disadvantaged married women who had to divide their time among many competing demands.

---

38 Rotundo, *American Manhood*, pp. 175–76, 267. John Tosh, "Domesticity and Manliness in the Victorian Middle Class: The Family of Edward White Benson" in *Manful Assertions: Masculinities in Britain since 1800*, ed. by Michael Roper and John Tosh (London: Routledge, 1991), pp. 44–73. Many women adopted a strategy of "superperformance" to achieve success in male-dominated professions. See Penina Migdal Glazer and Miriam Slater, *Unequal Colleagues: The Entrance of Women into the Professions, 1890–1940* (New Brunswick, NJ: Rutgers University Press, 1987), pp. 211–13.

39 Edward Shils, "The Order of Learning in the US: The Ascendancy of the University" in *The Organization of Knowledge in Modern America, 1860–1920*, ed. by Alexandra Oleson and John Voss (Baltimore: Johns Hopkins University Press, 1979), 19–47 (p. 32); Rotundo, *American Manhood*, pp. 175–76. In America, men reportedly were spending their leisure hours reading work-related publications rather than novels, plays, and poetry. By the turn of the century, male professionals were said to be focusing their social lives and friendships around their work. See Glazer and Slater, p. 175.

40 Shils, "Order of Learning", p. 33.

Around the same time, emerging standards of child rearing put pressure on women to spend more time with their children and be more actively engaged in their upbringing. During the nineteenth century, white middle-class family life in Britain and America was "adult-oriented," meaning that household schedules and routines were organized around the parents' activities rather than the children's.[41] Although the cult of domesticity and true womanhood glorified the woman's role as a mother, mothers in very well-to-do families and "solidly comfortable" middle-class families were not expected to spend a great deal of time with their offspring. Instead, it was understood that children would be cared for by servants and might see their parents for no more than an hour or two a day, at specifically-appointed times.[42] Such expectations made it easier for well-to-do working mothers to leave their children in the care of baby nurses, nursemaids, and governesses.

However, by the end of the nineteenth century, when colleges and universities in America began to offer courses in home economics, nutrition, and domestic science, middle-class women were told they should be more involved in caring for their children and bring scientific principles as well as maternal instinct to their efforts. Advice manuals and popular magazines spread the same message.[43] These new standards increased the challenges married women faced in managing households and families while pursuing a career.

Like other privileged women of their time, the wives in these dual career marriages employed teams of servants to help run their households and raise their children. They also enlisted help from female relatives — sisters-in-law, mothers, even daughters. Husbands sometimes pitched in, but an equitable division of household labor was not something these couples contemplated. The Palmers and the Webbs were childless (the Webbs by choice), but the Youngs had six children,

---

41 Marsh, pp. 36–40; Peterson, p. 104.
42 Patricia Branca, *Silent Sisterhood: Middle Class Women in the Victorian Home* (Pittsburgh: Carnegie Mellon University Press, 1975), pp. 74, 151; Perkin, pp. 96–97; Dyhouse, "Mothers and Daughters", pp. 29–34; James Walvin, *A Child's World: A Social History of English Childhood, 1800–1914* (Harmondsworth, UK: Penguin Books, 1982), pp. 99–100.
43 Stephen Mintz and Susan Kellogg, *Domestic Revolutions: A Social History of American Family Life* (New York: Free Press, 1989), pp. 121, 124; Solomon, *Educated Women*, pp. 85–87; Jane Lewis, *Women in England, 1870–1950* (Bloomington: Indiana University Press, 1986), xi.

and the Parsonses and the Mitchells each raised four children. (Two of the Mitchell children were adopted; two of Elsie and Herbert's sons died shortly after birth.) The emerging standards of child care did not deter these women from working, but they increased their anxiety and prompted several to make extraordinary efforts to spend time with their children and supervise their education and care. Like the "supermoms" of today, they took on seemingly unnecessary domestic or parenting tasks to show that they were traditionally "womanly" women despite being working wives.

Children complicated the juggling act significantly, but the prominence that men and men's work were given in the typical nineteenth-century home meant that a husband potentially posed a greater obstacle to a working wife than children did. Women were supposed to provide services and supports to men, not draw on them for themselves. Far from being valued, women's work outside the home was likely to be seen as deeply suspect, even unnatural. Although their earnings might be useful to the household, the women were typically not supporting families and not seen to be enhancing the family's reputation or status. Lacking the compelling motivation of economic need that pushed working-class women or middle-class widows into jobs, middle-class wives needed a different justification for their work. Self-fulfillment was not an acceptable rationale. Wives might claim to be serving a higher cause, responding to a calling, or simply making use of their talents and training, but their careers were more likely to be regarded — by themselves, as well as by others — as motivated by selfishness or unseemly personal ambition.[44] They might therefore be reluctant to ask for help or feel guilty about the sacrifices that other household members made on their behalf. And yet working wives needed support and assistance every bit as much as, if not more than, their husbands.

Breaking through the barriers of gender was difficult, even for these immensely talented and determined wives. When sorely pressed, they could be protective of their own needs, but they were often more inclined to appease than to confront unsupportive or grudging husbands. Few openly asserted that their work was as important as their husbands'

---

44 On women's justifications for pursuing a career, see Glazer and Slater, p. 104 and Carolyn Heilbrun, *Writing a Woman's Life* (New York: Norton, 1988), pp. 24–25.

work. Instead of complaining to their husbands about the extra burdens they had to shoulder, these wives — especially early in their marriages — were grateful and excited to have the opportunity to combine the roles of wife, mother, and worker. Visiting her own mother in 1905, Elsie Clews Parsons — a lecturer at Barnard College, settlement house worker, published scholar, and mother of two toddlers — wrote disparagingly to Herbert about her relatives' idle lives: "Mama and [cousin] Louise dress, i.e., bathe, curl, anoint, powder, manicure, etc., and think about dress all day long. Louise is incredible. She misses her adorable baby, & sews exquisitely, & she & Mama both play cards sometimes in the afternoon & off & on go out to lunch or dinner and that is absolutely all that happens to them [...]. It is an incomprehensible life to me and very sad."[45] It was only later in their marriages that Elsie, Grace, and Lucy began to express resentment of husbands who failed to appreciate the extraordinary efforts the women made to keep their households running smoothly, children cared for, and husbands happy while also producing important work of their own.

In an era when careers and professional work were increasingly defined as requiring specialized training, certification, and ascent up a hierarchical ladder, and increasingly associated with full-time paid employment in an institutional setting, these women blurred the distinction between amateur and professional that male professionals were trying to draw.[46] Elsie and Grace were highly credentialed scholars — PhDs at a time when very few men and even fewer women earned them[47] — who published in professional journals, were recognized as experts, and won academic honors and awards. But they were independent scholars, not college or university professors, and they

---

45   Elsie Clews Parsons to Herbert Parsons, September 20, 1905. APS.
46   On professionalism, see *The Organization of Knowledge in Modern America, 1860–1920*, ed. by Alexandra Oleson and John Voss (Baltimore: Johns Hopkins University Press, 1979); Burton J. Bledstein, *The Culture of Professionalism: the Middle-Class and the Development of Higher Education in America* (New York: Norton, 1976); J. W. Reader, *Professional Men, The Rise of the Professional Classes in Nineteenth Century England* (New York: Basic Books, 1966); and Harold Perkin, *The Rise of Professional Society: England since 1880*, 2nd edn. (London: Routledge, 2002). On the gendered underpinnings of nineteenth-century notions of profession and career, see Glazer and Slater, pp. 1–23, 209–45 and histories of women in specific professions.
47   Margaret W. Rossiter, "Doctorates for American Women, 1868–1907", *History of Education Quarterly*, 22 (Summer 1982), 159–83.

did not have paid jobs or institutional affiliations. Others of these wives pieced together paid employment opportunities, founded their own institutions, or pioneered new types of jobs (paid or unpaid) in social investigation and children's education. Having control over their schedules was critical to their ability to work.

These multi-talented wives wrestled with a second balancing act that few husbands experienced. They struggled not just to fit their work lives around their domestic responsibilities, but also to accommodate a variety of intellectual and cultural interests. Wanting to do many things with their time, the women challenged the emerging — male-driven — expectation that professionals should work increasingly long hours and focus their work increasingly narrowly. Elsie Clews Parsons transitioned from writing probing social commentary on modern mores to writing highly regarded scholarly ethnologies of indigenous peoples. Grace Chisholm Young wrote scholarly papers on pure mathematics during and after the time she was training to become a physician.

All five wives developed outlets for creative self-expression — writing fiction, composing poetry, publishing children's books and stories, chronicling their own lives and accounts of their marriages. Some workaholic husbands dismissed these activities as time-wasting distractions. Such judgments tended to reinforce the unequal division of labor within the household and confirm the man's sense of superiority: women who pursued multiple interests or allowed their work to be interrupted by household responsibilities were being "unprofessional" and therefore did not deserve to be taken as seriously or given the same support as their harder working, more highly focused husbands.

* * * * *

These five couples were variously successful in articulating and resolving the tensions and contradictions that made it so difficult to maintain a dual career marriage in their era — or in any era. The narratives that follow progress from the couples who had the most trouble accommodating the wife's independent career (the Palmers and the Youngs) to those who were most successful (the Webbs and the Mitchells). The deeply divided Parsonses — who managed to maintain two careers, but failed to satisfy each other's emotional needs — hold the middle ground. The Epilogue brings the story of dual career marriages up to the present and highlights the lessons that modern couples can learn from this earlier generation.

Individually, these narratives offer intimate, richly textured portraits of real couples struggling to balance work, love, leisure, and childcare over many decades of marriage more than a century ago. Together, they provide an enriched understanding of the persistence of patriarchal attitudes and behaviors, and a greater appreciation of the ways that professional standards intersect with notions of love and romance to shape marital roles and expectations in upper-middle class white homes. Seeing each of the marriages in the context of the other four sheds light on the constraints the couples faced, the choices they made, the progress they achieved in rewriting marital roles and relationships, and the conditions and supports that made it possible for them to succeed. Exploring the husbands' motivations and behaviors adds nuance and depth to the marital narratives.

Although dual career marriages have become the norm rather than the exception among the middle-class in America and Britain, modern wives still struggle against many of the impediments that constrained these five women. Despite the progress women have made in education and the workplace, gendered stereotypes persist in the public imagination. Ambition and forcefulness are still regarded as undesirable "masculine" traits in high-achieving women. Women win praise for being helpful, modest, and nice — while men are expected to be direct, assertive, and competitive. Masculinity is still strongly associated with earning a living. Husbands of very prominent women are counseled to show full support for their wives while also demonstrating they are not emasculated by the woman's success.[48]

The marital ideal of the angel in the house has lost its appeal, except among Christian conservatives. Men can now rely on secretaries, research assistants, and para-professionals to do many of the tasks that helpmate wives performed in the nineteenth century. Husbands are doing more in the home, especially more childcare, but women still

---

48   Emma Jacobs, "Secrets of Successful Dual-career Couples", *Financial Times*, October 13, 2019; Claire Cain Miller and Alisha Haridasani Gupta, "Why Supermom Gets Star Billing on Resumes for Public Office", *The New York Times*, October 14, 2020; Joan C. Williams, "How Women Escape the Likeability Trap", *The New York Times*, August 16, 2019; Sarah Lyall, "At Primary Debates and on Instagram, A Spouse Embraces His Campaign Role", *The New York Times*, August 20, 2020.

do the bulk of domestic work, and report spending an hour more per day on both childcare and housework than men do. Although growing numbers of men and women expect to have equitable marriages, in practice, many couples still give greater priority to the man's career than to the woman's. Working wives today are more likely than their husbands to make compromises that benefit a spouse's career but hurt their own — a trend that worsened during the Covid-19 pandemic of 2020–21. Such decisions penalize women at work and perpetuate the gender and pay gaps that contribute to power imbalances in the home.[49]

These five early dual career marriages illuminate the painful personal choices that dual career couples still encounter. Their example and inspiration are still needed today.

---

49 Claire Cain Miller, "Young Men Embrace Gender Equality, but They Still Don't Vacuum", *The New York Times*, February 11, 2020; Jessica Grose, "It's Not your Kids Holding Your Career Back. It's Your Husband", Slate.com, November 18, 2014; Avivah Wittenberg-Cox, "If You Can't Find a Spouse Who Supports Your Career, Stay Single", *Harvard Business Review Email Newsletter*, October 24, 2017, https://hbr.org/2017/10/if-you-cant-find-a-spouse-who-supports-your-career-stay-single; Patricia Cohen, "Recession with a Difference: Women Face Special Burden", *The New York Times*, November 17, 2020.

1. The Making of a Victorian Myth: Alice Freeman Palmer and George Herbert Palmer

Alice Freeman Palmer was a phenomenon in the nineteenth-century academic world. Only twenty-seven when she was named President of Wellesley College in 1882, Alice Freeman became a charismatic president and a talented administrator who reshaped the floundering women's college into a respected institution with a national reputation. In the process, she became "the most distinguished woman educator in the United States."[1] Nevertheless, when she married George Herbert Palmer, a philosophy professor at Harvard University, in 1887, she resigned from Wellesley, at his insistence. Five years later, she became the first Dean of Women at the University of Chicago, leaving George behind in Cambridge for weeks at a time to manage their household.

Yet, Alice's public image was not the pioneering woman who fashioned a dual career marriage for several years against great odds. Instead, her husband and her fellow educators, women as well as men, hailed her as a role model because she gave up Wellesley to marry George. They presented her life as a fairy tale: she, the beloved "Princess" of Wellesley, sacrificed her crown and career for the man she loved and lived happily ever after as queen of his heart and home. According to George's 1908 *Life of Alice Freeman Palmer*, Alice easily made the transition from college president to helpmate wife.[2] She was the

---

1   Ruth Bordin, *Alice Freeman Palmer: The Evolution of a New Woman* (Ann Arbor: University of Michigan Press, 1993), p. 113.

2   George Herbert Palmer, *The Life of Alice Freeman Palmer* (Boston: Houghton Mifflin, 1908).

       https://doi.org/10.11647/OBP.0318.01

epitome of an angel in the house but still managed to devote herself to volunteer activities that were as satisfying as, and more important than, her position at Wellesley. George's portrait of Alice shaped her public image for many decades. An immensely popular and influential book in its time, it sold more than 50,000 copies, was translated into multiple languages, and inspired numerous accounts of Alice's life, including a comic book version in the *Wonder Women of History* series in 1949.[3]

However, the letters Alice and George wrote to each other and the poetry Alice composed in secret tell a strikingly different story about her work and marriage. They suggest that the transition from president to wife, from college administrator to volunteer worker and behind-the-scenes educational advisor, was not easily made or eagerly sought. On the contrary, Alice spent several years after she married in paid employment, giving public lectures around the country as well as serving as dean at the University of Chicago. During these years, both Alice and George led demanding professional lives, and Alice's earnings made an important contribution to the household finances. Her work took her away from home for extended periods, and in her absence, George ran the household. Alice's professional activities created major tensions in the marriage. George encouraged her, but also incessantly pressured her to work less, so that she could spend more time at home with him. Ultimately, the strain of keeping George happy and meeting her professional obligations proved too much for Alice. She resigned from the University of Chicago, reduced her lecture schedule, and settled into the combination of domesticity and volunteer work that had proven unsatisfying during the first years of their marriage.

When scholars rediscovered Alice in the 1980s and 1990s, they began to challenge George's portrait of Alice and reexamine his role in her life and work. Most agree with him that Alice's influence on women's education expanded after she left Wellesley,[4] but they are quite divided

---

3   George Herbert Palmer, *Autobiography of a Philosopher* (Boston: Houghton Mifflin, 1930), p. 138; "Wonder Woman: Alice Freeman Palmer", *Wonder Women of History Comics*, 34 (March-April, 1949).

4   Barbara Miller Solomon, "Alice Freeman Palmer" in *Notable American Women: A Biographical Dictionary*, ed. by Edward T. James, Janet Wilson James, and Paul S. Boyer, 3 vols. (Cambridge, MA: Belknap Press, 1975–1982), III, pp. 4–8 (p. 6); Joyce Antler, *Lucy Sprague Mitchell* (New Haven: Yale University Press, 1987), pp. 55–57; Bordin, p. 285; Lois Kenschaft, *Reinventing Marriage: The Love and Work of Alice Freeman Palmer and George Herbert Palmer* (Urbana: University of Illinois Press, 2005).

over how to interpret her relationship with George. None do justice to the tensions that Alice's work created in the marriage or her struggle to maintain a professional career in the face of George's profoundly contradictory responses to her desire to work. The distortions in George's biography are the culmination of his efforts to deny these contradictions and make Alice into something she was not. She resisted his vision for some years, but in the end, succumbed, and settled for volunteer work instead of a professional position.

That decision should be seen as a compromise born of defeat rather than a triumphant synthesis or a preferred choice. The Palmers' marriage is best understood as a powerful illustration of how a dual career marriage strained the limits of nineteenth-century ideas about romance, marriage, gender, and professionalism. It was highly companionate, but George's desire to "share" masked his strong need to dominate and control. His sense of identification with Alice was so overwhelming, his desire for "oneness" so intrusive, that she found his loving attention suffocating, and sought employment, in part, to escape from it.

Upbringing, Education, and Wellesley

Alice Freeman's upbringing prepared her for a life of self-reliance, independence, and caring for others.[5] Her mother, Elizabeth, had taught school before she married and was only seventeen when she gave birth to Alice, the first of four children, in 1855. Alice always said that she and her mother "grew up together", but like many high achieving nineteenth-century women, she was closer to her father than her mother. When Alice was seven, James Freeman, a small-scale farmer in southwestern New York, left his farm and family in Elizabeth's care and went to Albany to study medicine at the Albany Medical College. After he graduated, James moved the family from the farm to the nearby village of Windsor, New York where he opened his medical practice.

Alice distinguished herself at the local academy, both as a student and a debater. At fourteen, she became engaged to one of her teachers, a graduate of Yale University. Eager to get more schooling, she broke off the engagement and convinced her parents to use the money they had

---

5   For Alice's early life, see GHP, *Life*, pp. 17–43, and Bordin, pp. 15–32.

saved for her younger brother's education to send her to college first. Practical considerations as well as a love of learning fed Alice's desire to attend college: she wanted to be able to support herself and her family. She promised that she would use her future income to pay for whatever education her siblings desired and would not marry until they were settled. Believing that co-educational schools were more academically rigorous than all-female colleges, she decided to attend the University of Michigan, which had begun admitting women two years earlier.[6]

Michigan's president James Angell was so impressed with Alice's intelligence and personality when he interviewed her on campus that he personally recommended her for admission. She had been poorly prepared academically, however, and had many academic "conditions" to be worked off. Alice lived up to Angell's faith in her. She quickly made up her deficits, established a solid academic record, and emerged as a student leader who was popular with both male and female students.

Family claims repeatedly interrupted Alice's education at Michigan. When her father suffered a serious financial reversal during her junior year, she spent a semester as the acting principal of a high school in Illinois so she could help support her family. Determined to make up the work she had missed at Michigan, Alice tried to study at home during the summer of 1875, but spent most of her time nursing her father and her sister, Stella. Nevertheless, she managed to graduate with her class in 1876, one of eleven women among sixty-five men.[7] Revealing the oratorical skills she would put to great use later in her life, she gave a stirring commencement speech on "The Conflict between Science and Poetry" that left her audience "spellbound."[8]

President Angell continued to mentor Alice, watching her progress and recommending her for teaching jobs. She taught for a year at a girls' boarding school in Wisconsin before becoming the principal of a public high school in East Saginaw, Michigan. These were hard years for Alice:

---

6   For the history of the University of Michigan and the experience of women undergraduates during Alice's era, see Bordin, pp. 42–45, and Barbara Miller Solomon, *In the Company of Educated Women* (New Haven: Yale University Press, 1985), pp. 50, 89.

7   E. G. Burrows, "Alice Freeman Palmer at Michigan", *Michigan Alumnus Quarterly Review*, 61 (Summer 1955), 321–28.

8   Arthur J. Linenthal, *Two Academic Lives: George Herbert Palmer and Alice Freeman Palmer: A Compilation* (Boston: privately printed, 1995), pp. 48–49.

her teaching loads were onerous, her health was poor, and money was a constant worry as she struggled to pay off her student debts and send money to her family. She began to work for a master's degree in history at the University of Michigan in the summer of 1877, but another family crisis intervened. After her father was forced to declare bankruptcy, Alice dealt with his creditors, rented a house for the family, and moved them from Windsor, New York to Saginaw.

During this troubled time, Alice received teaching offers from Wellesley College where several of her Michigan classmates were already teaching. Opened in 1875 by Henry and Pauline Durant, Wellesley was committed to developing healthy, vigorous, intellectual women. Determined to hire women faculty at a time when most colleges did not, Henry Durant, Wellesley's benefactor and virtual ruler, recruited widely to find qualified candidates.[9] Alice turned down an offer from Durant to be an instructor in mathematics in 1877, and two more in 1878, one to teach mathematics; the other to teach Greek. She continued to teach at the East Saginaw High School so she could remain with her family and nurse Stella, who was dying of tuberculosis. After Stella's death, in June 1879, Alice quickly accepted another offer from Durant, this time to be a professor of history, a position more in line with her academic interests and preparation.[10]

Alice arrived at Wellesley in the fall of 1879, just after the college graduated its first class.[11] She found the workload demanding and exhausting, but proved to be a popular teacher who inspired students and colleagues alike. She won Durant's respect by refusing to give in to him on a point of principle. When he wanted her to talk to a student about her religious faith with the intention of converting her, Alice refused,

---

9   Very few American universities offered PhD degrees before the 1880s. The first woman to earn a doctorate from an American university did so in 1877; three more women followed her in 1880. A small number of women pursued graduate training in Europe. By 1900, there were 288 women with doctorates in the US (Solomon, *Educated Women*, p. 134).

10   GHP, *Life*, pp. 78–82. Alice's offers from Wellesley are also recorded in AFP and GHP, "Chronicles of Two Lives", Wellesley College Archives, Alice Freeman Palmer Papers (AFP Papers).

11   Bordin, p. 101. See also Patricia Ann Palmieri, *In Adamless Eden: The Community of Women Faculty at Wellesley* (New Haven and London: Yale University Press, 1995).

saying she could not discuss religion with a girl she hardly knew.[12] After that, he worked with her on matters of school policy and administration. When he died in the fall of 1881, Alice, his hand-picked successor, was named acting president. The appointment became permanent the following March, a month after her twenty-seventh birthday.

Wellesley was in serious disarray and faced a very uncertain future when Alice took office. The college was operating in deficit; its academic reputation was compromised by its lack of rigor and close connections to evangelical Christianity; the faculty was demoralized, divided, and overworked; the students were unhappy. During her six year presidency, Alice reshaped the college through a combination of personal magnetism, skilled leadership, and astute management.[13] Her students found her "fascinating." One likened her to "a dancing star, all brightness, audacity, and leadership." Another attested, "Under her influence routine and drudgery were transfigured into something heroic." An alumna recalled, "When I saw her, I felt as if I could do things that I never dreamed of before."[14] Alice put Wellesley on a sounder financial footing and strengthened its academic credentials. She raising the entry requirements and academic standards, rationalized the curriculum and course requirements, hired better qualified faculty, and gave the faculty more decision-making authority. She transformed Wellesley from "a domestically oriented, religiously inspired college into a first-rate academic institution" and acquired a national reputation as an academic leader and spokesperson for women's education.[15]

Courtship, 1886–1887

Alice was at the height of her power and prestige as Wellesley's president when George Herbert Palmer, a Professor of Moral Philosophy

12 Palmieri, *In Adamless Eden*, pp. 26–27, citing Lyman Abbott, "Snapshots of My Contemporaries", *The Outlook*, August 24, 1921, 644. GHP, *Life*, p. 98.

13 For details, see Palmieri, *In Adamless Eden*, pp. 26–37.

14 Quoted in Patricia Ann Palmieri, "In Adamless Eden: A Social Portrait of the Academic Community at Wellesley College, 1875–1920" (unpublished thesis: Harvard School of Education, 1981), p. 107. A copy is in the Wellesley College Archives, AFP Papers.

15 Antler, pp. 29–30. See also GHP, *Life*, pp. 124–31; Caroline Hazard, *From College Gates* (Boston: Houghton Mifflin, 1925), p. 212; Palmieri, *In Adamless Eden*, pp. 36 and 128; and Bordin, p. 113.

at Harvard University, began to court her. They had been introduced at the home of a Harvard professor in December 1884, but it was not until the summer of 1886, when they met again at a dinner party, that a serious romance developed. After a few weeks, George was deeply in love with Alice and pressing her to marry him. He wooed her ardently and relentlessly, making it clear that she would have to leave Wellesley if they married.

In place of Wellesley, George offered Alice romantic passion, "womanly" fulfillment in domestic happiness, and the promise of a companionate marriage in which husband and wife would share common interests and activities. But she was loath to give up Wellesley and fearful that she could not be the kind of wife George wanted. Caught between competing loyalties and aspirations, she vacillated for nine months before agreeing to marry him. Unable to meet frequently or openly, George and Alice wrote each other two and three times a week, providing a vivid account of their painful struggle to resolve the marriage-career dilemma.[16]

When they began courting, George was 44, and Alice, 31. He was a widower, but the relationship was Alice's first experience of mature love. Honoring her self-imposed promise to help educate her younger siblings before she married, Alice had rebuffed romantic overtures from a number of fellow students and colleagues during college and her early years of teaching.[17] When she met George, she was no longer under that obligation.

In falling in love with George, Alice was responding to the ardent wooing of a man who attracted her physically, shared her cultural and professional interests and her strong religious faith, and revered her as

---

16 Transcripts of the Palmers' courtship correspondence, written between May 1886 and December 1887, were prepared for publication by Alice's sister, Ella Freeman Talmage. Many of the letters were published in Alice Freeman Palmer and George Herbert Palmer, *An Academic Courtship: Letters of Alice Freeman and George Herbert Palmer, 1886–1887* (Cambridge, MA: Harvard University Press, 1940). I read the transcripts of the correspondence in the Wellesley College Archives, Alice Freeman Palmer Papers, and checked them against the published letters to identify omissions and deletions. Like other scholars, I cite the typed transcripts in the AFP Papers in this chapter. The original manuscript letters, which I have consulted, and transcript copies are available at Harvard University, Houghton Library, 50M-199, George Herbert Palmer Correspondence (GHP Papers). See n"Note 69" below for information on the letters Alice and George wrote to each other after 1887.

17 GHP, *Life*, pp. 37, 69. Bordin, pp. 49–50, 76–78.

the epitome of the ideal woman. Like other nineteenth-century lovers, they read poetry together, went for long walks, exchanged flowers and keepsakes, and wrote often and intensely to each other about their feelings.[18]

George was a man of considerable learning and culture. He taught philosophy, but he had also taught Greek at Harvard, published a well-regarded translation of *The Odyssey*, and served as the curator of a university art collection. He was a confidant of Harvard President Charles Eliot, enjoyed many academic friendships, and was often consulted about faculty appointments at other schools. Throughout their courtship, Alice delighted in discussing her work with George and hearing his opinions and advice. When she arranged for him to give a series of readings from his translation of *The Odyssey* at Wellesley, she wrote to him, "Do you know how much it means to me? You come into my daily life then; you stand by me in my beautiful work here and have a part in it. It seems as if you belong to me in a new way."[19]

George was in robust health when Alice met him, but poor health had repeatedly interrupted his schooling. As a child, he had suffered from headaches and eye problems that required six operations. Forced to leave Andover Academy at the age of sixteen due to weak eyesight and granulated eyelids, he traveled in Egypt for a year with his brother and then worked in the family dry goods store. George's eye problems improved enough for him to enter Harvard College in 1860, but kept him out of the Civil War. He taught high school for a year after graduating from Harvard before entering Andover Seminary, where he studied philosophy as well as theology. Two additional years of study at the University of Tübingen in Germany were interrupted by illness. Back in America, George resumed his work at the Andover Seminary but had to give it up when he suffered what he called a "nervous collapse." He decided to become a professor rather than a minister, and was hired by

---

18   On courtship rituals, see Karen Lystra, *Searching the Heart: Women, Men, and Romantic Love in Nineteenth-Century America* (New York: Oxford University Press, 1989) and Ellen Rothman, *Hearts and Hands: A History of Courtship in America* (Cambridge, MA: Harvard University Press, 1987).

19   AF to GHP [December, 1886]. AFP Papers.

Harvard University as a tutor in Greek in 1870. By 1883 he was a full professor in the philosophy department.[20]

A year after he was hired by Harvard, 29-year-old George married Ellen Margaret Wellman, much to the consternation of both families. They were distressed by three things: Ellen, age 36, was seven years older than George; she had contracted tuberculosis; and she was a devout Swedenborgian while he and his family were Congregationalist. Both families eventually accepted the marriage, which was exceedingly happy, according to George. He described Ellen in the same formulaic, superlative terms he would use when he wrote about Alice. Ellen was "preeminent in fascination and accomplishments" and "exquisite in all things." They enjoyed "whole-hearted companionship" and always discussed consequential matters. She was an intellectual companion who shared George's interest in philosophy and a supportive helpmate who entered "completely" into his work. They traveled in Europe during the first year of their marriage, but as her health declined Ellen was mostly confined to home; for the last two years of her life, she could not speak above a whisper. After Ellen died in 1879, George moved into rooms in one of the Harvard residence halls.[21]

Temperamentally, the staid, reserved George was a marked contrast to the exuberant, outgoing Alice. He described his family as strict but loving and affectionate, and he remained close to several of his siblings as an adult. But he maintained that it was Ellen who taught him how to enjoy life.[22] Even so, his colleagues in later years were struck by the "order", "strict decorum", "restraint", and "dignity and reserve" of his life. At least one thought that George "had himself almost too well in hand" and "wished that he might occasionally let himself go."[23] Physically, Alice and George were mismatched in a way that upset nineteenth-century

---

20 George Herbert Palmer, *The Autobiography of a Philosopher* (Boston: Houghton Mifflin, 1930), pp. 9–10, 17–35. According to a US War Department Order, issued November 9, 1863 and published in *The New York Times* on November 15, 1863, men who suffered from seriously impaired vision and certain permanent diseases of the eyes and eyelids were exempted from the draft.

21 GHP, *Autobiography*, pp. 36–40.

22 Ibid. See also, Bordin, pp. 158–59, and Kenschaft, pp. 41–45. GHP to AF [June 15, 1887], AFP Papers.

23 Harvard University, Department of Philosophy, *George Herbert Palmer, 1842–1933. Memorial Addresses* (Cambridge, MA: Harvard University Press, 1935), pp. 65, 74, 41.

conventions of masculine men and feminine women. George was short
— only five feet, two inches tall — and slight, weighing less than 130
pounds. His face was dominated by a handlebar mustache and bushy
eyebrows which almost hid his piercing blue eyes. Nevertheless, George
had his own kind of magnetism. A colleague at Harvard noted that
he had "a personal force that made its impression" and numerous
acquaintances fell under the spell of his magnificent speaking voice.[24]
Alice's height is a matter of some dispute, but she appears to have been
quite tall for her day, and considerably taller than George.[25] She weighed
only 110 pounds when she graduated from Michigan and was down to
100 pounds at her wedding; living with George, she gained 40.

By the time he became involved with Alice, George had demonstrated
his interest in and sympathy for women's education. He lectured to the
female students enrolled at the Harvard Annex (later Radcliffe College)
and insisted that Annex students be admitted to a series of Greek
readings he gave at Harvard despite the administration's plan to limit
the audience to Harvard men. He also had a history of relationships
with intellectually inclined, well-educated, strong-minded women.
After Ellen died, he was romantically involved with Mary Whitall
Smith. The daughter of the Quaker Reformers Hannah Whitall Smith
and Robert Pearsall Smith, Mary was one of George's students at the
Annex and twenty-one years younger. Mary's brother, Logan, then a
student at Harvard, thought George's enthusiastic response to Mary
was unseemly for a professor of philosophy.[26] As George knew, Mary
was secretly involved with a London barrister, Benjamin Francis (Frank)
Costelloe; possibly she used George's interest to deflect attention away
from that relationship. Mary's redoubtable mother, a passionate believer
in the need for "perfect equality" between husband and wife, addressed
a very long letter to George describing in detail her views on the topic,
"On the Authority of a Husband." It is not clear whether she ever gave

24 Bordin, p. 159.
25 Possibly seeking to minimize the differences in their height, George wrote that
    Alice was of "medium height, a little below average." (Palmer, *Life*, p. 329.) At the
    time, the average American woman was 5'3". Records from the Class of 1876 at the
    University of Michigan put Alice's height at 5 feet 9 ½ inches, although it has been
    suggested that this could be a misprint for 5 feet 6 inches (Burrows, p. 321). It is
    hard to judge because photos do not show the two standing together.
26 Logan Pearsall Smith, *Unforgotten Years* (Boston: Little, Brown, 1939).

the letter to George, but she was immediately won over by him when he visited the Smith household in December 1884, the very month Alice and George met for the first time. Hannah was so impressed by George that she told Mary she was perfectly comfortable with the idea of having George as a son-in-law. However, Mary's engagement to Costelloe was soon announced.[27]

Hannah's endorsement notwithstanding, George's campaign to get Alice to resign from Wellesley suggests that he had absorbed many of the gender stereotypes and marital attitudes of his day. Instead of envisioning marriage as a partnership of equals, he seemed to want a wife who would make domestic life her first priority and be a constant helpmate to him. "Have you any such desire to be always at my side that studying how to help me could ever seem to you the greatest of duties, for which others might wait?," he pressed during one of Alice's periods of hesitation. George clearly felt that Alice could not play such a role if she remained at Wellesley. He had seen how Wellesley consumed her time and how their private life took second place to her work. He nobly, if grudgingly, tolerated the demands of her professional work during their courtship, but he was not prepared to devote a lifetime to doing so.

When their relationship reached a crisis point in December 1886, he begged her not to continue sacrificing her personal happiness and womanly nature to her public life:

> Your private life will tend more and more to shrivel, to be hidden, to be unsubstantially sentimental, while your public life goes its way more and more as a matter of business. I am sure you see these dangers. I see them more plainly than you, for I love you — that is I worship a glorious woman in you and believe that she is the one whom you were meant to be [...]. You think they are sacrifices which you are justified in making to a great institution. To me they look like suicide.[28]

George feared, too, that the presidency — with its long hours, ceaseless pressure, and constant anxiety — was taking a devastating toll on

---

27 See Barbara Strachey, *Remarkable Relations, the Story of the Pearsall Smith Women* (New York: Universe Books, 1982), pp. 79–81, and Tiffany L. Johnston, "Mary Whitall Smith at the Harvard Annex", https://berenson.itatti.harvard.edu/berenson/items/show/3030. Mary eventually left Costelloe and their two children to live with the art critic Bernard Berenson. See Chapter 4, p. 296.

28 GFP to AF, December 3 [1886]. See also, GHP to AF, March 16 [1887]. AFP Papers.

Alice's delicate health.[29] He had reason to worry about Alice's health. Her sister had died of tuberculosis, as had George's wife. During her first year at Wellesley, Alice had been forced to take a leave of absence when she developed a tubercular hemorrhage. She remained susceptible to colds and coughs, and during 1886 and 1887, her health was again deteriorating; in the spring of 1887 there was a false alarm about another hemorrhage. Nevertheless, in July 1887, a specialist declared there was no medical need for her to resign from Wellesley.[30]

Professional rivalry may also have contributed to George's desire to woo Alice away from Wellesley. George found Wellesley distinctly inferior to Harvard, but as a college president Alice enjoyed greater prominence and prestige than George did as a Harvard professor. (Neither he nor Alice ever directly acknowledged this, however.) She also made more money than he did: her annual salary was $4,000 in 1887; his was $3,500.[31] Within his own department, George's reputation was eclipsed by the brilliance of luminaries like William James and Josiah Royce. Recognizing that he was not "a system builder" and would therefore never be a great scholar, George devoted himself to criticism instead.[32] He was a popular teacher and published several well-regarded books on ethics as well as a translation of *The Odyssey*, but his own modest assessment of his scholarly talents has been generally accepted.[33] Knowing he was less illustrious than his colleagues at Harvard, it was probably galling for George to consider taking second place to his wife in the academic world. When Alice wrote that she was to receive an honorary degree from Columbia University — the first woman to be so honored by a major eastern university — George heartily congratulated her, but quickly noted, "I can't match your honors, but did I tell you that a month ago the Academy of Arts and Sciences asked me to become a member and that I declined?"[34]

---

29   GHP to AF [July 1886]; [November 15, 1886]; December 3 [1886]; [May 8, 1887] [May 22, 1887]. AFP Papers.
30   AF to GHP [July 10, 1887]. AFP Papers.
31   GHP, *Life*, p. 173.
32   GHP, *Autobiography*, pp. 124–25, 127.
33   Harvard University, *Palmer*, pp. 18, 26, 41. For a full discussion of George as a teacher and scholar and his standing within Harvard, see Kenschaft, pp. 173–81. See also the account of George's career at Harvard and the broad popularity of his courses by his colleague, Ralph Barton Perry, in Linenthal, pp. 435–36.
34   GHP to AF [January 30], 1887. AFP Papers.

George was adamant that Alice would have to give up Wellesley but did not insist that she would have to give up everything outside the home. Indeed, he argued that marriage to him would enhance and broaden her talents rather than diminish them. "[I]n my home you will be stronger for Wellesley, for yourself, and for every good purpose for which the Lord made you, than you can possibly by continuing longer a public functionary," he wrote her in the early weeks of their courtship.[35] George's choice of words — "my home" not "our home" — is telling. Months later, he again reassured her: "I would far rather you never came to me than that you should come and find your great powers in any respect lessened."[36] In his view, Alice would find greater freedom of expression and more outlets for her interests and talents in a home where she would be taken care of, protected from excessive demands on her time, and freed from the care and demands of running an institution.[37] Nevertheless, there was no attempt in the courtship correspondence to define what Alice's new work would be or how she would use her "powers" after leaving Wellesley. George's vision of the helpmate role Alice would play as his wife, and his insistence that he would support both of them financially, made it unlikely he would be eager for her to take on a new career.

Although George asserted that they were both impatient for her to lay down her responsibilities, their courtship correspondence shows that Alice gave up the presidency most reluctantly and only after considerable soul searching. Occasionally, when George pressed hard for a decision, she admitted to feelings of "hunger for a deeper, better life, of *homesickness* [meaning a desire for a home of her own], and dissatisfaction with the round of mere duty."[38] Having taken care of others for so long, Alice very probably looked forward to being tenderly cared for by George.

But at the same time she gloried in her work and knew she was making a valuable contribution to society. "Dear, there are so many things to be done for this College, from without and from within and to

---

35   GHP to AF, Friday am [summer 1886]. AFP Papers.
36   GHP to AF [December 4, 1886]. AFP Papers.
37   GHP, *Life*, pp. 175–77, 181–83.
38   AF to GHP [December 5, 1886]. Emphasis in the original. Similarly, AF to GHP [November 14, 1886]. AFP Papers.

be done at once. Help me to be worthy of them, and wise to know them
[...]. It is such good work to do!" she wrote to George.[39] She noted the
"fun" she had as a college president, the "continual delight" of the job,
how "interesting" she found the variety of responsibilities that made up
her work.[40] Nevertheless, she did not justify her reluctance to give up
Wellesley in terms of her own personal pleasure. Instead, she struggled
to determine whether she was meant to fulfill God's divine plan by
serving Wellesley or serving a husband.[41]

Like George, Alice had absorbed contemporary ideals about
marriage and wifehood. "I feel, more and more, that [marriage] is the
most beautifully blessed thing in all God's universe," she had written
to a friend who was preparing to marry in 1878.[42] She understood
that marrying George meant not only giving up Wellesley but also
submerging her life in his. Long before she met him, she had counselled
her friend about the satisfactions and difficulties of being a wife:

> *Keep happy* and grow in keeping another happy. Be unselfish, dear, and
> learn to *control* the woman's restless hunger. Let it only make you more
> tender and *sympathetic* and strong [...]. Then you will *feel* always that you
> are *bound up* together — that *everything* you do is *full* of the other. That it
> seems to me must be being *married* — and that you know is not the work
> of an hour — or a year.[43]

Alice had serious doubts about her ability to play that role and be
the kind of helpmate wife George wanted. "I am not sure that I could
supplement you as you have hoped. Perhaps we are too unlike," she
wrote him, intending to break off relations in September 1886.[44] Even after
she agreed to marry him, she continued to worry about her suitability
for the domestic life ahead. "I hope I shall not try your patience too

---

39   AF to GHP, November 14, 1886. See also, AF to GHP [September 24, 1886]. AFP
     Papers.
40   Quoted in GHP, *Life*, pp. 133–34. AF to GHP [May 24, 1887], AFP Papers. Hazard,
     p. 64.
41   AF to GHP [September 1, 1886]. AFP Papers.
42   AF to Lucy Andrews, August 24, 1878, AFP Papers.
43   Ibid. Emphasis in the original.
44   AF to GHP [September 1, 1886]. See also, AF to GHP [July 27, 1887]. Similarly, AF
     to GHP [March 14, 1887] [September 15, 1887] [November 17, 1887]; GHP to AF,
     September 14 [1887]). AFP Papers.

sorely, but ah! me, I wish I were more trained to home helpfulness," she cautioned George after their engagement was publicly announced.[45]

By temperament and experience, Alice did not seem prepared to play either a subordinate or a predominantly domestic role. Her upbringing, college life, and early teaching years had trained her to be self-reliant and self-sufficient. As Wellesley's president, she was the center of an admiring circle of students, faculty, and trustees and wielded virtually absolute power. George observed that her will was law, and reported, "whenever the little president raises her hand, the college hurries to obey."[46] She was accustomed to taking the initiative, making decisions, and seeing her directives carried out. Alice's closest associates and admirers recognized that her sweet and gentle manner masked an iron will and a strong temper, hardly the hallmarks of a submissive temperament.[47]

Neither Alice nor George was oblivious to the implicit power struggle that lay at the heart of their relationship. Their very first exchange of letters, in June 1886, highlighted the tension that would run throughout their marriage: his need to dominate, improve, and protect versus her desire to balance dependence with independence. Apologizing for "trying to steer" her, George admitted, "What I was born for is to set the crooked straight, and sometimes I find myself attempting to straighten what is already much straighter than I could ever make it." Alice replied, "If I did not respond to your wise counsels as gracefully as I should, it must be because I am used to giving advice rather than taking it." Nevertheless, she accepted his invitation to "become a girl again" and accompany him to Harvard's class day, promising that she would be "a most docile child."[48] Throughout their courtship and marriage, George would continue to treat Alice as "the little girl that I protect," someone who needed a wiser and stronger man to make decisions for her and intervene on her behalf.[49]

Images of male conquest and female submission recur throughout the couple's discussions of their relationship. George characterized his

---

45   AF to GHP [July 27, 1887]. AFP Papers.
46   GHP, *Life*, pp. 138–39.
47   Leila Sarah McKee Memoir, AFP Papers; GHP, *Life*, pp. 138–39; Hazard, p. 209; Lyman Abbott, "Alice Freeman Palmer — A Sketch" in "Knoll Papers", *The Outlook* (January 1916: 112), 86.
48   GHP to AF [June 3, 1886]; AF to GHP, June 7, 1886. AFP Papers.
49   GHP to AF [June 15, 1887]. AFP Papers.

courting in terms that suggest assault and plunder: "It is I who have broken through Wellesley walls and on me must fall the blame, if there is to be any," he exulted when their engagement was made public. "Tell people how you have had your home invaded and all your precious treasures stolen, and put them on the track of me the culprit." By suggesting that Alice had been overcome by brute force rather than choosing him of her own free will, George reduced her to an object and enhanced his sense of power. Indeed, his "possession" of her is a metaphor that occurs more than once in his letters.[50]

The power/submission motif figures prominently in the poetry Alice wrote years later about her courtship and marriage.[51] Several of these poems suggest that Alice found pleasure in submitting to a powerful man. In "The Surrender" she wrote of happily relinquishing herself to her "lord" and "king": "He is the lord of my new world,/ And new life has begun./ Take the scepter my king!/ All I am you have won." "Forbidden" expressed the delight a woman feels when her lover disobeys her and continues his pursuit after he has been instructed to stop. In "The Birthday" (which celebrated their betrothal night) she wrote admiringly: "Upon his face I saw such power/ As I had never known till now." In "Meeting" she marveled: "Oh, more than conqueror he seemed that day!" Alice's attitude was not unusual in an era when notions of romantic love cast women as submissive partners to heroic lovers who were their superiors in experience, intellect, and judgment — men who would guide and protect them.

Nevertheless, Alice was not prepared to submit to George in everything. In matters that touched only her private life, she tried to be compliant and accede to George's need to guide and control. When she discouraged him from visiting her at her parent's home in Michigan and he came anyway, she conceded: "I submit gracefully — as usual."[52] After they were engaged, she acquiesced in his decisions about renting,

---

50   GHP to AF, March 16 [1887]. AFP Papers.
51   George had the poems published in Alice Freeman Palmer, *A Marriage Cycle* (Boston: Houghton Mifflin, 1915). See below, p. 88. See also, Antler, p. 56 and Kenschaft, p. 202.
52   AF to GHP [August 16,1886]. AFP Papers.

furnishing, and decorating their first home in Cambridge.[53] She even had her seamstress remake several dresses that George did not like.[54]

But when her beloved Wellesley was at stake, Alice strenuously resisted George's attempts to take control. She repeatedly ignored his advice to work less, although she apologized for her "obstreperous ways" and for the inconvenience her presidency caused him.[55] Their most heated debate occurred when she insisted, for the sake of her work, on keeping their engagement a secret when George wanted to make it public. Their protracted exchanges show how determinedly Alice could hold her own against George when she chose to, how manipulative and patronizing he could be, and how willfully he ignored her forcefully expressed views when they conflicted with his.

When Alice finally agreed to marry George, in late January 1887, he wanted to announce their engagement immediately. She resisted, citing the negative effect the publicity would have on her and Wellesley. A month later, George pressed harder, but Alice held firm. She could not make a public announcement before going to Michigan to tell her parents in person. Nor could she work effectively if she had to attend to "the letters, the calls, the looks, the newspaper articles" which would follow a public announcement. Her advice to George reflected her own strength of character: "Dear, don't *allow* people to question you!"[56] George addressed his next letter to "dear perplexed Alice." He wanted to "throw my arms about you and protect you from all these troubles." Despite insisting that he would do whatever Alice wanted, he continued to ignore her clear articulation of her position and argued his own views.[57] Writing at two o'clock in the morning, she angrily responded,

> I do not see how it is *possible* to get through the spring term without doing the College some shameful injustice, or breaking down for lack of sleep. I don't like to emphasize *my* burdens here, but the unvarnished truth is that I have more than I *can* do well now without taking half my nights, and I am doing you no kindness by putting myself in the

---

53   AF to GHP [March 14,1887], [September 15,1887]; GHP to AF [September 15, 1887]; September 22, 1887; October 11, 1887; November 2, 1887. AFP Papers.

54   AF to GHP [October 4, 1887]; GHP to AF [December 19, 1887]. AFP Papers.

55   AF to GHP [December 5, 1886]; AF to GHP [March 13, 1887]. AFP Papers.

56   AF to GHP [January 17, 1887]; AF to GHP [February 24, 1887]. AFP Papers. Emphasis in the original.

57   GHP to AF [February 23, 1887], GHP to AF [February 25, 1887]. AFP Papers.

position which I cannot fill without injuring my health. And this plan does not seem to me feasible, from the health and home standpoint. Your case is different from mine, as you say. *Six hundred* people meet me in close relations every day, and my time is largely at their mercy.[58]

Alice proposed that she make an extended trip home to tell her parents, work on Wellesley affairs from Michigan, and inform a few people confidentially after her return. George concurred, and noted, both disingenuously and defensively, "My own life would be much less disturbed by allowing the matter to remain secret until summer. In urging you to disclose it I have had no thought of gains of my own."[59]

The question for George was not whether Alice would leave Wellesley, but when. Even after she agreed to marry, Alice was not completely reconciled to giving up Wellesley. In April, before anybody at Wellesley was told about the engagement, she and George discussed whether he could become president of Wellesley. The college's sectarian ties and low salary scale made it impossible to attract "a first class man" to the faculty and so it was filled with teachers "of second rank", George objected. In short, Wellesley was not good enough for him.[60] Moreover, he considered the idea an affront to his masculinity. "Nothing may be done looking to my leaving Harvard," he warned Alice. "I am sure you would feel it somehow humiliating to see me marry into a position. You would like to have me stand on my own feet. I do that here [at Harvard], and *you will stand by my side, my strong support*."[61] Once again, George was assigning Alice a helpmate role, not an equal partnership or support for her career. He added the formulaic, "But I will not insist. Do with me as you see fit." But he did not mean it and became increasingly resistant to the idea of leaving Harvard. Whenever anyone — Pauline Durant in May, several of the trustees in September — pressed to bring George to Wellesley, Alice loyally squelched the idea.[62]

Nevertheless, Alice was still looking for ways to stay at Wellesley. In early July, she thought it was possible that she and George could

---

58   AF to GHP [February 27, 1887]. AFP Papers. Emphasis in the original.
59   GHP to AF [February 28, 1887]. AFP Papers.
60   GHP to AF [April 21, 1887]. Similarly, GHP to AF [September 7, 8, and 14, 1887]. AFP Papers.
61   GHP to AF [April 21, 1887]. Emphasis added. AFP Papers.
62   AF to GHP, May 17, 1887. AFP Papers.

marry in the summer and live in Cambridge in the fall; she could help to "guide affairs" at Wellesley and possibly teach.[63] Later that month she tried, unsuccessfully, to convince George that they should at least live in Wellesley. Enthusiastic about the "perfect cottage" she had found, she eagerly envisioned George commuting to Cambridge while she stayed at home, reading his books, making his dinner, and going to Cambridge to attend his lectures. But it was not to be. George had already started looking for a house in Cambridge.[64]

In September, when several trustees were urging George to become president of Wellesley, he told Alice outright, "there is no question whatever about getting me. I have considered the subject for months, at first with inclinations not averse, and my decision is unalterable."[65] George would not come to Wellesley, but Alice stayed a semester longer as president than he would have liked.

In the end, Alice decided to marry George without challenging his expectations about her role as his wife. "I am confident that life with you would develop me into a nobler, larger character and life than any possible experiences alone," she wrote him shortly after their engagement was announced.[66] She left Wellesley without a clear idea of the work she would do as Mrs. George Palmer. "I am not ready to leave the College. I am not ready to be married. I have made no proper preparation. I have taken no training and my work here is not done. But I walk as happily as a child to a holiday — or any happy girl to meet her lover," she assured George a month before the wedding, reprising the submissive child theme that had marked their first exchange of letters.[67] The actual moment of change left Alice feeling stunned and disoriented. "The College life is all over! and I feel like an empty-handed lonely creature," she wrote George almost in despair two days before their wedding on December 23, 1887. She hastened to reassure herself, "But I have you, dearest! I say it over and over to quiet my heart."[68]

---

63 AF to GHP [July 10], 1887. AFP Papers.
64 AF to GHP, July 20, 1887. AFP Papers.
65 GHP to AF [September 7, 1887]. AFP Papers.
66 AF to GHP [July 27, 1887]. See also AF to Carla Wenckbach [July 29, 1887]. AFP Papers.
67 AF to GHP [November 17, 1887]. AFP Papers.
68 AF to GHP [December 21, 1887]. AFP Papers.

Marriage and Work, 1888–1892

A year and a half after her wedding, Alice was still disconcerted by the changes in her life. Passing through Wellesley by train on the opening day of the college in 1889, she wrote to George that her "sensations were too mixed for analysis." Yet she insisted she had no regrets. "I would not go back to the old days, sweetheart [...]. You are better, dear, than any college, to be your wife a higher place than 'The Princess' held in the days before you came, and made her a queen."[69] Nevertheless, the still-childless Alice was no longer content to lead a purely domestic life, as she had while she and George set up housekeeping in Cambridge and traveled through Europe during his sabbatical leave in 1888–89.

Their personal papers do not reveal why Alice and George, who were relatively old when they married (32 and 45, respectively), had no children. Alice loved children and was said to regret having none of her own.[70] While staying with her parents in 1894, she reported to George, "Father pathetically asks me where his grandchildren are, and I tell him it isn't my fault, so how do you feel now? When he comes East he may give you a scolding, and you'd better be very meek!"[71] It

---

69   AFP to GHP, September 7, 1889. Typed transcripts of the letters Alice and George wrote to each other after they married were prepared for publication for her sister, but never published. Typed transcripts of their correspondence from 1888 through June 1895, and from January 1901 through 1902, are in the Wellesley College Archives, Alice Freeman Papers, and Harvard University, Houghton Library, 50M-199, George Herbert Palmer Correspondence. Citations in this chapter refer to the transcripts in the Wellesley Archives for these years. Transcripts of the letters Alice and George wrote to each other between July 1895 and January 1901, available only in the George Herbert Palmer Correspondence, are cited in this chapter. I also consulted the original manuscript letters housed in the Houghton Library.

70   Alice's fondness of children: GHP, *Life*, p. 256; AFP to Robert Herrick, November 1, 1896, AFP Papers; AFP to GHP, December 15, 1901, AFP Papers. Regret in not having a child: Charles Eliot in George Herbert Palmer, *A Service in Memory of Alice Freeman Palmer* (Boston: Houghton Mifflin, 1903), p. 77. Sarah Lord Corson, a great-great-niece of George's, recounted that when her parents told George that they planned to marry, "he was pleased for them but urged them not to have children. There were more important things to do, he said." Email from Sarah Lord Corson to author, October 22, 2022.

71   AFP to GHP, April 25, 1894. A few months later, George wrote approvingly about a married couple he knew who sought medical advice about the potential effects of childbearing on the wife's health before deciding to have a child. GHP to AFP, October 23, 1894. AFP Papers.

is possible that George, who also had no children by his first wife, had a fertility problem. Or he may have feared the effect of childbearing on Alice's health. Alice's letters suggest that he did not much like infants, and one can imagine that he would not have been eager to share Alice with such a potentially demanding family member.[72]

Because she had no children, Alice felt free to devote her time to the education work that was important to both her and George.[73] Elected president of Women's Education Association and to leadership positions with the Association of Collegiate Alumnae (the forerunner of the Association of American University Women), Alice helped shape standards and supports for female college students and graduates. She was tireless in raising money for these national organizations, promoting the cause of higher education for women, and creating educational and employment opportunities for college-educated women. Her influence grew at the local as well as the national level. The governor of Massachusetts appointed her to the State Board of Education and named her to the five-member Board of Managers of the Massachusetts exhibit at the 1893 Chicago World's Fair. In charge of planning the state's exhibition on education, Alice made sure it featured women's education as well as men's. The lasting legacy of the Fair, she claimed, was that women were recognized as "human beings" not "peculiar people" who needed special treatment.[74] Alice remained a formidable power on the Wellesley Board of Trustees and numerous colleges and schools asked for her recommendations for female teachers and administrators and sought her advice about college governance and policy.[75]

These activities were not enough for Alice and she expanded her horizons by taking on paid employment in addition to her volunteer

---

72 Describing her delight in her infant niece, Alice wrote to George: "I don't think you would get tired of her [...] even you would want her for your own. You don't believe it, but you would." AFP to GHP, June 26, 1901. AFP Papers.

73 AFP, "Autobiographical Sketch 1900", written for a Harvard University time capsule, reprinted in Linenthal, pp. 14–16 (p. 14).

74 AFP, "Women's Education at the World's Fair" in *The Teacher: Essays and Addresses on Education*, by George Herbert Palmer and Alice Freeman Palmer (Boston: Houghton Mifflin, 1908), pp. 351–63 (p. 353). Originally published in *The Forum*, December 1891.

75 See Palmieri, *In Adamless Eden*, pp. 35–52, for Alice's continuing involvement in Wellesley.

work. In 1889, she began laying the groundwork for a new career as a paid public lecturer; she noted that the spring of 1890 marked the first time she was paid to give a speech. Between 1890 and 1892, she delivered more than one hundred lectures on women's education and women's domestic and public roles to schools, colleges, and women's organizations throughout the country.[76] From 1892 to 1895, she served as the first Dean of Women at the University of Chicago, travelling back and forth between Chicago and Cambridge.

During these years, Alice and George were living what would now be called a commuter marriage. These activities expanded Alice's reach and influence as an educator, brought in significant income to the household, and kept Alice away from home for weeks at a time. In her absence, George took on the many domestic tasks: he managed the household and servants, entertained guests, oversaw the annual canning and preserving, supervised the semi-annual moves between Cambridge and Boxford, and took charge of renovating and decorating several houses.

George did not reveal much of this in his biography of Alice, however. The focus of his portrait was the idyllic domestic life he and Alice led after she left Wellesley. He presented her as a lady of leisure who volunteered her spare time to philanthropic and educational causes (an acceptable role), not an accomplished educator who struggled after her marriage to find a professional outlet for her notable talents (a departure from the norm). He said almost nothing about Alice's work as a public speaker or her achievements at the University of Chicago. He emphasized that there was no financial need for her to work outside the home and stressed that most of her lectures and all her other activities after she left Wellesley, except for the Chicago deanship, were unpaid.[77] He also failed to mention how frequently Alice's work took her away from home. Instead, he insisted that her work in no way interfered with the domestic responsibilities that should concern a woman. He wrote:

---

76   Alice's speaking engagements during these years are listed in AFP and GHP, "Chronicles", AFP Papers.
77   GHP, *Life*, pp. 220–21, 260.

Her domestic cares were not less than those of ordinary women, nor less exquisitely performed. She did the usual amount of housekeeping, sewing, visiting, receiving guests, looking after the sick and poor, and attending social functions. In the occupations counted specifically feminine she even excelled. Yet after these were all beautifully accomplished there came those public duties to which she gave two thirds of her time.[78]

George was equally anxious to show that Alice's work had not hardened her or made her any less "womanly", although he believed that administrative work generally had that effect on women. According to George, Alice's "gentle" voice and "feminine and self-effacing" disposition distinguished her from the "strong and independent women, much unlike herself" who followed her as presidents of Wellesley.[79] His assessment reproduced unflattering stereotypes of female professionals, and conflicts with the way Alice portrayed herself in the letters she wrote to George about her work. There was nothing self-effacing or inconspicuous about the behavior she described; on the contrary, she revealed herself to be assertive, unyielding, and wholly effective. In short, George's portrait misrepresented Alice by omitting behavior that did not conform to the stereotype of "true womanhood" and ignoring the contradictions between her work life and her domestic life. His idealized portrait fails to capture the compelling complexity of Alice's character and circumstances and the struggle she went through to maintain an independent career.

George falsified himself as well. He presented himself as a conventional nineteenth-century husband who worshipped his wife and devoted himself to protecting and caring for her. He tolerated her outside activities because he shared her sense of duty, but he would have preferred having her all to himself, isolated in domestic bliss. Yet, in reality, George sometimes encouraged Alice to work because of the income she could earn. He also insisted he was happy to take on Alice's domestic role when she was away on business. On two occasions, he even asserted that a wife *should* contribute to the household income and

---

78 GHP, *Life*, pp. 312–13, 288, 290.
79 Ibid., pp. 231, 344. Similarly, p. 244. When Alice was working on the Women's Education Exhibit for the 1893 World's Fair, George wrote dismissively, "Of course those women's rights people will quarrel with everyone they see." (GHP to AFP, April 24, 1892. AFP Papers.)

not just be a "house body." Nevertheless, he simultaneously undermined her professional life by denigrating the institutions she worked for, repeatedly complaining about her absences, and pressuring her to cut her work short and return home to him.

These discrepancies challenge easy explanation. They reveal the huge fault lines that Alice's work created in the Palmers' relationship and the almost schizoid way they dealt with it. Accommodating Alice's work forced both Alice and George into roles that were antithetical to their deeply held notions about romance, marriage, gender, and power. And yet, they did not want to acknowledge this, even to themselves. As a result, they told contradictory stories about their relationship, their views on women's work, and the effect of Alice's work on their marriage — not just to the outside world, but also to each other. They also told conflicting stories at different points in time. The contradictions cannot be fully explained without understanding the stresses and strains that resulted from their effort to fit two careers into what was otherwise a very traditional relationship.[80]

Alice displayed great ambivalence about her lecturing. She delighted in the work and welcomed the opportunity to travel to new places, tour schools and colleges, renew old friendships, and forge new ones. She gloried in the acclaim that greeted her wherever she went. She wrote happily to George that she was introduced at the University of Michigan as "the most distinguished graduate of this or any other university" and was described as the "most talked about woman in Chicago."[81] On the lecture circuit in 1892, she was the guest of honor at "the most glorious reception ever heard of", featured in a local paper every day for a week, hosted as the guest of honor at a series of "elegant dinners and receptions", and toasted by the governor of Minnesota.[82]

And yet, she insisted she could not fully enjoy the work because she was so often away from George. She repeatedly resolved to give up

---

80 For a different view of the Palmers' marriage, see Kenschaft. My reading of George's personality and behavior is closer to Roberta Frankfort's characterization of him in *Collegiate Women* (New York: New York University Press, 1977), pp. 17–25, which discusses their courtship, but not their marriage.
81 AFP to GHP, May 31, 1890. AFP Papers.
82 AFP to GHP, April 22, 1892; AFP to GHP, April 26, 1892; AFP to GHP, April 29, 1892. AFP Papers.

the lecturing so she could stay at home with him. "Oh! my dear, this is miserable, simply miserable! [...] I wish all the world would leave us alone — I want nothing but you, just you! Next year we can make the house an excuse for shutting ourselves up together!" she vowed in the midst of her first successful lecture tour.[83] A month later, she promised, "One thing is certain. This year ends my public speaking career! I am going to play 'All the comforts of home awhile, and be only your wife.' "[84] She assured George, "[T]o be with you. That's all I want in this world. If people would let me be simply a selfishly happy wife, there is no doubt about the bliss of that state — never to be away from my beloved one, and to have time to think of him all I want when he is at work, and to talk to him all the rest of my life."[85] The following year, in the midst of yet another lecture tour, she resolved, "This is a foolish business. I am going to settle down and write instead of flying around the country."[86] In April 1892, she was again on the lecture circuit and again insisting, "I think I won't try this again."[87]

But Alice did not stop lecturing and did not stay at home. On the contrary, she increased the number of lectures she gave and the amount of time she was away from home. This suggests that despite her protests, Alice was eager to work, and eager to work away from home. The question is, why?

The Palmers enjoyed a deep intimacy that was both emotional and physical. But this intimacy came at a steep price for Alice. Their domestic life was framed by his idealized notions of womanhood and romance and her belief that a woman she should defer to her husband. This was both appealing and distressing for her. Despite the Palmers' rapturous descriptions of their mutual devotion and their unhappiness at being apart from each other, both had difficulty adjusting to marriage. The tensions created by George's need to dominate and Alice's desire for independence not only persisted but seemingly increased after they married. Their letters refer to "clashes" and "frictions." Each repeatedly

83 AFP to GHP, May 17, 1890. AFP Papers.
84 AFP to GHP, June 4, 1890. AFP Papers.
85 AFP to GHP, June 5, 1890. AFP Papers.
86 AFP to GHP, December 1891; similarly, AFP to GHP, November 12, 1891 and GHP to AFP, December 18, 1891. AFP Papers.
87 AFP to GHP, April 29, 1892. AFP Papers.

resolved to become a "better" wife or husband.[88] Instead of slipping easily into the domestic life that George depicted so movingly in his biography of her, Alice sometimes needed to escape from it and his efforts to control her life, efforts legitimized by his desire to achieve "oneness" with his beloved.[89] Work that took her away from home gave her opportunities to do that.

George's sense of oneness meant the establishment of the husband's hold over his wife rather than a genuine merger of two distinct personalities into a new, shared identity. Like many men of his time, he believed that a woman underwent a radical transformation under the influence of a lover or husband. When a young friend became engaged, he looked forward to seeing how the previously "unconquered girl" would be "shaped, adjusted, satisfied" by her fiancé.[90] During his own courtship, he had been pleased to see that Alice's letter writing style had changed in response to his influence, and he imagined that she was now only "partially [her]self when alone."[91] Alice's vision of oneness, in contrast, meant a companionship of equals.

Early in his courtship, George described the type of companionship he looked for with Alice: "a oneness of living, so that I may see all my thoughts through the mind of another and have all my drudgeries and successes transfigured and purified by making them yours." He hoped that he and Alice would become "as united in mind as in heart." Several months after they married, he elaborated, "I want you with me in all my thinking, in my scrutiny of the world, and in my intellectual enjoyment of it — just as truly as in my affections."[92] The repeated use of "me" and "my" are striking: *she* was to become a part of *him* and reflect his ideas

---

88 For example: GHP to AFP, April 26, 1889; September 8, 1889; June 17, 1891; September 25, 1892; April 6, 1894; October 7, 1894; AFP to GHP, April 30, 1892 and January 1, 1895. AFP Papers.

89 See Introduction, p. 12. Numerous historians document that nineteenth-century lovers experienced such a powerful sense of mutual identification that they felt they shared a common identity and sought to become "two souls in one." See Lystra, p. 42, and Stephen Mintz, *A Prison of Expectations: The Family in Victorian Culture* (New York: New York University Press, 1983), p. 133.

90 GHP to AFP, October 17, 1894. AFP Papers.

91 GHP to AF, March 18 [1887]. AFP Papers.

92 GHP to AF, Thurs am [July 1886]; GHP to AFP, April 29, 1888. AFP Papers.

and values. He would prove indefatigable in his efforts to mold Alice to his tastes.[93]

George's perfecting and controlling drives were especially evident during the selection, renovation, and decoration of the Palmers' homes. He fussed over the details of their domestic accommodations to a degree that sometimes amused and sometimes exasperated Alice. He repeatedly ensured that the major decisions about the rental or renovation of a house were made in Alice's absence. In 1890 while Alice was away visiting her parents, he abandoned the plan that he and Alice had agreed on for their next year's lodging and rented a different house instead.[94] She was concerned that his drive to achieve perfection would inconvenience their landlords, but she acquiesced, "You are to decide what you believe to be the wisest, and I shall be content."[95] She thereby set a pattern that would persist.

In 1891, George drew up plans and hired a carpenter to add a piazza to their country home while Alice was on a lecture tour.[96] It held 1,000 books and George used it as an outdoor study. In 1893, he negotiated the rental of a large house inside Harvard Yard ("the Quincy Street house") and then devoted several years and several thousands of dollars to renovating and decorating it. All the initial work was planned and executed while Alice was away from Cambridge. He explained to her, "I only hope I shall not commit you to things which if on the spot you would not approve. There are some grave decisions and I am obliged to incur them alone. It would be of no use writing to get your opinion, for they generally turn on the best compromise to be made between the opposing difficulties which close study of the conditions disclose."[97] On sabbatical in Europe in 1895, George spent the first two

---

93 George's notion of marital "oneness" did not require him to accompany Alice on her semi-annual trips to her parents in Michigan. He rarely went with her (often pleading lack of funds), and did not seem to have developed strong ties with her parents. He often expressed annoyance at the time and trouble Alice devoted to them.

94 AFP to GHP, May 22, 23, and 29, 1890. AFP Papers.

95 AFP to GHP, May 29, 1890. AFP Papers.

96 GHP to AFP, June 7, 1891. AFP Papers.

97 GHP to AFP, January 8, 1894. AFP Papers.

hours after their arrival rearranging all the pictures and chairs in their rented apartment in Paris.[98]

It was not unusual for late nineteenth-century middle-class American men, especially men who were interested in developing more companionate relationships with their wives, to take an interest in household decoration.[99] But the way George took over the decision making shows how patriarchal attitudes and behavior could persist in even the most companionate of marriages.[100] Setting up a home was something that George did *for* Alice rather than an activity that engaged them both. "Home is the place I have made for you," George boasted. He prided himself on his ability to create the surroundings that best expressed Alice's unique personality. "[The house] was built for you and thoughts of you shaped every transformation," he wrote to Alice. "No rooms in which I have ever met you are more distinctively yours," he maintained after he designed an office and waiting room for her in the Quincy Street house.[101] But the heart of the house was George's library, which displayed his art and his first editions of English literary classics.[102]

---

98 AFP to Robert Herrick, September 23, 1895. University of Chicago, Hannah Holborn Gray Special Collections Research Center, Robert Herrick Papers (RH Papers).

99 See Margaret Marsh, *Suburban Lives* (New Brunswick, NJ: Rutgers University Press, 1990).

100 A. James Hammerton, *Cruelty and Companionship: Conflict in Nineteenth Century Married Life* (London: Routledge, 1992) develops this theme in relation to British marriages.

101 GHP to AFP, January 5, 1894; [March 31, 1894]; April 12, 1894. AFP Papers.

102 Palmer, *Life*, p. 222; AFP to GHP, April 7, 1894; GHP to AFP, April 12, 1894. AFP Papers. George loved the house, in part, because it was the only residence inside Harvard Yard other than the President's house. George's obituaries note that the renovations cost $5,000 and were opposed by President Eliot, who warned that the university would soon need the house for other purposes. Nevertheless, George lived in the house until his death in 1933 ("G. H. Palmer Dead", *The New York Times*, May 8, 1933, p. 15; "George Palmer, Philosopher at Harvard Dead", *Herald Tribune*, May 8, 1933). The renovations cost more than George's annual salary at the time they were undertaken.

Fig. 1 Alice and George in George's library in their Quincy Street home. Wellesley College Archives, Alice Freeman Palmer Papers. Unknown photographer. Courtesy of Wellesley College Archives, Library & Technology Services.

Very likely, Alice was happy to have George occupied with something he enjoyed while she was off lecturing or at the University of Chicago. Quite possibly, she was happy not to squander her energies on so many domestic details. Perhaps giving in to George on domestic issues provided her with a bargaining chip to get more of what she wanted when it came to her work. Maybe she minded having him fashion so much of her life to his tastes. We do not know.

Even if she had wanted more say, Alice would have been no match for George when it came to house renovation and decoration. She had never decorated a house of her own, and her family had been beset by financial losses and insecurity. When George had visited her parents' home in Saginaw, he and Alice had laughed together over a "ridiculous" portrait that hung in her parents' bedroom. As the president of Wellesley, she lived in a suite of rooms in a student dormitory. George certainly had greater experience and interest in house decoration, and quite possibly more cultivated tastes. He grew up in a home where taste, refinement, and decoration were valued. Despite a modest income, his family spent "lavish" amounts of money on books, music, and "the dignified furnishings of the home," George recalled.[103] His family's country home in Boxford, about twenty-five miles north of Boston, where he and Alice spent every summer and many weekends, had been in his family for 200 years. It included over 100 acres of land, over half of them woodland. The house in which he and Alice occupied in Boxford was furnished with furniture of "ancient patterns" passed down by his New England forebears.

Alice's role in all this was largely passive. George's sentimental, romanticized vision of Alice in the domestic sphere could have come straight out of Coventry Patmore's "The Angel in the House", a poem they both admired and read aloud to each other.[104] As the angel in George's home, Alice had merely to grace the house with her presence. George "bowed" before her "perfection"; their home was "a kind of altar reared to [her] particular worship." She was "sweet to the core, fragrant and unperceived as mignonettes [small dainty flowers known for their perfume-like scent] in a sitting room, so unselfish and responsive."[105] Alice drew comfort from George because he was "so good and strong for me when I am weak and restless and full of oppression and pain."[106]

George described himself as a critic who appreciated what was adequate or harmonious and sought to bring it to perfection. He needed "something to begin and improve." Renovating houses gave him that opportunity. (He renovated five over his lifetime.) In Alice he had great raw material, so he sought to improve her too. He chose the books that filled the Palmers' homes and the clothes Alice wore in them. Alice sent her parents her multi-volume set of Charles Dickens' novels because

---

103 GHP, *Autobiography*, p. 4.
104 AFP to GHP, January 27, 1901. AFP Papers. As discussed in the Introduction, p. 7, Coventry Patmore's long narrative poem, *The Angel in the House*, first published in 1854, retained its popularity throughout the nineteenth century and set the standard for women as self-effacing, subservient wives and mothers.
105 GHP to AFP, June 1, 1890 and September 30, 1892. GHP to AFP, October 23, 1894. AFP Papers.
106 AFP to GHP, May 4, 1888. AFP Papers.

"George didn't like them."[107] When he criticized Alice's newly-made clothes before they were married, she had her maid remake them. He picked out on a new wardrobe for her on their first sabbatical trip to Europe in 1888–89. Years later, Alice dressed in "severe, handsome dresses" because George liked them, even though Alice herself thought they made her look like "a mooly cow."[108] It is hard not to think of her as another prop in the setting of his perfect home, another exquisite object to be possessed and treasured.

In the long run, George felt he and Alice had achieved his vision of marital unity. "She and I had become pretty completely one. Often my way of telling about her is to tell about myself," he proclaimed in his biography of Alice.[109] Alice too felt that she and George had become inextricably intertwined, but her reaction was far more ambivalent than his. While she rejoiced in her marriage and George's tender care, she knew that their "oneness" was purchased at the price of her individuality. Dearly as she loved George, she sometimes found his need to share and the intensity of their life together overwhelming, even suffocating. Work that took her away from home was welcome in part because it offered her an opportunity to be a person in her own right again.

There were hints of this during the Palmers' courtship. Before their engagement was announced publicly, Alice had written George, "Sometimes such great love as ours — yours and mine — sweeps me over that delicate line which decides the deepest joy and pain — and it seems to me my soul breaks away with — is it bliss or anguish? Is it longing or dread? — and flies into some strange unknown world, where I cannot yet go!"[110] Years later, Alice wrote a poem entitled "Myself" which expressed her wish to break the hold of their quiet domestic life, her need to be "alone and free", and her desire to test her own strength against new challenges. The last stanza in particular projects her dissatisfaction with the role of wife that robbed her of an independent existence, the "us" that eroded the "me."

---

107 AFP to GHP, April 12, 1892. AFP Papers.
108 AFP to GHP, September 2, 1889. AFP Papers. Lucy Sprague Mitchell, *Two Lives: The Story of Wesley Clair Mitchell and Myself* (New York: Simon & Schuster, 1953), p. 122.
109 GHP, *Life*, p. 16. Similarly, GHP to AFP, September 5, 1889 and September 30, 1892. AFP Papers.
110 AF to GHP [May 1887]. AFP Papers. This letter is not included in *An Academic Courtship*.

Oh, to be alone!
To escape from the work, the play,
The talking everyday!
To escape from all I have done
And all that remains to do!
To escape, — yes, even from you,
My only love, — and be
Alone and free!

Could I only stand
Beneath pale moon and gray sky,
Where the wind and the seagulls cry,
And no man is at hand,
And feel the free air blow
On my rain-wet face, and know
I am free, — not yours, but my own, —
Free and alone!

For the soft firelight
And the home of your heart, my dear,
They hurt, being always here.
I want to stand upright
And to cool my eyes in the air,
And to see how my back can bear
Burdens, — to try, to know,
To learn, to grow.

I am only you.
I am yours, part of you, your wife,
And I have no other life.
I cannot think, cannot do;
I cannot breathe, cannot see;
There is "us." There is not "me."
And worst, at your touch I grow
contented so![111]

This poem helps to make sense of Alice's willingness to take on work that required her to be absent from home. She accepted it, in part, because it gave her independence and freedom that being at home with George did not. Even George came to recognize that "packing a trunk" was as "necessary" to Alice as renovating a house was to him.[112] It is

---

111 AFP, "Myself", in AFP, *Marriage Cycle*, pp. 36–37.
112 GHP to AFP, January 15, 1895. AFP Papers.

doubtful, however, that he understood the emotions behind her need to be on the move.

George was as ambivalent as Alice about her work. Given that, by his own reckoning, she had been away from home for a total of two months over a nine-month period when she started lecturing, he was surprisingly enthusiastic about her early success. "I do not approve of your becoming a mere housebody; only of making that first," he explained. Congratulating her on "a very good first year" of lecturing, he urged her to expand her efforts:

> It was of consequence to make a public place for yourself now that the old eminence of Wellesley is removed. This place has been won. You have proved your power apart from office. Now the question will be to use that power with the most potent economy in the future. You will henceforth be welcome everywhere. This summer we will lay our plans about the sort of places to which you will go.[113]

Nonetheless, as his biography of Alice makes clear, George was not a public advocate of professional careers for married women. He supported her work for personal rather than ideological reasons. Historian Karen Lystra has argued that romantic love and the romantic ideal of oneness were powerful forces that helped nineteenth-century men transcend the patriarchal underpinnings of their society and develop more companionate relationships with the women they loved. Identifying so completely with a cherished loved one and vicariously feeling what the beloved felt helped men to overcome their selfish self-interest, according to Lystra.[114] George's support for Alice illustrates this phenomenon. His sense of oneness with Alice was so strong that he was convinced they had forged a joint identity and each was entwined with the other. He understood that lecturing was something she enjoyed, excelled at, and wanted to do. He was willing to let her work because he loved her and wanted her to be happy and use her talents.

Nevertheless, the effects of romantic love are limited and often short-lived. In George's case, self-interest provided an equally powerful and longer-lasting motivation. He was frankly delighted to have the additional income Alice brought home. Impressed by the $25 to $50

---

113 GHP to AFP, June 2, 1890. AFP Papers.
114 Lystra, pp. 229–37.

fee she earned per lecture, he jokingly threatened to retire and let Alice "carry both the glory and expense of the household" and instructed her not to give any lectures for free. Whenever he was annoyed by her absence, she reminded him that her efforts helped to pay for the house renovations and stock his library with first editions. When she thought about giving up the lecturing, she vowed, "I'll earn the money some other way."[115]

Obviously, the Palmers were not poor. Although George had always insisted that he could support Alice on his salary alone, the income she earned in speaking fees ($1,000 between January and October 1892) was very important to financing the lifestyle he desired. George readily admitted that he was given to extravagance while Alice was by nature exceedingly frugal. His salary at Harvard was $4,500 in 1893, and he earned additional money by teaching at the Harvard Annex and lecturing; the Palmers also had substantial investments.[116] Nevertheless, there were periodic concerns about meeting routine expenses, paying for the extensive and expensive house renovations that George undertook, and saving money for their sabbatical trips. In the spring of 1892, when Alice was on a lecture tour, George wrote frequently about being short of cash, and Alice was getting by on money loaned by her brother and economizing wherever she could.[117]

The benefits he derived from Alice's earnings did not stop George from complaining about her absences and pressuring her to return home. Angry that she prolonged a lecture trip when he had been counting on a "happy Sunday together after this barbaric absence", he accused her of sacrificing their home life so that others could "make money and renown out of you." A week later, he instructed her to refuse all social engagements in New York and return to Cambridge so they could enjoy an extra half-day together.[118]

---

115 GHP to AFP, May 21, 1890; GHP to AFP, May 23, 1890; AFP to GHP [April 1892]. AFP Papers.
116 GHP to AFP, April 10, 1892; October 17 [1894]; January 17, 1895. AFP Papers. Alice's earnings are recorded in AFP and GHP, "Chronicles", AFP Papers.
117 GHP to AFP, April 10, 16, 18, and 23, 1892; AFP to GHP, April 15 and 22, 1892. AFP Papers.
118 GHP to AFP, May 30, 1890 and June 7, 1890. Similarly, GHP to AFP, September 30, 1892. AFP Papers.

By the spring of 1892, when Alice and George were both offered jobs at the newly-founded University of Chicago, there were strains in their marriage. Returning from a western lecture tour and a visit to her parents in Michigan, she wrote to him,

> Off here in the northern forests, it does seem to me that I can never again have an irritable moment, or say an impatient word, or fail to make home happy and well-cared for. I wonder why it is I am so poor a wife, so ineffective and unamiable, when I am really in the home I love so, and long for even in half a day's absence. 'If I could once determine which is me!' I have been thinking a good deal about the year which is nearly over, as I have been traveling so many days and nights. I foresee, dear, that it will seem to you when you come to the summer vacation again, very much the same dreary failure that the other years since we came home from Europe have been. It is not what you want or like and I sometimes think we had better change it all. If only I could change myself! That is what is needed, I know, and I always fancy it will come — but it does not.[119]

Alice's despondency and self-doubt about her domestic life is a striking contrast to the confidence and exuberance she exuded when she wrote about her work. Nevertheless, she was prepared to sacrifice that work to please George. She proposed that, if they did not accept the Chicago offer, they should live for a year in their country home at Boxford. George could commute to his lectures and she would have "ample excuse for resigning from everything except Wellesley"; they could reduce their expenses, and she could devote herself to the "reading and writing" George often urged her to do.

The University of Chicago Deanship, 1892–1895

The offer from the University of Chicago was a generous one that recognized George's talents as well as Alice's. The school was scheduled to open in the fall of 1892 under the presidency of William Rainey Harper. Determined to make his new university the equal of Yale, Harper attempted to attract faculty from elite Eastern schools by offering them

---

119 AFP to GHP, April 30, 1892. AFP Papers.

unusually high salaries.[120] He wanted Alice to be Dean of Women and
Professor of History and George to chair the Philosophy Department. In
his *Life of Alice*, George reported that Alice was "from the first against
accepting the offer." She did not want to go, according to George,
because she was attached to their Cambridge home and his Harvard
roots, dubious about the scholarly opportunities available at Chicago,
and eager to remain near Wellesley. Moreover, she "perhaps dreaded
the wear and tear to which she would be exposed by another absorption
in college duties." For all these reasons, George wrote, the Palmers did
not want to accept Harper's offer, although their salaries would have
been considerably higher than what they were then earning.[121]

The Palmers' correspondence suggests a different scenario, however.
It was George, not Alice, who did not want to go to Chicago. She was
looking for a way to accept the deanship while he raised a litany of
objections centering on his concern that any position at Chicago would
be less important and prestigious than what he enjoyed at Harvard. He
also feared that the university, which was founded by Baptists, would
be too sectarian. Harper made the offer to the Palmers at their house in
Cambridge on March 12, 1892. They spent a week in Chicago in early
April during George's spring recess. He went home to Cambridge while
Alice visited her parents in Michigan, gave a few lectures, and returned
to Chicago to carry out her duties as one of Massachusetts' managers for
the World's Fair of 1893.[122]

Alice and George discussed Harper's offer at length in their letters
while she was away. George had nothing positive to say about the
appointment or the university. "I don't want to go," he wrote to Alice on
April 14.[123] Throughout the month, he continued to raise objections and
warned Alice not to encourage Harper. Alice, meanwhile, was clearly
attracted by the offer. The thought of the opportunities it could open for
women made her breathless with excitement.[124] While George's friends

120 Lynn D. Gordon, *Gender and Higher Education in the Progressive Era* (New Haven:
     Yale University Press, 1990).
121 GHP, *Life*, pp. 233–34.
122 AFP and GHP, "Chronicles", AFP Papers. He did not record that she returned to
     Chicago, but it is clear from the letters they wrote to each other in April, 1892 that
     she did.
123 GHP to AFP, April 14, 1892. AFP Papers.
124 AFP to Marion Talbot, March 16, 1892. University of Chicago, Hannah Holborn
     Gray Special Collections Research Center, Marion Talbot Papers.

advised him not to take the offer, Alice's urged her to accept, believing the deanship offered her a chance to accomplish even more for women's education than what she had done at Wellesley.[125] As a graduate of a co-ed university, Alice was eager to create a supportive community for women within a large university. She was also excited to think that she and George could "be together all the time after morning office hours and have the same kind of work."[126] It was only after the barrage of negatives from George that she wrote, "everyone urges you to come, and somehow I hate to think of it! I don't see how we can."[127] She was still ambivalent at the end of April: "I must say I long to get my hands on the Woman's College, but the next moment I long to stay in our own pleasant place."[128]

In the end, George was unwilling to relocate. When Alice returned to Cambridge on May 5, he informed Harper that he could not accept the University's offer.[129] But Alice continued to explore the possibility of taking the deanship on a part-time basis and leaving George behind in Cambridge. Over the next few weeks, she spelled out the "very strict" conditions under which she would accept the job, based on lengthy conversations with George: She would come to Chicago if she were paid $3,000 per year plus travel expenses, if she could limit her time on campus to ten to twelve weeks per year, and if Marion Talbot, a Wellesley faculty member and close friend, became an assistant dean. Alice insisted that she herself must be recognized as "dean all the time": all matters pertaining to the women's department at Chicago should be referred to her, even though she would be in residence for no more than twelve weeks each year. She told Harper that George was not happy with the proposed arrangement but "would not utterly refuse consent"

---

125 AFP to GHP, April 26, 1892. AFP Papers.

126 Ibid.

127 AFP to GHP, April 22, 1892. AFP Papers.

128 AFP to GHP, April 29, 1892. AFP Papers.

129 GHP, "Chronicles", AFP Papers. Telegram from GHP to William Rainey Harper, May 5, 1892, University of Chicago, Hannah Holborn Gray Special Collections Research Center, William Rainey Harper Papers. Letter from GHP to William Rainey Harper, May 5, 1892, University of Chicago, Hannah Holborn Gray Special Collections Research Center, Office of the President, Harper, Judson and Burton Administrations Records (UC, OPHJB), https://www.lib.uchicago.edu/ead/pdf/ofcpreshjb-0066-016.pdf. On May 7, 1892, *The Harvard Crimson* published a letter from GHP that explained his desire to remain at Harvard. Reprinted in Linenthal, pp. 95–96.

if her terms on salary, title, and an assistant dean were met. George himself wrote to Harper, in the margin of Alice's letter, "I hope you will return an emphatic 'no' to my wife's proposition."[130]

The salary Alice negotiated was high for an academic, especially a woman academic.[131] George felt that a lower salary "would be below her dignity" but Alice justified it as necessary compensation for the earnings she would forgo in lecturing and writing so that she could give her full attention to the University of Chicago. She wished she could be more generous about her salary, she wrote to Harper, but explained that "it is a very bad time for us [financially]" and the money was needed to meet their expenses.[132]

Harper accepted Alice's conditions. Although there were tussles with Harper over her title and duties, George let her go.[133] She took up her new post at the end of September 1892, a few days before the school officially opened. Though many Bostonians looked down on Chicago as a backwater provincial prairie town, not everyone shared George's reservations about the new university: Harper recruited notable scholars and several former college presidents in addition to Alice to the faculty.[134]

As one of President Harper's most trusted advisors during her first two years as dean, Alice was instrumental in making the University of Chicago a supportive and stimulating environment for women students. She established rigorous academic standards for the female students, ensured that they were fully integrated into the academic life of the

---

130 AFP to William Rainey Harper, May 28, 1892 and July 16, 1892. See also, AFP to William Rainey Harper, June 25, 1892 and July 6, 1892. UC, OPHJB, https://www.lib.uchicago.edu/ead/pdf/ofcpreshjb-0066-016.pdf.

131 See Bordin, p. 233.

132 AFP to William Rainey Harper, May 28, 1892. UC, OPHJB, https://www.lib.uchicago.edu/ead/pdf/ofcpreshjb-0066-016.pdf.

133 Alice was angry and dismayed when the university calendar announced she would be "Professor of History" and "Acting Dean." She feared the announcement put her and the university in a false position by not specifying that she would be in residence on a part-time basis. She did not intend to teach history and felt the university should hire women who were better qualified than she to do so. But in the end, she left the wording of her appointment to Harper. AFP to William Rainey Harper, August 3, 1892 and August 26, 1892, UC, OPHJB, https://www.lib.uchicago.edu/ead/pdf/ofcpreshjb-0066-016.pdf.

134 Backwater: Marion Talbot, *More than Lore: Reminiscences of Marion Talbot* (Chicago: University of Chicago Press, 1936), pp. 6–7. Scholars and college presidents: John W. Boyer, *The University of Chicago: A History* (Chicago: University of Chicago Press, 2015), p. 79.

university, and encouraged Harper to hire women faculty members and pay them good salaries.[135]

Judging by the accounts she sent George, Alice tackled her responsibilities with verve and assertiveness. Irritated by the slow pace of work on the women's dormitories, she "simply ordered things done, and made myself generally disagreeable."[136] She noted that her style was a decided contrast to that of the "sweetest-tempered, long-suffering" minister who had been in charge until her arrival. "He seems amazed, and after three days, relieved, by my vigor and temper," Alice informed George.[137] Finding that President Harper was "surprised and hurt" by her objections to his plans regarding the women students, she resolved to "tell him as little as I can, and take every bit of responsibility I dare to assume. I shall take even more in the future, for I will not be responsible for such common and vulgar living."[138] Nor was she shy about confronting Harper directly, or insisting that the university trustees and benefactors change arrangements that had been agreed to before she arrived. Soon she was describing her victories in arguments over building plans, establishing rules of conduct, and staffing the women's dorms. One of her fiercest battles with Harper was over his plan to have Associate Dean Marion Talbot manage the women's dormitory instead of hiring a matron and servants. "I asked plainly if they would expect [male professors] to add to their duties of dean or of Professor the work of a janitor in the men's building, and assured them that we were worth much more to them in other work than in training waitresses and answering doorbells," she reported to George, adding that she had been prepared to resign over the issue.[139]

Alice's accounts belie George's depiction of her as a woman whose "sweet lips" could not form the words "you shall", and who needed him to "fight off oppressors."[140] Far from shrinking from challenges, she thrived on them, as she had at Wellesley. "I *am* glad to be doing this work," she assured George. Sketching the magnitude of the tasks to be done

---

135 Trusted advisor: Bordin, pp. 250, 258. Environment for women: Gordon, *Gender*, p. 89. See also, Bordin, pp. 241–42.
136 AFP to GHP, September 23, 1892. AFP Papers.
137 AFP to GHP, September 25, 1892. AFP Papers.
138 Ibid.
139 AFP to GHP, September 29, 1892. AFP Papers.
140 GHP to AFP, September 25, 1892. AFP Papers.

and the difficulty of extracting the necessary money from the fiscally conservative trustees, she noted, "But the situation is interesting — and to be *conquered*. I am feeling very well, and cheerful."[141] A year later, her enthusiasm had not waned.[142] When she was back in Cambridge, she missed her Chicago work and was unhappy at not being able to oversee developments personally.[143]

When Alice started at the University of Chicago, George was pleased that she had found her "proper work" that made full use of her talents.[144] He had no regrets, however, about his refusal to join her. "From your letters I get an impression of second rate things all about you, and am glad we chose to stay in Cambridge," he wrote soon after Alice arrived in Chicago. Several weeks later, he commented, "It is as if a lot of green hands had undertaken to sail a ship."[145] The unspoken message was the same as when he refused to come to Wellesley: conditions which were perfectly suited to Alice's talents were insufficient for his.

Alice usually spent a month at the university in the fall and the winter and several weeks in the spring; she came out at other times as needed. George accompanied her for a week or ten days on some of these trips, but most of the time she was in Chicago, he remained in Cambridge. He initially insisted he was "quite ready to stand my full share of the hardship" that her absences would cause.[146] Convinced that they had forged a joint personality, he was confident that she took a part of him with her. "So away or near we are hand in hand," George comforted himself soon after Alice set off for Chicago.[147] While others might think what they saw was "all" Alice, George knew that he himself was "inextricably twined with it."

141 AFP to GHP [October 9, 1892], and September 25, 1892. Emphasis in the originals. AFP Papers.
142 AFP to GHP, October 3, 1893. AFP Papers.
143 AFP to Marion Talbot, October 30, 1892, University of Chicago, Marian Talbot Papers. Alice told President Harper that she wanted to do more for him and wished she could be more involved in university affairs when she was not physically present on campus. AFP to William Rainey Harper, December 1, 1892. UC, OPHJB, https://www.lib.uchicago.edu/ead/pdf/ofcpreshjb-0066-016.pdf.
144 GHP to AFP, September 25, 1892. AFP Papers.
145 GHP to AFP, September 30, 1892 and October 4, 1892. AFP Papers.
146 GHP to AFP, September 25, 1892; similarly, GHP to AFP, January 3, 1893. AFP Papers.
147 GHP to AFP, September. 30, 1892. AFP Papers.

Time away from each other also increased the sense of romance that was so important to the Palmers. After seven years of married life, George marveled that they had preserved the magic of courtship.[148] "To me you are always a subject of romance," he wrote Alice. "To see your step in the entry or to see you crossing a room is still to get a touch of fairyland." Alice wrote him that she could "never half understand how much I love and admire you until I am too far away to talk about it." He confessed, "I sometimes think these catastrophes [their separations] almost desirable, they reveal so how dearly we love each other. I see your loved figure more in our Boxford fields when you are away than when you are with me."[149] Moreover, he felt the role reversal that took place when Alice was away brought them closer together. "Is it not amusing how we exchange functions?" he asked during the first week she was in Chicago. "You sometimes run a college and I a kitchen, and again I appear as the director of youth and you of servants. It makes our partnership a rich one that we each can comprehend and even perform the other's tasks."[150]

Her first homecoming from the university in October 1892 was "a simple delight" and George sent his thanks for returning her in such good condition, Alice informed Harper.[151] Nevertheless, George's forbearance soon wore thin. Every quarterly trip for the first two years of Alice's time in Chicago involved an exchange of letters in which George angrily pressed her to come home while Alice pleaded that she needed to stay. Their correspondence in 1893 was typical. "I know how busy you are; but feel sure if you should wait to finish your business, I should never see you again," George complained after Alice had been away for ten days in the spring. Two days later, coping with the disruptions caused

---

148 George explained to his younger cousin, Robert Herrick, "After my wedding mother whispered to me as I kissed her goodbye, 'keep on courting, George' — a sagacious bit of advice, too little thought of." GHP to Robert Herrick, May 24, 1894, RH Papers. As discussed in Chapter 3, Herrick would later have a years-long affair with Elsie Clews Parsons.

149 AFP to GHP, March 1, 1891; GHP to AFP, August 27, 1901. AFP Papers.

150 GHP to AFP, September 23, 1892. AFP Papers.

151 AFP to William Rainey Harper, October 26, 1892. UC, OPHJB, https://www.lib.uchicago.edu/ead/pdf/ofcpreshjb-0066-016.pdf.

by a servant's illness, he insisted, "I really cannot wait much longer to see you." Four days later, Alice was back in Cambridge.[152]

Despite his good intentions, George came to resent both the domestic inconvenience and the lack of attention that Alice's absences caused him. He was happy planning menus, hosting friends and family, and orchestrating house renovations and decoration when she was gone, but he did not want to cope with servants' illnesses and feuds, or hire and train new servants.[153] Those tasks should be Alice's job, not his, he felt. And he was affronted when she missed a talk he gave as part of a prestigious lecture series at Harvard.

George acutely missed Alice's companionship. He drew his feeling of self-worth from his surroundings, and when she was not there to agree with and encourage him, he began to question his own importance. Left to his own devices, he suffered "a sense of my own worthlessness, and impotence" and began to feel that his "seeming dignity is a hollow sham."[154] Short partings increased the Palmers' affection for each other, but longer absences undermined their relationship.

The tensions resulted, on occasion, in open conflict. George wrote apologetically after an argument during Alice's first year at Chicago, "I fully recognize how difficult your situation is, pulled as you are in many directions [...]. Do not think I ever rudely blame you[,] darling." Nevertheless, his sense of injury was strong: "But when things seem to me to be drifting in a bad direction and I think I ought to pull you round to consider with me how the hard time may be stemmed, it makes me sore to do it. We are made to enjoy together; and then hard business exigencies arise, requiring us to balance conflicting considerations and to urge opposing claims, and both of us shrink from the seeming clash and by that very act make it greater."[155]

---

152 GHP to AFP, April 24, 26, 1893. See also, GHP to AFP, October 5, 1893; GHP to AFP, June 2, 1890. AFP Papers.

153 Illnesses: GHP to AFP, April 26, 1893; new servants: GHP to AFP, June 2, 1890. AFP Papers.

154 GHP to AFP, January 13, 1892 and April 11, 1894. See also, GHP to AFP, January 11, 1894. AFP Papers.

155 GHP to AFP, January 3, 1893. AFP Papers. On December 20, 1892, Alice had written a long letter to President Harper, laying out the personal difficulties (George's teaching schedule and the illness of several of his relatives) that would make it difficult for her to come to Chicago in early January and attend convocation as Harper now proposed. Instead, she hoped to come for several weeks in late January

The part-time arrangement created difficulties in Alice's job as well as in her personal life. Her attempts to schedule her Chicago terms of residence to suit George's schedule annoyed Harper without appeasing George, and she felt that her absences from the university reduced her effectiveness and left her poorly informed about what was happening on campus.[156] Letters were delayed, and people did not always follow up on the instructions Alice left. She did not always agree with President Harper, and let him know it. Over time, he became less likely to consult her about academic appointments and university policy and tended to treated her as more of a fundraiser than an advisor.[157]

Alice was dissatisfied enough to consider resigning from Chicago in the spring of 1894. She toyed with the idea of becoming the superintendent of schools for Boston. Friends urged her to return to Wellesley which was looking for a new president.[158] Yet when she broached the idea of resigning to George, he strongly opposed it. Arguing that it would be difficult to find another position that "could compare in power or dignity" with her work at Chicago, he urged her not to give it up and lectured her about professional responsibility:

> Every species of work has its hardships. And certainly you cannot feel these separations as more keenly than I do. But I do not know an occupation for you which presents so little hardship as this. It brings the least possible damage to ability, health, reputation, tastes. We have our living to make and our future to provide for. From time to time I want you to have a year of rest and I want to take it with you. But I do not want you to sit about the house at the absolute mercy of committees, callers, and alpaca women.[159] [...] That is not dignified. We have always held that in the best marriage both husband and wife should have a clear and serious profession and should cooperate in support of the family. If we had plenty of money, I should be unwilling to see you living without connected work. It is unwholesome for bodily and mental health. Rest is important and we can preserve three months for it in the summer, and if

---

with George. See also, AFP to William Rainey Harper, November 22, 1892. UC, OPHJB, https://www.lib.uchicago.edu/ead/pdf/ofcpreshjb-0066-017.pdf.

156 AFP to J. Laurence Laughlin, Thanksgiving Day 1892; December 21, 1892; and June 13, 1894. AFP to GHP, April 19, 1894 and January 15, 1895. AFP Papers.

157 Bordin, pp. 255–56.

158 AFP to GHP, April 2, 1894. AFP Papers.

159 In the late nineteenth century, women of taste and means wore alpaca dresses, made of very soft wool from sheep raised in Peru. George was undoubtedly referring to the women who donated to the many causes for which Alice raised funds.

we need more can take a year of it a year hence. The mode of your work of course you must settle for yourself. I do not insist on the Chicago post. I only say to you what you would say to Robert [Herrick] or to anyone who wasn't a woman. 'Don't give up a place which offers tolerably good work until you see your way to something better.' Because he is tired of a certain job a man doesn't drop it and trust to luck for the future.[160]

George's advice is startling. Given his complaints about Alice's absences, it is surprising that he did not leap at the chance to have her back home full-time. Moreover, his insistence that both husband and wife should have "a clear and serious profession" and contribute to the household income, along with his dismissal of volunteer work as undignified, make a powerful argument for dual career marriages that is completely at odds with his views when he was courting Alice. It is possible that George's ideas had genuinely developed, either in response to Alice's tutelage or as a result of seeing the effects of enforced idleness on her. But the attitudes he expressed in his biography of Alice suggest this was not the case.

George urged Alice to keep her job at the University of Chicago in 1894 not because, as his letter suggested, he had become an advocate of professional careers for married women in general, but because her salary was needed to pay for the renovations he planned for the Quincy Street house. Throughout the spring, he had been exceedingly anxious about how he would pay the large cost of the work he had ordered.[161] His letter should be interpreted as a challenge to Alice. Very likely, he was echoing what she had been saying to him for years to justify her career. He was, in effect, calling her bluff. The point was not lost on Alice. She agreed, rather unhappily, to remain at Chicago for another year.[162] George responded with relief. He sympathized with her dissatisfactions but insisted, "hard for us both as it is, it is easier than nothing" and launched into another discussion of their precarious financial position.[163]

George's letter was equally paradoxical on a second point. In stressing that he was giving Alice the same advice that she would give

---

160 GHP to AFP, April 4, 1894. AFP Papers.

161 GHP to AFP, April 3, 1894; AFP to GHP, April 5, 1894. AFP Papers.

162 AFP to GHP, April 7, 1894 and April 15, 1894. She had informed Harper on April 14 that she would stay for just one more year, she wrote to George on April 15, 1894. AFP Papers.

163 GHP to AFP, April 10, 1894. AFP Papers.

to a male colleague, he was telling her that if she wanted a professional career, she should act like a professional — that is, like a man. Yet he himself did not always treat her as a professional. He gave her verbal encouragement in her career but repeatedly denigrated the institutions and causes she worked for, tried to limit the amount of work she took on, and pressured her to return home. No male professional would be expected to interrupt his work and come home because his spouse was lonely, or counseled to cut back his working hours and delegate responsibility to others as George consistently urged Alice to do.

Discouraged by George's reaction, Alice told Harper in April that she was not interested in becoming Boston's School Superintendent. But a month later, after she returned to Cambridge, she was reconsidering. She assured Harper that she was committed to him and the University, but wondered whether he might prefer to use her salary for more important purposes. Reminding him that she would not stay longer than another year, when she and George planned to go abroad for his sabbatical leave, she urged Harper to tell her candidly whether she should remain at the University of Chicago, "especially now that such important work waits me here, if I were free to take it."[164]

Two days later, George sent his own letter to Harper, pressing him to tell Alice what she should do. He stressed the advantages of the Superintendent's job for the Palmers: it would be a permanent position, allow Alice to remain in Cambridge, and pay her $1,000 more than the Chicago deanship. (George was always eager to take advantage of financial opportunities.) But if Harper wanted Alice to stay, George assured him she would continue to work "delightedly" for the University. Harper's advice, scrawled on the back of George's letter was that she should "do both — to take the Boston work on the understanding that we will release her in one year."[165]

There is no further mention of the Superintendent's job in the Palmers' correspondence. Alice stayed at the University of Chicago for another year, but it was not a happy time for her. In late May, 1894, she had an acute attack of peritonitis (a dangerous infection of the soft lining of

164 AFP to William Rainey Harper, May 9 [1894]. UC, OPHJB, https://www.lib. uchicago.edu/ead/pdf/ofcpreshjb-0066-017.pdf.
165 GHP to William Rainey Harper, May 11, 1894. UC, OPHJB, https://www.lib. uchicago.edu/ead/pdf/ofcpreshjb-0066-017.pdf.

the abdomen) that left her unable to work and travel for several weeks.[166] Increasingly unhappy with President Harper's leadership, increasingly doubtful about her own effectiveness, and missing George more acutely, Alice began to look for ways to shorten her stays in Chicago.[167] George, heavily involved in the Quincy Street house renovations, became more stoical about her absences. He stopped urging her to cut her visits short and admitted that he found their separations far less painful than formerly, when he had been "incapacitated for work."[168]

Alice's letters to George in early 1895 suggest that she came to view her time at the University of Chicago as something of a failure. She was chagrined that her resignation, formally submitted in late December 1894 or early 1895, was greeted with silence from Harper.[169] Her letter of resignation noted that she had come to Chicago more often, spent more time there, and taken less compensation than originally agreed to, but she left with "keen regret" and "most happy memories" of serving with Harper. Others praised her work when they learned she was leaving, but Alice felt she was "not in favor" with Harper, and regretted that they had lost the "mutual confidence" that was essential to her role.[170] They clashed over staffing and academic requirements. He was "very annoyed" with her for having recommended a University of Chicago faculty member for a position at another university; she was put off by his "highhanded" management style and found him to be a "coarse, selfish person."[171] Her experience at Chicago undermined

---

166 AFP to William Rainey Harper, June 6, 1894 and June 13, 1894. UC, OPHJB, https://www.lib.uchicago.edu/ead/pdf/ofcpreshjb-0066-017.pdf. She felt pressured by Harper to resume work before she was fully recovered. AFP to J. Laurence Laughlin, June 13, 1894. AFP Papers.

167 AFP to GHP, April 19, 1894; AFP to GHP [October 9, 1894]. AFP Papers.

168 GHP to AFP, January 11, 1895. Similarly, GHP to AFP, January 11, 1894; September 30, 1894; April 1, 1895. AFP Papers.

169 AFP to GHP, January 3, 1895 and January 8, 1895. AFP Papers. In an undated letter sent to Harper, Alice told him her formal resignation was enclosed and provided him with an account of what she had accomplished at the University of Chicago in collaboration with others. AFP to William Rainey Harper [1895], UC, OPHJB, https://www.lib.uchicago.edu/ead/pdf/ofcpreshjb-0066-017.pdf. There is a copy or draft of a resignation letter, dated December 1894, in the GHP Papers.

170 Praise from others: AFP to GHP, January 8, 1895 and January 9, 1985. Not in favor: AFP to GHP, Friday morning [January 4, 1895?]. AFP Papers. See also, GHP to AFP, January 7, 1895. Mutual confidence: AFP to GHP, January 15, 1895. AFP Papers.

171 Very annoyed: AFP to GHP, Friday morning [January 5, 1895?]. Highhanded management: AFP to GHP, January 10, 1895. Coarse and selfish: AFP to GHP,

her professional confidence and made her more eager to return to a warm, supportive home environment. Possibly, too, George's increased willingness to tolerate her absences made her anxious to ensure that she remained central in his life.

Alice left the University of Chicago in April 1895, as she had left Wellesley, with no clear plan for future employment. A few weeks earlier both Palmers had been offered chaired positions at the University of Michigan by President James Angell, Alice's early mentor. George quickly replied that they could not accept. He was unwilling to leave Harvard's prestigious philosophy department, and did not want to forgo the generous pension for which he would soon be eligible, he explained.[172] After her experience at Chicago, Alice must have been reluctant to consider another part-time arrangement, however appealing it might have been to return to her beloved *alma mater*. Her departure from Chicago marks the end of her active professional career in academia and her full transition to volunteer activities supplemented with paid lecturing. But first the Palmers turned their sights to a sabbatical year in Europe.

Creating a Companionate Marriage

During the years that Alice lectured around the country and worked at the University of Chicago, one might conclude the Palmers came close to achieving Alice's ideal of companionate equality. Her work and travels proclaimed her to be an independent person in her own right, with interests and responsibilities separate from George and their home. George had to accept that that his own comfort and convenience

---

January 9, 1895. AFP Papers. Harper continued to disappoint Alice. She rearranged her busy schedule so she could give a speech at the University of Chicago's tenth anniversary celebration in 1901, but she was annoyed that Harper's invitation came just six weeks before the event. (William Rainey Harper to AFP, May 2, 1901; May 21, 1901; June 1, 1901. AFP to William Rainey Harper, May 7, 1901 and May 28, 1901. UC, OPHJB, https://www.lib.uchicago.edu/ead/pdf/ofcpreshjb-0066-017.pdf.)When the university did not award her an honorary degree, George observed, "If you had been half as famous and a man, [Harper] would have done so." GHP to AFP, June 21, 1901. AFP Papers.

172 GHP to James B. Angell, March 31, 1895. Bentley Historical Library, University of Michigan, James B. Angell Papers, http://quod.lib.umich.edu/a/angell/851644.0004.023/62.

did not necessarily come first. Many of the things George did for Alice were exactly the things helpmate wives did for their husbands in the nineteenth century.[173] When she was away from Cambridge, he answered her correspondence, met with her colleagues, represented her in meetings, and took care of the household. He drafted at least one of her speeches and edited her manuscripts. He prided himself on the role reversal that took place when she was in Chicago because it made him feel closer to her.

From the standpoint of creating a companionate marriage, George's efforts to share were admirable. But from the standpoint of establishing an equal marriage, they are alarming. For George, sharing was likely to mean shaping and molding Alice, doing things *for* her not *with* her, and leading her rather than making joint decisions. The Palmers' ideas of companionate marriage did not directly challenge Victorian norms of male dominance and female submission. On the contrary, George clung to the notion that every woman — even a strong and independent woman — was a child who needed a man's protection and guidance. Both Alice and George worked hard to restore the traditional balance of power that was undermined by her work.

At some level, both Alice and George understood that she had to have considerable autonomy in her professional life. When George felt President Harper was misrepresenting the terms of Alice's appointment at the University of Chicago, he urged her to make Harper rectify the error. But he acknowledged that it was her decision, not his.[174] When she was first considering resigning from Chicago, he advised against it, but conceded, "The mode of your work of course you must settle for yourself. I do not insist on the Chicago post."[175]

Nevertheless, George was as eager to impose his stamp on Alice's professional life as on her domestic world. When she expressed unhappiness with the way she was depicted in an official portrait that was being painted for Wellesley, he set off for New York to see the picture for himself; he intended to fire the artist if the portrait was not

---

173 See Introduction, p. 7 and M. Jeanne Peterson, *Family, Love and Work in the Lives of Victorian Gentlewomen* (Bloomington: Indiana University Press, 1989).

174 GHP to AFP, September 24, 1893. AFP Papers.

175 GHP to AFP, April 4, 1894. AFP Papers.

what he and Alice wanted.[176] Because he valued scholarship more than administrative work, and the written word more than the spoken word, George encouraged Alice to commit her thoughts to paper and not just give lectures and serve on committees.[177] Concerned about her health, he persistently admonished her to do less, conserve her energy, and get more rest.

He was particularly insistent — even intrusive — in his attempts to reduce her workload. Very early in their courtship, he — unbeknownst to Alice — lobbied the Wellesley Trustees to create a new position of dean to take charge of all the College's correspondence that required judgement and discretion, freeing Alice from a time-consuming task.[178] After they married, he pressured her not to take on causes and activities he did not think worthy of her, such as reading student theses and raising money for Italian immigrants.[179] When she became Dean of Women at the University of Chicago, he pressured her to resign from all her other activities except Wellesley, including her position on the Massachusetts Board of Managers for the World's Fair.[180] Two years later, he encouraged the Women's Education Association to elect someone other than Alice as its president.[181] Answering her correspondence when she was away, he turned down numerous requests for her to lecture without consulting her.[182] He repeatedly instructed her to reduce the social engagements that were part of her lecture tours and filled her evenings in Chicago, despite the fact that they provided opportunities for the networking and relationship building that were critical aspects of her working life.[183] When he joined her in Chicago (typically, not more than once a year), he instructed her to strictly limit the number of evenings they went out.[184]

---

176 GHP to AFP, December 16, 1889. AFP Papers.
177 GHP, *Life*, p. 9. GHP to AFP, May 16, 1890. AFP Papers.
178 GHP to AF [July 1886], AFP Papers. GHP to Mrs. Claflin [n.d.], GHP Papers.
179 GHP TO AFP, April 13, 1892. GHP, *Life*, pp. 254–55. Similarly, GHP to AFP, June 7, 1891. AFP Papers.
180 GHP to AFP, April 24, 1892; GHP to AFP, October 19, 1892; February 3, 1893; and November 24, 1893. AFP Papers.
181 GHP to AFP, January 15, 1894. AFP Papers. GHP, *Life*, p. 226.
182 GHP to AFP, February 8, 1893, and November 24, 1893. AFP Papers.
183 GHP to AFP, June 7, 1890; GHP to AFP, April 18, 1894. AFP Papers.
184 GHP to AFP, April 18, 1894; GHP to AFP, January 8, 1895 and January 12, 1895. AFP Papers.

George's attempts to protect Alice from stress and overwork and shoulder responsibilities for her were a way of reestablishing the husbandly dominance that was undermined by her professional life. His efforts were demeaning as well as constraining because they suggested that she was incapable of looking after herself or making wise decisions on her own. The clear implication was that he knew better than she what was right for her. "Every good woman is in danger of over-helpfulness," he wrote in his biography of Alice. "Recognizing this beautiful danger, after our marriage I constituted myself her watchdog and barked violently at whatever suspicious persons I saw approach. It pleases me to think that by such hostilities I cut off a quarter of her labors, the least important quarter."[185] He was undermining Alice's position as a professional trained to be independent and authoritative. But he saw his efforts as expressions of his tender, loving care.

Alice's reactions to George's need to control were complex. In the domestic sphere, she tended to defer to George without argument. Even if she disagreed with him, she acquiesced, using the traditional language of wifely submission and subordination. "You are to decide what you believe to be the wisest, and I shall be content," was a typical response.[186] She was less inclined to follow his lead professionally. George claimed in his *Life of Alice* that "although occasionally chafing under the restraint, she on the whole saw my usefulness [in limiting her activities] and rewarded me with adequate thanks."[187] However, on many occasions Alice simply ignored his instructions and did as she thought best. She stayed longer in Chicago or on a lecture tour than George liked (although not as long as she wanted to stay). She often failed to inform him about her travel plans. She accepted work projects and lecture invitations that he thought were a waste of time. She did not resign from all her other activities when she took the Chicago position in 1892, and she took on a new one: raising money to create an endowment for the Harvard Annex, with the understanding that it would be incorporated within Harvard University and the women students would receive Harvard degrees. (George was equally committed to this project, followed its progress closely, and represented her at meetings on its behalf when

---

185 GHP, *Life*, p. 319.
186 AFP to GHP, May 29, 1890. AFP Papers.
187 GHP, *Life*, p. 319.

she was in Chicago.)[188] Although Alice sometimes expressed interest in writing more (as George urged) and collaborating with him on a project, she never did. The one time George prevailed upon Alice, a brilliant extemporaneous speaker, to prepare for a lecture as he did — committing every word to paper, with extensive rewriting — rather than speaking from notes as was her custom, she gave the worst performance of her public speaking career. After that, she banned him from attending her lectures.[189]

Nonetheless, Alice never asserted that she had the *right* to make her own decisions or act independently when she and George disagreed. On the contrary, she undercut her displays of independence by the way she justified her behavior. Instead of claiming the prerogative to stay away until her work was completed, she told George that if knew the full circumstances, he would not object. "I am having a chance to do so much just now that I can never do again that you would say 'stay' if you were here," she assured him.[190] After receiving several "petulant" letters from him during her first weeks at the University of Chicago campus, she insisted it was duty rather than pleasure or ambition that kept her in Chicago.[191] She tried to deflect George's annoyance by flattering his vanity and emphasizing her own inadequacies. Noting how frequently the faculty and administration at Chicago observed that George's expertise would have solved many of the university's problems, she wrote, "It would have settled everything if you had come, and [put] everything right. I only fumble at trying to do what you would have been an expert at, and it gives me a great ache over it."[192] A double meaning is unmistakable: not only would it have "settled everything" for the university had George accepted Chicago's offer, it would also have made Alice's life much easier.

Alice was employing a strategy known as "reframing." Reframing occurs when a woman or man violates conventional expectations about gender roles and then redefines the behavior in a way that fits the accepted standards. By allowing gender roles to be simultaneously broken and

---

188 The women successfully raised the $250,000, but Harvard reneged on the agreement.
189 GHP, *Life*, pp. 257, 259; GHP to AFP, October 18, 1892 and April 21, 1902. AFP Papers.
190 AFP to GHP, October 10, 1893. AFP Papers.
191 GHP to AFP, October 18 and 19, 1892; AFP to GHP, October 21, 1892. AFP Papers.
192 AFP to GHP, October 21, 1892. Also, AFP to GHP, February 14, 1893. AFP Papers.

kept in place, reframing helps to reduce the violator's guilt and also protects her or him from criticism.[193] The concept of reframing helps to make sense of the contradictions that are so prominent in the Palmers' relationship — contradictions between what was done and what was said, and between the implicit and explicit messages embodied in the couple's behavior. The Palmers were reframing when George assumed a manager's role in Alice's work, announcing he would help decide where she would lecture, what activities she should take on, and the terms of her contract with the University of Chicago. Alice repeatedly asked for his advice on troublesome issues of college administration and used him as a sounding board for her ideas. Downplaying her own expertise, she frequently assumed the part of a helpless female vis-à-vis George. "I *need* you so," she wrote him during her first trip to Chicago. "I *can't* discuss all these great questions without you."[194] By asking for George's advice and guidance, belittling her own abilities, and praising his superior judgment and experience, Alice was acknowledging her inferiority and trying to restore the traditional gender-based balance of power. When George expressed interest in editing an article Alice was writing, he implied that she needed his help in order to make her writing sufficiently clear and forceful. The unstated assumption was that he was rescuing her, not merely polishing her material. In contrast, when a nineteenth-century wife performed the same tasks for an overworked husband, it was understood that she was relieving him of activities that were too tedious or too trivial for his concern, so that he could devote himself to more important work.

The way the Palmers handled Alice's earnings was another kind of reframing. What she earned was treated not as "her" money, although she had the legal right to it, but as "his."[195] Alice did not hesitate to note that, when she took on additional work, she was bringing home money to pay for his library and the painters' bills, expenditures that mattered a great deal to George.[196] For her, the money had a different meaning:

---

193 Lystra, pp. 142–43. Lystra limits her discussion of reframing to the way nineteenth-century courting couples represented their actions in letters to each other, but the concept can be applied to a range of behaviors.

194 AFP to GHP [October 9, 1892]. Emphasis in the original. AFP Papers.

195 Starting in 1855, Massachusetts allowed women the right to control their earnings, own and sell real and personal property, and make wills.

196 For example, AFP to GHP, January 11, 1894. AFP Papers.

it symbolized independence. Returning from a lecture, she proudly announced, "I have $25 in my purse which you did not put in, sir!"[197]

The Palmers also upheld the traditional power dynamic by assigning Alice's work secondary status compared to George's. After she left Wellesley, her work could be seen as less important than his because it was part-time and paid less. George always made it clear that her institutional affiliations and colleagues were far inferior to his at Harvard. Nor would he consider giving up his own prestigious position in order to open professional opportunities for her.

Most significantly, Alice did not try to carry over into her domestic life the kind of independence she exercised in her professional life. At home, she remained the model of a submissive wife. In the domestic sphere, their interactions were neither mutual nor equal. On the contrary, George used his interest in domestic concerns and household routines to shape Alice's tastes and impose his views on her. It was George who made the decisions and George's tastes that predominated in the Palmers' homes. Indeed, Alice may have been all the more willing to cede decision making in the domestic sphere because this arrangement left her freer to work and travel.

In the long run, the Palmers' attempts at reframing were only partially successful, and more successful for George than for Alice. Despite all evidence to the contrary, he continued to see her as the epitome of Patmore's "angel in the house" and refused to acknowledge the ways in which she failed to fit that image. Beset by pressures from two sides, Alice had a much more difficult time. The strain of trying to reconcile the role George expected her to play and the life she actually led was increased by the strain of trying to do a full-time job on a part-time schedule. She eventually succumbed to George's pressure, gave up paid professional positions, and settled into a life in which George and their home took priority over her volunteer activities. After Alice gave up her position at Chicago, she had few defenses against his intrusive devotion. In the end, George's concept of marital "oneness" overpowered her interest in creating a partnership of equals, each of whom contributed different strengths to a mutual life. Mutuality did not translate into a sustainable equality in the Palmer marriage because it

---

197 AFP to GHP, April 1, 1894. AFP Papers.

was overwhelmed by George's subtle but indefatigable efforts to shape and control Alice. Their marriage suggests that reframing was more effective as a strategy for masking occasional lapses from nineteenth-century gender stereotypes than in legitimizing long-term, on-going behavior that was fundamentally at odds with prescribed gender roles.

Domestic Life and Volunteer Activities, 1895–1902

The Palmers spent the first year after Alice left the University of Chicago traveling in Europe during George's sabbatical in 1895–96. After they returned to Cambridge, Alice devoted herself to a rich and expanding array of volunteer activities with national, state, and local education organizations, consolidating her position as the most influential force in women's education.[198] College presidents from all over the country — as many as four in a single day in March 1900 — came to the Quincy Street house to consult with her. She gave advice about administrative issues, academic standards and appointments, and student life. Using her extensive networks, she helped to place talented women in teaching and administrative positions in colleges and universities across the country.[199] She still gave lectures, mostly in the Northeast, and earned an average of $200 per month in lecture fees between October and March of every year between 1897 and 1900.[200]

As a Wellesley trustee, Alice continued to play a major role in setting the college's academic and administrative policy.[201] As a member of the Massachusetts State Board of Education, she helped raise standards in the state's teacher-training schools and became an effective advocate for public education in the state legislature. She worked on behalf of Italian immigrants and attending legislative hearings on a wide range of social issues that she believed teachers of inner-city children needed to address. As a leader of the Association of Collegiate Alumnae (ACA) and the Women's Education Association (WEA), she remained a

---

198 Influence: Solomon, "Alice", p. 6; Antler, pp. 55–57; Bordin, p. 285.
199 William H. P. Faunce, "Address" in Association of Collegiate Alumnae, *Alice Freeman Palmer: In Memoriam* (Boston: Marymount Press, 1903), p. 37; Antler, p. 55.
200 Lectures and earnings: AFP and GHP, "Chronicles", AFP Papers; AFP to Elizabeth Freeman, August 8, 1897, AFP Papers. AFP to GHP, February 1, 1897; October 13 [1897]; April 26, 1898, GHP Papers. AFP to GHP, December 13, 1901, AFP Papers.
201 Antler, p. 55. See also Palmieri, *In Adamless Eden*, pp. 36–47.

tireless advocate, spokesperson, and fundraiser for women's collegiate education. She worked with the staff of the Massachusetts Statistics Commission to develop data about the post-college life of female college graduates in order to debunk claims that higher education ruined women's health and chances of marrying.

Alice's days were packed with an exhausting schedule of appointments and calls with co-workers, educators, donors, college faculty and administrators; with committee meetings, legislative hearings, and board sessions; and with luncheons and receptions that doubled as business meetings. She shuttled back and forth between Cambridge, Boston, and Wellesley by train and subway. Sometimes she worked into the night and skipped social or cultural engagements so she could prepare a lecture, write a report, or catch up on letter writing. Like many prominent women of her day, she used her position as a hostess to advance the educational and civic causes she worked for. Between October 1899 and March 1900, she scheduled weekly "at homes"; hosted a reception for Radcliffe College's senior class and "a hundred ladies of special distinction"; held numerous suppers and luncheons, and gave five formal dinner parties. She did not shrink from the more humdrum tasks of volunteer work: she and a colleague hand-addressed 500 invitations for a fundraiser, and she advised Harvard faculty wives about acquiring silver tea sets and white tablecloths for college teas. She hemmed curtains while she conversed with callers.[202]

What Alice did not do was to become a champion for highly-educated, professionally-trained, middle-class wives who sought institutional positions or paid employment. She never publicly embraced the identity of a working wife or championed the interests of working wives in the way that she advocated for the needs of unmarried female scholars and teachers. As the chair of the ACA's fellowship committee, and President of the WEA, she raised scholarship money to send American college graduates to European graduate schools, at a time when very few universities in the US awarded the PhD degree. She emphasized that such support could protect women against the claims of a "sick brother" or a "lonely mother" — obligations that young women had

---

202 Her volunteer activities: AFP to GHP, October 13, 1897, GHP Papers. AFP to GHP, January 30, 1902, AFP Papers. GHP, *Life*, p. 8; AFP, "Diary March 1900" (written for a Harvard University time capsule), reprinted in Linenthal, pp. 157–98.

fewer defenses against than their male counterparts. She personally counselled a Wellesley graduate not to give up her newly launched career in order to care for a widowed brother and his child.[203]

Nevertheless, despite her own experience as a wife who struggled to carry out a demanding job and keep her husband happy, Alice did not seek to protect working wives from the claims of lonely or irritable husbands. Nor did she trumpet the life she lived as a professional and a wife. When she wrote a short autobiography for a time capsule documenting everyday life in 1900, she did not mention her years as Dean of Women at the University of Chicago — a striking omission.[204] Instead of focusing on opportunities for married women's employment, Alice's public addresses and published essays emphasized the unique contributions that well-educated, middle-class wives could make as volunteers for civic and social causes. Identifying these women as "the only leisured class in this country", Alice believed they had an obligation to "take on much of the unremunerated work of society, in education, in charity, in reform."[205] This was the message she wanted married women college graduates to put into practice, and this was the life she modelled after she left the University of Chicago.

In these years, the Palmers' life came closest to the way George portrayed it in his *Life of Alice*. Alice was very busy, but her volunteer activities did not make the same demands on George that her Wellesley presidency and her University of Chicago deanship had done. Despite her many commitments, she performed the expected role of a faculty wife: she hosted George's students and faculty colleagues, joined the requisite social clubs, and listened raptly to George's public lectures and the occasional sermons he preached at the university chapel.[206]

The letters Alice and George wrote to each other when they were apart indicate that the emotional intensity, physical passion, and romance of their early years persisted and gave both of them great happiness. "Our intimacy seems never to have been more tender or trusting than this fall. You never seemed to me more lovely in person

---

203 Undated letters to unnamed recipients, reprinted in GHP, *Life*, pp. 268–70, 273.

204 AFP, "Autobiographical Sketch (1900)", in Linenthal, pp. 14–16.

205 Alice Freeman Palmer, "What Women Can Do for the Public Schools", *The Independent* 50 (August 4, 1898), 301–04.

206 GHP, *Life*; Charles Herbert, "Mrs. Palmer as an Acquaintance", *Boston Evening Transcript*, December 10, 1902; AFP, "Diary March 1900", in Linenthal, pp. 157–98.

or character, or more exquisitely suited to make life rich and daily rejoicing," George rhapsodized in 1897. His letter crossed with her own paean of happiness, "What a beautiful life we do have! I think of it more and more, especially when I am away from you, and I long to be there again. It is simply exceptional, and I see that it is understood to be so, more and more. No one else is like you dear. No one."[207]

Others saw the Palmers' domestic life as blissfully tranquil. Lucy Sprague, lovingly referred to by Alice as "my only daughter," lived with the Palmers from 1896 to 1900 while attending Radcliffe College. Her portrait of the Palmers' home life highlights what George sketched in detail in his *Life of Alice* — a happy, loving couple united in work and play; evenings spent listening to George reading poetry and plays aloud (another guest marveled that George took all the parts when a Shakespeare play was read); summers and occasional weekends spent working on the grounds of their beloved Boxford home. Although Lucy remembered Alice as frequently "sputtering about something George would or wouldn't do," her account of the Palmers' home life gives no hint of hidden tensions or inner conflicts. She described Alice as a vibrant, capable woman, serious and fun-loving by turns, always ready for a "spree" no matter how busy her schedule. Lucy admired George and the intellectual atmosphere he created in the home, but she found him self-important and sententious, and thought his sister-in-law's nickname for him — "the little Almighty" — notably apt.[208]

Alice seemed to have created a seamless blend of volunteer activities and domestic life, but her characteristic ambivalence is still discernible. Although she extolled the life she and George lived in Cambridge, her accolades can sound flat, formulaic, and platitudinous. "I cannot imagine a happier or more interesting life than we live, in the place of all in the world where we wish to be, doing the work we wish to do," she wrote in her autobiographical summary for the Harvard time capsule in 1900. In contrast to George's rhapsodic accounts of summers at Boxford, Alice's description of her summer activities makes her sound like a

---

207 GHP to AFP, November 2, 1897; AFP to GHP, November 2, 1897, GHP Papers. GHP to AFP, June 16, 1901; AFP to GHP, June 24, 1901, AFP Papers. On their physical intimacy: GHP to AFP, January 23, 1901 and January 24, 1901. AFP Papers.

208 Mitchell, *Two Lives*, pp. 115, 121–23. All the parts: William Ernest Hocking, "Personal Traits of George Herbert Palmer" in Harvard University, *George Herbert Palmer*, p. 63.

woman who might have had too much leisure time. "In the summers, I have time for reading, writing, sewing and making jellies and preserves, — work of which I am very fond," she wrote. Her account of their life together suggests that she was living in George's shadow and his activities mattered more than hers. "Our interests are the same and we always share each other's work, — though he is essentially the scholar and I am not, but he has a rare gift of taking me into his many sided life." It is only in the accompanying record of her daily activities in Cambridge during March 1900 that the rich array of Alice's undertakings becomes clear, and her verve and vivacity shine through. In these daily entries, Alice the manager, planner, advisor, educator, fundraiser, and public servant, emerges from the shadows and dwarfs Alice the perfect wife and domestic companion.

The old tensions were not entirely resolved. George continued to pester Alice to curtail her activities and was irritated when she was away from home for too long. She continued to defer to him, repeatedly promising to be a "better" wife and apologizing for inconveniencing him with her activities, an unexpected visit from her mother, even a hospitalization.[209] She should be praised for all the things she had refused to do, she assured him: "The speeches I have not made, the meetings I have not presided over, the invitations I have not accepted, would make a long story."[210] Trying to fit her work around his convenience, she hosted an important luncheon on a day he was away so he would not be interrupted.[211] Eager to continue writing an article while George was visiting his brother, she suggested she should stay at Boxford by herself rather than join him. "Do stay as long as you can, and let me stay quietly here and work. Of course it would be much better for me to do so, but I will do whatever you say," she demurred. George assented, but asserted dominance by promising to "pull [the article] into shape" when he returned.[212]

---

209 Better wife: AFP to GHP, November 2, 1897, GHP Papers. Similarly: AFP to GHP, January 17, 1901 and June 24, 1901. AFP Papers. Mother's visit: AFP to GHP, July 18, 1899. GHP Papers. Hospitalization: AFP to GHP, September 6, 1901. AFP Papers.
210 AFP to GHP, April 12, 1897. GHP Papers.
211 AFP to GHP [August 14, 1900]. GHP Papers. She hosted a large luncheon and many other activities when he was away a few years later (AFP to GHP, January 30, 1902). AFP Papers.
212 AFP to GHP [August 12, 1900]; AFP to GHP [August 13, 1900]); GHP to AFP [August 14, 1900]. GHP Papers.

It was during these years that Alice wrote the poetry that described her courtship and marriage, including "Myself" (quoted earlier, p. 58), which suggests that she embraced the domestic focus of her marriage, but nevertheless lamented the loss of her independence. During her lifetime, these thoughts were deliberately hidden from the world and from George.[213]

In September 1902, the Palmers traveled to Europe for another of George's sabbatical leaves, accompanied by Lucy Sprague, who was helping George on his study of George Herbert, the English poet for whom he had been named. After crossing the Atlantic by cattle steamer, they traversed large areas of England, following in George Herbert's footsteps and gathering material for George's book. In November, in Paris, Alice began to suffer intestinal pains. The diagnosis was "intussusception of the intestine", a rare condition in which the intestine folds back upon itself, like the sections of a telescope. After weeks of illness, Alice was given a few hours to prepare for an operation that she knew was highly risky. Before leaving for the hospital, she instructed George about cancelling her future engagements and giving personal mementos to family and friends. Alice survived the operation but died in the hospital a few days later, on December 6, 1902. George was by her side, holding her hand.[214] She was forty-seven years old.

George arranged for a small memorial service in Paris and had Alice's body cremated, as she wished. He and Lucy returned to Boston by ship, with Alice's ashes, in late December. Lucy recalled that George talked incessantly about Alice throughout the journey. She sometimes fell asleep while sitting with him at night, and when she awoke he was still talking. When they docked in Boston, a weeping band of friends was waiting for them on the pier.[215]

During the next year, college presidents, deans, faculty members, and leaders of the major organizations she had served paid tribute to Alice at memorial services in Boston, Cambridge, and Chicago. Funds were raised to create living memorials (endowed scholarships and fellowships) and

---

213 Alice showed some of the poems, ones that described their life at Boxford, to George in 1901. She continued to work on them, refused to discuss them with him, and told him not go through the desk where she kept them locked up. See GHP, "Preface" in Alice Freeman Palmer, *Marriage Cycle*, x–xi.

214 GHP to Swinburne Hale, December 12, 1902, quoted in Linenthal, p. 218.

215 Mitchell, *Two Lives*, p. 133.

physical memorials (plaques, busts, statues, a ten-bell set of chimes at the University of Chicago) to perpetuate Alice's name and honor her work. Depicted as a pioneering woman who nevertheless exemplified women's traditional virtues of service to others, Alice was universally praised for being "a womanly woman and a scholarly woman", for "inspiring the best ideals of American womanhood", and for being the "embodiment of [the] welding of intellectual interests and love of home."[216] Caroline Hazard, president of Wellesley when Alice died, stressed that she "opened new doors for women and was among the first to pass through them. She reconciled the new and the old conceptions of women." President William Faunce of Brown University extolled her for being "an admirable synthesis of the older and newer ideals of womanhood." President Charles Eliot of Harvard claimed that Alice's "life and labors" were "the best example thus far set before American womanhood" because she "gave the most striking testimony she could give of her faith in the fundamental social principle, that love between man and woman and the family life which results therefrom afford for each sex the conditions of its greatest usefulness and honor and of its supreme happiness."[217]

Lucy stayed with George in Cambridge for many months and continued working with him on his book, which was published in 1905. She felt trapped by his "subtle ways of limiting my life" and "drained of all capacity to live except as his shadow" but found it impossible to break away from his grasping hold. Her published autobiography records his manipulative efforts to keep her by his side, strategies that seem perfectly consistent with his behavior towards Alice. The unpublished version recounts his attempt to convince Lucy to marry him (he was sixty-one; she was twenty-three) by insisting that otherwise he could not honor Alice's dying request that he "look after Lucy."[218] George's proposal shocked Lucy out of her lethargy and freed her from his influence. Alice's legacy to Lucy was longer-lasting: Lucy had a highly successful dual career marriage with Wesley Clair Mitchell, which is the focus of Chapter 5.

---

216 Association of Collegiate Alumnae, *Alice*, pp. 30, 35, 25.
217 Hazard, p. 208; Faunce in *Alice Freeman Palmer: In Memoriam*, p. 38; Eliot in GHP, *Service*, pp. 80, 76.
218 Mitchell, *Two Lives*, p. 133; Lucy Sprague Mitchell, Unpublished Autobiography in Columbia University, Rare Book and Manuscript Library, MS#0884, Lucy Sprague Mitchell Papers; Antler, pp. 84–85.

Tending the Flame

George's desire to shape Alice's image was as strong after her death as during her life. Anxious to keep her memory alive, tie himself to it, and introduce her to new admirers, he churned out a steady stream of material about Alice. He was not just the keeper of Alice's flame, but also the guardian of a particular image of her. He wanted everyone to know her as the ideal woman and wife as well as — perhaps even more than — the pioneering college president and university dean.

His privately printed volume of twenty-five portraits of Alice (1904) praised her for showing how "a deepened intelligence and wider knowledge of affairs may heighten the characteristic and ancestral traits of womanhood and greatly add to her charm."[219] The ten Scriptural verses he chose for her memorial carillon at the University of Chicago (1908) acknowledged she was "Great in Council and Mighty in Work" but also extolled her as "a gracious Woman", "Rooted and grounded in love," and noted "the sweetness of her lips increasing learning."[220] George's preface to his first volume of *The English Works of George Herbert* (1905) presented her as the ideal helpmate — an instigator, cheerleader, and muse, all rolled into one. "In reality, the book is only half mine," he wrote. "It was begun at [my wife's] instance, enriched by her daily contributions, sustained through difficulties by her resourceful courage, the tedium of its mechanical part lightened by her ever ready fingers."[221]

George knew that Alice might not have endorsed his efforts to keep her memory alive, but he plunged ahead. Acknowledging how difficult it had been to capture her spirit in his *Life of Alice Freeman Palmer* (1908), he admitted to a friend, "[H]ow angry she would be at my attempt! But if I can make more people love her, I shall not mind her wrath."[222] One reviewer hyperbolized that the book ranked second only to the Taj Mahal as a loving memorial to a dead wife.[223] George even found a way

---

219 Quoted in Linenthal, p. 551.
220 "Dedication of the Alice Freeman Palmer Chimes", *University Record of the University of Chicago*, 13:1 (July 1908), 9–17 (p. 17).
221 *The English Works of George Herbert Palmer*, ed. by George Herbert Palmer, 3 vols. (Boston and New York: Houghton Mifflin, 1905), I, xx.
222 GHP to Anne Whitney, 20 April 1908, quoted in Linenthal, p. 238, Note 1.
223 A. D. Dickinson, *The World's Best Books: Homer to Hemingway* (New York: Wilson, 1953), p. 265; quoted in Linenthal, p. 256, note 10.

to collaborate with Alice on a book, something they had talked about doing but never accomplished during her lifetime. *The Teacher: Essays and Addresses on Education* by George Herbert Palmer and Alice Freeman Palmer (1908) brought together twelve of George's speeches with four of Alice's.

Finally, George published forty-eight of Alice's poems in a volume entitled *A Marriage Cycle* (1915), despite the fact that she had asked him, in her final illness, to burn the poems after her death. He never considered destroying them, but he initially thought her record of their courtship and marriage was too intimate to publish in his lifetime. But after he consulted "four college presidents, four novelists, four poets, all persons of standing and social experience" and they encouraged him to publish the poems, he changed his mind. George found the quality of Alice's poems uneven, however. Many were very rough drafts, some did not scan, all lacked titles. Ever the critic and improver, he set to work to complete them. But realizing he could not do justice to them, he selected the best, gave them titles, and grouped them into themes. Fearful that Alice's poetry would otherwise be published in a fragmentary and disordered state, George published them, asserting, "To me it belongs to fix their final form."[224]

George used the profits from the sale of his books about Alice to stock his library of 3,000 first editions, most of which he eventually gave to Wellesley, along with $15,000 to create an endowment to pay for their maintenance. When a new edition of the *Life of Alice* was issued to honor Alice's election to the Hall of Fame of Great Americans in 1920, George arranged for the royalties to go to the Wellesley library. His generosity was a fitting effort to make restitution for having taken Alice away from the college, Katherine Lee Bates, a Wellesley graduate and professor, author of "America the Beautiful," pointed out in her introduction to the new edition.[225] George retired from Harvard in 1913, but continued to live in his beloved Quincy Street house until his death in 1933, at the age of ninety-one. His ashes were placed in Alice's memorial in the Wellesley chapel.[226]

* * * * *

---

224 GHP, "Preface" in AFP, *A Marriage Cycle*, ix–xvii.
225 See Linenthal, pp. 248–50.
226 Ibid., pp. 244–45.

The inevitable question is why George drew such fundamentally misleading portraits of Alice, himself, and their marriage in his *Life of Alice*. In part, he was self-deceptive. He saw in Alice what he wanted to see, and closed his eyes to behavior or beliefs that did not fit his preconceived, idealized image of womanhood. Thus, he ignored or misinterpreted situations that showed how forceful, independent, and authoritative she could be, and the pleasure she took in being in charge. He was particularly unlikely to register behavior that suggested Alice was not entirely happy with him or the domestic life that meant so much to him. If Alice expressed ambivalence about her work, what impressed George were her laments about being away from home, not the evidence that she delighted in her work and continued to accept jobs that kept her away from Cambridge. Such things were too painful for him to recognize, much less acknowledge to the world. George's characterizations were also self-serving. By concentrating on the satisfactions of their domestic life, he justified the marriage and enhanced his own value as the man who made the incomparable Alice Freeman happy. By stressing his role as Alice's advisor and protector, he also made a case for his masculine superiority and his importance in her life.

Alice herself contributed to this false portrait by encouraging George to see her as a woman who fit the mold of true womanhood. In her relations with him, she was essentially self-effacing and submissive. She appealed to him for guidance and advice although she was perfectly capable of administering a college on her own; she stressed how dependent she was on him when in fact she delighted in and longed for independence. When she was unhappy with her life, she blamed herself, not him. If her behavior deviated from expected gender norms, she tried to reframe her actions back into conformity. She did not articulate, except in her poetry, her desire to escape from his all-encompassing "oneness" and face challenges on her own. In short, she did not use her position as a working wife to challenge nineteenth-century norms of male superiority and dominance, and female inferiority and subordination, although she did promote companionate ideals.

Far more than the Palmers' personal relations were at stake in how Alice's image was presented to the world, however. Alice was an important public figure whose significance lay not only in her efforts to expand and improve women's educational opportunities, but also in the personal influence she wielded as an inspiration and a role model for educated women. For her contemporaries, Alice's great appeal lay precisely in her ability to blend public service with domestic life and maintain her "womanly charm." Her life provided reassurance to those who feared that educated women would not find fulfillment in traditional marriages; she became a model for young women who wanted a college education but feared being labeled "unwomanly." George was not the only one to stress these aspects of Alice's life. He echoed what Alice's fellow educators said about her in memorial services soon after her death.

Like George, Alice's colleagues believed that she had reconciled two traditions of womanhood and made her life a harmonious whole without stress or strain. In doing so, they raised false expectations for the future. In reality, the new and old styles of womanhood and wifehood did not mesh well in Alice's life. Her attempt to build a professional career after her marriage was fraught with contradictions and ambivalence, and created tension and conflict with George. Nor was it easy or wholly satisfying for her to settle into a life of domesticity and volunteer activity. To have stated this publicly, nonetheless, might have been detrimental to the causes for which she struggled.[227]

In an era when white women were just beginning to experiment with nontraditional roles, Alice's life was important as a model for educated and talented women who hoped to find fulfillment by supplementing marriages and motherhood with volunteer activities outside the home. It was important to George — and to Alice — to protect and perpetuate that image in order to advance the movement for women's education. Although she defended women's rights, supported women's suffrage, and fought fiercely for educational opportunities for women, Alice was not a radical and did not advance a feminist ideology. She promoted higher education for women and the involvement of women in public affairs as a means of enhancing, rather than displacing, their traditional roles as wives and mothers. She emphasized that women who went to

---

227 Jill Ker Conway, *True North: A Memoir* (New York: Knopf, 1994), pp. 151–52, discusses similar disparities in the lives and memoirs of women who were early college graduates and leaders in political and social reform movements during the Progressive Era. See also Carolyn G. Heilbrun, *Writing a Woman's Life* (New York: Norton, 1988), pp. 24–25, on the need for women achievers to offer themselves not as models for other women, but as "exceptions chosen by destiny or chance."

college would be better companions to their husbands and better guides to their sons (sons! not daughters!), run their households more efficiently, and bring their moral influence to bear in public service.[228] Although she spent several years as a working wife with a paid income, and pioneered a commuter marriage, Alice never championed professional careers for middle-class wives or talked about the difficulties she and others faced in attempting to blend marriage and career.

To have acknowledged the tensions between her different roles, questioned the happiness of her marriage, or explored the power dynamic between the Palmers would have undermined Alice's value as a symbol of feminine accomplishment. In the end, she, like George, was content to leave it to others to challenge the old stereotypes directly and implement a marital ideal that was egalitarian as well as companionate.

---

228 Alice Freeman Palmer, "On Women's Duties" (Warren, Ohio: National American Woman Suffrage Association, 1904). See also, Alice Freeman Palmer, "Why Go to College" in *The Teacher*, pp. 364–93 (pp. 364, 383–85).

2. A "Two Person Career": Grace Chisholm Young and William Henry Young

When Grace Chisholm argued against women's suffrage in a debate at her all-female English college in 1889, she was disdainfully dismissed by a female don as "one of those charming young ladies who marry the nice young man at the end."[1] Grace did marry — her mathematics coach, no less — but that was hardly the end of it. Along the way, she got a PhD in mathematics in Germany (one of the first awarded to a woman); trained to become a medical doctor; helped her husband, William Henry Young, with his mathematical research; won acclaim for her own mathematical studies; authored two children's books on scientific topics; wrote poetry and an historical novel; and raised six children in Germany and Switzerland.

Like many women of her generation, Grace found it easier to pioneer new roles for women outside the home than inside the home. She was a trail-blazing professional, but did not want to be seen as an ambitious "modern woman" who thought only of herself. She took as much pride and pleasure in creating a warm domestic environment as in developing an elegant mathematical proof or performing a skillful dissection. She successfully balanced her roles as homemaker and mother with the demands of her medical training. Her efforts to pursue an independent professional life while simultaneously helping her husband in his career proved more challenging. For years Grace managed to do both,

---

[1]   University of Liverpool Library, Special Collections and Archives, D.140, Papers of Professor W. H. Young and his wife Grace Chisholm Young (Young Papers). D.140/12/22, Grace's Cambridge Autobiography.

     https://doi.org/10.11647/OBP.0318.02

but ultimately she had to choose between supporting Will's work or advancing her own.

Becoming a Mathematician

Grace Chisholm was raised in an "eminently respectable", upper-middle-class household that valued education, intellectual achievement, and cultural accomplishment — qualities that would become touchstones of her own life. On her father's side, she came from a line of distinguished civil servants. Her formidable grandmamma on her mother's side was a "very rich, very placid, and very intellectual" lady who hosted many musicians of note in her London home.[2]

The youngest child of elderly parents — Henry William Chisholm was almost sixty when she was born in 1868; Anna Bell Chisholm was forty-five — Grace felt overshadowed by her two older siblings, and wished her parents were more demonstratively affectionate.[3] Her brother Hugh was considered brilliant. Her sister, Helen, who had had polio as a child, was regarded as a paragon of artistic sensibility and the personification of goodness and sweetness. (None of Helen's sweetness was shown to her, Grace complained.) In an era when children were supposed to be seen and not heard, she was frequently in trouble for being heard too much. Rambunctious and strong-willed, she felt both blamed and blameworthy. A frequent punishment was being locked in a bathroom. When she was very young, she reacted by crying and kicking at the door. But when she grew "older and bolder", she escaped by climbing out of the window and down the drain pipe.[4]

Grace showed an early interest and aptitude for mathematics. When she began to suffer from headaches, sleepwalking, and nightmares, the family doctor advised leaving her free to roam the grounds of her home

---

2   This account of Grace's childhood is based on her autobiographical writings (D.140/6/14/6 and D.140/12/1. Young Papers). See also, Ivor Grattan-Guinness, "A Mathematical Union: William Henry and Grace Chisholm Young", *Annals of Science* 29:2 (1972), 105–86 (pp. 106–10, 115–29), and D.140/2/2, R. C. H. Tanner Notes, Young Papers.

3   The Chisholms' first-born child suffered accidental brain damage and lived in a nursing home until her death at age twenty, according to Grace's son, Laurence. L. C. Young, "The Life and Work of WH and GC Young", formerly posted at http// www-history.mcs.st-and.ac.uk, pp. 1–18 (p. 6).

4   D.140/8/249, GC to WHY, June 2, 1896. Young Papers.

in Haslemere, Surrey, about 60 miles outside of London, and not giving her lessons unless she asked for them. The only subjects she wanted to study were mental arithmetic and music. After her father retired as head of the British Department of Weights and Measures in 1877, he encouraged her interest in geometry and helped her design three-dimensional models in his carpentry workshop.

When Grace turned ten, her mother decided it was time for Grace to be properly educated. The siblings' different educational experiences reflected the usual gender gap between boys and girls: expected to have a career, Hugh was sent to a public school and Oxford University.[5] Expected to devote themselves to charitable activities, amateur cultural pursuits, and domestic affairs, Grace and Helen had lessons with a governess. The girls were taught Latin and Greek, but Grace's mother vigorously opposed her desire to study medicine. Nevertheless, urged on by her husband, Anna Chisholm eventually allowed 21-year-old Grace to attend Girton College at the University of Cambridge where she won a scholarship to study mathematics in 1889.

In a college that had strong ties to the British feminist movement, Grace garnered little support when she argued against female suffrage in a college debate. Although her own mother was an early supporter of women's suffrage, Grace argued the opposition case "with diffidence but conviction."[6] In the light of her later life, her anti-suffrage views are not surprising.

It was a heady time for women to study mathematics at Cambridge. During Grace's first year, Philippa Fawcett, the daughter of feminist Millicent Fawcett and niece of Elizabeth Garrett Anderson (the first woman to qualify as a doctor in Britain), rocked the academic world by scoring higher than the highest-ranked man in the Cambridge Mathematics Tripos, the final examination for mathematics students. Fawcett's achievement challenged popular assumptions about women's intellectual abilities and made newspaper headlines throughout the world. Grace recorded the excitement that erupted when Fawcett's name and rank were announced.[7]

---

5   Hugh Chisholm became financial editor of the London *Times* and the editor-in-chief of the illustrious 1911 edition of the *Encyclopedia Britannica*.
6   D.140/12/22, Grace's Cambridge Autobiography. Young Papers.
7   Ibid.

Two years later, Grace had her own moment of glory. After being coached by William Henry Young, a young Fellow of Peterhouse College, she was ranked in the first class (top third) of scholars when she took Part I of the Tripos. One of 12 women and 112 men who took the exam in 1892, she was placed between the 23rd and 24th man. She scored another triumph a few days later when, on a dare, she and her friend, Isabel Maddison, took the final examination in mathematics at Oxford. The women sat for the Oxford exam unofficially, but Grace was again ranked in the first class (top third) of examinees, giving her what her brother called a "remarkable double first."[8] She returned to Girton for a fourth year to prepare for the more specialized second half of the Tripos examination. The only woman to take the exam in 1893, she was disappointed to be ranked in the bottom third of the fifteen examinees.[9]

Eager to continue her mathematics training, Grace had to look for opportunities abroad. She went to Germany to study with the illustrious Felix Klein at the University of Göttingen, one of the leading centers of pure mathematics in Europe. Undeterred by her mother's disapproval, Grace insisted her decision was a practical measure to ensure that she would be able to earn her own living if she needed to do so.[10]

Grace was one of a triumvirate of women — the other two were Americans — who arrived to study with Klein in 1893. A progressive educator as well as an innovative mathematician, Klein encouraged foreign women with excellent qualifications to audit classes at Göttingen and pressure the university to grant them degrees.[11] Grace was proud to be opening up opportunities for all women, but she pursued mathematics

---

8   Tripos Examination Results: D.140/12/16. Oxford exam: M. L. Cartwright, "Grace Chisholm Young", *Girton Review*, 31 (Easter 1944), 17–19 (p. 17); D.140/6/28c, Hugh Chisholm to GC, June 30, 1892. Young Papers.
9   Disappointment: D.140/6/39, GC to Frances Evans, June 14, 1893. Examination results: D.140/12/19. Young Papers.
10   D.140/6/34, GC to Helen Chisholm, February 17, 1893. Young Papers.
11   The three women were enrolled as "exceptions" at Göttingen. German champions of women's education encouraged foreign women to seek degrees in Germany because it was assumed that they would return to their native countries to find employment and not compete with German men for jobs. See Margaret W. Rossiter, *Women Scientists in America*, 3 vols. (Baltimore: Johns Hopkins University Press, 1982–2012), I, pp. 35–38. For Klein's efforts on behalf of women students, see Renate Tobies, "Internationality: Women in Felix Klein's Courses at the University of Göttingen (1893–1920)" in *Against all Odds: Women's Ways to Mathematical Research since 1800*, ed. by Eva Kaufholz-Soldat and Nicola M. R. Oswald (Cham, Switzerland: Springer, 2020), pp. 9–38.

out of love for the subject, not in order to make a feminist statement. She liked being treated as a colleague by the male faculty and students, but insisted that she and the other women students wanted "freedom" from "all unnecessary & conventional distinctions between men & women" rather than "equality" with men.[12] She was not a feminist, but knowing she was being judged as a representative of all women, she felt a "terrible" responsibility to set a good example by her behavior and scholarly accomplishments.[13] She eagerly asserted her identity as a woman as she became a scholar. She filled her letters to her family with accounts of her cooking, lacemaking, musical accomplishments, and social activities as well as her progress in mathematics.[14] Her anxious relatives were relieved to know she had not "sunk the woman in the scholar" but instead maintained the "qualities of the true and genuine woman."[15]

Feeling more "free and independent" than ever before, Grace vowed she would "move heaven and earth" to return to Göttingen for a third year and try for the PhD degree.[16] She was the first of the three women studying with Klein to finish her coursework and dissertation. Following his instructions, she went to Berlin in the spring of 1895 and successfully petitioned the Ministry for Culture for permission to take the oral examination, defend her thesis, and qualify for the doctoral degree. The only hitch was getting to the oral exam in April 1895. Assuming that a doctoral candidate would be a man, the cab driver who came to take Grace to her defense drove off with an empty cab after being told that there was no male boarder at her lodging. Grace had to run to the examination room on foot. She passed her defense *magna cum laude*, the first woman to win a doctorate in mathematics at a German university by completing the doctoral program and taking an oral examination.

---

12   D.140/8/3, GC to her family, November 5, 1893. See also, D.140/8/2, GC to Helen Chisholm, October 29, 1893. Young Papers.

13   D.140/8/60, GC to Anna Bell Chisholm, April 27, 1895. Young Papers.

14   Identity: GC to Helen Chisholm [June 4, 1894], and D.140/8/3, GC to Family, November 5, 1893. Activities: for example, GC to Helen Chisholm, D.140/8/73, June 30, 1895; D.140/8/67, May 12, 1895; D.140/8/41, December 20, 1894; D.140/6/2, GC to Helen Chisholm, October 24, 1893. Young Papers.

15   D.140/6/69, Gertrude Bell to GC, June 1, 1895. Young Papers.

16   Free and independent: D.140/8/11, GC to Frances Evans, December 23 [1893]. Vowed: D.140/6/52, GC to Frances Evans [February 25, 1894]. Young Papers.

When they heard the news, she and one of her American colleagues broke into a "war dance" of celebration for her landmark achievement.[17]

Courtship and Early Marriage

When she returned to her parents' home in London in the summer of 1895, armed with a doctoral degree and increased confidence, Grace found that her standing as a scholar clashed with her role as younger daughter in an upper-class home. She was offended by the efforts of her mother and sister to squelch her and keep her from talking in social gatherings. Although women had opportunities to teach in women's colleges and in all-girls' high schools, Grace was under no financial pressure to work, and there is no indication that she was looking for an academic post.[18] Her very conventional family would undoubtedly have been shocked had she sought paid employment. She herself felt that Cambridge dons did "enervating" work that stamped out "freshness and brilliance."[19]

Instead, Grace began to develop her dissertation into articles for publication. She sent a copy of her thesis to William Henry Young, the coach who had tutored her for Part I of the Tripos examination. When she visited Girton in the fall of 1895, they became so involved in discussing her experiences at Göttingen that Will forgot he had a roomful of students waiting for him.[20] They began to correspond and to meet, and he encouraged Grace to continue her mathematical work. In October he asked her to join him in writing a textbook on astronomy,

---

17 D.140/6/71, GC to Henry William Chisholm, April 27 [1895]. Young Papers. The Russian Sonia Kovalevsky (1850–1891) was awarded a PhD by Göttingen University in 1874, but without taking the oral examinations or thesis defense required of male candidates (she went on to have a brilliant career). Grace was the first woman to be awarded the PhD under the more stringent rules. See Lynn M. Osen, *Women in Mathematics* (Cambridge, MA: MIT Press, 1974), pp. 117–40.

18 On women's teaching opportunities, see Martha Vicinus, *Independent Women: Work and Community for Single Women, 1850–1920* (Chicago: University of Chicago Press, 1985), p. 127; Philippa Levine, *Victorian Feminism, 1850–1900* (Tallahassee: Florida State University Press, 1987), p. 38.

19 D.140/8/41, GC to Helen Chisholm [December 20, 1894], Young Papers. Rita McWilliams-Tullberg described the isolation and restrictions female dons suffered in their teaching and research careers at Cambridge in *Women at Cambridge: A Men's University Though of a Mixed Type* (London: Victor Gollanz, 1975), p. 105.

20 D.140/12/21, Grace's biographical jottings. Young Papers.

which was then a branch of mathematics and one of the subjects he taught at Cambridge. She agreed, but wanted to complete her own work before starting on his.[21] Solidifying her position as a mathematician, she joined the London Mathematical Society in January 1896.

A month later, Will abruptly proposed marriage. His impetuous behavior was characteristic, Cecily, the Youngs' oldest daughter, would note many years later.[22] According to family lore, Grace initially refused, insisting that she must remain single so she could provide for her mother and sister in the event of her elderly father's death. However, Will did not understand that he had been turned down, and Grace quickly changed her mind. Within a week their engagement was announced to family and friends, and Grace was describing herself as deliriously happy.

Acutely conscious that Will was "unlike any of the men of my circle", Grace was greatly relieved that her family appeared to like him.[23] By conventional standards, she was marrying down. Will's family was less distinguished and less financially well-off than hers. His father, Henry Young, was a grocer, who had left school at age fourteen. In England's class-conscious society, being "in trade" was not an acceptable occupation for a gentleman. Religion was another strike against Will when membership in the established Church of England offered social status, professional mobility, and educational opportunities unavailable to members of nonconforming religions. The second of six children and the eldest son, Will had had been brought up as a Baptist but converted to Anglicanism when he was an undergraduate at Cambridge. From the time he went to Cambridge, Will was self-supporting. When he married, his father had been on the verge of bankruptcy for several years. Will had taken over some of his investments and mortgages in order to keep him solvent; he also helped to support one of his sisters.[24] The Young family's personal interactions were as strained as its finances. Henry Young was a "bitter and difficult" person who suffered such serious indigestion that he took his meals separately from the rest of his family,

---

21 D.140/8/82, GC to WHY, October 13, 1895. Young Papers.
22 Grattan-Guinness, "Mathematical Union", p. 131 and D.140/2/2, R. C. H. Tanner notes. Young Papers.
23 D.140/8/135, GC to WHY, March 11, 1896; D.140/6/694a, GCY to WHY [October 18, 1903]. Young Papers.
24 D.140/29/12–64. Solicitor Henry Cooke's letters to WHY, especially18 April 1894 and 18 June 1896. Young Papers.

reading while he ate. He passed his fascination with travel and a facility for languages on to his son. He also bequeathed Will his irritability and impatience.

When they married, Will's academic achievements were less than Grace's. He had gone to the prestigious City of London School on scholarship and won important scholarships to Peterhouse College at the University of Cambridge.[25] He placed fourth in the Mathematics Tripos in 1884, but did not submit an essay for a prestigious prize in mathematics; instead he won a major theological prize. Will was a Fellow of Peterhouse College between 1886 and 1892, but no one advised him to do mathematical research or gave him helpful guidance. He made his living as a teacher, examiner, and coach at a series of prep schools and then at Girton College, where he had coached Grace.[26] He had increased his assets by investing in the stock market and saved a substantial amount of money.[27]

By choosing Will, a man whose social standing, class background, and professional status was lower than hers, Grace showed a disregard for convention. Instead of material success, he offered her romantic love and intellectual companionship. When she first brought him home, Grace would recall, her mother looked at her "with the mixture of

---

25   The headmaster of the City of London School was a friend of Will's father. Entrance
       was by competitive examination, and the fees were paid out of public funds. Unlike
       most public schools, it was a day school and had no religious test.
26   Grattan-Guinness, "Mathematical Union", pp. 110–15. D.140/2/2, R. C. H. Tanner
       notes. Young Papers.
27   According to Cecily Young (D.140/2/2, R. C. H. Tanner notes, Young Papers)
       and Grattan-Guinness, "Mathematical Union", p. 132, Will had 6,000 pounds in
       savings and investments that was put in a Trust when he married. (This is roughly
       equivalent to 188,000 pounds or $1 million today, using the CPI inflation calculator
       at https://www.officialdata.org/ to compare 1896 and 2021 values.) The financial
       records of the Youngs in the University of Liverpool archives are not clear about this.
       A week after the wedding, Will was advised that investments held by him, valued
       at 1,591 pounds in the Marriage Settlement, were both risky and low-yielding. The
       trustees recommended that Will and Grace sell them, even though it would mean
       a loss of capital. These might have been investments Will had taken over from his
       father. If the entire Marriage Settlement amounted to 6,000 pounds, this would have
       included Grace's portion from her family, as well as contributions from Will and his
       family. Grace's brother Hugh was a trustee, along with Henry Cooke, Will's solicitor
       and friend; under the terms of the Settlement, both Grace and Will had to agree
       when changes were made to any of the investments. See D.140/12/31a and b, Henry
       Cooke to WHY, 18 June 1896, and D.140/29/63, an incomplete copy of the Youngs'
       Marriage Settlement.

admiration and contempt that mother hens award to their special ugly ducklings." Grace was proud that she herself recognized Will's true value, even though he was "so unlike all my familiar pictures of the male being."[28] Although he had not yet accomplished very much, they both believed he would achieve great things. She found him more refined than other men of her acquaintance, meaning not more cultured, but more intellectual and more devoted to the life of the mind. She also valued him for not being set in his ways, and for being less egotistical than most men of her acquaintance. Many decades later, she again asserted that it was the breadth of his vision that first attracted her: he was the only person she had ever met who was not "cribbed, cabined, & confined."[29] Equally important, he encouraged her to continue with mathematics. Nevertheless, she counted on her "strong lover" to help her to become a better woman, "to fulfill the old ideals, not forsake them."[30]

Conscious of the class differences that separated her family and Will's, Grace agonized over the wedding preparations and the protocol for bringing the two families together. She herself may have looked down on Will's family. In later years, when Will's sister May lived with the Youngs, their daughter noted that Grace made fun of May's provincial manners.[31]

Grace's closest friend from Girton, Frances Evans, laughed at her for being ruled by the "bogey of impropriety" in planning the wedding, but Grace took such matters seriously.[32] On the big things that really mattered to her, she was courageous enough to do as she pleased. But she generally sought to portray herself in a very conventional light even when she deviated from traditional norms. She did not want to be gossiped about or criticized, especially by her family, and she was careful not to give offense when it could be avoided. Above all, she wanted to avoid conflict.

28 D.140/6/694, GCY to WHY, October 18, 1903. Young Papers.
29 D.599/1/1/1/6, Grace's notebook, entry dated 22–1–1931. University of Liverpool Library, Special Collections and Archives, D.599, Papers of Dr. R. C.H Tanner, including papers of her parents W. H. Young and Grace Chisholm Young (Tanner Papers).
30 D.140/8/146, GC to WHY, March 18 [1896]. Young Papers.
31 D.140/2/2, R. C. H. Tanner notes. Young Papers.
32 D.140/8/301, GC to WHY, June 6, 1896. Young Papers.

Will encouraged Grace to take on new roles and stand up to her family. He wanted her to become knowledgeable about his financial holdings and business transactions, meet with his lawyers, attend stockholder meetings, and find them a house to rent in Cambridge — activities which Grace's parents thought inappropriate for a young woman. Before her marriage, when Will and her mother advised different courses of action, Grace deferred to her mother.[33] But after she married, Grace would side with Will against her family.

The whirl of wedding preparations — shopping, sewing her trousseau, embroidering household linens, and making obligatory social calls — left Grace no time for mathematics, but she looked forward to getting back to work after her honeymoon.[34] Although some of her relatives thought she had been badly spoiled by her parents, Grace thought of herself as an ugly duckling or a Cinderella within the family unit. Enjoying the attention and gifts she received during her engagement, she seemed to feel she was coming into her own. Nearly 150 guests attended the wedding reception at her parents' London home in June 1896. Grace and Will made a handsome couple. Both were fit and athletic. Always self-conscious about her height, she repeatedly reminded him that he would need to stand "very straight," so he would not appear shorter than she when she stood erect in her long satin train.[35] As always, Grace clung to convention in the little things.

Vagabond Scholars

After a honeymoon in Switzerland and Italy, the Youngs settled into married life in Cambridge. Will continued coaching and worked on the astronomy textbook; Grace helped him and pursued her own mathematical interests. The pattern that would mark their lives — Grace balancing intellectual pursuits with housekeeping and childcare, Will focusing only on work and urging her to do the same — was quickly set. Grace informed Frances Evans, "However negligent I am of everything

---

33   D.140/8/232, WHY to GC, May 5, 1896; and D.140/8/201, WHY to GC, April 27, 1896. Young Papers.
34   D.140/8/105, GC to WHY, February 25, 1896; D.140/8/216, GC to WHY, May 2, 1896; D.140/8/301, GC to WHY, June 6, 1896; D.140/8/267, GC to WHY, May 27, 1896. Young Papers.
35   D.140/8/272, GC to WHY, May 28, 1896. Young Papers.

except 'the book' Will gets in a fever & talks of my many distractions. You must not think I am not very happy: I would like to have 'no distractions' & be able to work all day, but there are other things which however one puts them off have to be done in the end."[36] Pregnant in the fall of 1896, Grace devoted many happy hours to sewing and embroidering the baby's wardrobe, leaving little time to work with Will.[37]

The Youngs' relationship was romantic, passionate, and intense. On the first anniversary of their engagement, Grace gushed, "How could I know then that my love for you & yours for me were the biggest truths for us in the universe."[38] She found him "the most loving true & sympathetic of friends [...] as well as [the most] ardent of lovers."[39] They were personally happy but professionally frustrated. In the spring, Will's unsuccessful candidacy for an examinership in Wales forced the Youngs to take stock of their prospects. He was unhappy with his coaching work and both felt that the Cambridge mathematical tradition, which prepared undergraduates for intellectually arduous but unimaginative examinations, was too narrow and stifled creativity. Encouraged by Felix Klein, they decided to study in Europe with mathematicians who were exploring new branches of mathematics rather than refining a well-established body of knowledge.[40] Grace was familiar with this world from her days at Göttingen, but her insular and chauvinistic relatives were shocked and disapproving — "horrified", she noted.[41]

Grace and Will left England in September 1897, when their son Francis (called Frankie or Bimbo, an Italian word for male baby) was just three months old. Despite the dire predictions of Grace's relatives, the Youngs managed to make ends meet by living on savings, investments, and rental income. They regarded their new life as an exhilarating and productive adventure and relished the opportunities to travel, learn languages, and study mathematics. After spending a few

---

36   D.140/6/150, GCY to Frances Evans, September 3, 1896. Young Papers.
37   D.140/6/158, GCY to Frances Evans, January 1, 1897. Young Papers.
38   D.140/6/166, GCY to WHY, February 22, 1897. Young Papers.
39   D.140/6/158, GCY to Frances Evans, January 1, 1897. Young Papers.
40   For the contrasting intellectual environments in mathematics at Cambridge and Göttingen, see Joan L. Richards, *Mathematical Visions: The Pursuit of Geometry in Victorian England* (Boston: Academic Press, 1988), and Laurence Young, *Mathematicians and their Times*, North-Holland Mathematics Studies 48 (Amsterdam and New York: North Holland Publishing, 1981), p. 285.
41   D.140/6/172, GCY to Frances Evans, April 7, 1897. Young Papers.

months in Göttingen, they traveled through Italy. They arrived in Turin in November 1898, where they spent six months studying geometry with Corrado Segre, one of Italy's most eminent mathematicians. Will worked on a series of papers on the geometry of n-dimensional space, developing what Grace described as a new and "powerful" idea.[42] She acted as his "secretary and critic" and wrote a few papers of her own, applying the new mathematics she was learning to the theories developed in her dissertation.[43] By the end of 1899, she had published two papers, and Will had published four.

For brief periods, the Youngs shared domestic chores as well as intellectual pursuits. Often making do without servants, they initially treated housekeeping as an entertaining game. Not surprisingly, Grace soon took over the domestic work not done by hired help. Servantless in the fall of 1898, she bragged, "I did *everything*, & Will praised my cooking & I felt bursting with pride at the cleanliness of my kitchen & sitting room & bedrooms." She proudly reported how, on the opening day at the University of Turin, she made coffee, prepared lunch, dressed the baby, and did the washing up before rushing off to attend a lecture.[44] As always, she was anxious to convince her relatives and friends — and perhaps herself — that she was a model wife, mother, and homemaker despite being a mathematician.

At first, Grace found it difficult to give up the care of her son.[45] Nevertheless, after they went to Europe, she often hired a servant to help with Frankie, so she could work on mathematics and go on holidays with Will. Arriving to discuss mathematics with a renowned scholar in Italy, she nonchalantly handed the baby over to the maid "like an umbrella to be looked after." After their talk, Grace flung Frankie around her shoulder like a shawl, and she and Will went sightseeing.[46]

This freewheeling period soon came to an end. After Grace became pregnant in the late spring of 1899, the Youngs decided to settle in Göttingen where she had colleagues and friends. They continued their researches and Grace quickly established herself as part of the

---

42 D.140/6/222, GCY to Frances Evans, May 18 [1898]. Young Papers.
43 D.140/6/228, GCY to Henry William Chisholm, [n.d.]. Young Papers.
44 D.140/6/260, GCY to Frances Evans, November 16, 1898. Young Papers.
45 D.140/6/199, GCY to WHY [August 15, 1897]; D.140/6/207, GCY to Frances Evans, January 15, 1898. Young Papers.
46 D.140/6/214, GCY to Frances Evans, April 4, 1898. Young Papers.

university's international mathematical community. Mathematicians came to visit and talk shop with her, and Klein hired her, and eventually Will, to translate articles for his *Encyclopedia of Mathematical Sciences.*

Grace was cheerful and optimistic when she wrote to her family about her life in Göttingen, but to Frances Evans, whom she trusted not to "tattle", she revealed her anxieties and frustrations. Her main concern was to help Will realize the potential they both saw in him. "I shall not be really happy until his book is out," she admitted, vowing to do what she could to aid him. Convinced of Will's genius, she feared becoming like Xantippe, the famously shrewish wife of Socrates, who lost patience with her husband because she was "a perfectly ordinary woman, & quite incapable of appreciating the abnormal & wonderful & grand."[47] Grace drew inspiration from reading the biographies of great men, and felt a kinship with the poet Elizabeth Barrett Browning, who left England for Europe and sometimes railed against English critics who failed to appreciate her husband's literary talents.[48]

The Youngs prided themselves on having given up material comforts in order to live on a higher intellectual plane. Neither of them wanted to return to Cambridge, but they were increasingly worried about their finances. Will was in England for several weeks in December 1899, presiding over the entrance exam at the Rugby School to earn a little income, and visiting friends. Spending Christmas with Frankie in Göttingen and eight months pregnant, Grace was lonely and depressed. Will's return did not lighten her mood. On the eve of the new century, she resolved to free herself from her youthful dreams, and devote herself to her new life as a wife and mother.

> I feel that I shall throw overboard a lot of useless lumber with this old year, ties & regrets & the old life and be myself, wife & mother & let the rest go: that is what I mean by throwing off *youth*. I shall not any more let myself be persuaded into the wearying task of trying to reconcile new duties with what people are pleased to call *old*. Whether the old ones ever existed except in my imagination is I think open to doubt.[49]

---

47 D.140/6/318a, GCY to Frances Evans, December 10, 1899; see also, D.140/6/275, GCY to Frances Evans, February 28, 1899. Young Papers.

48 D.140/6/318a, GCY to Frances Evans, December 10, 1899. Young Papers.

49 D.140/6/328, GCY to Frances Evans, December 30 [1899]. Emphasis in the original. Young Papers.

Grace's determination was strong, but the decision was painful. Informing Frances of her resolution, she could not stop crying and sought to hide her tears from Will. She was steeling herself to throw off not just her personal ambitions, but also her ties to her English relatives and some English friends. She had never been close to her family, and her relationships with them deteriorated after she went to Europe. She felt they undervalued Will, discouraged her from visiting, and were petty about finances. When Grace's mother died, unexpectedly, in 1900, Grace felt they were partially estranged.[50]

Medicine or Mathematics?

The birth of Rosamund, called Cecily, in February 1900 forced the Youngs to adapt their lifestyle once again. They had already borrowed money from Grace's father, and with two children to support, they needed more income.[51] They decided that Will would resume his coaching work at Cambridge in the fall of 1900, where he was required to be in residence at the university for a total of twenty-two weeks over three terms. Convinced that Göttingen was less expensive than Cambridge and a preferable place to rear a family, they agreed that Grace and the children would remain in Germany and Will would go to Cambridge alone.

Will's return to Cambridge precipitated an equally dramatic change in Grace's professional life. Despite her resolution to give up old aspirations, Grace did not want to be just a wife and mother. A few months after Cecily's birth, she attended a dinner party at Felix Klein's home and was delighted when the other (male) mathematicians "made much" of her and made it clear that they expected more from her "than a thorough knowledge of housekeeping & the management of babies & a somewhat delicate husband with great thoughts and aims."[52] Knowing that Will could be away for eight weeks at a time, the Youngs felt Grace should have an intellectual outlet to keep her happy during his absences. By the time he left Göttingen in the fall of 1900, they had

---

50   D.140/6/419, GCY to WHY, 20 January [1901?]. Young Papers.
51   D.140/6/418, WHY to GCY, 19 January 1901. Young Papers.
52   D.140/6/336, GCY to Helen Chisholm, 19 May 1900. Young Papers.

agreed that she would start the medical training she had always wanted but had not pursued because of her mother's disapproval.

As a female student starting a medical curriculum at the University of Göttingen in 1900, Grace was less of an anomaly than she had been when she arrived to study mathematics in 1893. Although women could not officially enroll as medical students, they had been auditing medical classes at Göttingen University since 1895. Starting in 1899, they were allowed to take state-administered exams and could be licensed to practice medicine.[53] Although women's fitness for medical careers and the propriety of training them in co-educational classes were hotly debated topics in both Britain and Germany, Grace and Will were untroubled by such considerations.[54] The question they debated at length was whether Grace should pursue a medical career or help Will with his explorations in pure mathematics.

Will had hardly arrived in Cambridge before he reopened the discussion. Mistakenly thinking that Grace was having second thoughts, Will assured her there was no need to study medicine if she did not want to. "If we can keep the wolf from the door we shall probably all of us be much happier if you don't [study medicine]," he admitted. The alternative plan, a mathematical partnership with him, would come closer to fulfilling his vision of "the ideal life" than pursuing separate careers, he admitted. He outlined a course of work that would take eight to ten years to complete and require Grace "to work hard at bookwriting" while he was in England.[55]

Will continued to weigh the advantages and disadvantages of mathematics versus medicine even after Grace indicated she was very

---

53 Thomas Neville Bonner, *To the Ends of the Earth: Women's Search for Education in Medicine* (Cambridge, MA and London: Harvard University Press, 1992), and Patricia M. Mazon, *Gender and the Modern Research University: The Admission of Women to German Higher Education, 1865–1914* (Stanford, CA: Stanford University Press, 2003). Grace was one of thirty-seven women who studied medicine as auditors at Göttingen University between 1895 and 1908, the year when German women were allowed to officially matriculate in Prussian universities. (Bonner, *To the Ends*, p. 114.) After 1908, foreign students were still required to get the instructor's permission to attend classes.

54 Grace noted that the most prominent women doctors were married women. D.140/6/392, GCY to WHY, November 11 [1900?]. Young Papers.

55 D.140/6/371, WHY to GCY, October 19, 1900. His mistake: D.140/6/376, WHY to GCY, October 23, 1900. Young Papers.

happy with her new career.[56] Medicine might provide a better outlet for her talents than mathematics, and the income she could earn as a doctor would be helpful, he admitted. But his "other self" did not want Grace to embark on a medical career, admittedly for selfish reasons. "It objects to being away from you & would like to have you at its beck & call to save it some drudgery in the production of maths books & the like. It is inclined to object strongly at the notion that ten years hence it may only see you at certain stated hours of the day," he explained. But he did not think such feelings should stand in Grace's way if she really wanted to embark on a career in medicine.[57]

Will's letters had a powerful effect on Grace. After further reflection and discussion with friends, she decided to give up medicine. She informed Will: "If you and the children were not there I should do [medicine] certainly, I do not see that there is anything to deter me. I should be more glad to be able to do it now even than I should have been years ago."[58] Despite her deep desire to be a doctor, Grace could not free herself from the stereotypes of her time that taught women to put family before all else. "It is *no* sacrifice to me to give it up," she stressed. "The two determining factors are (1) that I want to help you with your work & (2) that I want to have a large hand in educating the children [...] I think I should have shattered my own idea of womanhood if I had allowed myself to be so completely taken from you & the children," she assured Will.[59]

After receiving this letter, Will quickly sent a telegram — an expensive and atypical method of communication between them — that specified: "Try medicine!" In his next letter, he countered her arguments against medicine and emphasized the benefits that could result: more income, perhaps enough for the family to live in England, and better care for the children's physical health. Downplaying her concerns about the children, he argued that she would be likely to spend more time with them than the average mother, and suggested that he might sometimes help with their care. But he stressed, as always, that she would have to let the servants do more. Struggling to overcome his own interests,

56   D.140/6/372, GCY to WHY, October 19, 1900. Young Papers.
57   D.140/6/373, WHY to GCY, October 20, 1900. Young Papers.
58   D.140/6/357a, GCY to WHY, October 22, 1900. Young Papers.
59   Ibid. Emphasis in the original. Young Papers.

he insisted that it would not be "fair" to ask for Grace's help in his work and he could advance without her assistance. Moreover, he felt the partnership role he envisioned for her — being at his "beck & call," saving him from the drudgery of preparing his work for publication — would not make sufficient use of her considerable talents. Moving from mathematics to medicine was the right course, he concluded. "[D]o it *because* of me and the children," he urged.[60]

Until this point in their discussion, Will seemed to be steering Grace to do mathematics with him. Very likely he was happy to reopen this possibility because his return to Cambridge set off new concerns about his future. Stimulated by the innovative mathematics that he was introduced to in Germany and Italy, Will had found the topic that would make his reputation. Klein had suggested that the Youngs familiarize themselves with the work of the mathematician George Cantor, and Will was quickly captivated by his work on set theory. Cantor's analysis of the nature of sets, the elements that make them up, and the correspondence between the elements in different sets, raised profound, somewhat metaphyisical, questions about mathematical concepts like continuity and infinity, and offered practical applications for measuring areas. Set theory is now regarded as one of the essential underpinnings of modern mathematics, but when Will began working on it, in the summer of 1900, it was a very controversial field of inquiry, not well known or highly regarded in England.[61]

When Will got to Cambridge, he found that no one was interested in the topics that excited him. The prospect of soldiering on alone in an academic environment that was, at best, indifferent to and, at worst, hostile to his mathematics must have been daunting indeed. Working with Grace would give him a partner who valued and understood his work; without her, he would be intellectually isolated. Given Will's temperament, this was not a recipe for success. His self-doubts returned.

Grace relied on Will's support and encouragement as much as he relied on hers. She had few if any models for combining marriage and

---

60 D.140/6/379, WHY to GCY, October 25, 1900. Emphasis in the original. Young Papers.

61 On the revolutionary nature of set theory, see Grattan-Guinness, "Mathematical Union", pp. 139–40, and William Dunham, *Journey through Genius: The Great Theorems of Mathematics* (New York: John Wiley and Sons, 1990), pp. 252–81.

motherhood with a career. As a dutiful wife, she felt she needed his blessing to embark on this new endeavor. Lacking female mentors, she had always been dependent on male approval: her father was her champion when she went to Girton College; Felix Klein was her champion in graduate school, and she continued to rely on his advice and contacts when she returned to Germany. In these letters, she did not tell Will what she wanted to do and try to convince him. Rather it was Will who framed the issues and guided the discussion, interpreted what Grace was saying, and made the case for her to go to medical school. In the end, he argued more forcefully on her behalf than she did.

At the same time that Will was supportive of Grace's efforts, he was also highly critical of her. He praised her "exceptional powers" but blamed her for being too emotional. "Grace is all ups and downs," he reminded himself. Chastising her for being too "impetuous" and "impulsive" — classic male complaints about female behavior — he warned her that such volatility might be harmful to her future patients.[62]

Despite her misgivings, Grace allowed herself to be persuaded by Will's arguments. Soon she was writing to him about how happy she was and how well her classes were going. Relieved that she would have a practical career to fall back on, Will sent her information about women's medical education and licensing in England. They agreed that she should take the London Matriculation Examination as a preliminary to taking the London Medical Examination needed to qualify to practice medicine back home.[63]

Balancing Medicine, Mathematics, and Family: 1901–1903

Will's ability to put Grace's interests above his own and treat her as someone deserving of equal consideration was lamentably intermittent and short-lived. His support for her medical training waxed and waned. The economic motivation for Grace to become a doctor — the hope that she could someday support the family — became less urgent

---

62   D.140/6/378, WHY to GCY, October 25, 1900. Young Papers.
63   D.140/6/383, GCY to WHY, October 29, 1900 and D.140/6/389b, GCY to WHY, November 4, 1900. D.140/6/391a, WHY to GCY, November 9, 1900 and D.140/6/393b, WHY to GCY, November 15, 1900. Young Papers.

after her ninety-two-year-old father died in January 1901 and left her an inheritance which they thought would provide an annual income of about 160 pounds. This was enough to sustain a lower-middle-class life style, but it was supplemented by Will's earnings and income from other investments and holdings.[64]

The prospect of more income eased the Youngs' financial burdens considerably. Feeling released from the enforced "penury" of their lives, they started to spend money more freely, and Will became more outspoken about the toll Grace's training took on her family.[65] He begged her, just after her father died, not to "sacrifice your husband & your children [...] to your medicine!" Reminding her of the distress he felt when he returned from Cambridge and saw her "tired face & the disorder around me", he bluntly challenged, "should we have allowed medicine to have come between us as it does?"[66]

Despite twinges of guilt, Grace stood firm about forging ahead with her medical training. "My own work is going on most satisfactorily &, whether it becomes a profession or not, will be invaluable to us all," she asserted a month after her father's death.[67] She passed several parts of the London Matriculation Examination in the summer of 1901, but needed additional work in Latin.[68] When a potential teaching job for Will in Australia fell through in 1902, she was relieved because she did not want to give up her medical work.[69] She steadfastly defended her time against interruptions from relatives. After her unstable sister-in-law, Ethel Young, had a breakdown in 1902 while she was living with the Youngs, Grace (with Will's encouragement) announced that a woman

---

64 Her inheritance: D.140/6/421, WHY to GCY, January 23, 1901; D.140/6/422a, WHY to GCY, January 24, 1901; D.140/6/423a, WHY to GCY, January 25, 1901, as well as multiple letters from Solicitor Henry Cook in 1901 and 1902 in D.140/29/12–53. Young Papers. Each Chisholm child received 1,448 pounds. For what it took to maintain a lower-middle-class life style, see F. S. Musgrove, "Middle Class Education and Employment in the Nineteenth Century", *Economic History Review* 12:1 (1959), 99–111. Supplemental income: D.140/6/1581, WHY to Mr. MacMahon, 25 August 1913. Young Papers.

65 They bought bicycles and a typewriter for Grace, and planned to travel more. D.140/6/561, WHY to GCY, 13 March 1902; D.140/6/547, GCY to WHY, February 18, 1902. Young Papers.

66 D.140/6/422, WHY to GCY, January 24 [1901]. Young Papers.

67 D.140/6/ 429, GCY to WHY, February 10, 1901. Young Papers.

68 D.140/6/461, WHY to GCY [June 1901]. D/140/24/2 Autobiographical notes by GCY on 1901–1902 (written in 1917). Young Papers.

69 D.140/6/597, GCY to WHY, 20 July 1902. Young Papers.

"as busy as I" could not provide adequate supervision, and the family would have to make other arrangements for Ethel's care. Grace did not want her own sister Helen to visit in 1902, because she could not afford to lose time from the lectures she was attending.[70]

But when Will needed her assistance, Grace dutifully struggled to provide it. When she started her medical training, they agreed she would no longer help him with his mathematical studies. Nevertheless, she was soon working with him again. Convinced that he needed to publish a book to be a serious job candidate and fearful that he would not finish one without her assistance, feeling guilty about her failure to be a helpmate wife, Grace offered to help "heart & soul as much as I can."[71] Pregnant in the fall of 1901 and not attending classes, she developed formulae for him, readied his papers for publication, and conducted his correspondence with other mathematicians.

Delighted to have her assistance, Will mapped out his plans for future publications and became increasingly proprietary about Grace's time.[72] Their third child, Janet, was born in December 1901. (Grace read Dante while waiting for her labor to begin.[73]) Two months later, Will admonished her, "Just now the [mathematical] work is *extremely important*. I don't like your not beginning before 3 p.m. & really don't see why this should be the case."[74] The following week he urged her not to do anything except mathematics, even though he was "disappointed & somewhat anxious at the nonresumption of the medical work."[75] This dual imperative — that Grace should devote as much time as possible to his work while advancing quickly through her medical training — was typical of Will's exhortations. She did her best to comply, but the pressure was grueling.

In the fall of 1902, when she was taking twenty-one class hours per week, Grace planned to devote three hours per day to mathematics late in the week and seven to nine hours per day to medicine early in the

---

70   D.140/6/579a, GCY to WHY, May 17, 1902. Young Papers.
71   D.140/6/429, GCY to WHY, February 10, 1901. Young Papers.
72   D.140/6/515, WHY to GCY, November 27, 1901. Young Papers.
73   D.140/6/521a, GCY to WHY, December 11 [1901]. Young Papers.
74   D.140/6/537, WHY to GCY, February 7, 1902. Emphasis in the original. Young Papers.
75   D.140/6/557, WHY to GCY, February 13, 1902. Young Papers.

week.[76] Will wanted her to prepare examination questions for him and work on his articles. Feeling overwhelmed, she offered to cut back on her medicine. When he did not insist, she persevered with her medical courses and took intense pleasure in them. She dreamed about anatomy, took pride in drawing connections between her botany and anatomy classes, and was surprised to learn that she had signed up for more chemistry classes than most medical students.[77]

During some weeks, she was too busy to help Will. When he pressed her for the exam questions, she reminded him that preparing for her London entrance exams took priority. "We must see that *nothing* interferes with this," she insisted, adding that it would facilitate her progress if he would leave Cambridge and stay in Göttingen with her and the children.[78]

Two weeks later, Grace's unmarried friend, Frances Evans, sent her a heartfelt tribute. "Your life is wonderful to me," Frances wrote, noting how exceptional Grace was in managing to "work out her own personal aims" while maintaining a loving home circle. "I meet devoted mothers & wives, but they can be nothing else — or I meet clever women with no home ties," she explained. Frances praised Will as well. "He has never tried to absorb your individuality and your career. Do you realise how wonderfully rare that is?" she queried.[79]

The reality was more complicated than Frances imagined. Will's career was a family enterprise, dependent on Grace's efforts as well as his. Time and again, his enthusiasm for Grace's medical studies warred with his ever growing desire for her help with his own work. As a result, he gave her frustratingly mixed messages. He repeatedly told her not to give up medicine, but insisted it should not interfere with the work she was doing for him.

His demands consistently undermined her progress, but Grace very rarely put her own needs first or expressed irritation. Instead, she did her best to accommodate him. Occasionally, she tried to protect her time by suggesting that she delay a visit to him in Cambridge or postpone a

---

76 D.140/6/619, GCY to WHY, November 13, 1902; D.140/6/620, GCY to WHY, 18 November, 1902. Young Papers.

77 D.140/6/619b, GCY to WHY, 13 November 1902. Young Papers.

78 D.140/6/622, GCY to WHY, November 26, 1902. Emphasis in the original. Young Papers.

79 D.140/6/627, Frances Evans to GCY, December 9 [1902]. Young Papers.

European holiday until she completed some portion of her own work. But she qualified her request by stressing "if you can spare me." Or she demurred, "I do not want to press it."[80]

The more pressure Will felt to advance his own career, the more likely he was to lose sight of the burdens he placed on Grace. Very occasionally, he apologized for driving her too hard. "I love you, my darling wife, admire you, respect you, reverence you too but all this does not prevent me letting you think of my comfort rather than your own!" he confessed in November 1904.[81] He also knew that he was overly critical of her and others.[82] But instead of sympathizing with her, he was more likely to berate her for failing to manage her time and her household efficiently.

When she started her medical training in the fall of 1900, Grace employed two servants to help with the children — Frankie, three years old, and Cecily, six months — and the housework. Nevertheless, believing that she could give the children better care than the servants, she arranged her schedule so that she could dress, bathe, and feed the children herself, spending several hours with them before they went to bed.[83] As the strain of doing both medicine and mathematics intensified, and the family continued to grow — Janet was born in December 1901, Helen (Leni) in September 1903, Laurence (Laurie) in July 1905, and Patrick (Pat) in March 1908 — Grace had to surrender more of the childcare and housekeeping. In addition to the servants, she had assistance from Will's younger, unmarried sisters. Ethel Young joined the household in May 1901 to help care for children. After she left in 1902, she was replaced by Mary Ann Young (Auntie May), who lived with the family for more than ten years. Even when she had help, Grace made time for her children. She wrote Will in the fall of 1902, "I did my daily quota of Physiology this morning before 7 AM. Cecily & Frankie were building castles in the bedroom. Janet was sitting on the fur hearthrug, nodding at me & laughing when I caught her eye, &

80 D.140/6/597, GCY to WHY, 20 July 1902. D.140/6/750, GCY to WHY, 6 February 1904. Young Papers.
81 D.140/6/848, WHY to GCY, November 28, 1904. Similarly, D.140/6/712, WHY to GCY, November 9, 1903. Young Papers.
82 D.140/6/416, WHY to GCY, January 18, 1901. Young Papers.
83 Better care: D.140/6/357, GCY to WHY, October 22, 1900. Schedule: D.140/6/389, GCY to WHY, November 4, 1900; see also, D.140/6/392, GCY to WHY, November 11 [1900]. Young Papers.

eating a biscuit."[84] On a day when a servant was off and Grace had sole charge of the children, she managed to make a dress for Cecily, read physics, and do mathematics for Will.[85]

The cost of this all-but-impossible balancing act was high. Grace was often physically exhausted and suffered from chronic and debilitating headaches. The headaches were attributed to a liver condition that later caused gall stones, but the stresses and strains of her life undoubtedly contributed as well.[86] In the midst of preparing for exams in the summer of 1902, while also working on Will's mathematics, she confessed to being "run down, off my feed, & got the blues."[87] In February 1904, when Will queried about the status of the work she was doing for him just after she had finished a set of exams, she responded rather sharply, "Really darling, I am too hard worked! but I am most anxious to get everything done & am very well & so are we all."[88] Such complaints were rare, however. For the most part, Grace undertook her multiple activities with enthusiasm and seemed to thrive on the challenges of her demanding life.

Will, in contrast, was anxious and frustrated. During most of the year, he was in England, trying to write papers on pure mathematics while coaching undergraduates at Cambridge University (1900–1904), conducting examinations at a variety of other schools, and serving as the Chief Mathematical Examiner for the Central Welsh [Education] Board (1902–1905), which administered examinations in primary and secondary schools and colleges throughout Wales. He was miserable in Cambridge. "[P]rivate teaching is very exhausting and unsatisfying [...]. It's awful here! Little knowledge, little time [crossed out] & much jealousy," he complained to Grace in November 1901.[89] Always sensitive to slights, he felt unappreciated and knew that he gained status by being the husband of "a distinguished woman."[90] Drained of will and enthusiasm, weakened by indigestion and minor physical ailments, he was often unable to work productively. He continued to apply for

---

84 D.140/6/615, GCY to WHY, October 29, 1902. Young Papers.
85 D.140/6/612, GCY to WHY, October 19, 1902. Young Papers.
86 D.140/2/2, R. C. H. Tanner notes. Young Papers.
87 D.140/6/590, GCY to WHY, June 30, 1902. Young Papers.
88 D.140/6/751, GCY to WHY, February 10, 1904. Young Papers.
89 D.140/6/501, WHY to GCY, November 5, 1901. Young Papers.
90 D.140/6/422, WHY to GCY, January 24 [1901]. Young Papers.

teaching positions in British universities and continued to be turned down.

Grace responded to his complaints, anxieties, and disappointments with stoic cheerfulness and redoubled her efforts to help him. "Let them give the readership & the examinership to Tag, Rag, and Bobtail. I really don't care a straw if you don't," she announced in November 1901.[91] She sweetly, but steadfastly, urged him not to lose heart, not to wallow in self-pity, and not to resign from Cambridge without having another position. Knowing that he needed "managing" (his term), she counselled him on his job searches and used her connections to influential scholars, friends, and relatives to get endorsements for him. She had to "drag" a testimonial out of Felix Klein for him in 1901, she told Will, because "nearly all our mathematical communications with him have been carried on through me."[92] She pushed Will, too, warning him that he would have to get himself "in harness" and work hard if they were to finish their book.[93] "Our honor is at stake," she reminded him, linking her professional reputation with his.[94] But she knew her own worth. When Will was thinking about giving a lecture on descriptive geometry in his effort to get the Welsh examinership in 1901, Grace advised him not to, because he did not know the topic and it would take him too long to learn it, even with her help. "*I* could lecture on it tomorrow if I was wanted!" she proudly noted.[95]

Helpmate Wife and Anonymous Partner

With Grace's help, Will produced numerous publications on set theory and its applications to various branches of mathematical analysis, including calculus. He had a profusion of ideas, and their work developed important theorems on problems of differentiation (constructing tangents) and integration (measuring areas under curves). Throughout their long collaboration, both Grace and Will persisted in treating her as the junior partner to her more illustrious, and ostensibly more gifted,

---

91   D.140/6/513, GCY to WHY, November 21, 1901. Young Papers.
92   D.140/6/504a, GCY to WHY, November 7, 1901. Young Papers.
93   D.140/6/499a, GCY to WHY, November 1, 1901. Young Papers.
94   D.140/6/429, GCY to WHY, February 10, 1901. Young Papers.
95   D.140/6/499a, GCY to WHY, November 1, 1901. Emphasis in the original. Young Papers.

husband. He referred to her as "the bottle washer" in his "experiments", the talented pupil who solved the problems that he, the teacher, set for her.[96] He claimed to have taught her set theory and persuaded her that she understood it well enough to help him.[97] She described herself as his "helper", "secretary", and "critic." Her role was to save him from much "drudgery" and the "troublesome and weary work" of preparing his manuscripts for publication.[98] She took notes while Will dictated, conducted his professional correspondence, and typed his manuscripts. She worked out the formulae to prove his theorems, found and corrected errors in his work, drafted early versions of some of his papers, and edited and rewrote others. In their accounts of the partnership, Will had the big ideas; Grace filled in the details and provided the structure and framework that defined his theories, freeing him to move quickly on to the next big idea.

Accepting Grace and Will's characterization of the partnership, their children portrayed Grace as an enabler and catalyst rather than a partner who contributed her own original insights to his work. Cecily, the Youngs' eldest daughter and a mathematician herself, explained,

> [M]y father had ideas and a wide grasp of subjects, but was by nature undecided; his mind worked only when stimulated by the reactions of a sympathetic audience. My mother had decision and initiative and the stamina to carry an undertaking to its conclusion. Her skill in understanding and in responding, and her pleasure in exercising this skill led her naturally into the position she filled so uniquely. If she had not had that skill, my father's genius would probably have been abortive, and would not have eclipsed hers and the name she had already made for herself.[99]

---

96   D.140/6/558, WHY to GCY, February 15, 1902; D.140/6/380, WHY to GCY, October 25, 1900. Young Papers.

97   D.140/6/4938, WHY to Patrick Young, October 31, 1931. Young Papers.

98   D.140/16/1, GCY, "Per Ardua ad Astra" (1917), p. 85; D.140/6/2244, GCY to Frances Evans, 4 October 1916; D.140/6/499, GCY to WHY, November 1, 1901; D.140/6/709, GCY to WHY, November 2, 1903. Young Papers.

99   Cecily Young (Tanner) to Professor Lida Barrett, circa 1968. Quoted in Sylvia Wiegand, "Grace Chisholm Young and William Henry Young: A Partnership of Itinerant British Mathematicians" in *Creative Couples in the Sciences*, ed. by Helena M. Pycior, Nancy G. Slack, and Pnina G. Abiram-Am (New Brunswick, NJ: Rutgers University Press, 1996), pp. 126–40 (p. 137). Similarly, D.140/2/2.1, R. C. H. Tanner notes. Young Papers. For Laurence Young's view of Grace's contribution, see Laurence Young, *Mathematicians*, p. 283 and Wiegand, "Grace Chisholm Young and William Henry Young", pp. 137–38.

In fact, Grace did much more than that. The Youngs' correspondence shows that she was a full intellectual partner, not just someone who carried out Will's instructions. Working out their views on set theory, they argued back and forth, questioned each other's reasoning, found mistakes in each other's work, and jointly carved out their approach. "I have not got a proof of this theorem yet from *our point of view*," Grace informed Will in the spring of 1902, emphasizing that the approach George Cantor, the father of set theory, had taken was one "*we* want to avoid."[100] Describing how she developed another proof, she explained, "it's what we planned except as regards the last step."[101]

Grace challenged Will, pushed him to think more deeply, expanded his vision, and improved their line of argument. She incorporated her own ideas into his work. Wanting to amend a paper that Will had already sent out for review, she explained,

> I see something new, & I want to alter the end materially & make it much simpler & more lucid & more consequential. I think even you yourself have not quite grasped the light which the intervals throw on derivation & I remember you doubted whether there was any process other than derivation, the process I call deduction. It is the fact that there is such a process & that I have not clearly brought this out in the final article of the paper on sets of intervals that make the reasoning there inadequate if not actually wrong.[102]

When Will questioned her proof, she continued to wrestle with it, ending up with "some *very* pretty work on overlapping intervals brought out by your criticisms & suggestions."[103] A year later, she assured him that the corrections she had made in another paper "were most necessary." She had fixed some mistakes and made the article "so lucid, so fundamental, [that it] leads to just what we want in the paper on sets of points."[104]

As part of the University of Göttingen's international community of mathematicians, Grace kept Will informed about what other mathematicians were doing and tested their reactions to the Youngs'

---

100 D.140/6/612, GCY to WHY, 19/10/02. Emphasis added. Young Papers.

101 D.140/6/578, GCY to WHY, January 22 [1902]. Young Papers.

102 D.140/6/611, GCY to WHY, 16/10/02. Young Papers.

103 D.140/6/619b, GCY to WHY [13/11/02]. Emphasis in the original; very is underlined multiple times. Young Papers.

104 D.140/6/647, GCY to WHY [4 May 1903]. Young Papers.

work.[105] She attended a weekly colloquium of mathematicians, and went out with the members afterwards to talk shop.[106] When a scholar who disagreed with the Youngs visited the university, Grace proposed that he give a talk to the colloquium so she would learn what others thought of him without revealing her own views. "See how the hard world is teaching your harmless dove the wisdom of the serpent," she warned Will.[107]

Grace's subordinate role in the Youngs' partnership was premised, in part, on the idea that Will was the more gifted mathematician. Awed by the mathematics he was doing in Italy in the late 1890s, she wrote a friend, "[Will] is so unlike most people that I find my greatest comfort & joy in reading about really great men; how often do I find his rare qualities, qualities which put him out of touch with ordinary people, reflected in those of the most celebrated people."[108] Years later, she still marveled at the originality of his mind and compared herself unflatteringly to him as well as to their sixteen-year-old son. Describing how Frankie developed a proof and discovered an error in her work, she wrote to Will, "I feel at once with him as I do with you, that I have to do with a mathematical power altogether beyond my own."[109]

Trapped in the gendered stereotypes of their time and uncomfortable with ideas of gender equality, Grace and Will failed to appreciate how much her thinking added value to his work. The belief that women could be excellent students but lacked the capacity for creative, original thought was seared deep into the Victorian mind.[110] Greatness in mathematics has traditionally been equated with genius, and the nineteenth-century world understood "genius" to be a characteristic of the male mind exclusively.[111] Early in the nineteenth century, the

---

105 D.140/6/611, GCY to WHY, 16/10/02. Young Papers.
106 D.140/6/619b, GCY to WHY [13/11/02]. Young Papers.
107 D.140/6/932, GCY to WHY, March 2, 1906. Young Papers.
108 D.140/6/318, GCY to Frances Evans, December 10, 1899. Young Papers.
109 D.140/6/1842, GCY to WHY, March 20, 1914. Young Papers.
110 Such attitudes die hard. Ben Barres, an acclaimed twentieth-century neuroscientist who spent the early years of his professional life as a woman, noted that when she was the only person in an MIT class to solve a particular problem on a test, the professor accused her of cheating, insisting that her boyfriend must have solved it for her (Neil Genzlinger, "Ben Barres, Neuroscientist and Equal-Opportunity Advocate, Dies at 63", *The New York Times*, December 31, 2017, A25).
111 See Claire G. Jones, *Femininity, Mathematics and Science, 1880–1914* (Basingstoke and New York: Palgrave Macmillan, 2009). Jones's illuminating exploration of the role

mathematician Mary Somerville (who worked at the intersection of mathematics, physics, and astronomy) trivialized her extraordinary talents by noting, "I have perseverance and intelligence, but no genius, that spark from heaven is not granted to the [female] sex."[112] In Grace's day, the male colleagues of the revered German mathematician Emmy Noether, awed by her formidable talents, adopted masculine nouns and pronouns when they talked to her or about her, as a way of indicating that her mind was as powerful as a man's.[113] Will bluntly told Grace that she was not a mathematical genius. "I value your help enormously up to a point. I do not believe, however, that your chief strength is in mathematics pure and simple. You can do everything well, & it is easy to do some things well, but mathematics is not one of those unless one has genius," he wrote her early in their collaboration.[114]

Recognizing Will's intellectual prowess was vital to the personal dynamic that fueled the Youngs' marriage. When he was elected a Fellow of the Royal Society in 1907, Grace rejoiced that he was fulfilling the promise of future success he had made when they became engaged.[115] The modern woman, "whatever her personal ambitions, really longs for a superior male mind, just as she admires the strength, & craves the protection of the complete man," she wrote in 1920.[116] Treating Will's work as more important than Grace's, and making his career their joint career righted the imbalance that had characterized their marriage at its start. Even when Grace challenged his conclusions or approach, she

---

that gender played in mathematics and science education and practice around 1900, and in the institutions and associations that supported them, provides an important context for understanding the career opportunities and dilemmas encountered by women of Grace's era. She and fellow Girtonian, Hertha Ayrton, a physicist and engineer, are featured in Jones's study.

112 Quoted in Teri Perl, *Math Equals: Biographies of Women Mathematicians and Related Activities* (Menlo Park, CA: Addison-Wesley, 1978), p. 91. Mary Fairfax Somerville (1780–1872) received strong support for her work from her second husband who helped her by searching for the books she needed, and copying and recopying her manuscripts.

113 Lynn M. Osen, *Women in Mathematics* (Cambridge, MA: MIT Press, 1974), p. 152. Albert Einstein noted that Noether (1882–1935) was regarded by leading mathematicians as "the most significant creative mathematical genius thus far produced since the higher education of women began." She studied at the University of Göttingen and later taught there, working closely with Felix Klein.

114 D.140/6/558, WHY to GCY, March 9, 1902. Young Papers.

115 D/140/24/1, Typed copy of GCY to WHY [March 1907]. Young Papers.

116 D.140/14/1, GCY essay, dated Xmas Day, 1920. Young Papers.

deferred to him and acknowledged his preeminence. Sending him the draft of a paper, she demurred, "I am rather pleased with it myself but think you are certain to improve it."[117]

Will's sense of superiority was bolstered by the fact that Grace's work habits conformed to neither the male-defined image of a professional in the late nineteenth century nor the more traditional concept of a highly gifted person with a calling. She emphasized the importance of balance and moderation and integrated her intellectual work with the demands of daily life.[118] Alarmed by the demands that Will's obsession with work and professional advancement placed on her and the children, she wrote in an undated fragment of a letter to Will that was possibly never sent:

> We must never go through another five weeks like last Christmas. Life was given to us to use & also to enjoy & whether you or I or someone else is the first person to publish some particular discovery is a matter of comparatively small importance. Far more important is that we should taste the full cup of life, enjoy it & be invigorated by it, rear healthy & capable children, & help carry on the world's business, & look our own fate calmly in the face.[119]

The equilibrium Grace struggled to achieve involved balancing different types of intellectual and cultural pursuits as well as work and family. In the midst of her medical studies and mathematical work, she managed to write children's books, compose poetry and fiction, and play music with her children. Such a broad range of interests did not serve Grace well in a world in which academic disciplines were becoming more specialized, dilettantism was frowned upon, and careers were supposed to be all-consuming. The notion that a professional career entailed total commitment, unstinting labor, and progressive advancement was born in late nineteenth-century England and America and reflected a

117 D.140/6/528, GCY to WHY, January 22 [1902]. Young Papers.
118 Modern day female mathematicians have commented on the persistence of such judgments and argued that their interrupted days have been a stimulant, not a deterrent, to their creativity and productivity. Margaret A. M. Murray, *Women Becoming Mathematicians: Creating a Professional Identity in Post-World War II America* (Cambridge, MA: MIT Press, 2000), pp. 151–98.
119 D.140/7/1.20, GCY to WHY, [n.d.], end missing. Young Papers. It is not clear whether Grace actually sent this to Will. She was rarely so directly critical of Will or so impassioned in challenging him.

distinctly male culture.[120] In contrast, the term "amateurism" connoted work that was "superficial, desultory" and associated with "less than a serious commitment, the pursuit of an activity for amusement and distraction."[121]

Will accepted these distinctions. He himself had dallied and focused too broadly when he was at Cambridge. In retrospect, he believed these habits contributed to his early lack of success as a mathematician and marked him as unambitious. When he wanted Grace's help, he could not tolerate distractions. He was not just making up for lost time; he was living the life he thought was required of a scholar. Nevertheless, Grace was a steadier and harder worker than Will. While he required ideal conditions in which to think and write, she applied herself efficiently and productively to the multiple tasks she undertook, coped with multiple interruptions, and often worked late into the night. Rejecting the Cambridge adage (developed by male scholars) that mathematics can be productively worked at for only six hours a day, Grace noted that she could profitably spend two or three hours reading mathematics after devoting a day to problem solving. Her notebooks are filled with notes and summaries of mathematical studies in English, French, German, and Italian.[122]

In Will's eyes, Grace also failed to measure up to the older ideal of work as a "calling," a service done in the pursuit of a higher good. He explained to their daughter Cecily, "The exceptionally intellectual person has a duty — that of developing the intellectual powers to the utmost limit, both for the sake of his own individuality & also for the possibilities it creates of contributing to the utmost extent to the intellectual & higher progress generally of mankind."[123] Dedicated to the pursuit of Truth, Will rode roughshod over anything that interfered with his work. Grace's failure to do the same — when she insisted on

---

120 See the Introduction to this volume, p. 19.
121 Burton J. Bledstein, *The Culture of Professionalism: The Middle-Class and the Development of Higher Education in America* (New York: W. W. Norton, 1976), p. 31. E. Anthony Rotundo, *American Manhood: Transformations in Masculinity from the Revolution to the Modern Era* (New York: Basic Books, 1993), pp. 175–76, notes that men typically approached their work with an all-engrossing "passion," and argues that the "habit of pouring heart and soul into their work [...] became a defining mark of American manhood" in the nineteenth century.
122 D.140/34/52–55, Notes by GCY in Small Notebooks. Young Papers.
123 D.140/6/3904, WHY to Cecily Young, May 12, 1927. Young Papers.

spending time with the children, refused to hire more household help, or allowed herself to be "distracted" by her other interests — fueled Will's sense of entitlement and superiority and justified the sacrifices he expected her to make on his behalf. She acquiesced without complaint, but it became harder for her to do so as time went on.

Grace was not only a subordinate partner but also an anonymous partner whose contributions were mostly hidden from the world. In private, Will gratefully acknowledged his reliance on her assistance. Their mathematical exchanges acted as "stimulants" that kept him "working and thinking."[124] Without her help, he felt lost. "Alone I can do nothing [...] my usefulness would be vitally attacked if you were not by my side strong & well," he wrote to her in 1903.[125]

Nevertheless, Will was conflicted about whether to publicly acknowledge Grace's help. He recognized that they should both be authors of the work they were producing in early 1902, but he feared that acknowledging Grace's work would hurt his chances of getting an academic job. Torn between equity and expediency, he opted for expediency. He laid out the problem for Grace:

> The fact is that our papers ought to be published under our joint names but if this were done we should neither of us get the benefit of it. No. Mine the laurels now & the knowledge. Yours the knowledge only.
>
> Do you suppose people will venture to say the laurels ought to be yours? No they would be very unwilling to allow that. They are on the horns of a dilemma. Each alternative annoys them. Divide and we are lost for they would pooh pooh both. Everything under my name now, & later when the loaves and fishes are no more procurable in that way, everything or much under your name. There is my programme. At present you can't undertake a public career. You have your children. I can and do.[126]

Will's assertion that no one would think the laurels ought to be Grace's was disingenuous and self-serving. Prejudice against women scientists women was strong, and prejudice against married women scientists was even stronger. Yet progress was being made. Not all prizes, honors,

---

124 D.140/6/553, WHY to GCY, February 15, 1902. Young Papers.
125 D.140/6/712, WHY to GCY, November 9, 1903; similarly, D.140/6/461, WHY to GCY [June 1901]. Young Papers.
126 D.140/6/553, WHY to GCY, February 15, 1902. Young Papers.

and outlets would have been closed to Grace. In February 1902, just when Will was thinking about an authorship policy for himself and Grace, the Royal Society, Britain's premier organization devoted to the promotion and improvement of science (including mathematics), rejected the first woman who applied for membership on the grounds that she was married. Hertha Ayrton had many publications and inventions in physics and electrical engineering, and the support of several (male) members of the Society, including her husband. But legal opinion ruled that the language of the founding charter, written in 1662, excluded married women because under English common law they were not deemed to be individuals with separate identities apart from their husbands.[127] No woman, single or married, joined the Royal Society until 1945.

The door of the Royal Society was barred, but the London Mathematical Society, founded in 1865, the preeminent association of mathematicians in Britain, had begun admitting women to membership in the 1880s and allowed them to give papers.[128] Grace had been a member since 1896. Moreover, when they published under their own names, married women as well as single women were winning recognition, prizes, and honors. Despite being denied membership in the Royal Society, Hertha Ayrton became the first woman to read her own paper at the Society in 1904, and was honored with its Hughes Medal in 1906, an award given to an outstanding researcher in the field of energy. Marie Curie famously won two Nobel prizes, in 1903 and 1911, as well as the Royal Society's Davy Prize.

Will's fear that neither he nor Grace would benefit if they published jointly because the world would "pooh pooh both" was equally disingenuous and self-serving. The greater likelihood was that he would get credit for his contributions but she would not get credit for hers. What twentieth-century scholars called "the Matilda effect" — the

---

127 Joan Mason, "Hertha Ayrton (1854–1923) and the Admission of Women to the Royal Society of London", *Notes and Records of the Royal Society of London*, 45:2 (1991), 201–20.

128 There were nine female members of the London Mathematical Society in 1895, about 4 percent of the total membership. In 1905, there were fourteen female members (15.5 percent). Claire Jones, "Grace Chisholm Young: gender and mathematics around 1900", *Women's History Review* 9:4 (2000), 675–91, https://doi.org/10.1080/09612020000200266. See also, Jones, *Femininity*, pp. 155–63.

longstanding habit of devaluing women's contributions in science and giving credit to men for work done by women — was already well-established. Then, as now, women struggled against the assumption that a woman who collaborates with a man provides assistance-type help while he does all the conceptual, original work. The history of collaborative couples in science is filled with relationships that fit — or were made to fit — that image. Wives' contributions have often been downplayed, unacknowledged, or hidden, due to a combination of institutional barriers, gendered stereotypes, social pressure, and personal choices.[129]

Faced with similar circumstances and dilemmas, some accomplished couples who were contemporaries of the Youngs — Marie and Pierre Curie, Hertha and William Ayrton, and Beatrice and Sidney Webb — made very different choices and found ways to honor the wife's achievements and contributions. They are striking exceptions to the general pattern. Had it not been for Pierre Curie's protests and avowals about his wife's role, Marie Curie would not have been a co-recipient of the Nobel Prize along with Pierre in 1903.[130] Nevertheless, the erroneous perception that Pierre discovered radium persisted. Hertha Ayrton, the wife who was rejected for membership in the Royal Society, wryly observed in 1909, "Errors are notoriously hard to kill, but an error that ascribes to a man what was actually the work of a woman has more lives than a cat."[131] A feminist and suffragette, Ayrton deplored that women's achievements were often overlooked "because no one will believe that

---

129 See Helena M. Pycior, Nancy G. Slack, and Pnina G. Abir-Am, "Introduction", in *Creative Couples in the Sciences*, pp. 3–35. The term "Matilda Effect" was coined by Margaret W. Rossiter in honor of Matilda J. Gage (1826–1898), an American suffragette and feminist, who described the habit of crediting men for work done by talented women in an 1870 essay, "Woman as Inventor." Margaret W. Rossiter, "The Matthew Matilda Effect in Science", *Social Studies of Science* 23:2 (May 1993), 325–41. See also, Nancy G. Slack, "Epilogue: Collaborative Couples: Past, Present, and Future" in *For Better or Worse? Collaborative Couples in the Sciences*, ed. by Annette Lykknes, Donald L. Optiz, and Brigitte Van Tiggelen (Basel: Springer, 2012), pp. 270–94.

130 American Institute of Physics, "Marie Curie and the Science of Radioactivity", https://history.aip.org/exhibits/curie/. If the Curies published separately, each highlighted the work the other had done to lay their common groundwork. See Helena M. Pycior, "Pierre Curie and 'His Eminent Collaborator Mme Curie'" in *Creative Couples*, ed. by Pycior, Slack, and Abiram-Am, pp. 39–56.

131 Letter to the *Westminster Gazette*, March 14, 1909, quoted in Mason, "Hertha Ayrton", p. 210.

if a man and a woman do a bit of work together the woman really does anything."[132] To avoid that problem, Hertha and her husband — William Ayrton, a professor of physics, electrical engineer, and staunch supporter of women's rights — agreed that they should not collaborate. "[H]e wanted me to get the full kudos for all I did, not only for my sake, but for the sake of all women," Hertha explained.[133] Beatrice and Sidney Webb, discussed in Chapter 4, also adopted more egalitarian views and practices in their long collaboration on social investigation and public policy reform.[134]

Because they lacked a feminist consciousness and were conditioned to expect female inferiority and subservience, it is not surprising that Grace and Will constructed a partnership that recognized his achievements and contributions and masked hers. Instead of addressing the problems Will identified, they helped to perpetuate them.

Authorship mattered greatly to Will in 1902 because he was struggling to get both an advanced degree and a university position. As a candidate for a Doctor of Science (DSc) degree from Cambridge University, he was required to demonstrate a capacity for original research. Co-authored publications might have made it harder to show this. Will's primary rationale was economic and pragmatic: he had to procure the "loaves and fishes" for his growing family, and publishing under his name alone would help him to do that. But he was also eager to enjoy the "laurels" of success and win prestige, honors, and awards. His sense of manly pride and masculine self-worth depended on career advancement and

---

132 Letter to the *Westminster Gazette*, March 14, 1909, quoted in Mason, "Hertha Ayrton", p. 216.

133 Ibid. Nevertheless, a very mean-spirited obituary of Hertha by Henry E. Armstrong (who had opposed her admission to the Royal Society) questioned her originality and suggested she owed more to her husband's influence than the couple thought. Armstong's obituary also criticized Hertha for not being the kind of domestic, helpmate wife who would have enabled William Ayrton to live "a longer and happier life and done far more effective work." (Henry E. Armstrong, "Mrs. Hertha Ayrton", *Nature*, 112 (1923), 800–1.) Ayrton's first wife, Matilda Chaplin Ayrton, who died in 1883, was one of the first English women to earn a medical degree. She continued to practice medicine during her marriage.

134 For additional examples, see *For Better or Worse? Collaborative Couples in the Sciences*, ed. by Lykknes, Optiz, and Van Tiggelen. Nancy G. Slack's "Epilogue: Collaborative Couples: Past, Present, and Future" (pp. 270–94) provides a useful assessment of the roles wives and husbands have traditionally played in collaborative efforts in science. She found that the men typically won the greater share of professional success when they collaborated with women.

affirmation from the outside world. Both he and Grace wanted him to step out of her shadow and be recognized as the brilliant thinker they believed him to be.

Convinced that his career was finally taking off, Will was acting with a new sense of urgency in 1902.[135] He had a topic he was genuinely excited about, unlike the astronomy book that had dragged on for five years and would never be completed. He was asked to review other mathematicians' work and contribute papers to European journals. To make the most of these opportunities, he told Grace, "we must flood the societies with papers."[136] To ensure his success, he wanted to publish their joint material under his name alone.

In this, as in so many aspects of their married life, Grace acquiesced to what Will wanted. They may have talked about their views on authorship when they were together, but they did not hash them out in their correspondence. She did not comment on his proposed policy in her letters.[137] Her silence may have been a form of protest, but it also signaled acceptance. Three weeks earlier, she had sent Will a draft of a paper that used material they had discussed together. She urged him to improve it, put his name on it, and then submit it for publication.[138] If she resented not being acknowledged as a collaborator in these early years, she never said so, and it was not evident to others. Grace's correspondence with the mathematician Max Dehn in 1906, about a theorem which Will had published in 1903, shows how joint their work was and how fully she was identified with and invested in it, even when the public credit went to Will. These letters also reveal how forcefully she defended their ideas against what she thought were undeserved critiques.[139] Nevertheless, whenever she had opportunities to publish on her own or as a co-author, she took them.

---

135 D.140/6/537a, WHY to GCY, February 7, 1902. Young Papers.
136 D.140/6/553, WHY to GCY, February 15, 1902. Young Papers.
137 Will specifically asked Grace to tell him when she received his letter, which he wrote on February 15, 1902. She replied on February 18, saying that she had received his letter on February 17. D.140/6/547, GCY to WHY, February 18 [1902]. Young Papers.
138 D.140/6/528, GCY to WHY, January 22 [1902]. Young Papers.
139 See Elizabeth Muhlhausen, "Grace Chisholm Young, William Henry Young, Their Results on the Theory of Sets of Points at the Beginning of the Twentieth Century, and a Controversy with Max Dehn" in *Against all Odds*, ed. by Kaufholz-Soldat and

The pragmatic reasons Will outlined would have made sense to Grace. She was as anxious for him to get a good job and win acclaim as he himself was. A better job would not only ease the Youngs' financial worries, but also, they hoped, allow the family to live together in England. She and Will would not have to be separated for weeks and months at a time.

In addition, Grace had her own reasons to remain anonymous, reasons that highlight the social constraints that limited female achievement in her day. As a well-brought-up Victorian woman, she had been taught not to seek praise or public recognition. When she was a graduate student at Göttingen University, she was reluctant to be interviewed by an English newspaper, fearing it was "not wholesome or desirable" to call public attention to herself. Informing her sister that she had passed her dissertation defense *magna cum laude*, Grace wrote, "I have heard things [about] myself which are so extremely flattering that they are not repeatable."[140] As a medical student, she recounted to Will the praise she had received from her anatomy professor but dismissed such "flattery" as "very naughty & a little like champagne." Repeating other compliments about her work to Will, she explained in her typically self-effacing way, "I tell you all this because I know it will please you probably more than it did me."[141] Downplaying her success, she assured Will that her relationship with him was more important than any academic achievement: "as for my husband, wouldn't I fly from every bit of flattery to nestle in his heart & be just his Baby again and no more."[142] (Because Grace did not like her given name, Will called her by her childhood nickname, "Baby", except when he was angry with her.[143])

Grace's concerns about being an ambitious woman were compounded by her desire not to outshine her husband. Will and the family unit mattered more to her than public acclaim. Her sense of identification

---

Oswald, pp. 121–32. See also, D.140/6/932, GCY to WHY, March 2, 1906. Young Papers.

140 D.140/8/61, GC to Helen Chisholm, 29 April, 1895. Young Papers.

141 D.140/6/383, GCY to WHY, October 29, 1900. Young Papers.

142 D.140/6/372, GCY to WHY, October 19, 1900. Young Papers.

143 D.140/2/2, R. C. H. Tanner notes. Young Papers. Patrick Young also reported that Will called Grace "Baby." D.140/2/4.1, Patrick Young to Ivor Grattan-Guinness, 1 November 1970. Young Papers.

with him was so strong that she experienced his success as her success. The satisfaction of work well done, the appreciation of her husband, and the admiration of her family and friends were sufficient reward, Grace maintained. She explained to her sister:

> I liked being *in cog.* [*in cognito*] to the outside world, & felt I had a perfect right to do so, husband & wife being one. I confess it seems to me a trifle 'ordinaire' to put my name with his on the title page. I don't want to be mistaken for the modern ambitious female, ambitious for herself & her own glorification. Our work has just been our work, as our children are our children.[144]

Grace's fear of appearing "ordinaire" — by which she meant "common" — suggests that her views were shaped by considerations of class as well as gender. As always, she did not want her family to think her actions were unbecoming for a woman of her upbringing and status.

Grace fully embraced the ideal that women found fulfillment in serving their loved ones. As a graduate student, she had expressed admiration for the "life of devotion and usefulness" that a friend derived from caring for her family.[145] When Will's unmarried sister gave up a job in order to "take charge of her motherless nephews & niece", Grace praised her for doing "the right thing."[146] Working with Will on a paper when she was a young bride, she rejoiced to find "there is so much for which I am needed." To her closest friend she confided, "it is *wonderful and delightful to me to feel how much I have helped & spurred* [*Will*] *on.*"[147] Twenty years after her wedding, Grace asserted that when a woman married, she "shut the door of personal ambition for herself, & passed through into another chamber where her life was to be merged with something broader & better."[148] She did not comment on whether she struggled to keep that door closed.

Assuming the role of helpmate wife eased Grace's guilt about pursuing an independent career and appearing to be ambitious for herself. Blaming herself for Will's failure to complete the book he had

---

144 D.140/6/872, GCY to Helen Chisholm, April 30, 1905. Young Papers.
145 D.140/6/63, GC to Frances Evans [October 1894]. Young Papers.
146 D.140/6/277, GC to Anna Bell Chisholm, March 5, 1899. Young Papers.
147 D.140/6/158, GCY to Frances Evans, January 1, 1897. Emphasis in the original. Young Papers.
148 D.140/16/1, GCY, "Per Ardua", pp. 2–3. Young Papers.

been planning to write when they married, she despondently queried whether others would think she had "failed in my task of being your helpmeet" by taking up medicine.[149]

Grace was following a well-established tradition by being a helpmate. In many upper-middle-class, intellectually elite households in nineteenth-century England, two spouses shared a single career — the husband's. Educated wives handled their husbands' professional correspondence, edited manuscripts, corrected galley proofs, prepared translations, took notes, and served as critics and sounding boards. In almost all cases, the wife's efforts were acclaimed by friends and relatives but not publicly acknowledged. These marital unions were characterized by intense affection and a strong sense of mutual satisfaction in the work.[150] The women's colleges at Cambridge also produced learned partners and helpmates for learned husbands. In Grace's circle in Göttingen, too, educated wives helped scholarly husbands with their correspondence and wrote out their manuscripts in neat handwriting.[151]

Like other couples who partnered in work, Grace and Will saw their mathematical collaboration as a tangible symbol of their love. Working together enhanced their sense of romance and helped them achieve the "oneness" that was the ideal of nineteenth-century couples. "There is nothing in the whole world for me without you, and it is only the feeling that I am helping you to develop your truest self and to show yourself as you are, that keeps up my spirits and energies in your absence," Grace wrote to Will.[152] He rejoiced in knowing that they were "rising *together* to new heights."[153] Her assistance increased his devotion. "I cannot tell you, my darling, how I admire, how I adore you, how grateful I am to you when I think of all you have done and are doing [...]. My best self is turned ever to the pole star of your love and self-sacrifice."[154]

---

149 D.140/6/429, GCY to WHY, February 10, 1901. Young Papers.
150 See M. Jeanne Peterson, *Family, Love, and Work in the Lives of Victorian Gentlewomen* (Bloomington: Indiana University Press, 1989), pp. 18, 166, 176–78.
151 Jones, *Femininity*, p. 48 notes the examples of Anna Klein, wife of Felix Klein (and granddaughter of the philosopher, Georg Wilhelm Friedrich Hegel), and David Hilbert's wife, Kathe.
152 D.140/6/496, GCY to WHY, October 30, 1901. Young Papers.
153 D.140/6/558, WHY to GCY, March 9, 1902. Young Papers.
154 D.140/6/712, WHY to GCY, November 9, 1903; see also, D.140/6/461, WHY to GCY [June 1901]. Young Papers.

Grace's role, background, and contributions were quite different from the typical helpmate wife of her day, however. She was a professionally trained mathematician with a PhD from a renowned center of mathematical research, fully capable of carrying out her own mathematical studies. Her insights and ideas were as valuable to Will as her secretarial and editing skills. She was also taking time away from her medical studies to help him. She accepted a secondary, subordinate, and unrecognized role in their partnership without complaint because she loved him and thought it was her wifely duty. But she deserved better, and Will knew it.

The Domestic Partnership, 1900–1913

Grace's subordinate role in the professional partnership with Will mirrored the role she was expected to play in their domestic partnership. In both spheres, she assumed the role of faithful lieutenant who executed Will's orders. In fact, because Will was away so much, Grace had to make many decisions on her own. Nevertheless, it was important to both Grace and Will that he was treated as the all-knowing, all-wise decision maker. Despite her intelligence, education, and force of mind, she looked to Will for guidance and protection. Living up to the virtues suggested by their names, both Will and Grace exemplified the nineteenth-century gender stereotype that posited male authority (will) against female acquiescence (grace).

Because he was so often absent from home, Will struggled all the harder to impose his ideas and opinions on the Youngs' domestic life. He trained Grace to do things the way he wanted them done and demanded a close accounting of her activities, expenditures, and general behavior. "Please don't draw any cheques except with my permission," he instructed her in 1901. "Though the money is to your credit, I want you to consult me about the spending of every penny of it."[155] Throughout their marriage, he bombarded her with unsolicited advice and detailed instructions about how to handle the servants, manage her time, improve her looks and dress, and bring up the children. Irritable and anxious by nature, he very frequently found fault with what she did.

---

155 D.140/6/501, WHY to GCY, November 5, 1901. Young Papers.

If she appeared to disregard his instructions, ignore his requests for information, or mismanage her responsibilities, he reacted with anger and sometimes with ridicule or contempt. He criticized the way she kept the household accounts, budgeted money, conducted the family's correspondence, and raised the children.

Grace deferred to Will because she loved him and felt deeply indebted to him. When Will promised, after her father died in 1901, to be both father and husband to her, Grace was deeply touched. "How much you have helped me, influenced me & moulded me beside your love! It is no empty form of words with me to speak of obedience and of your sanction. I could never be happy otherwise, and my will is in every respect yours," she proclaimed.[156] Several months later, she confided, "I love you dearest more than anything, & that means everything, because to please you means to do right and to think right."[157] Her insistence, "it is for you to decide for your wifie, & she will second your decision whatever it should be," applied to small as well as large matters.[158]

Nevertheless, Grace did not always agree with Will. Like other wives of her day, she found ways to circumvent his directives without challenging his authority. When she and Will disagreed, she expressed her objections in a way that indicated her willingness to obey him regardless.[159] When concerns about the children's health prompted Will to veto Grace's plans to bring them to England on holiday, she responded, "I think on this occasion dearest you are wrong, but of course I will not do anything against your orders."[160]

When Will was angry about something she did, Grace tried to appease him by humbly apologizing, expressing distress at his displeasure, or suggesting that there had been a miscommunication. When he criticized the arrangements she had made for the children's lessons, she meekly responded, "I am *so* sorry you think I have been slack, I have tried to do the nearest I could under the circumstances to what we had arranged."[161] On other occasions, she simply ignored his complaints and questions.

---

156 D.140/6/419, GCY to WHY, January 10 [1901]. Young Papers.
157 D.140/6/480, GCY to WHY, October 9, 1901. Young Papers.
158 D.140/6/750, GCY to WHY, February 6, 1904. Young Papers.
159 See the discussion of "reframing" in Chapter 1, pp. 77–80.
160 D.140/7/1.17, GCY to WHY [May 1906]. Young Papers.
161 D.140/6/980, GCY to WHY, October 31, 1906. Young Papers. Emphasis in the original.

She tempered her resistance with flattery and sweet talk. Always, the presumption was that Will knew best and was motivated by the best of intentions, and she should be guided by his example and wisdom. When she felt especially strongly about the need to convince him of a course of action, she framed her advice in terms of what a trusted friend or colleague thought he should do — rather than being insistent about what she wanted.

As a man and the head of the household, Will enjoyed privileges that other family members did not. Despite the Youngs' financial concerns, money was made available to pay for travel and vacations for him. Honey was too expensive for the whole family to enjoy, but a jar was kept for Will's personal use (for medicinal reasons, he told his son, Laurie).[162] He was rarely asked to shoulder household responsibilities, such as caring for the children or arranging care for his troubled sister, Ethel. Grace encouraged him not to come home when the household routines were disrupted by children's illnesses or other crises.

Will was "coddled", as he put it, but Grace was infantilized.[163] The Youngs' use of Grace's childhood nickname, Baby, with its connotations of weakness, dependence, and immaturity was telling. Both Grace and Will wanted him to shield her from disturbing news and distressing circumstances. "I cannot write a word about [world] events. Will does not let me read the newspapers as I get too upset by the horrors, but he just tells me any news," she wrote a friend during the Boer War.[164] Feuding with her brother and sister over financial issues after her father died, Grace begged Will to handle the increasingly acrimonious correspondence with her family. "[M]y dear strong rock, it is so sweet to feel I can hide myself in your caves when the world is cruel," she wrote in relief, grateful to have "a protector & an advisor who is much wiser and cooler than I am."[165] She complained about Hugh's "detestably proud overbearing nature"; Will found him "selfish and arrogant."[166]

---

162 L. C. Young, "Life and Work", p. 11.
163 Coddled: D.140/6/774, WHY to GCY, May 6, 1904. Young Papers.
164 D.140/6/343, GCY to Frances Evans, July 26, 1900. Young Papers.
165 D.140/6/536, GCY to WHY, February 6, 1902. Young Papers.
166 "Proud overbearing": D.140/6/521b, GCY to WHY, December 11, 1901. "Selfish and arrogant": D.140/6/572a, WHY to GCY, 20 March 1902. Young Papers. Janet Hogarth Courtney, who knew Hugh Chisholm from their student days at Oxford and later became a close friend, observed that Hugh had a "confidence of statement and assumption of superior knowledge which clung to him through life", giving

Far from smoothing things over, Will managed to insult Hugh and alienate other members of Grace's family when he questioned the distribution of the Chisholm household goods that Hugh had proposed. (Will also went to great lengths to convince Grace not to give away any of her inheritance to her sister, Helen.) Although Grace assured Will that her relatives were overreacting and misinterpreting what he had written, she urged him to take the high moral road and try to rectify the problem.[167]

But the damage was done. Hugh resigned as a trustee of the Youngs' marriage settlement, and relations between the siblings remained badly strained.[168] In 1904, Grace's cousin, Edith Bell, with whom Grace's sister Helen lived, wrote Grace that they hoped she would come for lunch when she was in London, but Will would not be welcome. "We do not wish to meet him again. The straight truth is that we none of us ever liked him, and always thought his influence on you regrettable; & his correspondence with Hugh quite determined Helen & me to avoid further intercourse with him."[169] The rift continued for many years, leaving Grace virtually isolated from her family in England and more dependent on Will's guidance and direction. She deeply lamented the "miserable estrangement" from her family, and the children's isolation from their English relatives, but she came to agree that Will had been right to curb her emotional and impulsive reactions.[170] Together they formed an indissoluble unit, united against both her unsympathetic, judgmental family and an academic world that failed to appreciate Will.

Knowing that she did not like confrontation, fearing that she was too inclined to do what others wanted, Will encouraged Grace to stand up for herself and not allow others to take advantage of her. Very occasionally, he even urged her to stand up to him. Debating where they should take a brief holiday when she was busy with her medical studies, he pressed, "You are to choose and you may choose anywhere *you like*, not what

---

him the appearance of arrogance, and at times, "the air of a Mussolini." Quoted in Denis Boyles, *Everything Explained that is Explainable: On the Creation of the Encyclopedia Britannica's Celebrated Eleventh Edition, 1910–1911* (New York: Knopf, 2016). Boyles notes that Hugh "exuded self-assurance."

167 D.140/6/579c, GCY to WHY, May 17, 1902. Young Papers.
168 D.140/29/53, Henry Cooke to WHY, 3 April 1902. Young Papers.
169 D.140/6/843a, Edith Bell to GCY, 11 November 1904. Young Papers.
170 D.140/24/2, Autobiographical notes by GCY, written in 1917, after the death of her oldest son. Young Papers.

you think I should like."[171] But she rarely asserted herself. Although she was the strength of the household, she served her loved ones without asking much for herself — especially for time to do her own work or for recognition from the outside world.

Progress in Mathematics and Medicine, 1903–1904

Even with Grace's help, Will's career advanced slowly. He hoped to earn a Doctor of Science (DSc) degree from Cambridge University in 1902, but he had to wait until 1903.[172] As evidence of original research, he had about twenty papers that had been published or submitted to academic journals beginning in 1897, written in German and Italian as well as English; many were papers that Grace had worked on with him. He secured a contract from Cambridge University in 1903 to write a textbook on set theory, but failed to get a Cambridge lectureship and a professorship at King's College, London, a post that Grace dearly wanted him to win.[173] Still bursting with ideas, he repeated his claim for her assistance. "It really seems to me that the efforts of both of us should in the coming year be directed to further improving *my* position," he informed her.[174]

Grace blamed Will's job difficulties on his failure to publish a book, but there were other problems. His specialty was of little interest to English mathematicians in the early twentieth century. His unusual career trajectory — producing no research for many years and moving abroad — made it hard for him to establish himself among more traditional British academics. In addition, as his letters indicate, Will could be difficult to get along with: sensitive, critical, impatient, and

---

171 D.140/6/793, WHY to GCY [5 June 1904]. Young Papers. Emphasis in the original.
172 The DSc degree recognized the recipient's ability to do original scholarship, as did the PhD, but was a less prestigious degree. Will explained that the DSc degree was "only awarded after many years of standing & after having done *conspicuous original work*" and claimed to be the youngest recipient in mathematics. (D.140/6/739, WHY to Mrs. Jeyes [n.d., 1903]. Emphasis in the original. Young Papers.) English universities did not award the PhD degree until after 1917. The first PhD in mathematics was awarded in England in 1924. See David Bogle, "100 Years of the PhD in the UK" (2018), https://discovery.ucl.ac.uk/id/eprint/10068565/.
173 D.140/4/720a, GCY to WHY, November 12, 1903. Young Papers.
174 D.1410/6/724, WHY to GHY, November 22, 1903. Emphasis added. Young Papers.

sure of his own opinions, he easily took offense and often rubbed people the wrong way.[175]

Grace made steady if slow progress in her medical training, but juggling her children and Will's work with her studies weakened her performance. When she began her medical training, she was confident that she could compensate for spending less time on her work than her fellow students by being more efficient.[176] But as she progressed, she felt increasingly at a disadvantage. She felt so far behind in her medical work in 1902 that she was reluctant to schedule a major exam because she doubted she "could get a first class except by cramming."[177] Early in 1904, she warned Will, "I do not know a fraction of what the others do, & unless I am able to study seriously next semester I shall come off very poorly."[178] Nevertheless, her time was repeatedly interrupted by Will's work and the children's needs.

Will suffered a major setback early in 1904, when he discovered that the innovative formula he developed to calculate areas under circles by using set theory — a major challenge in the field of integration — had been independently worked out two years earlier by the French mathematician Henri Lebesgue. Their techniques were different enough that Will could publish his approach, but the honor and glory of discovery went to Lebesgue.[179] Will withdrew his paper and rewrote it — with Grace's help — in the spring of 1904, just a few months before she was scheduled to take her medical qualifying examinations at the University of Göttingen. Her preparations for the exam were further interrupted when the three older children and Auntie May fell ill in June and the youngest child was teething. Noting that Leni "roared from 10 to 1 AM" one night, Grace wrote laconically, "I manage to work in scrappits."[180] She passed the Physikum at Göttingen, a preliminary examination that covered botany, zoology, anatomy, and physiology, but failed to get the high marks she desired.[181]

175 Grattan-Guinness, "Mathematical Union", p. 148. Laurence Young, *Mathematicians*, pp. 286–87.
176 D.140/6/392, GCY to WHY, November 11, 1900. Young Papers.
177 D.140/6/619, GCY to WHY, November 13, 1902. Young Papers.
178 D.140/6/750, GCY to WHY, February 6, 1904. Young Papers.
179 Grattan-Guinness, "Mathematical Union", pp. 142–43.
180 D.149/6/796, GCY to WHY, 15 June 1904. Young Papers.
181 D.140/7/1.13, GCY to WHY [?1904]. D.140/6/796, WHY to GCY, pc, July 24, 1904. Young Papers.

Having passed the Physikum, Grace became a candidate in medicine (abbreviated "Cand. Med."), the official term for a medical student in Germany, a title she proudly used along with her other academic degrees. Students typically took the Physikum after four semesters of study, but it took Grace, interrupted by pregnancies and Will's work, four years to complete the coursework. Another two to three years of course work lay ahead, followed by a year of clinical work. But first there was more mathematics to do with Will.

Mathematics Wins Out, 1905–1913

After years of being rejected for university teaching jobs, Will was hired as a Special Lecturer in Mathematics at the University of Liverpool in the fall of 1905. Founded in 1881 but not able to grant degrees until 1903, serving local students rather than a national elite, the university lacked the prestige and resources of the ancient universities like Cambridge and Oxford.[182] Will gave lectures, but he had no authority to shape the department and was not paid well.[183] He took the post because it was a step up from examining and coaching, and left him time for research. But he had barely arrived before he began to complain about the pay, his title, and his lack of influence, to the department chair as well as to Grace. No matter what Will was doing, his restless nature was rarely satisfied for long, a trait he himself recognized.

Will instructed Grace not to give up their home in Göttingen and contemplated resigning from Liverpool. He did not want the family to move to Liverpool, which he considered a cultural, social, and mathematical backwater; he also feared that the local industry made the city an unhealthy environment for children.[184] He stayed, but reduced his teaching load from three terms to two, so he had more time to research, write, and travel.[185] Will counseled Grace that she would be

---

182 Thomas Kelly, *For Advancement of Learning: The University of Liverpool, 1881–1981* (Liverpool: Liverpool University Press, 1981). Before 1903, University of Liverpool students were awarded degrees as external students at the University of London.

183 D.140/2/2, R. C. H. Tanner notes. Young Papers. Will earned a salary of 100 pounds for teaching two terms. Eventually his pay was increased to 150 pounds a year.

184 D.140/6/1069, WHY to GCY, February 28, 1907. Young Papers.

185 D.140/6/986, Draft letter of resignation, WHY to F. S. Carey, June 26, 1906. Young Papers. From January to late March 1907, Will did not teach but travelled in Italy.

better able to pursue her medical studies at Göttingen than Liverpool, but his claims for Grace's assistance with his mathematics increased.[186] He was no longer asking for her help, he was demanding it, without apology and without regard for the toll it took on her medical studies. "[I] am very anxious your lectures [in medicine] should not prevent the progress of mathematics work which seems to me now of quite the first importance," he wrote in September 1905, two months after the birth of their fifth child, Laurence (Laurie). The next week, he announced, "We must concentrate on the maths for the next few months — no time, I think for [medical] lectures."[187]

Between 1905 and 1907, Grace co-authored two mathematics textbooks with Will, worked with him on numerous articles that expanded their work on set theory, and wrote two science books for children by herself. Sparked by the work he was doing as a school examiner in Wales, Will was interested in writing textbooks with Grace in order to make money.[188] In 1905, they published *The First Book of Geometry*, a textbook that introduced solid geometry and geometric concepts to grade school students by teaching them to make models of solid objects by folding paper. Grace, who had a strong interest in educating children and extensive experience in geometric projection drawing and three-dimensional modeling — expertise that Will lacked — worked out the exercises by practicing them with their seven-year-old son. (Frankie referred to the volume as "our Geometry book", and redrew one of Grace's illustrations because he thought nobody would understand it.[189]) She produced almost 140 drawings to illustrate the

Grace did not join him until March because she felt the children needed her at home.
186 By 1905, women were enrolled as medical students at the University of Liverpool; the first woman, Phoebe Powell, graduated from its medical school in 1910. See Manuscripts and More, Special Collections and Archives at the University of Liverpool, "International Day of Women and Girls in Science, 11 February 2020", https://manuscriptsandmore.liverpool.ac.uk/?p=5137. Powell later married a doctor, had two daughters, continued to practice medicine, and taught pathology at the university as Phoebe Powell-Bigland. See "Obituary: A. Douglas Bigland", *British Medical Journal* (1938:1), 545. https://doi.org/10.1136/bmj.1.4026.545.
187 D.140/6/892, WHY to GCY, September 6, 1905; D.140/6/894, WHY to GCY, September 11, 1905. Young Papers.
188 D.140/6/826, WHY to GCY, October 17, 1904. Two years earlier, he had talked about writing textbooks with Grace and his sister Ethel. D.140/6/558a, WHY to GCY, March 9, 1902. Young Papers.
189 D.140/24/1, Diary Fragments from 1905, and 12 March 1907. Young Papers.

folding exercises and supervised the photographic illustrations; it is likely she wrote the entire text.[190]

In a departure from the policy Will had enunciated in 1902, Grace was listed as first author of *The First Book of Geometry*.[191] She was also co-author of *The Theory of Sets of Points*, published in 1906, an important book that introduced set theory to English readers and explained its relevance to numerous branches of mathematics.[192] Making her co-author was Will's idea, not hers, Grace assured her sister. Their son, Laurie, concurred: he later wrote that Will "occasionally slipped in her name in as co-author — she certainly did not."[193]

Perhaps Will thought acknowledging Grace as a co-author would help sell the books, given her reputation as a pioneering female mathematician and the potential appeal of a textbook for young children written by a mother who was also a scholar. Perhaps his conscience temporarily got the better of his ambition. Whatever the reason, they continued to highlight Will's work and minimize Grace's. The preface to *The Theory of Sets of Points*, which laid out the book's significance and accomplishments, was signed only by Will and used the singular pronoun "I" more often than the plural "we." When Grace applied, unsuccessfully, in 1905 for a research grant to study how mathematics was taught to youngsters in several European countries, she stressed that the work would be done "in collaboration with and under the direction of" her husband.[194]

Nothing more came of Will's interest in writing textbooks, but Grace published two science books for children under her name. *Bimbo* (1905) and *Bimbo and the Frogs* (1907) explained biology and reproduction in a narrative about an English family living in Germany that was closely

---

190 D.140/6/872, GCY to Helen Chisholm, April 30, 1905. Young Papers.
191 Grace Chisholm Young and W. H. Young, *The First Book of Geometry* (London: Dent, 1905). A German translation was published in 1908, and an Italian edition in 1911. It was translated into Yiddish in 1921, and subsequently published in Magyar and Swedish. Felix Klein was instrumental in getting it translated into German. See Tobies, p. 33.
192 W. H. Young and Grace Chisholm Young, *The Theory of Sets of Points* (Cambridge, UK: Cambridge University Press, 1906; repr. 2009).
193 D.140/6/872, GCY to Helen Chisholm, April 30, 1905. Young Papers. Laurence Young, *Mathematicians*, pp. 282–83.
194 D.140/6/869, Grace's Application for the Pfieffer Studentship, 1905.

modelled on the Youngs.[195] The explanations of cell theory and embryo development in humans and animals were elucidating, but shocking for some. Congratulating her on the publication of *Bimbo and the Frogs*, Grace's close friend, Frances Evans, admitted, "I don't know how much the folks I know will approve of its views — & of the knowledge it gives — much of which I myself was quite ignorant."[196]

After jointly publishing the geometry textbook and *The Theory of Sets of Points*, the Youngs reverted to producing a torrent of papers under Will's name alone. He published more than forty papers in 1907 and 1908, and was elected a Fellow of the Royal Society in 1907. Grace rarely submitted anything under her name alone. She was annoyed when a paper she submitted under her own name in 1907 was rejected for publication.[197] A year later, Will encouraged her to write a paper on a function that especially interested her, suggested how she should do one of the proofs, and told her to send it off in her own name.[198] From 1909 through 1911, when Will was back on the job market, the Youngs published four articles jointly, Will published forty-seven, and Grace published none.[199]

Grace's contributions were not entirely unrecognized in the mathematical community, however. George M. Minchin, who like Will was an examiner at the University of London, recommended Will for a teaching position at the University of Edinburgh in 1911. Writing independently to Will, Minchin acknowledged that he was really recommending "the Firm of W. H. Young and Co." which he knew relied on Grace's work as well as Will's.[200]

The flurry of publications and membership in the Royal Society were of little avail to Will's job search, however. He failed to win positions at universities in Glasgow (1909), Durham (1910), and Edinburgh (1912).

---

195 Grace Chisholm Young, *Bimbo: A Little Real Story for Jill and Mollie by Auntie Will* (London: Dent, 1905) and Grace Chisholm Young, *Bimbo and the Frogs: Another Real Story* (London: Dent, 1907). Bimbo, an Italian word for a male baby, is the nickname the Youngs gave Frank when they moved abroad.

196 D.140/6/1145, Frances Evans to GCY, November 13, 1907. Young Papers.

197 D.140/6/1067, GCY to WHY, February 27, 1907. Young Papers.

198 D.140/6/1169, WHY to GCY, July 2, 1908. Young Papers.

199 Author's calculations from the bibliography in Ivor Gratton-Guinness, "Mathematical Bibliography for W. H. and G. C. Young", *Historia Mathematica* 2 (1975), 43–58.

200 D.140/9/146, George M. Minchin to WHY, November 17, 1911. Young Papers.

Losing out at Edinburgh was a bitter disappointment for both Grace and Will — the university had hosted both of them during the application process — but they did their best to console each other.[201] Will was given the title of Associate Professor at Liverpool in 1912, but his work and pay scale remained the same.

Will's escalating demands effectively put Grace's long-term goal of practicing medicine on hold. After 1904, her medical work largely fades from sight, and is rarely mentioned in her correspondence with Will. Responding to his pressure, she seems to have shifted her primary focus from medicine to mathematics, a shift that would define the rest of her professional life. The amount of work she did with Will, the amount of time she was with him in England, the failure to mention her training in her letters — all suggest that Grace was not pursuing a medical degree with the same urgency and drive — or perhaps, the same support — as she had earlier in the decade, when the Youngs' letters are full of discussions about her courses, exams, and schedules. Prioritizing her role as a helpmate wife, she now fit her medical classes around the work she did for Will, rather than fitting his work around a grueling schedule of medical courses.

By 1905, Grace's medical courses seem to have become what Will had long suggested they should be — an intellectual outlet for her probing mind and an activity that kept her busy when he was not at home. Despite the many demands on her time, she took courses whenever she could and made progress in her medical studies. In the spring of 1906, when she was studying pathology with the celebrated Max Borst, Will complained that she was so "feckless," he feared she would poison herself doing a dissection.[202] But the dream of becoming a licensed doctor and having a practice of her own was receding.

In 1908, Grace turned 40, her sixth and last child, Patrick (Pat), was born in March, and the family moved to Geneva in the late summer. The Youngs said they left Germany to escape from the increasingly hostile anti-British sentiment that resulted from the Anglo-German arms race and imperial rivalries, and to find better educational opportunities for

201 D.140/40/5/1, Grace's Pocket Diaries, 22 February, 1912. Young Papers.
202 Feckless: D.140/6/959, WHY to GCY, May 11, 1906 postcard. Studying with Borst: D.140/24/1, Diary fragments. Young Papers. Max Borst, an expert in tumors, started teaching the University of Göttingen in 1905.

the children.[203] Moving to Geneva, where the university had a long history of educating women doctors and welcomed foreign students, ensured that Grace could continue her medical training, although that was not the impetus.[204] She matriculated as a medical student at the University of Geneva in the winter of 1908.[205] The rigorous medical curriculum typically took five years to complete.[206]

Will's mathematics continued to take precedence over Grace's medical studies, but she managed to fit some courses in.[207] Starting in 1908, she regularly spent six to eight weeks with Will in Liverpool during January and February and again in the fall. In some years she was with him during June as well. Nevertheless, she was registered for laboratory courses at the University of Geneva in 1910, and later reported that she had worked there for some years with the eminent Swiss surgeon, Charles Girard.[208] Grace's pocket diary for May 1913 is filled with notes, in French, on the pathology of gout. When Will went to India for six months that fall, Grace attended lectures given by Robert Hippolyte Chodat, a Professor of Medical and Pharmaceutical Botany at the University of Geneva, in the midst of working on articles with Will and learning about the philosophy of mathematics.[209]

---

203 Grattan-Guinness, "Mathematical Union", p. 147.
204 Will had thought about moving to Switzerland as early as 1904. D.140/6/784a, WHY to GCY, May 21, 1904. Young Papers.
205 Université de Genève, *Liste des Autorites, Professeurs, Etudiants et Auditeurs. Semestre D'Hiver 1908–1909*, p. 72 and *Liste des Autorites, Professeurs, Etudiants et Auditeurs. Semestre D'Hiver 1910–1911*, p. 56. https://www.unige.ch/archives/adm/documents-en-ligne/listes-des-autorites-professeurs-etudiants-auditeurs-et-laboratoires/
206 Between 1900 and 1910 Switzerland trained more women doctors than the United States and the rest of Europe combined. Bonner, *To the Ends*, Table 1, p. 62. Training length: Thomas Neville Bonner, *Becoming a Physician: Medical Education in Great Britain, France, Germany, and the US, 1750–1945* (New York and Oxford: Oxford University Press, 1995), p. 323. See also, Thomas Neville Bonner, "Pioneering in Women's Medical Education in the Swiss Universities, 1864–1914", *Gesnerus: Swiss Journal of the History of Medicine and Sciences*, 45 (1988), 461–73.
207 Université de Genève, *Liste*.
208 Laboratory courses: D.140/6/910, May Young to GCY, p.c., February 5, 1910, and Université de Genève, *Liste*, 1910. Studied with Girard: D.140/15/1, "Bimbo", and GCY letter, 19 November 1916, to the British military authorities seeking permission to go to France to nurse her son Frank, who was injured in a flight accident. She was informed by telegram, "Don't trouble wounded knee healing beautifully." Young Papers.
209 D.140/5/1 Grace's Pocket Diaries, May 4, 1913 and after. D.140/6/1636, GCY to WHY, October 31 [1913]. Young Papers.

Grace never became a licensed doctor. She wrote in a fellowship application in 1924 that she had completed all the course requirements for a medical degree, but "home duties" prevented her for completing the required hospital internship.[210] She left no account that explains when she finished her coursework, what circumstances prohibited her from doing an internship, or how she felt about the outcome of her long and arduous struggle to become a doctor. Will explained in 1940 that Grace had been prevented from doing her internship by his brother Alfred. According to Will, Alfred had peremptorily insisted that May leave the Young family and return to Germany to take charge of their sister, Ethel, rather than stay for an extra year so Grace could do her internship.[211] After May left, Will wanted to cut off the financial support he had been providing for Ethel.[212]

The truth is hard to uncover. May did leave the Young family in May 1913 and returned to Göttingen to live with Ethel. She informed Grace of her plans in March 1913, writing that she intended to make the move that October. She did not mention that Alfred played a role in her decision.[213] It is possible that forty-five-year-old Grace had hoped to leave May in charge of the children while she completed an internship, but there is no evidence of such a plan. Will's explanation was written almost thirty years after the event, when his mental and physical health was compromised, his sense of grievance was very strong, and not all of his recollections jived with the facts. The two brothers had long been at odds, and Will never forgave Alfred for taking the side of the Youngs' rebellious youngest daughter, Leni, when she moved out of her parents' house in the early 1920s. Blaming Alfred might have made it easier for Will to ignore his own role in blocking Grace's efforts to become a doctor.

---

210 D.140/12/36, GCY's Draft Application for the Yarrow Scientific Research Fellowship (1924). Young Papers.

211 D.140/12/5 Autobiographical Notes by WHY 1940, and the insert entered by Will on November 27, 1940 to Grace's pocket diary entry for May 31, 1913 (D.140/5/1). Cecily Young accepted Will's explanation and reproduced it in a summary of Grace and Will's lives (D.140/2/2). Young Papers.

212 D.140/6/1568, GCY to Herr Frank. Hostile relations between the brothers persisted into the fall of 1913. See D.140/6/1636, GCY to WHY, October 31, 1913. Young Papers.

213 D.140/6/1544a, May Young to WHY and GCY, March 5, 1913. Young Papers. May wrote that she was very sorry to leave, but referred to tensions in her relationship with Grace and Will over her supervision of the children.

Helpmate Wife Versus Hands-on Mother

Grace had hesitated to embark on her medical training in part because she would have less time with her children. Being Will's helpmate made it even more difficult for her to be a hands-on mother because he wanted her to devote so much time to his mathematical studies and stay with him in England. During her absences, Auntie May took charge of the children and the household with the help of several servants and eventually a governess.

Will had no doubts about whose interests were paramount. "I feel strongly that when you are not attending lectures your place is with me," he informed Grace in 1901.[214] Planning for her to come to Liverpool for six weeks in the spring of 1906, he pronounced, "The bairns could spare you as long as that."[215] In February 1911, he insisted that Grace remain in Liverpool instead of returning to Geneva when May felt overwhelmed by the children's illnesses and difficulties with the servants. During other of Grace's visits, May sent plaintive letters asking when Grace would return home and why she was staying longer than planned.

Grace occasionally balked at leaving home when she felt the children needed her. After spending six weeks with Will in Cambridge in the summer of 1901, she returned to Göttingen to await the birth of her third child in December rather than staying through the fall as Will wanted. In the summer of 1904, she put off a working holiday with Will because Auntie May and the children were ill. In 1907, she refused to meet him in Italy because she feared that, without her supervision, Frankie's schoolwork, music lessons, and general conduct would deteriorate. "Nothing but the children would keep me here now," she assured Will.[216] But most of the time, Grace tried to arrange her schedule — and the children's — to suit Will's convenience.

The difficulty Grace found in balancing her husband's needs against her children's needs was emblematic of a major shift in women's domestic roles after the start of the twentieth century. Throughout the nineteenth century, middle- and upper-middle-class white women were

---

214 D.140/6/454, WHY to GCY, May 10, 1901; see also, D.140/6/457, WHY to GCY, May 15, 1901. Young Papers.

215 D.140/6/907, WHY to GCY [November 27, 1905]. Young Papers.

216 D.140/6/1067, GCY to WHY, February 27, 1907. Young Papers.

taught to think of wifehood as their primary role and responsibility. Children of the British upper-middle class and aristocracy were typically cared for by domestic servants and spent very little time with their parents. Grace's own upbringing fit this model. Although she had her first lessons with her mother, she was mostly in the care of nursemaids and governesses (the Chisholms employed five maids), and rarely saw her mother during the day when she was very young.[217] Nineteenth-century homes, especially homes in which wives served as helpmates in their husband's work, were parent-centered rather than child-centered. Spousal relationships and work were more important than parental roles.[218]

The idea that well-educated mothers should be more directly engaged in childrearing began to take hold in the early decades of the twentieth century. In both England and America, mothers were encouraged to apply scientific principles to housekeeping and childrearing and expected to meet more demanding standards of "mothercraft."[219] Motherhood began to be seen as a scientific vocation that required intelligence and training rather than something that could be accomplished by intuition and natural inclination. By the 1920s, women in both England and America were told that raising their children should take priority over other concerns and obligations.

Grace was an heir to one tradition and a precursor of the other. Her childrearing was deeply informed by her knowledge of medicine and pedagogy. Fearing that her children would not get sufficient intellectual stimulation and the highest quality physical care without her direct involvement, she arranged her schedule in her first year of medical training so she could be with her young children at meals and bath time, and she often studied while they played around her. She planned, supervised, and arranged for their lessons and activities, but as her studies and her work for Will expanded, and she spent more time with him in Liverpool, she had to hand over more of their daily care to maids, governesses, and Auntie May.

When she was away with Will, Grace supplied menus for the household's meals and sent detailed advice and instructions about the

---

217 D.140/6/14/6 and D.140/12/1. Young Papers.
218 Peterson, pp. 103–04, 107–08.
219 See the Introduction to this volume, p. 20.

children's care. She expected caregivers to carry them out, apply the Youngs' rules, and instill the Youngs' values in the children. In Auntie May, she had a faithful caregiver and housekeeper, who, according to Cecily, the Youngs' oldest child, willingly carried out "all the decrees of the master of the house as interpreted by the mistress."[220] May's letters to Grace suggest that she found her brother's punishments too harsh, wanted the children to have more treats and pocket money, and wished that Grace would provide more variety in her weekly menus. But she nevertheless followed the parents' lead.

Will's parenting style was more characteristic of a mid-nineteenth-century patriarch than the domesticated husband and companionate dad that would emerge as an ideal in the 1920s in England and America.[221] As long as Grace was at the helm, he felt no need — or desire — to spend a great deal of time with his children, although he believed he was more involved in their upbringing than the typical father. With Grace's encouragement, he guiltlessly prioritized his work, his desire to travel, and his own comfort above spending time with his family. On occasion, with Grace's blessing, he chose not to come home when he had the opportunity to do so.

Physical absence did not stop Will from setting exacting standards for the children's upbringing. From the time the children were very young, his letters were full of observations and instructions about their health, behavior, leisure activities, formal education, and general development. No detail of the children's lives was too small to escape his attention. He specified the route they should follow on their daily walks; he instructed Grace to lengthen Frankie's lunchtime; he worried that Cecily's sewing projects would hurt her eyes, despite Grace's assurances that the stitches were large and the lighting sufficient. He fussed about their schooling, painstakingly planned a course of independent lessons to supplement the school curricula, corrected spelling errors and grammatical mistakes

---

220 D.140/2/3.1, R. C. H. Tanner Notes, Young Papers.

221 According to David Roberts, "The Paterfamilias of the Victorian Governing Classes" in *The Victorian Family: Structures and Stresses*, ed. by Anthony S. Wohl (London: Croom Helm, 1978), pp. 59–81 (pp. 59–60), Victorian fathers expected deference from their children, and children were taught to "worship" their fathers and accept their opinions as always right. Stephen Mintz, *A Prison of Expectations: The Family in Victorian Culture* (New York: New York University Press, 1983), pp. 12 and 111, argues that the father was the chief disciplinary figure and the embodiment of moral and intellectual authority in the Victorian home.

in their correspondence, and kept careful track of their academic progress.

Will loved his children deeply and worried greatly about their future, but he wanted their obedience and deference rather than intimacy or easy affection. When he was home, he ran the household as a "high-minded benevolent dictatorship", their eldest daughter, Cecily, recalled. He would "hold forth in anger [...] in fear that his authority was being undermined [...] he felt, in his own words, that he was 'captain of the ship' & it would go under if he was not implicitly obeyed, & also if he was not meticulously informed of the minutest details from which he could plan the destiny of all."[222] Cecily's younger brother, Laurie, described how decisions were made at one family meeting: everyone could speak, but Will dominated the conversation, and eventually the family came round to his way of thinking.[223] When Laurie was around seven years old, his father took him for long walks and lectured to him about mathematical sets. When the boy professed not to understand, Will stalked away in anger.[224]

Grace's letters to Will expressed her delight in a new baby, warm descriptions of the children's progress and activities, and accounts of happy times reading aloud, playing educational games, and practicing music with the children. She wrote poems and stories for them, amusing tales that featured the children as characters who interact with talking animals that teach moral lessons. She also wrote accounts of how the children solved scientific problems.[225]

Nevertheless, Grace was an exacting parent and a tough disciplinarian. (She once punished two servant girls who did not come back on time from an evening out by locking them into their bedroom.[226] She reprimanded another for flirting with students.) Grace's eldest daughter described her as a "highbrow" who did not "suffer fools gladly", but her sons found her more supportive and kind. Laurie noted her "characteristic look of intelligent sympathy, as if she was always ready to help someone else."[227] He recalled how "magnificent" she was

---

222 D.140/2/3, R. C. H. Tanner notes, Young Papers.
223 L. C. Young, "Life and Work", p. 10.
224 Ibid., p. 11.
225 D.140/14/1, GCY stories. Young Papers.
226 Laurence Young, *Mathematicians*, p. 235.
227 L. C. Young, "Life and Work", p. 14.

when two famous mathematicians arrived at their home in Switzerland to talk shop on the day the Youngs moved into new lodgings. (Will was away.) Grace excused herself for a short time, and came back with tea and freshly baked rock cakes (a family favorite, similar to scones) which she served on the family's best china.[228] Pat, the youngest child, revered his mother as a rare example of a woman who combined "brain power with deep feeling and undying loyalty."[229] Nevertheless, it was May to whom Cecily turned for warmth and nurturing. Unlike Grace and Will, Auntie May "believed in tempering severity with demonstrative affection," Cecily wrote.[230] She regarded May as a second mother, and as an adult, surmised that Grace might have been jealous of the children's relationship with May, even though the two women appeared to get along very well.[231]

Although Grace had hesitated to take up medicine for fear that she would be "sacrificing husband and children to a whim of my own", she wrote in 1917 that she had managed to get through her medical education "little by little without sacrificing home or mathematics."[232] She drew comfort from knowing that, even if she "had not been all to [her children] that other mothers are to their children, they do not resent it, & are far more loving than I could hope."[233] In fact, however, it was her work for Will, not her medical studies, that took Grace away from the children for extended periods.

Nevertheless, she and Will were outraged when Grace's relatives — that Greek chorus of disapproving commentary — criticized their "unusual" lifestyle in 1911. Grace responded indignantly, "[I]t has always been the path of duty & not that of pleasure that Will and I have chosen [...]. I have only done what any good woman would do. I have followed my husband's fortunes."[234] Will explained that Grace had always joined him during his English school terms, except when she

---

228 Ibid., p. 12.
229 D.140/6/5234, Patrick Young to WHY, August 8, 1934. Young Papers.
230 D.140/2/3.1, R. C. H. Tanner notes. Young Papers.
231 D.140/2/3.6, Cecily [Young] Tanner corrections for Ivor Grattan-Guinness, September 10, 1970. Young Papers. Cecily addressed May as "dear, dear mother" in a letter she wrote when she was twelve (D.140/6/1487, Cecily Young to May Young, November 8, 1912. Young Papers).
232 D.140/16/1, "Per Ardua", p. 64. Young Papers.
233 D.140/6/2358, GCY to Frances Evans, New Year's Day, 1917. Young Papers.
234 D.140/6/1288, GCY to Maud Bell, October 17, 1911. Young Papers.

could not leave their children. "When it was not possible [to be together], we were certainly deserving of pity, & not of blame," he protested.[235]

In fact, Will was away from home for longer periods than the Youngs cared to acknowledge. Sometimes he chose to be absent because his boisterous household interfered with his work or because his work wreaked havoc on family routines. He also insisted on indulging his wanderlust for foreign travel. "I can't be chained to a desk. I must have motion & change of scene in my life," he raged during one academic term.[236] Frequent separations did not mean that their ties were not strong or affection was wanting. On the contrary, like Alice and George Palmer (discussed in Chapter 1), Grace and Will felt their separations intensified their love. When Will was away, they wrote to each other daily — sometimes twice daily. Romance and passion were important parts of their relationship. Grace was thrilled when a good friend remarked that she and Will "have a recurrent honeymoon, & are like lovers when we are together."[237] Will imagined he was kissing Grace's ears and eyes when he wrote to her, and sent her 1,000 kisses by letter. He swooned before her, "the blood royal of womanhood." In January 1912, they worked all day on mathematics, and then crept downstairs at 11:30 at night, lit the Christmas tree lights, and danced together.[238]

Changes in the Partnership, 1913–1919

Grace and Will's lives changed dramatically in the fall of 1913 when Will became the first Hardinge Professor of Mathematics at the University of Calcutta in India. The three-year appointment allowed him to build a mathematics department, investigate mathematical education systems in other countries, and paid considerably more money than his position at Liverpool.[239] He sailed to Calcutta from Brindisi in October 1913 and returned home in April 1914. (Because they involved residencies

235 D.140/6/1291, WHY to Mrs. Gillim, November 5, 1911. Young Papers.
236 D.140/6/483, WHY to GCY, October 12, 1901. Young Papers.
237 D.140/6/604, GCY to WHY [October 6, 1902]. Young Papers.
238 D.140/5/1, Grace's Pocket Diaries, January 2, 1912. Young Papers.
239 The University of Calcutta paid Will 1,000 pounds a year, compared to the 150 pounds he received from the University of Liverpool for giving 53 lectures a year — after eight years of teaching there (D.140/6/1581, WHY to Mr. MacMahon, 25 August 1913, Young Papers).

at different times of the year, Will was able to hold the Calcutta and Liverpool appointments simultaneously. The University of Liverpool gave Will a more prestigious title — honorary Chair in Philosophy and History of Mathematics — but did not increase his salary or responsibilities.)

Not surprisingly, the long separation took a toll on the Youngs' relationship. Grace assured Will she was happy and busy, but she worried that he missed her less than formerly, and feared they were growing apart because he had so many new experiences she could not share. Will missed having her with him to discuss his ideas, act as his secretary, and purchase what he needed for daily living. But he repeatedly discouraged her from coming to India, telling her that she would not like the journey, the people, or the place. "I am very inclined to think it would be a *serious blunder* for you to come out to India even for a few months," he asserted.[240] Although Grace had told a cousin that she hoped to spend some time in India with Will, she did not argue the point or express a desire to join him in her letters.[241] Will was even happier that he had not brought his sons. Evincing the racism of his era and class, he admitted that he was filled with "horror" at the thought that one of their boys might marry a Eurasian and produce *"black"* grandchildren.[242]

While Grace fretted about her relationship with Will, he feared losing control over his family. He issued a steady stream of instructions about the children's education and activities, and berated Grace when things were not done to his specifications or he felt ill-informed about their activities. Sending their oldest son, Frank, a long list of Will's instructions, Grace sympathized, "I am afraid you will be tired of all these rules and regulations."[243] Very likely, she was projecting her own feelings about the strictures Will placed on her.

The household in Switzerland underwent many changes while Will was away. Auntie May's departure from the family at the end of May 1913, after ten years of helping with the children, was especially

---

240 D.140/6/1622, WHY to GCY [n.d, 1913], written while Will was on the ship to India. Emphasis in the original. Young Papers.
241 D.140/6/1588, GCY to Cousin Alick, August 29, 1913. Young Papers.
242 D.140/6/1716, WHY to GCY, 1 January 1914. Emphasis in the original. Similarly, D.140/6/ 1740, WHY to GCY, January 22, 1914. Young Papers.
243 D.140/6/1615, GCY to Francis Young, 7 October, 1913. Young Papers.

unsettling. Without her, Grace and the children struggled to get everything done. When the quality of Laurie's school work declined after May's departure, Grace told his teacher that she was too busy to supervise his homework as May had done. Twelve-year-old Janet took over the job.[244]

Replacing the children's German governess in the fall of 1913 — she too had been with the children for many years — was also difficult. Grace trained the new governess not to interrupt her when she was working, but Grace spent a lot of time managing the older children's schooling and extra-curricular lessons and nursing all the children through bouts of illness — activities that "sadly" eroded her work time, she told Will.[245] He, too, made many demands on her time. She prepared material on the relationship between Greek philosophy and mathematics for lectures he planned to give during the University of Liverpool's summer term. He wanted her help on a book about integration and a new edition of *Sets of Points* and expected weekly accounts of her progress.[246]

Grace was fully involved in formulating their ideas on all these topics. When Will thought she was going off in a wrong direction on a proof, he advised her to leave the rest for him, but she forged ahead.[247] She sent him many letters describing the work she was doing and what she was gleaning from reading the works of other mathematicians. He found her exploration of Greek philosophy and mathematics particularly insightful and planned to use it in a paper.[248]

Will's vacillations about whether to go first to Geneva or directly to Liverpool when he returned in the spring of 1914 must have reinforced Grace's fear that they were drifting apart. While she eagerly looked forward to the "heavenly weeks" they would have together after his return, he maintained that a few additional weeks of separation after

244 D.140/14/1. Young Papers.
245 D.140/6/1691, WHY to GCY, December 19, 1913. Young Papers.
246 *The Theory of Sets of Points* was out of print, but they had a contract for a new edition from Cambridge University Press. Neither it nor the book on integration was ever completed. Their daughter, Cecily (R. C. H. Tanner), worked with Ivor Grattan-Guinness to publish a second edition of *Sets of Points*, with a new preface and appendix, in 1972: W. H. Young and Grace Chisholm Young, *The Theory of Sets of Points*, 2nd edn. (New York: AMS Chelsea Publishing, 1972).
247 D.140/6/1686, WHY to GCY, December 15, 1913; D.140/6/1691, GCY to WHY, December 19, 1913. Young Papers.
248 D.140/6/1810, WHY to GCY, March 2, 1914. Young Papers.

such a long time apart would not matter.[249] In the end, he spent a few days in Geneva before going to the University of Liverpool. Grace stayed in Geneva and worked on turning his lectures into publishable articles.

Will was back in Geneva with his family when World War I broke out in August 1914. Forced to abandon his plans to study how mathematics was taught in various European countries, he remained at home until December 1914, when he returned to India. He was away for fifteen months, until April 1916. He was mostly in Calcutta, but he also travelled to Japan, other parts of the Far East, and the United States to study their university systems. On his return voyage to Europe, he visited South Africa and Spain. While he was away, the family moved to Lausanne, so Frank could live at home while he studied engineering at the University of Lausanne.

Living in neutral Switzerland while Britain was at war with Germany was difficult for Grace. Bursting with patriotism, she longed to contribute to the British war effort.[250] Her patriotic fervor led her to support Frank's desire to volunteer for military service in the fall of 1915 when he was eighteen, despite Will's repeated insistence that the boy should not enlist until he turned twenty.[251] During the first year Will was away, she and Frank happily followed his orders. But a "sudden change of circumstances" made them reconsider. Unable to reach Will, who was traveling in Japan and Ceylon, they acted on their own, confident that he would support their decision.[252]

Grace and Frank were most likely responding to two events. In May 1915, a German submarine torpedoed the *Lusitania*, a British ocean liner, killing 1,200 civilians. Grace was so upset after hearing the news in town that she could barely walk home.[253] The second event was the introduction of a new recruitment strategy by the British military in the fall of 1915, a last-ditch effort to avoid conscripting men into the armed

---

249 D.140/6/1641, GCY to WHY, November 14, 1913; D.140/6/1742, WHY to GCY, 25 January 1914; D.140/6/1806, 1807 and 1808, WHY to GCY, all dated March 1, 1914. Young Papers.

250 D.140/6/1905, GCY to Frances Evans, October 4, 1914. Similarly, D.140/6/2308, GCY to Francis Young, November 18, 1916. Young Papers.

251 The conscription policy, enacted in late January 1916 and implemented in March 1916, required single men ages 18–41 to serve. British subjects living abroad (as Frank was) were not conscripted until July 1917.

252 D.140/16/1, GCY, "Per Ardua", p. 255. Young Papers.

253 D.140/5/1, Grace's Pocket Diary, first week of May 1915. Young Papers.

forces. Under the Derby Scheme, as it was known, men could enlist as volunteers but defer active service until a later date. Recruitment efforts were intense, and recruiters went from household to household throughout England urging men to enlist.[254] Unable to reach Will, and presumably feeling pressure to act before the Derby Scheme expired in December, Grace and Frank decided they could not wait for Will's advice.[255]

Grace maintained that she had tried to do what Will would have done if he had been at home, but they were not in agreement on this issue. He did not share the passionate patriotism of his wife and son, and was much less susceptible to the pressure of public opinion. In a poem written on Christmas Day 1915, Grace encouraged young Englishmen throughout the world to "Go forth, our boys, at England's word!"[256] Frankie confessed that the German aggressions against civilians "made his blood boil."[257] But Will admired German culture and believed that "if Germany were to disappear it would be one of the greatest calamities which could befall the human race."[258] Nor did he want his son's extraordinary talents to be wasted as a cog in the British war machine.

Grace was as concerned as Will about Frank's future, but, influenced by British friends and family (including her perennially disapproving cousins), she feared that Frank would jeopardize a future career in Britain if he did not volunteer to serve in the war. She and Frank convinced each other that Will — who was 8,000 miles from Europe and had been away for more than a year — was too out of touch with British sentiment and

---

254 The Derby scheme was named after Edward Stanley, Lord Derby, who became Director-General of Recruiting on October 11, 1915. Frank's enlistment was encouraged by Grace's dear friend, Frances Evans. Grace may also have been influenced by her cousin Maud Bell. Maud corresponded with Grace in the fall of 1915 about Frankie's future, after Will had had an unpleasant encounter with other of Grace's Bell relations during his travels in the Far East. Reminding her how "spiteful" Maud was, Will advised Grace to throw her "meddling" letters into the fire and avoid being drawn into an epistolary dispute. D.140/6/2039, WHY to GCY, November 4, 1915; D.140/6/2056, WHY to GCY, November 23, 1915. Young Papers.

255 Some of Grace's letters were very delayed reaching Will when he was in Japan and Ceylon; others never reached him.

256 D.140/14/1, GCY, "The Great Recruitment." Young Papers.

257 D.140/15/8, GCY, "Frank: A Little Monograph Written by Request for Mrs. Evans [n.d.]." Young Papers.

258 D.140/6/2025, WHY to GCY, October 8, 1915. Young Papers.

European events to make a fully informed judgment. They confidently expected that he would see things differently when he returned.

And so, with Grace's blessing, Frank left his engineering studies in Lausanne and went to London in early December, intent on enlisting. After a few days, he decided to join the Royal Flying Corps. Knowing how opposed Will was, and having been instructed not to do anything without his permission, Grace was unwilling to let Frank sign up without his consent. When Frank cabled Will for permission, Will initially opposed the plan and expressed alarm at the family's "hysteria."[259] He eventually acquiesced, although he insisted he did not understand what he was agreeing to, and only consented because Grace asked him to do it "for her sake."[260]

Grace was uplifted by Frankie's enlistment, but for Will it was a catastrophe. Regarding Frank as "our eldest & best" child, Will had planned his future with great care. Now all the plans were wrecked and Frank's "career [lay] in Ruins," Will mourned.[261] Convinced that Frank had made a "terrible blunder", Will blamed Grace for disregarding his explicit "commands" and encouraging the boy.[262] Fearful that he would never see his son again, he fulminated, "Why oh why did you send Frankie to England against my express wishes?"[263] Will's latent misogyny quickly surfaced. "It's because women so often make decisions, without knowing all the facts, & influenced by their emotions, that the world goes wrong," he told Grace.[264] "A woman can never know the world as a man does, & she misses important bits of knowledge," he railed.[265] He accused her of disloyalty and criticized

---

259 D.140/6/2062, WHY to GCY, December 11, 1915. His letter to Frank was much softer in tone (D.140/6/2064, WHY to Francis Young, Letter No. 2, December 13, 1915). Young Papers.

260 D.140/6/2072, WHY to GCY, December 22, 1915; D.140/6/2074, WHY to Francis Young, December 22, 1915. Young Papers.

261 D.140/6/2104, WHY to GCY, January 12, 1916. Young Papers.

262 Blunder: D.140/6/2062, WHY to GCY, December 11, 1915. Commands: D.140/2091, WHY to GCY, January 1, 2016. Young Papers.

263 D.140/6/2075, WHY to GCY, December 26, 2015. Similarly, D.140/6/2091, WHY to GCY, January 1, 1916; D.140/6/2094, WHY to GCY, January 3, 1916, and D.140/6/2096, WHY to GCY, January 4, 1916. Young Papers.

264 D.140/6/2082, WHY to GCY, December 29, 1915. Young Papers.

265 D.140/6/2091, WHY to GCY, January 1, 1916. Young Papers.

her "precipitate and impulsive behavior" — denunciations that "upset [her] horribly."[266]

Will was somewhat mollified when the British military instructed Frankie to complete his engineering course in Switzerland and return to England in June 1916, when he would be nineteen and could enlist as an officer. Nevertheless, this contretemps heightened Will's fears about his family's growing independence. He became more reluctant to rely on the judgment of others and more determined to control the destiny of his other children.[267] Grace showed a positive and optimistic spirit to Frankie, but was greatly distressed by the "disharmony" and "mutual misunderstanding" that had developed between her, Will, and Frank.[268]

Confident that she and Frankie were right, Grace did not back down. In classic reframing mode, she told Will that, had he been fully aware of the circumstances, he would have made the same decision, and when he returned from India, he would see the wisdom of their action. After a month of heated exchanges, she put an end to the discussion by writing, "I am not going to say another word about this business till you come home, except that, trying as it all has been, I do not regret it, & that I am sure we shall all agree as to what is to be done when you come home."[269] Will agreed that they should stop discussing what had gone wrong and focus on planning for the future.

This was the most dramatic, but not the only indication of Grace's growing independence while Will was in India. She continued to assist him, but also developed her own mathematical work, and pushed Will in new directions. They debated their ideas, proofs, and theorems at length in their letters. Will was often critical of the work she was doing for him, but she forged ahead, and urged him to include some new ideas about probability, a topic she was independently discussing with

---

266 D.140/14/3, Typed Letters, Copy of WHY to GCY, January 12, 1916 with Grace's reaction added. Young Papers.

267 D.140/6/2089, WHY to Cecily Young, January 1, 1916, and D.140/6/2114, WHY to Cecily Young, January 19, 1916. Young Papers.

268 Optimism: D.140/6/2001, GCY to Frank Young, January 9, 1916. Grace's distress: D.140/14/3, Typed Letters, Copy of WHY to GCY, January 23, 1916 with reaction from Grace. D.140/16/1, GCY, "Per Ardua", p. 255 notes the "agony" Grace suffered when Will wrote she was disloyal. Young Papers.

269 D.140/6/2112, GCY to WHY, January 18, 1916. Young Papers.

another mathematician.[270] With her help, Will published eight papers under his own name between 1914 and 1916.[271] In a jointly authored paper, submitted a few weeks after his return from India in April 1914, they developed a theorem that became known as the Heine-Young theorem.[272] In addition, Grace won acclaim for five papers on the foundations of differential calculus, which were published under her own name in leading mathematical journals between 1914 and 1916. When she presented a paper at the centenary meeting of the Swiss Natural Science Society, in September 1915, she enjoyed "a most flattering reception" from an audience that included mathematicians, physicists, and medical scientists.[273] The Youngs also began to publish more co-authored papers. During 1916, after Will's return from India, they submitted four papers that were published under their joint names.[274]

As usual, we do not know how Grace and Will made their decisions about authorship, or why Grace began to publish more under her name alone and jointly with Will. Late in 1913, after each had published a paper, Will noted that he was more pleased to see Grace's paper in print than his own; perhaps this emboldened her.[275] Certainly, his lengthy absence gave her more opportunity to work on her own projects.[276] Whatever the impetus, the Youngs seemed, at long last, to be starting to implement what Will had promised in 1902: "Everything under my name now, & later when the loaves and fishes are no more procurable in that way, everything or much under your name."[277]

---

270 Will's criticisms: WHY to GCY, D.140/6/1952, February 8, 1915; D.140/6/1981, June 6, 1915; D.140/6/1965, March 12, 1915. Probability: D.140/24/3, GCY to WHY, January 10, 1914. Young Papers.

271 One article, published in 1914, acknowledged Grace's assistance in a footnote. Sylvia M. Wiegand, "Grace Chisholm Young", p. 248, and Grattan-Guinness, "Mathematical Bibliography", Entry 139.

272 Grattan-Guinness, "Mathematical Bibliography", Entry 143.

273 D.140/6/2016, GCY to Mrs. Carey, 20 September 1915. Young Papers.

274 Grattan-Guinness, "Mathematical Bibliography", p. 55.

275 D.140/6/1709, WHY to GCY, December 29, 1913. Young Papers.

276 Grace did not write an algebra textbook for use in India, as proposed by an Indian publisher who suggested she should write it under Will's "supervision." D.140/6/1978, K & J Cooper to WHY, 19 May 1915, following up an inquiry originally sent a year prior. Young Papers.

277 D.140/6/553, WHY to GCY, February 15, 1902.

Grace's publications solidified her scholarly reputation among mathematicians who were working to develop the modern theory of real functions and assured her a lasting legacy.[278] The distinguished mathematician M. L. Cartwright would later write, "In the opinion of many experts her work in this field is deeper and more important than her husband's."[279] Grace's name was given to a theorem she worked out in one of her published papers.[280] At the end of 1915, she won the Gamble Prize, awarded by Girton College to a graduate who had done outstanding research, for another paper. Noting that Grace had developed "one really very good theorem" in that prize-winning paper, the renowned mathematician G. H. Hardy cautioned the selection committee that using Grace's paper to judge the caliber of future entries might set an "extravagant" standard for the prize.[281] Two modern-day male mathematicians who have tried to assess Grace and Will's respective contributions have concluded that because their work was so entwined after they began to collaborate in 1901, it is impossible to determine who was responsible for what.[282] Even when the Youngs published separately and independently, their papers reflected their joint thinking, these scholars argue, extending to Grace the recognition that Will held back.

At last, Grace was winning recognition and honors that had been long denied her. But the timing of her success lessened her happiness in it. The Gamble Prize was awarded in the midst of the contretemps about Frank's enlistment, and she hesitated to send Will the news. A draft telegram asking Will to send his consent to Frank has several crossed out mentions of "Gamble Prize." When Will got the news of the award

---

278 M. L. Cartwright, "Grace Chisholm Young", *Journal of London Mathematical Society*, 19:75 (July 1944), 185–92 (p. 189).

279 Cartwright, "Grace Chisholm Young", *Girton Review*, p. 19.

280 Others were working independently on the same idea and shared credit with Grace. The theorem is known as the Denjoy-Young-Saks Theorem.

281 Quoted in Marjorie Senechal, *I Died for Beauty: Dorothy Wrinch and the Cultures of Science* (New York: Oxford University Press, 2013), p. 64. The Gamble Prize was awarded annually, but rotated triennially among disciplines. Reviewing the winning submission of mathematician Dorothy Wrinch in 1918, Hardy noted that her work was distinctly inferior to Grace's.

282 Andrew M. Bruckner and Brian S. Thomson, "Real Variable Contributions of G. C. Young and W. H. Young", *Expositions Mathematicae* 19 (2001), 337–58, https://doi. org/10.1016/S0723-0869(01)80019-0.

a few weeks later, Grace was disappointed that he did not respond enthusiastically about her achievement.[283]

Grace's opportunities for recognition in her own right were short-lived. When Will returned from India in the spring of 1916, brimming with plans to write a series of articles about university reform, Grace abandoned her own mathematical projects and slipped back into her accustomed role of helpmate wife. Once again, Will's work took precedence over everything else. "I am not allowed to do any housekeeping, & am up to my ears in papers," she reported in August.[284] She was still working "morning noon & night" on Will's projects in December and the grueling pace caused "a nasty little breakdown" in health and a recurrence of her debilitating headaches.[285]

Having experienced more independence during Will's time in India and proven her mettle as a mathematician in her own right, Grace found it more difficult to play the role of his assistant after he returned. She wrote despondently to Frances Evans, "The [domestic work] is good, the mathematics is Will's & so also good, but I fear my part in it is very mediocre; a good secretary could have done better."[286] Much of Grace's discontent arose from her thwarted desire to serve her country, especially after Frank began active duty as a second lieutenant in the Royal Flying Corps in July 1916.[287] This time he went to England with Will's backing, much to Grace's relief.

Nevertheless, Will soon began to pull strings to get his son reassigned to a job behind the lines, despite being told that the work Frank was doing was the most helpful he could do for the war effort, and he was very happy being "a mere pilot."[288] Grace typed the letters Will dictated,

---

283 Draft telegram: D.140/15/1. Will's response: D.140/6/2116, WHY to GCY, January 23, 2016. Grace's disappointment: D.140/24/3, Typed copy of WHY to GCY, January 23, 1916, with Grace's reaction added. Young Papers.
284 D.140/6/2210, GCY to Francis Young, August 24, 1916. Young Papers.
285 D.140/6/2342, GCY to Francis Young, December 19, 1916; D.140/6/1354, GCY to Francis Young, December 28, 1916. Young Papers.
286 D.140/6/2244, GCY to Frances Evans, October 16, 1916. Young Papers.
287 His call up, originally set for June 1916, was delayed by a month so he could take his final university exams.
288 D.140/15/1, Lt. Col. Wyndham to WHY, October 28, 1916; D.140/6/2366, Francis Young to WHY, January 6, 1917. Young Papers.

and wrote some of her own to potentially influential contacts. But she assured Frank she wanted him to manage his own career.[289]

With Frank in the Flying Corps, Grace's desire to offer patriotic service intensified. "I have been trying hard to do my duty as 'the older sister in the family of mathematicians' [...] I have been Will's secretary, & worked on my own small account, & the work is recognized, both in England & out of it. But, but all this while I would rather be with the Red Cross at the Front," she confessed to Frances Evans.[290] To Frankie, she lamented, "My duty is to play second fiddle, & do it all the time & all the time. I try to do it & I fail. I hope you will succeed, & I hope you will serve your country well [...]. I love to think you are actively serving England as I should like to do."[291] Grace's reference to playing second fiddle and repetition of the phrase "all the time and all the time" suggests she was finding her life more onerous than formerly. She started volunteering for three hours a week in an eye hospital, learning theory and getting practical experience.[292]

And then disaster struck. Frank was killed in action in February 1917, when the plane he was flying was shot down by the Germans. Both Grace and Will were devastated by the loss of their beloved son. Will felt Grace suffered a much greater personal loss, while he endured "the shattering of a whole chain of carefully laid plans" for Frank's future. Believing that Frank had rare talents, and determined to overcome the deficiencies of his own upbringing, Will had devoted himself to giving Frank the experiences, education, and advantages that would ensure his future success.[293] With Frankie's death, "the conventional triumphed yet once again & the unusual, the rare exception, was sacrificed," Grace wrote bitterly."[294]

---

289 D.140/6/2308c, GCY to Francis Young, November 18, 1916. Grace did not extend the same encouragement or sympathy to her rebellious daughter, Leni. Pleased that Will was trying to "manage" Leni after he returned from India, she noted, "Will certainly understands training his family, & if ever these girls get married, their husbands will have something to be grateful for." D.140/6/2222, GCY to Frances Evans, September 11, 1916. Young Papers.

290 D.140/6/2411, GCY to Frances Evans, February 6, 1917. Young Papers.

291 D.140/6/2342, GCY to Francis Young, December 19, 1916. Repetition in the original. Young Papers.

292 D.140/6/2308, GCY to Francis Young, November 18, 1916. Young Papers.

293 D.140/16/1, GCY, "Per Ardua", pp. 267–68, copy of a letter to an unidentified correspondent. Young Papers.

294 D.140/16/1, GCY, "Per Ardua", p. 282. Young Papers.

Her grief was intensified by the guilt she felt for having encouraged Frankie to enlist. In the rambling memoir she wrote about Frank shortly after his death, "Per Ardua ad Astra", she repeatedly told herself that Will did not blame her, but she continued to fear that he did.[295] Nevertheless, Grace held to the belief that, under the circumstances, she had made the right decision. And she took comfort from knowing that Frank had died a "heroic", even a "grand" death.[296] But Will's trust had been undermined. In future years, he would occasionally — and cruelly — remind Grace of the incalculable harm that resulted from her poor judgment. When they disagreed about the wisdom of moving back to England in the 1930s, he cautioned, "How afraid I am that you will take some irrevocable decision during my absence which like that about Frankie would go far to ruin our lives."[297]

Having lost Frank, Grace clung more closely to Will. Preparing to write her account of Frank's short life in 1917, she reread the letters she and Will had written to each other during the first decade of their marriage. It became clear to her as never before that Will had always had her best interests at heart and protected her against her own worst instincts and impulsiveness. She concluded that his loving care had failed in 1915 only because, when he "was not there to control, Frank and I had no natural protector to stand between us & personal feeling."[298] She did not consider whether she had been asked to sacrifice too much for Will over the years, and whether she needed protection against the incessant demands he made on her.

After Frank's death, Will again prioritized his professional advancement over Grace's. In May 1917, when he was contemplating resigning from the University of Liverpool, he bluntly informed Grace that a wife ought to put her husband's career ahead of her own. "A woman ought not to mind playing second fiddle, it is not really such a hardship," he claimed. Adding insult to injury, he pointed out that if

---

295 D.140/16/1, GCY, "Per Ardua," pp. 252, 255, 266. Young Papers. The title she gave the memoir of Frank's life, "Per Ardua ad Astra", meaning "through adversity to the stars" or "through struggle to the stars", was adopted as the motto of the Royal Flying Corps in 1913.
296 D.140/16/1, GCY, "Per Ardua," p. 255. Young Papers.
297 D.140/6/5299, WHY to GCY, August 3, 1935. In late 1939, when Will's behavior was becoming more and more erratic, he reproached Grace at length about Frank. D.140/6/5123, GCY to Janet Young, December 2, 1939. Young Papers.
298 D.140/24/2, Grace's Autobiographical Notes on 1901–1902. Young Papers.

Elizabeth Barrett Browning (with whom Grace had long identified) had helped Robert Browning "to express himself more clearly and exactly, and think more conscientiously, his work would have been infinitely better, and a great deal of her stuff would never have been published. Browning may have published two or three really good things herself and nothing lost," Will asserted. The phrase "playing second fiddle" echoes the sad refrain in Grace's letter to Frankie and suggests that this was not the first time she had heard this argument. She recorded Will's words in her notebook without comment, but it was a role that was becoming increasingly difficult for her to accept.[299]

A month later, in June 1917, Will won the London Mathematical Society's most prestigious prize, the de Morgan Medal, awarded for outstanding contribution to mathematics. He continued to turn out mathematical papers with Grace's help — mostly under his name alone[300] — but their productivity declined, and his relations with academia remained problematic. He did not return to India, and never fully finished his report on university education systems for the University of Calcutta.[301] He resigned from the University of Liverpool in the fall of 1919, partly because he did not like the terms he was offered — an extension of his existing salary and duties — and partly as a protest against the university's standards for awarding doctorates, which he thought insufficiently rigorous.[302]

The Young family felt they could not return to England unless Will got a post that paid enough to send the children to good schools. But Grace knew this was unlikely. "[British universities] have served us envy, hatred, & malice & uncharitability in the past & there is not the

---

299 D.599/16, recorded by Grace in a notebook, and dated 25.V.17. Tanner Papers.
300 They were co-authors of a paper published in 1923 and another in 1928. Grattan-Guinness, "Mathematical Bibliography", p. 57.
301 Grattan-Guinness, "Mathematical Union", p. 157.
302 Ibid., pp. 157–58. Kelly, *For Advancement of Learning*, pp. 154 and 526, lists Will as holding an honorary Chair in Philosophy and History of Mathematics from 1913 to 1919. According to the official announcement prepared by the University of Liverpool, Will was to be "Lecturer in Higher Analysis" with a salary of 100 pounds per session (D.140/6/2595, July 10, 1917, Young Papers). The undated draft letter of resignation Will dictated to Grace is a litany of the slights and injuries he felt he had received from the university (D.599/1/1/1/7, Grace's Notebooks, Tanner Papers). Another draft letter (D.140/15/1) protests the hiring of other men to positions in which Will has "special knowledge" as well as his criticisms of the PhD criteria. Young Papers.

slightest sign of them doing anything else in the future," she wrote, with unaccustomed bitterness, to Frances Evans.[303]

Later Marriage: the 1920s and 1930s

Will did get a better teaching position, but not one that met his family's needs. In the fall of 1919, he became chair of the Department of Mathematics at the University of Wales in Aberystwyth, a position that allowed him to hire staff, bring in visiting scholars, and develop a cohort of graduate students. Nevertheless, the school was a mathematical outpost in the hierarchy of British universities. The appointment did little to reduce Will's sense of injustice in never having won a post commensurate with his talents and his standing in the field. The eminent British mathematician G. H. Hardy agreed that Will deserved a more prestigious teaching position.[304] A year after he went to Wales, Will was elected president of the London Mathematical Society, a signal honor. Nevertheless, his reputation remained higher abroad than in Britain.

Although he was required to be in residence in Aberystwyth from September to May, Will decided not to bring his family with him because he needed solitude to work, and it would be too expensive to educate the children in England. "We must be content to be separate most of the year. The advantages are many," he informed Grace.[305] Nevertheless, he did not want to be left entirely to his own devices. When a move to a new house and a recurrence of gall stone problems made it impossible for Grace to come to Wales, their daughters went instead. Cecily spent two academic years with Will, acting as his assistant and keeping house for him; Janet spent one. Grace, back home in Switzerland, continued to work on the manuscript of a second edition of *The Theory of Sets of Points*, but it was never completed.

---

303 D.140/7/1.70, GCY to Frances Evans [probably 1918]. Young Papers.

304 See Grattan-Guinness, "Mathematical Union", p. 161. Hardy reiterated this view in G. H. Hardy, "William Henry Young, 1863–1942", Royal Society of London, *Obituary Notices of Fellows*, 4:12 (November 1943), 307–23, https://royalsocietypublishing.org/doi/10.1098/rsbm.1943.0005.

305 D.140/6/2850, WHY to GCY, November 18, 1919; similarly, D.140/6/2855, WHY to GCY, November 20, 1919; D.140/6/3120, WHY to GCY, March 12, 1922. Young Papers.

Will was outraged by any show of independence on Grace's part. Still convinced that he knew what was best for his family, and ever fearful that calamity would ensue if his wishes were not heeded, he heaped instructions and criticisms on Grace and the children. "The real difficulty," he wrote angrily to Grace when she was arranging to move the family to a new home outside of Lausanne in 1920, "has always been that I never give orders but reason & advice. And you have got into the way of disregarding anything but positive commands & you don't by any means always carry out these."[306] He upbraided her for acting "contrary to orders" and derided the decisions she made on her own.[307] "We are all fond of you, & proud of you, but we think you are inclined not to do the *intellectual* work that is needed to run a house, or a family, or a property with judgment & success," he wrote dismissively about her plans.[308]

Grace increasingly responded to Will's criticisms with silence, which added to his anxiety and irritation.[309] Occasionally, she protested. "I should like a few lines of news of yourself & not any directions or orders," she informed him in the mid-1920s.[310] More typically, she began to use her notebooks, and sometimes her pocket diaries, to vent her frustrations with him. From the late teens on, her reflections, observations, and criticisms of Will are sprinkled through the notebooks in which she took dictation from him, wrote notes on mathematical treatises, and worked out formulas and proofs. These occasional entries reveal what she was feeling and thinking while she exhibited a quiescent, obliging, self-sacrificing exterior.

Grace was beginning to see herself as a victim and longed for more affection from Will. In the fall of 1921, she noted that she had saved Will from many mathematical errors by being as stubborn as a donkey and digging in her heels — and he had "whacked" her for it. Two weeks later, she wondered whether he would have liked to have been born Louis Quatorze. She sadly concluded that she had been at her best during her

---

306 D.140/6/2941, WHY to GCY, May 18, 1920. Young Papers.
307 D.140/6/2894, WHY to GCY, February 2, 1920; D.140/6/2896, WHY to GCY, February 3, 1920. Young Papers.
308 D.140/6/1941, WHY to GCY, May 18, 1920. Emphasis in the original. Young Papers.
309 D.140/6/3071, WHY to GCY, May 21, 1921. Young Papers.
310 D.140/6/3453, GCY to WHY, March 29, 1925. Young Papers.

engagement and the early years of married life — a bleak commentary after twenty-five years of marriage.[311]

When she spent time with Will in Wales in 1923, Grace referred to herself as his "scapegoat."[312] To withstand his temper, she drew inspiration from a fourth-century Catholic saint, Monica, the mother of St. Augustine. After reading St. Augustine's *Confessions*, she wrote to her daughter, Janet,

> Saint Monica must have been a very wise & intellectual woman, an admirable wife & mother [...] [St. Augustine's] father was very hasty in temper & violent, but he never quarreled with Monica, because she was too wise & loving. Only when she differed from him she always managed to persuade him afterwards! Give Babbo [the Italian word for papa, which is what the children called Will] a big kiss for me & tell him I am going to try & be like Monica![313]

Will was incensed by any suggestion that he made too many demands on Grace. When his sister May told Grace she "was too unselfish" and urged her to take a much-needed vacation, Will sent a furious letter to Grace:

> What does [May] mean [by urging you to] 'strike for time off'? [...] have you not been your own mistress for years at a time? Just as if you had been looking after me while I was in India or Aberstwyth [...]. You disposed of your time as you chose, & had money enough all that time to take servants as many as you wanted.[314]

By the summer of 1923, 60-year-old Will was full of complaints about his work at the University of Wales.[315] He retired from teaching and joined Grace in Switzerland. During the first years of his retirement, the Youngs spent time together in their Swiss home, attended international mathematical conferences, and soaked in medicinal waters at German spas. When they took a lengthy trip to Canada and

---

311 D.599/1/1/1/7, Grace's Notebook of WHY dictations & oral notes, entries dated 5-IX-21 and 19-IX-21. Tanner Papers.

312 D.140/6/3219, GCY to Laurence Young, February 12, 1923. Similarly, D.140/6/3149 and D.140/6/3150, both GCY to Cecily Young, June 10, 1922. Young Papers.

313 D.140/6/3018, GCY to Janet Young, January 11, 1921. Young Papers.

314 D.140/6/3281, WHY to GCY [n.d., May 1923]; D.140/6/3278, May Young to GCY, May 22, 1923. Young Papers.

315 Draft letters in D.140/15/1, Grace's Pocket Diaries, dated January 15, 1923 and May 7, 1923. Young Papers.

the United States in 1924, Grace lectured on the concept of infinity at Bryn Mawr College, where Isabel Maddison, a friend from Girton and Göttingen days, taught mathematics. Between 1919 and 1929, Grace published six mathematical papers under her name, several of which explored the mathematics in Greek philosophy.

Fig. 2 Grace in 1923.
Courtesy of Sylvia Wiegand and
the American Physics Society.
CCBY ND-2.0.

Fig. 3 Will in 1920.
Photo by Walter Stoneman.
© National Portrait Gallery,
London.

Despite the honors and recognition he had received, Will's deep-rooted feelings of insecurity and rivalry persisted. The Russian mathematician, A. S. Besicovitch, who first came to England in 1924, recalled being asked by Will, "Are you one of those people who think my wife is a better mathematician than I am?"[316] Will did no further work in pure mathematics, but he gave occasional lectures and worked tirelessly to rebuild a spirit of international good will and collaboration as president of the International Mathematics Union and its successor organization, the International Congress of Mathematicians. He began to write a book on international finance, read Roman law and legal history, taught himself a number of European languages, and started to write

---

316 Quoted in Patricia Rothman, "Grace Chisholm Young and the Division of Laurels", *Notes and Records of the Royal Society of London* 50:1 (1996), 89–100 (p. 97), https://doi.org/10.1098/rsnr.1996.0008.

his autobiography. As always, he wanted Grace's help with all these endeavors. As always, he pressured her to spend more time on his work and less time on domestic chores and her own projects, and feared he had lost control of his loved ones. As late as 1937, he took Grace to task for going to England to help Cecily look for housing without consulting him first. A woman needs her husband's advice, he protested.[317]

Although Grace and Will enjoyed periods of warmth and affection in the 1920s and 1930s, stresses were mounting. It was easier for Grace to suffer Will's temper and devote herself to furthering his work and reputation when their relationship was passionate, emotionally fulfilling, and grounded in common interests and goals. After he retired, their interests were diverging and their personal relationship was deteriorating. When she was with Will, Grace tried to be a cheerful and supportive helpmate and caregiver. But to her children she expressed irritation about his incessant demands and constant interruptions. It took her three years to write an article on Plato's mathematical theories because she could work on it only in between Will's projects, she noted.[318] After several difficult weeks working with him on a major address, she complained, "writing up other people's ideas is much more trying than writing one's own."[319] Will's insistence on the "urgent" need to finish an article in 1931 turned the household into chaos. Four months later, Grace wrote in relief, "I am at last going ahead with my book [...] as long as Babbo was here I could hardly write at all."[320]

As they aged, Grace and Will chose to spend more time apart. Will indulged his wanderlust by travelling extensively on his own in Europe, Turkey, and Greece, in connection with his work as President of the International Congress of Mathematicians. He spent another six months traveling by tramp steamer in South America, and made frequent trips to England. By 1930, Grace and Will agreed that they preferred to take their vacations separately.[321] She often went to England or France to see

---

317 D.140/6/5427, WHY to GCY, January 8, 1937. Young Papers.
318 D.140/6/3217, GCY to Cecily Young, February 23, 1923; D.140/6/3240, GCY to Cecily Young, April 1, 1923. Young Papers.
319 D.140/6/4072, WHY to Cecily Young, with note from GCY, February 15, 1928. Young Papers.
320 D.140/6/4776, WHY to GCY, February, 20, 1931; D.140/6/4843, GCY to Cecily Young, June 5, 1931. Young Papers.
321 D.140/6/4523, GCY to Cecily Young, March 8, 1930. Young Papers.

her children and grandchildren, but she was also very happy staying in her Swiss home by herself.

In 1929, Grace branched out in a new direction and began writing an historical novel set in Elizabethan England. It interwove romance, adventure, and court intrigues, and also included Grace's speculations about the possible author of several plays attributed to Shakespeare. She circulated a draft of *The Crown of England* to several publishers in 1933, but none accepted it. She was working on revisions in 1935, but it was never published.

Grace was increasingly resentful about the way Will treated her, but she was still awed by his intellectual prowess. "Your mind like a butterfly hovers over all the flowers in turn. You are international & interscientific, there is no shutting you up in one nation or one science," she marveled as she wrote down his thoughts in 1931.[322] But as Will's focus narrowed, and his thoughts became more circumscribed, Grace's frustration grew. In 1935, she silently criticized him, interjecting reactions like "[Dear me! How dull he is!]" and "[This is meandering!]" as bracketed statements in the midst of pages of dictation about his boyhood and his approach to writing autobiography. Later, she dutifully transcribed his words, eliminated her interpolations, improved the writing, and turned out a very polished version of his thoughts.[323]

Repressing her thoughts and feelings undoubtedly took a strong psychological toll on Grace — all the more so because her feelings for Will were so conflicted. At times she seemed to seethe with anger and a sense of injustice at the way he treated her, but often she was loving and heartsick. The poetry she wrote in the 1930s captured this fundamental duality. "The Trot of the Scapegoat" balances her strong sense of mistreatment against her unflagging devotion to Will, deep dependence on him, and determination to care for him despite his temper. The Scapegoat comes when "the Master" calls, bears the Master's sorrow and gloom, and cheerfully awaits his commands. She flees when told to leave, and joyfully returns when the Master's mood "is serene and

---

322 D.599/1/1/1/7, Grace's Notebook of WHY dictations & oral notes, entry dated 22-1-31. Tanner Papers.

323 Ibid., entry dated 13–11–35. Tanner Papers. Polished version: D.140/11/5, Young Papers.

content."[324] Another poem — untitled, unfinished, and undated, but filed with materials from the late 1930s — reveals a darker and angrier side of Grace. After crossing out two milder stanzas, and struggling with the wording, she left a single stanza that reads:

> I love the man who reads to think & learn
> As to the critic, poisonous, sneering, smug
> I'd like him to shut up his ugly mug
> Or better still, depart & ne'er return.[325]

As a college student, Grace wrote that she composed poetry as a solace when she was depressed.[326] The raw emotion in this stanza is a sharp contrast to the sentimental expressions of many of her poems. The uncharacteristic coarseness of the language and harshness of her judgments are powerful and shocking — and very revealing.

Grace did not question that women should defer to male opinions and judgments, but during her fifties and sixties she began to acknowledge how difficult it was to be both a rigorously trained scholar and a woman who was expected to be subordinate to men. Conflicted herself, Grace gave a mixed message to her daughters. "We want you to be what hardly any modern unmarried woman of your age is, both sweet & gentle & loving & modest & also successful with a brilliant career of your own," she wrote her oldest daughter, Cecily. "But that is a very large order, it means *having & acting* on your own judgment & yet *distrusting* it & *giving way to* male opinions & desires. I am myself only very faintly realising the weakness & the strength of a really *great* woman." Once again, Grace drew inspiration from a religious model. "Remember how St. Francis lay down and made the monks walk over him," she advised Cecily.[327] It is not surprising that Grace's models for action were self-denying, self-sacrificing centuries-old saints, not modern, forward-looking, self-actualizing women.

Issues of gender, family obligation, and professional status became increasingly complicated for the Youngs as their daughters, as well as their sons, embarked on careers. Both Grace and Will had a preference for male children and were more pleased at the birth of a son than a

---

324 D.140/14/13, 1936. Young Papers.
325 D.140/14/1, [n.d.], filed with poetry written in the 1930s. Young Papers.
326 D.140/14/1, "My Poetry" [Dec. 31, 1890?]. Young Papers.
327 D.140/6/5494, GCY to Cecily Young, November 9, 1937; emphasis in the original. Young Papers.

daughter.[328] Although all their children were expected to attend college, pursue graduate training, and earn a living, Will admitted that he was more interested in planning his sons' careers than his daughters' and took the boys' successes and failures more to heart.[329] When Grace tried to calm his agitation over teen-aged Frankie's multiple spelling errors, pointing out that she herself was a poor speller, Will angrily responded, "Remember you are a woman & the fact that you spell wrong occasionally has not a tenth of the same importance."[330]

The children's lives and careers avoided many of the career-family tensions that had plagued Grace and Will's marriage. Both Cecily and Laurie earned higher degrees in mathematics and taught mathematics at the university level. Cecily did not marry until she was in her fifties and had no children. Laurie married and had six children. His wife was a stay-at-home mother, but her mother, Agnes Dunnett, was one of the first women to practice medicine in England; Dunnett became the sole provider for her husband and five children after her husband's business went bankrupt.[331] Janet was the only one of Grace's daughters to combine marriage, motherhood, and career. She had the life her mother once hoped for: after completing her medical training, she married and continued to practice medicine while raising two children. Leni, the family rebel, was the only child who did not earn a graduate degree and have a career; she left a graduate program in mathematics after she married. The mother of three, she proudly touted the virtues of domestic life and full-time motherhood.[332] Pat, the youngest child, earned a DPhil in chemistry and worked in chemical engineering and international finance. He married his secretary.

Grace and Will's belief that women were meant to support and serve men applied to daughters and sisters as well as to wives. Will expected his daughters to assist him when he was teaching in Wales in the early 1920s, and insisted on having Cecily's help at other times in the 1920s and

---

328 D.140/6/496, GCY to WHY, October 30, 1901; D.140/6/881, GCY to WHY, July 12, 1905; D.140/6/5375, WHY to GCY, August 9, 1936. Young Papers.
329 D.140/6/1495, WHY to Mrs. Pratt, November 22, 1912. Young Papers.
330 D.140/6/1611, WHY to GCY [October 1913]. Young Papers.
331 Sylvia Wiegand, "Grace Chisholm Young and Agnes Dunnett." Blog posted February 19, 2013, https://ggstem.wordpress.com/2013/02/19/sylvia-wiegand-grace-chisholm-young-and-agnes-dunnett/.
332 D.140/7/2.2, Leni Young [Canu] to GCY, September 23 [n.y.]. Young Papers.

1930s. Both he and Grace were offended if Cecily treated his demands as an imposition. In contrast, when Grace was ill during the winter of 1920, she and Will advised Janet not to interrupt her medical studies in order to care for Grace and manage the household in Switzerland.[333]

Laurie, the eldest surviving son, deserved special treatment, Grace and Will believed. In the late 1920s, when Laurie and Cecily were both studying mathematics at Cambridge University, she was drafted to proof, edit, and type his papers. Grace made it clear that it was Cecily's duty to help advance her younger brother's career. During the summer of 1931, when Will had already used several weeks of Cecily's time, Laurie wanted her to type the manuscript of his book, which was to be published by Cambridge University Press. Grace wrote to Cecily, "As for your work, of course we are proud of it, & glad you are forging ahead now. But we feel that from now to the time when Laurie's work has to be sent in, you ought to devote a great portion (if not all) of your time to his affairs."[334] Several years later, when Cecily was teaching mathematics at the Imperial College of Science and Technology at the University of London, Grace informed her that Laurie's "future [...] is all important, & any influence for the good which you [...] exercise on him & in his career will be gratefully recognized by us."[335] The children's unequal status was underscored when Will gave his entire collection of mathematics books to Laurie and none to Cecily.[336]

The rationale was the same that drove Will and Grace's unequal division of the laurels of their partnership: Laurie's work was considered more important than Cecily's because it was more important that he, a man, establish himself in a career. As the oldest surviving son, he was to be "the Head" of the family. The family honor and prestige would come from his professional success, not from his sisters' achievements. As the eldest daughter, Cecily was expected to be the "*centre* of the family" and exercise an "unselfish and attractive force" in its affairs, Grace stressed.[337]

---

333 D.140/6/3018, GCY to Janet Young, January 3, 1921; D.140/6/3017, WHY to Janet Young, January 4, 1921. Young Papers.
334 D.140/6/4868, GCY to Cecily Young, July 16, 1931. Young Papers.
335 D.140/6/5494, GCY to Cecily Young, November 9, 1937. Young Papers.
336 D.140/6/5490, Laurence Young to GCY and WHY, October 28, 1937; D.140/6/5494, GCY to Cecily Young, November 9, 1937. Young Papers.
337 D.140/6/5494, GCY to Cecily Young, November 9, 1937. Emphasis in the original. Young Papers.

The End of the Partnership

Will continued to win honors and acclaim, and Grace continued to defend him against criticisms and slights. In 1928, he was awarded an honorary doctorate by the University of Strasbourg and won the British Royal Society's prestigious Sylvester Medal, given to an outstanding researcher in mathematics. But when Cambridge failed to mark the fiftieth anniversary of Will's association with the university in 1932, Grace wrote to Laurie in distress, "I always feel indignant at any discourtesy, ingratitude, or want of consideration towards the noblest & most un-self-interested of men. Mind you always do your duty to your good father, who has been so neglected by those who owed most to him."[338] Nor would she tolerate any disrespect or criticism of Will from the children. On the contrary, she expected them to revere and defer to him as she did.[339]

As Will's mental health declined in the late 1930s, he became even more dependent on Grace's steadfast care. His behavior suggests that he may have been suffering from what would now be diagnosed as Alzheimer's disease: he was very forgetful, unable to perform ordinary tasks such as dressing himself, and increasingly erratic in behavior and temper. The children were scattered: Laurie lived in South Africa; Leni was in France; Cecily, Janet, and Pat were in England. Grace and Will discussed moving back to England, but remained in Switzerland.

Once again, the family was uprooted and divided by war. Janet's family was visiting Grace and Will in Lausanne when World War II broke out. Janet and her husband, Stephen Michael (a half-Jewish German who had changed his name from Siegfried and recently become a British citizen), quickly returned to England but left the children and their nanny, Nellie Green, with Grace and Will. As the war progressed, Janet urged her parents to come with the children to England. Fearful that his pro-German sentiments would cause him to be arrested in England, Will refused to leave. By early May 1940, Grace admitted that she was not the right person to care for Will in his decline, but she did not want other family members to sacrifice themselves in order to take

---

338 D.140/6/4982, GCY to Laurence Young, February 24, 1932. Young Papers.
339 D.140/6/5205, GCY to Jean Canu, July 21, 1934. Young Papers.

charge of him.[340] Two weeks later, she set off with her grandchildren, leaving Will in Switzerland in Nellie's care. Grace managed to get seats for herself and the two children on the last commercial flight from Paris to London before France surrendered to Germany.[341]

Although Grace had intended to return quickly to Will, the family decided, after the fall of France, that the journey would be too hazardous. Happy to be in England, but anxious about Will, Grace devoted herself to taking care of Janet's children. In November, she moved with them "to the wilds of Shropshire" to keep them away from air raids while Janet and her husband remained in London.[342] Will's mental and physical health continued to deteriorate. Nellie moved him into a nursing home, in June 1942, and left for England. Will died several days later, on July 7, 1942, at the age of seventy-eight. He and Grace had been married for forty-six years. In an obituary, the mathematician G. H. Hardy called Will "one of the most profound and original of the English mathematicians of the last fifty years."[343]

* * * * *

The two themes that had defined Grace's life — devotion to family and intellectual achievement — were still entwined at its end. Janet's daughter, Dorothy, has happy memories of playing and learning to read with her grandmother in England.[344] A tower of maternal energy and resourcefulness, Grace managed to get General Jan Smuts, the wartime prime minister of South Africa, to bring the baby booties she had knitted for Laurie's children to him in South Africa during the war.[345] Meanwhile, Grace's mathematical reputation and prominence were growing. In March 1944, the fellows of Girton College proposed to make her an Honorary Fellow in recognition of her distinguished and original work in mathematics.[346] But before the resolution could be acted

---

340 D.140/6/5832, GCY to Janet Young, May 2, 1940. Young Papers.
341 Grattan-Guinness, "Mathematical Union", p. 180.
342 D.140/6/5906, Janet Young to WHY, 12 November 1940; D.140/6/5982, Janet Young to WHY, 13 October 1941. Young Papers.
343 Hardy, "William Henry Young", p. 307. https://royalsocietypublishing.org/doi/10.1098/rsbm.1943.0005
344 Author interview with Dorothy Sampson, July 27, 1990.
345 Laurence Young, *Mathematicians*, p. 234.
346 Cartwright, "Grace Chisholm Young", *Journal of London Mathematical Society*, p. 191.

on, Grace suffered a heart attack, and died on March 29, 1944, at the age of seventy-six.

Grace's mathematical legacy similarly recognizes her strong commitment to family and mathematics. The London Mathematical Society currently awards two Grace Chisholm Young Fellowships a year to "mathematicians who need support when their mathematical career is interrupted by family responsibilities, relocation of a partner, or some other similar circumstance, making possible some continuous mathematical activity, so enabling the fellow to be in a position to apply for posts when circumstances allow."[347] The fellowships provide opportunity and support to individuals who have made choices similar to Grace's when faced with conflict between home duties and professional achievement. They are administered by the Women in Mathematics Committee of the Society, but men as well as women are eligible to apply.[348]

---

347 https://www.lms.ac.uk/grants/grace-chisholm-young-fellowships.
348 Grace and Will are also memorialized in the Grace Chisholm Young and William Henry Young Award established by their granddaughter, Sylvia Wiegand, and her husband, Roger, to support graduate student research in mathematics at the University of Nebraska, where both the Wiegands began teaching in 1972. Wiegand was the first woman to teach in the department. https://math.unl.edu/department/awards/graduate#young.

3. Separate Careers, Separate Lives: Elsie Clews Parsons and Herbert Parsons

Alice Freeman Palmer and Grace Chisholm Young failed to maintain their professional careers because they were constrained by their traditional views of love and marriage. Elsie Clews Parsons shattered those barriers. Born in 1874, she became an avowed feminist and a determined rebel. Her early life was a rebellion against her mother; her later life was a rebellion against her husband. As a wife, mother of four, PhD in sociology, college teacher and social critic turned anthropologist, Elsie boldly rejected old-fashioned values and behavior and struggled to rewrite the terms of early twentieth-century marriage and gender relationships. Offering a bold critique of marriage customs, she championed a broad set of marital reforms that anticipated practices advanced by second wave feminism sixty years later. Her life-long journey of self-exploration and cultural discovery led her from the glittering society of Newport, Rhode Island to the earnest reformism of Progressive Manhattan and Washington, DC; then to the bohemian, avant-garde world of Greenwich Village; and finally to the indigenous cultures of the American Southwest, Mexico, and Peru.

After a crisis in her marriage to Herbert Parsons, a lawyer and politician who served three terms in the US House of Representatives, Elsie began to construct — sometimes haltingly, often painfully, but always deliberately — a lifestyle more in keeping with her beliefs about the way women and men ought to live. Her vision of companionate romance and marriage placed work — the woman's as well as the man's — at the core of a relationship. She expected each partner to support the other's career — not just to tolerate it, but to encourage it, share it,

     https://doi.org/10.11647/OBP.0318.03

and create the conditions that would allow it to flourish. When Herbert failed to provide the engagement and encouragement she desired in her work, she turned to other men for intellectual stimulation and emotional support. In her affairs, as well as her marriage, she strove to make her partner's engagement in her work a foundation for romance and passion. Carving out a new standard, living up to it herself, and finding a male partner who would live up to it was not easy for Elsie, despite the clarity of her vision and her fierce determination to lead the life she wanted rather than the life others expected of her. Shaping her personal life around her work, leading a separate life from her husband, and having affairs made it possible for her to remain married and continue to work — but these strategies were not wholly satisfactory solutions to her marriage-career dilemma.

A Rebel in the Making

Elsie was brought up in a world of wealth and ostentatious social display. Her father, Henry Clews, Sr., a Wall Street banker, was a self-made millionaire. Her mother, Lucy Madison Worthington Clews, a Southerner by birth, had social standing and political connections. Their marriage was more of a business arrangement than a romantic union.[1] The Clews family — which included Elsie's two younger brothers, one of whom died in 1890, at the age of thirteen — wintered in New York and summered in Newport with the Astors and the Vanderbilts. Lucy's parties were noted in the Newport newspaper columns and she was dubbed "Newport's best-dressed lady."[2]

Elsie's rebellion against social artifice and the idle lives of Society women was as much a rebellion against her mother as rejection of a social system. Pampered, protected, and passionately interested in high society and fashion, Lucy Clews was the epitome of all that Elsie disliked about traditional womanhood. She brought Elsie up to be a dutiful

1   Lissa Parsons Kennedy, "Reminiscences of Elsie Parsons Kennedy." Interview by Allen Nevins, November 11, 1962. Columbia University, Rare Book and Manuscript Library, Oral History Archives at Columbia. Copies are in the American Philosophical Society Library, Elsie Clews Parsons Papers (APS) and the Rye Historical Society, Parsons Family Papers (RHS).
2   Peter H. Hare, *A Woman's Quest for Science: Portrait of Anthropologist Elsie Clews Parsons* (Buffalo, NY: Prometheus Books, 1985), pp. 27–28.

daughter and a decorative, compliant, and dependent lady like herself. "Adapt yourself [...] do not force any of your own ideas no matter how convinced you are of being right," Lucy admonished. "Be careful of your manners, & *your voice*."[3] Henry Clews's views of womanhood were equally traditional. Believing that a woman found her "crowning glory in homemaking and domestic life," he publicly deplored the "modern woman" who focused her energies and ambitions outside the home.[4]

Actively rejecting parental strictures, Elsie got in trouble as a youngster for playing with boys and going on "wild rides" on her horse. As an adolescent she defied her mother by not wearing a veil or a corset.[5] Offended by the hypocrisy of formal social life, she refused to exchange endearments, use affectionate greetings, or send thank you notes. When she insisted on going to college, she was condemned for being "selfish" for thinking about her own interests instead of "stay[ing] home [...] and be[ing] companionable to my mother."[6] It was only after Elsie created "quite a ruckus" that her more indulgent father finally gave his consent.[7]

Elsie enrolled at Barnard College in 1892, three years after it opened, and continued to live at home and accompany her mother to Europe every summer. Elsie worked hard at Barnard and also sparkled at balls, dinners, receptions, and weekend house parties.[8] Fearful that she would slip into a purposeless life, she reminded herself that an "intellectual life must be always of supreme importance" and her goal was "Accomplishment."[9]

---

3 APS, Lucy Clews to EC, August 28, 1888 and August 20, 1888. Emphasis in the original.
4 Quoted in Rosemary Levy Zumwalt, *Wealth and Rebellion: Elsie Clews Parsons, Anthropologist and Folklorist* (Urbana and Chicago: University of Illinois Press, 1992), p. 36.
5 ECP, *The Journal of a Feminist* with a New Introduction and Notes by Margaret C. Jones (Bristol: Thoemmes Press, 1994), p. 86. ECP's typed manuscript, "The Journal of a Feminist" (1913–1914), is in APS and quoted later in this chapter. "Journal of a Feminist" was not published during Elsie's lifetime.
6 APS, ECP, "Selfishness". While it was becoming acceptable for the daughters of the middle class to go to college in the early 1890s, daughters of rich and prominent families rarely did. See Barbara Miller Solomon, *In the Company of Educated Women: A History of Women and Higher Education in America* (New Haven: Yale University Press, 1985), p. 64.
7 Kennedy, "Reminiscences."
8 APS, EC to Sam Dexter, November 19 [1893] and December 13, 1893.
9 RHS, ECP, Journal 1893–1894.

During her sophomore year, Elsie enjoyed a close friendship with Sam Dexter, a twenty-six-year old Harvard graduate who shared her intellectual interests as well as her spirit of adventure and fun. The son of a wealthy and successful corporate lawyer in Chicago, he was pursuing a law career in Chicago when he met Elsie in the summer of 1893 in Newport. They maintained a lively correspondence, in which they discussed Elsie's "gay butterfly career", the books they were reading, and their views on women's suffrage.[10] Elsie's mother encouraged the relationship, which she regarded as a budding romance. The two families planned to travel together in Europe during the summer of 1894. But Sam died suddenly and unexpectedly that May, after a very brief illness.[11]

Scholarship, Courtship, and Civic Engagement: 1894–1900

Elsie mourned Sam but did not withdraw from her busy life. Returning to Barnard in the fall, she became more serious about her studies. She took up sociology, conducted field work in New York's immigrant communities, founded a chapter of the College Settlement Association at Barnard, and became active in the national organization.[12]

In late 1894, barely six months after Sam's death, she met Herbert Parsons at a weekend house party in Lenox, Massachusetts. A twenty-five-year-old lawyer with political aspirations, Herbert was instantly drawn to Elsie whom he found "charming, beautiful, and intelligent." More than twenty years later, he would recall that she was "regarded as a wonderful person because she was in college and enjoyed herself also."[13] Like both Elsie and Sam, Herbert came from a privileged

---

10   APS, EC correspondence with Sam Dexter, October–December, 1893.
11   Elsie preserved a lock of Sam's baby hair along with his letters. She and Sam's mother maintained a correspondence until Elsie married. Elsie's friendship with Sam's sister, Katherine, continued for decades.
12   Adapted from the model of Toynbee Hall in London, the settlement house movement that took root in America in the 1890s prompted middle-class women and men to live in communal residences in inner city neighborhoods and provide classes and other supports to the immigrant populations who lived in the area. The settlements in the College Settlement Association network were supervised and staffed by college-educated women.
13   APS, enclosure "for the children" in HP to ECP, May 12, 1918.

background. The son of a prominent and wealthy New York attorney, he was educated at elite private schools — St. Paul's School, Yale University, Harvard Law School — and spent a year studying at the University of Berlin. Although the two families lived within blocks of each other in Manhattan, Elsie and Herbert moved in different social circles. The Episcopalian Clews summered in Newport; the Presbyterian Parsons summered in Lenox, Massachusetts.

Elsie and Herbert quickly developed a close friendship, but she had no interest in a traditional romance. He joined her in the vigorous outdoor activities that she liked — ice-skating, bicycling, horseback-riding, and sledding — and escorted her to the concerts and plays he enjoyed. A keen sense of humor added to his appeal. Walking a difficult line between companionship and courtship, he adapted himself to her rules. He learned not to send her flowers after an argument; he refrained from dropping in unexpectedly to see her; he arranged their dates to fit around her schedule (which meant having to go on very early bicycle rides around the city); he avoided taking a chaperone along whenever he could.[14]

Like many gifted, ambitious, career-minded women in the nineteenth century, Elsie was reluctant to marry, even after she fell in love with a man who loved her and admired her accomplishments. Throughout five years of friendship with Herbert, she distinguished herself in her academic work and made steady progress through graduate school. She was elected to Phi Beta Kappa, and after graduating from Barnard in 1896, she enrolled (despite her mother's disapproval) in a master's program in sociology at Columbia University, two years after the school opened its graduate programs to women. She wrote her thesis on New York City's poor relief system after reviewing hundreds of case records, volunteered at New York's College Settlement, and became treasurer of the national College Settlement Association. In 1897, she was offered a paid position as headworker at the Friendly Aid Society's settlement house, but her parents objected so strenuously that she turned it down.[15] Elsie shrewdly turned the situation to her advantage by getting her parents to agree that if she lived in their home, she could work for a PhD

---

14 RHS, HP to EC, November 8, 1895; HP to EC, November 11, 1895.
15 RHS, Mary Ashley to EC, July 2, 1897.

degree at Columbia and would no longer be required to accompany her mother to Europe every summer.[16]

Elsie and Herbert's mutual interest in municipal government, progressive reforms, and civic philanthropy strengthened the bond between them. Although Herbert did not share Elsie's iconoclastic views on social norms, and was often too reserved for her tastes, he was a self-described reformer who favored quick action. Like Elsie, he chafed against his family's values and strictures while remaining tightly enclosed within the family circle. He worked in his father's law firm, but devoted himself to politics, to his father's disapproval and disappointment. Herbert's decision to ally with the progressive wing of the Republican Party, work against the Democratic Tammany Hall machine, and root out municipal corruption shocked his male relatives, who traditionally voted Democratic. The only son in a family of four daughters (a fifth sister died young), Herbert was familiar with many of the gender constraints that grated on Elsie.

Herbert was reliable, dependable, and safe. As their relationship developed, Elsie indulged the more adventurous, thrill-seeking side of her personality in her friendship with the famed architect Stanford White. Married and twenty years older than Elsie, the cultured, sophisticated, and fun-loving White enjoyed the company of young women and was very fond of Elsie. Herbert was greatly affronted when Elsie's mother would not allow her to go camping with him, his married sister and husband, and another friend in 1897. Lucy Clews feared the Parsons family would not be adequate chaperones, but allowed Elsie to attend a house party at White's Long Island home instead. Earlier that summer Elsie had gone to Canada on a camping trip with White, his wife, and another young female friend.[17]

Herbert was not a social rebel or an iconoclast, but he sympathized with and supported Elsie's scholarly aspirations and civic activities when others poked fun at them.[18] When she announced her plans to go

---

16   RHS, Lucy Clews to EC, September 21, 1897 and October 25, 1897.
17   RHS, HP to EC, July 28, 1897; Lucy Clews to HP, September 14 [1897]; HP to EC, September 1, 1897 and September 22, 1897.
18   One admirer who was given her graduate thesis to read commented, "P. H. D. Pretty Hard Drudgery!" (RHS, John Bost to EC, February 17 [1900]). Another told her it would take him longer to read it than it had taken her to write it (RHS, Henry Barbey to EC, December 13, 1899).

to graduate school, she was outraged by White's entreaty: "*Please* do not — why in the name of Heaven when you know you [are] young & lovely & intelligent and that everyone else knows it [...] — why must you go & waste any of it on a lot of musty-fusty & dusty old professors?"[19] In contrast, Herbert asked to read Elsie's PhD thesis on education policy in colonial America because he was genuinely interested in the topic. He provided her with statistics on municipal trends, helped her when she was running a boys' history club at a settlement house, and invited her as his guest to the annual meeting of the Legal Aid Society of which he was a director.[20]

Their relationship entered a new phase in the late spring of 1898, when Herbert, in an outpouring of patriotism, volunteered to fight in the Spanish American War. (He never saw action, but he was sent to a training camp.) While he was away, Elsie finally admitted that she was in love with him. "[N]o one has ever loved me the way I think you do, and it seems a wonderful thing," she wrote to Herbert.[21] Years later, recalling the "freedom and joy" she experienced when she fell in love with Herbert, she confessed, "There is nothing in the world, in my world, like the happiness of that feeling."[22] Nevertheless, she insisted she could never marry him. "You and I are both people of very firm ideals, I cannot marry you or it would be giving up my ideals [...] you must not go on loving me as you have done for it would be giving up your ideals," she explained.[23]

Elsie was opposed to marriage, in principle, because she saw it as a social institution that cultivated undesirable traits in both men and women. In her view, marriage inevitably fostered dullness, possessiveness, and dependence; she wanted freedom and adventure, not staid domestic routines and constraints. Occasionally, she felt more hopeful about marriage. After visiting a married cousin, she wrote Herbert, "It has thrown new light for me on matrimonial possibilities. They have been married 12 years and the romance persists as I have

---

19   RHS, Stanford White to EC [undated]. Emphasis in the original. Similarly, Stanford White to EC, 12 July 1897. He too teased her about her scholarly initials.
20   RHS, HP to EC, February 2, 1898.
21   APS, EC to HP, June 19, 1898.
22   APS, ECP to HP, June 7, 1909.
23   APS, EC to HP [n.d., probably 1898].

never seen it before."[24] But dining with newly married friends depressed her. "If I could advocate matrimony it would be on very different lines from what I see these people are talking. They have no imagination and no humor." If she were to marry, she informed Herbert, she would do it "just to show people how" a marriage should be constructed.[25]

Elsie feared that she and Herbert were too ill-matched to be happy together. Knowing that her "peculiar views" were too unconventional for him, she repeatedly expressed dismay at the thought she would "displease" or "disappoint" him.[26] She was equally conflicted about her own behavior. Her letters reveal a tension, for example, between her resistance to playing a "passive and receptive" role and her occasional, perhaps, unintentional, lapses into it. "I am feeling just now as dependent on you as ever you could wish me to be," she confessed in the fall of 1898.[27] The physical passion Herbert aroused in her made it hard for Elsie to assert her independence. She wanted Herbert to know she was "really hard and set." But she admitted, "I can't appear that way when you hold me in your arms. For I am not like that then."[28]

Although the tensions were mounting, Elsie and Herbert maintained their unsettled relationship for another year and a half. At times, she urged him to break off their relationship and find a more suitable partner, but whenever he seemed inclined to do so, she was greatly distressed.[29] Elsie's post-graduate school plans provoked a very serious rift in April 1899, when she was unexpectedly offered a newly created Hartley House fellowship to supervise student field work in Franklin Giddings' sociology course at Barnard. Pressed to decide quickly, she accepted, without discussing it with Herbert. When he reacted with dismay — he must have seen this as yet another obstacle to their marriage — she admonished him, "Don't say again that 'our paths in life lie wide apart.' It is not true."[30] Nevertheless, she again asserted that she could not marry him. "I have not changed

24 APS, EC to HP, May 21 [1898].
25 APS, EC to HP [August 15, 1898].
26 APS, EC to HP [August 15, 1898]; EC to HP, June 28, 1898; EC to HP [November 25, 1898].
27 APS, EC to HP [September 26, 1898].
28 APS, EC to HP, [n.d.]; similarly, EC to HP, July 13, 1899.
29 APS, EC to HP [October 3, 1898] and November 3, 1898.
30 APS, EC to HP [April 1899]. RHS, Franklin Giddings to EC, April 17, 1899.

my aversion to matrimony; indeed, it is stronger than ever, or rather I am more convinced than ever I shall never marry. For, although I love you better than I love or can conceive of loving anybody else, — moreover, if I had to choose between you on one side and all my family and friends on the other I would choose you — yet I should let you go entirely out of my life rather than marry you."[31]

Once again, Elsie announced that they should stop seeing each other, and urged Herbert to end the relationship.[32] There was a break, but by the end of June, they were back together and talking about marrying. The obstacles still seemed overwhelming to Elsie, but she was looking for ways around the difficulties. She assured Herbert, for example, that she would respect his religious faith, but because she did not share it, she could not worship with him.[33] (A staunch Presbyterian, he had seriously considered becoming a minister; she was an avowed atheist.)

Elsie was still struggling to find the right balance between love and work, dependence and independence, separation and connection — issues that would bedevil her for decades. Rejecting the nineteenth-century ideal of marital "oneness", she had warned Herbert not to become totally absorbed by her or by their joint life. "[D]on't tell me ever again, even lightly, that I came between you and your work," she protested. "In a high minded mood it would trouble me, and at other times it would give me a base satisfaction not good for me."[34] When he now expressed unhappiness about being apart from her, she responded, "Sweetheart, many of the happiest days of your life you are to spend without my presence. I wish it so [...] I could not bear to shut you off from everything."[35]

As they wrestled with their personal relationship, both Elsie and Herbert reached new professional milestones. Elsie was awarded her PhD in sociology in June, 1899; she published an article about her approach to sociological field work in *The Educational Review* and was asked to present a paper at the American Association for the

---

31   APS, EC to HP, April 29, 1899.
32   APS, EC to HP, May 22, 1899; June 21, 1899.
33   APS, EC to HP [July 20, 1899].
34   APS, EC to HP, June 30, 1898.
35   APS, EC to HP, July 17, 1899.

Advancement of Science.[36] In the fall, she started her position as the Hartley House Fellow. In November, Herbert was elected to his first public office as a Manhattan alderman (the equivalent of today's city councilman).

In early November 1899, Elsie was still protesting, "I am not fit to be your wife."[37] But at the end of the month, she finally agreed to marry Herbert, after what she described as "an anguished night" of "some hysteria." She announced her decision in language that echoed the formulaic surrender imagery expected of nineteenth-century women. "You won last night, my hero. In my heart of hearts, if not in my mind of minds, I think you are entirely right — and that I am entirely wrong. But please have patience with me," she begged.[38]

Elsie was not one to shrink from a challenge. Some years before, she had been upset when her brother accused her of being "afraid" to marry.[39] Giving up experiences was not part of her philosophy of living. Now she had the opportunity to show how marriage should be done, with Herbert a willing, if somewhat reluctant or dubious partner in the experiment. Herbert appealed to Elsie as an independent thinker who was knowledgeable about municipal affairs, an ambitious and hard worker, and a man of principle. It was reasonable to expect that marriage to him would keep her from sliding into the frivolous social life she wanted to avoid. He seemed to offer a promising blend of work and play, and appeared likely to be a companionate partner as well as a romantic lover.

But the primary reason Elsie married Herbert, it appears, is that, despite all their differences, she truly loved him and found it impossible to let him go. This was not a marriage of convenience or a pragmatic arrangement: it was a love match. But as Elsie understood only too well, it was a very risky undertaking. It is striking that, rather than breaking out of her wealthy and privileged world, as many of her career-minded compatriots did, the iconoclastic Elsie married someone from her own social class who was not entirely sympathetic to her unorthodox views and concerns.

36   RHS, William H. Hale to EC, June 7, 1899.
37   APS, EC to HP, November 1, 1899.
38   APS, EC to HP, November 27, 1899.
39   RHS, ECP Journal, 1893–1894.

Fig. 4 Elsie and Herbert on a camping trip with family and friends in 1900. Unknown photographer. American Philosophical Society Library, Elsie Clews Parsons Papers.

Elsie agreed to marry but not to give up her work. When their engagement was formally announced, her colleagues applauded her plans to continue with her professional and volunteer activities. The announcement in the *Herald Tribune* on May 30, 1900 described Elsie's activities and accomplishments in more detail than Herbert's. Barnard College trustee Annie Nathan Meyer enthusiastically assured her that the college would continue to pay her Hartley House Fellowship stipend.[40] However, some admirers feared she was backing away from what would have been a brilliant future. A Barnard faculty member lamented, "I am not going to congratulate you at all. You and Alice Duer were the two girls I had made up my mind would make great names for yourselves, and show women what they can do and now you just come down to the level of us ordinary mortals."[41]

---

40   RHS, Annie Nathan Meyer to EC, June 7 [1900].

41   RHS, A. R. Cross to EC, June 7 [1900]. Alice Duer, a Phi Beta Kappa graduate of Barnard College and friend of Elsie, married Henry Wise Miller in 1900, and moved with him to Costa Rica where his rubber business failed. After returning to New

Elsie spent the final weeks before her wedding in Newport. She was amused when her mother's staff gave her lessons in stocking and managing a house and taught her how to clean silver.[42] Back in New York, Herbert, aided by his older sister, Mamie, was making many decisions about furnishing, decorating, and provisioning their new home. Herbert was fussy, and did not always agree with Elsie's choice of china and silver patterns, lamps, and dining room furniture. Often, he and Mamie chose something that was grander and more ornate than what Elsie favored.[43] She genuinely seemed not to mind, and expressed relief that she did not have to spend more of her time on domestic details.[44]

Nevertheless, the hard won balance of her world was shifting. Acknowledging her growing dependence on Herbert, Elsie wrote, "There is nothing to put in the scale against you now — not even the Hartley House fellowship."[45] (It had been extended for a second year.) He assured her that their partnership would focus on work and accomplishment as well as personal happiness. "I want to make you happy & in that way if no other help you to accomplish real purposes," he promised. "I also believe that what we now plan is a truer & a fuller life, not only in its pleasures but also in its responsibilities, than that you ever contemplated."[46]

Elsie and Herbert were married at "The Rocks," the Clews's summer home in Newport, on September 1, 1900. Elsie was three months shy of twenty-five — too old to marry, according to her mother, who believed that a woman of twenty-five was likely to be "too set in her ways" to make a good wife.[47] Society notables, including the Astors and the Vanderbilts, attended the wedding breakfast, but the New York press

York in 1903 with their infant son, she became a successful poet, novelist, and screen writer. A feminist and a suffragist, she won fame for a collection of satirical poems entitled "Are Women People?", published in 1915. See Sue G. Walcutt, "Alice Duer Miller", in *Notable American Women 1607–1950: A Biographical Dictionary*, ed. by Edward T. James, Janet Wilson James, and Paul S. Boyer, 3 vols. (Cambridge, MA: Belknap Press, 1975), II, pp. 538–40.

42 APS, EC to HP, June 29, 1900; similarly, EC to HP, June 11 and June 14, 1900.
43 RHS, HP to EC, July 12, 1900; July 15, 1900; July 20, 1900; July 27, 1900; August 13, 1900.
44 RHS, Mary Parsons to HP, July 31, 1900.
45 APS, EC to HP, July 25, 1900.
46 RHS, HP to EC, July 28, 1900.
47 RHS, ECP Journal, 1893–1894

reported on Elsie's aversion to social display, interest in "serious" matters, and desire to keep the wedding "as simple as possible."[48] Elsie and Herbert had considered a honeymoon trip to Mexico but, knowing that Herbert might be nominated as a congressional candidate, they settled for a more sedate trip to New England. Their honeymoon ended abruptly when Herbert was nominated as the Republican Congressional candidate from a Democratic stronghold in Manhattan, a race he knew he could not win. They quickly returned to the city, where Herbert waged an exhausting but unsuccessful campaign.

Early Married Life, 1900–1904

Despite Elsie's reservations, the early years of the Parsons's marriage were very happy. Highly companionate, intense, and "accomplishful", their relationship fulfilled their vision of a marriage that incorporated meaningful work with personal pleasure. "Accomplishful" was the term Elsie and Herbert used to describe time spent in purposeful, productive endeavor that had good results. It was a touchstone by which they judged the value of their days; when they were apart, they kept each other informed about their accomplishful activities.

As she hoped, Elsie was showing others how marriage should be done. She broke through traditional constraints with gusto but tempered her iconoclasm with sympathetic consideration for Herbert. They avoided the dependence, possessiveness, and boredom that she feared marriage inevitably fostered.

Elsie began her second year as a Hartley Fellow a month after her wedding and was pregnant a few weeks later. Elsie and Herbert's reactions to the pregnancy and birth show the mutual support, easy camaraderie, and affectionate teasing that characterized their relationship. Both were delighted but sobered at the prospect of having a baby. Elsie seemed happier for Herbert than for herself. Informing him, she wrote, "This is very satisfying, isn't it? I want so much to help in bringing *everything* to you that you want, that I can't help being pleased."[49] Herbert expressed

---

48 *New York Herald*, September 2, 1900, quoted in Hare, p. 41.
49 APS, ECP to HP, December 4, 1900; emphasis in the original.

joy, but admitted, "I am so happy in the *e duobus unum* state that even a change to an *e tribus unum* seems to have perils."[50]

Herbert had reservations about Elsie's intention to meet with her Barnard students during her pregnancy, but did not tell her to stop. Knowing that his cautious approach made him seem like a "pettifogger" unable to see the big issue, he proudly queried, "Was I not discreetly silent?"[51] Undaunted, Elsie flouted the convention that kept pregnant women confined to the home, and, despite bouts of morning sickness, supervised her students' field work through the rest of the academic year.[52]

While Elsie wanted a boy, Herbert hoped for a girl. A daughter might do more than a son to advance the feminist causes Elsie cared about, he noted.[53] After Lissa was born in early August 1901 (two weeks late), Elsie, possibly with Herbert's help, produced an account of her birth, written from the baby's point of view. The journal, which includes only a few entries, provides an intimate glimpse into their marriage. Lissa hails the new century of womanhood and vows, "I'll teach [mother] to be glad I came and I'll be to her the best companion she could have, barring, of course, father." Observing that her parents "seem to like each other a great deal" and her father kisses her mother often, although rarely in front of other people, the baby reflects, "Love must be a wonderful, splendid thing."[54]

Elsie relished her new role. After visiting an unmarried friend in December 1901, she gushed to Herbert, "I wish that she had a *loving* husband and — a baby. But I naturally find myself wishing that for everyone to whom I wish well. A little bit of paradise on earth."[55] Nevertheless, she was back in the classroom at the start of the academic

---

50   RHS, HP to ECP, December 6, 1900; emphasis in the original.

51   Ibid.

52   RHS, ECP, 1900 Diary. RHS, Franklin Giddings to ECP, June 20, 1901.

53   RHS, HP to ECP, December 6, 1900.

54   RHS, "Diary of Elsie [Lissa] Parsons from the day of her birth, Tuesday August 6, 1901." The diary, which is in a box of Elsie's papers, has been attributed to Elsie. The handwriting appears to be Herbert's, although the style — text heavily annotated with footnotes — is characteristic of Elsie. The sentimental tone and language seem more like Herbert than Elsie. Possibly Elsie dictated it to Herbert, but he might have helped write it as a tribute to Elsie and Lissa and an expression of his love.

55   APS, ECP to HP, December 27,1901. Emphasis in the original. Similarly, ECP to HP, January 29, 1903.

year, two months after Lissa's birth. For the next four years, she juggled motherhood, teaching, and volunteer work with aplomb.

Elsie was promoted to Lecturer in Sociology at Barnard and took over Giddings' class in the fall of 1902, just about the time she became pregnant again. Her translation of French sociologist Gabriel Tarde's *Laws of Imitation* was published a month after her son, John, was born in August 1903. Tarde's seminal work analyzed the ways societies absorb and adapt parts of outside cultures, a topic that Elsie would continue to explore throughout her professional life.[56] She missed the annual fall meeting of the College Settlement Association in Boston because she was nursing John, but she was teaching her class at Barnard in October 1903.[57]

Elsie kept up a busy round of volunteer activities. She engaged in many of the causes and activities that college graduates of her day typically pursued, but she approached them in novel ways. She shocked co-workers at the College Settlement House with what they termed her "socialistic" views.[58] She raised money for and served as Treasurer of Greenwich House, the pioneering settlement founded by her friend Mary Kingsbury Simkhovitch. It replaced the religious philanthropy of the "lady bountiful" tradition with a nonsectarian, more scientific approach to working with poor families.[59] The Tenement House Commissioner commended Elsie's efforts to protect the safety conditions required by law in tenement homes.[60] She tried to get herself appointed as the first woman on the New York City Board of Education, but when Mayor Seth Low was reluctant to appoint a woman, she had to settle for an appointment on her local school board.[61] That experience was liberating: the evening Elsie attended her first school board meeting in 1902 was the first night she went out alone and unchaperoned, she would later write — a striking indication of how constrained the lives of upper-class unmarried women were in this period.[62] As a married woman,

56　On Elsie's interest in Tarde, see Desley Deacon, *Elsie Clews Parsons: Inventing Modern Life* (Chicago: University of Chicago Press, 1997), pp. 35–37.
57　RHS, Katherine Coman to ECP, November 5, 1903.
58　RHS, Florence Wardell to ECP, December 2, 1902.
59　C. C., "New Settlement Theory," *The New York Times*, August 24, 1902, p. 25.
60　RHS, Tenement House Commissioner to ECP, May 7, 1903.
61　RHS, Nicholas M. Butler to ECP, November 29, 1901; President of the Borough of Manhattan to ECP, March 6, 1902.
62　ECP, *Journal of a Feminist*, p. 94.

she enjoyed more freedom than she had as the sheltered daughter of a socially prominent and proper family.

Visiting her mother in Newport, Elsie took pride in the contrast between her busy life and her female relatives' lives of idle pleasure. "Mama and [cousin] Louise dress, i.e., bathe, curl, anoint, powder, manicure, etc., and think about dress all day long. Louise is incredible. She misses her adorable baby, & sews exquisitely, & she & Mama both play cards sometimes in the afternoon & off & on go out to lunch or dinner and that is absolutely all that happens to them [...]. It is an incomprehensible life to me and very sad," Elsie reported to Herbert.[63]

Herbert was meanwhile emerging as a force to be reckoned with in municipal politics and the progressive wing of the Republican Party. He earned his living as a lawyer, working in the firm headed by his father and his uncle. But his real passion, the activity that brought excitement and adventure to his life, was his political work.[64] As a Manhattan alderman from 1901 to 1903, he worked to reform city contracting procedures and to break the power of the Democratic Tammany Hall machine. Idealistic but shrewd, he supervised door-to-door organizing to turn out Republican votes and helped to create coalitions between Republicans and anti-Tammany Hall Democrats.[65] He failed to win nomination as a congressional candidate in 1902, but two years later he became the Republican candidate for Manhattan's Thirteenth Congressional District and went on to win the election.

Elsie and Herbert's professional lives were quite separate, but their mutual commitment to a progressive agenda for political and social reform gave them a common frame of reference and overlapping social and professional circles. Nevertheless, Elsie and Herbert approached their work quite differently. Herbert embraced politics as an opportunity to serve others and advance the general good, not as a pathway for fulfilling personal ambition. Inspired by a deep religious faith, he believed that "the most important thing in the world is service and

---

63   APS, ECP to HP, September 20, 1905.
64   Kennedy, "Reminiscences."
65   Zumwalt, pp. 63–65; RHS, William Parsons, Jr., "The Progressive Politics of Herbert Parsons" (unpublished undergraduate thesis: Yale University, April 30, 1965). William Parsons is unrelated to Herbert's family.

not self-aggrandizement."[66] When he failed to win the congressional nomination for his aldermanic district in 1902, he confessed to Elsie that he "had been suffering from too much Parsons" and was losing sight of his intention to serve but let others have the glory.[67] Throughout his political career, Herbert would win praise for his professional self-effacement, his willingness to remain in the background, and his ability to be "self-sacrificing and unselfish."[68] These traits kept Herbert from adopting the aggressive stance that many politicians exhibited in public life; in private life, they undoubtedly helped him to support Elsie without feeling threatened or displaced from center stage.

Unlike Herbert and many of her female contemporaries, Elsie did not justify her interest in working by appealing to a sense of service or religious duty. She was passionate about improving women's lives and liberating both men and women from outmoded constraints, but her major concern was self-fulfillment, not service to humanity. She worked because she had a personal need for occupation: research, writing, and teaching kept her busy and focused, and made her a happier and a more interesting person.[69] It also allowed her to escape from the household routines and conventional female activities that bored her. Far from shying away from personal notoriety, she welcomed and even cultivated it. At this point, her work ethic both impressed and puzzled Herbert. Later in their marriage, their different approaches to work would make for trouble.

In addition to her feminist views, a fortuitous set of circumstances helped Elsie to lead an "accomplishful" life and avoid the agonizing self-doubt that beset many well-to-do wives who worked outside the home. She was exceptionally fortunate in having an opportunity to teach at Barnard at a time when few colleges, including women's colleges, employed married women faculty and even fewer employed married

---

66 HP to Charles H. Pankhurst, December 16, 1907, quoted in William Parsons, Jr., "Progressive", p. 1. See also, Herbert's speech in *Report of Addresses at a Dinner Tendered to the Honorable Herbert Parsons, Hotel Astor, March 22, 1910*, and his notes for a speech to be given at Yale in 1908. All in RHS.
67 RHS, HP to ECP, October 5, 1902.
68 RHS, speeches by Henry L. Stimson and others in *Report of Addresses at a Dinner Tendered to the Honorable Herbert Parsons, Hotel Astor, March 22, 1910*.
69 RHS, Dolly Potter to EC [March 1, 1895], quoting Elsie. RHS, EC to Percy R. Turwell, June 12 [1895]; APS, ECP to HP, August 4, 1909.

women with children.[70] She was also fortunate to have a close friend who was similarly combining marriage, motherhood, and career. Mary Kingsbury Simkhovitch, Elsie's colleague at Columbia University and the Friendly Aid Society settlement, was allowed to keep her live-in position as head resident at the settlement when she married Vladimir Simkhovitch in 1899; but she was required to leave when their son was born in 1902.[71] When Mary founded and became the director of a new settlement, Greenwich House, later that year, she moved into it with her family.

Mary's exuberant correspondence with Elsie conveys the pleasure and pride both women took in forging new lifestyles that accommodated marriage, motherhood, and professional work. Sharing confidences about their pregnancies, husbands, children, and work, they encouraged and supported each other. Elsie was a generous friend who not only raised money for Greenwich House, but also helped Mary find a baby nurse, and arranged for Mary's children and nursemaid to stay at the Parsons residence in Lenox when Mary was feeling overwhelmed by work and childrearing.[72]

Elsie also had the financial resources to hire lots of domestic help. The offspring of two very wealthy families, she and Herbert had considerable inherited wealth and lived a very privileged, upper class life although they deliberately abandoned the more lavish lifestyles of their parents. In 1904, Elsie was running her household on $6,000 per year (around

---

70 For women faculty members, see Solomon, *Educated Women*, pp. 89–90. Barnard had a checkered history on this issue. Emily James Smith, Barnard's first dean, was allowed to retain the deanship after she married the publisher George Palmer Putnam in 1899. But she was forced to resign a year later when she became pregnant. In the summer of 1906, Harriet Brooks, a Barnard physics instructor, was asked to resign after she announced her engagement. Dean Laura Gill explained that the Barnard trustees expected a married woman to "dignify her homemaking into a profession, and not assume that she can carry on two full professions at a time." Quoted in Margaret W. Rossiter, *Women Scientists in America*, 3 vols. (Baltimore: Johns Hopkins University Press, 1982–2012), I, p. 16. Elsie was informed in 1907 that Barnard did not hire married women after she had recommended Alice Duer Miller and Mary Kingsbury Simkhovitch for positions (RHS, ECP to Nicholas Murray Butler, November 14, 1905; APS, S. B. Brownell to ECP, January 9, 1907).

71 Carroll Smith-Rosenberg, "Mary Kingsbury Simkhovitch" in *Notable American Women: The Modern Period*, ed. by Barbara Sicherman and Carol Hurd Green (Cambridge, MA: Belknap Press, 1980), pp. 648–50.

72 RHS, Mary Kingsbury Simkhovitch to ECP, May 20 [1902]; October 17 [1905]; October 29 [n.d.]; and Friday [1902].

$188,000 in today's money). Herbert gave her a personal allowance of $1,800 (equivalent to about $57,000 today), half of which she gave away. Her father provided her with an allowance of $2,500 ($79,000 today), which went into their savings. Elsie and Herbert gave away between a quarter and a third of their total income.[73]

The Parsonses lived in a five-story brownstone on East 35th Street in Manhattan, and had the use of Lounsberry, Herbert's father's thirty-acre estate in Harrison, New York which had a house with eight master bedrooms and ten servant bedrooms.[74] Elsie and the children spent summers in Newport, staying in the Clews's magnificent mansion perched on a rocky cliff above the ocean. In the late summer and early fall they stayed in a small house on the grounds of Stonover Farm, the Parsons family estate in Lenox, Massachusetts. (The main house had forty-five rooms.)[75] Herbert typically joined them on weekends. This schedule greatly reduced Elsie's housekeeping and hostessing responsibilities and gave her opportunities to sail, ride, and swim, activities which she loved. Their Manhattan household employed many servants, including several maids, a cook, a waitress, an occasional baby nurse, nursemaids, and other attendants for the children. Gardeners and chauffeurs were employed in other residences. In later years, Elsie would describe the moves between households as more complicated than the annual migrations of a native tribe.[76]

Like most women of her class, including her own mother, Elsie entrusted much of her children's care to baby nurses, nursemaids, and housemaids. She delegated the routine work, but not the planning and oversight. She kept close tabs on the children's development and conscientiously applied the principles of "scientific" mothering that became fashionable around the turn of the century. She maintained a meticulous record of Lissa's health and growth during her first year,

---

73 RHS, ECP to Herbert's father, John E. Parsons, September 23, 1904. Current value was calculated by using the CPI inflation calculator at https://www.officialdata. org/ to compare 1904 and 2021 values.

74 RHS, HP to Pease & Elliman, February 23, 1921.

75 Jennifer Huberdeau, "The Cottager: the Dismantling of Stonover Mansion", *The Berkshire Eagle*, July 25, 2018. https://www.berkshireeagle.com/archives/the-cottager-the-dismantling-of-stonover-mansion/article_87b1b558-c97b-5516-b128-5481972b8ba9.html. RHS, "Description of Stonover after Mary Parsons Died" [1940].

76 APS, ECP to her son, John E. Parsons, December 6, 1916.

documenting her daily intake of food and drink, size and weight, temperature and stool movements.[77] A handwritten "To Do" list offers a glimpse of Elsie's balancing act: a list of the work-related tasks to be finished before an upcoming trip fills one side of a sheet of paper; the reverse side lists the baby clothes and accessories needed for the journey.[78] Elsie filled her letters to Herbert with accounts of the children's activities. She could be a playful mother, pretending to be Lissa's horse, building a miniature garden with her, reading her stories and acting them out.[79]

Like other busy working mothers in the professional class who wanted to spend time with their children, Elsie found ways to work while a child played in the same room. When Lissa was four, Elsie was conscientiously training her to amuse herself while Elsie read or wrote by her side.[80] True to her feminist principles, Elsie was sorely disappointed when her children displayed the gender stereotyping she deplored. "John's masculine sense is already too developed for my liking. He often says boys do this, girls do that, etc.," she complained when John was three.[81] She was even more disheartened by Lissa's interest in clothes, makeup, jewelry, and "pretty things" — proclivities that Elsie blamed on Lucy Clews's unfortunate influence on her granddaughter.[82]

Elsie closely monitored the servants' behavior with the children and intervened when she thought their care was inadequate or their service lax.[83] She could be a demanding and critical employer, but many of her staff worked for her for years, and some saw her as a friend and confidante.[84] She had the highest regard and gratitude for the staff members who made it possible for her to minimize her role but maintain a smoothly running household.[85]

---

77   APS, Elsie's Journal of Lissa's health and growth.
78   RHS, ECP [n.d].
79   APS, ECP to HP, June 19, 1905; June 25, 1906; July 10, 1906.
80   APS, ECP to HP, October 3, 1905.
81   APS, ECP to HP, October 16, 1906.
82   ECP, *Journal of a Feminist*, p. 86.
83   APS, ECP to HP, June 14, 1904; June 18, 1904; February 24, 1907.
84   APS, Lena Frankfort to ECP, July 10, 1908. Similarly, ECP to HP, October 16, 1906.
85   APS, ECP to HP, May 28, 1903; ECP to HP, May 9, 1917. She left an annual annuity of $200 to Mary Carmody, who was employed periodically as a baby nurse and child care provider by Elsie over several decades (RHS, ECP's Last Will and Testament, May 26, 1938).

Herbert's assistance was also critical. Elsie was fortunate to have a husband who was supportive and understanding, if not always enthusiastic, about her activities. She greatly appreciated the ways Herbert "simplifie[d]" domestic life for her.[86] Before they married, he had taken on much of the responsibility for decorating, furnishing, and staffing their new home, and he arranged for weekly deliveries of fresh food from Lenox. When Elsie was in Lenox, he returned library books for her in Manhattan. When they traveled, he thought about the multiple pieces of luggage that were needed, ensured that all the locks had keys, bought the tickets, and made the hotel reservations. Sometimes he took charge of hiring new staff. Carrying out Elsie's detailed instructions, he contacted employment agencies, reviewed resumes, interviewed candidates, and hired a nursemaid for the children. (The process dragged on because he sometimes forgot to make the necessary phone calls or was too busy to call.)[87] Herbert also "simplified" Elsie's life by shielding her from her mother's interference and criticisms, spending time with Lucy when Elsie was out of the city, and acting as a "point man" in dealing with her family.[88] She reciprocated by intervening on his behalf with his father.

Elsie's approach to wifehood was as unconventional as her approach to motherhood. She was unusually candid in informing Herbert that she did not intend to make him the sole focus of her life or adapt to all his tastes and preferences. Her admission, "I miss you *awfully*, Herbert. You have become a part of every bit of me," was balanced by the parenthetical qualification, "Perhaps I ought to except a still lingering fondness for studying the development of the family, etc.", a reference to the importance she continued to place on her teaching and writing.[89] Explaining that she would not give up smoking cigarettes despite Herbert's objections, she acknowledged, "Theoretically, I suppose I ought to put your moral, intellectual etc. welfare, that is as I see it, first; but as a matter of fact I don't, except sporadically and remorsefully."[90]

---

86   APS, ECP to HP, May 28, 1903.
87   RHS, HP to ECP, June 20, 1904; June 22, 1904; September 28, 1905; September 30, 1905.
88   RHS, HP to ECP, October 4, 1905 and October 10, 1905.
89   APS, ECP to HP, June 16, 1902; emphasis in the original.
90   APS, ECP to HP, June 28, 1904.

Elsie tried to make Herbert happy, not because she felt her role as a wife required her to cater to and defer to him, but because she loved him.[91]

Despite their differences, Elsie and Herbert managed to maintain a delicate equilibrium in these early years together. There were disagreements, but no major stresses. For the most part, they treated each other with respect, sympathy, and understanding, even when they disagreed. Both displayed a strong sense of give and take, and an admirable ability to compromise. And both were highly appreciative of the efforts the other made.

For Herbert's sake, Elsie ran a household and took on a domestic role that did not appeal to her. She went through the motions of domesticity, and even signed a few letters to Herbert "your loving housewife" (undoubtedly with her tongue firmly planted in her cheek). But she made no effort to disguise the fact that she found the actual practice of homemaking tedious and boring.[92] Religion was another area of compromise. Although Elsie had warned Herbert that she could not worship with him, she occasionally went to church with him, to his great delight.[93]

On his side, Herbert tried to avoid being overly cautious and conventional. He gave Elsie freedom and space as well as affection and support. Despite his concerns, he did not try to stop her from teaching while she was pregnant. He preferred to have time alone with her on weekends, but realizing that he was being "selfish," he conceded, "Have your company if you will."[94] When they traveled in Europe in 1902, he acquiesced to her desire to ride in a "jaunty [public] cart" instead of waiting for a private conveyance to take them to their hotel.[95]

Nevertheless, Herbert could be irritable and impatient with Elsie over what he admitted were "little things", such as her chronic lateness and her failure to pay bills on time.[96] When he was morally outraged, he could be imperious and unforgiving. After an apparently heated discussion with Elsie and a guest about the children's upbringing, he

---

91 APS, ECP to HP, July 24, 1906 and October 21, 1907.
92 APS, ECP to HP, June 19, 1904.
93 RHS, HP to ECP, October 5, 1902.
94 RHS, HP to ECP, May 26, 1902.
95 RHS, HP Diary of 1902 trip.
96 Little things: APS, HP to ECP, May 21, 1905. Bills: RHS, HP to ECP, June 20 1902 and June 16, 1902. Lateness: RHS, HP to ECP, June 4, 1905.

refused to apologize to the guest because he felt he had to exercise his "sacred" "rights and duties" and protect his home. He angrily explained to Elsie,

> On the general proposition of what should go on in our own house I feel very strongly. I think we owe it to the children to have everything as happy, upright, clean, elevating & free from temptation as possible [...]. Much of their affection for & help from home will depend upon its having appeared moral in every way [...]. How you can hold your views I do not see for they are not the views of any educators and are condemned by the experience of ages.[97]

Elsie and Herbert's efforts to construct a companionate relationship around leisure activities caused some friction at this early stage, but would become more contentious in future years. For Herbert, a quiet domestic life spent with Elsie and the children was the most appealing aspect of marriage. "Perhaps I too much like possessions, but I did delight Friday in having you & the babe return home," he wrote Elsie. "Travel, & scenery & country & relatives are all very well but fail utterly when set over against our own house which is our home."[98] He regretted the frequent absences required by his legal work.[99] When he failed to be nominated as a Congressional candidate in 1902, he consoled himself by noting that a campaign would have required him to spend too much time away from his family.[100]

Elsie enjoyed their family life, but she also craved opportunities to escape from domestic routines and share more challenging activities and environments with Herbert. She delighted in the "invigorating life" they led for ten days of deer hunting in deep snow in the Adirondacks the first year they were married.[101] When they went to Europe in the summer of 1902 for almost two months, Herbert regretted leaving eleven-month old Lissa behind in the care of servants and Elsie's mother. He vowed that Lissa would come with them on future trips but Elsie, backed by Mary Simkhovitch, was adamant about getting away by themselves.[102]

---

97   RHS, HP to ECP, June 30, 1904.
98   RHS, HP to ECP, October 5, 1902.
99   RHS, HP to ECP, May 24, 1903.
100 RHS, HP to ECP, October 5, 1902.
101 RHS, ECP Diary, 1900.
102 RHS, HP Diary, 1902 trip. "I'm glad you are abandoning Lissa. Never too early to begin!" Mary encouraged Elsie (RHS, Mary Kingsbury Simkhovitch to ECP, June 27

Three years later, when Elsie and Herbert went on a Congressional trip to the Far East, Herbert contemplated not going when he found out that Lissa and John would spend several days solely in the care of servants before Elsie's mother returned from Europe.[103] But Elsie prevailed and they went.

Elsie's work was part-time and generally done during the hours Herbert was working. But the long hours he devoted to his law practice and his political work took a toll on Elsie. She was not happy when his electoral campaigns or his volunteer work with the Brick Presbyterian Church in Manhattan kept him from joining his family on weekends. She candidly admitted in 1903 that she would "not feel disappointed at all" if he lost a campaign because the job entailed "too much of a personal sacrifice."[104] A year later, she expressed even more forcefully the resentment she felt when his work precluded his spending weekends with her and the children. "I think the cost of a political career would be too great, altho' not in the way you think. In my eyes and *for me* there is no compensation or justification for the kind of wear you seem to have planned for yourself this month. I consider it a wrong. Incidentally, a wrong done to me. But that I know I cannot make you understand."[105]

Nevertheless, a month later Elsie was encouraging Herbert to run for Congress and agreeing that he should give up his legal practice and devote himself full time to politics.[106] At Herbert's urging, she wrote to his father, explaining that the loss of income would be of no consequence because they already gave away so much of their money and had enough assured income to cover their expenses. Moreover, because she held "certain views" it would be "extremely distasteful" to her to increase their scale of living in the future. Noting how important it was to Herbert to have his father's blessing, Elsie encouraged him to support Herbert's desire to give up the law. John E. Parsons did so,

---

[1902]). Elsie's baby nurse, in contrast, did not approve. As Lissa's amanuensis, she wrote a heartbreaking letter describing the pain the baby felt in being separated from her parents and her fear that they had gotten another daughter to replace her (RHS, Lissa Clews to ECP and HP, August 10, 1902).

103 RHS, HP to ECP, June 12, 1905.
104 APS, ECP to HP, September 14, 1903.
105 APS, ECP to HP, August 15, 1904; emphasis in the original. Similarly, ECP to HP, August 29, 1904.
106 APS, ECP to HP, September 22, 1904.

although not enthusiastically, and not without advising Herbert that a man did not need to consult with his wife before making such a career decision.[107]

Herbert gave up his law practice and ran for Congress. His victory in November 1904 opened a new era in their lives.

The Washington Years, 1905–1911

When Elsie and Herbert went to Washington, they were united and happy, full of promise and potential. When they left six years later, they were divided, depressed, defeated, and disillusioned.

Herbert's congressional term started in March 1905. Elsie finished her academic year at Barnard, and joined him on a two-month Congressional tour to the Far East before moving the family to Washington. Elsie seemed to take the move in stride and saw it as an opportunity to expand her work beyond sociology and settlement houses.[108] During her time in Washington, she studied the city's social rituals as an exercise in ethnography, read widely in ethnographic literature, and gathered ethnographic evidence about social mores and social taboos. Accompanying Herbert on official trips to Asia and the American West provided opportunities for her to learn firsthand about other societies and cultures.

As their world expanded, Elsie's vision grew. Herbert's stayed the same, but by comparison, seemed to shrink. As a public figure, he wanted and needed to play it safe. Increasingly, she shocked, embarrassed, and bewildered him. Increasingly, he disappointed her. The first hint of this came in the summer of 1905. Elsie described how he thwarted her ethnographic investigations as they traveled, first on their own to San Francisco, and then with the Congressional entourage in the Philippines, Japan, China, and Hong Kong:[109]

---

107 RHS, ECP to John Edward Parsons, September 23, 1904; John Edward Parsons to HP, October 3, 1904.

108 RHS, ECP, "My Washington Journal," March 1, 1905.

109 The official party included Secretary of War William Howard Taft, who was a former US governor of the Philippines; Alice Roosevelt; seven senators and twenty-four representatives and their wives. Herbert was valued for his knowledge of sugar production and tariff policy. (RHS, HP's account of the trip.)

He squirmed under the cross questioning I sent our driver in Salt Lake City through for information about the fast vanishing architectural traces of Mormon polygamy [....]. He refused to go at all to the Sunday cockfighting at Manila, and his disquiet and distress was so formidable when I started to Kodak a crucified criminal on the little rubbish strewn *cul de sac* of the public execution place at Canton that I had to forego getting what would have been the most interesting ethnographic document of our trade.[110]

After their return, Elsie published several hard-hitting articles about her experiences in the Far East and criticized the "race prejudice" that infused American actions in the Philippines.[111] Turning her attention to US society, she touted the benefits of employment outside the home for middle-class wives and promoted reforms that would support married women's work: flexible work schedules to accommodate child-bearing, convenient opportunities for nursing, lifting the social taboos that confined pregnant and nursing women to the home, and more sex education.[112] Both Herbert and her editor suggested she tone her work down.[113]

Elsie's reaction to Stanford White's shocking murder in June 1906 was potentially more provocative. White was shot dead by the jealous husband of a former chorus girl with whom he had had an affair and had allegedly raped. The sensationalist press coverage soon reported lurid accounts of White's involvements with underage chorus girls. But Elsie mourned her old friend and was quick to come to his defense. "Stanford was one of the noblest, most chivalrous & magnanimous men I have ever known, and I would like to say so on the witness stand [....] I could testify that I was never drugged in the tower room!" she asserted. Nothing came of her interest in testifying. But her past relationship with White and eagerness to speak on his behalf might have troubled the

---

110 RHS, ECP, "My Washington Journal", 1905.
111 Elsie Clews Parsons, "American Snobbishness in the Philippines", *Independent* 60 (8 February 1906), 332–33. Elsie Clews Parsons, "Remarks on Education in the Philippines", *Charities and the Commons* 16 (1 September 1906), 564–65.
112 Elsie Clews Parsons, "Penalizing Marriage and Childbearing", *Independent* 60 (18 January 1906), 146–47.
113 RHS, HP to ECP, October 2, 1905 and October 18, 1905. Hamilton Holt to ECP, June 13, 1906. Elsie sent a draft of "Penalizing Marriage and Childbearing" to Herbert, marking the direct references to birth control usage that the editor cut. See Deacon, p. 414, FN44.

more straight-laced Herbert, who had a public reputation to maintain as a member of Congress.[114]

The Storm over *The Family*

The publication of Elsie's first book in November 1906 — just a few weeks after Herbert was elected to a second Congressional term — certainly caused trouble for Herbert. Based on the lectures Elsie had given at Barnard College, *The Family: An Ethnographical and Historical Outline with Descriptive Notes, Planned as a Text-book for the Use of College Lecturers and of Directors of Home-reading Clubs* (New York: Putnam's, 1906) analyzed the evolution of the family as a social organization. Most of the 389-page book was a very dry, scientifically-grounded, footnote-laden compilation of information detailing the ways different cultures dealt with marriage, prostitution, rape, divorce, and related issues.

But in the final fifteen pages of the book, Elsie discussed "what ought to be" and advocated for "trial marriages" to give young couples an opportunity to live together before they contracted a legal relationship. Recognizing that most individuals reach sexual maturity before they acquire emotional maturity, confident that later marriages have a greater chance of happiness, and believing it was unrealistic to expect absolute chastity before marriage, Elsie supported "freedom of sexual intercourse for both sexes." Trial marriages should be embarked on with the expectation that they would be permanent, but unhappy couples who had no children could end them by mutual agreement, without social condemnation, she argued. *The Family* endorsed monogamy and denounced promiscuity and prostitution, but also supported liberalized divorce laws, remarriage for divorcees, equality

---

114 APS, ECP to Lewis Chanler, June 30, 1906, enclosed in ECP to HP, July 2, 1906. See also, APS, ECP to HP and HP to ECP, June 26, 1906; HP to ECP, July 2, 1906, and July 24, 1906; ECP to HP, July 26, 1906. For White's murder, the revelations about his sexual practices, and the trial of his alleged murderer, see Simon Baatz, *The Girl on the Velvet Swing: Sex, Murder, and Madness at the Dawn of the 20th Century* (New York: Mulholland Books, 2018), and Mary Cummings, *Saving Sin City: William Travers Jerome, Stanford White and the Original Crime of the Century* (New York: Pegasus Books, 2018).

within marriage, and more sex education and sexual freedom for women. Elsie dedicated the book to her daughter and son.

The Family set off a firestorm of outraged horror. Elsie's endorsement of "trial marriage" was denounced in pulpits and the press, often by people who admitted they had not read the book. Protestant ministers in New York preached Thanksgiving Day sermons condemning trial marriage as a "disgusting theory" and a "danger to married life." The book was "a menace to morality and the stability of society," the clergy fulminated.[115] The press coverage was vitriolic and inflammatory, and Elsie's identity as the wife of Congressman Herbert Parsons was always highlighted. Critics were offended that a woman with Elsie's education and social position could promote indecency and offer such "absurd, preposterous, diabolical" advice.[116] An anonymous (male) reviewer was offended by her cold, unfeeling, "rigidly scientific" tone.[117] One journalist advised Herbert to exercise more authority over Elsie, asserting, "If my wife were to advocate such principles as does Congressman Parsons' wife, she would have to choose another place to live pretty quickly."[118] Elsie did find a champion for her views in the Socialist press, but that may not have helped her cause.[119]

The media frenzy continued for weeks. A cartoon about Trial Marriage was blazoned on the cover of *Life Magazine* in December 1906.[120] Biograph released a twelve-minute long silent film entitled *Trial Marriage* depicting the unhappy life of a man who was inspired by a newspaper report on the book to embark on a series of "trial marriages."[121] A man on trial for seducing a fifteen-year-old girl defended his refusal to marry her by saying he believed in "Mrs.

---

115 *New York Daily Tribune*, November 30, 1906; *The New York Times*, November 30, 1906; *Evening Sun*, November 18, 1906, quoted in Hare, p. 11 and Zumwalt, p. 48. Clergy in Chicago also mounted a campaign against it. See William Kuby, *Conjugal Misconduct, Defying Marriage Law in the Twentieth-Century United States* (New York: Cambridge University Press, 2018), p. 151.

116 *Evening Sun*, November 18, 1906; *New York Herald*, November 18 and November 19, 1906. Quoted in Hare, pp. 11–12.

117 Quoted in Kuby, p. 152.

118 *World*, November 19, 1906. Quoted in Hare, p. 11.

119 *Daily People*, November 18, 1906.

120 Kuby, p. 155.

121 The film is intended to elicit sympathy for the unfortunate man who is reduced to tending babies, cooking meals, and doing housework by a succession of trial "wives." Popegrutch, *Century Film Project*: "Trial Marriage (1907)", https://

Parsons' theories." The judge lambasted the book and said it did not excuse the man's behavior.[122]

The scurrilous response to Elsie's book was a major political embarrassment for Herbert. Standing on the steps of their Washington home, he turned away a horde of reporters with a smile and the comment, "Mrs. Parsons has nothing to say, and will have nothing to say. Neither has Mr. Parsons."[123] We can only imagine what he said to Elsie in private.

Elsie enjoyed the attention her book attracted, but she was genuinely troubled about the potential damage to Herbert's political career. She wrote apologetically from New York, "I am afraid you have been having very disagreeable experiences on my account. The only thing that really pains me in the situation is the idea that I have interfered with your work, and that grieves me more than I can say."[124] As the chair of the New York County Republican Committee, Herbert had worked with President Theodore Roosevelt on electoral campaigns and won his trust and liking. Anxious to protect that relationship, Elsie sent a copy of her "unhappily notorious book" to Roosevelt, so he would know what the book was really like. "The public reception of the book has shown me that a writing wife is a distinct handicap to a politician and so henceforward in our family authorship is going to yield to statesmanship after as well as before elections," she assured Roosevelt, alluding to her decision to publish anonymously while Herbert remained in public office.[125]

It is not clear whether Elsie volunteered to stop publishing under her own name or whether Herbert asked — or told — her to stop. Publishing anonymously or pseudonymously was an obvious handicap for an emerging scholar and essayist, but Elsie never expressed regret or resentment about the decision.[126] There is a gaping hole in her

centuryfilmproject.org/2017/12/13/trial-marriages-1907. Elsie's picture and married name can be clearly seen in the shot of the newspaper in the film.

122 *World*, November 22, 1906. Quoted in Hare, p. 12.

123 *New York Herald*, November 19, 1906. Quoted in Hare, p. 13. Herbert was notorious for having nothing to say to the press. See "President Not to Interfere in States," *The New York Times*, July 29, 1908, p. 3.

124 APS, ECP to HP, November 21, 1906; ECP to HP, November 23, 1906.

125 RHS, ECP to President Theodore Roosevelt, December 22, 1906.

126 Elsie's mentor, Franklin Giddings, urged her not to make the "sacrifice" of ceasing to publish under her own name (APS, Franklin Giddings to ECP, December 10, 1906).

bibliography during the remainder of her time in Washington, but she read widely, observed carefully, and ruminated about the origins of social mores and the ways societies constrain their members. After Herbert left Congress, she published several books and many articles that drew on this material.

In the meantime, Elsie was more careful about publicly expressing her views but did not censor herself entirely. Enjoying a tête-à-tête with President Theodore Roosevelt at a White House dinner in March 1908, she engaged him in a one-hour conversation about prostitution, birth control, abortion, and divorce — a discussion many people would think "most immoral," Roosevelt noted.[127] Attending a meeting of the American Sociology Association in December 1908, Elsie proudly informed Herbert that her remarks on women's employment were well-received but did not get into any newspapers because she had "found a way to outwit the reporter."[128] This was fortunate, since the press might have had a lot to say about her assertion that economic dependence on her husband made a wife "approximate to the harem type."[129]

Elsie and Herbert weathered the public storm caused by *The Family*, but the contretemps took a heavy toll on their personal relationship. *The Family* exposed a side of Elsie that Herbert preferred to ignore. A deeply religious man, he did not read it because he feared he would find it offensive.[130] At the time Elsie did not complain, but years later, she would tell Herbert how hurt she was by his refusal to read and discuss the books she wrote.

Hamilton Holt, the *Independent* editor who had eagerly sought Elsie's articles, had no interest in publishing them without her byline. Her views were most valuable because of her "position" in society, he explained (APS, Hamilton Holt to ECP, November 22, 1906 and November 28, 1906).

127 RHS, ECP, "My Washington Journal", March 3 [1908].

128 APS, ECP to HP, December 29, 1908.

129 Elsie Clews Parsons, "Higher Education of Women and the Family", *American Journal of Sociology* 14 (May 1909), 758–63. This is the only work published under Elsie's name during the remainder of Herbert's Congressional career. Her second book, written while he was still in office, was published under a pseudonym in 1913: [John Main, pseud.], *Religious Chastity: An Ethnological Study* (New York: [n.p.], 1913).

130 APS, HP to ECP, August 7, 1912.

Political Wife

Personal tragedy added to Elsie and Herbert's troubles in Washington, when they lost two newborn sons in less than a year. The first boy died just two weeks after his birth, in April 1906; the second, born in February 1907, lived for less than two hours. In April 1907, Elsie was — unexpectedly — pregnant again. The pregnancy ended two months later, apparently terminated on the advice of her physician, who advised that a third pregnancy so soon after the previous two would be dangerous to her and the baby's health.[131]

Elsie was deeply depressed by the deaths of the two newborn boys. "[I]it seems to me that I shall never quite regain my old *joie de vivre* until I have, *we* have, a baby," she wrote Herbert four months after the death of the first child.[132] She noted how hard it was to be "brave," but drew comfort from Herbert's loving support.[133] Having serious work to accomplish was also restorative in her view. Had she not been able to apply herself to scientific work on a daily basis, it would have taken her longer to get over the first baby's death, she maintained in notes she prepared for a talk to the American Sociology Association in December 1908. Her remedy contradicted standard medical procedures of the day that recommended rest cures and inactivity for women who were ill or depressed.[134]

Throughout their Washington years, Elsie and Herbert were leading a more conventional married life than they did before or after. Without a teaching job, unable to publish under her own name, and often pregnant, Elsie had few professional outlets, while Herbert had a very

131 Elsie's doctor advised her how to bring on her menstrual flow, gave her pills, and recommended a curettage if necessary. It was scheduled for early May. In June, she was menstruating again. APS, ECP to HP, April 24, 1907 and June 25, 1907. APS, Dr. George Swift to ECP, April 26, 1907 and May 2, 1907.
132 APS, ECP to HP, August 20, 1906; emphasis in the original.
133 Brave: APS, ECP to HP, October 29, 1906. Comfort: APS, ECP to HP, September 1, 1909. When the second baby was born, Elsie was in New York and Herbert was in Washington. He talked to Elsie for forty minutes by phone, then took a train to New York. He returned to Washington by the noon train the following day (RHS, HP 1907 Diary, February 12 and 13, 1907).
134 APS, ECP's notes for her address, "Higher Education of Women and the Family", given to the American Sociology Society in December 1908. Both Elsie's doctor and Herbert recommended rest and relaxation rather than strenuous exercise and scholarly work when she went to the Adirondacks in the fall of 1908.

demanding job and worked very long hours. Such conditions were a recipe for marital disaster, she would later write.[135]

As a feminist, Elsie objected to women being relegated to exercising "wifely backstair influence" and playing a helpmate role.[136] "The sooner people get rid of the helpful wife theory, the sooner we shall have woman suffrage," she complained to Herbert in 1906.[137] Nevertheless, she was unhappy when she learned more about his political campaign from his co-workers than from him, and was hurt when he did not want her in the audience when he give a speech.[138] Whenever he did discuss his political work with her, Elsie's comfort and support was a solace to him.[139]

At a time when working very long hours was seen as a measure of masculinity, Herbert's fellow workers admired him for working sixteen and seventeen hours a day when he was chairman of the New York County Republican Party.[140] Nevertheless, the grueling political campaigns took a physical and emotional toll.[141] Herbert acknowledged that his business, social, charitable, and family interests all suffered during the long months he spent organizing Republican campaigns.[142] The final weeks of the 1907 campaign were so hectic that he advised Elsie not to join him in Manhattan because he would be too busy to see her. She came anyway, but on other occasions, she kept away when

---

135 Elsie Clews Parsons, *The Old Fashioned Woman: Primitive Fancies about the Sex* (New York: Putnam's, 1913), pp. 48–49.
136 APS, ECP to HP, January 8, 1907.
137 APS, ECP to HP, October 3, 1906.
138 Co-workers: APS, ECP to HP, October 29, 1906; speech: ECP to HP, October 25, 1906.
139 APS, ECP to HP, September 20, 1906; similarly, ECP to HP, October 13, 1907. APS, HP to ECP, October 9, 1907.
140 Masculinity: E. Anthony Rotundo, *American Manhood, Transformations in Masculinity from the Revolution to the Modern Era* (New York: Basic Books, 1993), pp. 176–77, 267. Work hours: RHS, William S. Bennett speech in *Dinner to Herbert Parsons, April 21, 1911 by his Constituents*.
141 A colleague recalled how an exhausted Herbert fell asleep while signing letters at his desk. Another noted that, after collapsing in a restaurant and being told by his doctor to give up the campaign, Herbert was back at his desk a day and a half later. RHS, speeches by Lloyd C. Griscom and Henry L. Stimson in *Dinner to Herbert Parsons, April 21, 1911 by his Constituents*; Henry L. Stimson, "Memorandum of Conversation with Henry D. Sayer, January 21, 1926," quoted in William Parsons, Jr., "Progressive Politics", p. 83.
142 HP to Charles H. Pankhurst, December 16, 1907, quoted in William Parsons, Jr., "Progressive Politics", p. 83.

he felt highly pressured.[143] In a touching demonstration of her love, she offered to adjust "my own time, the thing I most value" so he could enjoy more leisure time.[144]

By cleaning up the voter rolls and eliminating tens of thousands of fraudulent votes, Herbert's Republican organization scored major victories for the reform Republicans in the New York City municipal elections in 1906 and 1907. Herbert was hailed as the "master" of the Republican Party in New York County. But his inability to get the county Republicans to back William Howard Taft's presidential candidacy in early 1908 was a blow. In August 1908, Herbert was considering not running for reelection, fearing that Progressives were fighting a losing battle and he would eventually be "thrown out" anyway. Praising his work, Elsie encouraged him not to leave Congress. "As for me, there would be both advantages and disadvantages in your withdrawing from politics. Our social life would be so much duller that I should want to get some amusement out of writing and I should be free to do so. On the whole, I should be disappointed if you declined renomination to Congress," she concluded.[145] Despite the constraints his Congressional position placed on her, and the amount of time he devoted to his electoral work, Elsie was largely content with the life they were living in Washington. She willingly made the sacrifices required of her, and found compensating gains in new projects.

Nevertheless, in the fall of 1908, Elsie, now thirty-four, was feeling unhappily "middle-aged" and starting to exhibit a new restlessness.[146] She went off on a six-week vacation of swimming, canoeing, and horseback riding in the Adirondacks when Herbert was too busy to accompany her. While she was away, she enjoyed a week-long flirtation with a twenty-three-year old medical student, Reginald Fitz.[147] Basking

143 APS, ECP to HP, October 23, 1907; August 19, 1904; October 16, 1906; March 26, 1908; March 30, 1908.

144 APS, ECP to HP, July 11, 1906.

145 APS, ECP to HP, August 10, 1908.

146 APS, ECP to HP, April 24, 1907; APS, Lucy Clews to ECP, November 4 [1908].

147 Elsie corresponded with Fitz for a few months and tried to interest him in making another trip to the Adirondacks. But his conventional "Boston spirit" prohibited him from venturing "too far from civilization" alone with her (APS, Reginald Fitz to ECP [1908?]). He graduated from Harvard Medical School in 1909, and Elsie renewed her friendship with him in Boston during the summer of 1911 (APS, ECP to HP, June 16, 1911).

in the tonic effect of the young man's admiration, she teasingly informed Herbert, "you can be jealous, a little."[148] In her mind, it was all harmless fun. As she had told Herbert several years earlier, she was monogamous by nature. "I seem to have a monogamous instinct just as I have brown hair; & I don't pride myself on having either," she assured him.[149]

The Imaginary Mistress

Elsie returned from the Adirondacks refreshed if not rejuvenated. Herbert was reelected in November 1908. At the beginning of 1909 she was pregnant again, and still acting like a very conventional wife. She attended Congressional debates and hearings on the bills Herbert sponsored, and hosted teas and dinners for him.[150] They dined and danced at the White House and the British Embassy, and developed a friendship with the Huntington Wilsons.

Herbert had become friendly with Wilson, an Assistant Secretary of State, and his wife, Lucy, during the summer of 1908, when Elsie and the children were in Newport. He enjoyed dining and walking with them, and mentioned them frequently in letters to Elsie. During the winter and spring of 1909, the two couples took canoe rides, walks, and sightseeing trips together, and saw each other often at dinners and parties.[151]

Elsie had assured Herbert that her flirtation with Reginald Fitz was harmless, but she did not feel that way about Herbert's friendship with Lucy Wilson. The Wilsons had no children and their marriage appeared to be strained. Herbert remarked on their frequent "spats."[152] Jealousy had long been an issue for Elsie. As early as 1898, when Herbert had paid a midnight call to her friend Alice Duer (later Miller), Elsie was surprised — and dismayed — to discover that she had a "jealous disposition."[153] Now it came out in full.

---

148 APS, ECP to HP, October 2, 1908.
149 APS, ECP to HP, July 26, 1906.
150 RHS, ECP, "My Washington Diary", January, February, and March 1909.
151 RHS, ECP, "Washington Diary." APS, Lucy James [Wilson] to HP, March 28, 1918. F. M. Huntington Wilson, *Memoirs of an Ex-diplomat* (Boston: Humphries, 1945), https://babel.hathitrust.org/cgi/pt?id=uc1.$b541385&view=1up&seq=1&skin=2021.
152 APS, HP to ECP, July 19, 1909.
153 APS, EC to HP, June 30, 1898.

By mid-June 1909, after watching Herbert's behavior very closely, Elsie was convinced that he had fallen in love with Lucy.[154] Herbert assured Elsie she had no reason to be jealous, but continued to sing Lucy's praises. Unable to shake what she called her "obsession" with Lucy, Elsie, who was about five months pregnant, suffered intensely. She was angry when Herbert made light of her fears. She was angry when he took them seriously. When she was not angry, she was depressed.[155] Herbert added to Elsie's distress by often being irritable or preoccupied when they were together.[156]

Elsie agonized over her behavior as well as Herbert's. In theory, she believed that "interest in the other sex at large shakes you up out of any settled, sodden conjugality and was therefore desirable."[157] But, in practice, Herbert's desire to spend time with Lucy Wilson left Elsie feeling aggrieved, angry, and hurt. Consumed by jealousy and suspicion, she could not keep her emotions in check. She was appalled to find herself making scenes, spying on Herbert, and bursting into tears. Without a professional outlet, Elsie had little to distract her. "The trouble with me is the lack of a time-compelling job. I always knew that my character couldn't stand against idleness. Lately I have taken to copying mss. in which there is no mental effort, but which keeps me occupied, and I am much better off," she informed Herbert.[158]

Herbert, Jr. — a healthy baby — was born in October 1909, but the Parsonses' marital difficulties persisted. Just seeing Lucy's name in a letter pushed Elsie into unpleasant musings that reduced her "to a wretched state." In February, 1910, in a letter with many blotches and cross outs, she instructed Herbert not to tell her when he had been with the Wilsons and not ever to mention Lucy's name in his letters.[159] Accusing him of being "a poor psychologist", she warned him that it was impossible "to joke obsessions away." But when he was silent about Lucy, Elsie read between the lines and found other evidence of

---

154 APS, ECP to HP, June 18, 1909; HP to ECP, July 24, 1909; ECP to HP, August 23, 1909.
155 APS, ECP to HP, August 23, 1909.
156 Her distress: APS, ECP to HP, July 19, 1909. His irritability: APS, HP to ECP, July 18, 1909; ECP to HP, July 19, 1909; HP to ECP, August 9, 1909; HP to ECP, August 1, 1909.
157 APS, ECP to HP, July 27, 1909.
158 APS, ECP to HP, August 4, 1909.
159 APS, ECP to HP, February [n.d.], 1910.

his infatuation. "You haven't the art to keep her out of your letters even when you don't mention her," she railed.[160]

Lucy would remain a thorn in Elsie's side for many years. The wound mostly festered out of sight, but from time to time, Elsie's unhappiness would flare into open conflict with Herbert. Years later, she wrote several fictionalized accounts of the Lucy Wilson episode that more fully reveal the toll it took on her marriage. Her unpublished short story, "The Imaginary Mistress", begun in 1913 and rewritten in 1915, draws heavily from the Parsonses' letters as it charts the disintegration of a marriage that mirrors her own. Lois, Elsie's fictional counterpart, believes that her husband, Anson, has fallen in love with another woman, although he refuses to acknowledge it. Like Elsie, Lois suffers from a jealous obsession with the other woman, who is named Alice.[161]

The title, "The Imaginary Mistress", is particularly suggestive. For Elsie, the term alludes to the husband's unwillingness to act on his desire and make the woman he loves his mistress. But for the reader, there is another possibility: that Anson/Herbert is not in love with Alice/Lucy and his supposed feelings are a construct of Lois/Elsie's imagination. Lois considers this explanation, but dismisses it. Like Elsie, she is convinced that her husband is in love with another woman but too timid to consummate the relationship. For this, he earns Lois's pity and contempt. Similarly, Elsie's 5-page play, "In New York State", written during 1914 and 1915, depicts a dramatic confrontation between a jealous wife and a husband who remains faithful to her despite being in love with another woman.[162]

It is impossible to know whether Herbert had an affair with Lucy or if he was in love with her. There is no extant correspondence between them in 1909–1910, and no documentation — other than Elsie's and Herbert's letters, and Elsie's fiction — about the relationship. Certainly, there must have been a strong emotional tie between Herbert and Lucy. Years later, Lucy would tell Herbert that the time she spent in Washington from the summer of 1909 through the spring of 1910 was the "happiest" period

---

160 APS, ECP to HP, Saturday AM [n.y.].
161 APS, ECP, "The Imaginary Mistress", pp. 7, 10, 11, 14, 15.
162 APS, ECP, "In New York State."

of her life between 1904 and 1915.[163] For Herbert to have seen so much of Lucy, over so many years, despite the difficulties it created in his marriage and the pain it caused Elsie, suggests that her company was exceedingly important to him. But his personality and upbringing make it highly unlikely that, even if he had a strong attraction to Lucy, he and she had a physical relationship. Elsie herself was convinced that they did not.

Herbert was an extremely religious, highly principled, deeply moral man. He was brought up as a strict Presbyterian, a tradition that frowned on pleasure, encouraged sexual repression, and promoted adherence to virtue and duty. As an undergraduate at Yale, he contemplated becoming a minister; throughout his life he was a regular churchgoer and involved in church administration and leadership. In both public and private life, he was driven by a keen sense of duty. He could be priggish, even prudish; he was sometimes moralistic and moralizing. He took the staff of Greenwich House to task for holding a fundraising entertainment on a Sunday evening in violation of his religious principles; he was horrified when Elsie let the children see her nude; he thought it was harmful for young men to know about brothels; he was offended when Huntington Wilson swore in front of Lucy. He was so uncomfortable with Elsie's views on sex, marriage, and pre-marital cohabitation that he did not want to read *The Family*.

Unlike Elsie, Herbert believed in the institution of marriage. According to her, he thought that unhappily married people should simply learn "to make the best of it." He was not introspective or inclined to analyze his feelings. As a politician, he was notorious for being unreadable and unfathomable. These views, beliefs, and habits were likely not only to have kept Herbert from acting on his feelings, but also to have protected him from the self-knowledge that he was in love with a woman who was not his wife. Elsie also suggested that the appeal of romantic yearning and virtuous self-sacrifice would have been powerful motivators for Herbert. He was a man of integrity, not a hypocrite.

What mattered was that Elsie believed Herbert was in love with Lucy, not whether her suspicions were justified. When her obsession began in the summer of 1909, Elsie was very much in love with Herbert,

---

163 APS, Lucy James [Wilson] to HP, March 28, 1918. The Wilsons married in 1904 and divorced in 1915.

and her happiness was very much entwined with his. "What I had most cared for I had lost," Lois mourns in Elsie's short story. "The old sense of oneness with him that I had ridiculed as a conjugal tradition but which had been a profound and joyful reality for me had disappeared," she laments. Decades later, discussing her daughter's unhappy marriage, Elsie paid tribute to the happiness of her early relationship with Herbert by remarking, "[anyone] who did not have the experience of eight or ten years of fairly comfortable living with another person was missing one of the big things in life."[164]

It was particularly galling for Elsie to think that Herbert had fallen for a woman of Lucy's "type." In "The Imaginary Mistress", Lois/Elsie describes Alice/Lucy as "a quiet, self-effacing person, but charmingly dressed, pretty, and possessed of a delightful voice." She maintained a "beautiful house," and was "in every way a woman of taste." The woman who captivates the husband in Elsie's short play "In New York State" is scornfully characterized by the wife as being the type of woman who would "like being the head of your house — even if she weren't in love with you" — that is, a woman who enjoyed playing hostess and maintaining a gracious and decorative home.[165] In Elsie's eyes, Lucy epitomized the womanly ideals she herself had rejected: helplessness, domesticity, unthinking adherence to social conventions, selfless devotion to a man. Similarly, Herbert's fictional alter egos — chivalrous males who serve and protect their lady love — fit the romantic ideal that Elsie had always scorned.

In fact, Lucy, the heir to the Dun (of Dun and Bradstreet) fortune, was not quite the domestic nonentity that Elsie suggested. Although Lucy was renowned as a gracious hostess, she was also an accomplished pianist. Planning to have a career as a concert pianist, she had gone to Vienna to study with the man who taught Paderewski. Ill health had forced her to give it up. Lucy was also exceedingly beautiful. Portraits by John Singer Sargent and others depict her as softly feminine, almost ethereal. (Photographs of Elsie, in contrast, show her to be much firmer of jaw, resolute, strong, and determined.) Lucy was well-traveled and familiar with the non-European world. She and her husband had lived

---

164 ECP, "Imaginary Mistress", pp. 10 and 18. APS, Ralph Beals to Peter H. Hare, July
      31, 1978.
165 APS, ECP, "In New York State."

in Japan when he was an attaché at the American Embassy, and they had traveled in the Balkans and Turkey as well as the Far East. Far from being shy and retiring, Lucy boldly (and successfully) lobbied Secretary of State Elihu Root to procure a promotion for Huntington.[166]

While Elise wrestled with jealousy, Herbert was beset by another problem that caused him to weep aloud and lose sleep, and undoubtedly contributed to his preoccupation and irritability. His father, the legal counsel and a director of the American Sugar Refining Company, popularly known as the Sugar Trust, was under a federal investigation for allegedly illegal business practices undertaken by the Trust. Knowing that John E. Parsons, one of New York City's most prominent lawyers, was likely to be indicted, and fearing that an indictment "would kill" the eighty-year-old man, Herbert offered to help him and was prepared to resign from political office. But Parsons did not want his son to be involved.[167] On July 1, 1909, Parsons and six other directors of the Trust were indicted for conspiracy in restraint of trade. If convicted, they faced possible jail terms. All the defendants pleaded not guilty and were released without bail. A series of legal appeals delayed their trial until March 1912. After it ended in a mistrial, due to a hung jury, the government delayed for another six months before dropping all the indictments.[168]

Although Herbert repeatedly asserted that he himself had never done any work for the Trust or profited from it, he was potentially tainted by his father's problems.[169] An editorial in the *New York Sun* in November 1909 claimed that Herbert was in the pay of the Sugar Trust and had used his position as Chair of the Republican Committee of New York County to aid the Trust and protect the indicted men.[170]

---

166 New York Community Trust, "Lucy Wortham James" [n.d.], https://nycommunitytrust.org/wp-content/uploads/2018/03/Lucy-Wortham-James.pdf. See also, Huntington Wilson, *Memoirs*. Elsie and Herbert would have met the Wilsons in 1905, when the Taft Congressional tour was entertained at the American Embassy in Japan.

167 APS, HP to ECP, June 24, 1909. Herbert's father was the legal mastermind behind the establishment of the trust.

168 A separate civil case with a different set of defendants ended in a settlement in March, 1909. The Trust paid millions of dollars in fines and back payments for customs fraud.

169 RHS, HP to Hon. Charles A. Culberson, February 11, 1909; HP to Phillip P. Campbell, December 7, 1909 and December 16, 1909.

170 "The Cancer of a Republican Administration", *The Sun*, November 7, 1909.

Republican candidates won important victories in New York City municipal elections in the fall of 1909, but the election of Tammany Hall's mayoral candidate was a setback for Herbert and the reform politicians.

Late in January, 1910 Herbert abruptly resigned as Chair of the Republican Committee. His years of public service were praised at a dinner given in his honor, but questions about his relationship to the Trust persisted. In April, he and his father were sharply attacked in a debate in the House of Representatives. Herbert stood loyally by his father, and was given a standing ovation by the chamber.[171] Elsie provided little support for Herbert during this difficult time. Years later, she regretted that she had, in her words, "failed" Herbert by not being more sympathetic when he had been so troubled about his father's case.[172]

In the midst of these personal and professional problems, Elsie and Herbert traveled to the American southwest in the summer of 1910. While Herbert conducted the official part of his trip as a member of the House Committee on Public Lands, Elsie spent a week camping and traveling on horseback with a guide in what was called "Indian country", an experience that whetted her appetite to study the Native American cultures of the southwest.

Traveling separately, both Elsie and Herbert were moved by the rugged beauty of the landscape. But when they traveled together in the Grand Canyon and Yosemite, in the company of a guide, the differences in their perspectives and temperaments became painfully obvious. On their second day on the trail, Elsie lost her wedding ring when she slipped it off before swimming, left it in a towel, and shook out the towel after her swim. Despite hours of searching, Elsie and Herbert could not

---

171 Paul deForest Hicks, *John E. Parsons, An Eminent New Yorker in the Gilded Age* (Westport and New York: Prospecta Press); *The New York Times*, December 17, 1909, p. 6; *The Independent* 17 (July-Dec.1909), p. 57; RHS, *Report of Addresses at a Dinner Tendered to the Honorable Herbert Parsons, Hotel Astor, March 22, 1910*; William Parsons, Jr., "Progressive." "Scores Sugar Trust", *Washington Herald*, April 15, 1910, p. 2. *US Congressional Record*, April 14, 1910, 4695–706. Rep. Rainey (D-Illinois) claimed that "the sugar trust by a system of false weights has stolen millions from the US treasury and its officials still go about in private yachts, posing as respectable citizens."

172 APS, ECP to HP, June 16, 1913.

find the ring.[173] No conscious act of Elsie's could have sent a clearer message about her growing ambivalence about her marriage.[174]

Over the next week, she upset Herbert by being headstrong and reckless on the trail.[175] She went "dashing ahead" on a very perilous road, took a wrong turn, got seriously lost, and later slept along the bank of a rushing river. Herbert, as usual, played it safe. He maintained a steady pace on the trails, carefully followed the guide, retreated to safer ground for sleeping, and fussed about the delays in their schedule.[176] When Elsie and Herbert finally had a frank discussion about the problems in their marriage, in the summer of 1912, their painful memories of that 1910 trip loomed large.[177]

After that trip, Elsie slipped, somewhat uncomfortably, back into domestic life. Earlier in the summer, she had been spending five to six hours a day doing lessons with the children and "bullying the whole household most painfully" in her effort to make the children more self-reliant.[178] After her return, she resumed teaching Lissa and John reading, story writing, and mapmaking, a challenge she found harder than teaching college students.[179] Her candid accounts of her difficulties show how incapable she was of sentimentalizing motherhood and how uncompromisingly honest she was with both herself and Herbert. Regretting that she had lost her temper with Lissa, Elsie ruefully acknowledged, "She provokes me to a desire for physical violence and leaves me amazed with myself — I now understand wife-beating — given a certain kind of wife."[180]

Increasingly, Elsie seemed to be turning to male friends to provide the strenuous physical activity and intellectual companionship for which Herbert seemed to have little time or interest. Congressman

---

173 RHS, HP, Diary date book, 1910 and HP, Diary of 1910 Western Trip.
174 Sigmund Freud discussed the significance of a lost wedding ring in *The Psychopathology of Everyday Life*, trans. A. A. Brill (New York: MacMillan, 1915), p. 235. I am indebted to Barbara Fisher for this citation.
175 APS, HP to ECP, August 7, 1912.
176 RHS, HP, Diary of 1910 Western Trip.
177 APS, ECP to HP, August 6, 1912; APS, HP to ECP, August 7, 1912.
178 Hours per day: APS, ECP to HP, June 27, 1910. Bullying: APS, ECP to HP, June 26, 1910.
179 APS, ECP to HP, September 8, 1909; similarly, APS, ECP to HP, June 27, 1910.
180 APS, ECP to HP, October 29, 1910. Other instances of Elsie's efforts at self-control and her chagrin at losing her temper with Lissa: APS, ECP to HP, October 28, 1910; March 18, 1911; and June 11, 1911.

Andrew Peters, a friend of both Elsie and Herbert, was a willing companion in 1909 and 1910. (On more than one occasion, he was taken to be her husband.[181]) The witty, erudite, aristocratic, married British diplomat George Young was a particular favorite while he was working in Washington between 1910 and 1912. He took as much delight as Elsie in their lively intellectual discussions, canoe and horseback rides, and sightseeing expeditions.[182]

Herbert lost his Congressional seat in the November election in 1910, a defeat that left him feeling "churlful."[183] After five years in Washington, the Parsonses prepared to return to New York. In December, Elsie was pregnant again. Eager for an adventure before succumbing to the constraints imposed by another pregnancy, she spent a month sailing in the Bahamas with Kirk Brice, a friend she had known for many years, when Herbert was unable to join her. Careful to avoid gossip and scandal, Elsie and Kirk cabled separately to make hotel reservations, refused to share the only available sleeping room on a train to Florida, and slept in separate staterooms. But they also enjoyed moonlit sails and swims and overnight side trips, Elsie reported to Herbert.[184]

When his Congressional term ended in March 1911, Herbert returned to New York to resume his legal practice, while Elsie stayed in Washington so the children could finish the school year. To head off her jealousy of Lucy Wilson, Elsie encouraged Herbert to widen his social circle and see other women in New York.[185] She adopted a similar approach with her circle of male friends. Convinced that Herbert was incapable of feeling jealous, Elsie wrote freely to him about her

---

181 APS, ECP to HP, August 13, 1909. Peters served in Congress (1907–1914), as Assistant Secretary to the Treasury (1914–1918), and Mayor of Boston (1918–1922). After he married Martha Phillips in 1910, the two couples remained friends. The Peters were invited to Lissa's wedding in 1922 and Elsie and her younger sons went sailing with them in the 1920s.

182 Elsie's feelings for George Young: APS, ECP to HP, March 10, 1911 and April 18, 1911. His feelings for her: APS, George Young to ECP, May 17, 1912.

183 RHS, John Edward Parsons to HP, November [9], 1910, quoting the telegram Herbert had sent announcing his defeat. John Edward Parsons regretted that Herbert had become a "victim" in the election.

184 APS, ECP to HP, February 7, 1911, and ECP to HP, Saturday [1911].

185 APS, ECP to HP, March 7, 1911.

activities and her feelings for her male companions. She insisted, both at the time and afterward, that her flirtations were rare, and none were serious. Her trips and outings were simply a device to distract her from her unhappiness and keep her from making demands on Herbert that he could not or would not fulfill, she assured him.[186] She expected her accounts to be believed. But she never accepted Herbert's assertions that he did not love Lucy Wilson.

Elsie felt sobered by "the tremendous responsibilities" she and Herbert faced in raising their children, but their different approaches to childrearing and religion drove them further apart in the spring and summer of 1911.[187] Herbert let Elsie know how hurt and angry he was when she — in Lissa's presence — contemptuously noted that he was a churchgoer.[188] He was shocked when eight-year-old John began to use bad language and Elsie did nothing to stop it.[189] He was outraged that she let the children see her in the nude. Elsie explained, "Nudity *per se* has never stimulated any sex feelings in me. But a sunset, waves, singing, a jest, do."[190] Herbert's angry response indicates his contempt for Elsie's radical social views and experiments. "Why think that John a boy should be like you & unlike other boys!" he expostulated.

> I am frequently astonished at your novel propositions entirely self-made, not based on the views of those most experienced & almost universal reason and belief, but in direct opposition to them without reason [...] what I am wont to call your lack of knowledge of human nature. I want what is best for the children, new or old, but I trust the old until real reasons are given for the new.[191]

Worn out by childcare responsibilities and domestic routines, Elsie scheduled numerous outings and several weekend trips with a variety of male and female friends in the spring of 1911. She had an unexpected

---

186 Lack of jealousy: APS, ECP to HP, July 27, 1909. Rationale for trips: APS, ECP to HP, February 7, 1911; ECP to HP, 1911, n.d; ECP to HP, June 16, 1911. APS, ECP to HP, August 6, 1912.

187 Tremendous responsibilities: APS, ECP to HP, March 30, 1911.

188 APS, HP to ECP, May 1, 1911.

189 APS, HP to ECP, October 4, 1911.

190 APS, ECP to HP, July 26, 1910.

191 APS, HP to ECP, July 27, 1910.

overnight stay with George Young, when they missed the last train back to Washington after a day of sailing on Chesapeake Bay.[192]

Herbert may or may not have been jealous of Elsie's male friends, but he was not happy about the time she was spending away from the children. He snidely observed, "You must have a very competent governess to look after your children when you are away & bring them up so charmingly."[193] This suggests that anger and resentment — and concerns about the children — smoldered beneath his customary forbearance. (Elsie did not employ a governess, but she had the trusted Miss Carmody to look after the children in her absence.)

As a working father, Herbert had little time to be with the children. He tried to reserve Sundays for his family, and he occasionally took the children on special outings.[194] But when he expressed regret that he was not free to spend more time with the children, Elsie drily observed, "I doubt you would enjoy having the children so constantly with you for 2–3 weeks as you do for 2–3 days."[195]

In July 1911, a month before her sixth and last child, McIlvaine, was born, Elsie wrote to Herbert from Newport that she had fallen asleep considering whether he "wouldn't be happier and second better off married to one of [Lucy's] type" than to her. The dream she had that night — in which she was wearing a "flaming scarlet dress in a picture gallery" and an admirer was "sitting upright in a bed declaring that he was in love with me" — suggests that she was beginning to contemplate a more flamboyant role for herself, that of a femme fatale rather than a devoted wife and mother.[196] Her longstanding aversion to marriage as an institution deepened. "[S]o many sins flourish under its protection, and so many virtues are found incompatible with it," she wrote despondently to Herbert.[197]

---

192 Worn out: APS, ECP to HP, June 12, 1911. Weekend trips: APS, ECP to HP, April 24, 1911 and ECP to HP, June 16, 1911. Overnight with Young: ECP to HP, April 24, 1911.
193 APS, HP to ECP, May 10, 1911.
194 RHS, HP letter regarding speaking request at Yale University [1910]. After Lissa had had a tooth pulled in 1910, Herbert took her to meet President Theodore Roosevelt in order to cheer her (Kennedy, "Reminiscences").
195 APS, ECP to HP, August 22, 1911.
196 APS, ECP to HP, July 12, 1911.
197 APS, ECP to HP, July 25, 1911.

Replacing an Emotional Easy Chair

Having another baby and moving the family back to New York later in 1911 did not ease the strains between Elsie and Herbert. The tensions that had been building for years finally flared dramatically in August 1912 when they were both in Newport. After an argument that began in person, Elsie finally forced Herbert to talk about the problems in their marriage. The discussion continued over several days by letter after Herbert returned to New York. Elsie began by laying out her "theory" that Herbert had "been in love with Lucy Wilson these three years — on & off." She explained:

> Just how much you have yourself realized it, I don't know, but about the fact itself I have never been uncertain. I believe it has made no difference in your feeling for me, that you care for me now as much as you ever did. In fact, as you once told me, that you enjoy my company even more after having been with her. As far as I can see too she does you good.
>
> So in my better moments I have honestly wanted you to see as much of her and as intimately of her as possible. But try as I will, and during the last three years I have resorted to many devices, I still have despicable moments which I don't understand in the least.[198]

Herbert dismissed Elsie's notions as "bosh" and accused her, as usual, of "exaggerating matters."[199] Elsie was stung by his dismissive response to her effort to be open and honest.[200] In the ensuing discussion, they acknowledged what had been clear for several years: although Lucy Wilson was the precipitating cause of the marital crisis, she was by no means the only problem. Both Elsie and Herbert focused on their failure to be sufficiently "companionate" with each other, although each had a different perception of what marital companionship entailed. Herbert felt Elsie had changed in ways that puzzled and distressed him. He did not "understand" her growing need for "travel, [and] things new & unconventional."[201]

Elsie agreed that they had become increasingly disconnected, both emotionally and intellectually. "I think we have always had a different

---

198 APS, ECP to HP, August 4, 1912.
199 APS, HP to ECP, August 6, 1912.
200 APS, ECP to HP, August 7, 1912.
201 APS, HP to ECP, August 4, 1912.

theory of companionship, although it is only within the last two or three years that it has been apparent to you," she explained. "It is my new experiences, my new ideas, and feelings, my fresh impressions of persons and places that I have wanted to share with you. The more interesting or exciting or delightful a thing was the more I wanted you in connection with it." She wanted a relationship in which both partners would take an interest in the other's activities and talk freely about their respective work. Differences of opinion should be openly discussed, not hidden or ignored. Elsie had hinted at this during their courtship and had long chastised Herbert for being too uncommunicative about his work. But she had never before expressed the pain she felt when he failed to show interest in her work. Now she wrote:

> Do you realize that apart from the family and the routine of life all my energy and a very large part of my interest have gone into writing which you have never shown the slightest interest in? [...] to have you absolutely out of so large a part of my life is cutting. It isn't that I want your agreement. Any kind of criticism or ridicule of the ideas themselves would be welcome. Then there is so much in talk that I have to constantly repress because I know it would put you out with me.[202]

Herbert's response could not have assuaged Elsie's concerns. He had not read all of *The Family* out of "cowardice": he feared he would find the contents too distasteful. But he resolved to make amends and read it.[203]

Elsie was also wounded by Herbert's disinterest in finding "companionship in new places" with her. "Tolerance" of her enthusiasms and the freedom to explore them on her own or with others were as much as he could promise; he did not intend to involve himself in her new pursuits. She could travel but he had no intention of joining her. He offered practical reasons for his reluctance. He traveled weekly for his law practice; he could not afford to take so much time off; he wanted to spend as much time as possible with the older children while they were still living at home. (John and Lissa were ten and twelve at this time.) But "cowardice" was a problem here, too, Herbert confessed. Ever since the Yosemite trip, he had been "afraid" to take another trip with her.[204]

---

202 APS, ECP to HP, August 6, 1912.
203 APS, HP to ECP, August 7, 1912.
204 Ibid.

His attitude did not bode well for their future. The relationship they had enjoyed for the first decade of their marriage had been very satisfying, but it was no longer enough for Elsie. She wrote:

> [U]ntil about three years ago although I had short times of much unhappiness I was very happy in your companionship and made the most of your theory of companionship — a kind of emotional easy chair.
>
> Not that I haven't been happy during this time in our *institutional* companionship. I like easy chairs very often myself. Our relation is still the chief thing in the world to me and it seems grotesque to even have to tell you so.[205]

Herbert's concept of companionate marriage was still quite limited, although more advanced than many men of his era. He offered Elsie independence, but would not become part of her new life. She did not want his patronizing tolerance; she wanted his companionship and engagement. The "emotional easy chair" Elsie had happily shared with Herbert was becoming a strait jacket that confined and constrained rather than comforted. As they reestablished themselves in New York, they needed to find a different mode of relating if they were to move forward together.

In the meantime, Elsie imposed yet another rule about Lucy Wilson. Struggling to honor her belief in marital freedom, protect herself from jealousy, and avoid future emotional scenes, Elsie told Herbert she did not want him to mention Lucy in his letters, but he should feel free to spend time with her. Elsie would not accept invitations from Lucy for herself, but would pass them along to Herbert. "The idea that you should not see her whenever you want is most repugnant to me," she stressed.[206]

An Unclassifiable Woman, 1913–1920

Elsie reshaped her work and marriage in bold ways after she returned to New York. While Herbert picked up his life pretty much where he had left off in 1905, she developed new friends, new interests, and new professional outlets. She became a member of Heterodoxy, a pioneering feminist consciousness-raising organization; a contributor to

---

205 APS, ECP to HP, August 5, 1912, emphasis in the original.
206 APS, ECP to HP, August 26, 1912.

opinion-shaping journals like *The Masses* and *The New Republic*; and an accomplished anthropological field researcher.[207]

Free to express her opinions and use her own name, Elsie published four books and a stream of popular and scholarly articles between 1913 and 1916.[208] Writing what she called "social propaganda", she explored how societies seek to shape and control their members by stamping out individuality. By studying her own society as an ethnographer would look at an unfamiliar culture, she revealed the roots of "modern" customs and behavior, and challenged popular assumptions about the distinctions between "primitive" cultures and more "advanced" societies. By exposing the often hard-to-see mechanisms of social control in everyday life, she hoped to free individuals — especially women, but also men — from the insidious effects of social classification. Elsie's books help to explain her personal iconoclasm and her desire to break away from social artifice and convention. "The more thoroughly a woman is classified the more thoroughly she is constrained," she proclaimed. Her pronouncement, "the new woman means the woman not yet classified, perhaps not classifiable" was a fitting credo for her own life.[209]

Noting that marriage forced women to be intellectually, economically, and emotionally dependent on their husbands, Elsie denounced it as "the most satisfactory device yet worked out for the control of one adult by another."[210] She supported women's suffrage, but was more concerned about the subtle but powerful ways that social custom constrained a woman's freedom in daily life.[211] "It's more important to women to get rid of their petticoats than to get a vote. And it's still more important

---

207   Herbert returned to his family's law firm (although his father no longer headed it), resumed the philanthropic endeavors that were family traditions, and continued to support the Progressive institutions and causes he had championed before 1905. He served on the boards of the Memorial Hospital (which his father had helped to found) and Greenwich House, run by Elsie's old friend, Mary Kingsbury Simkhovitch.

208   ECP, *The Old Fashioned Woman, Primitive Fancies about the Sex* (New York: Putnam's, 1913); *Fear and Conventionality* (New York: Putnam's, 1914); *Social Freedom: A Study of the Conflicts between Social Classifications and Personality* (New York: Putnam's, 1915); and *Social Rule: A Study of the Will to Power* (New York: Putnam's, 1916).

209   ECP, *Social Rule*, pp. 56–57.

210   Ibid., pp. 45–46.

211   ECP, "Feminism and Conventionality" in *Women in Public Life*, ed. by James P. Lichtenberger. Special Issue of *Annals of the American Academy of Political and Social Science*, 56 (November 1914), 47–53 (p. 48).

for them to get a good job," she argued in *The Journal of a Feminist*.[212] She focused on eradicating the everyday constraints on women's inner freedom: "checks upon going about alone, clothes that hinder movement, censorship of ideas and feeling, endless little sex taboos."[213] Herbert, in contrast, was an enthusiastic proponent of women's suffrage and worked closely for its passage with the leaders of the New York State movement. Elsie was also an advocate for birth control at a time when that was a very radical act. She presciently observed that the opportunity to separate sex and parenthood by controlling childbearing was nothing short of revolutionary.[214]

In Washington, Elsie had been a lone voice, a "crank" who stood out for her iconoclasm.[215] In New York, others felt similarly about the things she cared about and experimented with alternative lifestyles. As a member of Heterodoxy, she was part of a sympathetic and scintillating circle of feminists, intellectuals, social experimenters, and bohemians who challenged social and marital norms, debated the tenets of feminism, and lead unconventional lives. The writers and intellectuals she came to know at *The New Republic* and *The Masses* were equally committed to freeing the individual from societal constraints, outmoded standards of behavior, and the trappings of bourgeois marriage.[216] In these circles, Elsie emerged as a sly observer and witty chronicler of

---

212 ECP, *Journal of a Feminist*, p. 67.

213 Ibid., p. 46.

214 Ibid., p. 40. See also, ECP, "Feminism and Sex Ethics", *International Journal of Ethics*, 26 (July 1916), 462–65; and ECP, "When Mating and Parenthood are Theoretically Distinguished", *International Journal of Ethics*, 26 (January 1916), 207–16. For a public speech, see APS, "Society Told of Birth Curb", newspaper clipping from the *Chicago Tribune* on a talk ECP gave in 1917. For Elsie's support of Margaret Sanger's efforts to disseminate information about birth control in 1916, see Margaret Sanger, *Margaret Sanger: An Autobiography* (New York: Norton, 1938), pp. 188–89.

215 RHS, ECP, "Washington Journal."

216 For Heterodoxy, see Nancy F. Cott, *The Grounding of Modern Feminism* (New Haven: Yale University Press, 1987), pp. 43–45; Judith Schwarz, *Radical Feminists of Heterodoxy, Greenwich Village, 1912–1940* (Norwich, VT: New Victoria, 1986); and Joanna Scutts, *Hotbed: Bohemian Greenwich Village and the Secret Club that Sparked Modern Feminism* (New York: Seal Press, 2022). Margaret C. Jones explores the articles and milieus of the female writers and editors of *The Masses*, many of whom were members of Heterodoxy, in *Heretics and Hellraisers: Women Contributors to The Masses, 1911–1917* (Austin: University of Texas Press, 1993), pp. 1–21, 28–53. For Elsie's work in particular, see pp. 34–39, 48–49. See also, Leslie Fishbein, *Rebels in Bohemia: The Radicals of the Masses, 1911–1917* (Chapel Hill: University of North Carolina Press, 1982).

sexual and social mores and feminist beliefs and practices. A forerunner of 1970s feminists, she understood that the personal and the political were inextricably linked.

Elsie was also laying the groundwork for a career as a professional anthropologist. Two solo trips to the Southwest, in 1912 and 1913, reinforced her desire to become a serious student of Native American culture. Under the leadership of Franz Boas, a professor at Columbia University and curator at the American Museum of Natural History, anthropology was being transformed into an academic discipline that required formal training, rigorous standards of proof, and extensive field research.[217] Elsie allied herself with a group of young anthropologists — among them Pliny Goddard, Robert Lowie, and Alfred Kroeber — who were trained by Boas and exercised considerable influence in the discipline. These pioneering anthropologists provided her with social as well as intellectual companionship and encouraged her to make the transition from writing social propaganda to writing scholarly anthropological treatises. By 1918 she earned Boas's interest and support as well.[218]

All the while, Elsie was struggling to develop a new set of ground rules for her own marriage. During what she called the "year of misery" that followed the confrontation of August 1912, her ambivalence about Herbert and her marriage was as strong as ever.[219] Although he had urged her, "Write me *anything* [....] Don't repress," she still felt stifled by his disapproval. "I don't want to love you merely as I do a child, & if I can't talk freely to you & *be myself* to you that is what it will come to," she wrote despondently to him in January 1913.[220] And she still felt pushed aside by Lucy's continuing presence in Herbert's life.

---

217 For Boas's role in the early history of anthropology, see Margaret Mead and Ruth L. Bunzel, *The Golden Age of American Anthropology, 1880–1920* (New York: George Braziller, 1960), p. 400, and Marvin Harris, *The Rise of Anthropological Theory: A History of Theories of Culture* (New York: Thomas Crowell, 1968), pp. 250–54.

218 Boas's support: APS, ECP to HP, December 28, 1918. ECP's correspondence with all these men is in APS, and she mentioned them in her letters to Herbert. On their importance to her as anthropologists and friends, see Deacon, pp. 145–63; and Zumwalt, pp. 163–81.

219 Year of misery: APS, ECP to HP, June 16, 1913.

220 APS, HP to ECP, August 7, 1912; APS, ECP to HP [January 13, 1913]. Emphasis in the originals.

Elsie tried to honor her resolution that Herbert should be free to spend time with Lucy as long as he did not mention her in person or in letters. When Elsie left on a solo trip to Mexico early in 1913, she encouraged him to see Lucy. Herbert, who had been hired as Lucy's lawyer, was drawing up her will; they had many business meetings and a few dinners during the month Elsie was away.[221] Nevertheless, Elsie was incensed when she could not avoid Lucy after her return and discovered that Herbert had arranged for Lissa to spend several days with the Wilsons in Washington. Berating Herbert for creating such a "messy situation", she scolded, "You do mismanage appallingly, and you seem incapable of learning."[222] She instructed him to make a new rule: "Whenever L. W. is in evidence (i.e., when E. C. P. cannot get out of the way in time) and for one week afterwards do not make love to E. C. P. at all. First you stimulate and then you inhibit E. C. P.'s feelings & it is that which during the last half year has made her so often go to pieces."[223] Referring to herself in the impersonal third person and instituting a rule were Elsie's way of depersonalizing the situation and distancing herself from the pain Herbert's behavior caused her. She warned him that if they began "to dislike each other", they would have to "part for good."[224]

More misery followed. In June, 1913 Elsie spent a day in tears, wishing that she and Herbert could "get back to our old simple loving relation." She resolved to "be more loving" and avoid the behaviors that annoyed him.[225] "I will wear a hat in town. I won't talk 'theories' — what else?" she queried a week later.[226] During the rest of the summer, she seemed unsettled — anxious for new experiences and eager to get out of her domestic easy chair. In July, she jumped at an opportunity to report on women's reactions to the Balkan War as a special correspondent for two

---

221 RHS. Herbert's billable hours and business meetings with Lucy are recorded on worksheets for his office in January and February 1913. Dinners with Lucy are recorded in his calendar diary for these months. Elsie's alter ego in "The Imaginary Mistress", her fictionalized account of Herbert's relationship with Lucy, resents that her husband becomes her rival's business manager even though she consented to the arrangement (p. 13). Elsie may have felt the same emotions after Lucy hired Herbert to be her lawyer.
222 APS, ECP to HP, February 13, 1913.
223 APS, ECP to HP, February 15, 1913.
224 APS, ECP to HP, February 14, 1913.
225 APS, ECP to HP, June 16, 1913.
226 APS, ECP to HP, June 23, 1913.

New York newspapers. Expecting to go to Athens and Constantinople, she arranged to travel with her friend George Young, the British diplomat, who was also reporting on the war.[227] When her assignment was cancelled after a second war broke out, she quickly scheduled a fall trip to study Native American cultures in the American Southwest.

In Elsie's fictionalized accounts of the Lucy Wilson episode, written between 1913 and 1915, her alter egos finally rid themselves of their "obsession" with the other woman, after years of unhappiness, by ceasing to love their husbands, a development the unperceptive husbands never notice.[228] Elsie was very likely describing her own experience of falling out of passionate, romantic love for Herbert. After the summer of 1913, she appeared to have her emotions under control and no longer expressed a longing for Herbert or their past life. Instead, she was constructing a new life that did not revolve around him. Herbert, meanwhile, continued to do legal work for Lucy Wilson, and handled her divorce from Huntington Wilson in 1915.

Having fallen out of love with their husbands, Elsie's fictional counterparts grow troubled by the hypocrisy their marriages represent. The unnamed female protagonist in "In New York State" wants her upright husband to continue to live with her while taking the other woman for his mistress. Knowing that he is too conventional to do that, she urges him to divorce her and marry the other woman. A divorce would give her "freedom from the insincerities of our present mode of life." But he — predictably — shies away from the public embarrassment of having to prove adultery in order to obtain a divorce. In "The Imaginary Mistress," Elsie's alter ego, Lois, is contemptuous of her husband's "conventional ideas" about marriage and fear of scandal. She regards her husband's rectitude as a fault not a virtue, and pities him for his "self-suppression."[229] Unhappy about living a lie, she urges her husband to divorce her. When he refuses, she abruptly leaves him and moves to Mexico, where she becomes a successful archeologist and hosts a famed salon.

---

227 APS, ECP to HP, July 23, 1913. With characteristic disregard for others' convenience, Elsie asked Herbert to book her sailing to Europe, and prevailed upon Young to travel earlier than he had originally intended.

228 APS, ECP, "In New York State"; ECP, "Imaginary Mistress", pp. 17–18.

229 APS, ECP, "Imaginary Mistress", pp. 7–8, 12–13, 16–17, 20.

Elsie and Herbert never discussed divorce in their letters, but surely they talked about it. Elsie, who believed that the legal, societal, and religious restrictions on divorce and remarriage should be relaxed, would certainly have considered it, if not argued for it; Herbert, undoubtedly, would have opposed the idea. Elsie explored the topic at length in *The Journal of a Feminist*. Amos, the character based on Herbert, believes it is permissible for married partners to separate but not to remarry. Cynthia, the diarist who expresses Elsie's views, thinks that the right action depends on the circumstances. Couples might wisely choose to stay together for the sake of their children, but she finds Amos's view that unhappy couples should remain married and "make the best of it" both pointless and absurd.[230]

Elsie had always insisted that she was monogamous by nature; her ideal was a passionate relationship that was exclusive so long as it was fulfilling and truly loving. Finding herself unhappily married to a man who did not believe in divorce, seemingly no longer in love with him, and much sought after by other men, Elsie needed a new model for marital behavior.

In the summer of 1913, she was receiving amorous letters from Grant LaFarge, a prominent New York architect.[231] She had known LaFarge for many years, and they were part of the same social set in Newport. In late July and August 1913, he appeared to be pressing Elsie to have a sexual relationship, but seemed willing to accept whatever terms she proposed.[232] In October, he was writing to her about his views on sex and his reactions to a short story she wrote, presumably "The Imaginary Mistress". He lamented that it offered no vision of a sexual relationship that was "entirely mutual, equal, fully shared."[233] In the spring of 1914, they spent more than a month together traveling in Europe.[234]

---

230 ECP, *Journal of a Feminist*, p. 12.

231 Christopher Grant LaFarge (1862–1938), the eldest son of the artist John LaFarge, married Florence Bayard Lockwood in 1895. His firm, Heins and LaFarge, planned the original design of the Cathedral of Saint John the Divine, the buildings of the Bronx Zoo, and the architecture of the first subway line in New York City. His oldest son, Oliver, became a noted anthropologist and an advocate for the Native Americans of the Southwest.

232 APS, Grant LaFarge to ECP, 29 July [1913]; 19 August [1913?]; and Tuesday [1913?].

233 APS, Grant LaFarge to ECP, 14 October [1913].

234 APS, ECP to HP, April 27, 1914 and May 3, 1914. Elsie was using the money her father gave her as an allowance to pay for the trip, she explained to Herbert.

We do not have Elsie's letters to Grant, but we can trace her thinking about extra-marital affairs in Cynthia's ruminations in several journal entries dated November and December 1913 in *The Journal of a Feminist*. (Grant appears as a married man who no longer loves his wife — or she him — and who has already had an affair.) Although Cynthia's ideal (like Elsie's) is a relationship of exclusive passion, she sees no value in maintaining "moribund" relationships merely for the sake of the past. Believing that most husbands can be satisfied with routine and unthinking sex a few times a month, she is comfortable with the idea that a woman can take a lover while continuing to have a sexual relationship with her husband.

It is impossible to document when Elsie's relationship with Grant, which lasted for almost ten years, became an affair, but there is no reason to doubt that it did. Unlike Herbert, Elsie had no moral qualms about having an affair. She had been faithful to Herbert because she loved him, not because of her marital vows, institutional bonds, or societal expectations. Once she fell out of love with him — assuming that the situations she described in "The Imaginary Mistress" and "In New York State" are true to life — she had no reason not to have an affair. She was too comfortable with sexuality, too much part of an avant-garde world, and too eager to grasp experiences to hold herself back when she felt no moral repugnance at the idea.[235]

Realigning her life and establishing a new *modus vivendi* with Herbert was nevertheless painful. Elsie never wrote directly about that process. But what she wrote a decade later, about situations when a woman or man has an ongoing affair but continues to maintain a relationship with her or his spouse, sheds light on her affairs and her relationship with Herbert.[236] She vehemently rejected the term "adultery" as a "vicious catchword." She also objected to the term "sharing" which implied that women were property to be owned. She was more accepting of "trios",

---

235 Earlier, she might have been hesitant if a situation she describes in "The Imaginary Mistress" is accurate. When Elsie's alter ego Lois travels in Mexico (as Elsie did in January 1913), a lingering sense of loyalty to her husband keeps her from responding to the kisses of a man she meets and travels with. Lois thinks there would be nothing wrong with such a physical relationship, but she foregoes it because she knows it would hurt her husband "to the quick."

236 University of Chicago, Hannah Holborn Gray Special Collections Research Center, Robert Herrick Papers (RH Papers), ECP's notes for Chapter "Pigeon Cove" in "Tides", the book she and Robert Herrick were writing in the mid-1920s.

but cautioned, "[t]here is 'nothing desirable' about that [...] it is an emergency measure against disaster. And I don't see how outsiders can ever determine the amount of disaster it may preclude — or involve." Nevertheless, Elsie thought trios were very common situations, and perfectly natural, almost inevitable, when "either husband or wife comes to love the other in a parental kind of way."[237] Her description of trio arrangements as fraught and difficult, born out of a sense of desperation, undoubtedly describes her own experience. No wonder she was so unyielding with Herbert and so unaccommodating to others' schedules during the mid- and late- 1910s.

Rewriting the Rules of Marriage

As she wrestled with the problems in her own marriage and explored marriage customs in other cultures, Elsie struggled to articulate how modern couples could keep relationships vital and passionate, protected from the stultifying effects of domestic routines, proprietary habits, and formulaic behavior. Reciprocity, mutual responsiveness, candor, and sincerity were essential to any meaningful relationship, she argued.[238]

Expanding on the themes she had written about in *The Family* in 1906, Elsie championed opportunities for women to express their sexuality, practice birth control, and engage in premarital and extramarital sex. Believing that marriages should derive legitimacy from the relationship between a couple rather than the sanction of church or state, she supported easing divorce laws and relaxing the social stigma that attended divorce. Elsie's remedies for the ills of marriage were provocative for a woman of her class and background, but they were emblematic of what many leading social rebels, intellectuals, and artists — including members of Heterodoxy and writers at *The Masses* — were saying, writing, and doing about marriage in the 1910s and 1920s.[239] Her

---

237 Ibid.
238 ECP, *Social Freedom*, pp. 32–33; ECP, *Fear and Conventionality*, pp. 152–53; ECP, "Feminism and Sex Ethics", pp. 462–65.
239 For the backgrounds, connections, and views of leading "sex radicals" and other marriage reformers in the 1910s and 1920s, and Elsie's place among them, see Claire Virgina Eby, *Until Choice Do Us Part: Marriage Reform in the Progressive Era* (Chicago and London: University of Chicago Press, 2014), and Christina Simmons, *Making Marriage Modern: Women's Sexuality from the Progressive Era to World War I*

connections to these groups provided her with inspiration and support, as well as opportunities to publicize her views.

Marriage "imposes conditions fatal to passion," Elsie believed. A husband, knowing he can get what he wants at any time, stops taking trouble to get it, and his "uncourted wife" becomes passive and passionless, "at best only a friend, at worst a jealous proprietress." The "complementary institution" of adultery was just as lethal to passion, Elsie warned, noting that lovers could be institutionalized as easily as husbands, and long term affairs were just as likely as marriages to sink into unthinking habit.[240]

To keep passion alive, Elsie recommended that couples eliminate routine, spend time apart, and find ways to express their individuality. "The daily familiarity we so insist upon in marriage of itself would take the edge off any spiritual intimacy, dulling responsiveness. A degree of loneliness is essential to fervor," she asserted.[241] Convinced that domestic routines had an enervating effect on passion, she urged modern couples to follow the eighteenth-century example of Mary Wollstonecraft and William Godwin and experiment with keeping separate apartments while married.[242]

Maintaining separate social lives was another strategy to avoid boredom and keep relationships fresh. "Conjugal detachment is essential to conjugal attachment," Elsie had informed Herbert in 1910.[243] Couples should spend time together because they enjoyed each other and had common interests, not because society found it convenient to treat them as a unit. To eliminate what she called the "tagger-on spouse problem", Elsie argued in the *New Republic* in June 1916 that married individuals should be sent separate invitations to social events; a host should not be obligated to invite both partners when he or she wanted to see only one.[244]

(New York: Oxford University Press, 2011). Most of these champions of change were white, heterosexual, middle-class or upper-middle-class intellectuals who addressed a white middle-class audience, but Simmons also writes about the views and marriages of middle-class Black reformers during this period.

240 ECP, *Journal of a Feminist*, pp. 43–44.
241 ECP, "Feminism and Sex Ethics", p. 464.
242 ECP, *Journal of a Feminist*, p. 48.
243 APS, ECP to HP, June 30, 1910.
244 ECP, "Must We Have Her?", *New Republic*, 10 June 1916, 145–46. The New York *Evening Telegram, Evening Herald*, and *Evening Sun* all ran stories about Elsie's article. The newspaper clippings are in APS.

The major problem Elsie wrestled with was how a woman could preserve her independence when she was in love with a man. "How are women to live *with* men, not *without* men like the ruthless fighters for institutional freedom, and not in the old way *through* men?" Elsie agonized.[245] Recognizing that there was "a marked impulse to subjection in the normal woman," she warned against letting a love relationship become a woman's entire existence.[246] "That monstrous alternative of the Nineteenth Century, Work-instead-of Love is by no means slain," she lamented.[247]

To avoid "self-surrender" and preserve her "inviolable" core, a woman had to find a focus for her energy and imagination that had nothing to do with the man she loved. This required "intellectual work or indeed any work that is interesting and exacting." In Elsie's view, having a job would allow a woman to maintain her individuality and independence, and help her to build a stronger relationship with a man:

> Hitherto the work of women has been considered only from the economic standpoint, or from the point of view of making her economically independent of men [...]. It is time now to consider her work as a safeguard of her spiritual independence — a preservative of her integrity, a means of discipline. It is only through work one can be quite sure one is taking life at first hand, and it is only by taking life at first hand, by being the spiritual equal of her lover that a woman may preserve a free and passionate life with him, a life of mutual joys and satisfactions, a life aglow through their imagination.[248]

Elsie put these ideas into practice in her own life. By 1915, she was adamant that she and Herbert should lead quite separate domestic and social lives. The Parsonses' multiple homes — in Manhattan, Lenox, and Harrison, New York — helped Elsie maintain the physical distance she desired.[249] Increasingly, she and Herbert stayed at different residences. If either wanted to spend time with the other, it had to be arranged in advance. They still had a sexual relationship, since there was a pregnancy

---

245 APS, ECP, "Journal of a Feminist" mss., p. 53 (ECP, *Journal*, p. 46). Emphasis in the original.
246 Ibid.
247 APS, ECP, "Journal of A Feminist" mss., p. 56 (ECP, *Journal*, p. 48).
248 APS, ECP "Journal of a Feminist" mss., p. 54. (ECP, *Journal*, p. 47.)
249 Herbert inherited Lounsberry in Harrison from his father in 1915.

scare in 1915.[250] Their professional activities also kept them apart. Elsie went off for weeks of field work several times a year. Herbert traveled for his law practice and rented a house in Albany in 1915 when he was a member of the Constitutional Convention that was rewriting the New York State constitution. "How strange you all are about where you live!" their oldest son, sixteen-year-old John, observed in 1919, noting that Elsie was at Lounsberry, Herbert was in an apartment on the Upper East Side, and Lissa was in midtown.[251] Elsie travelled frequently and freely, but not with Herbert. After another unhappy trip visiting several National Parks with their older children, in the summer of 1914, she and Herbert did not travel together for seven years.[252]

"I can't help thinking that freedom rather than consideration is the basis of a real relation between two persons," Elsie told Herbert, explaining why he had no "*a priori* claim" on her evenings just because they were married.[253] She frequently turned down his proposals to do something together.[254] Nevertheless, she took offense if Herbert forgot that they had made plans or expressed a preference to garden rather than to do something with her. And she was hurt when Herbert was invited to parties for the pro-suffrage set hosted by her friend Alice Duer Miller, while she was not.[255]

Despite Elsie's belief in marital freedom, Herbert's continuing relationship with Lucy Wilson still had the power to wound. Elsie was uncharacteristically vitriolic when she discovered that he had spent part of a weekend at Lenox motoring with Lucy and the Parsons children in the spring of 1915, while he was working on Lucy's divorce case. "Keep your 'cat' out of the family life, just for your own fun," she instructed him, echoing the anger she felt when she returned from Mexico in February 1913 and found that Herbert had arranged for Lissa to spend a weekend with the Wilsons in Washington.[256]

---

250 APS, ECP to HP, September 17, 1915 and October 5, 1915.

251 APS, John E. Parsons to HP, December 9, 1919.

252 Elsie apologized to Herbert for being "cranky" during the trip, but felt he had arranged it to suit his style of travel rather than hers. APS, ECP to HP [July 31, 1914].

253 APS, ECP to HP [April 5, 1915]; similarly, ECP to HP, April 21, 1915 and April 24, 1915.

254 APS, ECP to HP, November 2, 1916. RHS, telegrams from ECP to HP, November 6, 1916 and November 19, 1916.

255 Hurt: APS, ECP to HP, November 15, 1916.

256 APS, ECP to HP, May 26, 1915.

Escape Artist

"Interesting and exacting work" was the antidote Elsie recommended
to counterbalance a woman's unfortunate tendency to "self-surrender"
when she was in love. It was also her strategy for overcoming the
unhappiness of her marriage. From the mid-teens on, Elsie structured
her life to accommodate her work rather than fitting her work around
the needs of her husband and children. In the summer of 1915, she
embarked on the intensive field research on the Pueblo dwellers that she
had been "hankering" to do for years.[257] She published her first scholarly
articles on the culture of the Pueblo after making a second research trip
to New Mexico later that year. By 1918, she was spending at least a
month every year in the southwest studying indigenous cultures, and
a month or longer in the Caribbean or the southeast coast of the United
States documenting the spread of folktales from the islands to the US
mainland. She published frequently and widely in scientific journals and
held numerous offices in professional associations of anthropologists.[258]

Anthropology filled Elsie's need for adventure, physical challenges,
and discovery of the new and exotic. Unimpeded by trains, tourists,
and an anxiously protective husband, she slept outdoors in all kinds
of weather, rode horseback for hundreds of miles over rough terrain
(armed with a loaded revolver), and survived earthquakes and
poisonous snakes.[259] She came to prefer the company of the "negroes
and Indians" she met on her research trips to the people she socialized
with back East.[260]

Elsie's changing relationship with Herbert gave her the impetus and
the freedom to spend a great deal of time in the field. After her marriage
soured, she felt no obligation to create a home for Herbert. "New York
seems drearier than ever, & this 'keeping house' more abominable,
when there's no point in keeping it — for anybody," she complained in

---

257 APS, ECP to HP, August 31, 1915.
258 Elsie received a "starred" listing in *American Men of Science* in 1927, an indication
     that she was a recognized leader in the anthropology profession (Rossiter, *Women
     Scientists*, I, p. 289; Table 10.4, p. 293). For accounts and assessments of Parsons's
     career in anthropology, see Deacon, and Zumwalt.
259 She pitied Herbert for seeing the country only through the glass windows of a train.
     APS, ECP to HP, February 16, 1918.
260 APS, ECP to HP, November 21, 1917. See also, APS, ECP to Tony Luhan (husband of
     Mabel Dodge Luhan), April 11, 1932.

1913 and in later years.[261] Her youngest children, born in 1909 and 1911, were still quite young when she started her anthropological expeditions. As they grew older, she increased the amount of time she spent in the field. When she was home, Elsie secluded herself so she could work undisturbed every morning. If she was immersed in her work, she turned down requests from Herbert and the children to spend time with her, and largely put the family out of her mind.[262] When Herbert noted how much he valued letters from home when he was stationed in Europe, Elsie expressed surprise. "When my own interest is much absorbed, in the Southwest, for example, I don't care much for letters, in fact I forget people," she confessed. A weekly telegram telling her that everything was all right at home was sufficient for her.[263]

Although Elsie employed many household servants, she relied increasingly on Herbert and her daughter Lissa to help out. According to Mac, their youngest child, Elsie and Herbert negotiated an arrangement in the teens whereby he agreed to take more responsibility for the older children while she had primary responsibility for the younger ones.[264] Herbert became a very engaged father. He attended family ceremonies, holiday celebrations, athletic events, and school functions (including Lissa's high school graduation) that Elsie missed. He went on camping trips with the two older children, and took them (along with Elsie's mother) to Europe in 1921. With help from his sister, he planned Lissa's 1921 wedding.[265] When she and John came home to visit, he turned down professional and social engagements so he could spend his evenings with them.[266] Lissa fondly remembered the pleasure she and her father took in staying up late to gossip about the politicians they

---

261 APS, ECP to HP, December 17, 1913. Similarly, APS, ECP to HP [April 15, 1915] and November 21, 1917.
262 APS, ECP to HP, November 2, 1916; ECP to her son, John E. Parsons, May 14, 1918, May 16, 1918, and May 18, 1918. Elsie looked forward to Herbert's return from the army in 1919, but was prepared to miss his homecoming if it conflicted with a rescheduled research trip to the Southwest with Boas.
263 APS, ECP to HP, October 17, 1918.
264 Desley Deacon, 1994 interview with McIlvaine Parsons (Deacon, p. 462, note 5).
265 Wedding and 1921 trip: APS, HP to ECP, July 7, 1921. 1921 trip: RHS, HP to State Department, May 9, 1921; HP Memo for Office, May 6, 1921. Wedding planning: RHS, HP file: Correspondence re Yale Club 1921, and Herbert's annotations on an invitation list for Lissa's wedding in RHS, HP, Folder: Fifth Division.
266 RHS, HP to Mary Kingsbury Simkhovitch [n.d., 1920]; HP to Frank F. Barth, August 24, 1924.

knew.[267] Herbert also did a lot for the younger boys in the early 1920s: he escorted them to boarding school, made sure they were properly outfitted, visited them, and arranged for their travel back home. He corresponded at length with the boys' schools about their curriculum and performance, hired tutors, and took the boys on vacations.[268]

Herbert's involvement with the children, unusual for a man in this era, served his purposes as well as Elsie's.[269] Doing more with the children gave him opportunities to counter her iconoclasm and expose them to the values, standards, and experiences that were important to him. Both Lissa and Elsie counted on Herbert to provide Lissa with connections to the social world that Elsie scorned.[270] After accompanying Lissa to a dance on Upper Fifth Avenue in 1918, Elsie felt "quite like an immigrant mother who does not know her daughter's set."[271] Herbert worried that Herbert, Jr. and Mac were not getting an adequate education at the experimental day school that was very likely Elsie choice.[272] The boys started attending Herbert's alma mater, St. Paul's School, in 1923 when they were fourteen and twelve; John was already enrolled there.

Taking charge of renovating and decorating their homes similarly provided opportunities for Herbert to counter Elsie's untraditional tastes. Elsie, who had always claimed incompetence about furnishing and decorating a house, was happy to turn those responsibilities over to Herbert.[273] In addition, he made travel arrangements for all the family members and dealt with Elsie's relatives when they were too much for her.[274] Even Herbert's secretary contributed to Elsie's freedom by taking

---

267 Kennedy, "Reminiscences", p. 21.
268 RHS, HP correspondence in the 1920s with the Lincoln School, St. Paul's School, and Herbert Jr.'s tutor, Edward P. Furber; and plans for trips and arrangements for Herbert Jr.'s summer camp.
269 For men's roles in childrearing, see Robert L. Griswold, *Fatherhood in America: A History* (New York: Basic Books, 1994).
270 APS, ECP to HP, January 14, 1919.
271 APS, ECP to HP, April 15, 1918.
272 RHS, HP correspondence with St. Paul's School in 1922. APS, HP to ECP, July 7, 1922.
273 APS, ECP to HP, October 12, 1911; February 24, 1916; March 21, 1918. Elsie's house in North Haven, Maine, purchased after Herbert died, was the only residence that reflected her tastes, according to her grandson David Parsons, who noted that its Southwestern décor is strikingly different from the Parsons's other homes. Author interview with David M. Parsons, July 2010.
274 Herbert informed Elsie's brother, Henry Clews, about Lucy Clews's failing health when Elsie could not think of what to say, and took the younger boys to visit Henry

care of personal tasks that a more traditional wife — or a wife who was more often at home — would have done.[275]

Lissa, who was always more domestically inclined than her mother, also filled in, not always happily. When the servants were not on duty, she cooked.[276] During the spring and fall of 1918, she took charge of the household and her younger brothers for several weeks while Elsie was in the southwest and Herbert was in Europe with the US army.[277] She also managed the household accounts for several years, a responsibility she disliked intensely.[278]

When she was home, Elsie played a typical maternal role — reading bedtime books with the younger boys, giving them swimming lessons, making a riddle book with Mac, escorting Lissa to dances.[279] But her pacifist views, liking for "negroes and Indians", and refusal to wear a hat embarrassed her older children, especially in front of their friends and their friends' mothers.[280] Her relationship with Lissa, her temperamental and intellectual opposite, was fraught for many years and repeated much of the generational conflict that characterized Elsie's relationship with her own mother. Elsie remained deeply disappointed that Lissa was not a feminist.[281]

Elsie's lifestyle from 1915 on was, in part, an adjustment to a troubled marriage. But it was more than that. She was implementing her ideas about protecting women's freedom, expressing individualism, and preserving love and passion. She would apply the same rules in

---

in France. (RHS, HP to Henry Clews, Jr., June 2, 1924 and undated cable; HP Vacation Memo, June 28, 1924.)

275 Herbert asked his legal secretary to give instructions to his Manhattan housekeeper (RHS, HP to Miss Doran, July 18, 1917; July 12, 1917; and July 13, 1917) and to send a birthday telegram to Lissa (August 6, 1917). Doran helped with arrangements for Lissa's wedding and mailed out the invitations (RHS, HP Folder: Correspondence re Yale Club 1921).

276 APS, ECP to HP, March 17, 1917 and March 20, 1917.

277 APS, Lissa Parsons to HP, February 2, 1918, and September 11, 1918; Kennedy, "Reminiscences," p. 21.

278 APS, Lissa Parsons to HP, September 26, 1919; June 22, 1920; February 28, 1921.

279 APS, ECP to HP, February 3, 1918; ECP to HP, April 15, 1918; ECP to HP, October 16, 1918.

280 APS, ECP to HP, June 17, 1917; John E. Parsons (son) to HP, April 9, 1917 and April 23, 1917; ECP notes for lecture on "Social Conventions."

281 Lissa dropped out of Bryn Mawr College after a year, married in 1921 when she was twenty, and had her first child a year later. Not a feminist: APS, Ralph L. Beals to Peter H. Hare, July 31, 1978 and December 19, 1978.

her romantic relationships with other men, holding both herself and them to high standards of behavior. After years of compromises and accommodations, she was constructing exactly the life she felt a modern woman should lead. When a male friend asserted that women were not meant to be scientists and it would be impossible for Elsie to escape from writing "social propaganda," Elsie proudly announced to Herbert, "Well, I have escaped, & forever."[282] She was escaping, not only from the strictures men placed on women professionals, but also from the constraints of a traditional marriage focused on domestic life.[283]

Gypsy, Goddess, Witch

In the 1910s and 1920s, Elsie turned to other men to find the intellectual companionship and romance that Herbert failed to provide. The architect Grant LaFarge, the anthropologist Alfred Kroeber, the novelist Robert Herrick, and the playwright Clarence Day all paid court to her, expressing their love in poetry and prose as well as letters. They wooed her with wit and charm, and romanticized her as something other worldly, exotic, even magical. To LaFarge, she was "my beloved Gypsy Queen" or an exotic mermaid. Herrick likened her to the lion-headed Egyptian goddess, Sekhmet. Kroeber called her a "lovely witch."[284]

Herbert had failed Elsie, not only by seeming to succumb to the charms of another woman, but also by being unable — or unwilling — to share her interests and discuss her unconventional views. Now entering her forties, she deliberately chose partners who showed a genuine interest in the work she was doing and the settings in which

---

282 APS, ECP to HP, November 6, 1918. The friend was Meredith Hare, whom Elsie had known since college days.

283 Elsie wanted to create opportunities for other women as well. She chastised her male colleagues for not awarding fellowships to women and expressing anti-feminist views (APS, ECP to A. L. Kroeber, March 26, 1929). She used her own money to fund a month of field research for a young scholar and mother who was caring for three stepsons and an infant daughter. The recipient, Esther Schiff Goldfrank, contrasted Elsie's support with Boas's opinion that motherhood was more important than anthropology. See Gloria Levitas, "Esther Schiff Goldfrank" in Ute Gacs et al., *Women Anthropologists: Selected Biographies* (Urbana: University of Illinois Press, 1989), pp. 120–26.

284 APS, Grant LaFarge to ECP, 24 July 1918; APS, A. L. Kroeber to ECP [1919?]. Sekhmet: quoted in Blake Nevius, *Robert Herrick: The Development of a Novelist* (Berkeley: University of California Press, 1962), p. 301.

she did it. None of these relationships is well-documented. Few of the men's letters to Elsie, and almost none of hers to them, have survived. We do not know how she felt about the men, but we know something about how she approached the relationships and how her partners felt about her.

The men who figured most prominently in Elsie's life after 1913 were, up to a point, supportive work partners and enthusiastic travel companions.[285] She embarked on a joint project with each of the men — another touchstone of romance and intimacy in her Greenwich Village milieu, which celebrated creative collaborations between lovers. Nevertheless, she did not let her romantic attachments interfere with her research or writing schedules. Nor would she surrender the freedom to come and go as she pleased and see whomever she wanted.

Grant LaFarge, the architect who played a major role in Elsie's life from 1913 into 1922, shared her love of the outdoors and her interest in Native American lore, camping, and canoeing.[286] He designed the log cabin where she wrote at Stonover Farm, and eagerly supported, discussed, and shared in her work.[287] At the very beginning of their relationship, he imagined a "fascinating little vision" of work done together.[288] Later, he happily recalled trips when she had worked while he fished. Dreaming of future trips where they would work side by side, he hoped "to do that work which more than any other brings me reward; to surround your work with pleasure, ease, with happiness; perhaps even with romance?"[289] When he accompanied her to the southwest, he made drawings, paintings, and photographs of the indigenous cultures she studied. They collaborated on *American Indian Life* (1922), a collection of native tales retold by leading anthropologists

---

285 The author Clarence Day (1874–1935), severely crippled by rheumatoid arthritis, was a close friend but apparently never a lover. After he published an affectionate sketch of Elsie as an intrepid folklorist (Clarence Day, "Portrait of a Lady", *New Republic*, July 23, 1919, 387–89), he explained, "I couldn't have done it just the way I did if I hadn't loved you [...]. I don't mean that I love you like a madman, or a husband, or anything. But I do love you more than as a friend." (APS, Clarence Day to ECP [1919?]) Day also expressed frustrated love for Elsie in light verse (APS, Clarence Day to ECP [n.d.]).

286 See Oliver Lafarge, *Behind the Mountains* (Boston: Houghton Mifflin, 1956). APS, ECP to HP, April 27, 1914.

287 Cabin: Kennedy, "Reminiscences", p. 24.

288 APS, Grant LaFarge to ECP, Tuesday, [n.d., 1913?].

289 APS, Grant LaFarge to ECP [n.d.].

that she edited and he illustrated.[290] They seem to have parted ways in 1922, but there is no surviving record that explains how or why this happened.

Shared work interests stimulated Elsie's relationships with Alfred Kroeber and Robert Herrick in their early stages, but both men ultimately felt that her devotion to her career was an insurmountable barrier to the intimacy they desired. A professor at the University of California at Berkeley, Kroeber was one of the anthropologists in Boas's inner circle who had encouraged Elsie to make a career in anthropology. Widowed in 1913, he was a leading anthropologist and a cosmopolitan intellectual, handsome, charismatic, and charming.[291] A strong friendship and the beginnings of a romance blossomed between him and Elsie in 1918, when he was on leave from the University of California and Herbert was in Europe with the US army. Alfred spent a good deal of time in Lenox and made himself popular with Elsie's children by teaching them "outrageous" forms of poker; he and Elsie were flattered to be asked to join John and his friends on a camping trip.[292] Alfred seems to have made a sexual overture to Elsie during the summer but had been rebuffed. He continued to write her affectionate letters and assured her she remained "#1" on his scorecard, although he knew he was lower down on hers.[293] (Both LaFarge and Day were also sending Elsie love poems and love letters during the summer of 1918.)

In the fall of 1918, Elsie and Kroeber went together to the Zuni pueblo in New Mexico where she studied the ceremonies and he, the language; they planned to write a joint paper on the comparative ceremonialism of the Pueblo peoples. Elsie wrote Herbert that she found the trip enjoyable and helpful for her work.[294] But Alfred was disappointed that she seemed more interested in her work than in him. He lamented,

---

290 ECP, ed. *American Indian Life: By Several of Its Students* (New York: Huebsch, 1922).
291 Two years younger than Elsie, he entered Columbia College in 1896 and earned his PhD under Boas in 1901. See Julian H. Steward, *Alfred Kroeber* (New York: Columbia University Press, 1973), and Theodora Kroeber, *Alfred Kroeber: A Personal Configuration* (Berkeley: University of California Press, 1970).
292 Trip with John: APS, ECP to HP, June 14, 1918. Outrageous poker games: Kennedy, "Reminiscences."
293 APS, A. L. Kroeber to ECP, July 23, 1918 and August 6, 1918.
294 APS, ECP to HP, September 26, 1918.

Haven't you made it a little hard for me, Elsie, to be as interested in you as I did want to be? Perhaps it was a defense, or an antipathy reaction produced by myself, that made you put work in the foreground when I was surely more interested in Elsie the person than in Elsie the anthropologist. Before long I got the impression that you wanted nothing between us but shop.[295]

The collaborative project was never finished, and their friendship waned after Alfred returned to Berkeley, although they saw each other from time to time in New York.[296]

By the time Elsie became involved, in the fall of 1923, with Robert Herrick, a popular and critically acclaimed novelist, she was quite explicit about how she expected a romantic partner to relate to her work. She wanted what she had never gotten from Herbert. "Each is to contribute to the systematic pursuits of the other, and with real interest not merely with patience and long-suffering," she explained as they were preparing for a long trip in 1925. The dividends of such behavior would be substantial, she assured Robert. "By showing her that he is really interested in her doing good work, not merely tolerant of her working, and that he wants to contribute to her work as work she is sure to feel a spontaneous kind of gratitude that may surprise him by its expressiveness," Elsie promised.[297]

For a time, the relationship provided what Elsie sought. Robert, a widower with a grown son, accompanied her on lengthy research trips to the Southwest, the Caribbean, and Mexico. They had many interests in common: modern womanhood, marriage, and gender relations were central themes in his novels, and he was knowledgeable about race relations and Caribbean island cultures.[298]

They planned to collaborate on a book (tentatively titled "Tides") that would contrast the sexual experiences and perspectives of an older couple like themselves (Robert was fifty-seven and Elsie, forty-nine,

---

295 APS, A. L. Kroeber to ECP, Tuesday [n.d., likely fall 1918]. More on his disappointed hopes: APS, A. L. Kroeber to ECP, October 9, 1918; December 12, 1918; and February 22, 1919.
296 APS, A. L. Kroeber to ECP, January 26, 1920 and May 24, 1920.
297 RH Papers, ECP to RH, "Memorandum for Travel in the World and in Life."
298 Herrick's early books are regarded as perceptive illustrations of changing social mores in America in the early twentieth century. See Nevius, viii–ix, and Christopher Lasch, *The New Radicalism in America, 1889–1963: The Intellectual as a Social Type* (New York: Alfred A. Knopf, 1966), pp. 39–43.

when their affair began in 1923) with those of a younger generation. For the youth perspective, they would draw on the lives of their adult children. Elsie had long been interested in the role a novelist could play in promoting new norms of social behavior.[299] Now she had an opportunity to see such work at close hand and help to shape it. She wrote comments on Robert's drafts and contributed chapter outlines and notes for their joint book.[300] In one of the scenes she wrote, the female character who represents her tells her lover, who is based on Robert, "it's more fun talking to you than to anybody."[301]

Although Robert would come to see their relationship as exceedingly one-sided, it was nevertheless stimulating for his work as well as for Elsie's. He had a reputation for basing his plots and characters on the lives of the people he knew, and Elsie provided him with enormously rich material at a time when he felt his career was at its lowest ebb.[302] The novel he had published in 1922 — his first in seven years — had not been well-reviewed and sold poorly.[303] When he met Elsie, he was fearful of being displaced by younger writers with fresher ideas. With her, he found new focus and new energy. He produced *Wanderings* (1925), a book of four lengthy short stories, including "The Adventures of Ti Chatte" and "Stations of the Cross"; *Chimes* (1926), a novel about the early years of the University of Chicago; and early versions of the material that was meant to be in "Tides", but would eventually be used in *The End of Desire* (1932). All these books explored modern womanhood, and all featured Elsie as a major character. In addition, he wrote numerous drafts of "The Story of Jessica Stowe," fleshing out the personality of the female character who embodied Elsie, in different guises and under different names, in the fiction he published between 1925 and 1932.

Robert was deeply in love with Elsie and fascinated by her as the epitome of a modern woman. In his depictions, she is beautiful, charming and alluring, adventurous and physically fearless, relentless

---

299 ECP, *Journal of a Feminist*, pp. 44–45. Herrick felt similarly about the role of the novelist. RH Papers, "What Women Say about Themselves."

300 RH Papers, "Tides." Typescript text with handwritten notes by ECP.

301 RH Papers, ECP notes for the chapter entitled "Pigeon Cove."

302 RH Papers, "Diary of an Intravert [sic]."

303 RH Papers, Alfred Harcourt to RH, August 2, 1922 and November 26, 1924; RH to Robert Morss Lovett, April 20 [1924].

in challenging convention and old-fashioned thinking — but also aloof, independent, insistent on her individuality, ruthless in getting her own way, reprehensibly focused on her work, and impervious to the pain she causes others. His fiction and diaries chart the progress of their affair and his changing view of her as their relationship deteriorated. As he grew more frustrated, and more despairing about their future, his depictions of Elsie became harsher and more unflattering. In the end, he portrayed her as a model of modern womanhood that was to be avoided rather than emulated.

Elsie envisioned a companionate relationship with Robert that would free both of them from traditional gender roles and allow them to preserve separate identities. But having no models for the kind of connection she aimed for, she acted what others regarded as the male part. Robert saw a role reversal and resented taking on the traditionally female role. Writing about Elsie as the model for the character Jessica Stowe, Robert described her "manlike" qualities: she does exactly as she pleases with no consideration for others, puts her work above all else, and brings more passion to her science than to her relationships. He knows that if she were a man these traits "would have been considered wholly admirable."[304] But as the lover of such a woman, he feels distressed and demeaned by her behavior. He chafes at taking on the supporting role that the wives and female partners of male professionals of this era were conditioned to accept. His diaries record a litany of complaints: he has to cater to her whims, follow her lead, fit himself around her convenience and schedules. She does not give him the time, attention, or sympathy that he craves. And yet, he finds it impossible to resist her charms.

In another reversal of traditional gender roles, Elsie focused on her work, while Robert focused on creating the conditions in which she could work. At first, he happily took charge of the logistical arrangements for their trips, arranging for their food and lodging, and hiring and outfitting their boats. But less than a year into their relationship, he likened himself to a "kept lover, always on tap when she wanted and ignored the rest of the time." The experience of "subordinating myself to her somewhat whimsical will, taking whatever she feels like giving"

---

304 RH Papers, "The Story of Jessica Stowe", pp. 68–69.

left him feeling "degrade[d]."[305] Affronted by Elsie's "very great absorption in her professional work — and her vanity about it and all its perquisites," he became increasingly resentful about serving as her "housekeeper, cook, and manager" — tasks he had voluntarily taken on in the hope of making himself indispensable to her.[306] Struggling with impotence in 1924, a problem he blamed on Elsie's "emotional sterility," he feared he could not satisfy her sexually.[307]

Robert summed up his understanding of the part he was expected to play in Elsie's life shortly before they sailed to the West Indies in February 1925. He believed he was supposed to "efface himself when not wanted by Dr. E. C. P." and "subordinate all and any of his interests to the pursuit of Folk Lore [and] assist in every possible way the accomplishment of the objective of the Field Trip, — especially in regard to arranging for transportation, accommodations, baggage, etc." In addition, "when Dr. P is occupied with folklore" he was "not in any way to obtrude upon her notice, nor expect attention, consideration, personal or amatory."[308] Robert's choice of verbs is revealing: he was to efface, subordinate, not obtrude. In short, he felt he was expected to be wholly submissive to Elsie — yet another reversal of traditional gender roles. By addressing her in an impersonal memo and referring to himself and her in the third person, Robert was imitating Elsie's style. She responded with a memorandum of her own, but she softened the effect by using their pet names. Explaining that he should not feel "she is being perverse and indifferent when she declines to play with him", she warned that "clashes of time and place may have to be met by temporary separations to which no emotional meaning is attached."[309] Her explanation did little to reassure him or quell his resentment.

Robert's growing hostility to Elsie was also fueled by professional jealousy. She was in demand as a social critic even after she switched her main focus to anthropology, while Robert, who wrote about many of the same themes, felt unappreciated. She contributed an article for *The Nation*'s series on "Our Changing Morality" and gave an address ("Is

305 RH Papers, "Diary of an Intravert [sic]", January 24, 1924, January 27, 1924, and February 4, 1924.
306 Ibid., January 24, 1924.
307 Ibid.
308 RH Papers, RH to ECP, "Field Trip, Number Three", 1925.
309 RH Papers, ECP to RH, "Memorandum for Travel in the World and in Life", 1925.

Monogamy Possible?") at the public dinner the magazine hosted in 1924. Robert, who attended as Elsie's guest, admired her performance but sourly dismissed the evening as a "half-baked journalistic concoction."[310]

More fundamentally, their conflict grew out of their contrasting ideas about love. Elsie explicitly rejected the nineteenth-century ideal of "oneness" that expected a woman to submerge herself in the beloved and find her identity and purpose in loving him. She wanted "Tides" to illustrate how the love between a woman and a man produces a new sense of joint identity. Her theme for the chapter on "Creation" was: "The sense of life created as a child by both, nourished by both, shared in by both, making something in which both participate something which is held in common, but is not a merging, submission of one to the other."[311] A chapter on "Union" would show that "the unitary idea of merged personality — is fundamentally false. Not only is such a complete absorption of one personality by another or the transformation of two personalities into one impossible, it would be a dreary and impoverished state of being."[312]

Early in their relationship, Robert had expressed similar views. In 1923, he wrote about love as "a union of souls, yet a jealous preserving of individuality [...]. It is, in reality a doubling of life and purpose with a single unity of feeling."[313] Nevertheless, his fiction and journals suggests that he believed love has to be all encompassing and all absorbing, and that the woman has to submit to the man. Each of his male protagonists wants to be a romantic hero whose love awakens his beloved to sexual delight, melts the harshness and iciness of her personality, and transforms her into a true woman — a woman who is gentle, loving, and nurturing. Like so many men and women of this era, Robert seemed unable to free himself from this romantic ideal of a strong man who overpowers a weak, dependent woman.

The dramatic tension in his fictional accounts of his affair with Elsie arises from the protagonist's attempts to break down what Thomas Lapin, the hero of "The Adventures of Ti Chatte" calls the "terrible self-sufficiency" of his lover, subsume her, and transform her through his

---

310 RH Papers, "Diary of an Intravert [sic]", January 24, 1924.
311 RH Papers, "Tides" [1925].
312 RH Papers, Chapter "The Ebb", in "Tides" [1925].
313 RH Papers, "Passion, Love, Marriage — all or none?" (1923).

love.[314] In Herrick's view, these relationships fail because the woman cannot love or give of herself, not because the hero asks too much. The independence of the heroine in "The Stations of the Cross" elicits in the narrator a physical and violent compulsion to bend her to his will. He feels driven by the need

> to discover this glowing inner coal of passion within himself, to penetrate her cool aloofnesss — to possess and exult. The very whiteness and coldness of the woman, denying him, refusing to be drawn into the circle of his will, to become one with him [...] now tempted him to violence. He looked steadily, stilly at her, like a serpent. And she met his gaze as if fascinated by some new power, feeling herself drawn irresistibly out of her isolation into the circle of his will.[315]

In Robert's notes for the book that became *Chimes*, the poet who loves Jessica Stowe Mallory, the character modelled on Elsie, finally recognizes the futility of his love because "he did not elicit the woman he dreamed from the actual Jessica and he fails to persuade her [,]the actual Jessica[,] to find her fulfillment in or through him."[316] He ultimately recoils from the woman's "exaltation of work above love" and her insistence on preserving a sense of self, independent from him. This theme is replayed in *The End of Desire*, Robert's final novel about Elsie. The heroine, Serena Massey, is a thinly disguised Elsie; Arnold Redfield, her lover, is based on Robert. Massey, a highly successful psychologist, is "aloof," "cool," and "self-contained." Redfield, a professional colleague, is both angered and wounded by the recognition that she and he "are not 'one': she the individualist, had never let him forget that for a moment!" In contrast, Redfield feels a "complete absorption" in Massey.[317]

In a reversal of traditional gender roles, Redfield does for Massey what a woman typically does for a man. While she fits him into a busy schedule of professional engagements, family responsibilities, and travel, he sacrifices all his other interests, including professional opportunities, so he is free to see her whenever she desires. He devotes himself to providing the "cherishing care of her person and her spirit, which he

314 RH, "The Adventures of Ti Chatte" in *Wanderings* (New York: Harcourt Brace, 1925), p. 211.
315 RH, "Stations of the Cross" in *Wanderings* (New York: Harcourt Brace, 1925), p. 87.
316 RH Papers, "Jessica at Fifty."
317 RH, *The End of Desire* (New York: Farrar and Rinehart, 1932), pp. 6–7, 281–82, 286.

had made a cult."[318] While she works on her scholarly articles, he types her manuscripts and sees to lunch; when they travel together, he makes all the practical arrangements and devotes himself to providing for her comfort. He has an ulterior motive: he practices subordination in order to create dependency and establish power and control.

Robert's growing antagonism colored his depiction of Elsie the professional as well as his portrayal of Elsie the woman. Although he initially admired Elsie's work, the more he felt controlled by her, the more he denigrated it. When he began writing about Elsie as the character Jessica, he planned to make her a brilliant research scientist, distinguished by her intellectual passion and her "selfless" dedication and commitment to her work. But he ultimately decided to portray Jessica as "a curious second rate scientist without an originating idea, but industrious as a gather [sic] of facts." He likens her absorption in "computation, proof reading, summary cross referencing" to the sewing or knitting that occupies other women.[319]

Herrick's ambivalence about Elsie's career, his vision of "oneness," his desire to make himself indispensable and forge intimacy out of her weakness and dependence, are reminiscent of George Herbert Palmer's relationship with Alice Freeman Palmer. (See Chapter 1.) George, a cousin of Robert Herrick's mother, was an early mentor to Robert. The novelist knew both George and Alice well: he was a frequent guest at Boxford, a colleague of Alice's at the University of Chicago, and their travel companion in Europe in 1895. Both Alice and Elsie are featured in *Chimes* (1926), Robert's novel about the early years of the University of Chicago.[320] Alice (transposed to a widow instead of an absentee wife) appears as the beloved Dean of Women, Edith Crandall. Crandall's warmth, generosity of spirit, old-fashioned ideals and womanliness contrasts with the "intellectual passion" and "emotional sterility" displayed by Jessica Stowe Mallory, the married psychology scholar who is based on Elsie.

Herrick was not the only man who felt threatened by Elsie's self-reliance and saw her as unwomanly despite her charm and beauty. The

---

318　Ibid, p. 279.
319　RH Papers, "The Story of Jessica Stowe", pp. [2], 69; "Jessica Stowe, 3rd version."
320　RH, *Chimes* (New York: Macmillan, 1926). RH Papers, Robert Morss Lovett to Allen T. Hazen, February 24, 1947.

images that Elsie's lovers and admirers used to describe her — mermaid, witch, goddess — suggest menace as well as magic. Mermaids lure men to their death; witches are evil; goddesses ruin the lives of mere mortals. Such beings are dangerous because they are not bound by the ordinary conventions of civilization. Elsie's male admirers also found her deficient in the stereotypically female traits of compassion and tenderness. LaFarge avoided turning to Elsie for comfort when he was depressed, explaining, "I'm in that primitive male state where I want petting & I've a feeling that you have no use for such critturs."[321] Kroeber characterized her as a woman hardened by experience, "scarred" by "her long fight for self-preservation."[322] In the aftermath of their trip to Zuni, he felt it necessary to remind her to be "kind" and not "harsh" with him.[323]

Robert was hardest on Elsie. He presents her, in the character Serena Massey in *The End of Desire*, as a woman who takes but never gives. She is heedless of how her behavior affects those closest to her (her family as well as her lovers) and indifferent to the inconvenience that others suffer on her behalf; she uses her admirers and then discards them. He views her efforts to balance her time between her lover, her family, and her work as reprehensibly egocentric; he equates her reserve and self-sufficiency with frigidity. He depicts her as a woman devoid of softness or tenderness, despite her charm and sexual appeal. He expressed the same mixture of attraction and distaste in his journal when he compared Elsie to the Egyptian goddess Sekhmet. "Sekhmet [...] the lion-headed one, was worshipped more in fear than in love. She was stern, ruthless, remote from human feebleness of will and purpose. Inexorable — and yet a woman and lovely! Like my Sekhmet [...]. Something more than mere woman, something less, too."[324] "Ruthless", "brutal", "hard" are recurring epithets in Herrick's descriptions of Elsie.[325]

Both Herrick and Kroeber admired Elsie's accomplishments and enjoyed the intellectual stimulation she provided. But they were put off by her independence and resented having to compete with her work for her attention. Not surprisingly, their subsequent romantic

---

321 APS, Grant LaFarge to ECP [n.d., 1913?].
322 APS, A. L. Kroeber to ECP, Christmas [1920?].
323 APS, A. L. Kroeber to ECP, Christmas [1920?] and February 12, 1921.
324 Quoted in Nevius, p. 301.
325 RH Papers, "Forward to Jessica", pp. 1–3.

partners were quite different from Elsie. In 1926, when he was fifty, Alfred Kroeber married one of his graduate students, a twenty-nine-year-old widow with two small children. Theodora Kracaw Kroeber gave up anthropology when they married so she could devote herself to her family and support her husband's career. Alfred Kroeber's (male) biographer describes her as "an ideal wife" whose devoted care was instrumental in Alfred's professional success. Among other things, she served dinner to their four young children in their rooms "rather than impose them on Kroeber." Theodora pursued her own successful career as a writer and anthropologist only after the children were grown and Alfred had retired.[326]

Herrick's subsequent romantic history was an equally emphatic rejection of Elsie and her values. After their affair ended, he retreated to the pampering care of his devoted housekeeper, and then had an affair with a married woman who did not have a career. He continued to write unflattering portraits of career women in his novels and praised the kind of woman he dubbed the "Gretchens" of the world — women who understood what it meant to sacrifice their work for a loved one, especially a man.[327]

Many of the men and women Elsie knew in Greenwich Village underwent similar struggles and ultimately failed to free themselves from the old-fashioned concepts of love and gender that they railed against in their journalism and fiction. Max Eastman, Floyd Dell, and Hutchins Hapgood, for example, initially sought female partners who were talented, intellectual, and independent. But after tempestuous relationships with such women, Eastman and Dell each settled for a woman who gave up her own aspirations and happily devoted herself to making him a home and supporting his career.[328]

---

326 Steward, *Alfred Kroeber*, pp. 18–19, 22; Grace Wilson Buzaljko, "Theodora Kracaw Kroeber", in Gacs et al., pp. 187–93. See also, Theodora Kroeber, *Alfred Kroeber*.

327 RH Papers, "My Last Book" (January 1928). For his life and relationships after parting from Elsie, see Nevius, pp. 311–27.

328 See Ellen K. Trimberger, "Feminism, Men and Modern Love" in *Powers of Desire* by Ann Snitow et al. (New York: Monthly Review Press, 1983), pp. 131–52. "I'll be anything you want me to be — sister, sweetheart, secretary, slave — I'll be your mother if that is what you want," the Russian artist Eliana Krylenko promised Max Eastman. After they married, Eastman proudly reported that she "kept house, typed my manuscripts, and washed my shirts in a cold well." Krylenko continued

In contrast, Elsie stuck to her principles and tried to get her male partners to honor them. That this proved no easier with her lovers than her husband shows that patriarchal beliefs and behaviors were as deeply embedded in the psyches of individuals as in the institutions of early twentieth-century life. As Elsie would learn, a simple reversal of gender stereotypes and activities engendered its own problems and was potentially no more satisfying than a more traditional division of work and domestic activities.

War on the Home Front

Elsie's relationship with Herbert remained strained throughout the teens. He knew when she was traveling with a man, but her letters never discussed her relationships with the men, and he did not comment on them. As a passionate and long-term pacifist, Elsie was both outraged and pitying when Herbert volunteered at the age of forty-eight for a job with the US army in the summer of 1917.[329] She had vociferously denounced American involvement in the war, railed against the militarism and jingoism that swept the country, and protested the suppression of free speech on academic campuses and in the press.[330] Herbert called their Lenox home the "headquarters of pacifism."[331]

Commissioned as a major, Herbert expressed the masculine love of war that Elsie deplored. He welcomed the challenge of "doing one's job to the limit" and reveled in the "excitement" war service brought to his life.[332] He spent six months at the Army Training College before sailing to France in January 1918 where he was attached to the Headquarters of the Fifth Division of the US Infantry. One of the few officers who spoke German, he interrogated German prisoners of war in France, and

---

to paint, but only as a hobby. "I love to see you play at all kinds of work so vividly," Eastman observed with patronizing approval (Trimberger, p. 146). For a positive portrait of how the writers Hutchins Hapgood and Neil Boyce managed to combine work and love in their marriage, see Eby, pp. 135–69.

329　APS, ECP to HP, August 21, 1917.
330　See Hare, pp. 107–21, and Deacon, pp. 184–86.
331　HP to ECP, June 11, 1917, quoted in Hare, p. 108.
332　APS, HP to ECP, June 20, 1917; HP to ECP, November 21, 1917; HP to the children, January 25, 1918.

went to Germany with the army of occupation after the armistice. He returned to the States in March 1919.[333]

Elsie and Herbert had a number of angry exchanges about the war while he was in Europe, but they eventually found some accommodation. By the summer of 1918, she had relaxed her ban against military dress in her home and moderated her denunciations against the war.[334] Away from the family, Herbert waxed nostalgic and sentimental. Writing to the children on Mother's Day 1918, he described how he and Elsie met and fell in love, and he praised the "foresight and intelligent care" she had invested in their upbringing.[335] Shortly before his division was expecting to see action in September 1918, he wrote Elsie a heartfelt farewell letter that expressed his love and made clear that he valued her for what she valued in herself: "So grateful too have I been for the stimulation to honest effort & the challenge to straight thinking you have always been, even if at times I may not have seemed appreciative of it."[336]

The longer Herbert was in Europe, the more critical he grew of the army's emphasis on bureaucracy, rank, and obedience — views that would have resonated with Elsie.[337] Convinced that wars had to be prevented as well as waged, he resigned from the Republican Party in September 1920 when it failed to support the League of Nations. This ended his political career and earned him public denunciations from prominent Republicans, including a cousin who was his law partner.[338] Unpopular but principled actions were Herbert's hallmark. He refused to be associated with a fundraiser for Greenwich House because it involved a Sunday night theatrical performance, a practice that violated his religious principles.[339] He did not join the American Bar Association in 1913 because he believed it excluded lawyers of color.[340] Nevertheless,

---

333 RHS, HP memos to his office, January 25, 1918 and November 15, 1918.
334 Relaxed the ban: APS, ECP to HP, August 20, 1918.
335 APS, HP to the children, enclosure in HP to ECP, May 12, 1918.
336 RHS, HP to ECP, September 10, 1918.
337 APS, HP to ECP, November 20, 1918.
338 RHS, HP to Chairman of the Joint Committee on Printing, September 1, 1925 and clipping from *The New York Times*, October 18, 1920.
339 RHS, HP to Mabel F. Spinner, October 4, 1919.
340 RHS, HP to Charles A. Boston, July 16, 1913 and July 18, 1913.

he was aghast when he learned that Elsie brought a Black man home to tea in 1921.[341]

Herbert said that his law practice and volunteer activities kept him very busy, but time may have hung heavy on his hands after he gave up his political work.[342] He admitted to being lonely and welcomed visits from family members when Elsie was away.[343] He developed a passion for horticulture and landscaping, and did much of the gardening at Lounsberry and Stonover Farm himself.[344] He remained very fussy about things being done right and fired off letters of complaint about trains that were delayed, overcrowded, or overheated; telegrams that were not delivered on time; shipments of Lenox produce that were not properly packaged; and department store orders that were improperly filled.[345]

During the 1910s and 1920s, Herbert enjoyed a friendship with Vira Boarman Whitehouse, a woman more like Elsie than like Lucy Wilson. Born in 1875, Vira was a debutante and Southern belle who grew up in New Orleans and attended Sophie Newcomb College. She married the stockbroker Norman de R. Whitehouse and had one daughter. She was a member of Heterodoxy, President of the New York State Woman's Suffrage Party, and a proponent of birth control. As a suffragist leader, she raised large donations from wealthy men, implemented an expensive advertising campaign, and linked the suffrage cause to the war effort.[346] In 1918, she became the director of the Swiss Office of the US Committee on Public Information, which combatted German propaganda and promoted American war aims in Europe. Her book,

341 Their son, John, described Herbert's agitation to Elsie. APS, John E. Parsons to ECP, January 26, 1921.
342 RHS, HP to Col. Goodson, November 20, 1922.
343 RHS, HP to John E. Parsons, January 20, 1924.
344 Descriptions of Herbert's gardening interests and activities abound in his correspondence in the 1920s in RHS. For example, HP to T. A. Havemeyer, January 15, 1920; HP to Charles Berndt, April 22, 1922.
345 RHS: Trains: HP letter of December 27, 1916. Merchandise: HP to Wanamakers, January 2, 1922 and January 4, 1922. Produce: HP to Stonover staff, 1925. Postal service: HP to Post Office [October 1915].
346 Although the *New Republic* and other contemporary sources credited her with winning New York State's endorsement of women's suffrage in 1917, Vira and the wealthy women she worked with were successfully "airbrushed" out of many accounts of the struggle, Johanna Neuman argues in *Gilded Suffragists: The New York Socialites Who Fought for Women's Right to Vote* (New York: New York University Press, 2017), p. 142.

A Year as a Government Agent, detailed the obstacles she encountered as
the first woman to hold such a position. In 1921, she bought a leather
business, reorganized it, made herself president, and managed it for
eight years before selling it.[347]

Vira and her husband had attended Elsie and Herbert's wedding,
but her close relationship with Herbert developed when both were
active in the women's suffrage movement. They often appeared on the
same public platforms and participated in the same back room strategy
discussions. She also served with Herbert on the board of Greenwich
House.[348] At the end of 1915 and beginning of 1916, he dined frequently
with her, during a time when Lucy Wilson seems to have faded out of
his personal life after her divorce in November 1915.[349]

Wartime service took both Vira and Herbert to Europe in 1918–1919.
The summer after Herbert returned from the war, Vira asked for his
legal advice about suing *The New York Times* for publishing articles that
she believed were a deliberate effort to make her look "ridiculous."[350]
(He advised her not to sue.) Two letters in Herbert's files suggest their

347 Schlesinger Library, Harvard University, Papers of Vira Boarman Whitehouse,
    "Finding Aid"; Lauren Claire West, "The Uneasy Beginnings of Public Diplomacy:
    Vira Whitehouse, the Committee on Public Information, and the First World
    War" (unpublished MA thesis 4718: Louisiana State University, 2018). https://
    digitalcommons.lsu.edu/gradschool_theses/4718/
348 The Whitehouses were listed as guests at Elsie and Herbert's wedding in 1900. See
    "Miss Clews is Married", *The New York Times*, September 2, 1900. Vira served with
    Herbert on the Board of Greenwich House in 1914. (Tracy Briggs, "Twenty Years
    at Greenwich House" (unpublished PhD thesis: The University of Toledo, 2008),
    https://www.proquest.com/openview/f8c206869eee0373717a42fec748b050/1?pq-
    origsite=gscholar&cbl=18750) In 1916, Herbert gave a speech at a Cooper Union
    meeting on women's suffrage that Vira presided over as Chairman of the New York
    State Woman Suffrage Party (RHS, HP 1916).
349 RHS, HP Diaries, 1915 and 1916. After her divorce, Lucy took the name Mrs.
    Lucy Wortham James, and maintained an apartment in New York and a house in
    Newport. She served on the boards of both the Memorial Hospital and Greenwich
    House along with Herbert in the 1910s and 1920s. He rarely recorded appointments
    with her in his engagement calendars after her divorce. She wrote him several letters
    in 1918 when he was serving with the US army in France and she was in England.
    In one very long, very rambling, somewhat incoherent letter written while she was
    sailing back the States, she nostalgically recalled happy times in Washington during
    1909 and 1910 — the period when Elsie was overcome with jealousy of Lucy. Lucy
    posed two direct questions: "Do you want letters or do they irk you?" and "What
    address?" (APS, Lucy James to HP, March 28, 1918.) There are no additional letters
    from Lucy in Herbert's papers, but they continued to serve together on the boards
    of the Memorial Hospital and Greenwich House after he returned from Europe.
350 RHS, HP memos to Vira Boarman Whitehouse, June 19, 1919 and June 20, 1919.

relationship was affectionate. Vira wrote from Newport, "I've seen Mrs. James. She is lonely but so very fragile she makes me feel like a great coarse over-healthy fat woman over-flowing with vitality. I suppose there is no use to ask you to come up for a Sunday? I wish you could. Yours — until 1957 — was it? Vira B. W." Herbert responded that he was spending his weekends in Lenox, but expected to be in Newport on weekends in August. "What would my family say if I stayed away now, for a weekend visit to a fat lady in Newport? And one who is against the GOP."[351] (The "Mrs. James" Vira mentions was very likely Lucy Wilson.)

Herbert frequently mentioned Vira in his letters to Elsie in the 1920s, noting when they dined together or attended concerts and plays. It is impossible to know whether their relationship was a friendship or an affair. There is no evidence to suggest that Elsie suffered the pangs of jealousy over Vira that she had endured over Lucy.[352] Elsie would not have approved of Vira's decision to win support for women's suffrage by linking it to support for the American war effort. But she might have been pleased that Herbert chose a companion who was an activist and a feminist who rejected the idea that a woman's place was in the home.

Rapprochement between Elsie and Herbert

Despite their differences and despite — or possibly because of — their other attachments, Elsie and Herbert's relationship improved in the early 1920s. Their letters became chattier, more affectionate, and less angry. Instead of coming up with reasons to avoid seeing Herbert, Elsie accepted his invitations and proposed additional occasions to be together. They stayed more frequently at the same residence, had more of a joint social life, and took their younger sons on joint vacations. Traveling in the southwest, Nova Scotia, and Europe, they shared staterooms and hotel rooms. Nevertheless, Elsie fiercely guarded her freedom to come and go as she pleased. She frequently did not let her family know when she would be returning from a field trip; she repeatedly informed

---

351 RHS, Vira Boarman Whitehouse to HP, July 10, 1919; HP to Vira Boarman Whitehouse, July 14, 1919.
352 However, in keeping with her "principle of not crowding family life", Elsie decided not to attend an event at St. Paul's School when she learned that Vira would be accompanying Herbert to it (APS, ECP to John E. Parsons, June 3, 1921).

Herbert that her plans to join him had changed or were likely to change
at the last minute; and she often tacked a separate trip for herself on to
a family vacation.[353] And she continued to take trips with Grant LaFarge
and with Robert Herrick.

During this more tranquil period, the Parsons recaptured the habits
that had enriched their early marriage: they were respectful of each
other's concerns, found compromises that honored their differences,
and tried to please each other. After visiting her mother before leaving
on a lengthy field trip, Elsie reported to Herbert, "[I] called on Mama
yesterday to say goodbye and please you both."[354] They also recovered
some of the teasing affection that characterized their first years together.
Informing a friend about the schedule for a proposed visit from him and
the younger boys, Herbert noted that Elsie's plans were still up in the air.
"If there are Indians, colored people or Hindus she will prefer to spend
her time folk-loring them," he warned.[355] Herbert tried to take the sting
out of the younger boys' criticisms of Elsie by recounting how other sons
treated their parents during his recent visit to St Paul's School.[356]

Now, as earlier, the Parsons were most powerfully connected through
their roles as parents. Mutual concern about the older children — Lissa's
unhappy marriage and John's future as a lawyer — and mutual delight
in the younger boys' exploits brought them closer together.[357] Other
developments also eased tensions. Herbert's willingness to accept Elsie's
rules about her work and relationships, his increased involvement
with the children, his loving tributes from Europe, the difficulties that
developed in Elsie's other relationships: all undoubtedly helped to make
Elsie more appreciative of Herbert. She would later tell their eldest son,
John, "There was never anything like Father's welcome. I always wanted

---

353 Social life and living arrangements: RHS, HP to Major J. B. Barnes, March 9, 1922,
     and undated telegrams from ECP and HP. Trips together: RHS, HP memo to ECP,
     June 27, 1922; HP Vacation Memo, June 28, 1924. Separate trips for Elsie: RHS: HP
     to Henry Clews, Jr., 1923; HP to Charles Sheldon, June 12, 1923 and July 8, 1923, and
     HP memo to ECP, June 27, 1922.
354 RHS, ECP to HP, Thurs AM [n.y. 1925?].
355 RHS, HP to Charles Sheldon, June 12, 1923, and July 8, 1923.
356 RHS, HP to ECP, November 12, 1923.
357 Younger boys: RHS, ECP to HP, Sunday [n.y.]; [August 18, 1925] and [August 21,
     1925]. Lissa's marriage: RHS, Lissa to HP, April 10, 1924; July 29 [1924]; August 12
     [1925]. John's future: Lissa to HP, May 21, 1925.

to come back to it. He was so plainly glad to have me back and was so much nicer than other people I might have been seeing."[358]

In the midst of this rapprochement with Elsie, Herbert suffered a freak accident. In September 1925, when he was showing his youngest son, Mac, how to ride a new motorbike, the vehicle overturned, landed on top of Herbert, and ruptured his kidney. Elsie was in Lenox with the family when the accident occurred. She spent the next two days at the hospital with Herbert, who was conscious until close to the end. Herbert, Jr. reported that the only time he saw Elsie cry was when she returned to tell the family that Herbert had died.[359]

Nevertheless, Elsie did not reveal her emotions in public. The town of Lenox put on something like a state funeral for Herbert. All the shops in the town closed; church bells tolled fifty-five times, one for each year of Herbert's life; Stonover employees carried his casket; and local residents turned out en masse.[360] Elsie, who felt that "death has always meant the end", chose not to attend. On the day of the funeral, she and the younger boys lunched with Walter Lippmann, a founding editor of *The New Republic* who had served with Herbert in Europe in World War I. Lippmann said that Herbert's name was never mentioned during the meal.[361] Had she been on her own, Elsie noted, she would have taken off for the southwest as soon as Herbert died. She stayed long enough to get her sons off to school, but missed the christening of Lissa's second child.[362]

Elsie's Final Years

Herbert's death upended Elsie's life in very significant ways. It removed a critical source of emotional ballast. With Herbert gone, she spent more time with the family and became more involved in the children's lives. The year after Herbert died, she bought a house in North Haven, Maine, which became her home base in summers. During the rest of the year,

---

358 APS, ECP to John E. Parsons, September 4, 1930.
359 RHS, Elsie's account of Herbert's death, dated September 22, 1925. Seeing Elsie cry: Hare, p. 66.
360 "Services for Parsons Here and in Lenox," *The New York Times*, September 19, 1925. There was also a service for Herbert at the Brick Memorial Church in Manhattan.
361 Funeral and lunch: Hare, p. 167; friendship: Kennedy, "Reminiscences".
362 ECP to Mabel Dodge Luhan, October 13, 1925, quoted in Zumwalt, p. 92. See also Deacon, p. 300.

she made her home with her children and relied on female relatives to take care of her domestic needs. From 1927 to 1935, she lived mostly with John and his wife Fanny at Lounsberry, where Fanny happily ran the household. After Lissa remarried in 1935 and moved to Lenox, she and Elsie developed a closer relationship. Elsie spent time with her every fall, and moved into Lissa's Manhattan apartment, sharing it with her son, Mac, for a few years. Lissa helped manage the apartment, and Elsie also had the services of two maids and a secretary.[363]

Elsie's relationship with Robert Herrick deteriorated after Herbert's death. Between 1926 and 1928, they spent time together in New York, New England, and Maine, and he accompanied her on lengthy and adventurous research trips to Egypt and the Sudan, the Caribbean, and Majorca. His "angry feeling of smothered resentment" that he was "being used as a convenience" intensified. His efforts to win her over by serving as "housekeeper" when they traveled "went for naught," he complained.[364] He wanted to spend more time with her, and even marry her, but this is not what she wanted. She was busy with her work, more involved with her children, and wary as ever about the deleterious effects of marriage.[365] Their affair ended sometime in 1928, when Robert was writing *The End of Desire*, his final, highly unflattering, account of Elsie and their relationship.

Elsie, who did not read the novel before its 1932 publication, contemptuously dismissed it as bad portraiture and a "dull book."[366] She complained to her eldest son, John, "Why a woman described directly as self-centered does not marry a man described indirectly as self-centered is to him a theme. Besides you are wondering all the time why he wanted to marry such a prig and why he felt so sorry for himself." She found Robert's depictions of her mother and her children "perverse and grotesque" and hoped they would not recognize themselves. If she felt betrayed and hurt by Robert's hostile portrait, she did not dwell on

363 For Elsie's domestic arrangements, see Hare, p. 140, and Deacon, pp. 353, 367.
364 RH Papers, "Leaves from the Diary of a Wanderer," 1926, 1927.
365 Deleterious effects of marriage: ECP to Mabel Dodge Luhan, May 8, 1923. Copy in APS.
366 Herrick finished writing *End of Desire* in 1930, but had trouble finding a publisher due to concerns that the book would cause a scandal and the female protagonist (Elsie) would be easily identifiable. One editor advised him to publish it under a pseudonym. RH Papers, RH to Robert Morss Lovett, 18 May 1930; 24 May 1930; and 22 March 1931; Nevius, pp. 305–06, 319–20.

it, although she admitted, "It does leave a bad taste in my mouth about the writer, and I am not surprised that even if he did not think it was portraiture he was disinclined to see me while he was writing it."[367]

Elsie's anthropological explorations took her to the Caribbean, the southwest, Central America, and South America in the 1930s and 1940s, but her traveling companions were younger colleagues or her sons. She went on many field trips alone. She had at least one more romance, but it did not go well. Her only account of it, written in a draft letter to an unidentified recipient, probably in 1929, suggests that the man was younger, less experienced, and rather naive.[368]

All the while, Elsie's professional success and reputation grew. She published her major contributions to anthropology in the late 1930s — *Mitla, Town of Souls* (1936) and *Pueblo Indian Religion* (1939). At the end of 1940, she was elected president of the American Anthropological Association, the first woman to hold that office and head a major scientific organization in the United States, according to her journalist son, Mac.[369]

Elsie returned to New York from two months of field work in a remote Ecuadorean village in late November 1941. Busy as she was with meetings, anthropological work, and seeing family and friends, her thoughts turned to Herbert. "There are times when I miss Father awfully. This is one," she wrote her son, Mac, in early December, just days before she fell ill with appendicitis.[370] Despite all the disappointments and pain of their marriage, her bond with Herbert persisted sixteen years after his death.

A colleague described Elsie as being in good spirits and apparent good health on the evening of December 10, when she attended a council meeting of the American Ethnological Association. The next day, she was in the hospital undergoing an appendectomy. She seemed to be making a good recovery, and planned to attend the annual meeting of the American Anthropological Association at the end December, when her presidential term ended. On December 19, she took a turn for the

---

367 APS, ECP to John E. Parsons, April 3, 1932.

368 The letter is quoted in Deacon, p. 320.

369 McIlvaine Parsons, "Dr. Elsie Clews Parsons in Dead," *New York Herald Tribune*, December 20, 1941.

370 ECP to McIlvaine Parsons, December 7, 1941; quoted in Hare, p. 66, and Deacon, p. 380. According to Deacon, the original letter was retained by McIlvaine Parsons.

worse and died, at the age of sixty-six.[371] She had already written her presidential address, which anthropologist Gladys Reichard read to the meeting. In keeping with the instructions she had given her family, Elsie was cremated and had no funeral, religious service, or gravestone.[372]

The legacy of Elsie's "accomplishful" life lies not just in her contributions to anthropology, but also in her trenchant social critiques, feminist perspectives, and resolute efforts to construct a personal life that accommodated both passion and work. The challenges she faced were compounded by the fact that she rarely had a partner who shared her vision. Unlike Alice and Grace, each of whom adjusted her career to accommodate a husband, Elsie was prepared to jettison her relationship with a man rather than give up her productive work life. The two marriage narratives that follow show the greater potential for change when both partners were committed to constructing a marriage grounded in mutual support for each other's work.

---

371 Gladys Reichard to A. L. Kroeber, December 19, 1941; Gladys Reichard to Herbert Parsons, Jr., 12 January 1942. Quoted in Zumwalt, p. 329. Elsie's death was variously attributed to an embolism, uremia, and pulmonary thrombosis. See Hare, p. 167.
372 APS, ECP Memo to Lissa, February 11, 1940.

4. A Partnership of Equals: Beatrice and Sidney Webb

The extraordinary partnership that Beatrice Potter and Sidney Webb embarked on when they married in 1892 spanned almost fifty years and left a lasting mark on British sociology, social welfare policy, and public administration. Born in 1858 and groomed for a high society marriage, Beatrice grew up believing that love and career were incompatible goals for a woman. She married the lower class Sidney, a Fabian Socialist and a clerk in the Colonial Office, because she believed he would be the ideal partner for her work. Their partnership was fundamentally egalitarian and showcased Beatrice's talents as much as Sidney's. They wanted their relationship to be a model for others.

Instead of having children, the Webbs wrote books together. They investigated social and economic issues, campaigned for sweeping changes in education and social policy, sat on government commissions, and founded the London School of Economics. They are buried together in Westminster Abbey, the only non-Royal couple to be so honored. The Webbs were a deeply devoted couple who became "singularly at one in heart and intellect," Beatrice wrote.[1] But their seemingly idyllic union was marred for many years by Beatrice's yearning for a more romantically compelling partner than Sidney and her sublimated

---

1   Beatrice Webb, Diary, 12 January 1934. https://digital.library.lse.ac.uk/objects/ lse:rut323dac. Beatrice's manuscript and typescript diaries (along with the Webbs's letters) are archived in the London School of Economics and Political Science, British Library of Political and Economic Science, Passfield Papers. I cite the digitized manuscript diaries in the London School of Economics Digital Library. If the digitized link fails to load or key pages are missing or unreadable, I cite the digitized typescript copies. Dates are consistent with those in *The Diary of Beatrice Webb*, ed. by Norman and Jeanne MacKenzie, 4 vols. (Cambridge, MA: Belknap Press, 1982–1985), an indispensable resource for scholars as well as general readers.

    https://doi.org/10.11647/OBP.0318.04

passion for the dominating politician Joseph Chamberlain, whom she had earlier hoped to marry.

Upbringing

The eighth child in a family of nine surviving daughters, Beatrice Potter grew up in a world of wealth, influence and privilege, among "a class of persons who habitually give orders."[2] Both her grandfathers were members of Parliament. Her father, Richard Potter, lost the fortune he inherited, but made another as a railway investor and director. The Potter household upheld many gendered stereotypes of male and female roles but deviated from others. Beatrice described her father as "the only man I ever knew who genuinely believed that women were superior to men, and acted as if he did."[3] He treated his wife and daughters as confidantes and asked for their advice in his business dealings, although he generally did not follow it.[4] According to Beatrice, his "love for his children was more like that of a mother than a father", and it was he, not her mother, who provided "the light and warmth of the home."[5] She and her sisters remembered Richard Potter as loving and affectionate, but there was another, darker side to his personality: he had a strong authoritarian streak, and sometimes treated his loved ones with contempt, cruelty, and bullying.[6] Beatrice herself recognized that her father controlled the family destinies; the household "lived where it suited him to live, and he came and went as he chose."[7]

The Potters' union was a love match, and Beatrice wrote that Richard "worshipped" his wife. Nevertheless, during most of her married life, Lawrencina Potter was a disappointed and dissatisfied woman. The daughter of a Member of Parliament who had raised her to be

---

2   Beatrice Webb, *My Apprenticeship* (Middlesex, UK: Penguin Books, 1971; first published, 1926), p. 65.
3   Ibid., p. 35.
4   Barbara Caine, *Destined to Be Wives: The Sisters of Beatrice Webb* (Oxford: Clarendon Press, 1986), p.16.
5   Love: BP to SW, 30 December 1891, London School of Economics and Political Science, British Library of Political and Economic Science, Passfield Papers. "Light and warmth": BW, *Apprenticeship*, p. 35.
6   Caine, pp. 15, 16, 19–20.
7   BW, *Apprenticeship*, pp. 35, 36.

"a scholar and a gentlewoman," Lawrencina expected that Richard Potter would enter Parliament and they would build a life around their mutual interests in politics and religion. This hoped-for ideal was never realized, however. Instead, Richard had to earn his fortune and spent long periods away on business trips while Lawrencina remained at home, incapacitated by frequent pregnancies and ill-health. Although she enjoyed the friendship of several of England's leading intellectuals, her intellectual aspirations were largely unfulfilled, and her time was spent caring for her growing family and maintaining the large houses that Richard Potter rented for the family. She published one novel, but it was not well received.[8]

Lawrencina was further disappointed in being the mother of daughters rather than sons. After her only son died at the age of two (Beatrice was six), Lawrencina largely withdrew from the family's social life. Isolating herself in her bedroom, studying foreign grammars and religious texts, she relied on her daughters to serve as housekeepers, hostesses, and traveling companions for their father. Lawrencina's unhappiness made it difficult for her to provide much affection to her children. All the Potter daughters found Lawrencina to be cold, stern, and difficult to please, but Beatrice in particular felt unloved and displaced by her mother's affection for her younger brother and her younger sister, who became the pet of the family.[9] Beatrice would later write with sympathy about her mother's difficult life and blighted intellectual aspirations, but she did not seem to see a connection between her mother's frustrated ambition and her own ambivalence about marriage and childrearing. Not feeling much sympathy with or affection from her sisters, Beatrice grew up lonely and unhappy in the midst of her large family.

The Potter household provided a rich environment for Beatrice's intellectual development if a crippling one for her emotional growth. Her parents enjoyed the friendship of prominent scientists, philosophers and politicians — Herbert Spencer, Thomas Huxley, and Sir Francis Galton were frequent guests — and the girls were encouraged to read widely and discuss intellectual topics. Lawrencina

---

8   Ibid., pp. 37–41; Caine, p. 24.
9   BW, *Apprenticeship*, p. 36; Caine, p. 27.

arranged for their education with great care. Tutors taught them classical languages, mathematics, music, history, and geography; they were sent to finishing schools, and had extensive opportunities for foreign travel.[10] Her younger sister was being tutored for the entrance examinations for Oxford University in the late 1870s, but Beatrice was not encouraged to develop academic interests.[11] "Beatrice is the only one of my children who is below average in intelligence" was Lawrencina's early judgment.[12] Because she was frequently ill, the only formal schooling Beatrice received was a few months at a boarding school when she was seventeen. But she read widely on her own, and won the special attention and affection of Herbert Spencer, the philosopher and sociologist who was a close friend of both her parents. The interest and encouragement he paid to Beatrice — teaching her his ideas about the scientific categorization of human society, evaluating her philosophical essays, and comparing her favorably to the young George Eliot — were critical to her intellectual development.

Despite the unconventional aspects of their upbringing, Beatrice and her sisters were groomed to take their place in the world as the wives of men who were successful in business, politics, and the professions. Each spring, the Potters rented a house in London so the girls could attend the balls, dinners, and parties that constituted the London "Season"; they officially "came out" and were presented at Court. Although two sisters had flirted with unconventional lifestyles, by the time Beatrice was in her early twenties her older sisters had all made traditionally "good" marriages to upstanding, successful, mostly wealthy, men. Not all the sisters had happy marriages, but all were conventional wives, bearing and raising children, supervising their children's education, managing large households, and devoting themselves to their husband's well-being.[13]

---

10   Caine, pp. 35, 43–44.
11   Ibid., p. 41.
12   BW, *Apprenticeship*, p. 36.
13   See Caine, pp. 59–61, 68, 76–77. Theresa Potter gave up her desire to study nursing in the face of familial opposition in 1874. Kate, the second oldest child, rejected two proposals of marriage in the mid-1870s, lived apart from the family in London, and volunteered with Octavia Hill's Charity Organization Society. She married Leonard Courtney, a Liberal Member of Parliament, in 1883, when she was thirty-five.

Leading a Double Life, 1882–1885

Beatrice's halting rebellion against family models and expectations started when she was twenty-four, just a few months after her mother's death in 1882. Her diary records both her reservations about participating in a social life designed to result in marriage to a prominent man and her growing ambition "to lead a life with some result" of her own, despite the obvious obstacles. Influenced by Herbert Spencer, she was interested in using scientific principles to understand how human society was organized.[14] Intent on writing a book, she embarked on a rigorous course of study so she could learn observation and experimentation, become competent in numerical evidence, and develop a literary style. She read philosophy, mathematics, and literature, and arranged to be taught biology and physiology. Her resolution was sorely tested as family responsibilities claimed more and more of her time. As the older of two unmarried daughters, she was obliged to act as her father's hostess, supervise his households in London and the country, and take charge of her younger sister. Nevertheless, she managed to study for three hours a day before the rest of the household arose at eight o'clock.

Reconciling what she would later term the "rival pulls" of family affection and intellectual curiosity was no easy task.[15] Beatrice resolved to conduct herself in such a way that her family would have no cause for criticism: "Now my honest desire is to appear commonplace and sensible so that none of my dear kind family will think it necessary to remark to themselves or to me that I am otherwise than ordinary; to be on the right side of ordinary is the perfection of prudence in a young woman, and will save her from much heartburning and mortification of spirit."[16] But four months later she raged, "At present I feel like a caged animal, bound up by the luxury, comfort and respectability of my position. I can't get the training I want without neglecting my duty."[17]

Beatrice dissembled at social gatherings as well as at home. She attended the events of the London Season in the spring of 1883 as though in camouflage, deliberately trying to mask the intellectual side of her

---

14   Diary, 13 August 1882. https://digital.library.lse.ac.uk/objects/lse:diy675wal
15   BW, *Apprenticeship*, p. 133.
16   Diary, 25 November 1882. https://digital.library.lse.ac.uk/objects/lse:diy675wal
17   Diary, 31 March 1883. https://digital.library.lse.ac.uk/objects/lse:diy675wal

nature. "[I]t is a curious experience" she wrote in her diary, "moving about among men and women, talking much, as you are obliged to do, and never mentioning those thoughts and problems which are your *real life* and which absorb, in their pursuit and solution, all the earnestness of your nature."[18] Beatrice's determination to hide her real interests from her "dear kind" family and their social world suggests a healthy instinct for selfpreservation. But it also reflected her own deep ambivalence about her intellectual aspirations: Despite the pleasure she derived from her studies, Beatrice was beset by doubts about her capacity for intellectual work and the propriety of her efforts. Her diary entries vacillate between a belief that she could accomplish something of real worth if only she could "devote myself to one subject", and an equally pervasive fear that her writing was hopelessly "amateurish" and her thoughts too subjective.[19] Having no opportunity for advanced schooling and being forced to work in virtual isolation, she had no way to judge the value of her work.

Beatrice herself was somewhat repelled by her ambition. Brought up in a society that valued women more for the pleasantness of their personalities than for the sharpness of their minds, she faulted herself for being self-promoting rather than self-effacing, assertive rather than compliant, selfish rather than self-sacrificing. Explaining her attempts to keep her "intellectual" life "hidden from the world", Beatrice admitted, "in my heart of hearts I'm ashamed of it."[20] She had begun to question the traditional female role, but she was reluctant to cast it aside altogether. On the eve of the London Season in 1883, she struggled to decide whether she should *"give myself up* to Society, and make it my aim to succeed therein" or do only as much as duty required and spend the bulk of her time on her studies. In the end, she resolved to devote herself to the "cultivation of social instincts" because it was the more conventional option. "It is going with the stream, and pleasing my people [...] it is *taking* opportunities instead of *making* them; it is risking less and walking in a wellbeaten track in pleasant company [...] and

---

18   Diary, 24 April 1883. Emphasis in the original. https://digital.library.lse.ac.uk/ objects/lse:cal528buz

19   Diary, 24 March 1883. https://digital.library.lse.ac.uk/objects/lse:diy675wal

20   Diary, 24 April 1883. https://digital.library.lse.ac.uk/objects/lse:cal528buz

lastly, and perhaps this is the reason which weighs most with me, there is less presumption in the choice," she wrote in her diary.[21]

Eager to learn more about the lives of the urban poor, Beatrice volunteered with the social reformer Octavia Hill's Charity Organization Society in the East End slums in the spring of 1883, replacing her older sister, Kate, who left the Society when she married. Founded by Hill in 1869, the Charity Organization Society had made volunteer charity work an acceptable activity for a well-to-do unmarried woman. But Beatrice's motivation was far from conventional. Trained to distinguish the "deserving" poor from the "undeserving" poor, COS workers were expected to help the families and individuals who seemed capable of bettering themselves; the volunteers dispensed moral advice as well as other forms of assistance to those deemed worthy of aid. Beatrice was less interested in improving the morality and lifestyles of individual families than in learning about the underlying causes of poverty and unemployment.[22]

In the fall of 1883, Beatrice carried her exploration of social conditions farther afield. She spent a few weeks in the working-class village of Bacup in northern England — a very different experience of poverty from that in London's slums. Although the family she stayed with was distantly related to her mother, Beatrice lived with them under an assumed identity, passing herself off as a working girl from another village so she could more easily win their trust and more closely observe their lives and their religious, social, and cooperative organizations.[23] Her experiences in London and Bacup fired Beatrice's enthusiasm for hands-on social investigation. In January 1885 she became a rent collector and manager of the newly opened Katherine Buildings, near the docks in London's East End. Operated by the COS, they housed a very poor population of dock workers and casual laborers. Beatrice and a female co-worker were responsible for selecting the tenants, keeping the rent accounts, and evicting tenants who created disturbances or fell behind in their rent. Beatrice began compiling detailed information about the

---

21 Diary, 22 February 1883. Emphasis in the original. https://digital.library.lse.ac.uk/objects/lse:diy675wal

22 Deborah Epstein Nord, *The Apprenticeship of Beatrice Webb* (Amherst: University of Massachusetts Press, 1985), pp. 122–23; BW, *Apprenticeship*, p. 186.

23 On the importance of assuming different identities in Beatrice's life, see Nord, pp. 154–55.

residents' families, work histories, and housing and emigration patterns, and had plans for collecting similar information from residents in other buildings.[24]

These activities expanded Beatrice's world beyond the narrow circle of her family and social class. She moved freely about London, traveling between the opulence of the West End and the squalor of the East End neighborhoods, and developed a network of unmarried women friends among the volunteers and writers whom she came to know in London. Well aware that her interest in social analysis rather than traditional social work set her apart from her female peers, Beatrice was eager to present a more conventional image to the outside world. She was exhilarated by her new freedom, but still desirous of being treated "as a pleasant ordinary women." She reassured herself as much as her father, "An interesting hardworking life, with *just a touch* of adventure is so delightful, so long as one does not get stamped with that most damaging stamp: 'Eccentricity.' "[25]

An All-consuming Passion, 1883–1886

The ambivalence Beatrice manifested during the mid-1880s as she vacillated between the typical life of an upper-middle-class woman and the pioneering life of an unmarried working woman was exacerbated by her equally ambivalent relationship with Joseph Chamberlain. A Cabinet minister and leader of the radical wing of the Liberal Party, Chamberlain combined a commanding personality, a keen intelligence, and good looks with wealth, social position, and political power. When Beatrice met him at a dinner party at the end of May or beginning of June 1883, he was forty-seven, twice widowed, and reportedly looking for a new wife. Beatrice was twenty-five, wellconnected, intelligent and wealthy, but far less experienced in courtship and still uncertain whether she wanted to devote her life to marriage or work. She fell passionately in love with Chamberlain but was unwilling to stifle her independent spirit and become the type of compliant, self-effacing woman that his domineering personality required in a wife. She spent four years

---

24   Nord, pp. 138–39 and 144–46.
25   BP to Richard Potter [? August 1885], Passfield Papers. Emphasis in the original.

agonizing over whether she would accept a proposal if it came and fighting off depression whenever it appeared that there would be no proposal. Even after Chamberlain married in 1888, Beatrice was unable to free herself from her obsession with him.

The Potter-Chamberlain relationship has fascinated Beatrice's biographers but the details of their encounters are not always clear. Chamberlain left no account of the relationship and Beatrice's diary entries are frequently oblique and leave many gaps.[26] Her initial reaction to him was ambivalent: "I do, and I don't like him," she wrote in her diary.[27] As they saw more of each other at various at social events in London during the summer of 1883, Beatrice's interest grew. She spent a week at Chamberlain's London residence in September 1883, as the guest of his daughter. Apparently believing herself to be under inspection as a matrimonial candidate, Beatrice continued to express ambivalence to her sisters and in her diary.[28] When Chamberlain spent several days at her father's home in January 1884, his unequivocal statements about the subordinate role he expected his wife to play and Beatrice's reluctance to accept such a position created doubts on both sides, and caused Beatrice much heartache.[29] By May 1884 Beatrice was convinced that she had "loved and lost", but the story was by no means over.[30] She acknowledged that Chamberlain "had been the wiser of the two" for not pursuing the relationship, but she sank into a severe depression that lasted several months. Repeatedly berating herself for not being the compliant female that Chamberlain wanted, Beatrice despaired at

---

26 Kitty Dobbs Muggeridge, the daughter of Beatrice's younger sister Rosalind, wrote that, according to family accounts, Joseph Chamberlain was once seen hurrying away from the Potter house in London, "pale-faced and distraught", while Beatrice was found inside in tears, sobbing that she had just refused him. Kitty Muggeridge and Ruth Adam, *Beatrice Webb, A Life 1858–1943* (New York: Knopf, 1968), p. 93. There is no other evidence that Chamberlain proposed to Beatrice, and her diary entries and correspondence with her sisters suggest otherwise.

27 Diary, 3 June 1883. https://digital.library.lse.ac.uk/objects/lse:cal528buz

28 BP to Mary Playne [October 1883], in *The Letters of Sydney and Beatrice Webb*, ed. by Norman Mackenzie, 3 vols. (Cambridge, UK: Cambridge University Press, 1978), I, p. 17. Diary, 26 September 1883; 5 November 1883; New Year's Eve 1883. https://digital.library.lse.ac.uk/objects/lse:cal528buz

29 Beatrice recorded their differences in considerable detail in her Diary, 12 January 1884. https://digital.library.lse.ac.uk/objects/lse:cal528buz

30 Diary, 9 May 1884. https://digital.library.lse.ac.uk/objects/lse:cal528buz

finding personal happiness, and strove to dull her pain through the "narcotic" of her work with the Charity Organization Society.[31]

A renewal of contact at the end of January 1885 — after Beatrice had taken on the management of Katherine Buildings — left her just as unsure about Chamberlain's intentions and her own desires.[32] They did not meet again until late July 1885, when one of Beatrice's sisters hosted a picnic in an attempt to move the issue towards a resolution. Beatrice, humiliated by what she took as Chamberlain's arrogance and disdain, would later recall that day as "the most painful one of my life."[33] Stung by Chamberlain's apparent indifference, Beatrice contemplated not seeing him again.[34] But in November 1885, she discussed her feelings for Chamberlain with his sister (whom she was visiting), and was bluntly informed, "The brother had never thought of me."[35] Still Beatrice could not free herself from her obsession with Chamberlain. On two occasions — once by letter in March 1886, and once in person in July 1887, when he again came as a guest to her father's house, at her invitation — Beatrice told Chamberlain himself that she loved him.[36] During their conversation in 1887, she rebuked him for suggesting they should remain friends when their relationship was so painful to her, and insisted that they not see each other again.[37] This time, her resolution held. Chamberlain traveled to America a few months later, as the head of a diplomatic trade mission. He returned to

31   Diary, 28 July 1884. https://digital.library.lse.ac.uk/objects/lse:cal528buz. "Narcotic" of work: Diary, 8 March 1885. https://digital.library.lse.ac.uk/objects/lse:tag606voq

32   Diary, 29 January [1885], and [1 February] 1885. https://digital.library.lse.ac.uk/objects/lse:tag606voq

33   Diary, 12 [22?] May 1886. https://digital.library.lse.ac.uk/objects/lse:yom975poh

34   BP to Mary Playne [?late July 1885], in *Letters of Sidney and Beatrice Webb*, I, pp. 36–37.

35   Beatrice did not write about this painful conversation in her diary until five months later, on 6 March 1886. https://digital.library.lse.ac.uk/objects/lse:yal805mem

36   By letter: Diary, 6 March 1886 and 15 March 1886. https://digital.library.lse.ac.uk/objects/lse:yal805mem. In person: Diary, 9 June 1887, 8 August 1887 [?August 1887]. https://digital.library.lse.ac.uk/objects/lse:yom975poh. See also, the comment Beatrice wrote on the letter Chamberlain sent her on 7 August 1887, quoted in *Diary of Beatrice Webb*, I, p. 211, and editor's notes, pp. 208–11.

37   Beatrice tore the 1887 entries (between June 1 and August 11) describing these events out of her diary in 1887 and sealed them up, along with several letters from Chamberlain. She did not reopen the packet until May 1890, when she added a note explaining what she had done (Diary, May 1890 note penned at the end of manuscript vol.14, https://digital.library.lse.ac.uk/objects/lse:zib295pim). See also, *Diary of Beatrice Webb*, I, editor's notes, pp. 208–11, 333.

England in March 1888, secretly engaged to Mary Endicott, the twenty-three year old daughter of the US Secretary for War.[38] Beatrice did not meet Chamberlain again until 1900, but his hold on her imagination persisted.

Beatrice was well aware that she was drawn to Chamberlain against her better judgment, a realization that in no way reduced the power of his attraction. She characterized her struggle as a conflict between "the intellectual and the sensual", between Reason and Emotion, between "principle [and] feeling."[39] She knew that she and Chamberlain held incompatible views and understood that if they were to marry, she would have to give way to him. In Beatrice's view, Chamberlain was "a despot" who ran his household as dictatorially as the political machine he headed in Birmingham. She believed that he wanted a wife who would be completely subordinate to him and not hold — or at least not express — independent opinions. She did not try to hide either her incapacity or her disdain for such a role. What he characterized as "intelligent sympathy" in a woman, she termed "servility"; he angered her by his attempt to assert "absolute mastery" in his conversation and social relations with her; she disappointed him by refusing to yield and openly disagreeing with him.[40] She recognized, too, that if she married him, she would be forced to give up her intellectual aspirations and accept the traditional role of a woman who lived through — and for — her husband. As his wife, she would need to "separate, even more than I do now, my intellect from my feeling [...]. I should become par excellence the mother and the woman of the world intent only on fulfilling practical duties and gaining practical ends," Beatrice warned herself.[41] Her family and friends confirmed her assessment; most cautioned her against marrying Chamberlain. Such a marriage would

---

38 History WestMidlands, "The Mistress of Joseph Chamberlain's Highbury — Mary Endicott Chamberlain" (podcast, November 25, 2019), https://historywm.com/podcasts/mary-endicott. Chamberlain wooed Mary in a traditional manner, sending her red roses after their first meeting.

39 Diary, 10 December 1886, https://digital.library.lse.ac.uk/objects/lse:yom975poh; BW, *Apprenticeship*; BW, Diary, New Year's Eve, 1883, https://digital.library.lse.ac.uk/objects/lse:cal528buz

40 Diary, 12 January 1884. https://digital.library.lse.ac.uk/objects/lse:cal528buz

41 Diary, 16 March 1884. https://digital.library.lse.ac.uk/objects/lse:cal528buz

be "a tragedy — a murder of your independent nature," her sister Kate counselled.[42]

Beatrice devoted much thought and heartache over many years trying to understand why, despite this basic incompatibility, she was so attracted to Chamberlain. In part, she saw a union with Chamberlain as an opportunity to increase her own "prestige" and "importance." She candidly acknowledged: "Ambition and superstition began the feeling. A desire to play a part in the world, and a belief that as the wife of a great man I should play a bigger part than as a spinster or an ordinary married woman."[43] Playing a helpmate role to Chamberlain "would not have been a happy life, but it might have been a noble one," she mused.[44] Beatrice's conviction that she could accomplish more as a political hostess than through her own work reflected both her personal insecurity and the position of women in the 1880s. Powerful women in their own right were the rare exception; public prominence and influence was far more easily acquired through marriage to a prominent man. Her self-doubts were exacerbated by the contrast between Chamberlain's political prominence and her own obscurity. She saw him as an "extraordinary man," and always referred to him as "the Great Man." She, in contrast, was merely "an ordinary young woman" still unsure whether her intellectual gifts were sufficient to fulfill her aspirations.[45]

Beatrice's obsession with Chamberlain reflected more than just displaced ambition. She responded to him with an almost overwhelming physical passion. The discovery of her own sexuality transformed Beatrice's life. "The woman's nature has been stirred to its depths," she wrote a year after meeting Chamberlain. The intensity of her feelings was devastating: "Last of all came — passion — with its burning heat, an emotion which had for long smoldered unnoticed, burst into flame, and burnt down intellectual interests, personal ambition, and all other selfdeveloping notions," she marveled.[46]

---

42   Kate Courtney to BP, July 1885, written after the disastrous picnic she hosted on
      Beatrice's behalf, quoted in *Diary of Beatrice Webb*, I, editor's note, p. 135.
43   Diary, 22 April 1884. https://digital.library.lse.ac.uk/objects/lse:cal528buz
44   Diary, 28 July 1884. https://digital.library.lse.ac.uk/objects/lse:cal528buz
45   Diary, 16 March 1884. https://digital.library.lse.ac.uk/objects/lse:cal528buz
46   Diary, 15 October 1884. https://digital.library.lse.ac.uk/objects/lse:tag606voq

Chamberlain elicited Beatrice's passion, in part, *because* of the masterful way he conducted himself and the dominance and superiority he exuded. She wrote in her diary:

> Joseph Chamberlain with his gloom and seriousness, with absence of any gallantry or faculty for saying pretty nothings, the simple way he assumes, almost asserts, that you stand on a level far beneath him and that all that concerns you is trivial; that you yourself are without importance in the world except in so far as you might be related to him: this sort of courtship (if it is to be called courtship) fascinates, at least, my imagination.[47]

Chamberlain embodied a key element of the Victorian ideal of masculinity — mastery — and Beatrice found this sexually exciting. She compared his working of the Birmingham crowd at a political rally to the way a man established power over a woman. After seeing the crowd's reaction to his speech, she reported in her diary, "It might have been a woman listening to the words of her lover! Perfect response, unquestioning receptivity. Who *reasons* with his mistress? The wise man asserts his will, urges it with warmth or bitterness, and flavours it with flattery and occasional appeals to moral sentiments."[48] For a Victorian woman, even an independently-minded one, the idea of being attached to another, stronger personality was compelling even though — indeed, *because* — it meant submerging one's own personality in another's. Alice Freeman Palmer struggled with the same issue, and Elsie Clews Parsons thought that a woman's tendency to lose interest in everything but her lover was one of the most damaging aspects of being female.

The attributes that Chamberlain wanted in a wife — submission, selfsacrifice, obedience — were the very virtues that Victorian women were taught to cultivate. Beatrice did not live up to this ideal, but instead of rejecting it, she blamed herself for failing to meet it. Insecure about her talents, uncertain about committing herself to an unconventional lifestyle, and struggling to define herself as a professional, Beatrice found the idea of marriage to Joseph Chamberlain appealing because it offered a ready-made identity and well-defined responsibilities: it would provide her with a "settled and defined occupation" without

---

47 Diary, 16 March 1884. https://digital.library.lse.ac.uk/objects/lse:cal528buz
48 Diary, 16 March 1884. Emphasis in the original. https://digital.library.lse.ac.uk/objects/lse:cal528buz

requiring her to pioneer a new role.[49] If she married Chamberlain she would acquire prominence through his position and become the type of woman her family and social world admired. The part of Beatrice that clung to the traditional and disdained the unconventional welcomed this, but the part of her that longed to make a significant contribution of her own rebelled against the subordination and vicariousness of such a relationship.

So painful were the seemingly mutually exclusive choices — losing her independence or losing Chamberlain — that Beatrice remained in a paralysis of indecision for years. She repeatedly asserted that the issue was over and done with, only to return to it again and again in her diaries, questioning, reevaluating, reinterpreting her own behavior as well as Chamberlain's. Her inability to resolve her feelings or end the ambiguity of the relationship was an added source of unhappiness. "Doublemindedness has run right through — a perpetual struggle between conscience on the one hand and feeling on the other — I had not the courage to follow either to the bitter end — hence my misery," she wrote in the spring of 1886.[50]

Embracing a Career, 1885–1890

After the humiliating visit from Chamberlain in the summer of 1885, when he treated her with rudeness and indifference, Beatrice resolved to embrace a future of work with courage and determination, and planned to record her progress with care.[51] Nevertheless, the uncertainty with Chamberlain had undermined her confidence in herself as a worker as well as a woman. "[M]y intellectual faculty is only mirage, I have no special mission," she had despaired in 1884.[52] The prospect of spending her life as an unmarried career woman filled her with dread.[53] Apart

---

49   Diary, 9 May 1884, and 22 April 1884. https://digital.library.lse.ac.uk/objects/lse:cal528buz

50   Diary, 6 March 1886. https://digital.library.lse.ac.uk/objects/lse:yal805mem

51   Rudeness and indifference: Diary, 12 [22?] May 1886. https://digital.library.lse.ac.uk/objects/lse:yom975poh. Resolved: Diary, 7 August 1885. https://digital.library.lse.ac.uk/objects/lse:tag606voq.

52   Diary, 9 May 1884. https://digital.library.lse.ac.uk/objects/lse:cal528buz

53   Diary, 5 November 1883. https://digital.library.lse.ac.uk/objects/lse:cal528buz; 19 November 1884, https://digital.library.lse.ac.uk/objects/lse:tag606voq; and 28 May 1886. https://digital.library.lse.ac.uk/objects/lse:yom975poh

from the inevitable loneliness, she feared a lifetime of work would "unsex" her and cultivate "masculine qualities" and "masculine interests." Writing to her father, she drew a harsh portrait of "the working sisterhood" of women who were shut out from "matrimonial career[s]": they were "exceedingly pathetic" women who exercised their "somewhat abnormal but useful qualities" while leading "lives [...] without joy or lightheartedness."[54]

The frequent discussion of the relationship between work and gender in Beatrice's diaries in the 1880s underscores how troubling she found this issue. Her concerns echo the judgments of Victorian scientists and philosophers about the female mind and the unnatural and harmful effects of intellectual work on women. Herbert Spencer, Beatrice's early mentor and intellectual champion, was a prominent contributor to the debate, and his views likely exercised a powerful influence on her. In *The Principles of Sociology* (1876) Spencer argued that the division of labor that led men to earn a living and women to take care of the home was the most "progressive" and efficient method of social organization. He understood that since women outnumbered men in Victorian England, some women would be forced to earn a living, but warned:

> no considerable alteration in the careers of women in general can be or should be, produced, and *further*, that any extensive change in the education of women, made with the view of fitting them for business or professions would be mischievous. If women comprehend all that is contained in the domestic sphere, they would ask no other.[55]

Beatrice compiled a long list of the ways middle-class working women transgressed gender norms. She was particularly appalled by women who gave public addresses. When she attended a lecture by Annie Besant, the social reformer and women's rights activist, Beatrice admired her skill but recoiled from the spectacle of a woman speaking in public. "[T]o *see* her speaking made me shudder. It is not womanly to thrust yourself before the world. A woman, in all the relations of her life, should be sought."[56] Female administrators were "unsexed" because they

---

54   BP to Richard Potter [early November 1885]. Passfield Papers.
55   Quoted in Carol Dyhouse, *Girls Growing Up in Late Victorian England* (London: Routledge and Kegan Paul, 1981), pp. 152–53; emphasis in the original.
56   Diary, 27 November 1887. Emphasis in the original. https://digital.library.lse.ac.uk/objects/lse:yom975poh

exercised "justice, push and severity" in their work. "Learned women" had no outlet for their emotions. Rent collectors and charity workers were more acceptable because they were guided by "feeling more than thought" and could develop "the emotional part of their nature."[57] She most "revered" the "unknown saints" (such as her sister, Kate) who devoted themselves to good works but sought no recognition for their efforts.[58] Unable to free herself from cultural stereotypes that defined her ambition and talents as "abnormal", Beatrice looked for careers where women could excel by bringing a *"woman's temperament"* — meaning feeling and empathy — to their work. Solving social problems was one of those areas, she believed.[59]

Shattered by the painful encounter with Chamberlain in July 1885, Beatrice resolved to establish herself in such a career and recover from her attachment to him. The winter of 1885–86, when her struggle began in earnest, was a particularly bleak period, both personally and professionally. When her father suffered a major stroke in early December, Beatrice left London to become his caretaker in his country home. Distraught over Chamberlain, denied the opportunity to work, and forced to spend her time "companionizing a failing mind", Beatrice despaired about her past and future.[60] "I am never at peace with myself now — the whole of my past life looks like an irretrievable blunder, the last two years like a nightmare!" she agonized in her diary.[61] Deeply depressed, she contemplated her own death and wrote out instructions for how her possessions should be distributed if she were to die.[62]

Nevertheless, as Beatrice would later realize, this period of enforced isolation was critical to her professional development.[63] Freed from the distractions of London's social life and the demands of managing Katherine Buildings, she studied economics and history in order to understand the unemployment and poverty she had encountered in London, and began to put her thoughts into writing. Her almost suicidal

---

57   Diary, 12 August 1885. https://digital.library.lse.ac.uk/objects/lse:tag606voq
58   BP to Richard Potter [early November 1885]. Passfield Papers.
59   Ibid. Emphasis in the original.
60   Diary, 19 December 1885. https://digital.library.lse.ac.uk/objects/lse:tag606voq
61   Diary, 11 February 1886. https://digital.library.lse.ac.uk/objects/lse:tag606voq
62   BP, Testamentary Letter, January 1, 1886, in *Letters of Sidney and Beatrice Webb*, I, p. 50.
63   BW, *Apprenticeship*, p. 289.

depression did not lift until she had a small professional success. When she submitted a letter to the editor of the *Pall Mall Gazette*, the journal published it as a short article, entitled "A Lady's View of the Unemployed at the East", under her name, in February 1886. "A turning point in my life," she scrawled above the note from the Gazette's editor before pasting it into her diary.[64]

Seeing her work in print and knowing that people (including Chamberlain) were reading and discussing her opinions gave Beatrice hope and courage.[65] Her friendship with Charles Booth soon provided her with an opportunity to delve more deeply into social issues. Booth, a wealthy merchant, shipping company owner, and social researcher, was married to her cousin Mary, and Beatrice had known and admired him for years. In the spring of 1886, he embarked on an ambitious exploration of poverty and employment in London. The massive study (eventually entitled *Life and Labour of the People in London* and published between 1889 and 1903 in seventeen volumes) broke new ground by combining quantitative data on employment and unemployment, wages, rents, and household size with observations on the daily routines and personal circumstances of London's poor.[66] Aware of the information Beatrice had compiled on the Katherine Buildings tenants, and her interest in the methodological challenges of studying poverty, Booth asked her to join the small committee that was advising him on the study design in the spring of 1886 (just weeks after she told Chamberlain how she felt about him).[67] A year later, she became one of the researchers on Booth's project.

---

64 Diary, final pages of mss. vol. 7 (February 1886), https://digital.library.lse.ac.uk/objects/lse:tag606voq. The article was published in the *Pall Mall Gazette* on February 18, 1886. Beatrice's diary entry of 27 March 1886 also identifies the acceptance of her article as a "turning point [...] a small sop to my almost wrecked ambition." https://digital.library.lse.ac.uk/objects/lse:yal805mem

65 Chamberlain wrote to Beatrice asking for more details on her thinking, precipitating an awkward exchange of letters that ended with her informing him, "I could not lie to the man I loved" (Diary, 6 March 1886. https://digital.library.lse.ac.uk/objects/lse:yal805mem).

66 Nord, pp. 155, 181–84. See also the discussion of the methodology on the London School of Economics website: https://booth.lse.ac.uk/learn-more/what-was-the-inquiry.

67 Diary, 17 April 1886. https://digital.library.lse.ac.uk/objects/lse:yom975poh. BP to Mary Booth [?March 1886] and [?early March 1886] in *Letters of Sidney and Beatrice Webb*, I, pp. 55–56.

Beatrice spent the summer of 1886 completing the first of several lengthy essays on economic history and theory. She worried that she would be thought "conceited" because of the forceful way she stated her views. "It is this hopeless independence of thought that makes my mind so distasteful to so many people and rightly so," she reflected, "for a woman *should* be more or less dependent and receptive."[68] Nevertheless, she resolved to remain true to herself, and circulated the paper for review and comment among her friends.

Having arranged for her sisters to take over Richard Potter's care for four months a year, twenty-eight-year-old Beatrice returned to London in the spring of 1887 to begin an investigation of poverty in Tower Hamlets in the East End for Booth. She spent several weeks observing workers at the docks, gathering information about dockside employment, compiling statistics, and interviewing laborers, their families, and employers. In striking contrast to the tortured selfdenigration of earlier years, she wrote with new confidence in her diary, "I see more reason for believing that the sacrifices I made to a special intellectual desire were warranted by a certain amount of faculty [...]. I feel power, I feel capacity."[69] It was not just bravado.

Several months later, the *Nineteenth Century*, a monthly journal that encouraged the exchange of ideas among the intelligentsia, published an article by Beatrice about the dockworkers. She aimed to provide local color and context, not just bare statistics, to explain the worker's lives. "[I]t is *the* work I have always wanted to do, the realization of my youthful ambition," Beatrice rejoiced.[70] More successes followed. Her editor at the *Nineteenth Century* urged her to write two additional articles for publication. Already committed to Booth to study the system of "sweated" labor that paid women for piecework tailoring done in shops or at home, Beatrice resolved to "dramatize" her account by

---

68 Diary, 14 September 1886; emphasis in the original. https://digital.library.lse.ac.uk/objects/lse:yom975poh

69 Diary, 30 March 1887. https://digital.library.lse.ac.uk/objects/lse:xih515bal. See also, Diary, 22 January 1887. https://digital.library.lse.ac.uk/objects/lse:yom975poh

70 Beatrice Potter, "The Dock Life of East London", *Nineteenth Century*, 22 (October, 1887), 483–99. Local color: BW, *Apprenticeship*, p. 301. Diary, 30 September, 1887. https://digital.library.lse.ac.uk/objects/lse:xih515bal. Emphasis in the original.

learning the tailoring trade and writing about the working conditions from the inside, as she had done when she wrote about life in Bacup.[71]

When she returned to the East End in the spring of 1888, Beatrice added sewing lessons to days full of interviews, observations, and statistical analysis. After she acquired some basic skills, she dressed herself as a working class woman, adjusted her accent, and sought employment as a "trouser hand." She worked in one establishment for two consecutive days, and several other employers hired her for a few hours of work.

Beatrice was not a very accomplished seamstress, but she was making a mark as a social investigator. In May 1888 she gave evidence as an expert witness before the House of Lords Commission on the Sweating System. Several months later, she published two articles about sweated labor in the *Nineteenth Century*. The first was a straightforward analysis about the employment and living conditions of sweatshop workers in the tailoring trade. The second, entitled "Pages from a Work-Girl's Diary" was her personal account of working in the sweating industry, which generated a wider readership. Her confidence grew and she again believed she had "a special mission" to help solve the social questions of her day.[72] Still working for Booth, she began a study of London's Jewish immigrant community.

Despite her professional success, Beatrice's inner battles persisted. Determined to devote her life to the well-being of others, she struggled to rid herself of vanity, egotism, and ambition. Nevertheless, her efforts to achieve "selfrenunciation" were painful and halting.[73] Denied an outlet for her "strong physical nature," she had to sublimate her sexual feelings. "If I were a man, this creature would be free, though not dissolute, in its morals, a lover of women," she acknowledged. "[But] as I am a woman: these feelings, unless fulfilled in marriage which would mean destruction of the intellectual being, must remain controlled and

71 Diary, [August?]1887. https://digital.library.lse.ac.uk/objects/lse:xih515bal
72 Beatrice Potter, "East London Labour", *Nineteenth Century*, 24 (August, 1888), 161–83; Beatrice Potter, "Pages from a Work-girl's Diary", *Nineteenth Century*, 25 (September, 1888), 301–14. Diary, 5 May 1888. https://digital.library.lse.ac.uk/objects/lse:yom975poh
73 Diary, 21 January 1887, 22 January 1887,5 February 1887. https://digital.library.lse.ac.uk/objects/lse:yom975poh

unsatisfied, finding their only vent in [...] religious exaltation."[74] A few years later, Beatrice noted that celibacy was "as painful to a woman [...] as it is to a man."[75] Shortly thereafter, she berated herself for feeling sexually attracted to a man she did not otherwise care for: "How one despises oneself, giving way to these feelings (and over thirty too — it would be excusable in a woman of twenty-five), but that part of a woman's nature dies hard. It is many variations of one chord — *the supreme and instinctive longing to be a mother.*"[76]

The battle to crush her ambitious nature was equally hard fought. "[B]efore my work can be perfectly true, vanity and personal ambitions must die [...] I must love my work and not myself," Beatrice admonished herself in the summer of 1886, articulating a theme that would echo repeatedly in her diaries.[77] Two years later, she was forced to admit: "Selfconsciousness and vanity [...] are still the great stumbling blocks of my nature."[78]

Expunging Chamberlain from her consciousness was even harder. Throughout the 1880s, Beatrice's unrequited love sounded a contrapuntal refrain of despair, anguish, and humiliation against the rising chorus of her professional achievements. New encounters with Chamberlain and bitter memories of past confrontations threw her into periodic bouts of severe depression. The pride she took in her early publications was undercut by the two humiliating exchanges with Chamberlain in 1886 and 1887 when she confessed that she loved him. When he did not reciprocate, she was as chagrined by her own behavior as she was pained by his indifference. Try as she might, she could not free herself from the spell of the man she had come to view as her "evil genius."[79] In an apparent effort to rip Chamberlain out of her heart and mind after their exceedingly painful meeting in the summer of 1887, she tore out the diary entries describing it and sealed them up with the last letters he sent her.[80]

---

74   Diary, 10 December 1886. https://digital.library.lse.ac.uk/objects/lse:yom975poh
75   Diary, 7 March 1889. https://digital.library.lse.ac.uk/objects/lse:tus438hic
76   Diary, 4 June 1889. Emphasis in the original. https://digital.library.lse.ac.uk/objects/lse:tus438hic
77   Diary, 11 July 1886. https://digital.library.lse.ac.uk/objects/lse:yom975poh
78   Diary, 21 August 1888. https://digital.library.lse.ac.uk/objects/lse:yom975poh
79   Diary, 27 March 1886. https://digital.library.lse.ac.uk/objects/lse:yal805mem
80   She did not reopen the packet until May 1890, when she added a note explaining what she had done (Diary, May 1890 note penned at the end of manuscript vol.14,

Marriage, spinsterhood, and Chamberlain were still very much on her mind throughout 1888. When her younger sister became engaged early that April, Beatrice stoically accepted being "the old maid of the family."[81] Reading unofficial reports of Chamberlain's engagement to Mary Endicott in the press in late April was far more devastating: Beatrice felt as though she had been stabbed.[82] She felt comforted when her work was going well, but became severely depressed whenever she doubted its value or her abilities. In September she and a female friend in London laughed together over a popular magazine's depiction of the hardworking, earnest, cosmopolitan life of The Glorified Spinster — "a new race of women not looking for or expecting marriage." But when she quoted the article's description of the "self-dependent, courageous, and cool headed" Glorified Spinsters in her diary, Beatrice observed pityingly, "Ah, poor things."[83]

Chamberlain's marriage in November 1888 was the cruelest blow. Rumors of the engagement had circulated since April, but it was not officially announced until November 7, just eight days before the ceremony.[84] After reading newspaper accounts of the wedding, which took place in Washington, DC, Beatrice suffered "a week of utter nervous collapse" that left her unable to work. Several more weeks of "exquisite mental torture" followed. Nevertheless, she did her best to get back to research and writing. By year's end, she was again taking solace in her growing sense of competence in her chosen craft.[85]

There was no turning back. The first volume of Booth's *Life and Labour of the People in London*, which included three chapters by Beatrice, was published to considerable acclaim in April 1889. "[A] great success," she wrote happily in her diary.[86] Feeling secure enough as a researcher to strike out on her own, Beatrice decided to study working-class

---

https://digital.library.lse.ac.uk/objects/lse:zib295pim). See also, *Diary of Beatrice Webb*, I, editor's notes, pp. 208–11, 333.

81   BP to Mary Playne [?9 April 1888], in *Letters of Sidney and Beatrice Webb*, I, p. 63.

82   Diary, 26 April 1888. https://digital.library.lse.ac.uk/objects/lse:yom975poh

83   "The Glorified Spinster", *MacMillan's Magazine*, 58 (September 1888), 371–76. Diary, 3 September 1888. https://digital.library.lse.ac.uk/objects/lse:yom975poh

84   The secrecy was intended to avoid political fallout from the trade agreement that both Chamberlain and Mary's father were involved in negotiating when the couple met (History WestMidlands, "Mistress").

85   Diary, 29 December 1888. https://digital.library.lse.ac.uk/objects/lse:yom975poh

86   Diary, 21 April 1889. https://digital.library.lse.ac.uk/objects/lse:tus438hic

cooperative organizations, a topic she had become interested in during her 1883 visit to Bacup and which the editor of the *Nineteenth Century* encouraged her to investigate. She rejected the advice of the renowned economist Alfred Marshall to study "the unknown field of female labor," a topic which he believed only a woman could do well and for which he thought Beatrice was especially well-suited. He praised her abilities, but warned her off the subject she had chosen. "A book by you on the Cooperative Movement I may get my wife to read to me in the evening to while away the time, but I shan't pay any attention to it," he told her dismissively in March 1889.[87]

Alfred's wife, Mary Paley Marshall, was a former student of his, an author, and a college don. She wrote about and taught economics, but seemed to efface herself completely during her marriage to him.[88] Hearing Alfred Marshall assert that marriage required the submission and devotion "body and mind of the female"; listening to his declamations against strong, independent women; and seeing the devoted ministrations of his "gentle, unassuming [wife], who sits by his side, selects his food, and guards him from obtrusions" made a strong impact on Beatrice, who wrote detailed entries about her encounters with the Marshalls in her diary.[89]

Observing the Marshalls' interactions must have reinforced Beatrice's growing sense that she had been right to resist Chamberlain's efforts to dominate her. But the anguish of losing him remained. Recalling the pain of her last meeting with him two years before, she resolved in July 1889 to devote herself to a "life of loneliness and work", so that others could experience "the peaceful joy" she herself had lost.[90]

Despite Marshall's warning, Beatrice was convinced she had found a career that would allow her to express her womanly nature and in

---

87   BW, *Apprenticeship*, p. 351. Emphasis in the original. Beatrice reported the conversation in detail in her Diary, 8 March 1889, but this quotation from Marshall is not in the original diary entry or the Typescript copy.

88   See John Maynard Keynes, "Mary Paley Marshall, 1850–1944" in *Cambridge Women: Twelve Portraits* ed. by Edward Shils and Carmen Blacker (Cambridge, UK: Cambridge University Press, 1996), pp. 73–92.

89   Diary, 8 March 1889 and 7 June 1889. https://digital.library.lse.ac.uk/objects/lse:tus438hic

90   Diary, 29 July 1889. https://digital.library.lse.ac.uk/objects/lse:tus438hic. She ripped the next eight pages of commentary on Chamberlain out of her diary; they have not survived. See *Diary of Beatrice Webb*, I, editor's note, p. 288.

which her gender would be an asset. She could infuse her "female" sensibility into her investigations by focusing on "feeling" and the human context behind the statistics. As a woman, she felt she was more readily trusted than a man, more able to put interviewees at ease, and better able to get information from them. Such considerations helped to allay her deepseated fears about the "masculine" aspects of her work and personality. At the same time, she relished the unconventional friendships and social interactions she developed with male trade unionists and cooperative society leaders in the course of her investigations.[91]

Nevertheless, Beatrice somewhat perversely allied herself with the champions of traditional womanhood by signing a well-publicized petition against female suffrage in 1889. Although she soon realized that her anti-suffrage stand was a mistake, she did not endorse female suffrage until 1906. Twenty years after that, she finally explained her early opposition: she felt she did not need a vote because she herself had never "suffered the disabilities assumed to rise from my sex." On the contrary, she believed her gender had given her distinct advantages in the late 1880s when few men of her socio-economic class had the freedom to pursue a career of "disinterested research" as she had done, and male magazine editors were eager to publish articles by women because they were a novelty that attracted readers.[92]

As Beatrice grew more confident about her talents and her ability to bring a female perspective to her work, she began to value aspects of her character that had once troubled her. Now she viewed her perseverance and forcefulness as strengths that would help her achieve her goals rather than merely "disagreeable masculine" traits to be deplored.[93] Instead of viewing the celibacy required of unmarried women as a repudiation of their womanhood and motherhood, she accepted it as a way for strong

---

91   Diary, 25 March 1889; 7 June 1889. https://digital.library.lse.ac.uk/objects/lse:tus438hic

92   Beatrice Webb, *Our Partnership*, ed. by Barbara Drake and Margaret I. Cole (New York: Longmans, Green, 1948), p. 361. BW, *Apprenticeship*, pp. 353–55.

93   Diary, 12 April 1886, and 30 September 1887. https://digital.library.lse.ac.uk/objects/lse:yom975poh "Disagreeable masculine": Diary, 8 March 1889. https://digital.library.lse.ac.uk/objects/lse:tus438hic

women to focus "the special force of womanhood, motherly feeling" into public work, enabling them to accomplish things men could not.[94]

Beatrice also began to see a new pattern in her life, one that gave more legitimacy to her intellectual aspirations. She had initially portrayed herself as a victim of circumstances who joined the "working sisterhood" out of necessity rather than choice. In the first agony of Chamberlain's rejection, she had cried: "I have not despised the simple happiness of a woman's life; it has despised me and I have been humbled so far down as a woman can be humbled. My way in life has been chosen for me."[95] Now she concluded that work had always been her destiny. The Chamberlain episode began to look like a regrettable interlude that had distracted her from the true focus of her life: "If only I had been true to my ambition! I tried to push it from me, and to clutch at other things, but all in vain," she lamented.[96]

By the end of the decade, Beatrice had undergone an important transformation. Despite unhappiness, personal setbacks, and great insecurities, her identity as a social investigator and a "glorified spinster" had jelled. She was no longer a wealthy Society woman who dabbled in social work and studied social policy in her spare time; she was a professional "brainworker," a published author whose opinions were sought by reformers, politicians, and the press. She embraced — not just tolerated — her life as an unmarried working woman. Recording her father's desire to see his "little Bee married to a strong man", she unapologetically observed in November 1889, "he does not realize that she has passed away, leaving the strong form and determination of the 'glorified spinster'" in her place.[97] Believing once again that she had a special mission and the skills and discipline to accomplish it, Beatrice faced the future with equanimity. "My whole thought and feeling have drifted far into the future. It is for future generations, for their noble happiness that I live and pray," she wrote, somewhat melodramatically, in the spring of 1890.[98]

---

94 Diary, 29 August 1887. https://digital.library.lse.ac.uk/objects/lse:xih515bal
95 Diary, 4 April 1886. See also, Diary, 10 December 1886. https://digital.library.lse. ac.uk/objects/lse:yom975poh
96 Diary, 25 December 1887; also, Diary, 30 March 1887 and 30 September 1887. https:// digital.library.lse.ac.uk/objects/lse:yom975poh
97 Diary, 26 November 1889. https://digital.library.lse.ac.uk/objects/lse:tus438hic
98 Diary, 5 May 1890. https://digital.library.lse.ac.uk/objects/lse:zib295pim

Courtship, 1890–1892

Beatrice's hard-won equilibrium was thrown off balance by her friendship with Sidney Webb, a rising star in the British Fabian Society. They were introduced in January 1890, when Beatrice was researching workingmen's organizations and a mutual friend recommended Sidney as a knowledgeable source. When they met, each already knew and admired the other's work. Beatrice had described Sidney's contribution to *Fabian Essays on Socialism* as "by far the most significant and interesting essay" in the volume; he thought her chapters in Booth's *Life and Labour of the People in London* were the only ones with literary merit.[99] Their first conversation convinced her that her views on alleviating poverty made her a socialist, although she had not previously thought of herself in those terms.[100] Intrigued, Beatrice invited him to dinner to meet the Booths. Despite his Cockney pronunciation, "shaky" use of "Hs", lack of eloquence, and unkempt appearance, she found Sidney "a remarkable little man" and decided, "I like the man."[101] Her friends were less impressed.

Sidney had none of the privilege, wealth, and social connections that Beatrice inherited. Born in 1859 to lower-middle-class parents, he had made his way in the world by virtue of his formidable intelligence and unflagging capacity for hard work. His father was an accountant who was active in local politics; his mother ran a hairdressing shop in an unfashionable section of central London. As their means allowed, they invested in their sons' education. They scraped together enough money to send Sidney and his older brother to a private academy in London, and both boys had two years of schooling in Switzerland and Germany in the early 1870s.[102] When he returned to London at the age of sixteen, Sidney had to earn his living. He worked as an office clerk by day and took classes at night, distinguishing himself with many prizes

---

99   Webb, *Apprenticeship*, p. 401.
100   BP to SW, May 2, 1890. Passfield Papers.
101   Diary, 13 February 1890. See also, Diary, 26 April 1890. https://digital.library.lse.ac.uk/objects/lse:zib295pim
102   Royden J. Harrison speculates in *The Life and Times of Sidney and Beatrice Webb, 1858–1905: The Formative Years* (Houndmills, UK: MacMillan, 2000), pp. 7–8, that the boys were sent abroad for schooling during a troubled time at home, when their father very likely had an affair and an illegitimate child, possibly with a live-in servant.

and honors. After finishing second in the competitive examinations for the civil service in 1883, he was hired by the War Office, and advanced to become a clerk in the Colonial Office. He earned a law degree from University College, London, and was called to the Bar in 1885.

Like Beatrice, Sidney had been unhappy in love. During 1884 and 1885, he was romantically attached to a woman named Annie Adams, and expected that they would marry. When their relationship ended in the summer of 1885, he was deeply depressed.[103] Like Beatrice, he tried to bury himself in work in order to forget his pain. More than three years later, when his friend Edward Pease, a fellow Fabian, became engaged, Sidney acknowledged that "an old wound, which still embitters me, was torn open and bled." He lamented that many of his friends had married in recent years, while he himself remained single and lonely.[104]

All the while, Sidney devoted his passion and energy to the reform clubs and political societies that proliferated in London in the 1880s. In 1885, he joined the fledgling Fabian Society, which aimed to abolish poverty through legislative and administrative reforms, establish communal control of production and social life, and convert the British public and governing class to its socialist agenda with a barrage of facts and statistics. Quickly emerging as a leader, he formed friendships with a number of men who would make their mark on British culture and politics. All were instrumental in introducing and popularizing the concept of democratic socialism in Britain. In demand as a pamphleteer, lecturer and debater, he impressed his audiences with the breadth and depth of his knowledge and his total recall of facts. Hearing Sidney give a public address for the first time, the great Irish playwright and fellow

---

103 Adams married Corrie Grant, a barrister and former journalist who would eventually become a Liberal MP. Sidney wrote to Graham Wallas and Bernard Shaw in July and August 1885 about his great unhappiness and Adams's decision to marry someone else. See *Letters of Sidney and Beatrice Webb*, I, editor's note, p. 86, and *Selected Correspondence of Bernard Shaw: Bernard Shaw and the Webbs*, ed. by Alex C. Michalos and Deborah C. Poff (Toronto: University of Toronto Press, 2002), p. 7. Sidney identified Adams's future husband as "Corrie-Grant-Woodstock" in a letter to Wallas, but Woodstock is the bye-election he lost in July 1885, not part of his name. See "Lord Churchill Wins", *The New York Times*, July 4, 1885, p. 1.
104 SW to Marjorie Davidson, 12 December 1888. Passfield Papers.

Fabian, George Bernard Shaw, who became a life-long friend, described him as "the ablest man in England."[105]

Both Beatrice and Sidney were outsiders in the professional worlds of their day, Sidney by virtue of his class, Beatrice by virtue of her gender. This gave Sidney some sympathetic understanding of Beatrice's efforts to establish herself a social investigator and writer, and helped him to be more supportive of her efforts. It might have made her more understanding of his situation, but she always saw class as a greater disability than gender and was put off by Sidney's lower-class accent and demeanor and shabby clothing.

Beatrice and Sidney corresponded after she left London to resume caring for her father in March 1890; she invited him to visit for a day and sought his advice on her work. She valued his friendship, but noted his many faults in her diary: "His tiny tadpole body, unhealthy skin, lack of manner, cockney pronunciation, poverty, are all against him [...]. This self-complacent egotism, this disproportionate view of his own position is at once repulsive and ludicrous."[106] Sidney was 5'4", and his head was too large for his body. But his intellect, knowledge, and commitment to the social and political issues that she cared about appealed to her immensely. In May 1890, she suggested he travel with her and a few friends to the Co-operative Congress in Glasgow. As they strolled through the city, Sidney told Beatrice he was in love with her, upsetting the delicate balance of their relationship. After what she called a "critical twenty-four hours" had passed, she insisted, during another sunset walk, that she could offer him nothing but friendship. They agreed to a "working compact": they would continue to discuss their work and give each other advice and guidance, but Sidney would refrain from displays of emotion.[107]

Deeply in love with Beatrice, Sidney tried in vain to suppress his feelings and treat her as a colleague; whenever he forgot himself, she drew back. He found her *"ravissante."* She found him so "personally

105 Quoted in Jeanne MacKenzie, *A Victorian Courtship: The Story of Beatrice Potter and Sidney Webb* (New York: Oxford University Press, 1979), p. 62.
106 Diary, 26 April 1890. https://digital.library.lse.ac.uk/objects/lse:zib295pim
107 Diary, 23 May 1890. https://digital.library.lse.ac.uk/objects/lse:zib295pim

unattractive" that she doubted whether she could "submit to a close relationship."[108] Months of trial and tribulation resulted.

Still defining life in terms of either/or choices — love or work, reason or emotion, private happiness or public service — Beatrice was resigned to living a life in which emotions played no part. Characterizing herself as a woman "forged into a simple instrument for work" she warned Sidney, "Personal happiness to me is an absolutely remote thing; and I am to that degree 'heartless' that I regard everything from the point of view of making my own or another's life serve the community more effectively."[109]

Sidney was determined not to let personal happiness elude him. He urged Beatrice not to live in the past lest she succumb to "the growing numbness of emotional death."[110] He played on her fear of becoming "hard" and "self-willed" — that is, unwomanly — if she chose a professional life over a personal relationship. Using the same arguments that George Herbert Palmer had used to woo Alice Freeman, he warned her against sacrificing everything else for her intellectual work: "You would lose your subtle sympathy [...]. You would have dried up 'warmheartedness' in order to get Truth — and you would not even get Truth. Do not crush out feeling [...]. I cannot believe that you will commit this emotional suicide."[111]

Sidney offered Beatrice a life in which she could enjoy love *and* work, rather than continually pitting them against each other. He assured her that work would form the basis of their life together and pledged that each would contribute to the other's projects. "I will *make* you help me, and I will insist on helping you — our relationship shall be judged solely by the helpfulness to each other's work. Forgive me, if I say that I believe that if we were united we could do great things together," he claimed.[112] If they worked together, they would show that 1 plus 1 added to 11, not 2. "We have the ideas which can deliver the world [...]. Shall we continue to count each for one or is there no way of making our forces

---

108 *Ravissante*: SW to BP, 29/7/90. Unattractive: BP to SW [?8 October, 1890], referring to her reaction to him in Glasgow in May 1890. Passfield Papers.

109 BP to SW [?29 May 1890]. Passfield Papers.

110 SW to BP, 11–12 October 1890 (Letters in Diary Notebook). Passfield Papers.

111 SW to BP, 30 May 1890. Passfield Papers.

112 Diary, 23 May 1890. Emphasis in original. https://digital.library.lse.ac.uk/objects/lse:zib295pim

count for eleven? You have it in your hands to make me, in the noblest sense, great. I, even I, have it in my power to help your own particular work," he asserted.[113] "[*T*]*ogether we could move the world!*" he encouraged her, in stark contrast to Chamberlain's condescension and dominance.[114]

Nevertheless, Beatrice was still "haunted [...] day and night" by the memory of Chamberlain. Less than a week after striking her compact with Sidney in 1890, she reread her 1887 diary entries about Chamberlain, which she had sealed up with his letters.[115] She continued to follow Chamberlain's life and political career with feverish interest, gleaning details about him from newspapers and the gossip of friends. Later in the summer of 1890, she was mortified to find herself waiting outside a London museum for hours, hoping to catch sight of Chamberlain.[116]

As intellectual comrades, Beatrice and Sidney shared a great deal. Each had expertise that the other found useful. Sidney helped Beatrice develop practical proposals for solving the problems of sweated labor, explained theoretical economics to her, and introduced her to his fellow Fabians. Although she did not join the Fabian Society until the summer of 1892, she advised Sidney on how to increase its influence, instructed him about the English Poor Law, and helped to set up meetings between the Fabian leaders and the progressive wing of the Liberal Party.

On a more personal level, she corrected Sidney's pronunciation and suggested how he should dress and conduct himself in society.[117] He was quite willing to put himself in her hands. "Now tell me of other faults. Do you not realise that your real *Fach* [expertise] in life is to 'run' me?" he encouraged.[118] "I am trying to think of my vowels!" he proudly reported.[119]

Acutely aware that he was not her match in looks or social position, Sidney exhibited none of Chamberlain's domineering masculinity. When he learned that Beatrice would inherit considerable wealth when

---

113 SW to BP, 16 June 1890. Similarly, SW to BP [?4 December 1890]. Passfield Papers.
114 SW to BP, 30 May 1890. Passfield Papers. Emphasis in the original.
115 Diary, May 1890 note penned at the end of manuscript vol.14, https://digital.library.lse.ac.uk/objects/lse:zib295pim. See also, *Diary of Beatrice Webb*, I, editor's notes, pp. 208-11, 333.
116 Beatrice recorded this humiliating event in her diary on 1 December 1890. https://digital.library.lse.ac.uk/objects/lse:zib295pim
117 BP to SW [11 August 1890]; BP to SW [?September 1890]. Passfield Papers.
118 SW to BP, 16 June 1890. Passfield Papers.
119 SW to BP, 19 September 1890 (Letters in Diary Notebook). Passfield Papers.

her father died, he felt the imbalance in their relationship more keenly and suffered "a pang of wounded pride."[120] But he did not think her wealth should be an insurmountable bar to their relationship. In place of worldly riches, he offered her devotion, support, and encouragement, and dedication to the causes she believed in. He assured her he had no interest in trying to control her or absorb her life into his. "I can be in love without any desire for possession [...]. I am absolutely in your power," he wrote abjectly.[121]

Beatrice was troubled by Sidney's willingness to put himself so completely in her hands. Asking for his help in working through Alfred Marshall's *Principles of Economics*, she wrote, "In that case I shall be at your feet, and not you at mine, a wholesome reversal of the [usual] relationship — more in keeping with the relative dignity of Man and Woman [...] which will relieve the one-sided strain of our relationship."[122]

Nevertheless, she felt buoyed by their burgeoning friendship. She wrote appreciatively in her diary in the fall of 1890, "[Sidney] is certainly extraordinarily improved and becoming a needful background to my working life and I the same to him [...] the beauty of the friendship is that it stimulates the work of both."[123] And yet, only a few days later, she recoiled when he made an off-handed remark that seemed to assume they would marry. His presumption jolted her into seeing how impossible their situation was. Heart sore, she wrote Sidney a devastating letter, telling him she had tried to love him, but failed. Chamberlain's hold on her was too great, she explained, without identifying him by name. She had been "desperately in love [...] passionately attached to him" for six years and doubted she could care for anyone else. "The other man I loved but did not believe in, you I believe in but do not love," she wrote in anguish. She could not become engaged to a man she did not love. Trying to soften the blow, she announced, somewhat histrionically, "I am doing more than I would do for any other man — simply because you are a Socialist & I am a Socialist." She concluded by offering a modicum of hope, promising, "I will try to love you."[124] The

120 SW to BP, 29/7/90. Passfield Papers.
121 SW to BP, May 30, 1890. Passfield Papers.
122 BP to SW [11 August 1890]. Passfield Papers
123 Diary, 2 October 1890. https://digital.library.lse.ac.uk/objects/lse:zib295pim
124 BP to SW [?8 October 1890]. Passfield Papers

painful mixed messages she sent to Sidney reflected her own strong ambivalence about their relationship.

Sidney likened the unexpected letter to "an earthquake" but remained hopeful that she would be won over by seeing how much their combined work could contribute to the service of Humanity.[125] "I have love enough for two," he assured her.[126] More anguished letters followed. Her friends' disapproval increased Beatrice's resistance. "He is not enough of a man: You would grow out of him," Charles Booth warned her.[127]

In early December, when Sidney was recovering from a bout of scarlet fever, Beatrice confessed she still did not love him and was certain she could never love him. The still "open wound" that Chamberlain had inflicted left her incapable of loving. "I came out of that six years agony [...] like a bit of steel. I was not broken but hardened," she explained. Because she did not love Sidney, she could not "make the stupendous sacrifice of marriage."[128] She was even more adamant in her diary. "Marriage is to me another word for suicide," she wrote. "I cannot bring myself to face an act of *felo de se* [suicide] for a speculation in personal happiness. I am not prepared to make the minutest sacrifice of efficiency for the simple reason that though I am susceptible to the charm of being loved, I am not capable of loving. Personal passion has burnt itself out."[129]

Sidney was crushed, but accepted her decision with good grace. He wrote her several tender, gentle, loving letters and returned all of hers as she requested. "He has behaved *nobly*," Beatrice noted approvingly.[130] He hoped she would be happy, but warned her, "It does seem very difficult for a woman to go on leading a lonely life, without wifehood or motherhood, without unconsciously losing much of 'warmheartedness,' without sinking into sourness and narrowness."[131]

125 SW to BP, 7 PM [8 October 1890]. Passfield Papers.
126 SW to BP, Sunday 12 October [1890], Passfield Papers.
127 Diary, 22 October 1890. https://digital.library.lse.ac.uk/objects/lse:zib295pim?id=1 se%3Azib295pim
128 BP to SW [?7 December 1890]. Open wound: BP to SW [?8 October 1890]. Passfield Papers.
129 Diary, 1 December 1890. https://digital.library.lse.ac.uk/objects/lse:zib295pim?id= lse%3Azib295pim
130 Diary, 31 December 1890. https://digital.library.lse.ac.uk/objects/lse:zib295pim?id =lse%3Azib295pim. Emphasis in the original.
131 SW to BP [13?] 14 December, 1890. Passfield Papers.

Beatrice thought it would be better if they parted completely, but agreed to Sidney's desire to remain friends. She insisted that they could no longer be "intimate" friends, and could not write anything to each other that could not be read by somebody else.[132] Under these restrictions, they wrote less frequently for the next several months, and their correspondence became stiff and formal. They exchanged information about their work and asked each other for career advice, but their easy camaraderie was gone. Sidney was contemplating leaving the Colonial Office and earning his living as a journalist; Beatrice was looking for the topic for her next book. His letters were morose and dispirited; her emotional state is unknown because she wrote very little in her diary, and Sidney later burnt many of her letters. They did not meet in person between early January and April, when a sympathetic mutual friend brought them together by suggesting that Sidney would be the ideal person to help Beatrice write a summary of the first of the public lectures she was scheduled to give on cooperative organizations.[133] (Apparently, she had overcome her former aversion to women speaking in public.)

Their friendship restored through their work on the summary, Beatrice and Sidney traveled together with a mutual friend to the annual Cooperative Congress in May 1891, as they had the previous year. Sidney tried his luck again, and this time Beatrice did not withdraw. She explained her change of heart in her diary: "[Sidney's] resolute patient affection, his honest care for my welfare, helping and correcting me, a growing distrust of a self-absorbed life and the egotism of successful work (done on easy terms and reaping more admiration than it deserves), all these feelings are making for our eventual union, the joining together of our resources, mental and material, to serve together the 'commonwealth.'"[134] Her decision was the result of rational calculation rather than overpowering emotion. "My engagement was a very deliberate step each condition thought out thoroughly," she wrote in her diary at the end of 1891.[135] Several

---

132 BP to SW, Sunday [14? December 1890]. Passfield Papers.
133 BW, *Apprenticeship*, p. 407.
134 Diary, 31 May1891. https://digital.library.lse.ac.uk/objects/lse:zib295pim?id=lse%3Azib295pim
135 Diary, 27 December 1891. https://digital.library.lse.ac.uk/objects/lse:bin716wef

years later, she admitted, "[I]t was reason and not love that won me, a deliberate judgment on the man's worth and almost coldblooded calculation of the life I could live with him and he with me."[136]

Beatrice and Sidney left the cooperative congress without a clear resolution of their relationship, but with the expectation that they would marry. The "years of dull misery, with flashes of veritable agony" can "end in Work and Love", Beatrice wrote with cautious optimism in her diary.[137] They shared their first kiss in London, and in June they spent three weeks in Norway with two other Fabians. When they returned, they were secretly engaged.

Loneliness and a desire for companionship were factors in Beatrice's calculation, but work considerations were paramount.[138] Her determination to make her marriage serve her work shocked her friends and family, but Sidney understand and felt the same.[139] Sharing her sense of mission and devotion to work, he too viewed their union as a "consecration of our lives to the service of Humanity."[140] Such assertions left Beatrice confident that marriage to Sidney would "not wrench me from my old life, simply raise it to a higher level of usefulness."[141]

Beatrice did not pretend that Sidney excited her passion as Chamberlain had done. "I am not 'in love,' not as I was," she admitted in her diary when she and Sidney were on holiday in Norway.[142] She was acutely conscious that she was not making the "good" marriage that she had been groomed for. For a woman of her upbringing, marrying a man like Sidney was an act of bravery, boldness, and hope. "The world will wonder," she wrote a month after they became secretly engaged. "On the face of it, it seems like an extraordinary end to the once brilliant Beatrice Potter [...] to marry an ugly little man with no social ambition

---

136 Diary, 24 May 1897. https://digital.library.lse.ac.uk/objects/lse:hus734mos
137 Diary, 31 May 1891. https://digital.library.lse.ac.uk/objects/lse:zib295pim?id=lse%
    3Azib295pim
138 Diary, 6 June 1891, and 20 June 1891. https://digital.library.lse.ac.uk/objects/
    lse:wip502kaf
139 Shocked family and friends: BP to SW, 20 August 1891; BP to SW [?8 December
    1891]. Passfield Papers.
140 Diary, 20 June 1891, https://digital.library.lse.ac.uk/objects/lse:wip502kaf; SW to
    BP, 9 October 1890. Passfield Papers.
141 Diary, 20 June 1891. https://digital.library.lse.ac.uk/objects/lse:wip502kaf
142 Ibid.

and less means, whose only recommendation, some will say, is a certain pushing ability."[143]

Knowing that her marriage to Sidney would "griev[e] the old man past enduring," Beatrice insisted that their engagement had to remain a secret while her father was alive.[144] In the meantime, she suffered her sisters' criticisms about her lifestyle and work, and their concern that she would make a "bad" marriage.[145] She and Sidney told only a few close friends about their engagement.

Both Beatrice and Sidney were determined to pioneer a new style of marriage. "[W]e have a great responsibility laid upon us. Not only has each of us faculty and the opportunity of using it, but both together — the two united for a true marriage of fellowworkers — a perfect fellowship: it is for us to show that such a marriage may be durable and persisting," Beatrice wrote the summer they became engaged, asserting that the challenge made both of them "grave and anxious."[146] In fact, Sidney, more exuberant by nature, viewed their future with excitement. "Be it ours to prove to ourselves at any rate, that we are human beings of equivalent freedom and joint lives. What a chance we have!" he exulted.[147]

Sidney did much to allay Beatrice's fears during their year-long engagement. Theirs would not be a "chattel marriage" in which the wife became a possession of the husband, he promised. He did not want to absorb Beatrice's life or work into his, he repeatedly noted. If she ever felt he was acting out of "heedless selfishness" or "overpowering" her, she must let him know.[148] Because she was "a Sun" in her own right, with her own solar system, they would need to move in tandem, without becoming either "sun & planet" or "planet & satellite," Sidney warned. "When two solar systems come together it is a big thing!" he encouraged.[149] He purposefully planned for a collaboration that would support their

---

143 Ibid. See also, Diary, 21 January 1892. https://digital.library.lse.ac.uk/objects/ lse:bin716wef

144 Diary, 31 December 1890, https://digital.library.lse.ac.uk/objects/lse:zib295pim? id=lse%3Azib295pim, and 15 July 1891, https://digital.library.lse.ac.uk/objects/ lse:bin716wef. See also, BP to SW, 7 December l890. Passfield Papers.

145 BP to SW [20 August 1891], 3 January 1892 [?January 1892], and [?8 January 1892]. Passfield Papers.

146 Diary, 7 July 1891. https://digital.library.lse.ac.uk/objects/lse:bin716wef

147 SW to BP, 5 December/91. Passfield Papers.

148 SW to BP, 31 October 1891, Passfield Papers.

149 SW to BP, 30 May [?1891], Passfield Papers.

mutual independence, develop each other's strengths, and upset the conventional gendered division of labor. Her role would be to think and inspire, he told her; he would help her write more efficiently, and attend to proof-reading and fact-checking so she had more time to think. They would take turns serving as each other's private secretary. He looked forward to standing for Parliament in the future, but lamented that she could not be a Member of Parliament instead of him.[150] He presciently warned her that she would need to recant her opposition to women's suffrage. Occasionally, less enlightened views crept into his letters. He noted that he loved her all the more for her faults of "willfulness" and "ambition", before conceding that those traits were not actually faults.[151]

Despite his encouragement, Beatrice remained defensive about her desire to be both social investigator and wife. Explaining her preference for work over "domestic details," she mused, "I do not despise those details, but it is no use forging a fine instrument with exceptional effort and then discarding it for a rough tool. It may have been misdirected effort to make the instrument, it may be a mistake to transform the woman into a Thinker, but if the mistake has been paid for, one may hardly throw away the result."[152]

Still tending to see the world in either/or terms, lacking models of women who managed to couple marriage with professional life, Beatrice continued to feared that her work or her husband would suffer. "Every now and then I feel I have got into a hole out of which I can't struggle. I love you — But I love my work better. It seems to me that unless I give up my work I shall make a bad wife to you. You cannot follow me about the country, and I cannot stay with you," she lamented in the fall of 1891, when she was spending long periods out of London researching trade union archives and interviewing trade unionists.[153] Signaling that she was not prepared to cut back on her research so they could have more time together, and acknowledging that she needed another year to complete her research, she candidly informed him, "We need not love each other the less because with both of us, our work stands first and

150 SW to BP, 22 September 1891, Passfield Papers.
151 SW to BP, 25/5/91, Passfield Papers.
152 Diary, 7 July 1891. https://digital.library.lse.ac.uk/objects/lse:bin716wef
153 BP to SW, Saturday [12? September 1891]. Similarly, BP to SW, Xmas Day 1891. Passfield Papers.

our union second."[154] Sidney readily confirmed that work and duty were more important than personal pleasure. "We could not love each other so well, loved we not our work and duty more," he agreed.[155] He assured her she could be both a good researcher and a good wife, but unselfishly pledged, "I would infinitely rather endure to lose you for a year rather than have you neglect your work for my sake."[156]

Although she was increasingly happy in his company, there were aspects of Sidney's personality and looks that remained unappealing to Beatrice. He tried repeatedly to send a photograph of himself that was acceptable to her. She returned the first, admonishing, "It is too hideous for anything [....] let me have the head only — it is the head only that I am marrying."[157] He had more photos taken, according to her directions, but feared she would be disappointed. Warning her that nothing could make his face appear handsome, he pointed out, "I could not love you anymore if I were perfect in form."[158] He sent her one of the new pictures with apologies for his "ugliness" and later joked about their "Beauty and the Beast" relationship.[159] She continued to advise him on his pronunciation and clothing. "You can improve!" she encouraged.

Working directly with Sidney allayed more of Beatrice's concerns. They spent a few days in August working together on material she was gathering for her book on trade unions, and had another two weeks of joint work in October. They worked long hours with frequent interruptions for "intervals of 'human nature'", as Beatrice referred to what was most likely kissing and cuddling — a reassuring indication that Sidney's appearance did not pose an insurmountable bar to physical intimacy.[160] "It is very sweet this warm and close companionship in work," she observed in August.[161] Their fortnight of hard work and

---

154 BP to SW [?12 September 1891]. Passfield Papers.

155 SW to BP, 14/9/91. Passfield Papers.

156 SW to BP, 14/9/91. A second letter, written the same day (dated 14 Sept/91), reiterated his willingness to put her work ahead of their personal pleasure. Passfield Papers.

157 BP to SW [20 August 1891]. Passfield Papers.

158 SW to BP, 1 September 1891; her directions: SW to BP, 7/9/91. Passfield Papers.

159 Photo: SW to BP, 23 Sept/91; Beauty and the Beast: SW to BP, 3 Nov/91. Passfield Papers.

160 Human nature: Diary, 11 August 1891, 19 August 1891, and 10 October 1891. https://digital.library.lse.ac.uk/objects/lse:bin716wef

161 Diary, 11 August, 1891. Ibid.

"blessed" companionship in October made Beatrice very happy. But as old fears were laid to rest, new ones emerged. Convinced that her early success was the result of transforming her anguish over Chamberlain into productive energy, Beatrice soon began to worry that a happy marriage would make her less productive and too dependent on Sidney.

Despite their increasing closeness, Beatrice and Sidney had few opportunities to be together in the fall and winter of 1891–92. When she was not caring for her father, she was rushing off to industrial towns in northern England to review trade union records, interview trade unionists, and attend union meetings. Sidney resigned from the Colonial Office in September 1891, intending to work as a journalist and help Beatrice with her book, but was soon caught up on his own activities. Despite his good intentions, he was often unavailable to help Beatrice, as he struggled to meet journalistic deadlines, complete a busy lecture schedule, and wage a hard-fought electoral campaign for a seat on the London County Council.

Sidney was mostly in London, but also had engagements in other cities. They met when they could: on railway platforms in various towns, before their trains took off in opposite directions; in hotels, if their schedules permitted a longer stay in the same city. Beatrice, who thought of herself as an "investigator living the life of a bohemian", took pride in the "daring unconventionality" of their hotel meetings.[162] When Sidney joined her for two weeks to work on the trade union book in the town of Tynemouth, she "coolly" hired a private sitting room in her hotel so they could work undisturbed. Sidney slept in a different hotel, but posed as her private secretary. They churned out masses of material, while also making time for "human nature" without the hotel guests being any the wiser.[163]

They handled their separations well and kept each other informed of all they were doing. Their correspondence (especially Sidney's daily missives) teemed with work-related discussions: strategic analyses of key political and social issues, accounts of whom they saw and what was said, mutual advice about what to say or write or do about particular topics.

---

162 Bohemian: Diary, 27 December 1891. Daring unconventionality: Diary, 25 September 1891. https://digital.library.lse.ac.uk/objects/lse:bin716wef

163 Diary, 10 October 1891. https://digital.library.lse.ac.uk/objects/lse:bin716wef

Although Beatrice was determined to focus on work rather than their personal lives, their relationship was not without romance. Beatrice sent flowers from her father's garden to spark memories of special times between them; Sidney saw her face in his imagination, kissed her picture before going to bed, remembered the smile on her lips and how beautiful she had looked in the blue silk dress she wore in Norway. Their marriage would be not a "foolish gust of passion" but a great and enduring love, a "holy friendship," he promised.[164]

Although he is often portrayed as a humorless grinder of facts, Sidney revealed another side of his personality in the daily letters he wrote to Beatrice during their engagement. He discussed literature and art, described scenic views, and wrote her gossipy, amusing anecdotes about people they knew. He was sympathetic to Nora in *The Doll's House*, but appalled by Mary Costelloe's "*wickedness*" in leaving her husband (Sidney's friend and fellow Fabian, Frank Costelloe) and two children to go off with Bernard Berenson.[165]

Their relationship overturned upper-class conventions in another major way. Beatrice paid Sidney's electoral expenses for the London County Council (LCC) seat, and planned to use her inheritance to pay for the bulk of their living expenses once they were married, freeing Sidney from having to earn a living. He gratefully accepted her financial support and admitted that it relieved him of considerable anxiety.[166] Reliant on her intellectual and financial assistance, he stressed that he would be "the Member for Potter" on the LCC and dutifully gave her an accounting his expenditures.[167]

Throughout the fall and winter, he continued to soothe Beatrice's anxiety about being a "'professional' wife", as she termed her future role.[168] He assured her that her calculated approach to work and marriage did not make her "unwomanly" (as one of her friends had charged), and promised, "It is possible to have at the same time great love, keen

---

164 SW to BP, 1/3/92. Passfield Papers.
165 SW to BP, 1/9/91, 14/9/91, emphasis in the original. Passfield Papers. Before she married Costelloe, Mary Whitall Smith had been romantically linked with George Herbert Palmer, her professor at the Harvard Annex in 1884. See Chapter 1, pp. 36–37.
166 SW to BP, 9 Sept. 1891; BP to SW [?8 December 1891]. Passfield Papers.
167 SW to BP, 9 Dec/1891. Passfield Papers.
168 BP to SW, Xmas Day [1891]. Passfield Papers.

desire for work, and a great sense of responsibility."[169] Responding to her persistent fear that a change of name and change in status from spinster investigator to married woman would be "disastrous" for her trade union investigations, he was prepared to delay their wedding until she completed more research.[170]

Despite herself, Beatrice was increasingly happy with her new life. When she saw Chamberlain and his wife from a distance at a railway station during one of her research trips in the fall of 1891, she was relieved she was not with him. "I shuddered as I imagined the life I had missed," she wrote in her diary.[171]

When she finally informed her sisters about her engagement, several days after Richard Potter died on New Year's Day 1892, Beatrice warned them that Sidney was "small and ugly" and lacked savoir faire, social position, and wealth.[172] Having been prepared to break with her sisters if they opposed the marriage, she was relieved that the family "behaved with benevolence and good sense" in accepting Sidney, even if they did not like him or his Socialist politics.[173] Beatrice found it hard to put aside her own class prejudices when she visited Sidney's sister and widowed mother in their "dingy", "crowded", "lower middle class" home. But happiness and love helped her overcome her discomfort in their "ugly and small surroundings."[174]

Sidney had many detractors and few champions among Beatrice's friends and extended family. She was tainted by her adhesion to Socialism as well as her attachment to Sidney. The Booths virtually dropped her after they learned of her engagement although they resumed their friendship by the wedding.[175] Herbert Spencer, offended by her Socialist ties, no longer wanted her to be his literary executor.[176]

---

169 SW to BP, 9 Dec/1891; BP to SW [?8 December 91]. Passfield Papers.

170 Disastrous: BP to SW [?early January 1892]. See also, BP to SW [?12 September 1891]; SW to BP, 14/9/91, and 14 Sept/91. Passfield Papers.

171 Diary, 21 October 1891. https://digital.library.lse.ac.uk/objects/lse:bin716wef

172 BP to Laurencina Holt (written in late December, mailed in early January 1892), in *Letters of Sidney and Beatrice Webb*, I, pp. 382–84.

173 Break: BP to Mary Playne [early January 1892], in *Letters of Sidney and Beatrice Webb*, I, pp. 384–85. Benevolence and good sense: Diary, 21 January 1892. https://digital.library.lse.ac.uk/objects/lse:bin716wef

174 Diary, 21 January 1892. https://digital.library.lse.ac.uk/objects/lse:bin716wef

175 Dropped: Diary, 27 December 1891. https://digital.library.lse.ac.uk/objects/lse:bin716wef

176 Diary, 21 January 1892. https://digital.library.lse.ac.uk/objects/lse:bin716wef

Beatrice's brother-in-law, Leonard Courtney, a Liberal MP, told her that she would have been an ideal candidate to serve on the Royal Commission on Labour (which he headed) were it not for her Socialist views.[177] The general reaction to the engagement was so critical that Beatrice wondered in retrospect whether she would have had the "courage" to marry Sidney had not at least one valued friend recognized that he "was essentially distinguished in character and intelligence."[178] Beatrice had detractors, too. H. W. Massingham, a journalist friend of Sidney's who was unaware of the engagement, advised him to marry a wealthy woman, but to steer clear of Beatrice Potter lest he discover that he "had bitten off more than you could chew." Massingham added, "Don't marry a clever woman, [because] they're too much trouble."[179]

After their engagement became public, Sidney battled on in his campaign to win a seat on the London County Council while Beatrice continued her exploration of trade unions. After his victory in March 1892, he took over two important committees and began to work on plans for overhauling London's technical education system. A newly confident Beatrice, feeling less in need of his help (she had hired a male secretary, much to the dismay of her sisters and brothers-in-law), told Sidney to focus on his work instead of helping her with her book.[180]

By the time she and Sidney married, in a civil ceremony at the St. Pancras Vestry Hall, in July 1892, Beatrice was increasingly optimistic about her chances of blending personal happiness with professional success. She may not have felt the same passion that she had felt for Chamberlain, but Sidney had become essential to her and they loved each other "devotedly." "Never did I imagine such happiness," Beatrice wrote in early May.[181] "The only thing I regret parting with is my *name* — I *do* resent that," she complained to Sidney three weeks before the

---

177 BP to SW [undated, between letters of January 1 and January 3, 1892]. Passfield Papers. Beatrice had been lobbying for the position. See *Letters of Sidney and Beatrice Webb*, I, editor's note, p. 278.

178 Diary, 24 May 1897. https://digital.library.lse.ac.uk/objects/lse:hus734mos. The friend was Alice Stopford Green, widow of historian John Richard Green, and herself a writer. Beatrice often stayed with her when she was working in London, and Green had been instrumental in bringing Beatrice and Sidney back together in the spring of 1891.

179 SW to BP, 15/9/91. Passfield Papers.

180 BP to SW, 5 May, 1892. Similarly, BP to SW [?March 1892]. Passfield Papers.

181 Diary, 4 May 1892. https://digital.library.lse.ac.uk/objects/lse:bin716wef

wedding.[182] On the day of the ceremony, she again lamented, "Exit Beatrice Potter. Enter Beatrice Webb, or rather (Mrs.) Sidney Webb for I lose alas! both names."[183] The newlyweds spent their honeymoon in Ireland and Scotland, happily researching trade unionism. They were away for eight weeks, but devoted only a few days to the sightseeing that would have constituted a more conventional wedding trip.

Adjusting to Marriage and the Working Partnership, 1892–1902

The Webbs's partnership lasted for more than fifty years and produced a remarkable body of work and a deeply devoted couple. They worked together as researchers and writers, activist reformers, practicing politicians, policy advisors, behind-the-scenes manipulators, and educators. They aimed to construct "a science of society" and translate their findings into practical reforms in social policy and public administration. They published highly regarded studies detailing the evolution of working class organizations and English local government. They wrote scores of books and articles proposing fundamental reforms in social policy and governmental institutions. They left a legacy in the administrative structure of London's educational system, the socialist platform of the British Labour Party, and the design of the post-World War II British welfare state. They helped mold several generations of civil servants and policy analysts through their work with the London School of Economics and Political Science and the *New Statesman*, both of which they helped to found. Beatrice believed they fulfilled Sidney's prediction that they would be more productive by working together than apart. She maintained they were "welded by common work and experience into a complete harmony of thought and action" and were "singularly at one in heart and intellect."[184]

---

182 BP to SW [?1 July 1892], emphasis in the original. Passfield Papers.

183 Diary, 23 July 1892. https://digital.library.lse.ac.uk/objects/lse:bin716wef. There were precedents for not taking a husband's name in British feminist circles, according to Philipa Levine, "'So Few Prizes and So Many Blanks': Marriage and Feminism in Later Nineteenth-Century England", *Journal of British Studies*, 28 (April 1989), 150–74 (p. 157). But Beatrice was not part of those circles.

184 Welded: Diary, 16 July 1921. https://digital.library.lse.ac.uk/objects/lse:ras535xan. Singularly at one: Diary, 12 January 1934. https://digital.library.lse.ac.uk/objects/lse:rut323dac

Fig. 5 Beatrice and Sidney at work around 1895. Unknown photographer. LSE Image Library/1385. London School of Economics and Political Science, British Library of Political and Economic Science.

Although Beatrice characterized herself from the start of her marriage as an extraordinarily fortunate wife who delighted in the "perfection" of her relationship with Sidney and the great happiness of their daily life, she was, in fact, deeply ambivalent about her husband and her work throughout the first decade of their marriage.[185]

The root problem was that her sensual, passionate nature was not fully satisfied by Sidney. During their courtship, Beatrice had made it brutally clear that he did not excite her sexually. Indeed, she may have chosen to marry him, in part, because he did not arouse her passion. Convinced that passion and romance were antithetical to serious, intensive "brainwork", she felt confident that her relationship with Sidney would not supplant her interest in work or undermine her commitment to social reform. Having spent the years after the rupture with Chamberlain trying to suppress her sexual yearnings, she had

---

185 Diary, 1 December 1892. Similarly, Diary, 21 June 1893, and Christmas Day, 1893. https://digital.library.lse.ac.uk/objects/lse:bin716wef

convinced herself that it was heroic and ennobling to subordinate her physical nature in order to devote herself to work that would contribute to the good of society.[186]

As Beatrice herself admitted, marrying Sidney was an act of renunciation, not self-indulgence. Referring to Sidney as a comrade and companion suggests they had a collegial working relationship rather than a passionate partnering. Addressing him as her "darling boy" when she wrote to him during their engagement and marriage suggests she took maternal pride in shaping him and advancing his career.[187] Both designations suggest she gave him affectionate devotion, tender and loving care — but not erotic, passionate love. "With intellectual persons love is the passion for warm enduring affection and intimate mental companionship," she reflected after five years of marriage.[188]

At times, Beatrice's sensual side rebelled, leaving her physically debilitated, emotionally drained, and deeply depressed. The outward signs were flagging interest in her work and recurrent daydreaming about Joseph Chamberlain, who remained for her a symbol of passion and romance. He began to appear in her fantasy life in July 1893, just a year after her wedding. Despite her claims of being "triumphantly happy" with Sidney, she was still dazzled by Chamberlain's "extraordinary personality" and political gifts, although she increasingly questioned whether he was using them for self-aggrandizement rather than to advance the general good.[189] Brooding about him, she lost her zest for work. She followed his career, and struggled to keep her imagination in check. In March 1896, despite her avowals of being "absolutely happy with Sidney", she could not shake Chamberlain from her thoughts.[190]

186 Beatrice reviewed her reasoning at length in her Diary on New Year's Day, 1901. https://digital.library.lse.ac.uk/objects/lse:nef769qal
187 She remarked on the "maternal tenderness" she felt for Sidney in Diary, 20 June 1891. https://digital.library.lse.ac.uk/objects/lse:bin716wef Elsie Clews Parsons observed that when one spouse "comes to love the other in a parental kind of way", the marriage was in trouble. See Chapter 3, p. 229.
188 Diary, 14 January 1898. https://digital.library.lse.ac.uk/objects/lse:hus734mos
189 Diary, 30 July 1893. https://digital.library.lse.ac.uk/objects/lse:bin716wef
190 Diary, 28 March 1896. https://digital.library.lse.ac.uk/objects/lse:hus734mos

Beatrice felt she had conquered her "morbid troublings" by the beginning of 1897.[191] She kept them at bay during 1898, when she and Sidney spent nine months traveling in America, Australia, and New Zealand, gathering information about the structure and practices of local governments. But after they were back in England, her thoughts returned to Chamberlain, who was drawing considerable press attention as Colonial Secretary during Britain's involvement in the Boer War in South Africa. "When I am at work I do not feel otherwise than happy and fortunately am well and can work my six hours. But after dinner when the cigarette is done I either feel depressed or my cursed habit of sentimental castle-building leads me to harp back to the past," she confided in her diary.[192]

Intellectually, Beatrice knew she had made the right choice in marrying Sidney and devoting her life to their joint work. "We have a constant delight in our daily life of search after truth and loving companionship, far away from personal ambition, competitive struggle, and notoriety. I should have hardened and coarsened if I had been subject to the strain of a big flashy social position. The sweet little person that he [Chamberlain] chose is far better suited to be his wife," she reminded herself in the fall of 1899, at a time when she felt she and Sidney had almost no political influence.[193] Beatrice's rationalizations were of little avail. During the spring of 1900, her "foolish daydreams" about Chamberlain were again interfering with her work.[194] She knew that her tender affection for Sidney, and his devotion to her, was real and heartfelt. But her more passionate, romantic self still yearned for a different type of intimacy with a more commanding and important man. She probed her contradictory emotions in her diary:

---

191 Diary, 18 January 1897. https://digital.library.lse.ac.uk/objects/lse:hus734mos
192 Diary, 15 June 1899. https://digital.library.lse.ac.uk/objects/lse:nef769qal
193 Diary, 10 October 1899. https://digital.library.lse.ac.uk/objects/lse:nef769qal. Beatrice made the same point about becoming "hardened and coarsened" in a conversation with Chamberlain's sister in 1902 (Diary, 15 February 1902). Mary Endicott, the "sweet little person" that Chamberlain married in 1888, was the perfect political wife, according to Pat Jalland, *Women, Marriage, and Politics, 1860–1914* (Oxford: Oxford University Press, 1988), pp. 229–31. Jalland notes that Mary gave Chamberlain uncritical support and never voiced her own opinions. She was not a total cipher, however. When Chamberlain was felled by a stroke in 1906, she conducted his political business in order to hide the extent of the damage he suffered.
194 Diary, 22 May 1900. https://digital.library.lse.ac.uk/objects/lse:nef769qal

Just as it was the worst part of my nature that led me into passionate feeling for Chamberlain so it was the best part of my nature which led me to accept Sidney after so much doubt and delay. And certainly, just as I was well-punished for the one, I have been richly rewarded for the other course of feeling and conduct. And yet, notwithstanding this conviction, I find my thoughts constantly wandering to the great man.[195]

A chance meeting with Chamberlain on the terrace of the House of Commons in July 1900 increased Beatrice's unhappiness. During their lengthy conversation, she felt they were being watched and judged.[196] When she heard rumors, a few weeks later, that Chamberlain's marriage was in trouble, Beatrice battled against "a terrible depression."[197] She was distraught by the thought of Chamberlain's misery, and feared — even though she knew her concern was "morbid and exaggerated" — that some people were blaming her for his marital difficulties. "And to think that I am over 40, and he is over 60! What an absurdity," she chastised herself.[198]

Beatrice was in great anguish throughout the summer and fall of 1900, and unable to shake off thoughts of Chamberlain. His political mastery was on display in Parliamentary debates and public meetings, and his speeches were widely reported in the press during the general election of October 1900, which turned on the issue of the Government's prosecution of the war. Framed as a vote of confidence in the Government's conduct of the Boer War, and Chamberlain's actions as Colonial Secretary, the election resulted in a landslide victory for Chamberlain and the Conservative Party. Beatrice turned a brave face to the world, and to Sidney, who knew nothing of her struggle.[199] But she was so miserable that, on a working vacation with Sidney in Yorkshire in the fall of 1900, she sometimes went off by herself to the moors to weep. Decades later, she described what she went through as a "nervous breakdown."[200]

---

195 Ibid.
196 Diary, 4 July 1900. https://digital.library.lse.ac.uk/objects/lse:cav667nar
197 Diary, 19 October 1900. https://digital.library.lse.ac.uk/objects/lse:cav667nar
198 Diary, 16 November 1900. https://digital.library.lse.ac.uk/objects/lse:cav667nar
199 Diary, New Year's Day, 1901. https://digital.library.lse.ac.uk/objects/lse:nef769qal. Similarly, 9 December 1901. https://digital.library.lse.ac.uk/objects/lse:bex452giv
200 Diary, 14 April 1927. https://digital.library.lse.ac.uk/objects/lse:dut736noc

Beatrice's battle with depression and obsession lasted for another year. She periodically announced that she was cured, only to suffer another relapse. Throughout 1901, which she described in her diary as the most unsatisfactory year since her marriage, she felt that "the sensual side of my nature seemed to be growing at the expense of the intellectual."[201] Nevertheless, she routinely described herself — in her diaries, and in letters to Sidney and others — as a happily married woman who had found the perfect mate and lifestyle. "Sometimes Sidney and I feel that we can hardly repay by our work the happiness and joy of our life. It seems so luxurious to be able to choose what work one will do according to one's faith in its usefulness and do that work in loving comradeship," she asserted in the midst of the period when she would slink off alone to weep.[202] On a day when she could not shake Chamberlain from her thoughts, she wrote to Sidney, "I don't like being away from my boy, but I lie awake and think how much I love him and how glad I am to have married him [...]. To have found a comrade who also believes in [building up a science of society] is extraordinary good luck."[203]

During this difficult time, the Webbs went off on another working vacation. Lying alone in the hot sun on a rocky beach on the Dorset coast, when Sidney had been called back to London for a day, Beatrice's thoughts turned to sex and motherhood. Watching the waves ebb and flow on the beach, she described the "music" made by the withdrawing waves as "a sound of infinite sweetness and sadness, like the inevitable withdrawal of a lover from the mistress he still loves." Languidly considering whether a woman "should marry the same man, in order to have babies, that one would select as joint author" and whether "a man or a woman [ought] to have many relations with the other sex or only one," she decided the answer was "one lover, not only in the letter but also in the spirit." Beatrice dismissed her thoughts as "noonday dreaming [...] with no bearing on my personal life" but she could not shake her sensuous mood. She continued:

201 Diary, 9 December 1901. https://digital.library.lse.ac.uk/objects/lse:bex452giv
202 Diary, 25 September 1900. https://digital.library.lse.ac.uk/objects/lse:foj709hir
203 BP to SW [?22 May 1900], in *Letters of Sidney and Beatrice Webb*, II, p. 131. Diary, 22 May 1900. https://digital.library.lse.ac.uk/objects/lse:nef769qal

I move and lie full length on the beach and watch the marvelously tinted wave break on the pink pebbles and then withdraw itself with a sweet low moan [....]. I remember I am well over forty, growing grey and somewhat wrinkled. I get up, shake myself mentally from sunshine dreams: Tomorrow I must plan out the chapter on the 'Select Vestry' otherwise it won't be ready for [Sidney] to write on Thursday.[204]

Beatrice's speculations about having two lovers, the erotic imagery of the waves lapping on the shore and withdrawing "with a sweet low moan", her abrupt transition from reveling in physical sensation and daydreams to the no-nonsense work of planning a chapter on select vestries: all are powerful testimony to her sexual and emotional repression.[205]

Beatrice's feelings of unfulfilled womanhood were exacerbated by the Webbs' decision not to have children. Convinced that the functions of "brainworker" and mother were essentially incompatible, Beatrice believed that a woman had to choose one or the other, a choice that was deeply painful for her. Accepting the societal view that motherhood was a woman's crowning achievement, she felt that "intellectual" women who did not have children "thwart[ed] all the purposes of their nature." In keeping with early twentieth-century views on eugenics, Beatrice also worried that the Britain's gene pool would suffer if intellectually gifted couples and members of the upper-classes failed to reproduce.[206] Nevertheless, having worked so hard and made so many sacrifices to shape her intellect into "an instrument for research," Beatrice believed that it was imperative to protect that investment. Fearful that motherhood would destroy her intellectual acuity, she opted not to have children, and Sidney agreed. Her summary judgment, written on New Year's Day 1901, a few weeks before her forty-third birthday, was "on the whole I do not regret the decision, still less does Sidney."[207] Nevertheless, a few

---

204 Diary, 24 April 1901. https://digital.library.lse.ac.uk/objects/lse:bex452giv
205 Some of Beatrice's contemporaries also thought about the benefits of having one partner for sex and another for intellectual activities. See Ruth Brandon, *The New Women and the Old Men: Love, Sex and the Woman Question* (New York: Norton, 1990) and Judith R. Walkowitz, "Science, Feminism and Romance: The Men and Women's Club, 1885–1889", *History Workshop Journal*, 21 (Spring 1986), 37–59.
206 See Caine, p. 116, for Beatrice's criticism of companionate couples who chose not to have children. For her connections to the early twentieth-century eugenics movement in Britain, see Donald MacKenzie, "Eugenics in Britain", *Social Studies of Science*, 6 (1976), 499–532.
207 Diary, New Year's Day, 1901. https://digital.library.lse.ac.uk/objects/lse:nef769qal

months later, during her contemplation of her life choices on the beach in Dorset, she asked herself, "Are the books we have written together worth (to the community) the babies we might have had?"[208] The Webbs would refer to their pet projects — the London School of Economics, the *New Statesman*, the Poor Law Report, their book about Soviet Russia — as their "children." These achievements were compensation, but perhaps not wholly satisfactory substitutes, for flesh and blood offspring.

Coming to Terms with the Working Partnership

Everything about the Webbs's life was arranged to maximize their ability to work. Neither Beatrice nor Sidney had an interest in making their home a showpiece of Victorian domesticity. Their London domicile was chosen for its proximity to Parliament. Their dining room doubled as a workroom, its walls lined with books. Their living room was set up like a public meeting space, with long banks of seats fitted into alcoves, and no sofa.[209] Beatrice spent several weeks shopping for wallpaper and furnishings when they moved in, but happily left the day-to-day details of housekeeping and food preparation to servants, who ran the household with little supervision.[210]

In their first years together, the Webbs did not go out much, entertained few people other than their families and Sidney's Fabian friends, and rarely went to the theatre or concerts. Beatrice immersed herself in research and writing; Sidney worked with her, but also devoted long hours to the London County Council, the Fabian Society, and the London School of Economics. Vacations, too, were work opportunities, mostly devoted to reading and writing interspersed with walks and hikes. (During a three-week vacation in 1901, Sidney made his way through twenty-six books borrowed from the London Library.[211])

Sidney was the perfect work partner, capable of unflagging effort and long hours of focused attention, morning, afternoon, and night.

---

208 Diary, 24 April 1901. https://digital.library.lse.ac.uk/objects/lse:bex452giv
209 *Diary of Beatrice Webb*, II, Introduction, pp. 13–14.
210 For example, Diary, 24 May 1897, https://digital.library.lse.ac.uk/objects/lse:hus734mos; 11 May 1923, https://digital.library.lse.ac.uk/objects/lse:lec463nir; 18 July 1926, https://digital.library.lse.ac.uk/objects/lse:beg266zey. BW to Mary Hankinson, 10/5/10, in *Letters of Sidney and Beatrice Webb*, II, p. 345.
211 Diary, 24 April 1901. https://digital.library.lse.ac.uk/objects/lse:bex452giv

He "is perpetually working," Beatrice reported in 1901 — very likely with a mixture of awe and exasperation. She herself could work no more than six hours per day. Sidney did not share her cultural interests, and discouraged her from accepting social engagements that might distract her from the next day's work or tire her out. These habits increased the Webbs's output, but limited their companionship to a narrow sphere. They also made it difficult for Beatrice to pursue her interest in music, literature, and religion, and find outlets for her sociability. In 1893, in the midst of brooding about Chamberlain, she yearned for "a wider culture" of art and literature.[212] During her severe depression in 1901, she craved music and religious outlets.[213]

Accustomed to working on her own, highly ambitious but greatly insecure, Beatrice was sometimes frustrated by Sidney's critical scrutiny, probing analysis, and dry writing style. After she spent five days writing a lecture in 1893, she was upset when Sidney felt it needed more work and offered to help her. His reaction caused a "little bit of a tiff" and left her feeling mortified and angry. They spent another four days working together on a new draft. Relying so much on Sidney's help undermined Beatrice's confidence and made feel like a parasite. She was similarly unnerved by the constructive criticism and rewriting that Sidney's fellow Fabians provided on draft chapters of their book.[214]

This was not the only occasion when the Webbs's collaboration became acrimonious. They argued so much over one chapter of *Industrial Democracy* in 1897, that they agreed to focus temporarily on separate sections of the book.[215] At other times, they resolved their arguments with "a shower of kisses."[216] All in all, Beatrice felt that the collaboration took a considerable mental and emotional toll. "How could we do it, if working together were not, in itself, delightful," she reflected.[217]

She also felt constrained and oppressed by the dryness of their material and prose style. She wrote despondently in the summer of 1894, "Not getting on with our [trade union] book. It is a horrid grind, this analysis — one sentence is exactly like another — the same words, the

---

212 Diary, 30 July 1893. https://digital.library.lse.ac.uk/objects/lse:bin716wef
213 Diary, 9 December 1901. https://digital.library.lse.ac.uk/objects/lse:bex452giv
214 Diary, 17 September 1893. https://digital.library.lse.ac.uk/objects/lse:bin716wef
215 Diary, 27 August 1897. https://digital.library.lse.ac.uk/objects/lse:hus734mos
216 Diary, 18 January 1897. https://digital.library.lse.ac.uk/objects/lse:hus734mos
217 Diary, 10 November 1902. https://digital.library.lse.ac.uk/objects/lse:won715bor

same construction, no relief in narrative [...]. I feel horribly vexed with myself for loitering and idling as I do morning after morning, looking on while poor Sidney drudges along."[218] Six months later, although the work was going better, Beatrice expressed her desire to write a novel as a way of having a "fling": "I want to imagine anything I damn please without regard to facts as they are [...]. I want to try my hand at an artist's work instead of mechanics. I am sick to death of trying to put out hideous facts, multitudinous details, exasperating qualifications in readable form."[219] At work on the first volume of their massive study of local government in 1901, she found herself "brooding" over religious questions and reading about psychology, theology, and the lives of the saints. "The one subject my mind revolts at is local government," she admitted.[220] Significantly, the recurring episodes when Beatrice could not motivate herself to work or argued with Sidney about their work coincided with the times she was unable to stop brooding about Chamberlain.

Starvation Therapy

Beatrice maintained that she cured the deep depression that began in 1900 by "starvation."[221] Taking the advice of a celebrated doctor who believed diet was the key to healthy living, she became a vegetarian late in 1901, put herself on an exceedingly strict diet, and precipitously lost weight. She recorded her food intake and health symptoms in her diary. After several months, her weight stabilized, her eczema was healing, she slept better, and she could concentrate and work for longer hours. Her mood improved, and she was able to keep her thoughts and emotions under control. "I am no longer plagued by foolish fancies and absurd daydreams," she wrote in relief in late April 1902.[222] Her later diaries contain no more regrets about her childless state or yearning ruminations about Chamberlain, although she continued to follow his career with interest. (Chamberlain suffered a severe stroke in 1906 and died in 1914.)

---

218 Diary, 10 July 1894. https://digital.library.lse.ac.uk/objects/lse:kac646sis and https://digital.library.lse.ac.uk/objects/lse:wip502kaf

219 Diary, 1 February 1895. https://digital.library.lse.ac.uk/objects/lse:kac646sis

220 Diary, 2 January 1901. https://digital.library.lse.ac.uk/objects/lse:bex452giv

221 Diary, 14 April 1927. https://digital.library.lse.ac.uk/objects/lse:dut736noc

222 Diary, 25 April 1902. https://digital.library.lse.ac.uk/objects/lse:xas833lok

Beatrice would remain an abstemious, even a faddish eater, rigorously limiting how much she ate and denying herself all rich foods and stimulants like coffee. The "starvation" therapy was more than physical: she was also starving her emotions by repressing the sensual and imaginative side of her nature in her life with Sidney.

Other lifestyle changes that began in 1902 very probably contributed to Beatrice's recovery and helped to resolve her ambivalence about her marriage. She derived enormous satisfaction during their first decade of their marriage from their professional success and the conviction that their star was rising. Sidney had pushed through important educational reforms on the London County Council. They had published several books, founded the London School of Economics, and were sought out as experts. "No young man or woman who is anxious to study or to work in public affairs can fail to come under our influence," Beatrice rejoiced in 1898.[223] But in 1900 and 1901, she felt they were largely isolated from the country's political leadership and spent most of their time with the "intellectual proletariat."[224]

By 1902, the Webbs were making deliberate efforts to increase their influence and gain support for their ideas by widening their social and political circles. They hosted eight to ten, occasionally as many as twenty-five, politicians, civil servants, and intellectuals at dinners and luncheons in their home on a weekly basis. Beatrice's upbringing and family background had groomed her to be a political hostess, and that was the role she would have played as Chamberlain's wife. The Webbs's guests may have left hungry for better quality meals and more generous portions, but they were likely sated by the discussions of social and political issues.[225] Beatrice shone in dispensing brilliant conversation. Sidney could weigh in and bask in her glow. He gained standing and recognition in political circles, and so did Beatrice. With an expanded social and intellectual world, she had more scope for her sociability and her keen interest in human personality. All this must have helped her accept the sacrifices she had made to marry Sidney. The autumn of 1902

223 Diary, [?] March 1898. https://digital.library.lse.ac.uk/objects/lse:hus734mos
224 Intellectual proletariat: Diary, New Year's Day, 1901. https://digital.library.lse.ac.uk/objects/lse:nef769qal
225 Beatrice's niece, Kitty Muggeridge, recalled the frugal meals Beatrice served. See Muggeridge and Adam, p. 15.

was "thoroughly satisfactory", she pronounced.[226] "I am frightened at my own happiness," Sidney confessed.[227]

The psychological battle Beatrice had waged for ten years was over. During the course of 1902, she settled into the routine of her married life and no longer wrote with yearning in her diary about the things Sidney could not offer. In 1903, she reflected, with seeming sincerity, "A woman who wanted a husband to spend hours talking to her or listening to her chitchat would find [Sidney] a trying husband. As it is we exactly suit each other's habits. Long hours of solitary brooding is what I am accustomed to and without which I doubt whether I could be productive [...]. I have my thoughts and he has his book, and both alike go to complete and fulfill our joint task."[228] In 1904, she paid a call on Chamberlain's wife, and then lunched with Sidney and both Chamberlains, without recording any distress or brooding.[229]

A Partnership of Equals

After 1902, the partnership with Sidney became the mainstay of Beatrice's emotional life. Over the next four decades, she extolled the happiness she and Sidney found in each other and their work without expressing the dissatisfactions of earlier years. On their forty-seventh wedding anniversary in 1939, she proudly asserted, "[W]e have been one and indivisible, in work and in rest, at home and abroad, in our private life and our public career."[230] The Webbs came to identify so completely with each other that they found it difficult to function apart. During one separation, Sidney lamented, "I get on with my various tasks with difficulty, missing my inspiration, my companionship and my joy! It is really terrible to think how dependent I am on your constant presence."[231] Beatrice observed in 1907, "Apart, we each of us live only half a life; together, we each of us have a double life."[232] In 1934, when

---

226 Diary, [?] December 1902. https://digital.library.lse.ac.uk/objects/lse:won715bor
227 Diary, 7 June 1902. https://digital.library.lse.ac.uk/objects/lse:xas833lok
228 Diary, 4 August 1903. https://digital.library.lse.ac.uk/objects/lse:xij627rup
229 Diary, 10 June 1904, 17 June 1904. https://digital.library.lse.ac.uk/objects/lse:xij627rup
230 Diary, 23 July 1939. https://digital.library.lse.ac.uk/objects/lse:tul234dab
231 SW to BW, 22 April 1908, in *Letters of Sidney and Beatrice Webb*, II, p. 298.
232 Diary, 21 June 1907. https://digital.library.lse.ac.uk/objects/lse:wur719qow

Sidney spent five weeks in the Soviet Union — the longest they had been separated — Beatrice suffered "acute emotional starvation" and felt she was "living a half-life."[233]

The sense of unity that fueled the Webbs' marriage and working partnership was as strong as that of any couple previously discussed. However, there was a fundamental difference in the way the Webbs experienced that unity. In the Palmer and Young relationships, and in Robert Herrick's romantic ideal, "oneness" meant that the man's interests and activities absorbed the woman and made it difficult for her to sustain a career of her own. In contrast, the Webbs achieved "oneness" without either partner being submerged in the other, and without rooting the relationship in male mastery and female subordination. Although Beatrice and Sidney talked about being "one," they spoke as frequently about the "jointness" of their personal and professional and partnership. The distinction is subtle but highly significant: "jointness" suggests a coupling and an adding together, while "oneness" connotes the absorption of one person by another. Beatrice's characterization of Sidney as "the Other One," and Sidney's idiosyncratic arithmetic ("in our case, $1 + 1 = 11$") reinforces the idea that their unity was achieved by adding two personalities together to jointly create a new one rather than simply submerging a weaker personality into a stronger one. "[N]either of us is outstandingly gifted; it is the '*combinat*' that is remarkable," Beatrice observed.[234]

The Webbs's collaboration and marriage has inspired many portraits and analyses. Most accounts highlight the partnership's unity rather than its egalitarian aspects. Beatrice is generally portrayed as the more brilliant, more creative, more original thinker, and by far the more colorful and masterful personality. Sidney is often depicted as a plodder who was ill-equipped to take the initiative or oppose Beatrice if they disagreed.[235] Norman and Jeanne Mackenzie, the editors of Beatrice's

---

233 Diary, 27 September 1934. https://digital.library.lse.ac.uk/objects/lse:rut323dac

234 Diary, 25 September 1933. https://digital.library.lse.ac.uk/objects/lse:tol638hey

235 Lisanne Radice, *Beatrice and Sidney Webb, Fabian Socialists* (New York: St. Martin's Press, 1984) is an exception. She argues that Sidney was the "more gifted" partner to whom Beatrice owed an immense intellectual debt (pp. 4–6). A recent analysis finds that the Webbs had a more egalitarian division of labor than two other couples (Bernard and Helen Bosanquet, and Victor and Sybella Branford) of their day who were similarly engaged in social investigation and improvement efforts. See Eileen Janes Yeo, "Social Science Couples in Britain at the Turn of the Twentieth Century:

diaries, argued that she was the guiding force in the marriage and Sidney was "happy to defer to Beatrice in all the policies of the partnership." Characterizing Sidney as a civil servant *par excellence*, trained and happy to implement the plans of his superiors, they suggest that he played a similar role with Beatrice, serving as "an untiringly loyal and immensely able instrument of her will."[236]

Certainly, Sidney was not an overbearing, authoritarian, controlling Victorian husband. This does not mean, however, that Beatrice dominated him. To view the Webbs's relationship as merely an inversion of the traditional model of dominant male and subservient female oversimplifies what was in fact a highly complex and mutually supportive collaboration. Their partnership fostered an egalitarianism that was manifested in three principal aspects of their work: the process of writing their books and developing their positions; the ways in which they influenced each other; and the diversity of roles each played over the long course of their partnership. Their union was a remarkable accomplishment for their own day, or for any time. Its success owed as much to Sidney as to Beatrice.

The Writing Partnership

Beatrice's diaries make clear how much intellectual give and take was involved in forging a partnership that enabled the Webbs to speak with a single — often overpowering — voice and function like "two typewriters clacking as one."[237] Beatrice may have chosen the topics for their books and led the research effort, but she did not control the writing or determine their conclusions unilaterally. In the early years of

---

Gender Divisions in Work and Marriage" in *For Better or Worse? Collaborative Couples in the Sciences*, ed. by Annette Lykknes, Donald L. Optiz, and Brigitte Van Tiggelen (Basel: Springer, 2012), pp. 220–44. As Nord, pp. 1–14, points out, the unflattering, almost caricatured, portraits of the Webbs written by H. G. Wells and Beatrice's niece, Kitty Muggeridge, focus on the ways Beatrice and Sidney violated the gender stereotypes of their day.

236 *Diary of Beatrice Webb*, IV, Introduction, xiii.

237 Speaking with a single voice: Margaret Cole, *Beatrice Webb* (London: Longmans, Green, 1945), p. 138; Muggeridge and Adam, p. 15; Kingsley Martin, "The Webbs in Retirement" in *The Webbs and Their Work*, ed. by Margaret Cole (London: Frederick Muller, 1949), pp. 285–301 (p. 297). Typewriters clacking: A. G. Gardiner, quoted in George Feaver, "Introduction" to BW, *Our Partnership* (Cambridge, UK: Cambridge University Press, 1975), xxiii.

the collaboration, she took the first cut at organizing the material and outlining the chapters, but much of the writing was left to Sidney.[238] He did not adopt her ideas automatically, and her preliminary thinking and outlining were subject to frequent, often drastic, sometimes acrimonious, reworking once he began to write the text. Beatrice described the process of writing their book on local government in 1901:

> The first three days I spent struggling with the first draft of the first chapter rearranging each section and, when I had rearranged it, submitting it to Sidney. Then he would begin (I sitting by his side) to rewrite it, both of us breaking off to discuss or to consult our material. Indeed this constant consultation of our 'specimens' is the leading feature of our work [...]. One of us will object 'that is not so' or 'that is not always the case' and then forthwith it becomes a question of evidence.[239]

They hammered out their understanding of the English Poor Law in much the same way in 1902. Beatrice explained:

> For a whole month I played about with propositions and arguments, submitting them, one after another, to Sidney, before we jointly discovered our own principles of Poor Law administration [...]. It is a curious process, this joint thinking; we throw the ball of thought on to the other, each one of us resting, judging, inventing in turn. And we are not satisfied until the conclusion satisfies completely and finally both minds [...]. It is experimentation, and constantly testing the correspondence between the idea and the fact [...]. I do most of the experimentation and Sidney watches and judges the results, accepting some, rejecting others. It is he who finds the formula that expresses our conclusions.[240]

In later years, the division of labor changed somewhat, but the final product was no less collaborative. While they were working on *A Constitution for a Socialist Commonwealth of Britain* in the late teens, Beatrice wrote that she was "designing the separate chapters and dictating a rough draft and redictating until it expresses my mind, and then Sidney correcting all of it and adding sections to it after discussion with me — the finished product representing the combined thought of 'the Webbs.' In the end we never disagree!"[241] She stressed, "Neither of

---

238 *Letters of Sidney and Beatrice Webb*, II, ed. note, p. 15.
239 Diary, 24 April 1901. https://digital.library.lse.ac.uk/objects/lse:bex452giv
240 Diary, 10 November 1902. https://digital.library.lse.ac.uk/objects/lse:won715bor
241 Diary, 5 July 1919. https://digital.library.lse.ac.uk/objects/lse:buh232top

us would have written the book alone — it is the jointest of joint efforts."[242]
Their dear friend, George Bernard Shaw, who worked closely with them
on many projects, remarked that the Webbs's thinking was so entwined
he could never tell whether Beatrice or Sidney had written a particular
sentence.[243]

Mutual Influence

The give and take that defined the Webbs's intellectual partnership is
also evident in the ways they shaped and molded each other. Beatrice
persuaded Sidney to serve on the London County Council instead of
seeking a Parliamentary seat in the early 1890s. She thought his talents
would be put to better use on the local panel and he needed more
political experience; she also did not want to lose his help in writing
their books.[244] Noting his subsequent success in advancing the Fabian
concept of municipal socialism at the LCC, she proudly asserted,
"With his life I am more than satisfied. The work he is doing, creating
machinery for collective action, is the work I desired to see him do [...].
This combination of practice and theory is, I think, the ideal life for
him."[245] When Sidney was considering becoming a Labour candidate
for Parliament in 1920, Beatrice convinced him it was the right move at
the right time.[246]

---

242 Diary, 11 May 1920. https://digital.library.lse.ac.uk/objects/lse:buh232top
243 See George Feaver, "Two Minds or One? The Mills, the Webbs, and Liberty in British
   Social Democracy" in *Lives, Liberties and the Public Good: New Essays on Political
   Theory*, ed. by George Feaver and Frederick Rosen (Houndmills, UK: Macmillan,
   1987), pp. 139–72 (p. 150). Edward Pease, General Secretary of the Fabian Society
   for many years, and Leonard Woolf also found it impossible to distinguish Beatrice's
   and Sidney's respective contributions to the Webbs's joint work. Edward R. Pease,
   The History of the Fabian Society (New York: Barnes and Noble, 1963), p. 212; Woolf
   quoted in Radice, p. 324.
244 SW to BP, 17 Sept/91. Passfield Papers. See also, *Letters of Sidney and Beatrice Webb*, I,
   ed. note, p. 405. Beatrice doubted that Sidney was "a first rate political instrument"
   or would become a political "leader", by which she meant "an acknowledged
   chief." Diary, 7 July 1891, and Diary, 1 December 1892. https://digital.library.lse.
   ac.uk/objects/lse:bin716wef
245 Diary, 30 July, 1893. https://digital.library.lse.ac.uk/objects/lse:bin716wef. Despite
   her happiness in Sidney's success, her thoughts returned to Chamberlain while she
   wrote this entry in her diary.
246 Diary, 8 June 1920. https://digital.library.lse.ac.uk/objects/lse:buh232top

Beatrice also took credit for advancing Sidney's career by smoothing his rough edges and creating opportunities for him to interact with leading politicians and intellectuals. "The perfect happiness of his own life has cured his old defects of manner — he has lost the aggressive self-assertive tone, the slight touch of insolence which was only another form of shyness and has gained immensely in persuasiveness," she noted a few years after they married.[247] Years later, she observed approvingly, "All asperity and harshness has left him [...] he is less of a doctrinaire than of old, more of an investigator [...]. And I think the 'setting' I have given him of simple fare and distinguished friends suits him, both in reputation and taste."[248]

Sidney was happy, even grateful, to accept Beatrice's guidance on these matters, but he did not always defer to her or look to her to tell him what to do. He initiated and led several of their joint projects. The educational reforms he achieved as chairman of the Technical Education Board of the London County Council (1892–1910) — a scholarship ladder for bright working class boys, a system of polytechnics and technical institutions to provide a practical education for poor children, a reorganization of the degree programs at London University — owed little to Beatrice.[249] He discussed his ideas with her, and enlisted her help in organizing some local vestry elections. But the details of the reforms and the strategies for moving them through the LCC were his. His work for the Fabian Society was a continuation of what he was doing before his marriage; Beatrice did not become active in the leadership of the Society until 1912. And it was Sidney, not Beatrice, who took the lead in developing the London School of Economics and the *New Statesman*, two of the Webbs's most important intellectual "offspring."[250] In 1924, she would have preferred to have him working with her rather than serving in the Cabinet, but she acknowledged that the decision to leave public office was his to make, not hers.[251]

247 Diary, Christmas 1895. https://digital.library.lse.ac.uk/objects/lse:hus734mos
248 Diary, 22 March 1901. https://digital.library.lse.ac.uk/objects/lse:bex452giv
249 Cole, *Beatrice*, p. 85.
250 Feaver, "Introduction" to BW, *Partnership*, xxx–xxxi. *Letters of Sidney and Beatrice Webb*, II, ed. note, x. Diary, 21 September 1894. https://digital.library.lse.ac.uk/objects/lse:kac646sis. Cole, *Beatrice*, p. 85.
251 Diary, 2 May 1924. https://digital.library.lse.ac.uk/objects/lse:fim518vor

Sidney also molded Beatrice, although his influence may not always have been beneficial. She refused many social invitations because he insisted they would only exhaust her and distract her from her work.[252] Occasionally, he discouraged her from giving public lectures.[253] Most significantly, he had a stifling effect on Beatrice's creativity and imagination. He not only imposed a dry statistical tone in their manuscripts, but also squelched her interest in individuals and personalities. Resuming her solitary diary writing after keeping a joint journal with Sidney during their nine-month trip to the United States, Australia, and New Zealand in 1898, Beatrice complained that she had "lost the habit of intimate confidences." She explained, "One cannot run on into self-analysis, family gossip, or indiscreet descriptions, if someone else, however dear, is solemnly to read it then and there; I foresee the kindly indulgence or tolerant boredom with which he would decipher the last entry and this feeling would, in itself, make it almost impossible to write whatever came into my head at the time of writing without thought of his criticism."[254]

At times, Beatrice felt that Sidney's mere presence had an inhibiting effect on her diary writing. "When Sidney is with me I cannot talk to the 'Other Self' with whom I commune when I am alone — 'it' ceases to be present and only reappears when he becomes absent," she wrote in 1904.[255] Twenty years later, Beatrice noted that she had not written in her diary for nine weeks, in part because "Sidney has been here and I can never write in his presence."[256]

Changing Roles Throughout the Partnership

Beatrice and Sidney's partnership was not a collaboration in which two people worked together to advance the career of one, and the dominant and subordinate positions were clear from the start. On the contrary,

---

252 For example: Diary, [?] June 1904, https://digital.library.lse.ac.uk/objects/lse:xij627rup, and 14 October 1905, https://digital.library.lse.ac.uk/objects/lse:nin225zok

253 For example: BW to Edward Pease [18 April 1893], in *Letters of Sidney and Beatrice Webb*, II, p. 5.

254 Diary, 5 February 1899. https://digital.library.lse.ac.uk/objects/lse:nef769qal

255 Diary, 16 October 1904. https://digital.library.lse.ac.uk/objects/lse:xij627rup

256 Diary, 12 February 1925. https://digital.library.lse.ac.uk/objects/lse:siq946mib

both the Webbs played a variety of shifting roles. At times, one assumed the leadership position or the more public role, while the other took on a more subordinate, behind-the-scenes, "helpmate" role. Then they reversed positions. Their revolving roles are another marker of the fundamental egalitarianism in their relationship. As Beatrice herself recognized, she "needed to be 'leader' in some respects and servant in others" in order to be fully happy in marriage.[257]

When they married, the Webbs anticipated that Beatrice would be the thinker and Sidney the pragmatic reformer and politician. She expected to live the life of a "recluse" while he would provide her with "an open window into the world."[258] For the first thirteen years of the marriage, they followed this plan. Sidney helped Beatrice with their books (always published under both names), but he also served on the London County Council and spearheaded the founding of the London School of Economics as a college of public administration. The Webbs did not involve themselves much in running the LSE, but it would provide a welcoming environment and opportunities for both female faculty and female students and became known for a more informal, less hierarchical style than older, more traditional universities like Oxford and Cambridge.[259]

In the early 1900s, Beatrice expanded the Webbs's narrow domestic circle by hosting what amounted to a political salon. Determined to "permeate" the major political parties with their reform agenda, they invited carefully selected politicians, civil servants, and intellectuals to luncheons and dinners and fed them information about specific projects and proposals. They believed their efforts succeeded in getting Sidney's proposals for restructuring local education administration written into the Conservative Education Act of 1902/3 and adopted by Parliament. They were proud to be seen as effective and unscrupulous "wirepullers" who wielded influence behind the scenes.[260]

---

257 She said this to Joseph Chamberlain's sister, Clara Ryland. Diary, 15 February 1902. https://digital.library.lse.ac.uk/objects/lse:xas833lok

258 Diary, 1 December 1892. https://digital.library.lse.ac.uk/objects/lse:bin716wef

259 See Maxine Berg, *A Woman in History: Eileen Power, 1889–1940* (Cambridge, UK: Cambridge University Press, 1996), pp. 142–44.

260 Others have questioned the effectiveness of their tactics and pointed out that they often backed the wrong candidates. See *Letters of Sidney and Beatrice Webb*, II, editor's note, ix–x.

Their lifestyle changed more dramatically when Beatrice was appointed to the Royal Commission on the Poor Law in November 1905. For the next seven years, she played the lead public role while Sidney cheerfully took on the role of behind-the-scenes partner. "Just now our usual positions are somewhat reversed: it is he who sits at home and thinks out the common literary work, it is I who am racing around dealing with men and affairs," Beatrice noted in her diary in 1907.[261] Dissatisfied with the direction the chair of the commission was taking, she conducted a separate investigation of the workings of the Poor Law, with help from Sidney and four paid research assistants. Together she and Sidney hammered out the principles of a new system to replace the existing but outmoded methods and institutions to help the poor. Beatrice drew strength from Sidney's emotional support and encouragement as well as benefiting from his technical expertise. He proved invaluable to her in reviewing the mounds of evidence, formulating reform proposals, devising strategies for dealing with her fellow Commissioners, and writing the dissenting Minority Report.[262] "I tremble to think how utterly dependent I am on him — both in his love and on his unrivalled capacity for 'putting things through,'" she acknowledged in her diary.[263]

---

261 Diary, 3 May 1907. https://digital.library.lse.ac.uk/objects/lse:wur719qow

262 The ambitious plan outlined in the Minority Report, of which Beatrice was the principal author, would have replaced the old poor law relief system with separate programs to aid the sick, the aged, and the unemployed. Reflecting the Webbs's structural view of the problems, the proposed reforms were intended not just to alleviate the effects of poverty, but to prevent it from occurring. Many of the core principles and central recommendations of the Minority Report were reflected in Walter Beveridge's *Social Insurance and Allied Services*, better known at the Beveridge Report (1942), which became the blueprint for the social welfare system that Britain adopted after World War II. See Lucinda Platt, "Beatrice Webb, William Beveridge, Poverty, and the Minority Report on the Poor Law" (February 23, 2018), https://blogs.lse.ac.uk/lsehistory/2018/02/23/beatrice-webb-william-beveridge-poverty-and-the-minority-report-on-the-poor-law/, and Jose Harris, "The Webbs and Beveridge", in *From the Workhouse to Welfare: What Beatrice Webb's 1909 Minority Report Can Teach Us Today*, ed. by Ed Wallis (London: Fabian Society, 2009), pp. 55–64.

263 Diary, 18 February 1907. https://digital.library.lse.ac.uk/objects/lse:wur719qow. See also, BW to SW [?14 November 1907], in *Letters of Sidney and Beatrice Webb*, II, p. 276. Jose Harris notes in "The Webbs and Beveridge" that Beatrice could not have written the report without the work Sidney did in predigesting the technical details of poor law administration. Harris also argues that if Sidney had been a member of the Commission, he would have been better than Beatrice at managing the personal dynamics among the Commission members and succeeded in getting agreement around a Majority Report that incorporated the Webbs's principles.

Beatrice assumed an equally public position as chairman of the National Committee for the Break-Up of the Poor Law, the pressure group the Webbs launched in 1909 to mobilize public support for the reforms outlined in the Minority Report. Directing a paid staff, thirty to forty volunteers, and over 400 lecturers, Beatrice discovered unsuspected talents as a manager, organizer, and lecturer. She relished being in a position of authority.[264] She also enjoyed an expanded sense of "oneness" with Sidney, who resigned from the LCC to write pamphlets and give lectures for the campaign to create a new welfare system.[265] "Our comradeship has never been so complete. Hitherto, we have had only one side of our work together — our research and book writing. But this last year we have organized together, spoken together, as well as written together," she wrote enthusiastically.[266]

Beatrice was especially grateful that Sidney was willing to support her without claiming credit for himself. "He has been extraordinarily generous in not resenting, in the very least, my having nominally to take the front place, as the leading minority commissioner, and ostensible head of the National Committee," she wrote appreciatively in her journal.[267] A few years later, when he did not want to be listed as co-author of a jointly written article, she marveled, "He seems to be wholly devoid of vanity or personal ambition, he never feels he does not get his [just] desserts."[268] Yet, she had done the same for him, declining to put her name on pointedly political article they wrote jointly to promote the idea of guaranteeing a "national minimum" of education and welfare. "I believe in mere 'wife's politics'; only in research do I claim equality of recognition!" she asserted.[269]

After the Webbs ended the unsuccessful Poor Law agitation in 1912, Beatrice assumed a leadership role in the Fabian Society, helping to develop its policy agenda and running its Research Department. Sidney remained a key figure in the Fabian leadership, worked on the Webb's ongoing study of English local government, and continued to write and

264 Diary, New Year's Eve, 1909. https://digital.library.lse.ac.uk/objects/lse:won715bor
265 Diary, 15 May 1909; 27 May 1910; 14 November 1909. https://digital.library.lse.ac.uk/objects/lse:won715bor
266 Diary, New Year's Eve, 1909. https://digital.library.lse.ac.uk/objects/lse:won715bor
267 Ibid.
268 Diary, 25 September 1915. https://digital.library.lse.ac.uk/objects/lse:cij556jub
269 Diary, 8 June 1904. https://digital.library.lse.ac.uk/objects/lse:xij627rup

lecture on British social policy. In 1913, he took the lead in founding the *New Statesman*, a national weekly journal of leftist opinion which the Webbs always referred to as one of their "children."

Having focused on domestic social policy and paid little attention to European politics and diplomacy, the Webbs found themselves emotionally and intellectually unprepared for World War I and largely sidelined in British political circles when the war broke out.[270] By mid-1916, Beatrice was in a state of severe depression and nervous collapse, horrified by the carnage and suffering caused by the war, and depressed by the realization that she and Sidney had no influence over the Britain's wartime leaders.[271] Showing the classic symptoms of neurasthenia (physical and mental exhaustion, irritability, and headaches), she found it difficult to work on their usual studies. Instead, she began a new endeavor: transcribing her diaries in preparation for writing an autobiography that would tell the story of her life and work prior to her marriage. She rallied in 1917 and 1918, when she was appointed to several government committees that discussed plans for reconstructing British society after the war. Struggling to get some of her Poor Law proposals adopted by a government committee charged with improving local government, she reluctantly stopped working on her autobiography.

Sidney emerged as a prominent public figure in the late teens. As an influential member of the Labour Party Executive — Beatrice dubbed him the party's "intellectual leader" — he wrote much of the party's new constitution and was instrumental in getting it to adopt a Socialist platform in 1918. He sat on a government commission charged with considering the future of the mining industry, including working conditions, wages and hours. In 1922, he won a seat in Parliament, as a Labour MP for Seaham Harbor, a mining district in northern England. Two years later he was appointed President of the Board of Trade and became a Cabinet Minister. The Labour Party was in power for only ten months in 1924, but Sidney kept his Parliamentary seat until 1929.

While Sidney was in Parliament, Beatrice turned back to writing her autobiography, and played a conventional helpmate role in his career:

---

270 Diary, 31 July 1914, https://digital.library.lse.ac.uk/objects/lse:mod807hoq, and the note Beatrice added in August 1918 in the typescript diary, https://digital.library.lse.ac.uk/objects/lse:vat325giy

271 Diary, 14 April 1927. https://digital.library.lse.ac.uk/objects/lse:dut736noc

she answered his correspondence, wrote a newsletter to his female constituents, campaigned with him, and served as his political hostess. Her willingness to put Sidney's work ahead of her own makes her sound like the most subordinate of nineteenth-century wives. "My first duty is cooperating with Sidney's parliamentary work," she asserted, even though she knew she would have little time or energy for her own writing and found her new role rather tedious.[272]

Beatrice regretted that they were working on parallel tracks rather than on a joint project. "[H]e has interests about which I know little, and I am absorbed in creative writing in which he has no part but that of a kindly and helpful critic of style," she lamented when he was in the Cabinet.[273] Hard at work on her autobiography, she took little interest in the Labour Government and the issues that had previously absorbed her. "The concrete questions which I have investigated — trade unionism, local government, cooperation, political organization, no longer interest me: I dislike reading about them, thinking about them, talking about them, or writing about them," she admitted in her diary.[274]

The realization that Sidney did not value her autobiographical writing distressed Beatrice. "[T]here is something about it that he not exactly resents, but which is unsympathetic [to him...] the whole thing is far too subjective, and all that part which deals with 'my creed' as distinguished from 'my craft' seems to him the sentimental scribblings of a woman only interesting just because they are feminine," she maintained.[275] Writing a public account of her life and work before her marriage was immensely important to Beatrice. It was her attempt to come to terms with her own personality, the forces that had shaped her, and the dualities that defined her life. It also provided an outlet for the creative imagination that she had bottled up for almost thirty years of writing fact-filled analyses of British government and social policy. By showing her to be a sensitive observer of individuals and a woman of feeling as well as intellect, the publication of the autobiography, entitled

---

272 Diary, 9 February 1923, https://digital.library.lse.ac.uk/objects/lse:ras535xan. Diary, [?28] January 1924, and 9 February 1924. https://digital.library.lse.ac.uk/objects/lse:fim518vor

273 Diary, 28 June 1924. https://digital.library.lse.ac.uk/objects/lse:fim518vor

274 Diary, 10 July 1924. https://digital.library.lse.ac.uk/objects/lse:fim518vor

275 Diary, 19 March 1925. https://digital.library.lse.ac.uk/objects/lse:siq946mib

My Apprenticeship, in 1926 radically altered Beatrice's public image.[276] This was a side of her that Sidney had never fully appreciated, and one that she had learned to keep hidden from him.

After the Labour Party lost power in November 1924, Sidney kept his seat in Parliament but resumed the writing partnership with Beatrice. They published the last of their ten volumes on British local government in 1929, the year the Labour Party was voted back into power. Sidney had not run for re-election, but was made a baron, given a seat in the House of Lords, and joined the Cabinet as Secretary of State for the Dominions and Colonies. Both of Sidney's Cabinet posts had been held by Joseph Chamberlain, Beatrice noted in her diary.[277]

Beatrice self-sacrificingly assumed a helpmate role once again, although she knew her own work would become "scrappy and incompetent" as a result.[278] But she refused to accept the title of "Lady Passfield" and be presented at Court.[279] Sidney retired to private life in 1931 after the Labour Party lost the General Election, and the Webbs, now in their seventies, took on several new projects. Beatrice started writing the second volume of her autobiography, an account of the Webbs's marriage and joint work, which she called "Our Partnership." The Webbs spent two months in Soviet Russia in 1932, and embarked on a study of the Soviet economy and government. Beatrice in particular saw Russian Communism as the triumph of socialism in action, and the Webbs enthusiastically endorsed it as a model for other socialist societies. When *Soviet Communism: A New Civilization?* was published in the fall of 1935, Beatrice and Sidney triumphantly hailed it as their last and biggest baby.[280] In fact, the book was severely critiqued by many who felt the Webbs had been taken in by Soviet propaganda.

Beatrice's prediction that *Soviet Communism* would be their last major work was prophetic. Sidney suffered a stroke in January 1938, at the age of eighty, and never fully recovered. Beatrice mourned the end of their

---

276 See Nord, pp. 8–9, and G. D.H. Cole, "Beatrice Webb as an Economist", in *Webbs*, ed. by Margaret Cole, pp. 267–82 (pp. 276–77).

277 Diary, 6 July 1929. https://digital.library.lse.ac.uk/objects/lse:var297foh

278 Diary, 2 October 1929; 16 June 1930; see also, 27 December 1929. https://digital.library.lse.ac.uk/objects/lse:var297foh

279 Diary, 20 June 1929, 29 June 1929, and 6 July 1929. https://digital.library.lse.ac.uk/objects/lse:var297foh

280 Diary, 15 November 1935. https://digital.library.lse.ac.uk/objects/lse:kuk362nid

working partnership. "I cannot march alone," she despaired.[281] Miserable without Sidney's companionship and support, Beatrice arranged for his care, nursed him tenderly, and prepared for her own death. She kept on writing, but as her own health deteriorated, she asserted that she would welcome death but did not want to leave Sidney on his own.[282] She died first, at the age of 86, in April 1943. Sidney followed in October 1947. (The second volume of Beatrice's autobiography, posthumously edited at Sidney's request by Barbara Drake and Margaret Cole, was published as *Our Partnership* in 1948.[283]) At the suggestion of Bernard Shaw, Beatrice's and Sidney's ashes were buried together in Westminster Abbey, the only non-Royal couple to be so honored. Beatrice would have been pleased by this striking tribute to the jointness of their life and the importance of their work.

Explaining the Partnership's Success

The Webbs's partnership succeeded not primarily, as the Mackenzies have suggested, because Sidney conducted himself like a civil servant committed to carrying out the will of the more powerful Executive, but because he was a collaborator by temperament and political conviction. A civil servant supports a hierarchical power structure and division of labor, while a collaboration suggests a more equal relationship in which all work together for a common vision and common goal. Advancing the work of a committee of which one is a member, a decision-maker, and a fellow strategist is different from being a civil servant who simply executes what another thinks up.

Determined that they would have "equivalent freedom and joint lives", Sidney conscientiously applied his collectivist political principles to his domestic life. Years before he met Beatrice, he explained his philosophy of collaboration and marriage to Marjorie Davidson, the fiancée of his friend and fellow Fabian, Edward Pease. "My own theory of marriage does not involve the merging of personalities," Sidney wrote,

---

281 Diary, 25 January 1938. https://digital.library.lse.ac.uk/objects/lse:wid939bez

282 Diary, 8 April 1939, https://digital.library.lse.ac.uk/objects/lse:tul234dab; 13 September 1942, https://digital.library.lse.ac.uk/objects/lse:ril779lef; 25 March 1943, https://digital.library.lse.ac.uk/objects/lse:cej353yic

283 Webb, *Our Partnership*, ed. by Barbara Drake and Margaret I. Cole (London: Longman's, Green, 1948). It provides a detailed account of their work through 1911.

> My theory of life is to feel at every moment that I am acting as a member of a c[ommi]ttee, and for that c[ommi]ttee. I aspire *never* to act alone, or for myself. This theoretically combined action involves rules, deliberation, discussion, concert, the disregard of one's own impulses, and in fact is Collectivism or Communism [...]. This need not imply that I am in favour of "merger" or even of Communism in marriage, let it be a mere partnership. But let the partners, in every detail, act in and for the partnership.[284]

Sidney's collectivist philosophy is essential to understanding the success of the Webb's partnership and marriage. As a man who valued collective deliberation and discussion, Sidney did not approve of a marriage in which the wife made decisions for the husband any more than one in which the husband made decisions for the wife. Dismayed to learn that Davidson was unilaterally making decisions that affected both her and Pease, Sidney warned against "the evil effect" of such a practice, which he characterized as "merely the old bad theory of marriage inverted."[285]

The deference Sidney learned as a civil servant undoubtedly helped him to work well with Beatrice, but an equally important preparation was his collaboration with George Bernard Shaw. Sidney and Shaw formed what Shaw called "a committee of 2"; along with Graham Wallas, they were leaders of the infant Fabian Society years before Beatrice entered Sidney's life.[286] Like Beatrice, Shaw was a more compelling, complex, and creative personality than Sidney. Shaw later wrote that the wisest thing he ever did was to force his friendship on Sidney and create "a committee of Webb and Shaw." To Sidney he admitted, "When we met, you knew everything I didn't know, and I knew everything you didn't know."[287] The Shaw-Webb relationship, like the collaboration between Beatrice and Sidney, was an intellectual partnership distinguished by its complementarity and equality, rooted

---

284 SW to Marjorie Davidson, 12 December 1888. Passfield Papers. Emphasis in original.
285 Ibid.
286 Similarly, the collaboration of Marie and Pierre Curie, which resulted in a shared Nobel Prize for Physics in 1903, was preceded by Pierre's research partnership with his elder brother, Jacques, and facilitated by Pierre's "honest and modest nature." See Helena M. Pycior, "Pierre Curie and 'His Eminent Collaborator Mme Curie': Complementary Partners", in *Creative Couples in the Sciences*, ed. by Helena M. Pycior, Nancy G. Slack, and Pnina G. Abir-am (New Brunswick, NJ: Rutgers University Press, 1996), pp. 39–56.
287 Quoted in Harrison, *Life*, p. 24.

in affection, and fueled by a mutual sense of enhanced power, insight, and influence. Royden Harrison describes it as an "equal relationship" in which Sidney "renounce[d] personal power in favour of a pervasive, self-effacing influence."[288] A biographer of Shaw called the two men "an ideal couple."[289] The fact that Sidney had enjoyed such a relationship with another man helped free him from any sense that such a role was demeaning or emasculating. It also made it easier for him to relate to Beatrice as a colleague without typecasting her as a woman and a wife.

Sidney's background and upbringing also helped him to accept nontraditional gender roles. His mother owned and managed a hairdressing shop, and at times was the family's principal breadwinner. Upper-middle-class norms of gender roles and domestic life had no attraction for Sidney. He had not grown up in that world, and he did not aspire to be part of it. On the contrary, as a socialist, he questioned its fundamental premises and principles. Nor was he awed by Beatrice's wealth and social standing, an imbalance that might have posed problems for a more traditional — or less confident — man. Sidney was supremely self-confident and comfortable with who he was and what he was trying to accomplish. He had little of the self-doubt and self-criticism that plagued Beatrice.

While Sidney seemed genuinely indifferent to gender norms and questions about the distribution of power in their marriage, Beatrice continued to wrestle with them. She always insisted that Sidney was the dominant force in the partnership while she was merely the "nominal" head or "ostensible leader", even when she assumed the more public role. "Fortunately, in spite of his modesty, everyone knows that [Sidney] is the backbone of the Webb firm, even if I do appear, on some occasions, as the figurehead" was her characteristic assessment.[290] In *My Apprenticeship*, she described Sidney as "the predominant partner of the firm of Webb."[291] Dismissing fellow Fabian H. G. Wells's judgment that Sidney lacked "will-power and capacity", Beatrice asserted, "I am much more [Sidney's] instrument than he is mine."[292]

288 Ibid., p. 25.
289 Hesketh Pearson, *G.B.S.: A Full Length Portrait* (Garden City, NY: Garden City Publishing, 1942), p. 60.
290 Diary, New Year's Eve, 1909. https://digital.library.lse.ac.uk/objects/lse:won715bor
291 BW, *Apprenticeship*, p. 398.
292 Diary, 15 July 1906. https://digital.library.lse.ac.uk/objects/lse:nin225zok

Beatrice wanted Sidney to be recognized as the more important half of the partnership, in part, because she thought that a woman who controlled or outshone her husband transgressed the natural order. She felt inferior to Sidney because, having absorbed societal views on gender and intelligence, she believed that men were innately superior to women in brain work.[293] "I do not much believe in the productive power of women's intellect; strain as she may, the output is small and the ideas thin and wire-drawn from lack of matter and wide experience. Neither do I believe that mere training will give her that fullness of intellectual life which distinguishes the really able man," she wrote two years after her wedding.[294] She repeatedly emphasized the ways in which Sidney's intellectual capacity exceeded hers. "He is stronger brained than I am, can carry more things in his mind at once," she noted when they were struggling to write a particularly difficult chapter.[295] "Sidney can do about four times as much as I, whether measured in time or in matter" was her characteristic judgment.[296] While she could work no more than five or six hours a day for an extended period without provoking a nervous collapse, he routinely spent almost all his waking hours working. Beatrice always took care to acknowledge how dependent she was on his help.[297]

Beatrice also considered Sidney the better, or at least, the more facile writer because he wrote quickly and easily while she produced a text only after laborious rewriting and editing.[298] Only in one area did Beatrice claim superior talents. "In the use of documents [Sidney] is far more efficient than I, but in manipulation of witnesses with a view of

---

293 BW to Graham Wallas [?mid-July 1897], in *Letters of Sidney and Beatrice Webb*, II, p. 55, remarked on the "the essential inferiority of the woman."
294 Diary, 25 July 1894. https://digital.library.lse.ac.uk/objects/lse:kac646sis. Herbert Spencer's early influence on Beatrice may have been at least partly responsible for this. He believed that the female brain had "somewhat less of general power or massiveness" than the male brain, and therefore lacked "the power of abstract reasoning and that most abstract of emotions, the sentiment of justice." Quoted in Cynthia Eagle Russett, *Sexual Science: The Victorian Construction of Womanhood* (Cambridge, MA: Harvard University Press, 1989), p. 119.
295 Diary, 27 August 1897. https://digital.library.lse.ac.uk/objects/lse:hus734mos
296 Diary, 22 February 1906, https://digital.library.lse.ac.uk/objects/lse:nin225zok; see also, Diary, 24 March 1908, https://digital.library.lse.ac.uk/objects/lse:wur719qow
297 BW to SW, April 26, 1908, in *Letters of Sidney and Beatrice Webb*, II, pp. 302–3. See also, BW to SW [29 April 1908], Ibid., p. 307.
298 BW to Frederic Harrison, December 28, 1897, ibid., p. 59.

extracting confidential information, his shyness and scepticism [about using it] gives me the advantage. And I am more ruthless in the exercise of my craft when he is not there to watch," she acknowledged.[299]

Despite Beatrice's insistence that "everyone knows that Sidney is the backbone of the Webb firm", some did not see the partnership in that light. When H. G. Wells published an exaggerated and unflattering portrait of the Webbs and other Fabians in his novel, *The New Machiavelli*, in 1911, he depicted Beatrice as domineering and subjugating and Sidney as "almost destitute of initiative." Beatrice took the characterizations in stride. After reading the serialized version of the novel in 1910, she remarked, "we read the caricatures of ourselves [and others] with much interest and amusement. The portraits are very clever in a malicious way."[300]

Nevertheless, Beatrice's assessment of their personalities suggests she too might have seen their relationship as an inversion of contemporary gender norms. She contrasted Sidney's selfless nature, moral goodness, and self-effacing personality — stereotypically "feminine" attributes — with her egotism, self-will, and aggressive vanity — stereotypically "masculine" traits. Similarly, the "shyness" she noted in Sidney when he interviewed witnesses is more typically considered a "feminine" trait, just as her "ruthless" interviewing style would more typically be described as "masculine." Her description of the way Sidney managed her also suggests a gender role reversal: "It will be delightful to get back to our 'dovecote', and be again with my darling old boy — who twists his strong-minded wife round his little finger — by soft sounds and kisses."[301]

* * * * *

Staying in 1927 in the house where she had lived before her marriage, Beatrice remembered the anguish she had experienced forty years earlier as she struggled to choose between love and career. Now she rejoiced in having found a solution for that dilemma. "If I could have foreseen an old woman of seventy striding across the common with forty years of successful literary work and thirty-five years of a perfect marriage,

---

299 Diary, 28 April 1899. https://digital.library.lse.ac.uk/objects/lse:nef769qal

300 Diary, 5 November, 1910. https://digital.library.lse.ac.uk/objects/lse:won715bor

301 BW to SW [late Sept. 1892]. Passfield Papers.

and both work and love continuing, how high-spirited and happy I should have been," she mused.[302] In the final decades of her long life, her deep satisfaction in having successfully combined love and work was a frequent refrain in her diaries. "We have had a good life together; we leave finished work, and the one who is left behind for a few more years of life will have as consolation, the memory of a perfect marriage. What more can a human being expect or demand?" she asked.[303] More than a decade later, she repeated, "We have lived the life we liked to live and we have done the work we intended to do, in blessed partnership. What more can mortals want?"[304]

In fact, Beatrice had, at times, wanted more: a more passionate love, such as she had felt for Chamberlain; a partnership that allowed her to express her creative, imaginative side; motherhood and flesh-and-blood children. Her attempt to combine marriage and work was not a perfect solution to the marriage-career dilemma. On key issues, she failed to free herself from the either/or thinking that made her life so difficult as a young woman. Nevertheless, in the context of nineteenth-century ideas about love and romance, forging "oneness" that did not require a woman to subordinate herself to a man and gave as much prominence to her achievements as to his, is a significant advance. In these respects, Beatrice and Sidney came closer to achieving the synthesis of independence and intimacy that many dual career couples were seeking. The American educator, Lucy Sprague Mitchell, and her economist husband, Wesley Clair Mitchell, discussed in the next chapter, came closer still.

---

302 Diary, 28 July 1927. https://digital.library.lse.ac.uk/objects/lse:dut736noc
303 Diary, 9 August 1922. https://digital.library.lse.ac.uk/objects/lse:ras535xan
304 Diary, 10 June 1935. https://digital.library.lse.ac.uk/objects/lse:kuk362nid

5. Having It All: Lucy Sprague Mitchell and Wesley Clair Mitchell

While most women of her generation and class opted for work or marriage, Lucy Sprague Mitchell came close to "having it all." Both she and her husband, Wesley Clair Mitchell, were acclaimed writers, teachers, and institution builders, she in progressive education, he in economics. Lucy wrote a pioneering book about children's use of language and co-founded the celebrated Bank Street College of Education, which still trains teachers in the curricula she pioneered. Wesley, one of the foremost economists of his generation, produced groundbreaking analyses of business cycles and developed quantitative indicators of the US economy.

In addition to their distinguished careers, the Mitchells had a fulfilling marriage and raised four children, two of whom were adopted. Lucy wrote about their relationship, careers, and family life in *Two Lives: The Story of Wesley Clair Mitchell and Myself*, published in 1953, five years after Wesley's death. Her message — as relevant today as it was in the 1950s — was that both wives and husbands need to adopt new behaviors to make such marriages work. She showed that it was possible for a wife and mother to pursue a career when her husband supported her efforts and helped to raise their children.

When they married in 1912, the Mitchells were determined to construct a dual career marriage, and for the most part, they succeeded admirably. They were more effective than many couples in balancing career and family demands, navigating between marital intimacy and independence, and reshaping the typical gendered division of labor within the home. But their results were not flawless and the process

    https://doi.org/10.11647/OBP.0318.05

was not painless. No dramatic demarcations or crises threatened their marriage, but there were stresses, dissatisfactions, and disappointments.

Their relationship shattered conventional gender stereotypes and challenged traditional notions of masculinity, love, and romance. Breaking the mold proved easier for Wesley than for Lucy. Comfortable with himself, Wesley was not very troubled by the way their lives deviated from the norm. But Lucy had deeply internalized many conventional notions of gender roles. It took her years to appreciate that the man she initially found to be too weak and passive was a tower of quiet strength and a model husband for an ambitious woman.

Early Lives

Lucy's upbringing in the 1880s provides a sharp contrast to the domestic life she and Wesley created in the 1910s and 1920s. Born in 1878, Lucy was the fourth of six children of Lucia and Otho Sprague, a wealthy Chicago merchant. Her childhood was troubled and unhappy, marked by her father's repressive parenting, the deaths of two younger brothers, an older sister's emotional instability, her father's struggle with tuberculosis, and her mother's withdrawal and depression. Lucy described the Sprague household as the epitome of a Victorian family in which an authoritative husband and paterfamilias ruled over a submissive family. Otho, who was ten years older than his wife, made all decisions for the family, and strictly disciplined the children in accordance with his puritanical religious beliefs. Lucy and her siblings recited Bible verses at breakfast. Frivolity and time-wasting were frowned upon, as were bright colors and displays of emotion. Punishments were frequent. Lucy blamed her father for stifling her mother's impulsive, fun-loving nature and artistic spirit. The result was a depressed wife and mother, and highly anxious children who carried a strong sense of personal failure and guilt.[1]

Lucy found herself retreating into "an inner world" of her own creation and often felt like an "on-looker" in her own life. Writing stories and poems was a secret pleasure that she viewed as a secret

---

1 This description of Lucy's childhood and upbringing is based on her book, *Two Lives: The Story of Wesley Clair Mitchell and Myself* (New York: Simon & Schuster, 1953), pp. 30–51.

vice. Considered too nervous to go to school, she was schooled at home. Like many precocious daughters, she educated herself by reading the books in her father's library. She also learned by listening to the conversations of his business associates and the cultural and civic leaders who came to the Sprague home in the early 1890s. Having made a fortune by establishing a chain of wholesale grocery stores, Otho moved as easily in Chicago's civic arena as in the realm of big industry, big business, and big finance. The Spragues entertained many of the luminaries who flocked to the Chicago World's Fair in 1893, as well as members of the faculty and administration at the newly founded University of Chicago.[2]

Lucy admired the energy and ambition of her father and his business associates, but began to question their politics and values, especially her father's equation of success with making a lot of money. She was fortunate in having female mentors. Jane Addams, founder of Hull House, offered alternative values and an alternative model of success for the impressionable teenager. Alice Freeman Palmer, who sometimes stayed with the Sprague family when she was in Chicago, befriended Lucy and provided her with another, very different, model of female achievement. (Alice's dual career marriage is discussed in Chapter 1.)

Lucy's life became harder after she moved with her parents to Southern California in 1893, when she was fifteen. After years of battling tuberculosis, Otho became a virtual invalid who insisted on very exacting care; Lucia became more withdrawn, sometimes going for a week without speaking. Lucy spent several long, miserable months serving as the family nurse, housekeeper, and fill-in cook before she was enrolled at the Marlborough School in Los Angeles.[3] She boarded at the school during the week and returned home on weekends to resume her caregiving duties. The school was a lifeline for Lucy, providing her with a solid education and an opportunity to be with girls her own age. She blossomed and formed friendships that lasted for decades.

---

2   LSM, *Two Lives* (*TL*), pp. 58, 59, 64–66.
3   Lucy wrote that she did this for a year (*TL*, p. 110). Joyce Antler, *Lucy Sprague Mitchell: The Making of a Modern Woman* (New Haven: Yale University Press, 1987), p. 37, explains that it was about six months.

Miserable at the prospect of returning home after she graduated in 1896, Lucy sent her older sister, Mary, a despairing letter announcing her desire to go to college. Mary, who had married Adolph Miller, an economics professor at the University of Chicago, did not offer any help. But she shared Lucy's letter with Alice Freeman Palmer when the two couples met in Paris. Alice immediately proposed that Lucy live with her and George and attend Radcliffe, and persuaded Lucy's parents to agree.

Lucy's life changed dramatically when she lived with the Palmers. They provided a warm, loving, and happy home that was as nurturing as it was stimulating. She became a surrogate daughter to the childless Alice, who introduced her as "my only daughter." Going on "sprees" with Alice, listening to George read poetry, conversing with the Harvard faculty who came to dinner, and meeting the educational leaders who arrived from around the country to consult with the Palmers gave Lucy an education that was as important as the formal classes she took at Radcliffe. Alice's support and example were especially consequential. "No one who lived with Alice Freeman Palmer could believe that an intellectual career must make a woman unwomanly — or unfeminine, either," Lucy noted in *Two Lives*.[4] Alice's ability to combine an "eager zest for life" with a light touch in wielding formidable executive ability made a deep impression on Lucy.[5] She always regarded Alice as "one of the great people of the world," and maintained that no one other than Wesley wielded a stronger influence on her life.[6]

Lucy experienced her first romance during her college years. She fell in love with Joe, a "blonde charmer" who was a young, financially insecure cousin of George, and a frequent visitor to the Palmer home in Cambridge. Joe was in love with her, but the relationship ended disastrously in her senior year when he was found to be peddling lewd photographs to Harvard students. He claimed he was selling them to make enough money to marry Lucy. Advised by George to jump bail after his arrest, Joe fled to Mexico. He wrote to Lucy, asking her to send

---

4   LSM, *TL*, p. 193.
5   LSM, *TL*, p. 73.
6   LSM, manuscript chapter on her Chicago years. Columbia University Library, Rare Book and Manuscript Library, MS#0884, Lucy Sprague Mitchell Papers (LSM Papers). Lucy wrote a draft of an unpublished autobiography (UA) in the 1940s, and later incorporated revised sections of it into *Two Lives*, published in 1953.

him money since she had so much of it. His "bitter, recriminating" letter shocked her more than his involvement in selling the pictures.[7]

After she graduated from Radcliffe in 1900, Lucy's life was again taken over by her family's needs and expectations. She spent the summer of 1900 in Maine, caring for her psychologically fragile sister, Nancy; she lived with a cousin in Chicago during the winter and officially "came out" in Chicago Society. Throughout the spring and summer of 1901, she devotedly nursed her mother, who came to Chicago to be treated for cancer of the abdominal membranes. After Lucia died in the fall of 1901, Lucy returned with her father to Pasadena. Depressed and desperate for something to do, she started to train as a landscape gardener. When she fell seriously ill several months later, relatives brought her back to Chicago.

Once again, Alice came to Lucy's rescue: She invited Lucy to travel in Europe with her and George during his sabbatical year, and help out with the book he was writing about his namesake, the English poet George Herbert. The trip began happily in the fall of 1902, but ended in tragedy. After several weeks in England, the trio moved on to Paris, where Alice fell ill with an intestinal blockage. Days later, she died after an emergency operation. (For details, see Chapter 1, p. 85.) Her last words to George were "Take care of Lucy."[8]

Grief-stricken, Lucy returned to Cambridge with George and lived in his house for many months. Greatly depressed by the deaths of Alice and her own mother, struggling against George's dependence on her, Lucy felt rudderless and trapped. She supplemented her work on his book with graduate courses and a part-time job as a secretary to the Dean of Radcliffe College, but she felt unable to take control of her life. George had fashioned "a vise even stronger than Father forged for me," she realized, one that left her "drained of all capacity to live except as his shadow."[9] It was not until George proposed marriage, claiming he wanted to fulfill Alice's instruction to look after her, that Lucy was able to break free. The shock of his inappropriate proposal — she was twenty-three, he was over

---

7 LSM, *TL*, pp. 125–26.
8 LSM, *TL*, p. 132.
9 LSM, *TL*, p. 133.

sixty — and distortion of Alice's dying request finally galvanized Lucy to take action.[10]

Once again, the academic world provided her with a lifeline. Lucy left Cambridge when President Benjamin Wheeler of the University of California at Berkeley offered her a position at the college, intending that she would become its first Dean of Women. Wheeler had gotten to know Lucy during the summer of 1903 when she was visiting her sister, Mary, and brother-in-law, Adolph Miller, who was teaching at Berkeley. Writing about Wheeler's offer more than forty years later, Lucy stressed how both were taking a major risk: each had only a vague notion of what she would do as dean, and she had no training for the job. Wheeler proposed that she come to Berkeley and get to know the school and its students; after a year or so, he and she could jointly develop her position as Dean of Women. She agreed, but insisted — at George Palmer's urging — that she also be given some teaching responsibility.[11]

Lucy arrived in Berkeley in the fall of 1903 and spent several years as an assistant adviser, taking courses, and teaching a few of her own before being appointed Dean of Women and Assistant Professor of English in 1906. As dean, Lucy organized social and cultural activities and club houses for the female students, none of whom were housed on campus. She tried to broaden their horizons by taking them on field trips to San Francisco, training them in the elements of self-government, and informing them about employment possibilities in fields other than teaching.[12]

It was at Berkeley that Lucy got to know Wesley Clair Mitchell, although they had met in 1900 or 1901 at a dinner given by the Adolph Millers in Chicago. (Robert Herrick, the relative of George Herbert Palmer and friend of Alice who would become Elsie Clews Parsons's lover in the 1920s, was a guest at the same dinner.[13]) Unlike Lucy, Wesley grew up in a warm and loving home where parents and children shared common interests and activities and delighted in talking to each other about them.[14] His father, John Wesley Mitchell, a physician,

---

10   LSM, "Unpublished Autobiography" (UA), LSM Papers. Lucy did not mention George's marriage proposal in *TL*.
11   LSM, *TL*, pp. 133–34; LSM, UA. LSM Papers.
12   LSM, *TL*, pp. 194, 198, 207, 210. See also, Antler, pp. 100–5.
13   LSM, *TL*, p. 99. For Herrick's relationship with Elsie Clews Parsons, see Chapter 3.
14   LSM, *TL*, p. 28.

never recovered from the leg wound he suffered in the Civil War and eventually became an invalid. In contrast to Lucy's submissive mother, Wesley's mother, Lucy Medora McClellan Mitchell (Medora), to whom Wesley was very close, was a strong advocate of women's rights. Born in 1847, she supported women's suffrage and practiced birth control after she had seven children in eleven years. Believing that women should have "a controlling voice in their own life interests", she assumed considerable responsibility for the household as her husband's health deteriorated.[15] John Mitchell made a series of bad business investments, and money was a constant worry. Nevertheless, Medora, who had studied at Oberlin College and taught school before her marriage, made sure that her daughters as well as her sons had opportunities for post-secondary education.[16]

Like Lucy, Wesley had shouldered a lot of family responsibilities at an early age — "far too early," he would tell her. Even as a youth he was "earnest and serious."[17] Compared to Lucy's circles in Chicago, his world growing up in Decatur, Illinois was narrow and small. But it widened considerably when he became an undergraduate at the newly opened University of Chicago in 1892. After graduating in 1896, he did a year of graduate study in economics at the University of Halle in Germany, and then returned to the University of Chicago to complete his PhD degree. He worked for a year at the Census Office in Washington, DC before joining the economics department at the University of Chicago in 1900. His first book, based on his doctoral dissertation, was published in 1902.

Courtship: Mastering a "Primitive" Woman

Adolph Miller, Lucy's brother-in-law, brought Wesley to Berkeley in late 1902, about nine months before Lucy arrived. His course on "Economic Origins" was one of the first she took at the university, and they met frequently at the homes of mutual friends. He had made a

---

15   LSM, *TL*, p. 27; Medora Mitchell to WCM [late 1911 or early 1912], and June 18, 1912. LSM Papers.
16   Wesley's older sister, Beulah, attended and then taught at the Art Students League in New York.
17   WCM to LS, October 18, 1911. LSM Papers.

good impression on her in Chicago, but seeing more of him in Berkeley, she decided he was he was intellectually advanced but socially and emotionally immature.[18]

Neither Lucy nor Wesley was prepared for the dramatic events that changed their relationship in May 1907. Arriving at a fancy dress party in a gypsy costume, Lucy mesmerized the guests by dancing a spontaneous and lengthy gypsy dance. Adolph Miller reprimanded her for forgetting "her position" and dancing with abandon. But Wesley was enchanted and — by his own admission — fell completely in love with her. He quickly sent her two poems which expressed great admiration for her. Two weeks later, he wrote her a letter telling her he loved her and wanted to marry her. Lucy — shocked and perplexed — claimed to be emotionally attached to another man and wrote a firm refusal. Instead of pressing his case, Wesley retreated.[19]

Lucy did not tell anyone about this incident; Wesley confided only in his older, married friend Sarah (Sadie) Hardy Gregory, who also knew Lucy. Over the next few years, Lucy and Wesley saw very little of each other. He immediately buried himself in writing the draft of a book on the money economy. After spending five months working for the US Immigration Commission in San Francisco in 1908, he headed east to teach at Harvard University. When he returned to Berkeley in the fall of 1909, Lucy was about to leave to spend the academic year 1909–1910 in Berlin with Berkeley President Benjamin Wheeler and his family.

Both Lucy and Wesley were back in Berkeley in the fall of 1910. They could not avoid meeting, but Wesley felt very awkward in her company.[20] Nevertheless, in the spring of 1911, he was arranging hiking expeditions that Lucy joined. Their relationship took another dramatic turn when they spent five weeks camping in the Sierra Mountains with

---

18 LSM, *TL*, p. 143.
19 This paragraph is based on LSM, *TL*, pp. 213–14; the Mitchells' courtship letters; and the letters Wesley wrote to Sarah Hardy Gregory on May 11, 1907; May 16, 1907; and June 7, 1907. He sent drafts of the two poems — "The Dancer" and "Heart's Quest" — to Gregory, asking her advice on the wording and the rhymes. Typescripts of the letters and poems are in Columbia University, Rare Book and Manuscript Library, MsColl\Mitchell, Wesley Clair Mitchell Papers (WCM Papers). Neither Wesley's proposal letter nor Lucy's response has survived (*TL*, p. 214).
20 WCM to Sarah Hardy Gregory, May 17, 1911. LSM Papers.

mutual friends in the summer of 1911. Their entourage included three walkers, four riders, a cook, a packer, and seventeen horses and mules carrying supplies.[21] Lucy found Wesley to be a different personality in the mountains than in the valley — more fun-loving and less serious, bolder and more adventurous, even something of a strong, protective hero. Twice he rescued her from danger, by ordering her to climb a tree while he chased off a herd of cows, and by coming back for her in the midst of an electric storm after she had gotten separated from the group. "Never will I forget him as he came leaping down those boulders in that wild storm," she wrote forty years later in *Two Lives*.[22] To mark their new relationship, Lucy gave them new names. She dubbed him "Robin" as a reminder of the great outdoors and his perpetually rosy cheeks. She became "Alta", a reference to high mountain peaks. Lucy would call him Robin for the rest of his life, but Alta did not stick. Wesley went by many names: his parents, siblings, and early friends, used his middle name, Clair, although his mother often called him "Bonnie" in reference to his looks. To his professional colleagues and the friends he made in New York, he was Wesley.

They returned from their trip "deeply in love", according to Lucy. Nevertheless, like many career-oriented women, she hesitated to marry. Her struggle to overcome the marriage-career dilemma was complicated by uncertainty about her career path. She had told President Wheeler in the summer of 1909, a few months after her father died, that she intended to leave the deanship within a few years.[23] Feeling that academia was too much of an ivory tower, she turned down offers from Nicholas Murray Butler, President of Columbia University, to become Dean of Barnard College.[24] By the fall of 1911, she still was not sure what she wanted to do.[25] Undaunted by her blossoming relationship with Wesley, she left Berkeley in October for a previously planned four-month trip to New York where she shadowed several prominent women as they went about their work so

21   LSM, *TL*, pp. 216–17.
22   LSM, *TL*, pp. 220–21.
23   LSM, *TL*, p. 204.
24   LSM, *TL*, p. 210; Nicholas Murray Butler to LS, May 28, 1909; July 12, 1909; August 31, 1909; and July 14, 1910. LSM Papers.
25   LSM, *TL*, p. 210.

she could understand what they did.[26] She gathered information about emerging employment opportunities for her Berkeley undergraduates, but also explored possibilities for herself and made valuable contacts with leading female professionals.

Lucy and Wesley exchanged more than sixty letters while she was away. Like other nineteenth-century couples, they were engaging in the courtship ritual of "testing" their suitability as life partners by exploring their personalities and their ideas about marriage.[27] They confessed their worst faults, voiced their greatest fears, and probed to see their loved one's reaction to these revelations. The testing process was common, but their concerns were very different from most couples of their day. Lucy was testing two things in particular: how supportive Wesley would be as the husband of a wife who worked outside the home, and whether he was forceful enough to be the kind of "masterful man" she desired for a husband. The first issue was more easily resolved than the second. Lucy did not yet understand that the kind of support she was looking for was unlikely to come from a man who epitomized conventional notions of masculinity.

Lucy's experiences in New York gave her a renewed sense of purpose, a greater appreciation of her talents, and a clearer focus for her ambition. She felt she could hold her own among the female leaders she was meeting, and found that her ideas about education interested philanthropists and journalists. Despite her lack of training, she felt the equal of the women she was spending time with in New York and confident that she had the potential to be one of the "big, educational constructors."[28] All this strengthened her desire to work after she married. She put Wesley on notice: "[W]hat is a necessity is that I have an outlet, a use for my own constructive force — & I think, though I am not certain, that that would have to be wider though not deeper than my

---

26   The women Lucy shadowed included Lillian Wald at the Henry Street Settlement (where Lucy roomed with Florence Kelley); Mary Richmond at the Charity Organization; Pauline Goldmark, who was conducting a social survey; and Julia Richman, who was working on education in the public schools. Lucy also volunteered with the Salvation Army. (LSM, *TL*, pp. 208–9.)

27   See Karen Lystra, *Searching the Heart: Women, Men, and Romantic Love in Nineteenth-Century America* (New York: Oxford University Press, 1989).

28   LS to WCM, October 29, 1911. See also, LS to WCM, November 3, 1911 and November 8, 1911. LSM Papers.

home. This, theoretically, you would approve of. But practically, would you? Could you? Would I?"[29]

Nevertheless, she assured him that his work would have precedence over hers. "If I marry you, your work and your standards shall prevail [...] if your work is not more important than mine (leaving aside the most important of all which is *our* work, our home, and our possible children), why then, I do not wish to marry you."[30]

As her ambitions grew, Lucy became more insistent that her future partner would have to support her work. "This is the genuine, the unquenchable, the vital me & you must reckon with it if you would reckon with me," she warned Wesley.[31] Describing her desire to fight injustice, "straighten out the human mess", and leave a legacy that would outlive her, she asked Wesley whether he was sure he wanted "a wife who is urged by such passionate intensity."[32] He took her seriously and encouraged her to think big and aim high. "Your letter about your budding interests and your plans for future work pleases me to the core of my heart," he assured her.[33] A few days later, he elaborated:

> Your need of work is to me one of your most splendid qualities. I not only admire but also sympathize with it, because it answers my expanding need. To stifle it would be to cut off the sweet source of happiness to you and helpfulness to others. If marriage threatened such a result you certainly ought not to marry. Furthermore I agree most heartily that the home in and of itself would not give adequate scope to your distinctive energies. You have proved your fitness to serve a larger circle, & you ought not willfully to make it narrow.[34]

Knowing how important work was to him, he accepted that Lucy would feel the same, and applauded her determination. "On the critical issue I am perfectly clear — I should be prouder of you for holding to your constructive work, for marrying *like a man* without narrowing your sphere & usefulness," he wrote.[35]

29 LS to WCM, October 29, 1911. LSM Papers.
30 Ibid.
31 LS to WCM, November 3, 1911. LSM Papers.
32 LS to WCM, November 8, 1911. LSM Papers.
33 WCM to LS, November 3, 1911. LSM Papers.
34 WCM to LS, November 6, 1911. LSM Papers.
35 WCM to LS, November 3, 1911. Emphasis added. LSM Papers.

Wesley was able to bring a sympathetic understanding to the problem because his friendships with several women enlightened him about the difficulties highly educated women encountered when they married and lacked a professional outlet, and the challenges they faced if they tried to maintain a career after they married. His closest friend and confidante in Berkeley, Sarah Hardy Gregory, had been a Fellow in Economics at the University of Chicago when he was an undergraduate. Sadie had experienced her own version of the marriage-career dilemma and agonized for years about marrying Warren Gregory, a lawyer from a prominent and wealthy San Francisco family. She taught briefly at Wellesley College before she married him in 1896. Constrained by societal expectations, Sadie did not work after she married, but she struggled to find an outlet for her formidable intellectual gifts.[36] When Wesley was writing the material that would be incorporated into his magnum opus, *Business Cycles*, she served as his intellectual sounding board and critic. She read the chapters he churned out in the late spring of 1907, just after Lucy rejected his precipitous marriage proposal. Both Sadie and Wesley derived immense satisfaction from this arrangement, and it made him optimistic about the pleasures of sharing his work with a future wife.[37]

From his friend Dorothea Rhodes Lummis Moore, Wesley knew something about the challenges couples faced in dual career relationships. Dorothea had gone to medical school and practiced medicine during her marriage to the journalist Charles Lummis. Five years after they divorced, she married Ernest Carroll Moore in 1896. When Ernest taught at Berkeley between 1900 and 1906, Dorothea was head of the South Park Settlement in San Francisco and working for reforms in the juvenile court system.[38]

---

36   Sadie and Wesley had a conversation about the difficulties these social norms created for intellectually-inclined women who married well-to-do men with successful careers. WCM, Diary Appointment Book, September 3, 1907. WCM Papers. Wesley made daily entries in his Diary Appointment Books from 1905–1948. They are an invaluable source of information about his and his family's activities.

37   For more on Wesley's friendship with Sadie and the help she provided him in 1907, see below, pp. 397–399.

38   The difficulties Dorothea's career caused in her first marriage to Charles Lummis are discussed in Lystra, pp. 207–13, and Regina Markell Morantz-Sanchez, *Sympathy and Science: Women Physicians in American Medicine* (New York: Oxford University Press, 1987), pp. 126–27. Dorothea and Wesley corresponded for years after each

The only downside Wesley contemplated if Lucy were to have a career of her own was the likelihood that she would be too busy to help him with his work. He would have liked her advice on the manuscript of *Business Cycles* in the fall of 1911, but knowing the many demands on her time, he did not think it "fair" to ask for her help. But he wanted to work with her in the future: "To feel that we are working together will be a joy to me. And won't it be to you? Could we do anything which will bring us closer together in the most delightful & lasting fashion?" he asked. He was convinced that her "keen insight, well-proportioned judgment [...] & excellent literary taste" would greatly improve the final product. "Together we can make it much better than I can make it alone, or aided only by the criticisms of professional friends & Sadie Gregory," he assured her.[39] (At this time, Lucy knew little about the assistance Sadie had provided. But she would be greatly troubled to discover, forty years later, just how much help Sadie had given Wesley.)

Despite the fact that that they knew "few married couples who attempt and still fewer who succeed" in pursuing separate work, Wesley was confident that he and Lucy would succeed and have a stronger marriage as a result. "Neither wishes to throw the whole burden of managing our common life upon the other, neither wishes to absorb the other's whole life," he noted. "Each of us can feel a just pride in what the other accomplishes. And this feeling will enable us to make what to others might be a bar separating them in sympathy a bond uniting us — a bond re-inforcing our love and steadying the life we build together."[40] By helping each other in their work, he insisted, they "would pull together & in the end I fancy that we'd find we had a common load."[41]

Wesley's efforts to convince Lucy he took her work seriously were bolstered by the practical support he offered. When she announced that New York would be the best location for her work, he replied that moving to New York would also be helpful to his career.[42] When she

---

left Berkeley, and saw each other when Dorothea visited New York. Ernest Moore would later become Vice President and Provost of the University of California, Los Angeles.
39 WCM to LS, November 15, 1911. LSM Papers.
40 WCM to LS, November 6, 1911. LSM Papers.
41 WCM to LS, October 18, 1911. LSM Papers.
42 LS to WCM, October 29, 1911; WCM to LS, November 6, 1911. LSM Papers.

said she might need to return to New York for six weeks on her own in the spring, he agreed that work and duty sometimes had to take precedence over personal pleasure. However, he did not want her to spend a year alone in New York, because he felt that at their relatively advanced ages, they should not delay too long before starting a family.[43]

Wesley's solution for the problem of raising children when a woman worked was hiring help to attend to the children's routine care.[44] He did not propose that he would take on any household responsibilities, but Lucy had reason to believe that he would help out in emergencies. While she was in New York, Wesley devoted a great deal of time to helping his sister, Eunice, and her family when Eunice was ill and her husband was away. Both Wesley and Sadie Gregory kept Lucy informed about the help Wesley provided, despite the toll it took on his writing.[45]

Wesley found it easier to ease Lucy's doubts about his willingness to support her work than to overcome her fear that he would not be "a masterful man." She was immensely ambivalent about what she wanted in a man and a marriage. She assumed that if they married, she and Wesley would have a marriage of "companionable equality."[46] But she criticized him for not being more commanding and assertive. Despite her independence and ambition, she was susceptible to the romantic ideology and gender stereotypes that portrayed men as masterful and in charge and women as submissive and dependent. Lucy repeatedly expressed a desire to be conquered by Wesley; she wanted to feel compelled to offer him "the homage which your soul demands of hers."[47] Similarly conditioned by societal stereotypes, Alice Freeman Palmer, Grace Chisholm Young, and Beatrice Webb were other ambitious women who wanted to be overwhelmed by a powerful, heroic man.

43 WCM to LS, December 14, 1911. See also, WCM to LS, November 6, 1911. LSM Papers.
44 WCM to LS, November 6, 1911. LSM Papers.
45 WCM to LS, October 23, 1911; November 6, 1911; November 7, 1911; November 10, 1911; November 12, 1911. Sarah Hardy Gregory to LS, November 8, 1911. See also, WCM to Medora Mitchell, December 3, 1911. All in LSM Papers.
46 LS to WCM, December 18, 1911. LSM Papers.
47 LS to WCM, November 20, 1911. LSM Papers.

Lucy began questioning Wesley's forcefulness as soon as she left for New York. Explaining that she found him "academic" and "unaggressive," she reminded him how he had meekly accepted her rejection of his declaration of love in 1907 and made no effort to change her mind. "A man of more force — not intellectual or even emotional, but more force in meeting the world & whipping it into line would have persisted & insisted," she pointed out.[48]

She continued to hammer the point throughout the fall. "Your character, your lovableness & your intelligence appeal to me convincingly. In those three great essentials I acknowledge you my superior & find yielding easy," she wrote. "But there is a subtle something which I have & which you lack — a something which kept me from considering the possibility of marrying you for many years [....]. It is called — when we force ourselves to name it 'personality.'"[49] Lucy struggled to clarify what she meant. She was talking not about "character" but about "something quite different: something which conquers tho' it does not deserve to, a something which compels tho' it does not command, a something which apparently wins without effort [... something that] stands for a real if intangible power."[50] The key point, for Lucy, was that she had this intangible source of power and Wesley did not.

Deeply ambivalent about her own powerful "personality", Lucy wanted a partner who would help keep it in check, and she was not sure Wesley would be equal to the challenge. "[My personality] must be guided or it will run riot. Can you do that without breaking its spirit? I doubt if anything but personality can control personality. I doubt if intelligence or character can ever really curb the impetuous rush without bruising & mutilating the intangible wild thing," she cautioned.[51]

She conceded that they would be "very happy", "far happier than most", if they married. But still she hesitated, knowing that "in my soul I should not be humbled. I should not feel the best had come to me. I should not feel that to serve you was the greatest privilege that had come

---

48 LS to WCM, October 26, 1911. LSM Papers.
49 LS to WCM, December 2, 1911. She used almost exactly the same language in her letter of December 18, 1911, but substituted "sweetness" for lovableness. LSM Papers.
50 LS to WCM, December 2, 1911. LSM Papers.
51 Ibid.

to me."[52] Lucy's reservations show that at some deep emotional core she was, as she put it, a very "primitive" woman. Feeling that Wesley had no understanding of female psychology, she explained to him:

> A woman always feels a rush of gratitude, founded on humility, that she is given to serve a man. She bows with proud humbleness before the masculine creature she acknowledges as her lord, her leader [...]. The fact remains that *your masculinity* does not compel me. It is not a thing to be reasoned about: it is a thing to be felt [...] I am too much the primitive woman to be satisfied without this sense of leadership, this feeling that my husband is a 'masterful man' [...]. Character you have and I honor you; intellect you have & I admire you; Sweetness of nature you have and I love you: but leadership, mastery, personality you have not & you do not compel me.[53]

Lucy was brutally candid in telling Wesley that she feared her desire for children would lead her to marry "a man whose personality is less than mine & whose conquest of me was due not to dominance of his soul over mine but to the cowardice of my own soul."[54] She was equally honest in admitting that she did not love him as fully as she knew she could love a man.[55] She was referring to her relationship with her college boyfriend Joe, whom she described in her unpublished autobiography as "the one human being I might have loved enough to make me forget myself."[56] Knowing that Wesley did not expect or elicit such a loss of self was deeply troubling to Lucy.

Her doubts about Wesley's "masculinity" did not mean that she found him physically unappealing. "I want you with all the quivering

---

52 LS to WCM, December 18, 1911. LSM Papers.
53 Ibid. Emphasis added. The reference to female psychology comes from LS to WCM, October 26, 1911. LSM Papers.
54 LS to WCM, December 2, 1911. Lucy's fear that she might marry in order to have children was hinted at in a "Round Robin" letter she wrote to her Radcliffe classmates on the train to New York in October, 1911. She described her longing to have a child in a poem, "The World's Gifts", which she enclosed in LS to WCM, December 3, 1911. When Wesley took this as a sign that her resistance was weakening, she assured him that the poem was written "in an impersonal frenzy" with "no thought of you or any man." (LS to WCM, December 18, 1911.) After Wesley's death, she recalled how fearful she had been that her desire to have children might have prompted her to marry a man she did not love. LSM, "Robin" (November 20, 1948), pp. 12–13. All in LSM Papers.
55 LS to WCM, November 27, 1911 and December 18, 1911. LSM Papers.
56 LSM, UA, quoted in Antler, p. 86.

longing of a passionate woman — I want the sound of your voice, the touch of your hand, and your lips, the whole of you. If I were with you, I would put my arms around you and come close," she wrote.[57] Wesley was equally attracted to Lucy, but reminded her, "There is so much more in both of us and between both of us than passionate longing to be in each other's arms."[58]

Lucy's doubts were compounded by knowing that her friends did not think Wesley was a suitable mate for her. She was painfully aware that she would be "marrying down" by choosing Wesley. "You do not compel *my* world. The people you draw to you are not *my* people. You need to be interpreted to be understood by those who instinctively choose me as their own," she lamented.[59] Planning to go camping with Wesley in the Yosemite when she returned to California, Lucy insisted that her friends, not his, should accompany them. "I want to decide [the marriage question] when my kind of people are with me to keep me conscious of *my* background," she explained.[60]

What bothered Lucy were not the differences in their material circumstances, but the differences in their social worlds. Her self-defined milieu was a world of achievers, players on a big stage. Her father, a self-made millionaire, was a pillar of Chicago's civic and cultural life. She went from his home to the Palmers' home where she met many of the nation's academic leaders. In New York, she felt comfortable in the company of women who were carving out new professions and heading new institutions. The men and women Lucy identified as part of her world when Wesley was wooing her — Marion

57 LS to WCM, November 8, 1911. LSM Papers.
58 WCM to LS, November 15, 1911. His passion for her: WCM to LS, November 14, 1911 and November 26, 1911. LSM Papers.
59 LS to WCM, December 2, 1911, emphasis in the original. Similarly, LS to WCM, December 18, 1911. LSM Papers.
60 LS to WCM, November 22, 1911, emphasis in the original. LSM Papers.

Jones Farquhar,[61] Benjamin Wheeler,[62] and Adolph Miller[63] — were people who assumed their own importance and made others respond accordingly. She wanted to be surrounded by people who made things happen. Less successful individuals were not only weak but dull.

Lucy wanted to live in a world of luminaries, and she was not sure Wesley would provide entrée to it. As he himself admitted, his social circles constituted a "very small world." The people he described as his intimates — his family, Sadie Gregory, Dorothea Moore, and the economist Thorstein Veblen — were not people in prominent positions, but people he was drawn to because he thought he could help them.[64] (Although Veblen is more famous today than anyone in Lucy's social world, in his own day he was a controversial figure and thinker who was let go from one academic position after another.[65]) Wesley's own career trajectory may also have given Lucy pause. He had shown promise, and was sought after for academic jobs, but at the age of thirty-seven he had yet to make a major intellectual contribution to economics. Lucy was also

61   Lucy and Marion Jones Farquhar (1879–1965) had been intimate friends since they were roommates at the Marlborough School in their teens. Marion was the daughter of Senator John Percival Jones of Nevada who made a fortune in silver mines and railroads and co-founded the city of Santa Monica. Lucy visited the family in their home where she met many prominent people. Marion won several US tennis titles and, in 1900, two Olympic medals in tennis. She married architect Robert D. Farquhar in 1903, had three sons, and lived in Greenwich Village. After their divorce, she became a well-known violinist and voice coach. (LSM, *TL*, pp. 112–14; https://www.olympedia.org/athletes/2736.)

62   Benjamin Wheeler, President of the University of California at Berkeley from 1899 to 1919, led the school through an unprecedented period of physical growth and expansion and consolidated the power of the university president at the expense of the faculty. During the year Lucy spent with Wheeler and his family in 1909–1910, when he was a visiting professor at the University of Berlin, Wheeler was treated as an important dignitary by Prussian society and politicians. Lucy accompanied the Wheelers to state dinners, social occasions, and university functions. The Berkeley faculty opposed Wheeler's "autocratic" ways and forced him out of office in 1919. (LSM, *TL*, pp. 205–7; "Days of Cal: A Brief History of Cal: Part 2", www.bancroft. berkely.ed/CAlHistory/brief-history.2.html)

63   Adolph C. Miller married Lucy's older sister, Mary, in 1895. In 1902, he became a Professor of Economics at Berkeley with responsibility for developing its College of Commerce. He left Berkeley when he was appointed Assistant Secretary of the Interior in 1913. In 1914 he became one of the original members of the Board of Governors of the Federal Reserve (www.millerinstitute.berkeley.edu/page.php).

64   WCM to LS, December 7, 1911. LSM Papers.

65   For Veblen's checkered career and Wesley's efforts to help him, see Elizabeth Walkins Jorgensen and Henry Irvin Jorgensen, *Thorstein Veblen, Victorian Firebrand* (Armonk, NY: Sharpe, 1999).

quite ambivalent about the academic arena as a venue for achievement. She felt that academia was too much of an ivory tower and too many academics were pedants. Nor did she want to live in a world which she feared would never take her seriously because she lacked an advanced degree.[66]

Wesley tried various stratagems to counter Lucy's arguments and concerns. By the middle of November, he had become more assertive about expressing his opinions as truth and more likely to treat her as a weak female who needed his strong masculine guidance and protection. He described her as "a brave honest little girl" and insisted, "Oh, little one, you do need my help in solving this problem, whether that help would prove serviceable in the future or a burden."[67] Noting that it was she "who most needs help — the one whose inner strength is less — the one whose fluttering spirit is more likely to fail midst the storms of life," he suggested that together they could develop a plan of action for her future work. He even proposed a specific topic for her to research.[68]

Lucy was outraged when Wesley suggested she lacked perseverance and focus. "I must say that my spirit has never 'fluttered in the storm of life.' If I have steered an unsteady course, it has not been from lack of courage or lack of vision," she protested.[69] Nor was she inclined to accept Wesley's advice about the future direction of her work. Ignoring his suggestion that she take up philanthropy, she developed her own plan, her "vision" she called it, for incorporating sex education and community values into a public school curriculum.[70]

None of this seemed to bother Wesley. He applauded her plan and made no further effort to guide her. Nevertheless, he refused to accept

---

66 LS to WCM, December 25, 1911. Her lack of training: LS to WCM, October 29, 1911. LSM Papers. Her negative view of academia: LSM, *TL*, p. 211.

67 WCM to LS, November 18, 1911; LS to WCM, November 20, 1911. See also WCM to LS, December 16, 1911 in which he refers to her as "such a satisfactory girl!". LSM Papers.

68 WCM to LS, December 5, 1911. LSM Papers.

69 LS to WCM, December [12?], 1911. LSM Papers.

70 Lucy sent him an outline of her plan for educating women and girls about sex, but later noted that her ideas "had crystalized and broadened." (LS to WCM, December 20, 1911, LSM Papers.) On the train from New York, she wrote two papers: one that detailed her views on sex education, and one on educational innovations to address the needs of "The Whole Child." LSM, *TL*, pp. 210–11.

Lucy's judgment that because he lacked "personality", he lacked mastery and leadership. "There is a considerable force within me which does not fear your force or acknowledge its own inferiority," he assured her. He conceded that many of her friends "would always consider me a queer stick, & wonder why so fine a woman threw herself away on such a person." But he argued that she was too courageous and independent to let herself be swayed by people who "would laugh at you for making an eccentric choice." Moreover, he promised, "[T]hose who really matter 'will understand & value me.'"[71]

Wesley did not agree that he would be the weaker partner if they married. Countering her charge that he lacked "leadership, mastery, and personality," he outlined an alternative vision of leadership as proof of his "virility." His mastery was expressed in his role as a pioneer and explorer rather than in commanding others.

> Your world is made up of men & women who are captains of bands doing work in the well-settled busy land of the present. You feel in yourself the capacity to be such a captain — to sway the interests of your contemporaries & to work out your visions in the lives of men & women. Now I am not fond of this kind of life. The land of the present strikes me as a most unsupportable place for the mass of men [...]. So I leave the land of the present & go forth into the land of the future as an explorer [...]. Such an explorer is, if you like, no leader [...] he can do better work if he travels alone.[72]

Old-fashioned leaders saw someone like himself "as a visionary, an unpracticed person, one not to be trusted with the direction of affairs", Wesley admitted. In his view, it was the captains of industry and trade who "lack vision, courage, insight." He asked Lucy to join him in carving out new ideals and promised that if she did, she would no longer think he lacked virility. Wesley's vision of a pioneering leader struck a responsive chord in Lucy but did not erase all her doubts. "It may be I am too much of an explorer by temperament to follow anyone's trail even yours, or it may be that I do not feel you are a sure-guide, that I have not found *my* leader. I do not know. But something there is that

---

71   WCM to LS, December 7, 1911. LSM Papers.
72   WCM to LS, December 2, 1911. LSM Papers.

rises in inexplicable pride & refuses to let me make the last surrender," she responded.[73]

When they set off for Yosemite, Wesley was confident that his sense that Lucy belonged to him would triumph over her feeling that he could not "dominate" her. He was right, but several more weeks went by before Lucy finally agreed to marry him. Adolph Miller offered Wesley his congratulations but informed him that the family was "somewhat divided" over the engagement. Lucy believed the Millers disapproved of her choice.[74]

Planning for their new life together, Lucy and Wesley decided to resign from Berkeley and move to New York, although though neither had a job there. During a hectic spring, Wesley completed the manuscript of *Business Cycles*, and Lucy produced an elaborate Greek pageant, written, acted, and danced by Berkeley's women students. They married on May 8, 1912 in a simple ceremony attended by a few family members and close friends, despite her relatives' desire for a fancier and larger wedding in Chicago.[75] After stops in Chicago and New York, the Mitchells left for a seven month working honeymoon in Europe. On the trip, they corrected the proofs of Wesley's manuscript, attended lectures, and met with leading economists (including Beatrice and Sidney Webb). Lucy visited schools in England and attended meetings of the London County Council, which oversaw local education.[76]

Lucy's doubts were allayed enough for her to marry. Balancing their very different personalities, finding a satisfying outlet for her ambition, and integrating professional life with family life would be the work of years not months. In the process, Lucy had to rethink her ideal of manhood and reconcile her assumptions about marital equality with her desire to submit to a more powerful male.

---

73 LS to WCM, December 29, 1911. Emphasis in the original. LSM Papers.
74 Adolph Miller to WCM, February 1, 1912; LSM, UA. LSM Papers.
75 WCM to Medora Mitchell, March 10, 1912; Medora Mitchell to WCM, April 1, 1912. LSM Papers. His parents were unable to attend the ceremony.
76 LSM, *TL*, pp. 232–34.

Career Building and Family Building

When they returned to New York in December 1912, Lucy and Wesley set to work to build their careers. Wesley turned down offers from Cornell University and Yale University, and began teaching economics at Columbia University in the fall of 1913. After *Business Cycles* came out in September 1913, he was recognized as the leading authority on using statistical empirical data to analyze economic trends. His reputation assured, he was promoted to full professor in 1914.[77]

Lucy meanwhile worked hard to establish her credentials as a progressive educator. She took classes, volunteered as a visiting teacher, and helped to develop and administer a psychological testing instrument for the Board of Education. She refined her ideas about using schools to teach sex hygiene and promote community values, while learning about educational experiments in other parts of the country and developing relationships with progressive education leaders in New York City. She would later describe her "fumbling" efforts to define a focus, but her activities were in fact driven by powerful internal logic, fierce determination, and strong ambition.[78]

Lucy's preparations paid off in the spring of 1916, when a large grant from a wealthy, philanthropically-minded cousin enabled her to launch the Bureau of Educational Experiments (BEE). (The name was a form of "polysyllabic intimidation," Wesley teasingly observed.[79]) Lucy spent two weeks finalizing the plan with Wesley and Harriet Johnson, an educator she had worked with on several projects, but the outlines had been brewing in Lucy's mind throughout her time in New York. The BEE's purpose was to marry what researchers were learning about child development with the approaches teachers were using in experimental schools — two related but independent fields when the BEE was founded.[80]

Lucy would later describe the early years of the Bureau as one of the most exciting and stimulating periods of her life. With the grant, the BEE was able to fund its own research projects, gather and disseminate

---

77 LSM, *TL*, p. 241.
78 Fumbling efforts: LSM, *TL*, pp. 249–50.
79 LSM, *TL*, p. 252.
80 LSM, UA, Chapter 14, LSM Papers. LSM, *TL*, p. 222.

information about experimental efforts around the country, and support efforts to apply the learnings to educational practice in experimental schools. In October 1916, Lucy started teaching at Caroline Pratt's Play School, giving her an opportunity to engage directly with young minds and put her ideas into practice.

Building a family presented a parallel challenge during these career building years. Lucy was thirty-three when she married, and Wesley was thirty-seven — old to be starting a family. When Lucy did not become pregnant, they decided to adopt — an unusual step for members of her social class. After a few months of working with an adoption agency, they brought home an eight-month-old boy at the beginning of February 1914. As champions of progressive education, whatever concerns they might have had about his future were allayed by their belief that character was molded by environment rather than heredity.[81] Nevertheless, they hesitated to name the boy after family members, and debated whether he should call them "aunt" and "uncle" rather than "mother" and "father."[82] In the end, they named the baby John McClellan Mitchell (Jack), incorporating Wesley's father's given name and his mother's maiden name, and Jack called his adopted parents "mother" and "father."[83] Five months after his adoption, Lucy was pregnant; she gave birth to Sprague in March 1915. Wanting more children, the Mitchells adopted again. Two-month-old Marian (Marni) joined them in April 1917. Lucy gave birth to Arnold, their fourth and last child, less than a year later, in February 1918. (Sprague and Arnold were both given family names from Lucy's side.)

---

81 They were reassured by what John Dewey wrote about nature and nurture. WCM to LSM, March 13, 1914; LSM to WCM, March 15, 1914. LSM Papers.

82 LSM to Medora Mitchell, February 1, 1914 and February 9, 1914. Believing that "environment is much more than heritage", Wesley's parents enthusiastically welcomed their grandson and wanted him to call them grandma and grandpa (Medora Mitchell to LCM, February 4, 1914). Lucy's upper-class relatives were more concerned about the potentially harmful influence of heredity. Cautioning that "blood will tell", Lucy's Aunt Nan advised her to thoroughly investigate the baby's "pedigree." (Nancy Atwood Sprague to LSM, February 3 [n.y.]. See also, A. Sprague to LSM, February 14, 1914. All in LSM Papers.

83 Lucy wrote a charming adoption story for Jack and noted that he accepted it without question when she told it to him in 1918. LSM Papers.

Fig. 6 Lucy and Wesley with their four children in 1918. Unknown photographer. Lucy Sprague Mitchell Papers, Rare Book and Manuscript Library, Columbia University in the City of New York.

Lucy's happiness was complete. After years of struggle and doubt, she had a successful career, a loving and loved husband, and four thriving children. Both she and Wesley felt "a kind of miracle had come to us."[84] But their busy, happy life was not simply the product of privileged entitlement and random good fortune. It was also the result of very hard work.

Managing a Four-ring Circus

Wesley made good on the assurances he had given Lucy about the importance of her work and his willingness to help her. Over the long course of their marriage, he provided consistent and enthusiastic support, contributed substantive input, and shouldered childrearing responsibilities without complaint. Without his involvement and encouragement, Lucy insisted, she could not have accomplished what she did.[85]

Wesley was actively engaged in Lucy's work at the BEE. He worked with her and Harriet Johnson on the initial plan, served as treasurer and a trustee, and was a member of its governing body until 1931. His expertise in quantitative measurement and analysis was especially valuable. He attended monthly Board meetings, sat on the hiring and membership committees, wrote funding proposals, advised on legal and financial matters, and connected the fledgling organization to experts in various fields. At the annual year-end party, held in the Mitchells' home, he generally gave an address on some aspect of social science that related to the bureau's work.[86] The BEE was very much a family enterprise — significantly, one that was grounded in Lucy's work, not Wesley's. He also joined her at Caroline Pratt's Play School, where he taught carpentry.

Wesley was as eager to help out with their children as with the BEE. He was especially unusual among the fathers of his time because he engaged in their care and development when they were infants and toddlers. According to Lucy, he defined the childcare challenge they faced as "a family problem shared by fathers" not a wife's responsibility

---

84   LSM, *TL*, p. 259.
85   LSM, *TL*, p. 259.
86   LSM, *TL*, pp. 274, 368. Bank Street College Archives (BSCA), Records of the Bureau of Educational Experiments (BEE), Working Council Minutes and Reports. See also, WCM, Diaries, WCM Papers.

alone. The key, they agreed, was for husbands to become more involved in domestic life. This had to occur, Lucy warned, without any feeling that "masculine dignity has been outraged."[87]

The Mitchells tried to arrange their schedules so that at least one of them was with the children at meals, bath time, and pre-bedtime play.[88] Wesley routinely read to the children and told them stories. When baby Marni took two bottles a night, he and Lucy took turns getting up to feed her.[89] When Lucy was away, he made special efforts to be home at mealtimes and bedtime.

Both parents scheduled their lives to maximize work time and family time. When the children were infants and toddlers, they were put to bed around 6:30 PM and slept for twelve hours, allowing both Lucy and Wesley significant time for other activities in the evenings.[90] Lucy held many evening meetings in their home, and often provided her colleagues with dinner beforehand. Wesley read and wrote late into the night, frequently after Lucy was asleep.[91]

Although Wesley was an unusually engaged father, the Mitchells' domestic life was not an equal division of labor, nor was it intended to be. Lucy, who had desperately wanted to be a mother and made the education of children her life's work, spent far more time with the Mitchell children than Wesley did. She got up at 6 AM to breastfeed or give juice, but worked in bed — sometimes in the company of a child — before the family ate breakfast together at 8 AM.[92] She nursed the children when they were ill, took them to medical specialists in other cities, and sometimes took a child on a special vacation. When there was a new baby, she cut back to part-time teaching so she could nurse the baby and spend more time with the older children. Wesley might have shared some of Marni's nighttime feedings, but it was Lucy who routinely bathed and changed her.

---

87 LSM, UA, Chapter 30, "A Backward Look", p. 10.
88 LSM, *TL*, p. 258.
89 WCM to Medora Mitchell, June 23, 1917. LSM Papers.
90 Reports on the Mitchell children, written for their schools, some by Lucy, some by Wesley: Arnold (November 26, 1919 and May 23, 1922); Marni (December 15, 1920 and May, 1922). LSM Papers.
91 BEE Working Council Minutes, BSCA. WCM, Diaries, WCM Papers.
92 LSM, *TL*, p. 259.

When the children were very young, and Lucy was working at the BEE and the Play School, she deliberately structured her life so that there were few boundaries between her professional and domestic worlds. Physically, socially, even financially, her work life and home life were fully integrated. Her world looked like a chaotic four-ring circus, she would explain, but it was an organic whole, and each aspect contributed to and strengthened the others. The unifying focus was children.[93]

Lucy's balancing act was greatly facilitated by the physical connections between her work life and her domestic life. She operated the BEE out of her home in its first years, and her closest colleagues and friends lived within a short walk of each other in Greenwich Village. The mews of the Mitchells' Greenwich Village townhouse provided the play yard for Pratt's Play School, and the school eventually acquired additional space from the Mitchells. In 1921 the Mitchells bought and refurbished six houses, three on West 12th Street and three on West 13th Street, which had adjoining back yards. The BEE and its Nursery School occupied most of one house on West 13th Street. Pratt's Play School, eventually renamed The City and Country School, was housed in the other buildings. The Mitchells lived in a large apartment that took up the top two floors of the houses on West 12th Street. Their apartment had its own, separate entrance, but could also be accessed from the school. Teachers and students moved freely between the two during the day. These arrangements allowed Lucy to breastfeed her children and see them at intervals throughout the day.[94]

Lucy worked in the midst of her family. She chose not to have a study of her own until the children were older, when she took over what had been the playroom in their summer residence in Greensboro, Vermont; later she created a study on the third floor of their Greenwich Village home. Before that, she said she scribbled her experimental children's stories at the dining room table, in the subway, or on a bus.[95] (She never took taxis.) It was typical that Lucy tried to catch up on her work

---

93   LSM, *TL*, pp. 271–72.
94   LSM, *TL*, pp. 255, 484. Irene M. Prescott, "Lucy Sprague Mitchell: Pioneering in Education", An Interview Conducted by Irene M. Prescott (Berkeley: University of California, 1962), https://digicoll.lib.berkeley.edu/record/217139?ln=en. A copy, entitled "Reminiscences of Lucy Sprague Mitchell. Oral history, 1960", is in the Columbia University, Rare Book and Manuscript Library, Oral History Archives.
95   LSM, *TL*, p. 259.

correspondence on a Sunday morning while playing with Marni and the two older boys. Wesley, meanwhile, sat alone in his splendid study, writing about economics.[96]

There were a few significant periods early in the marriage when Wesley was not around to lend a helping hand. When they were in California during the summer of 1915, he went off on a three-week camping trip with friends. Lucy was unable to join him because she was hobbling about on crutches, due to a knee injury. She stayed behind with two maids to take care of four-month old Sprague and two-year old Jack, entertain Wesley's family and other house guests, and prepare a paper on her views on educating children about sex, which she was to deliver to a conference in San Francisco in early August. Although Lucy encouraged Wesley to enjoy himself, what she wrote about the family's activities in letters to him and in daily entries in his diary suggest that she was greatly stressed and more than a little resentful of his absence.[97] She apologized for sending him a "rather woeful" letter at the start of his trip, but continued to write him detailed accounts of the domestic difficulties she encountered. She also made it clear that the demands of household, children, and guests left her little time or energy to focus on her talk. As a result, she was greatly disappointed in the final product.[98]

Wesley did not again go off by himself on a pleasure trip. But there were times when his work took him away from the family for extended periods. From early 1918 into 1920, he typically spent three days a week in Washington, DC. He was employed by the War Industries Board where he became Chief of the Price Section, with responsibility for estimating the need for key materials, tracking imports, and setting prices.[99] Wesley's weekly commute began in February 1918, just ten days before Lucy gave birth to their fourth child. He was in New York for Arnold's birth, but returned to Washington two days later. Lucy, deeply involved in the BEE and the Play School, remained in New York with four-year old Jack, three-year old Sprague, one-year old Marni, and newborn Arnold. Throughout the spring, Wesley took the midnight

---

96   WCM to Medora Mitchell, June 23, 1917. LSM Papers.
97   She made the daily entries in his diary while he was on his camping trip, July 14-August 8, 1915. WCM, Diary, 1915, WCM Papers.
98   LSM to WCM, July 25, 1915; August 4, 1915; August 5, 1915. LSM Papers.
99   LSM, *TL*, pp. 296–97, 301; WCM, Diaries, 1918–1920, WCM Papers.

sleeper train to Washington on Wednesday nights. He returned to New York on the Saturday night sleeper, arriving home in time for Sunday morning breakfast.[100]

During these years, Wesley struggled to establish a satisfactory balance between his professional life and his family life. He took a leave of absence from Columbia so he would be free to volunteer for war-related work in Washington, DC, as many experts in various fields were doing. He turned down a job offer in Washington in the fall of 1917 because he thought it would require too much time away from his family.[101] The position he accepted early in 1918 was more manageable, but still put a great deal of pressure on him and Lucy. (In the summer of 1918, he refused another assignment that would have kept him in London through the end of the war.[102]) Like many women who juggle part-time work with family responsibilities, Wesley was sometimes frustrated by not having more time to give to a job he found stimulating and challenging. The work "is all excitement — one corner turned & another in sight at the same instant," he wrote to Lucy.[103] "Life [in DC] continues to be exciting. Indeed I am in a mood to demand excitement & to make it when it doesn't offer itself," he announced.[104] To his mother, he confided, "The great difficulty is that I can be there but half the week."[105] Anxious to protect his work time in Washington, he resisted moving a meeting of the BEE's Trustees from Sunday to Saturday.[106]

Nevertheless, when a domestic crisis arose, Wesley made himself available to Lucy without complaint or hesitation. In the summer of 1918, he accompanied the family to their summer property in Greensboro, Vermont and then returned to Washington. A week later, Lucy had to cope with what Wesley described as "a chapter of accidents": two of the children and the most dependable of the maids were ill, and two other members of the household staff had sprained their wrists cranking the engine that pumped water for the cottages. Wesley rushed back

---

100 Wesley's weekly commutes are documented in WCM, Diaries, 1918–1920, WCM Papers; his letters to his mother and Lucy, and WCM to W. E. Hocking, April 9, 1918. LSM Papers.
101 WCM, Diary, November 2, 3, and 4, 1917. WCM Papers.
102 WCM to LSM, August 1, 1918. LSM Papers.
103 WCM to LSM, June 14, 1918. LSM Papers.
104 WCM to LSM, August 20. 1918. LSM Papers.
105 WCM to Medora Mitchell, March 12, 1918. LSM Papers.
106 WCM to W. E. Hocking, April 9, 1918. LSM Papers.

to Greensboro to help, despite Lucy's insistence that he did not need to come. He returned to Washington after a week, where he devoted a great deal of time to hiring a professional nurse who was willing to endure the very rustic living conditions at Greensboro.[107]

Patriotic duty continued to push against family responsibility. "I should not be going back to Washington if I did not feel it every man's duty to aid all he possibly can in getting the country organized," Wesley explained to his mother when he returned from his emergency week in Greensboro. "In some ways my past researches have given me special training for it, & I must not leave unless family reasons make absences from home too much of a sacrifice for Lucy & the children. It is a hard choice even now."[108] For the rest of the summer, Wesley split his time between Washington, where he was working ten-hour days, and Greensboro. Scheduling his visits was another challenge as he tried to minimize the disruption to his office, while maximizing his usefulness to Lucy.[109] Any extra time he took off would have to be made up later, he warned. When he was not able to get away from his office, Wesley commiserated about how difficult things were for Lucy, expressed concern for her well-being, and lamented that he could not be with her and the children.[110]

At the end of the summer, Wesley's job was expanded and extended under a new department, the Central Bureau of Planning and Statistics.[111] Excited about the new work, which involved writing a history of prices during the war, he assured Lucy that the job would give him time to be with her and the children. He continued to commute between Washington and New York for another year and a half, prolonging this unusually difficult period for the family.

This was the only period of their marriage when Wesley repeatedly urged Lucy to curtail her activities so she did not wear herself out and become ill. Always before, he had assured anxious relatives, his mother

---

107 WCM to Medora Mitchell, June 23, 1918; WCM to LSM, June 24, 1918. LSM Papers. Wesley was also eager to protect Lucy from the claims of her relatives. After the death of her aunt, he informed the Sprague family that someone other than Lucy would have to deal with the family affairs because she was already overburdened (WCM to LSM, June 28, 1918. LSM Papers).
108 WCM to Medora Mitchell, June 23, 1918. LSM Papers.
109 WCM to LSM, July 24, 1918. LSM Papers.
110 WCM to LSM, July 20 [1918]; August 1, 1918; June 14, 1918. LSM Papers.
111 WCM to LSM, August 15, 1918. LSM Papers.

in particular, that Lucy was not "overdoing" or endangering her health by working too hard. Now, Wesley advised Lucy to do less, and rejoiced when she agreed.[112] His concern was double-edged: he was genuinely worried about Lucy's health and the strain she was under, but he also must have feared the toll on his own work if she fell ill and he had to deal with family emergencies.

We do not know how Lucy felt about the fact that Wesley was away so much between 1918 and 1920. Her letters to him have not survived, and she was unusually circumspect when she wrote about this period in *Two Lives*. Her few extant letters from the time suggest that she tried to take the difficulties in stride and gloss over the hardships. Nevertheless, her acknowledgement to a friend that "to manage four babies and nurse one is rather taxing!" seems like a veiled complaint.[113] Lucy had a great deal of household help, but she and the children were often ill. It was a critical time for her own work, as she and her colleagues struggled to develop an effective organizational structure for the BEE, develop its research agenda, set quality standards for the work it funded, and launch the BEE's own nursery school.[114]

There were many reasons why Lucy might have accepted Wesley's absence without complaint or resentment. His part-time absence was clearly preferable to his being away all the time. She did not want to move to Washington. She may have agreed about the claims of war and patriotic duty. Very likely she was pleased to see Wesley become more assertive about the way he approached his work. Perhaps she welcomed the opportunity to demonstrate that his work was more important than hers, as she had insisted it should be.

Several things suggest, nevertheless, that the separation took a toll on the Mitchells' relationship. Lucy was not waiting like a loyal Penelope or a heartsick housewife for Wesley's weekly return from Washington. Nor did she go out of her way to see to his comfort. On the contrary, when he

---

112 WCM to LSM, December 25 [1918], and February 22 [1919]. After Sprague's birth in 1915, Medora expressed anxiety "lest Lucy's ever urgent ambition leads her to too early exertion." (Medora Mitchell to WCM, April 7, 1915). In 1918, she advised Wesley to "be prompt with safeguards against [Lucy's] too great ambition, and unlimited enthusiasm." (Medora Mitchell to WCM, May 18, 1918). All in LSM Papers.
113 Letter fragment from LSM, June 14, 1918. See also, Lucy's "Round Robin" letter to her Radcliffe classmates, October 6, 1924. LSM Papers.
114 BEE, Working Council Minutes, 1918 and 1919, BSCA.

arrived home on a Sunday morning, she was often not there. Typically, she was staying at Caroline Pratt's country property. Sometimes she took one or two of the children with her. Often she extended her stay into the early days of the week, when Wesley was at home. If Lucy remained in New York, Caroline was likely to be with her when Wesley arrived. She dined often with the Mitchells, went to the theatre with them, and frequently popped in for "a chat" with Lucy.[115] Lucy used her weekend getaways with Caroline to work on the stories that she would publish in *The Here and Now Storybook* and as a source of rest and relaxation. She may also have been trying, perhaps subconsciously, to indicate displeasure with their commuting marriage.

Wesley might be faulted for being away from home for long stretches of every week while the children were so young. Nevertheless, he took only a part-time wartime job in Washington; he did not complain about the significant wear and tear entailed in his weekly commute; he willingly rearranged his schedule to come to Lucy's assistance when domestic crises arose. None of this should be downplayed. His behavior was a radical departure from the way many men of his day — including many of the husbands featured in this book — behaved. Moreover, when he was in New York, he voluntarily chose to adjust his work schedule so that he could spend more time with the children, and Lucy could have more time to work.

A Real Worker at Last

Both Lucy and Wesley expanded their professional horizons and achievements in the 1920s, during the second decade of their marriage. On leave from Columbia University, Wesley helped to launch two major research organizations that advanced his vision of using quantitative information to develop economic indicators and shape national policy. As a founder and the first Director of Research at the National Bureau of Economic Research (NBER), a post he held from 1920 to 1945, he oversaw work that deepened his analysis of business cycles and applied quantitative measurement to studies of national income and other

---

115 Wesley's arrivals and departures and Lucy's comings and goings are noted in WCM, Diaries, 1918–1920. WCM Papers.

topics. As a founder and board member of the Social Science Research Council (SSRC) between 1923 and 1945, he was instrumental in bringing quantitative statistical analysis, as well as a more inter-disciplinary focus, to the study of social problems. He joined with other progressive educators in opening the New School for Social Research in 1919, and taught there for several years before returning to Columbia. A non-traditional school for adult learners that promoted the free exchange of ideas and interrogation of major social problems, the New School assembled a faculty of scholars and artists who were reformers and activists as well as teachers.[116]

Lucy took off in a different direction. Although the BEE amassed an extensive base of observational records and quantitative data on students in progressive schools and used the information to understand children's developmental stages, Lucy increasingly found outlets for her creative energies by writing stories and books for children, developing innovative school curricula, and training others in her methods. Her pathbreaking *Here and Now Storybook*, published in 1921, provided a theoretical discussion of how children between the ages of two and seven acquire and use language, along with a collection of children's stories, written by Lucy, that applied her theoretical framework. The stories were intended to expand children's understanding by helping them to explore the world around them and make sense of their own experiences and environments. Based on children's actual experience of the real world — the "here and now" — Lucy's stories were a departure from both the fantasy-based tales and didactic moral tales that made up the bulk of children's literature at the time.[117]

When the book was received as "a serious professional contribution" by the education community, Lucy felt that she had become "a real worker", at last. "I was beginning to grow up professionally as well as personally. I knew it and Robin knew it too," she noted.[118] Newly confident, she next developed an innovative social studies curriculum for children aged eight to twelve. It combined information about the

---

116 Judith Friedlander, *A Light in Dark Times: The New School for Social Research and Its University in Exile* (New York: Columbia University Press, 2019), pp. 6–13, 49–50, discusses the early history of the school and Wesley's role in it.

117 LSM, *Here and Now Storybook* (New York: Dutton, 1921). LSM, *TL*, pp. 284–85.

118 LSM, *TL*, p. 288.

history, geography, and science of different places and different periods with poetry, narrative prose, and layered and detailed maps.

As Lucy became more involved in teaching and moved the Bureau's focus away from quantitative measurement towards the exposition and application of educational theory in books, curriculum development, and teacher training, there was less reason and fewer opportunities for Wesley to be directly involved in her work. Nevertheless, he remained a trusted advisor, lecturer, and trustee at the BEE, knowledgeable about what Lucy was doing, cognizant of organizational stresses and strains, and familiar with the personalities who worked with her.[119]

When they did not work directly together, Lucy stressed that she and Wesley talked "endlessly" about his work and hers.[120] Although the specific content of their work was quite different, their approaches had much in common: a mutual interest in collaborative, cross-disciplinary work; a conviction that they were breaking new ground; and a commitment to theoretical work that had practical application in the real world. These were strong points of connection that increased the sense that they were pulling a common load. Lucy reported that Wesley read everything she wrote, and she read all of his less technical writing, which amounted to a substantial body of speeches and addresses. Their letters to each other are full of information about their respective endeavors and plans for future work. Wesley's diaries record when he was reading her books and articles, and when she was reading her stories aloud to him. He valued her reaction as a literary stylist and lay reader, and felt her suggestions improved his writing.[121] When they were courting, he had identified this as the role he hoped she would play and tried to convince her that she was uniquely qualified to do it.

Connecting over Their Work

Even when he was not directly involved in Lucy's professional life, Wesley took vicarious pride and pleasure in her accomplishments. He reported on her activities in his diaries, and described them in letters to his parents and siblings. He was an enthusiastic audience for all her

---

119 For the shift of focus at the BEE, see Antler, pp. 290–93.

120 LSM, *TL*, p. 249.

121 WCM to LSM, December 29 [1918]. LSM Papers.

books. After reading an early version of the material she would publish
in 1921 in the *Here and Now Storybook*, he applauded, "You certainly are a
versatile creature my dear — combining a theory of how to write stories
that a psychologist might envy [...] with the fire that delights a child,
the faculty in rhyming of a bard & the sketching of an artist's happy
moments."[122] He was equally enthusiastic about the reception of *Horses
Now and Long Ago* (1926) which embodied Lucy's innovative approach
to teaching children what she called "human geography." He wrote:

> You are a radiant creature, and in time I expect to see a school system
> organizing itself in ordered fashion round the classics which you are
> producing one after another. Time may come when even those stuffy
> foundation people will see that they were mistaking academic moons
> for the real sun, because the real sun was rising in a part of the heavens
> unexpected by them.[123]

Wesley also accommodated Lucy's work by welcoming her colleagues
and friends into the Mitchells' domestic life. Her closest colleagues —
Caroline Pratt, Jessie Stanton, and Harriet Johnson, along with Johnson's
partner and child, and Marion Farquhar and her three sons — formed
an extended family group that became the core of the Mitchells' social
life. They shared meals, holiday celebrations, travel, and children's
activities and outings in the city, the Mitchells' weekend homes, and
their summer retreat in Greensboro. Having feared that "her world"
would not take to Wesley, Lucy was pleased to find that her New York
friends became his friends too.[124]

Involvement in the children's upbringing remained an important
part of Wesley's support throughout the 1920s. Although the Mitchells
employed as many as five maids, and occasionally a baby nurse who
helped with the children's physical care, Wesley continued to help out.
He wrote detailed reports on the children's activities and personalities
for their teachers, and attended parent-teacher meetings and other
activities at their schools. As the children grew older, he escorted
them to doctor's appointments, birthday parties, and music lessons,
and spent time talking about their health and development with

---

122 WCM to LSM, December 25 [1918?]. LSM Papers.
123 WCM to LSM, Thursday morning [Aug 1926?]. LSM Papers.
124 LSM, "Robin" (November 20, 1948). LSM Papers.

various specialists. He took a band of children by train for a day at the Mitchells' Long Beach Island cottage to celebrate Sprague's birthday in April 1923. When the boys were teenagers, Wesley frequently helped them with their science, math, and German homework.[125]

But it was Lucy who organized the children's schedules, took charge of moving the family between their Greenwich Village home and their weekend and summer residences, and searched for the best high schools for the children. Wesley helped out, especially in emergencies, but he irritated Lucy by not anticipating what needed to be done and not responding to problems without being prompted. Like other male professionals, when he worked at home he was isolated in a study where he was not to be disturbed. Lucy reported that the Mitchell children learned to respect Wesley's privacy when he was working, and even the youngest child knew he was not to be interrupted. He interacted with the children at regularly scheduled breaks. Late in the morning, he left his study and peeled an apple which he shared with any child who was around.[126] In Greensboro, he stopped writing in mid-afternoon and then worked on carpentry projects in his workshop; the children, each of whom had a set of small-sized tools, were encouraged to join him.

Nevertheless, Wesley tolerated interruptions well. He would stop his work and chat with any child who wandered into his domain. His youngest son, Arnold, later recalled the special times he had with Wesley in his study when he got home from school before his older siblings.[127] Lucy maintained that she was always interruptible for her children, but the neighbors' children at Greensboro saw a different side of her: they remembered her scolding them for making too much noise and chasing them off the property when she was trying to work.[128]

Crafting a work-family balance that satisfied Lucy as well as Wesley was no easy task. His work-related absences could be very difficult for her. She was most likely to complain when she felt overwhelmed by family problems and unable to get her work done — an indication of how much she relied on his help and good sense. When Wesley was

---

125 WCM, Diaries, WCM Papers. School Reports on the children, LSM Papers.
126 LSM, *TL*, p. 317.
127 LSM, *TL*, p. 264.
128 Interruptions: LSM, *TL*, p. 315. Neighbors' children: Antler, p. 276.

away for three weeks at the annual meetings of the SSRC in August 1926, Lucy described an "explosion" she had with eleven-year-old Sprague and numerous problems with the car. Noting that she was "unwell" — a reference to menstruation — and feeling "like the very devil," she concluded, "I miss you woefully & resent your giving the time unless it's awfully worth *your* while."[129] In 1928, Wesley left for his annual SSRC meeting just six days after Lucy returned from a lengthy trip to Europe with the two older boys. Lamenting that he would be away for three weeks, Lucy repeatedly asked when he could get back to Greensboro for a weekend visit. He replied that he would "shoot home the very first minute I can & stay until I am dragged back" but was unable to give her a specific date.[130]

A few years later, when Wesley was working on economic analyses for a National Planning Board created by President Franklin Roosevelt, Lucy sent him several letters from Greensboro detailing a host of problems with their now teen-aged children that made it impossible for her to get any work done. She concluded, "perhaps it's mean to wish you had been here."[131] Wesley expressed sympathy but had no intention of rushing home and thereby "deserting a pair of devoted colleagues at a critical moment." Unless there was a family emergency, Wesley felt that obligations to colleagues weighed as heavily as obligations to family, and he expected Lucy to understand that.[132] Whenever Lucy was away, Wesley assured her that everything was fine, and urged her to stay away for as long as she liked, finish whatever she was doing, and get a good rest.[133]

Lucy appreciated that Wesley took on more domestic chores than many men of his era did, but she held him to a high standard and often let him know when she was irritated or frustrated by his behavior. What bothered Lucy was not that their household roles were unequal, but that Wesley failed to see how unequal they were and took much

---

129 LSM to WCM, August 25, 1926; emphasis in the original. LSM Papers.
130 LSM to WCM, August 24, August 27, and September 3, 1928. WCM to LSM, August 28, 1928. LSM Papers.
131 LSM to WCM, June 19, 1934. Similarly, LSM to WCM, June 25, 1934. LSM Papers.
132 WCM to LSM, June 26, 1934. Similarly, WCM to Beulah Chute, November 30, 1939. LSM Papers.
133 For example: WCM to LSM, February 2, 1920; March 4, 1925; and June 29, 1928. LSM Papers.

of what she did for granted.[134] They sometimes had quite different perceptions about how much each contributed to household tasks. Wesley noted in his diary that he and Lucy "got supper together as usual" on Sunday evenings when the maids were off as though he were an equal partner in the effort. Lucy's perspective was that Wesley was rather useless in the kitchen and did virtually nothing except make the cocktails.[135]

Like Grace Chisholm Young, Lucy felt her husband failed to appreciate the effort she put into keeping their complicated household running smoothly. Unlike Grace, she was inclined to let him know when his behavior irritated or angered her. In the long account of their life together, which she wrote just three weeks after Wesley's death, as a personal communication to him, Lucy observed, "I did get mad at your unawareness of work that was not desk work." The inequity involved in planning the meals, transporting the food on the train, and then cooking dinner when they arrived for a weekend in Stamford, even though she had been working just as hard as Wesley throughout the week, made her irritable, Lucy admitted.[136]

Nevertheless, Lucy imposed many of these maddening unequal burdens on herself. Despite her irritation, she did not push Wesley to take on household tasks unrelated to childcare. Instead of trying to teach him to be more helpful in the kitchen, she made sure he did not need to get his own meals. When she was away from Greensboro for three weeks in 1926, she put twelve-year-old Jack in charge of preparing the meals, with eight-year-old Marni and seven-year-old Arnold as his helpers. Recalling this incident, a colleague observed that Lucy "always treated Robin as though he was somewhat helpless."[137] Years later, when she no longer had household help, Lucy arranged for someone to get meals for Wesley when she was away. Making his own breakfast was noteworthy enough to be recorded in his daily diary.[138]

---

134 LSM, "Robin", p. 22. LSM Papers.
135 WCM, Diary, October 17, 1915, WCM Papers. LSM, "Robin", p. 23. LSM Papers.
136 LSM, "Robin", pp. 22–23. LSM Papers.
137 Charlotte Winsor, in Irene M. Prescott, "Interview with Charlotte Winsor, Irma Black, and Barbara Biber" (1962). LSM Papers.
138 WCM, Diaries, May 12, 1942; April 23, 1943; August 31, 1943. WCM Papers.

Constructing a Companionate Marriage: "Talking All the Time"

The Mitchells' marriage was highly companionate. Wesley was her "best friend" as well as her husband, Lucy wrote after he died.[139] "For many, love of children or love of work/is a substitute for the caring and sharing in marriage./But not for me!" she proudly proclaimed in a poem she wrote fifty years after their wedding.[140] During their first years together, Lucy and Wesley shared a rich social and cultural life. They hosted many dinners and parties, attended the theatre and art exhibits, read books and poetry aloud to each other, and travelled to New Orleans, California, and Chicago. Lucy was delighted to discover that Wesley knew how to "play" and was more willing to do so than she had imagined.[141]

Sharing activities made them richer. When Wesley went to an art exhibit by himself, or read a book he thought Lucy would enjoy, he wanted to repeat the experience with her.[142] When she was away, his days were busier than usual, but he found them "empty." Without her, he said, "They have no radiance — no life."[143] He sometimes went shopping with her, and had an eye for spotting dresses and scarves in her preferred style.[144] They read poetry and books aloud to each other throughout their marriage.

Both Lucy and Wesley were engaged in planning and designing their homes in Greenwich Village, their summer compound in Greensboro, and their weekend retreats in Long Beach Island and Stamford, Connecticut. Lucy, who had wanted to study architecture, drew up the initial plans for the complex of small cabins in Greensboro, and she and Wesley spent months laboring over the details. They worked together to design a study for Wesley in each of their homes, and the bookcases that held his extensive book collection.[145] The carpentry projects Wesley,

---

139 LSM, "Robin", p. 27. LSM Papers.
140 LSM, "Caring and Sharing," January 31, 1963. LSM Papers.
141 LSM, *TL*, p. 235.
142 WCM to LSM, March 16, 1914 and March 17, 1914. His mother informed Lucy that Wesley need to share an experience with a loved one in order to fully appreciate it. Medora Mitchell to LSM, March 19, 1912. LSM Papers.
143 WCM to LSM, March 15, 1914. Similarly, WCM to LSM, June 4, 1920. LSM Papers.
144 LSM, *TL*, p. 255.
145 Greensboro: LSM, *TL*, p. 307. Studies: LSM, "Robin", pp. 19–20. LSM Papers. The Stamford study was especially challenging, requiring over 100 sketches.

a skilled amateur carpenter, undertook in Greensboro also involved joint planning, especially when Lucy did the finishing, painting, and stenciling. His attention to detail matched hers: he described his design for a lamp in eleven separate letters to her.[146]

Caring for young children changed the Mitchells' routines but reinforced their sense of togetherness. In contrast to many wealthy households, the children ate their meals with their parents from a very early age. Both Wesley and Lucy spent time with the children before they were put to bed, and Wesley, as well as Lucy, read to them and told them stories; sometimes he also pitched in at bath time. He joined her in Christmas shopping, wrapping, and decorating when the children were young. For years, they hosted at least fourteen people, and sometimes as many as twenty-six, for Thanksgiving and Christmas dinners.[147] (Household help, of course, made this possible.)

Shared enjoyment of their children, shared concerns about their health and well-being, and shared planning for their activities and futures added to the Mitchells' sense of companionship as the children grew up. Nevertheless, the Mitchells' notions of togetherness did not require them to do everything together. When they were courting, Wesley had predicted their marriage would be stronger because neither felt the need "to absorb the other's whole life."[148] After they married, they met the challenges of managing time apart as well as time together, and balanced intimacy with independence more successfully than many dual career couples.[149]

As individuals who married later in life, the Mitchells were accustomed to having independent time and separate friendships; as dedicated professionals, they were used to being absorbed in work projects. As their children grew older, Lucy and Wesley's efforts to maximize work time and family time meant that they often divided their parenting duties and followed different schedules on weekends: they took the

---

146 LSM, *TL*, p. 132.

147 WCM, Diaries. WCM Papers. Holiday dinners: LSM, *TL*, p. 265.

148 WCM to LS, November 6, 1911. LSM Papers.

149 Marcus Collins, *Modern Love: Personal Relationships in Twentieth-Century Britain* (Newark: University of Delaware Press, 2003), pp. 114–19, notes that in the 1950s, couples who felt they had successfully achieved greater intimacy through greater companionship in shared activities often complained about feeling suffocated and claustrophobic from too much togetherness.

children on separate outings in the city, and came and went at different times, sometimes even on different days, to their weekend home. Time together was even more limited during the week. Lucy had many evening meetings as well as full work days.[150] When she did not have meetings, she was often tired and went to bed early. Wesley stayed up later, reading and working after she and the children were asleep. Their time at Greensboro, where they went every summer from 1916 to 1947, was restorative: they shed their administrative and teaching responsibilities, focused on their writing, and spent more time with the children and with each other. Lucy found the Greensboro summers idyllic, which may explain her frustration when Wesley left to attend several weeks of SSRC meetings. Her idea of heaven was being at Greensboro with "Robin at work and I at work / Robin and I sharing and loving to share."[151]

Lucy and Wesley enjoyed their separate activities, but found it essential to talk to each other about them. "I have so *much* to tell," Lucy observed when she was traveling in Europe without Wesley.[152] When he spent a year teaching at Oxford University in England in 1931–1932 and she stayed in New York to keep Bank Street's Cooperative schools afloat in the wake of the Great Depression, she noted, "I miss talking things over with you terribly."[153] The day Lucy arrived in Oxford for a visit, Wesley wrote in his diary, "Talking all the time. Happy." — a rare expression of his feelings.[154] Wesley always took vicarious pleasure in hearing about Lucy's activities — her "adventures" he called them — and made note of them in his diaries and his correspondence with his mother and sisters.[155]

Conversely, when the Mitchells did not talk, their relationship suffered. Writing to Wesley on the eve of their twentieth wedding anniversary in 1932, Lucy acknowledged there had been periods when they had "stopped talking — stopped much give & take." But, she insisted, these were mere "episodes in loving intervals of companionship."[156]

---

150 When Wesley proposed that they go to the theatre, she agreed with enthusiasm, but listed five evening engagements within an eight day period that limited her availability. LSM to WCM, February 1, 1924. LSM Papers.

151 LSM, "Today I Fell to Thinking" (March 12, 1950). LSM Papers.

152 LSM to WCM, July 2, 1928. LSM Papers. Emphasis in the original.

153 LSM to WSM, December 6, 1931. LSM Papers.

154 WCM, Diary, January 3, 1932. WCM Papers.

155 Her adventures: WCM to LSM, November 1, 1935, and October 15, 1939. LSM Papers.

156 LSM to WCM, May 7, 1932. LSM Papers.

Forging a More Egalitarian Marriage

The Mitchells' marriage was not only highly companionate, but also more egalitarian than many. Although there was no equal division of domestic responsibilities, Lucy's needs, interests, and commitments were taken as seriously as Wesley's. Household routines, family activities, and social life were structured around her work as much as his. She was not expected to play a traditional helpmate role to advance Wesley's career. When an interviewer remarked on how unusual Wesley was in permitting her to devote so much of her time to her work, Lucy responded that there was never a question of his "permitting" her to do anything; that was not the way their relationship worked.[157] He did not try to impose his opinions and tastes on her or mold her to his image of womanhood. He was supportive and facilitative of her work, without being directive or controlling. "In our long married life, Robin never once took the attitude that the way to help me was to put his judgment on me. He helped me but he did not try to reform me. He just accepted me," Lucy wrote appreciatively in *Two Lives*. He could do this, she came to realize, because he "had not a trace of the masculine infallibility which had afflicted the older men who had influenced my life."[158]

Wesley gave Lucy more support for her work than she gave to him. She was not a traditional helpmate or, as she phrased it, a "guardian" wife.[159] She helped proofread the tables and text of *Business Cycles* on their honeymoon, and she occasionally made charts, proofread, and typed for Wesley during their early years together. But these were mere "practical chores" that neither she nor Wesley thought worth her while after she found a clear direction for her own work. Once she established her own busy career, "Robin would not have accepted this kind of help from me, nor would I have offered it," Lucy stressed.[160]

Nor did she uproot herself or her own work in order to advance Wesley's career. She and the children did not accompany him to Washington during the years he worked there in the late 1910s and early 1920s. She did not move with him to England when he was a visiting

---

157 Prescott, "Lucy Sprague Mitchell", p. 149.
158 LSM, *TL*, p. 236.
159 LSM, Draft *TL*, Chapter VI, p. 17. LSM Papers.
160 LSM, *TL*, p. 249.

professor at Oxford University in 1931–32, although she rearranged her schedule so she could spend two months with him.

The Mitchells entertained Wesley's friends, but it was Lucy's friends and colleagues and the organizations she was affiliated with that dominated their social life. She rarely attended his classes or went to his office.[161] There were practical reasons for this. Lucy's work and social life were anchored around their home in Greenwich Village, while Wesley's professional world was more remote from the family center. Her schedule was exceptionally busy; as a working wife and mother, she did not have time to be an active partner in Wesley's work. He could devote more time to her endeavors, in part, because he did not have as much responsibility for the children and the household. In many dual career marriages, it was not unusual for the husband to serve as his wife's partner, champion, facilitator, editor, manager, or promoter. A working wife, in contrast, often had little direct involvement in her husband's work.

The difference in the assistance the Mitchells provided to each other, especially in the early years of their marriage, did not trouble them. Wesley was genuinely interested in and happy to be involved in Lucy's work at the BEE and always made time for it. He was grateful for whatever help she gave him and did not seem to mind that she was less engaged in his work. As discussed later, it was only after he died, when Lucy discovered how much assistance his friend Sadie Gregory had given him at an earlier stage in his career, before he married, that Lucy began to question whether she ought to have done more to help him.

Lucy and Wesley's relationship was a major shift from the power dynamic of a traditional nineteenth-century marriage. Several things helped them make this transition successfully. They benefitted from the changing context of American life: by the time they embarked on their second decade of marriage in the 1920s, ideals of companionate marriage were more widespread, and a growing proportion of middle-class wives and mothers were in the labor force, although the total

---

161 Lucy wrote that when Wesley held his seminars for his advanced students at their house, she sometimes sat in on them or joined the students afterward for beer and sandwiches (*TL*, p. 386). The only time Wesley recorded Lucy's attendance at one of his lectures was in 1914. Lucy did not see his NBER office until shortly before his retirement in 1945. (WCM, Diary, January 12, 1914 and May 24, 1945. WCM Papers.)

number remained small. Lucy herself was part of a 1926 study of 100 college graduates who were married and working outside the home; like Lucy, many of these women were mothers.[162] But there are more significant reasons why Lucy and Wesley were unusually successful in structuring a marriage that supported two independent careers.

Wesley's financial indebtedness to Lucy was an unacknowledged but undoubtedly powerful motivator. Like many ambitious wealthy women, Lucy "married down" in both social and economic terms. Her inherited wealth supported the work she did in New York and financed their multiple homes. It also provided Wesley with a freedom and lifestyle he had not previously enjoyed. Because he helped to support his family and pay for his younger brothers' educations and business investments, Wesley felt compelled to take the highest paying job offer he received in the years before he married.[163] After he and Lucy married, he left the University of Berkeley without having another position, spent seven months in Europe, and did not teach again until the fall of 1913. Leaving a teaching job without having secured another was quite unconventional, he told his parents.[164] But he assured Medora that the money he sent them every month was his "own", not Lucy's.[165]

The Mitchells also drew strength and inspiration from having many like-minded friends and colleagues. When they were courting, both Lucy and Wesley noted that they had no good models for the type of marriage they envisioned. The Palmers did not count, Lucy maintained, because they had no children.[166] (Given how strongly she criticized George's desire to be obeyed, self-importance, and manipulative tendencies, it is possible that she came to question how supportive a husband he was to Alice.) The social and professional circles the Mitchells formed in New York and Greensboro included numerous dual career couples who were pursuing separate careers and raising children.

---

162 Virginia MacMakin Collier, *Marriage and Career: A Study of One Hundred Women Who are Wives, Mothers, Homemakers, and Professional Workers* (New York: Bureau of Vocational Information, 1926).

163 LSM, *TL*, p. 185; WCM to LS, October 18, 1911. LSM Papers. WCM to Sarah Hardy Gregory, June 16, 1908 and June 21, 1908. WCM Papers.

164 WCM to Medora Mitchell, March 10, 1912. LSM Papers.

165 WCM to Medora Mitchell, July 9, 1913. LSM Papers.

166 WCM to LS, November 6, 1911; LSM, Draft Chapter 30, "A Look Backwards", p. 10. LSM Papers.

Wesley's closest friend in New York was fellow Columbia economist Vladimir G. Simkhovitch, who was married to Mary Kingsbury Simkhovitch, the founder and director of the Greenwich House Settlement. Wesley and Vladimir, who had met as graduate students in Germany, talked often at Columbia, played chess together, and consulted each other on professional issues.[167] Mary, a close friend of Elsie Clews Parsons, worked through her two pregnancies and moved her family into Greenwich House Settlement when she opened it in 1902.[168] Wesley sat on the Board of Greenwich House with Herbert Parsons, taught at the New School in the same years as Elsie Clews Parsons, and enjoyed chatting with Elsie when he saw her at wedding in 1937. Mary was involved in several BEE projects, and the Mitchells and the Simkhovitches socialized as couples.[169]

Several other women who worked with Lucy were wives and mothers. Helen Thompson Woolley, a University of Chicago PhD, collaborated with Lucy on developing and fielding a psychological survey of public school children. She spent a month in the Mitchells' home in 1915, leaving her husband and her two young daughters behind in Ohio.[170] Psychologist Leta Stetter Hollingworth was involved in several BEE projects, as was her husband Harry Hollingworth, who taught psychology at Barnard College.[171]

The Mitchells' circle of intimates in Greenwich Village included women who challenged traditional notions of womanhood by forming unconventional households and personal relationships as well as by

---

167 WCM, Diaries, WCM Papers.

168 See Chapter 3, p. 192, and Caroll Smith-Rosenberg, "Simkhovitch, Mary Kingsbury," in *Notable American Women: The Modern Period*, ed. by Barbara Sicherman and Carol Hurd Green (Cambridge, MA: Belknap Press, 1980), pp. 648–51.

169 WCM, Diaries. WCM Papers.

170 See Rosalind Rosenberg, *Beyond Separate Spheres: Intellectual Roots of Modern Feminism* (New Haven: Yale University Press, 1982), pp. 81–83. See also, Elizabeth Scarborough and Laurel Furumoto, *Untold Lives, The First Generation of American Women Psychologists* (New York: Columbia University Press, 1987), pp. 199–202.

171 Banned from teaching in the New York City public schools because she was married, Leta Hollingworth earned a PhD from Columbia in 1916 and taught psychology at Teachers College. Her husband, Harry Hollingworth, not only supported her career but also wrote a biography of her. See Victoria S. Roemele, "Hollingworth, Leta Anna Stetter" in *Notable American Women: A Biographical Dictionary*, ed. by Edward T. James, Janet Wilson James, and Paul S. Boyer, 3 vols. (Cambridge, MA: Belknap Press, 1975–1982), II, pp. 206–8; Rosenberg, pp. 84–86; and Harry Hollingworth, *Leta Stetter Hollingworth: A Biography* (Lincoln: University of Nebraska Press, 1943).

working outside the home. Lucy was especially close to Harriet Merrill Johnson, a co-founder of the BEE and the first director of its Nursery School. Johnson and her partner, Harriet Forbes, adopted a baby girl from Russia. Caroline Pratt, the founder of the City and Country Day School and one of Lucy's dearest friends in the late teens and early twenties, lived with a female companion, Helen Marot.[172] Elisabeth Irwin, who founded an alternative, experimental public school, and worked closely with Lucy on several projects, lived in an openly lesbian relationship with Katharine Anthony. They raised two adopted daughters.[173]

These couples wrestled with many of the same career-life choices as Lucy and Wesley. Their lives, writings, and professional endeavors offered critiques, both implicit and explicit, of traditional marriages and family life. Believing that children would be better off if they were not in the constant care of a mother, the women devoted their lives to developing the kinds of institutions — high quality nursery and primary schools with progressive curricula — that enabled women to enter the workforce with less guilt and anxiety about their children. Wesley's involvement in the New School introduced the Mitchells to additional individuals who were experimenting with alternative life styles.[174]

The families who spent their summers at Greensboro and formed a tight-knit social community included still more dual career couples — Agnes and Ernest Hocking, Clive and Elizabeth Lewis Day, Frank and Amey Watson. Agnes Hocking and Elizabeth Day, both married to academics, were founding teachers and administrators of pioneering progressive schools. They began their work around the same time

---

172 Pratt and Marot lived together from 1901 until Helen's death in 1940. Marot also carried out several projects for the BEE. See Mary E. Hauser, *Learning from Children, The Life and Legacy of Caroline Pratt* (New York: Peter Lang, 2006).

173 Lillian Fadiman, *To Believe in Women: What Lesbians Have Done for America* (New York: Houghton Mifflin, 1999), p. 29; "Elizabeth Irwin, Long an Educator", *The New York Times*, October 17, 1942. Patricia Aljberg Graham, "Irwin, Elizabeth Annette" in *Notable American Women*, ed. by James, James, and Boyer, II, pp. 255–57.

174 Notably, Elsie Clews Parsons, Emily James Putnam, and Alvin Johnson. Wesley remained on the Board of Directors of the New School after he stopped teaching there in 1922; Lucy eventually replaced him on the Board. See Friedlander, p. 50 and Note 26, p. 386.

that Lucy launched the BEE and started teaching at the Play School.[175] They too struggled with many of the same challenges as the Mitchells. Elizabeth Day loved teaching but admitted that the demands of managing both the school and her household made her "always tired and frequently cross" — a characterization that Lucy could identify with. Agnes Hocking often voiced regrets about not being a full time mother, but always insisted she did not want to give up her career.[176] Winifred Rieber, another friend from Berkeley days, had a flourishing career as a portrait artist. She often left her husband and children behind in California when she took off to paint a commissioned portrait.[177] Rieber painted several portraits for the Mitchell family and stayed as a guest in their Greenwich Village home.

Friendships of this sort were rare among the other couples featured in this book. Knowing so many other couples who were juggling careers, households, partners, and children contributed to Lucy's growing sense of confidence. That Wesley as well as Lucy had close friends who were similarly situated was particularly unusual. Both Mitchells could draw comfort from the fact that they were not completely alone or aberrant in their efforts.

---

175 The Hockings and other Harvard couples founded a progressive, experimental school for their children in 1915; it later became the Shady Hill School. Agnes Hocking taught English and poetry at Shady Hill, and served as its administrative head during its early years. Ernest Hocking taught philosophy at Harvard and was an early Trustee of the BEE. See Edward Yeomans, *The Shady Hill School: the First Fifty Years* (Cambridge, MA: Windflower Press, 1979). Elizabeth Lewis Day, married to Yale professor Clive Day, was a mother when she purchased a private school in 1916. Having overcome Clive's objections to her working full time, she was the school's principal between 1916 and 1938 and also taught English and drama ("The Hopkins School: Celebrating 350 Years" at www.hopkins.edu). Amey Eaton Watson was former social worker, a PhD sociologist, and social activist. Her position as an Instructor at the University of Utah was terminated when she married Frank D. Watson in 1913. She subsequently taught at the Pennsylvania School for Social and Health Work and earned her PhD at Bryn Mawr in 1923, when she was the mother of three boys. A fourth son was born in 1924. Amey did field work and wrote several reports for the Women's Bureau at the US Department of Labor. Frank Watson taught at Haverford College. See Amey Eaton Watson, "Illegitimacy: Philadelphia's Problem and the Development of Standards of Care" (1923) and *Household Employment in Philadelphia* (1932).
176 Antler, pp. 278–79.
177 Dorothy Rieber Joralemon, "Too Many Philosophers", *American Heritage Magazine*, 31 (October/November 1980), https://www.americanheritage.com/too-many-philosophers#1.

Shared Visions at Work and Home

Both Lucy and Wesley were consciously trying to adopt marital roles and behaviors that they thought were important for future generations. This was a mutually shared vision rather than something one partner tried to impose on the other. Wesley argued the point in their courtship letters. Lucy made it a major theme in *Two Lives*. They were not bohemians or radicals, but they were visionaries who were as pioneering and collaborative in the workplace as in the home. Their behavior in one sphere reinforced their behavior in the other, and brought them closer together.[178]

Colleagues noted that Lucy was deeply "unconventional" in her thinking. She described herself as "half Gypsy."[179] Her decision to marry Wesley flew in the face of her upbringing and defied the expectations of her friends and relations. He challenged convention by moving to New York without the assurance of a job. The Mitchells' decision to adopt a baby was sufficiently unusual for a family of their wealth and social standing that the *New York Times* wrote a news article about the adoption.[180] After they had a biological child, the Mitchells flaunted convention again by adopting a second baby.

They were pathbreakers in the workplace as well as in the home. The progressive education that Lucy advanced was an intentional break with nineteenth-century educational theory and practice. The BEE's efforts to develop scientific evidence and measures of children's developmental stages and link them to experimental efforts in the classroom were highly innovative. Lucy's *Here and Now Storybook* was hailed as "epoch making" and "revolutionary" and she encouraged

---

178 Historian Eric Rauchway places the Mitchells' marriage in the broader context of American Progressivism, arguing that they, and other married couples like them (notably, Dorothy Whitney and Willard Strait, and Mary Ritter and Charles Beard) used their ideas about family and social obligation as the basis for educational, economic, and social reforms that would liberate individuals and society from traditional roles, social conventions, and gender norms. See Rauchway, *The Refuge of Affections: Family and American Reform Politics, 1900–1920* (New York: Columbia University Press, 2001), pp. 2–12, 20–22, 94–121, 126–57, 173.
179 Prescott, "Interview with Winsor, Black, and Biber." LSM Papers.
180 "Waifs Find Good Homes," *The New York Times*, April 1, 1914. See also, Antler, p. 231.

and supported other innovative writers of children's literature.[181] She continued to adapt and invent throughout her career — developing a pioneering social studies curriculum in the 1920s, forging a teacher training college out of a cooperative network of experimental schools in the 1930s, incorporating her progressive educational philosophy into several New York City public schools in the 1940s. She went on a five-month trip to Asia when she turned sixty in 1938 because she felt she was getting stale and wanted to spark her creativity.[182]

Wesley similarly broke new ground in economics, as he had intended to do.[183] His study of *Business Cycles* (1913), which built a new theoretical system out of quantitative evidence and empirical observation, was regarded as a "landmark" publication that had "revolutionary consequences" for the study of economics. The projects he headed at the National Bureau of Economic Research (NBER) from the 1920s into the 1940s, which developed national economic indicators out of quantitative data sources, were equally pioneering.[184]

Collaborative decision-making was another hallmark of their work and a marked contrast to Lucy's father's style of authoritarian leadership. As the Director of Research at NBER, Wesley excelled in getting businessmen, labor leaders, statesmen, and scholars to agree to a common research agenda and reach a uniform interpretation of the evidence. His colleagues found him to be "magnanimous in sharing credit" and praised him for having "taught us to work together and help one another." His work at the SSRC was similarly focused on getting experts in different disciplines to work collectively in pursuit of common goals.[185] In his final months, he had a recurring nightmare in which he was responsible for the construction of a medieval cathedral, but could

---

181 Epoch-making: Elizabeth Jenkins in *Journal of Home Economics*. Revolutionary: Harold Ordway Rugg in *Journal of Educational Psychology*. Both quoted in Antler, p. 253. Encouraged other writers: Anna Holmes, "The Radical Woman Behind 'Goodnight Moon'", *The New Yorker*, February 7, 2022, 16–22, https://www.newyorker.com/magazine/2022/02/07/the-radical-woman-behind-goodnight-moon.

182 Prescott, "Lucy Sprague Mitchell".

183 WCM to LS, October 18, 1911. LSM Papers.

184 National Bureau of Economic Research, Press Release (May 12, 1952) announcing the publication of *Wesley Clair Mitchell: The Economic Scientist*, ed. by Arthur F. Burns. See also, Arthur F. Burns, "Wesley Clair Mitchell, 1874–1948" [n.d.], and Frederic C. Mills, "Wesley Clair Mitchell, 1874–1948" [n.d.]. All in LSM Papers.

185 Arthur F. Burns to LSM, November 3, 1948. "Resolution Adopted by the Executive Committee of Board of Directors of National Bureau of Economic Research,

make little progress because there was no spirit of cooperation among the workers.[186]

Collaborative leadership that stimulated "joint thinking" and promoted cross-disciplinary work was a foundation of Lucy's educational "credo" as well.[187] The BEE went through numerous reorganizations and protracted debates in its early years as Lucy and her colleagues struggled to find an organizational structure that reflected and advanced this collaborative vision.[188] The BEE's Cooperative School for Student Teachers (CSST), better known as the Bank Street College of Education, also embraced collaborative and cooperative management structures and decision-making.[189] Lucy's collaborative approach was reflected in her working relationships as well as in the BEE's management structures. Colleagues described her as stimulated by intellectual give and take, quick to incorporate co-workers' suggestions into her thinking and writing, and happy to work anonymously behind the scenes to advance the BEE's objectives.[190]

Both Lucy and Wesley brought the same collaborative, cooperative approach to their marriage and strove to avoid what they referred to as "executive" behavior in the home. Wesley was as anxious to foster cooperative traits in his children as in his professional colleagues. Concerned about six-year-old Sprague's competitiveness and aggression with other children, Wesley turned to his son's teachers for help, explaining, "I don't like struggles for personal ascendancy & I don't acquit myself well in them when they are unavoidable [...] I shall be glad of anything that gives a more cooperative turn to Sprague's dealings with others."[191] When Lucy was traveling in Europe with the two older boys in 1928, Wesley was uncomfortable about issuing directives to the younger children and household staff in order to prepare the Greensboro complex for the summer.[192] When he was teaching at Oxford, Lucy sent

---

November 16, 1948"; Mills, "Wesley Clair Mitchell" [n.d.]; WCM to Robert Redfield, October 24, 1939. LSM Papers.

186　LSM, "Robin", p. 24. LSM Papers.

187　BEE, Chairman's Report, 1921–22 and 1922–23, BSCA. LSM, UA, LSM Papers.

188　BEE, Working Council Minutes, 1918–1921, BSCA.

189　LSM, *TL*, pp. 469–72.

190　Prescott, "Interview with Winsor, Black, and Biber", LSM Papers. Lucy's continuing commitment to collaboration: LSM, *TL*, p. 547.

191　WCM, School Report on Sprague Mitchell, February 6, 1921. LSM Papers.

192　WCM to LSM, June 17, 1928. LSM Papers.

him a series of letters detailing her conflicting thoughts about whether she and the children should join him in Europe and what kind of new car to buy. He weighed in, but insisted that the decisions were up to her.[193] Lucy was equally troubled about having to take command when decisions about schedules needed to be made, and family members and guests could not decide on a course of action. "Life has been viciously executive for me," she complained to Wesley after one such episode in Greensboro.[194]

Coming to Terms with a New Type of Man

Despite their shared values, creating a pioneering marriage that met their emotional needs and enabled them to pursue independent careers proved easier for Wesley than for Lucy. His letters and diaries reveal none of the resentments or frustrations that men like George Herbert Palmer, William Henry Young, and Robert Herrick experienced as the partners of career-oriented women. Wesley did not feel his masculinity was compromised by taking on a greater role in the children's upbringing, supporting Lucy's career, or making decisions with her. But Lucy struggled to reconcile his behavior with her socially-determined sense that men should be powerful, assertive, and dominating.

Like Sidney Webb, Wesley was a natural partner, a collaborator by temperament as well as conviction. He explained to Lucy before they married, "I detest the feeling of anger which serious opposition rouses in me, and I am always ready to let others do as they like in small matters rather than waste time in trying to persuade them that my ways are better."[195] Professional colleagues and personal friends alike characterized Wesley as an "encourager" and "sympathizer", and praised him for his "kindness", "gentleness", "sweetness", "modesty", "simplicity", and "humility."[196] These attributes, more often associated with self-effacing nineteenth-century women than domineering nineteenth-century men, help to explain how Wesley could be so

---

193 WCM to LSM, April 24, 1932. LSM Papers.
194 LSM to WCM, June 22, 1934. LSM Papers.
195 WCM to LS, October 18, 1911. LSM Papers.
196 These words occur again and again in his obituaries and the sympathy letters Lucy received after his death. LSM Papers.

generously supportive of Lucy. He treated her the same way he treated everyone.

Wesley could also draw on the example of his parents' marriage and values, particularly the influence of his mother, to whom he was very close. Medora Mitchell had taught Wesley important lessons about women's rights, intellectual abilities, and aspirations. Impressed by Lucy's "energy" and "vigor," Medora encouraged her son to play an enabling role in his marriage. "[G]ive her strength and poise and rest by your very presence — by oiling the cogs, and helping to bring the things to pass as she may wish," she advised.[197]

As Lucy recognized and envied, Wesley had a unity of character that she lacked. Untroubled by self-doubt or guilt, he accepted himself as readily as he accepted others. His values, beliefs, and personality all drove in a similar direction, reinforcing and strengthening him. Comfortable with himself, he was comfortable with others.

For Lucy, temperament, belief, and upbringing were more at war with each other. She described herself as a "scientist by conviction" not by "temperament."[198] The same distinction applied to her approach to leadership. Despite her faith in the value of collaborative decision-making, she often took charge. At home, she made the decisions and arrangements that kept her complicated household running smoothly. To ensure that things got done, she had to issue orders and establish routines. She played a similar executive role at the BEE and the City and Country School where she handled the practical details that kept the organizations in operation: raising funds, balancing the budget, purchasing supplies, paying the bills. Lucy did not like being an administrator, but she knew she had the requisite skills to run an organization well. In this aspect of her work, one colleague observed, she was "the Boss."[199]

Lucy could be imperious and sometimes seemed to feel entitled. She issued a lot of orders when she travelled, and expected family

---

197 Medora Mitchell to WCM, March 4, 1912, in response to his letter of February 27, 1912. For his devotion to his mother, see also WCM to Medora Mitchell, May 12, 1912. LSM Papers.

198 LSM, *TL*, xviii.

199 Lucy's administrative skills: LSM, *TL*, p. 288. The Boss: Barbara Biber in Prescott, "Interview with Winsor, Black, and Biber." LSM Papers.

and colleagues to smooth her way and make arrangements for her.[200] Brilliant, charismatic, and driven, she failed to appreciate that others had to struggle to accomplish much less. Children, colleagues, and students could find it difficult to live up to her exacting standards. Perhaps Wesley did as well.

At home, Lucy was quick to express annoyance or anger, although she might be apologetic or embarrassed about it afterward. After one set-to with Wesley when she set off on a work-related trip, she apologized for her "horrid" behavior and asked for assurances that he still loved her.[201] When Wesley was absent from home, her letters reported her frustrations with domestic woes, family members, and houseguests. Blaming one irritable mood on her menstrual cycle, she apologized to Wesley, "Glad you are to miss this for once!"[202] Looking back on their marriage after Wesley's death, Lucy was filled with guilt about her anger and impatience. A poem she wrote in 1951 lamented, "temper flares in the same old way." Another expressed regret that she had not been "more adequate and gentle."[203]

Lucy was an immensely charismatic, supportive, and inspiring leader and teacher, well-loved by her colleagues, student teachers, and the children she taught. But she could also be a taskmaster. "Many a meeting opened with Lucy giving us an arithmetical account of all the hours, added up into days, she had been forced to waste while she waited for us, her tardy colleagues," a BEE staff member recalled.[204] She could also be harsh with underlings: she berated a janitor who mixed up the slides she had prepared for viewing.[205] Even her peers found Lucy intimidating. Henry Rieber, married to the artist Winifred Rieber and

---

200 When Lucy stayed longer than expected on a trip to Florida, Wesley and her colleagues went to a great deal of effort to find a substitute speaker for a talk she was scheduled to give (WCM to LSM, February 20, 1934, LSM Papers). When she went to California to help Arnold find a house in 1947, Lucy instructed Wesley's sister, Beulah, to supply the name of a hotel and a rental car agency because "We all have to get started the minute we arrive." She also wanted Beulah to mail a letter for her (LSM to Beulah Chute, August 22, 1947, LSM Papers).

201 LSM to WCM, May 29, 1914. LSM Papers.

202 LSM to WCM, October 3, 1916. LSM Papers.

203 LSM, "I Sometimes Think" (Christmas, 1951); "Today I Fell to Thinking" (March 12, 1951). LSM Papers.

204 Barbara Biber in *Lucy Sprague Mitchell: An Hour of Remembrance* (New York: Bank Street College of Education, 1967), p. 20. LSM Papers.

205 Antler, p. 321.

later a good friend, recalled an early encounter with Lucy at Berkeley that "scared the life" out of him.[206] Lucy herself regretted that she often lost her temper and expressed herself more forcefully than she should have when she worked with Elisabeth Irwin, head of the Little Red Schoolhouse, on a public school adaptation of the BEE's curriculum.[207]

These incidents, many of which occurred when people caused her to waste precious time, reflected the intense pressure Lucy felt as a working wife and mother. Her upbringing made her immensely sensitive to what she called the "sin" of wasting time; the many demands on her as a teacher, chairman of the BEE, author, wife, and mother of four, exacerbated her distress. Despite her anxieties and feelings of inadequacy, Lucy's experience of entitlement and privilege gave her an expectation that others should do things for her. While Wesley's upbringing reinforced and strengthened his companionate and sharing traits, her background provided lessons on behavior that was to be avoided rather than emulated.

Lucy's conflicting ideas about what she wanted in a man and a marriage were harder to resolve. When they were courting, she assumed she and Wesley would have a marriage of "companionable equality." But she faulted Wesley for not being more commanding and assertive, and she found it difficult to envision a satisfying relationship in which the man would not be more powerful, more important, more masterful, and more "compelling" than the woman. Wesley was one of the rare men of Lucy's acquaintance who encouraged her to be independent and did not expect her to live vicariously through him. Yet he was so different from her expectations of a "manly" man that she repeatedly called his masculinity into question and hesitated to marry him.

To come to terms with Wesley, Lucy had to redefine her notions of masculinity and rethink the attributes that characterized a "good" husband and a strong leader. In part through Wesley's example, and in part through the evolution of her own philosophy of leadership, she was able to free herself from her longstanding attraction to big personalities and strong leaders of a traditional type. She came to see that Wesley was a stronger man than she had initially thought. As a result, he could support, encourage, and help her, without trying to direct her or control

---

206 Henry Rieber to LSM, June 30, 1944. LSM Papers.
207 LSM, *TL*, p. 422.

her. For Lucy, this was transformational. "With you I learned to respect my work. You respected it. You respected me. Guilt and shame, lack of self-confidence evaporated and I accepted myself," she wrote in her musings about their relationship after he died.[208] "I began to use what powers, what talents, what abilities I had instead of trying to ignore or suppress them," she explained in *Two Lives*.[209] Wesley could give her freedom and encouragement precisely because he lacked a traditional male ego and made no claims for "masculine infallibility" and privilege.[210]

In Lucy's new understanding, what had once seemed like faults and weaknesses began to look like virtues and strengths. She came to see Wesley as a model husband, better suited to the needs of a twentieth-century woman than the powerful and domineering men she had admired growing up. She also came to appreciate that his supportive personality reflected, not a lack of ego, but a healthy self-confidence that did not require him to be the center of attention or establish ascendancy over others.

Over time, Lucy became more disparaging of those who did not exhibit Wesley's collegial, supportive behavior. When she wrote her autobiography in 1944, she was sharply critical of men like her brother-in-law Adolph Miller who were convinced of their own infallibility. She remembered Miller as a "ponderous", pontificating, thirty-five-year-old, "giving the world his infallible opinions in well-rounded sentences." And yet, when she and Wesley were courting, Lucy had faulted him for not being more like Miller. It took her years — and Wesley's help — to break "the spell of Adolph's infallibility," she admitted.[211] Her brother, Albert, a Chicago businessman and city controller, was cut from the same cloth. Convinced that he knew what was best for everyone, he grew "sullen and hurt" when his advice was ignored, Lucy observed.[212] She even faulted George Herbert Palmer for his characteristic self-importance, concurring in the judgment of his sister-in-law who dubbed him, "The Little Almighty."[213]

---

208 LSM, "Robin", p. 26. LSM Papers.
209 LSM, *TL*, p. 541.
210 LSM, *TL*, p. 236.
211 LSM, UA, p. 12. LSM Papers.
212 LSM, UA, p. 107. LSM Papers.
213 LSM, *TL*, p. 100.

Lucy was equally critical of women whom she thought were too authoritarian or too demanding. In the 1920s, she fell out with two of her closest friends — Caroline Pratt, the founder of the Play School (later the City and Country School), and Marion Farquhar, her roommate at the Marlborough School — over this issue. Pratt, whom Lucy regarded as "a kind of genius", was immensely influential in Lucy's understanding of child development.[214] They worked closely together at the Play School, and their professional collaboration blossomed into a personal friendship. But time and again, Caroline proved unsupportive of Lucy's innovative research, writing, and teaching. When she refused to let Lucy use the records of students she had taught at the City and Country School, Lucy was unable to complete a book that was half written. Having her project end this way was as painful as suffering a stillbirth, Lucy reported.[215] Caroline's refusal to account to the BEE for the projects it funded at her school was another source of tension. Lucy stopped teaching in the City and Country School in 1928 and renegotiated her financial support for the school a few years later. They could no longer work together because Pratt was the kind of leader who insisted on having her own way. "She clipped my wings," Lucy explained.[216]

The treatment Lucy received from her friend Marion Farquhar in the early 1920s was equally hurtful. When Lucy spent several months in a glassed-in room on the roof of the Mitchells' brownstone after being erroneously diagnosed with tuberculosis, Marion never came to visit and did not even write Lucy a letter. Lucy's sense of abandonment was acute. Reflecting on the "strangeness" of her friend's behavior, she realized how one-sided their friendship had become: Marion thought of her only as an appreciative audience for Marion's exploits. The two women continued to take trips together and attend social gatherings in each other's homes, but Lucy no longer felt the same self-sacrificing devotion. Their friendship ended abruptly in 1941 for reasons that are not clear.[217] Such painful experiences with trusted friends undoubtedly

---

214 LSM, UA, p. 408. LSM Papers.

215 LSM, UA. LSM Papers.

216 LSM, *TL*, pp. 410–14. For more on Pratt's work, personality, and relationship with Lucy, see Antler, pp. 244–46, and Hauser, *Learning*.

217 Lucy's account of Marion's behavior (referred to as Vivian) in her unpublished autobiography is very raw and anguished; she did not mention it in *TL*. On the abrupt end of their friendship, see Antler, Note 45, p. 403.

increased Lucy's appreciation of Wesley's steadfast support and affection.

In addition, Lucy came to realize that Wesley had a stronger personality than she originally thought. As his career advanced, he exhibited a more assertive "make things happen" style that contrasted with what Lucy had earlier called his "unaggressive academic" approach to life. As he gained prominence and recognition in his field, she could take vicarious pleasure in his career success. And through her own work, she came to understand that the collaborative leadership he exercised at NBER and SSRC, the social science research organizations he helped to found in the 1920s, was ultimately more effective than her father's style of issuing commands and making all the decisions. Redefining her notion of leadership enhanced Wesley's image.

Wesley's ability to keep Lucy on an even keel was especially important. She was a woman of strong emotions who was given to dramatic outbursts. She described her life in terms of "searing" experiences and responded to people and events with an intensity that could be overwhelming.[218] Overcome by the breathtaking views from the summit of the Sierra Mountains in 1911, she was frustrated when her fellow campers, Wesley included, did not respond in kind. "In a grandiloquent gesture I swept my arm towards that shimmering vision below us. 'You look at that unmoved!' I shouted and retired to a rock of my own, sobbing violently. I hadn't an inhibition left at 14,503 feet," she wrote in her unpublished autobiography.[219]

Lucy could be as "histrionic," as she characterized it, in her daily life.[220] In contrast, Wesley strove to avoid emotional exchanges and defuse emotional scenes. "He disapproved of emotional intensity in discussions — even when it did not take on a personal tone — lest it be strong enough to prevent any real meeting of the minds. I have seen Robin exercise a kind of unobtrusive, calming influence in many

---

218 Lucy coped with "searing memories" of her beloved Alice Freeman Palmer after Alice's death in 1902 (LSM, UA. LSM Papers). In 1938, she enjoyed five months of "searing experiences" that changed her life when she traveled in Asia. (LSM, Notes on rereading the diary of her trip. LSM Papers.)
219 LSM, UA. LSM Papers.
220 LSM, "Robin", p. 27. LSM Papers.

meetings," Lucy wrote.[221] He had an equally calming effect on her. He could withstand the force of her emotions without responding in kind.

Although Wesley sometimes disappointed her by not being sufficiently sensitive to her emotional needs, Lucy appreciated his ability to rein her in and help her maintain equilibrium. Early in their marriage, she apologized profusely for being "horrid" to him while he was "as usual sweet and dear" to her. Already, she appreciated the effect of his soothing influence. "You may cure me sometime—at least I used to be worse, didn't I?" she inquired.[222] Several years later, after venting her frustration with a houseguest in a letter to Wesley, Lucy concluded, "I need you sweetheart, to keep me poised. Dear, dear boy — I could never exist without you."[223] In response to Lucy's increasingly agitated letters about the US economic crisis and its toll on the Bank Street network of cooperative schools and the Mitchells' finances in the early 1930s, Wesley sent soothing counsel and analyses from England that made the situation seem less dire.[224]

This is what Lucy had said she wanted in a husband: someone who could hold her more flamboyant, effervescent, and emotional personality "in check" without breaking her spirit. She had feared that Wesley would not be able to do that because he had no inclination to dominate. She discovered that he could calm her without trying to control her. He did not share her dramatic reactions to people, places, and events, but he tolerated them and even derived a vicarious sense of pleasure and excitement from them. This pattern was established early and is fundamental to understanding their relationship. Wesley fell in love with Lucy the night she performed a spontaneous gypsy dance at a party in Berkeley in 1907. The dance shocked Lucy's brother-in-law, but something in Wesley responded to and yearned to share Lucy's passionate approach to life. Although he would sometimes recoil from what he "gently" referred to as Lucy's "dramatic way", he admired her intensity and enthusiasm.[225] She made his life more vibrant and more fun. "We are most eager for your return — not because we lack anything

---

221 LSM, *TL*, p. 387.
222 LSM to WCM, May 29, 1914. LSM Papers.
223 LSM to WCM, October, 1916. LSM Papers.
224 WCM to LSM, April 16, 1932. LSM Papers.
225 Her dramatic way: LSM, "Two Me's" (October 1960); his admiration: LSM, "Stand By Me Dear, Stand By Me" (November 12, 1962). LSM Papers.

we esteem necessary to our comfort, like swept floors, but because we have a better time when you are with us," he wrote when she was away.[226] The house seems "uninteresting without you," he reported during another of her trips.[227] And he always looked forward to seeing what she would do next.

By seeing Wesley's gentleness as an expression of strength rather than weakness, Lucy came to understand that he was a force to be reckoned with. "I might so easily have wrecked a lesser man — and a lesser man might have wrecked me, too," she observed.[228] Nevertheless, she took pains to show in *Two Lives* that Wesley was not weak or spineless. The compromises they made in their marriage were not all "mushy concessions" on Wesley's part, she pointed out. When a fellow economist asserted that the "C." in Wesley's name stood for compromise, Lucy countered that he was willing to fight for what he believed in, but he picked his battles carefully and did not enjoy the fight.[229] And she stressed that anything he did to help out at with the children, he did voluntarily, because he wanted to, rather than because she required it.

Lucy also used various strategies to show that, as important as her career was, Wesley's career was more so. She contrasted her "fumbling" and "groping" attempts to establish herself as an educator and develop the BEE to Wesley's seemingly effortless ability to secure academic and research positions after he left the University of California, Berkeley. She stressed how critically important he was to her career, not only by encouraging and supporting her, but also by applying his expertise — in scientific measurement, economics, and finance — to her work. "I have many half formed ideas both for farming & for Bureaus & for my own work. I *wish* you were here. Not only I need you but the whole community needs some such leadership as you could give. We're very messy in our thinking," Lucy wrote when Wesley was away at Oxford and she was struggling to keep Bank Street and its network of cooperative schools from financial collapse.[230]

---

226 WCM to LSM and Arnold Mitchell, July 4, 1930. LSM Papers.

227 WCM to LSM, June 4, 1920. LSM Papers.

228 LSM, *TL*, p. 236.

229 LSM, *TL*, p. 234.

230 LSM to WCM [April, n.d.], 1932. Emphasis in the original. LSM Papers.

All this suggests a lingering need on Lucy's part to convince herself as well as the rest of the world that a man whose outstanding traits were gentleness, supportiveness, and a desire to get people to work together could still be successful, strong, and masculine. The new model husband who made it possible for his wife to work embodied a new style of masculinity. Wesley understood this from the start; Lucy came to realize it only gradually.

Motherhood and Career: Stresses and Satisfactions

Lucy portrayed the pleasures and challenges of being a working wife and mother very differently than many of her contemporaries did. Although her life was "hectic", she wrote in *Two Lives*, "I loved it. I thrived on it." She gloried in "a wonderful life" that was enriched by "desire, zeal, righteous indignation, enjoyment, [and] hard work."[231] She wanted the world to understand that married women might choose to work outside the home because they "enjoy having a profession, enjoy tackling an intellectual or a social or a business or an art problem, enjoy contacts with people and with thinking that they would never have if they thought their place was steadily and exclusively in the home."[232] She made this point not only on her own behalf, but on behalf of all working mothers. She did not see herself as unwomanly or unfeminine. Nor did she see herself as a bad wife or a bad mother.

Lucy was equally forthright in writing about the hardships entailed in juggling the BEE, classroom teaching, and writing books while raising four children and being married to a man who had an equally demanding career. "Women who carry responsibility for both home and jobs are still in conflict. A mother who takes a job in the world as it is now organized really has two jobs, and she has to be both strong and smart to carry them both adequately," she cautioned.[233] She acknowledged that working mothers are often anxious and exhausted, and conveyed the pain involved in ceding a child's care to someone else. Under doctor's orders to stop breastfeeding her youngest child when he was eight months old, Lucy wrote that she felt like "an outsider" when

---

231 LSM, *TL*, p. 540, and LSM, UA. LSM Papers.
232 LSM, UA, "Chapter 20, Looking Backwards and Forward", p. 8. LSM Papers.
233 Ibid. Similarly, *TL*, p. 542.

she saw the mutual devotion the baby and his nursemaid lavished on each other.[234]

Lucy wanted to be as much a part of her children's lives as a mother who did not work outside the home. Like Grace Chisholm Young, she set a standard of "supermomism" for herself. She seemed to feel she had to do not just as much as, but more than, a non-working mother would do. She embroidered and sewed her children's clothes; made doll clothes; darned socks and mended torn clothing while she sat in meetings. When the children were sick, she slept in their rooms so she could tend to them during the night. She also took on the care of her friends' children. Weekends and summers were generally spent with at least one additional child, and usually several; Polly Forbes-Johnson, the adopted daughter of Harriet Johnson and her partner, Harriet Forbes, spent so much time with the Mitchells that she was treated as an honorary fifth child and called Lucy and Wesley "mother" and "father." Marion Farquhar's three sons spent a great deal of time with the Mitchells. One lived with the Mitchells when he was recovering from a tubercular hip in the 1920s, and Lucy supervised his care.[235]

Anxious to present herself as a mother who welcomed opportunities to spend time with her children and made enormous sacrifices to do that, Lucy sometimes minimized how much domestic help she had and the role that others, including Wesley, played in the children's upbringing, and how much her work took her away from home.[236] Occasionally, she fudged facts, explaining that her absence from the family — the days she spent at the Shady Hill School in 1927 and her decision not to accompany Wesley to Oxford in 1931 — was motivated by the needs of a child rather than the demands of her work.[237] Returning to New York

---

234 LSM, School Report on Arnold Mitchell, November 26, 1919. LSM Papers.

235 Polly: WCM to Beulah Chute, May 31, 1938. Marion's son: LSM, UA. LSM Papers.

236 We learn more details about Wesley's involvement in the children's care from his diaries and letters than from *Two Lives*.

237 In 1927, Lucy spent three days a week in Boston, teaching her new geography curriculum at the Shady Hill School, taking Marni with her. The plan evolved, Lucy wrote in *TL* (p. 422), to benefit Sprague, who had become too dependent on her while he recuperated from an accident. But Wesley's diaries for 1927 (WMC Papers) and Lucy's Round Robin letter to her college classmates (December 18, 1927, LSM Papers) suggest that the opportunity to teach the geography curriculum at Shady Hill was the driving force behind her absence from home. In 1931, Lucy instructed Wesley to explain to his British colleagues that she was unable to join him for his year as a visiting professor at Oxford due to a son's illness, rather than because she

after a visit to Oxford, she assured Wesley, "I hate leaving you in Oxford. Not that you need *me*. But I rather think you need a *wife!*"[238]

"What happens to the children, especially to young children, when both parents work is the *real* problem. Concern for their children is what makes it so difficult for a working mother and keeps her anxious and usually tired," she acknowledged in *Two Lives*.[239] Nevertheless, Lucy's primary focus in that book was the toll the juggling act took on the mother, not the children. She was less attuned to the difficulties the children of working mothers experienced. Because her professional life focused on children's development, she was convinced that working made her a better mother. "Trying to learn what children are like helps any mother with her children. I know I made many mistakes with my children. But I believe I would have made even more without my work," she asserted.[240]

That was not the view of her children, however. Lucy's biographer, Joyce Antler, who interviewed Lucy's three sons in the late 1970s, reports they felt like "guinea pigs in the laboratory of progressive education" and resented Lucy's career. They remembered her as emotionally remote and thought she had not been deeply involved in their lives. They felt much the same about Wesley as a father, but did not blame him so much. Several of the children felt they had received more loving care from — and as a result, had developed a stronger emotional bond with — Mollie Cotter Casey, who worked for the Mitchells for many years. She was hired as a maid and eventually became a trusted and loving housekeeper who took charge of the house and children when Lucy was working. Mollie openly expressed her affection for the children, and they loved her in return. Arnold described her as his "real mother." All the Mitchell children found it difficult to live up to what they saw as their parents' very demanding expectations and lofty example. Tensions

---

was needed at Bank Street (LSM, "Robin", p. 19, and LSM to WCM, May 7, 1932, LSM Papers). Lucy similarly explained in *TL*, p. 388, that Arnold's health was the reason she did not go to Oxford for the year.

238 LSM to WCM, February 24, 1932. LSM Papers. Emphasis in the original.
239 LSM, *TL*, p. 542, emphasis in the original.
240 LSM, *TL*, p. 540.

and resentments persisted after the children became adults. Lucy's relationship with her only daughter Marni was particularly difficult.[241]

This does not negate the loving efforts Lucy made to ensure her children's health, well-being, and happiness. It suggests rather, that just as wives and husbands are likely to have different versions of the same marital narrative, so there are two perspectives on a parenting relationship—the child's and the parent's.[242]

Complaints about emotionally distant parents were not uncommon among the children of early career women; nor were they uncommon among other children of this era, especially those brought up in wealthy and prominent families, even when the wife did not work.[243] Despite Lucy's interest in child development, both she and Wesley adopted childrearing policies, common to their own day, that seem unduly harsh to a later generation. Lucy threw cold water on Jack's face to get him to stop screaming when he was five. The children were sent from the table when they were too silly, "whiny" or "uncontrolled." A nursemaid shut eighteen-month old Arnold in a closet to break him of throwing tantrums. When Sprague would not stop crying when it was time to go to bed, Lucy spanked him; when he continued to cry, the maid shut him in a closet. Lucy became impatient with Marni when she dressed too slowly.[244] Wesley, unhappily but conscientiously, spanked a four-year-old visiting child for bedwetting.[245] The Mitchell children were reacting to these behaviors as well as to Lucy's work and the pressures of her demanding schedule. Marni and Jack's relationships with their parents were further complicated by the fact that they were adopted.

Lucy acknowledged that there were tensions with her children, but overall she presented a very rosy picture of the Mitchells' domestic life. This was not just a defense mechanism; it was characteristic of her optimistic approach to life. Nevertheless, she seems to have been particularly self-absorbed and self-protective about her parenting. While this may have damaged her relationships with her children, it also

---

241 Antler, pp. 360–62. On Lucy's relationship with Marni, see Mollie [Cotter Casey] to LSM [December, 1958], and LSM, "Another Christmas — 1958." LSM Papers.

242 Phyllis Rose remarked on the "his" and "her" versions of marital narratives in *Parallel Lives, Five Victorian Marriages* (New York: Vintage, 1984), pp. 6–7.

243 See Chapters 2 and 3.

244 LSM reports and notes on the children. LSM Papers.

245 WCM, Diary, August 31, 1914. WCM Papers.

helped to free her from guilt and allowed her to offer encouragement to those who believed mothers should have careers and fathers should be more involved in childrearing.[246] She could take pride in knowing that she herself had contributed to the institutions and learning that would provide more adequate care for children outside the home. She could also be confident that the care her own children received outside the home was of the highest quality.

Lucy's accounts of the early years at the BEE and the City and Country School and summers at Greensboro — times when her personal and professional lives were intimately fused — are so vividly and lovingly sketched in *Two Lives*, that they dominate the reader's understanding of how she balanced family and career. She was less forthcoming about how much she was away or busy, especially in later years when the children were still at home. She did not mention, for example, the weekends she went away with Caroline Pratt to write her stories for children, the vacations they went on together, or the times she was away visiting other schools, giving lectures, or attending professional meetings — activities that are recorded in Wesley's diaries and in the Mitchells' correspondence. In 1927, Lucy was away from home for three days a week, while she was teaching at the Shady Hill School in Massachusetts. Later in the 1920s and early 1930s, when she was teaching at the Little Red Schoolhouse in Manhattan, working with teachers and staff at CSST's network of progressive schools, and giving seminars at the BEE, she was out of the house on most weekdays and Saturday mornings, as well as several evenings a week. In 1931, her schedule was so packed that she had very little time to spend with Arnold, the only child at home. She felt badly about that, but she did not cut back on her work. Nor did she report how busy she had been in *Two Lives*.[247]

Despite some exaggerations, omissions, and blind spots, Lucy's picture of the way she and Wesley fit their work into their family life is mostly honest and certainly caring. Neither she nor Wesley engaged in the mythmaking that George Herbert Palmer did when he wrote his *Life of Alice Freeman Palmer*. Both Mitchells were committed to the idea that men and women had to behave differently if women's efforts to work

---

246 LSM, *TL*, p. 543.
247 LSM to WCM, October 18, 1931 and November 22, 1931. LSM Papers. Sprague and Marni were both in boarding school; Jack was with Wesley in England.

were to succeed. For the most part they applied those beliefs proudly and straightforwardly in their daily lives.

Later Years

Lucy drew an idyllic portrait of the Mitchells' marriage in *Two Lives*, describing their long happy years together, united by work and children, shared activities, and unfailing support for each other. Nevertheless, there were times, especially later in their marriage, when Wesley's propensity to immerse himself in his work made her feel that he was not sufficiently attentive to her and the children. After his death, she wrote a poem describing how she could tell at "a glance" whether he was focused on statistics or on her.[248] Wesley seemed especially withdrawn during the children's adolescence, she noted.[249] He often chose not to attend the weekly dances the teenagers held in the Greensboro barn, chaperoned by parents. When he did show up, he frequently sat in a corner and played chess.[250] Instead of joining the family for movie outings and musical evenings, he sometimes holed up in his study to read after dinner.[251]

Wesley's emotional reserve increased Lucy's sense of distance. He "was so sane, so controlled himself — and always had been — that he sometimes failed to notice the emotional difficulties some child was facing. He took it for granted that all the rest of us, *including myself*, were equal to managing our difficulties alone," Lucy wrote in *Two Lives*, signaling how dependent she had become on his emotional support and sage advice.[252] When her editor proposed that she soften this judgment, and mentioned specific ways to do so, Lucy refused. The editor's suggested changes were "simply not true," Lucy insisted.[253]

Wesley was all too aware of his inclination to withdraw. In 1934, he wrote to a close friend from Berkeley days, "Life has been so full of pressing obligations of late that I feel in the danger of losing all

---

248 LSM, "Statistics or Me" (December 26, 1951). LSM Papers.
249 LSM, *TL*, pp. 481–82.
250 LSM, *TL*, p. 483.
251 WCM, Diaries, March 19, 1936; November 26 and 27, 1937. WCM Papers.
252 LSM, *TL*, p. 482, emphasis added.
253 Unidentified editor's comments on a draft of *Two Lives*, with Lucy's handwritten responses. Emphasis in the original. LSM Papers.

human contacts in the midst of efforts to improve social conditions. That would be a horrible fate and it is one to which an unfortunate with my temperament might really succumb."[254] To fellow economist Joseph A. Schumpeter, he confided, "my next volume is getting a hold upon me that is slightly terrifying at times. Like you I feel occasionally that I am not a human being but a machine for turning out technical copy."[255]

Wesley's customary restraint and withdrawal were especially troubling for Lucy as she and Wesley aged. Disappointed by his calm reaction to her distress when she suffered a detached retina in December 1945, she turned to her Bank Street colleagues for sympathy and sustenance.[256] A year later, he failed to comprehend how frightened she was when a spasm in a cerebral blood vessel caused a temporary memory loss.

Retirement posed new hurdles. Wesley retired from Columbia in 1944 when he turned seventy; a year later, he resigned as Director of Research at NBER and from other posts, although he continued to work on NBER projects. Struggling to discern meaningful patterns in masses of statistical data and explain them in his customary elegant and precise prose style, Wesley was pleased to spend more time in Stamford where he could write undisturbed. Lucy started to write her autobiography, an activity she enjoyed immensely. Twenty years earlier, Wesley, a voracious reader of all forms of literature, had read Beatrice Webb's autobiography, *My Apprenticeship*, aloud to Lucy, to their mutual enjoyment.[257] Perhaps Beatrice's exploration of the development of her craft and credo, and the social and familial context of her upbringing, provided a model and inspiration for Lucy. Wesley was confident she would produce "a most interesting document" and pronounced the opening chapter "charming."[258]

In 1946, the Mitchells gave up their New York apartment and made Stamford their permanent home. Wesley was happy that they saw

---

254 WCM to Dorothea Moore, January 27, 1934. LSM Papers.

255 WCM to Joseph A. Schumpeter, November 18, 1936. LSM Papers.

256 LSM, *TL*, pp. 498–99. The long account of her recovery from the detached retina is in LSM Papers and *TL*, pp. 499–504.

257 WCM, Diaries, March and April, 1926. WCM Papers. *My Apprenticeship* is discussed in more detail in Chapter 4, pp. 321–322.

258 Most interesting: WCM to Beulah Chute, April 1, 1944, LSM Papers. Charming: WCM, Diary, March 27, 1944. He read additional chapters of Lucy's autobiography in April 1944, August 1944, and February 1945. WCM, Diaries, WCM Papers.

little of other people because he had more time to work.[259] But Lucy, who depended on interactions with colleagues, found it hard to be in Stamford, cut off from her friends and activities, more or less isolated with a husband who was content to "work, work, work, with almost no interruptions." Although she had thought moving to Stanford was a good idea, she came to feel that it pushed her towards retirement before she was fully ready.[260] She and Wesley still spent one night a week in Manhattan, allowing her to attend meetings on various projects at the BEE, but this was not enough for Lucy.[261]

Wesley suffered a heart attack in September 1947 when he was seventy-three, but made a good recovery. Two months later, he became the first recipient of the Francis A. Walker Medal, an award given every five years by the American Economic Association to the living American economist whose career had made the greatest contribution to economics.[262] Lucy and their son, Jack, were in the audience when Wesley received the medal.

Wesley's second heart attack, in August 1948, was far more serious. When Lucy suggested hiring a professional nurse, Wesley initially demurred. But after giving it some thought, he agreed, observing, "I don't suppose you're getting much writing done." His reaction was characteristic, Lucy explained: "He did not think in terms of anxiety or illness but in terms of protecting my work."[263] After a few weeks, Wesley realized he would not be able to work again and resigned from all of his NBER projects. It was at this point, Lucy believed, that he lost his will to live. He refused food, water, and medicine, and died after several days in the hospital, in late October 1948.

Immediately after Wesley's death, Lucy experienced what she described as a period of profound "dislocation." In her grief and loss, her inner stability evaporated and she "regressed" to an earlier stage in her life, before she married Wesley, when she had been consumed by anxiety, insecurity, and guilt. She got through it by reliving her

---

259 WCM to Beulah Chute, December 2, 1940. Similarly, WCM to Beulah Chute, October 3, 1941; January 4, 1943; August 1, 1944. LSM Papers.

260 LSM, *TL*, p. 504.

261 WCM to Beulah Chute, November 30, 1947. LSM Papers.

262 American Economic Association, https://www.aeaweb.org/about-aea/honors-awards/walker-medalists.

263 LSM, *TL*, p. 529.

experiences, and reviewing and reassessing her years with Wesley. She spent the first weeks after his death writing a long account of their marriage, in the form of a letter addressed directly to him. In it, she poured out her love and admiration for him, but also noted behavior that frustrated or disappointed her.[264]

Several months later, Lucy started gathering material to use in writing his biography. She wanted to write a book that would describe Wesley the man as well as Wesley the renowned economist. Finding it difficult to discuss his life and work without writing about their life together, she finally decided to tell both their life stories, incorporating material from the autobiographical memoir she wrote in the mid-1940s as well as his papers and correspondence.[265] Wesley might have approved: in 1946, he read a pre-publication copy of *Our Partnership*, Beatrice Webb's account of her life and work with Sidney, with great interest and discussed the potential audience for an American edition of the book with his son, Arnold, who worked in publishing.[266]

Two Lives: The Story of Wesley Clair Mitchell and Myself, published in 1953, traces Lucy's and Wesley's lives before they met, discusses their independent careers, and describes their life together as spouses and parents. Along with the Bank Street College of Education, this portrayal of a dual career marriage is Lucy's legacy for future generations. She was fortunate not only in being able to live a new style marriage, but also in being able to articulate the vision she shared with Wesley and to point the way for others. Believing that dual career marriages would become more common in the future, she emphasized the satisfactions and advantages of such unions, and the need for both men and women to adopt new roles to overcome the challenges. Solving "the family problem" required new behaviors from husbands and fathers as well as wives and mothers, Lucy insisted.[267] Advertising copy stressed that Lucy's accomplishments "were made possible by a husband who believed thoroughly that a wife and mother could also be a professional

---

264 LSM, "Robin". LSM Papers. This account of the Mitchells' marriage was written about three weeks after Wesley died.

265 LSM, *TL*, pp. 546–47. LSM to Arnold Mitchell, January 18, 1951. LSM Papers. Arnold was enthusiastic about the new approach.

266 WCM, Diaries, October 28, 1946 to November 6, 1946. WCM Papers.

267 LSM, *TL*, pp. 539–42.

woman."[268] Readers, especially women who hoped to combine work outside the home with marriage and motherhood, found the book inspirational. "I will be recommending it often!" the married dean of Radcliffe College, Lucy's alma mater, assured her.[269]

Nevertheless, Lucy had to wrestle with some personal demons when she was writing *Two Lives*. Throughout their marriage, Wesley was more involved in Lucy's work and provided her with more support and engagement than she offered him. She felt no guilt about this while he was alive. But after he died, she was deeply disconcerted to discover, when she read his correspondence with Sarah Gregory, that Sadie had provided Wesley with a very different type of intellectual support before he and Lucy married. Lucy began to question whether she might have done more to help Wesley, and whether, by doing less, she had lost an opportunity for greater intimacy with him.

Sadie, a wife and mother who did not work outside the home, was a trained economist who served as a sounding board and critic for Wesley between 1907 and 1911, while he was writing the book that would become *Business Cycles*. She gave him substantive feedback on the manuscript, helped him to articulate and focus his themes, and advised him about his career.[270] Inspired by her interest, he valued her encouragement and emotional support as well as her technical understanding and advice. Sadie was also the only person who knew about his passion for Lucy and his unsuccessful proposal to her in 1907.

When he had first known the brilliant, beautiful, and charming Sadie when she was a Graduate Fellow at the University of Chicago in 1894,

---

268 Written for the Book of the Month Club, April 6, 1951. LSM Papers.
269 Berenice Brown Cronkite to LSM, November 27, 1953. LSM Papers.
270 Lucy included lengthy extracts from Wesley's correspondence with Sadie in *Two Lives*, pp. 165–79. Typescripts of these letters, and others that he wrote to Sadie between 1905 and 1908, are in the WCM Papers. Sadie destroyed the originals of many letters after sending transcripts of them to Lucy. (Sarah Hardy Gregory to LSM, October 16, 1950. LSM Papers.) Wesley addressed Sadie as "dear mentor" and "Sadie the Wise" and referred to her as his "best friend" (WCM to Sarah Hardy Gregory, June 17, 1907; June 24, 1907; June 16, 1908. WCM Papers). In 1908, when he was torn between accepting a job at the University of Chicago or negotiating a higher salary from the University of California, Berkeley, she drafted a letter for him to send to President Wheeler (WCM to Sarah Hardy Gregory, June 16, 1908; June 21, 1908; November 9, 1908. WCM Papers).

Wesley had regarded her with "secret adoration."[271] Their friendship, renewed after Wesley came to Berkeley, where Sadie and her husband had a second home, continued for the rest of his life, and Sadie's interest in his career remained strong. Visiting New York in 1914, she went to hear him lecture, accompanied by Lucy — one of the rare times Lucy attended one of his lectures. Sadie went to see his office at NBER in 1936; Lucy did not see it until 1945, shortly before Wesley retired as NBER's research director.[272] Over the years, their friendship was strengthened by periodic visits between the two families (both before and after Sadie was widowed in 1927), the long talks they had during these visits, and the support each family gave to the other's children. In the 1930s, Wesley tore open a letter from Sadie with excitement when he recognized her handwriting on the envelope.[273] The last time he saw her, in 1948, he noted that her eyes were still "as bright blue as in the 1890s."[274] Sadie and Wesley's devotion and concern for Thorstein Veblen, the radical economist who had taught both of them at the University of Chicago, and their efforts to help him were other strong bonds.[275] But the foundation was the mutual satisfaction each derived from their work on Wesley's early manuscript. In the Mitchells' marriage, in contrast, the intimacy born of close intellectual collaboration was experienced more through Wesley's involvement in the work of the BEE than through Lucy's role in his activities.

Learning after Wesley's death how much Sadie had contributed to *Business Cycles*, and knowing how comparatively little she herself had done by merely helping to proofread the text, Lucy realized that the tribute Wesley paid her in that book — "But more than all others, my wife has shared in the making of this book" — was undeserved. "If I had known then what I know now, I should not have permitted him to say this," she wrote in a draft of *Two Lives*.[276] Lucy's editor counseled her, "It is for you and for you only to decide whether *your own feelings*

271 WCM to Sarah Hardy Gregory, March 23, 1934, quoted in Jorgensen and Jorgensen, Note 4, p. 225.
272 WCM, Diaries, January 12, 1914; January 17, 1936; May 24, 1945. WCM Papers.
273 WCM to Sarah Hardy Gregory, March 23, 1934, quoted in Jorgensen and Jorgensen, Note 4, p. 225.
274 WCM, Diary, June 5, 1948. WCM Papers.
275 See Jorgensen and Jorgensen, pp. 125–26, 173–74, 180–81.
276 LSM, Draft TL, LSM Papers.

about Robin's friendship with S. G. (as you realized this more fully after Robin's death) belong in the book." Resisting the editor's suggestion to introduce Sadie earlier in the book, Lucy wrote, "I have rewritten this 3 or 4 times & I am *sure* [underlined twice] I should not discuss their friendship until I take up his and my relationship."[277] If in her grief and disorientation after Wesley's death, Lucy felt retrospectively jealous of Sadie's relationship with Wesley, it cannot have helped that Lucy's son Jack inquired in 1950 whether Arnold had named his new baby Gregory after "father's close friend."[278]

Acknowledging the help she had given Wesley was a sensitive issue for Sadie as well as for Lucy. For Sadie, this must have brought back painful memories of her time at the University of Chicago when she had unwittingly become the center of a marital contretemps between the economist Thorstein Veblen and his first wife, Ellen Rolfe Veblen. That crisis was precipitated when Veblen acknowledged Sadie's help, but not Ellen's, in producing his translation of an economic study in 1895. (Ellen helped with the translation; Sadie helped with proofreading.)[279]

Sadie provided Lucy with copies of Wesley's letters, but preferred to remain anonymous and played down her contribution to *Business Cycles*. Wesley "would have gone steadily on in his development in any case," she pointed out.[280] But Lucy decided to identify Sadie and reprint lengthy extracts from Wesley's letters to her to explain the evolution of

---

277 Unidentified editor's comments on a draft of *Two Lives*, with Lucy's handwritten responses. Emphasis in the original. LSM Papers.

278 John McClellan Mitchell to LSM, April 30, 1950. Arnold Mitchell had spent several holidays with the Gregory family after he moved to California. LSM Papers.

279 Veblen's infatuation with Sadie Hardy (later Gregory) and its effect on his unhappy marriage are discussed in Jorgensen and Jorgensen, pp. 39–64, and detailed in the letters they reprint. Sadie left the University of Chicago in the fall of 1895 to teach economics at Wellesley College, a position about which she was deeply ambivalent. She was equally torn about marrying Warren Gregory, who had pursued her for years, and to whom she was secretly engaged. A few weeks into the semester, she had a physical and mental collapse which left her unable to work. In February 1896 — months after she had left Chicago and set a date for her wedding to Gregory — Veblen confessed to Sadie that he had loved her from the day he first saw her. A month later he informed Ellen about his feelings for Sadie and began to press for a divorce. He assured Ellen that his relationship with Sadie was platonic, and Sadie felt there was nothing she should be embarrassed about in her relationship with Veblen. She married Gregory in April 1896, but Ellen's jealous misery and rage persisted. This was the first of many contretemps in Veblen's troubled first marriage.

280 Sarah Hardy Gregory to LSM, June 26, 1949. LSM Papers.

his economic thinking. Lucy did not publicly acknowledge her sense that she did not deserve Wesley's accolade in *Business Cycles*, but she struggled to justify her own, lesser contributions to his work. She could not offer the same type of assistance as Sadie, Lucy repeatedly stressed in *Two Lives*, because she was not a trained economist. Moreover, by the time she and Wesley married, he no longer needed the detailed technical advice and encouragement that Sadie had provided. Most importantly, he valued Lucy's work too much to expect her to lavish such time-consuming attention on his manuscripts. She concluded that she may have best facilitated Wesley's work by giving him the space and time he needed do his writing, and keeping others from interrupting him.[281]

Lucy was describing a very traditional wifely role, one that often diminished rather than added to spousal intimacy. This essentially negative appraisal seems too harsh, and undercuts her claim that she and Wesley developed their sense of "pulling a common load" by talking to each other "endlessly" about their work. Her assessment might accurately characterize their later years, when Lucy felt Wesley was withdrawing into his work, but it does not capture the long, jointly productive decades of their middle years. That Lucy would write this suggests that she might have begun to question whether she had done enough for Wesley, or that she might have come to regret that he had not needed her more.

* * * * *

Lucy lived for almost twenty years after Wesley died. She did not teach again, but she continued to write and publish accounts of her educational work. At the age of seventy-five, she began a three year stint as Acting President of Bank Street. When that ended in 1955, she moved to Palo Alto, California and bought a house just a few blocks from the home of her youngest son Arnold and his family. She saw them on a daily basis, and traveled across the country to visit her other children and grandchildren. Lucy continued to reflect on and write about her life experiences, especially her life with Wesley and the process of growing old; many of her written musings and poems were addressed to Wesley.

---

281 LSM, *TL*, p. 249.

Even in old age, Lucy had to wrestle with conflicts between her career and her family. Her sons were well launched in life, but Marni suffered from chronic alcoholism. When Marni required surgery and almost died from repeated hemorrhages in the spring of 1958, Lucy returned to New York to be with her during her four months of hospitalization. She went home to California in July only after Marni was out of danger. A month later, a heart attack put eighty-year-old Lucy in the hospital and severely curtailed her mobility. When the University of California at Berkeley announced that Lucy would be awarded an honorary doctorate of letters at the end of September, her doctors told her that she could attend the ceremony but not walk in the procession or participate in the celebratory luncheon. Tragically, Marni died in Stamford just a few days before the ceremony, after suffering another hemorrhage. Mollie, the Mitchells' beloved caregiver and housekeeper, was with her at the end. Marni's funeral took place on the very day Lucy's honorary degree was awarded. Lucy grieved for Marni, but weakened by her own health problems, remained in California, and received her honorary degree in person.[282] It seems a cruel irony that Lucy, who struggled so hard to balance work and family life, should have been confronted with such a stark choice between the two so late in her life.

After several years of declining health and flagging capacity, but continuing engagement in writing projects and reflections about the aging process and her own life, Lucy died of a heart attack in October 1967, at the age of eighty-nine.

Free to Be Herself

The Mitchells' companionate marriage was based on a different vision of love than the traditional romantic ideal. Lucy described Wesley not as a romantic lover but as "a perfect companion." She wrote, "I cannot imagine a more perfect companion than Robin, whether he was gay or serious. For, though he was so stimulating, he was at the same time a most *comfortable* person to be with, by which I mean he was just himself and content to let others be themselves."[283] When they were courting,

---

282 See Antler, pp. 349–50. Lucy poured out her grief and love for Marni in a poem, "Another Christmas — 1958." LSM Papers.

283 LSM, *TL*, p. 506, emphasis in the original.

she assumed that a strong romantic hero could become an equal partner in a companionate marriage. Over time, she discovered these two ideals were incompatible.

We know that the traditional vision of romantic love was immensely attractive to Lucy when she was deciding whether to marry Wesley. We also know that — at times — Wesley could be too reserved and too absorbed in his work for Lucy's tastes. Did she sometimes want a different type of partner, someone whose intensity and passion could match her own? Was there an emotional core that did not get tapped in their relationship?

The answer to these questions is undoubtedly, yes, at least at times. There are hints that Lucy was sometimes troubled by a lack of romance in her life after they married. She wrote in *Two Lives* that she was "really touched" to receive a telegram from Wesley when they were apart on their twentieth wedding anniversary, suggesting that she expected an anniversary greeting. But when she "tore it open", she was disappointed to find that he merely advised her to "use your own judgment" about purchasing a new car.[284] Lucy herself may have contributed to the lack of romance and sentimentality in their relationship. After Wesley died, she blamed herself for not being more expressive about her love for him during their final years together.[285]

Wesley's deficits might have caused Lucy occasional regret or irritation, but they did not produce the type of deep depression that Beatrice Webb suffered during the first decade of her marriage. Both Mitchells were wise enough to accept each other's imperfections; they realized they each had what they termed "the flaws of their virtues."[286] Wesley may sometimes have shied away from the heat of Lucy's emotions, but he accepted them as the flip side of the intensity that he admired in her and vicariously enjoyed. And Lucy knew that Wesley's

---

284 LSM, *TL*, p. 325. The Mitchells generally avoided sentimental anniversary rituals. They celebrated their first anniversary by planting flowers together, but after a few years they spent the day working, as they preferred (WCM, Diaries, WCM Papers). On a few occasions, they forgot their anniversary altogether. They sometimes forgot the children's birthdays, at least those of Jack and Marni, the two adopted children (WCM, Diary, June 1, 1917, WCM Papers. WCM to LSM, February 1, 1917; LSM to WCM, February 6, 1934. LSM Papers).

285 LSM, "Robin", and the poems she wrote to Wesley in the 1950s and 1960s. For example, "The Cycle of Fear" (November 10, 1960). LSM Papers.

286 LSM, "Robin", p. 222. LSM Papers.

ability to support and encourage her was linked to his reserve and his willingness to let others have the limelight. Despite herself, she liked having the appreciative audience that Wesley provided. Although she was somewhat embarrassed by what she called her "exhibitionist tendency", she welcomed attention and enjoyed being the star of her own drama.[287] Sharing center stage with a more extroverted personality might have caused other, more serious difficulties in her marriage, as it did in her friendships with Caroline Pratt and Marion Farquhar.

The Mitchells were also wise enough not to expect that all their emotional needs could be met by one person. Lucy looked for stimulation, both intellectual and emotional, outside her marriage. Not in affairs, not from other men, but in intense friendships with female colleagues and friends: not only with Pratt and Farquhar, but also with Harriet Johnson, co-founder of the BEE and the first head of the BEE's Nursery School, and Jessie Stanton, who became the head of the Nursery School after Johnson's death in 1934. Wesley's lifelong friendship with Sadie Gregory may have provided a similar outlet for him.

Lucy's friends and colleagues were not only included in the Mitchells' social life, but also integrated into their living arrangements. Jessie Stanton occupied a separate apartment in the Mitchells' Greenwich Village brownstone after their children went off to college; Harriet Johnson and Harriet Forbes purchased land from the Mitchells and built themselves a house on the Mitchells' farm in Stamford; visiting friends stayed for weeks at the guest cottage at Greensboro. When Lucy and Wesley started taking annual trips together during the Columbia exam period in the 1930s, each brought a friend along as a companion. Friends, not Wesley, accompanied Lucy on the numerous European trips she took over the years. In the 1940s, she sometimes felt unhappily isolated with Wesley when they retired to Stamford.

The steadfast support Wesley provided to Lucy should not be undervalued, however. Early death had claimed many whom Lucy loved most: her two younger brothers died before she was fifteen; her fifty-one-year old mother died in 1901 when Lucy was twenty-seven; Alice Freeman Palmer, Lucy's beloved surrogate mother, died a year later at the age of forty-seven. Others who were important to Lucy

---

287 Exhibitionist tendency: LSM to Arnold and Jean Mitchell, January 18, 1954. LSM Papers.

used her for their own advantage: she had to break free from them in order to do what mattered to her. Joe, her first love, turned on her when she would not send him money when he fled the country after selling pornographic pictures. "Two selfish old men", as Lucy characterized them, had tried to control her and kept her from getting the professional training she desired. Her father had not wanted her to go to college or get a job, and Lucy never forgave him for exposing her to tuberculosis by insisting that she nurse him through his illness. After Alice died, George Herbert Palmer established an emotional stranglehold over Lucy and tried to manipulate her into devoting her life to him. Marion Farquhar and Caroline Pratt failed Lucy as well.

But Wesley remained constant and true, always there for Lucy even if, at times, a bit dull or abstracted. He genuinely had Lucy's best interests at heart, acted on them, and enabled her to act on them as well. His reliability, support, and independence were fundamental to her ability to have a life that encompassed work, children, and domestic happiness. A more traditionally masculine or romantic man would have made it harder for her to pursue an independent career. Married to Wesley, Lucy was free to be herself.

Epilogue

The roots of patriarchal marriage are deeply embedded in social and economic structures. What disadvantages women in the home, disadvantages them in the workplace — and vice versa. For the current generation of dual career couples, as for this pioneering generation, finding the right balance of work and family typically requires more painful personal choices from women than from men.

As the Palmers, the Youngs, the Parsonses, the Webbs, and the Mitchells learned, addressing only one side of the marriage-career divide will not solve the interrelated problems. The Webbs and the Mitchells, the two couples in this early generation who were especially successful in establishing a more equitable balance of marriage and career, were committed to rewriting the rules of professional life as well as married life. They were as collaborative in their workplaces as in their homes. They founded new types of research organizations and educational institutions, applied research in new ways, explored new questions, and developed new sources of information. Many of these organizations became welcoming havens for women professionals and dual career couples.[1]

These two-pronged efforts reinforced the values the Webbs and the Mitchells espoused in their work and domestic lives in ways that strengthened both. Elsie Clews Parsons's efforts to shape her marriage and affairs in accordance with her feminist beliefs were more problematic.

---

[1] Notably, the New School, the London School of Economics, the Fabian Society, the Bank Street College of Education, and the network of cooperative schools it organized. Claudia Goldin and Larry Katz, distinguished economists who are married to each other, met through their work at the National Bureau of Economic Research in the 1990s. They jokingly refer to NBER as the "National Bureau of Economic Romance" (Peter J. Walker, "Time Traveler: Profile of Harvard Economist Claudia Goldin", *IMF Finance and Development*, December 2018, 40–43, https://scholar.harvard.edu/files/goldin/files/imf_people_in_economics_0.pdf).

          https://doi.org/10.11647/OBP.0318.06

She had few opportunities to apply these values in the workplace, although she did try to move her colleagues in that direction. The wives in the more traditional couples — the Palmers and the Youngs — experienced unsettling tensions between their work roles and domestic lives. Unable to break free from conventional gender stereotypes, Alice and Grace deferred to their husbands at home, bowing to their authority rather than asserting their own, and found multiple ways to limit the effects of their revolutionary careers on their roles as wives.

What was needed to bring about major and lasting change in the marriages of this early vanguard of dual career couples was a conscious commitment to more equality in the home and the workplace, and a simultaneous assault on both fronts. A similar approach would prove critical in enabling large numbers of middle-class wives to carve out professional careers in the 1980s and 1990s, long after Alice, Grace, Elsie, Beatrice, and Lucy died. But it would take decades of struggle before that was accomplished. Waves of apparent progress were followed by periods of retrenchment, backlash, and new hurdles. Throughout the lifetimes of these five women, and for decades afterward, middle- and upper-class white women who wanted to combine marriage and career faced enormous professional and personal obstacles. To succeed, they had to be unusually talented and fiercely determined super-achievers.

Later generations of middle-class working wives and mothers wrestled with the same challenges and painful personal decisions as these early women professionals did. In both the workplace and the home, they were bucking cultural norms that continued to define middle-class womanhood in terms of motherhood, wifehood, and homemaking, and expected women to be supportive and deferential to men.

The 1920s–1940s

Although the number of female professionals grew fairly steadily but slowly from the 1920s through the 1960s, women made up only a tiny proportion of what remained an overwhelmingly male professional world in America and Britain during this period.[2] As a result, even

---

2   Women made up between 4 percent and 6 percent of doctors, between 1 percent and 3 percent of lawyers, and between 22 percent and 26 percent of college and university teachers in the US during these decades. See Nancy F. Cott, *The Grounding of Modern*

highly trained and credentialed women in law, medicine, science, and academia were marginalized into lower paying, less prestigious jobs and venues, with limited opportunities for advancement, higher status, and higher pay.[3]

Married women encountered even more obstacles than single women. In the United States, the propriety of careers for married women was hotly debated throughout the 1920s in newspapers and magazines, women's colleges and alumnae associations, and women's organizations.[4] From the mid-1920s into the 1940s, public and private employers — school boards; government agencies at the local, state, and federal levels; colleges and universities; and businesses — adopted marriage bars, anti-nepotism rules, and more informal methods of discrimination to keep married women out of white collar and professional jobs.[5] In Britain, the Civil Service, the British Broadcasting Corporation, local government councils (who hired doctors as well as teachers), and private firms had marriage bars in place from the 1920s

---

Feminism (New Haven: Yale University Press, 1987), Table 7.1, p. 291. Women comprised about 20 percent of British doctors in 1944, 14 percent of college and university faculty in England in 1931, and 2 percent of solicitors in 1957. See Wendy Moore, *No Man's Land: The Trailblazing Women Who Ran Britain's Most Extraordinary Military Hospital During World War I* (New York: Basic Books, 2020), p. 296; BBC News, "75 Years of Women Solicitors," December 19, 1997; Lady Hale, "100 Years of Women in the Law: From Bertha Cave to Brenda Hale", Speech at King's College, London, 20 March 2019; and Fernanda H. Perrone, "Women Academics in England, 1870–1930", *History of Universities* 12 (1993), 339–77, https://scholarship.libraries.rutgers.edu/esploro/outputs/journalArticle/991031549861904646.

3 Women's marginalization is an important theme in the histories of women in these professions. See Regina Markell Morantz-Sanchez, *Sympathy and Science: Women Physicians in American Medicine* (New York: Oxford University Press, 1985); Mary Roth Walsh, *Doctors Wanted: No Women Need Apply* (New Haven: Yale University Press, 1977); Virginia G. Drachman, *Sisters in Law: Women Lawyers in Modern American History* (Cambridge, MA: Harvard University Press, 1998); Cynthia Fuchs Epstein, *Women in Law* (Garden City, NY: Anchor, 1983); Margaret W. Rossiter, *Women Scientists in America*, 3 vols. (Baltimore: Johns Hopkins University Press, 1982–2012); Helen McCarthy, *Double Lives, A History of Working Motherhood* (London: Bloomsbury, 2020).

4 See Cott, *Grounding*, pp. 181–211; Lois Scharf, *To Work or To Wed, Female Employment, Feminism, and the Great Depression* (Westport, CT: Greenwood, 1985), pp. 22–32; Morantz-Sanchez, *Sympathy*, pp. 319–29.

5 See Claudia Goldin, "Marriage Bars: Discrimination against Married Women Workers, 1920s to 1950s", National Bureau of Economic Research Working Paper 2747 (October 1988), https://www.nber.org/system/files/working_papers/w2747/w2747.pdf; Scharf, pp. 43–110; Rossiter, I, pp. 141–42, 195–97.

until the mid-1940s.[6] Marriage bars prohibited employers from hiring married women or retaining women employees who married. Anti-nepotism rules, designed to protect institutions from hiring unqualified relatives of staff members, in practice excluded wives from jobs for which they were highly qualified. These discriminatory practices became more widespread in the 1930s, when they were promoted as a way to maintain jobs for male wage earners who were supporting families. But they started before the Great Depression, continued afterward, and were especially common in highly feminized fields like teaching and clerical work. They reflected a strong white middle-class cultural bias against working wives and mothers, not just a desire to protect men's jobs.[7] Their message was clear: a married woman's place was in the home.

Because of their family obligations, married women were considered to be less reliable as workers than their male colleagues or unmarried women. Male resistance was fueled by the assumption that women would marry and leave the profession, wasting their expensive training and denying scarce opportunities to (more deserving) men. This concern reflected a career model, based on male experience, which required long, uninterrupted years of full-time work. The male model ignored evidence showing that some married women professionals followed a different career trajectory by taking time off when their children were young and working additional years later in their careers.[8] Rather than adjust their model, or introduce more family-friendly policies in professional offices, men chose to limit women's entry into the professions or avoided hiring them.

Efforts to keep middle-class women in the home came not only from the professional world, but also from escalating expectations about women's roles as wives, mothers, and homemakers. From the 1920s on, children were seen as the greatest impediment to combining marriage and career.[9] While it had been acceptable, even desirable, to delegate

---

6   Mary Ann C. Elston, "Women Doctors in the British Health Services: A Sociological Study of their Careers and Opportunities" (unpublished PhD dissertation, University of Leeds, 1986), pp. 312–58, https://etheses.whiterose.ac.uk/247/1/uk_bl_ethos_375527.pdf; McCarthy, *Double*, pp. 139–53.

7   Cott, *Grounding*, pp. 209–11; Scharf, pp. 80, 105–6, 142–43.

8   Walsh, pp. 252–54.

9   Virginia MacMakin Collier, *Marriage and Career: A Study of One Hundred Women who are Wives, Mothers, Homemakers and Professional Workers* (New York: Bureau of Vocational Information, 1926), p. 116. Viola Klein, *Britain's Married Women Workers*

housework and child care to servants in the Victorian era, by the 1920s, middle-class mothers were expected to spend more time with their children and personally fulfill the more exacting standards of "scientific mothering" that were being taught in colleges. A precipitous decline in the availability of household servants in the interwar years increased the pressure on middle-class women to be hands-on mothers and homemakers.[10] A heavy reliance on servant care for their children set many upper- and middle-class working mothers apart from their peers who did not work outside the home.[11]

Despite the obstacles and shibboleths, growing numbers of women professionals felt they could combine marriage and career rather than having to choose between them. The percentage of women working in professional jobs in the US who were married doubled from 12 percent in 1910 to just under 25 percent in 1930, and continued to climb as younger professionals supplanted the women of an earlier generation who had chosen career over marriage.[12]

Domestic Accommodations

For decades, dual career marriages upset household routines by changing women's roles and behavior but did not ask much of men, except forbearance. From the 1920s through the 1950s, studies of middle-class wives who had careers outside the home identified supportive husbands as a key condition that made it possible for them to work, even

(London: Routledge & Kegan Paul, and New York: Humanities Press, 1965), pp. 18, 52; Judith Hubback, *Wives Who Went to College* (London: William Heinemann, 1957), p. 79. See also Cott, *Grounding*, pp. 197–98; Morantz-Sanchez, *Sympathy*, p. 321; Drachman, pp. 245–46.

10 Studies that document higher standards of childrearing and homemaking coupled with a decline in servants are strikingly similar in the US and Britain. See Cott, *Grounding*, pp. 165–70; Martin Pugh, *Women and the Women's Movement in Britain, 1914–1999*, 2nd edn. (New York: St. Martin's Press, 2000), pp. 83–85, 220; Deirdre Beddoe, *Back to Home and Duty: Women between the Wars, 1918–1939* (London: Pandora, 1989), Chapter 1 and p. 103; Hubback, *Wives*, p. 7; Margaret Marsh, *Suburban Lives* (New Brunswick, NJ: Rutgers University Press, 1990), pp. 137–38,145; McCarthy, *Double*, pp. 41, 158–59.

11 Ninety of the one-hundred middle-class wives with careers whom Collier surveyed in 1926 employed servants to take care of their homes and children, at a time when less than 5 percent of American households had domestic servants (Cott, *Grounding*, pp. 196–97).

12 Cott, *Grounding*, Table 6.3, p. 183.

if the men provided little more than sympathy and encouragement.[13] (Good health, training and work experience before marriage, short and flexible hours of work, household assistance, and reliable arrangements for child care were also important.) Husbands pitched in from time to time, but outside of feminist circles, there was little expectation that they should play a substantial role in homemaking or childrearing. Certainly not that they should share childrearing and domestic tasks equally. Or that a husband should be prepared to sacrifice his own career for the sake of his wife's work.

An exceptional husband might turn down a high-level position at a university that could not accommodate his wife because of anti-nepotism rules, take a job at a less prestigious university if it would be advantageous to his wife's career, or leave a university that ended his wife's employment after they married.[14] But such incidences were rare. More commonly, women made the compromises in order to advance the man's career, an approach that reinforced traditional assumptions about men's and women's roles.

Married couples who worked in the same field often worked in partnership with each other, a strategy that made it easier for the wives to combine work and family. Some of these collaborations may have come closer to the Webbs's egalitarian partnership than to Grace Chisholm Young's subordinate relationship with her husband, but the model of a more gifted male being assisted by a devoted, supportive, detail-oriented woman persisted. Helpmate partnerships with a husband were promoted as a way to ease the tensions highly-educated women encountered when they tried to balance career and family.[15]

---

13 Collier, pp. 81–86, 113, 121. Anne Byrd Kennon, "College Wives Who Work", *Journal of the American Association of University Women*, 20 (June 1927), 100–5. Hubback, *Wives*, pp. viii, 95, 159; Klein, p. 77.

14 For examples of husbands who made career sacrifices, see Rossiter, I, pp. 195–97, and Claire Palay, "Lea Miller's Protest: Married Women's Jobs at the University of Washington", HSTAA 105 (Winter 2010) https://depts.washington.edu/depress/women_uw_lea_miller.shtml.

15 Ethel Puffer Howes advocated for this in the 1920s (Cott, *Grounding*, p. 203) and Judith Hubback did so in the 1950s (Hubback, *Wives*, p. 47). An example from the 1940s is Helen Murray Free, who worked with her husband Alfred Free on developing a breakthrough diabetes test. She credited him with having the ideas, while she was the technician. Despite their highly productive partnership in the lab which he headed, their employer, Miles Laboratories, transferred her to a different division for several years, in accordance with the company's anti-nepotism policy.

Middle-class marriages in general were becoming more companionate and affectionate, as husbands and wives shared more interests and spent more leisure time together. Surveys of middle-class wives who worked in the 1920s, which were widely commented on in the popular press, found that their marriages were more companionate, and the spouses were happier for being able to share professional interests as well as family activities.[16] But being more companionate was no guarantee these dual career marriages were more equal: that required commitment and intentionality on the part of both spouses.

Professional Accommodations

Middle-class white women who combined marriage and career in these decades fell back on the same strategies that the women in the early generation utilized. To better accommodate their families, many sought part-time work, jobs with flexible hours, work that could be done at home, or work that focused on children's well-being or development. Those who worked fulltime were supported by a number of household staff. Some created more accommodating work environments by partnering with their husbands, establishing their own practices or businesses, or working in organizations headed by women. (Marriage rates were historically higher among women doctors and lawyers than in other professions because these women could establish their own practices, often in partnership with a husband, a male relative, or another woman.[17]) Other wives worked in unpaid positions or as independent scholars and researchers. Sometimes these were welcome choices that eased the challenges of caring for family and home while pursuing a career. Sometimes they were forced choices that resulted from discrimination in the professional world, constraints imposed by

---

Denise Gellene, "Helen Murray Free, 98, Chemist Who Developed a More Efficient Diabetes Test", *The New York Times*, May 4, 2021, A20.

16 More companionate in general: Cott, *Grounding,* pp.156–57; McCarthy, *Double,* pp. 12–13; Pugh, pp. 224–26. More companionate and satisfying marriages among middle-class couples with working wives: Collier, pp. 81–86, 121; Kennon, p. 100. On the potential and difficulties of dual career marriages among women lawyers, see Drachman, pp. 211–21, 241–47; among women doctors, Morantz-Sanchez, *Sympathy,* pp. 136–38, 324–28.

17 Drachman, pp. 179–80; Morantz-Sanchez, *Sympathy,* pp. 136–37.

husbands and families, or the limitations of work environments that did not welcome women or make accommodations for working mothers.[18]

Too often, these approaches limited the wife's opportunities in the workplace. They trapped many women in lower-level positions or relegated them to the margins of professional work. They foreclosed opportunities for advancement, higher pay, and recognition. They also reinforced traditional gender stereotypes that depicted men as creative thinkers and leaders, and women as detail-oriented implementers and helpmates. They helped to keep working wives in traditional roles and secondary positions in the home as well as the workplace.

In professional and white collar offices, female employees typically became helpers, enablers, secretaries, and assistants, while men were directors and bosses. This hierarchy did not challenge the traditional gender mold. The problem for women professionals was that they *were* breaking the mold: by virtue of their training, they were men's equals, not their inferiors. But both society and individual couples found ways to curtail and counteract the effects of these changes rather than embracing new roles or directly confronting old stereotypes.

Outside of feminist circles, there was little public questioning, until the 1960s, of the patriarchal underpinnings of married life or workplace routines that made it so difficult for women professionals who were trying to straddle both worlds. The feminist movement was weakened and fragmented in America and Britain during and after the 1920s, and many middle-class wives who worked distanced themselves from feminism. They looked upon the difficult decisions that women had to make as painful personal choices rather than structural and systemic problems that could be addressed by collective action.[19]

---

18   These strategies are documented in the surveys of middle-class working wives conducted in the 1920s and 1950s and the histories of women in law, medicine, science, and academia cited previously. Cott, *Grounding*, pp. 189–208 and McCarthy, *Double*, pp. 139–53, provide helpful overviews.

19   For post-1920 feminist views on combining career and marriage in the US, see Scharf, pp. 21–42; on the role of feminism in Britain after 1920, see Pugh, pp. 235–65. Cott, *Grounding*, pp. 232–39, and McCarthy, *Double*, p. 153, also discuss the tensions between feminism and professionalism in these decades. The studies of college-educated wives who worked outside the home in Britain and the US all stressed that solutions needed to be individual and personal; the authors distanced themselves and their subjects from what they referred to as old style feminism. See Collier, p. 34; Kennan, p. 102; Hubback, *Wives*, pp. 83, 85, 87; Klein, p. 77.

The 1950s and 1960s

The 1950s was a particularly difficult period for middle-class American women who wanted both marriage and a career. In a disheartening replay of what had happened in Britain after World War I, female doctors and scientists who had made significant professional advances during World War II were pushed aside and sidelined when men returned from war service and tried to reclaim the world of science as a male preserve.[20] Once again, women were expected to retreat to domestic life.

As Betty Friedan explained in her immensely influential best-seller, *The Feminine Mystique* (1963), middle-class culture in 1950s America was shaped by a powerful domestic ideology that taught women their primary responsibilities were to be wives, mothers, and homemakers, and they should find fulfillment in those roles.[21] Women's magazines, advertising campaigns, and advice manuals like Dr. Benjamin Spock's best-selling book on infant and child care (first published in 1946) reinforced the message. The ideal of the male breadwinner supported by a full-time homemaker wife who raised the children was the model around which white middle-class life was organized. Smaller percentages of women earned college degrees and PhDs in the 1950s than in previous decades. White women married earlier, moved to the suburbs, and had more children. (As Stephanie Coontz points out, Friedan was writing about the lives of white women, and ignored the significantly different experience of Black women. Much higher proportions of middle-class Black women, especially upper-middle-class Black women, worked outside the home in the 1950s, whether they were mothers or childless.[22])

---

20 For the backlash in Britain, see Elston, pp. 289–308, and Moore, pp. 276–90. For the US experience, see Rossiter, II, pp. xv–xviii, 27–49.

21 Betty Friedan, *The Feminine Mystique* (New York: Norton, 2013), originally published in 1963.

22 Stephanie Coontz, *A Strange Stirring: The Feminine Mystique and American Women at the Dawn of the 1960s* (New York: Basic Books, 2012) notes that 64 percent of Black upper-class mothers worked outside the home in the 1950s, compared to only 27 percent of white upper-class mothers (pp. 121–38). The higher their social class, the more likely Black women were to work outside the home. In contrast, mothers in the upper middle-class were the least likely social group of white women to have jobs. See Coontz, and also Bart Landry, *Black Working Wives: Pioneers of the American Family Revolution* (Berkeley: University of California Press, 2000). He

The percentage of women professionals who were trying to combine marriage and career continued to grow, although the total numbers were still very small.[23] Despite signs of progress, such women still faced major obstacles. Marriage bars were lifted, but anti-nepotism policies continued. After decades of not employing married women, women's colleges began to retain women faculty who married; they also started to hire married women for tenure-track positions. But these schools were also, increasingly hiring male faculty members and paying them more than they paid women.[24] Ambitious women found a compelling champion in Millicent McIntosh, married mother of five, who became head of Barnard College in 1947 when her youngest child was eight. Featured on the front cover of *Newsweek Magazine* in 1951, "Mrs. Mac" became a national spokesperson for the idea that women could be good wives and mothers while simultaneously enjoying a career.[25]

Male prejudice against female professionals remained strong. The demand for science workers exploded in the 1950s and 1960s, but women scientists continued to be pigeonholed into jobs as men's assistants — positions for which they were overqualified, and which did not offer opportunities for recognition or advancement. Coed colleges and universities hired relatively few women.[26] Similar difficulties beset women doctors and lawyers, often leaving them underemployed, underutilized, and underpaid.[27]

argues that middle-class Black couples pioneered an ethic of dual earner marriages in nineteenth-century America.

23 Rising marriage rates among women scientists: Rossiter, II, p. 114. Among women lawyers and doctors: Drachman, pp. 179–80 and Table 9, p. 257.

24 Rossiter, II, pp. 220–34.

25 Karen W. Arenson, "Millicent McIntosh, 102 Dies; Taught Barnard Women to Balance Career and Family", *The New York Times*, January 5, 2001, and Karen W. Arenson, "Feminist's Centennial", *The New York Times*, November 19, 1998. Bob McCaughey, "Mrs. Mac" (Blog: July 24, 2017), https://blogs.cuit.columbia.edu/ram31/documents/6-tough-times-depression-war-other-distractions/deans-presidents/millicent-c-mcintosh/.

26 Rossiter, II, pp. 122–28, 149–64.

27 Walsh, pp. 255–60. Morantz-Sanchez, *Sympathy*, pp. 339–85. Although she was ranked in the top 10 percent of her Stanford University Law School class, the only job offer Sandra Day received when she graduated in 1952 was as a legal secretary. After she married John Jay O'Connor in December 1952, she volunteered to do legal research and write memos for the San Mateo county attorney's office, working for no pay and sharing space with a secretary. It was months before she was paid for her work. See Evan Thomas, *First: Sandra Day O'Connor* (New York: Random House, 2019), pp. 43 and 52. Ruth Bader Ginsburg encountered similar discrimination

Fears of "wastage" continued to disadvantage women who sought professional training and jobs. Male-dominated work environments made few if any accommodations (part-time jobs, maternity leaves, rehiring guarantees) to ease the burdens on working mothers, and some adopted practices and policies that made it more difficult for them.[28] In contrast, women's colleges began to develop programs and supports for highly-credentialed women graduates who had taken time off to rear children and wanted to reenter the workforce.[29]

Middle-class women in Britain also heard very mixed messages about working outside the home in the 1950s.[30] The traditional middle-class model of working husband and stay-at-home housewife and mother was touted in popular culture, and reinforced by the well-publicized views of male psychiatrists. Stressing the critical importance of the maternal-child bond, these experts raised fears about the dire consequences of juvenile delinquency and other maladjustments if women abandoned their pre-school age children and worked outside the home.[31]

In spite of these alarmist warnings, the exploding demand for women's labor in Britain encouraged older wives, both middle-class and working-class, to return to the labor force after their children were grown, and even consider working part-time while their children were in school. Surveys of well-educated middle-class women identified a minority who were successfully combining careers and motherhood, and others who wanted to work if they could find appropriate part-time jobs. These studies, which were widely reported in the popular

when she, the mother of a three-year-old, graduated in a tie for first place in her class at Columbia Law School in 1959. No private firm made her a job offer. No federal district judge in New York would hire her as a law clerk until a Columbia Law School professor threatened to stop referring Columbia graduates to him as law clerks in the future. See Jane Sherron De Hart, *Ruth Bader Ginsburg* (New York: Knopf, 2018), pp. 76–81.

28 Some medical schools in the 1950s required pregnant women and new mothers to take time off from their studies (Walsh, p. 255).

29 Maggie Doherty, *The Equivalents: A Story of Art, Female Friendship, and Liberation in the 1960s* (New York: Knopf, 2020) discusses the path-breaking role the Radcliffe Institute for Independent Study, launched in 1960, played in advancing older women's careers.

30 Stephanie Spencer, *Gender, Work and Education in Britain in the 1950s* (Houndmills, UK: Palgrave MacMillan, 2005). McCarthy, *Double*, pp. 232–34.

31 John Bowlby, author of *Childcare and the Growth of Love* (1953) was the major proponent. McCarthy, *Double*, pp. 247–49, discusses the powerful influence of his ideas. Klein, pp. 147–49, provided a cogent refutation of Bowlby.

press, also showed that middle-class husbands were more approving of working wives than husbands in the lower social classes. The men voiced more reservations than their wives acknowledged, however.[32]

Newly recognizing the value of maternal instincts and experience, "caring" professions like teaching, social work, nursing, and medicine, under pressure to meet the demands of the expanding welfare state and the National Health Service, began to develop part-time jobs and retraining opportunities to bring older middle-class mothers back to work in the UK. Older women and women with school age children were also recruited for low-paying, unskilled jobs. But professions traditionally dominated by men — the law, the senior civil service, the financial industry — continued to uphold the career model of full-time work with no major breaks, and made few if any accommodations for married women.[33] By 1966, women still made up only 9 percent of the higher professions in Britain, an increase from just 5 percent in 1921.[34]

The question of whether marriage and career were incompatible roles for middle-class women was hotly debated in the British popular press, just as it had been during the 1920s in America. Like the American studies of working wives in the 1920s, surveys conducted in Britain in the 1950s and 1960s emphasized the satisfactions of dual career marriages among the educated middle-class elites, finding that shared work interests and shared family activities made these couples more companionate.[35]

The obstacles experienced by these highly privileged women — women who were overwhelmingly college graduates from middle-class backgrounds, married to men who had similar backgrounds and who worked in business or professional jobs — were of a different order than the difficulties encountered by their working class and immigrant counterparts who lacked their resources and were mostly low-wage factory workers, personal helpers, care givers, and cleaners.[36]

---

32   Higher support among husbands in higher social classes: Klein, p. 67. Less support than wives credited: Klein, pp. 62–65. See also, Hubback, *Wives*, pp. 37–38. Press coverage: Helen McCarthy, "Social Science and Married Women's Employment in Post-War Britain", *Past and Present* 233 (November, 2016), 269–305 (pp. 288–98), https://doi.org/10.1093/pastj/gtw035.
33   McCarthy, *Double*, pp. 264–79; Elston, pp. 384–88.
34   Pugh, p. 288.
35   Klein, pp. 60–62, 78–79; Hubback, *Wives*, pp. viii, 85, 95, 159, 146.
36   McCarthy, *Double*, pp. 289–320; Pugh, p. 288.

Supporters of careers for middle-class wives did not challenge other gendered stereotypes that defined middle-class marriage. Homemaking and childrearing were still assumed to be the woman's responsibility. Wives who worked outside the home were still expected to take care of the home and children, make whatever adjustments and compromises were required, and navigate between the perilous shores of self-assertion on the job and self-deprecation in the home. Husbands were praised for offering support and encouragement, but not expected to provide much substantive assistance. If they experienced a conflict between career and family, British women were told to put family first.[37]

"A Quiet Revolution": The 1970s and After

A widespread assault on the patriarchal underpinnings of middle-class marriages and workplaces took hold in the 1960s and resulted in momentous changes. Fueled in part by second wave feminism, women made new and stronger demands for equity in education, the workplace, and the home. In the 1960s and early 1970s, they won legislative protections and legal redress against problems that had long been treated as personal and individual but were newly seen as structural and systemic. Legislation supported the principle of equal pay for equal work, prohibited discrimination by sex in education and employment, and put an end to admissions quotas, marriage bars, anti-nepotism rules, and other practices that disadvantaged women in the workplace.

Starting in the 1970s, white middle-class women flooded into professional schools and graduate schools in record numbers. Intent on having careers, they married later, had smaller families, and stayed in the work force after they had children.[38] In the twenty-first century, women have outnumbered men in medical schools and law schools in

---

37 Hubback, *Wives*, pp. 93,159; Klein, p. 18. A frustrated career woman who took second place to her husband, Judith Hubback was keenly sensitive to navigating the tensions between women's work roles and family roles, and understood the need to make compromises for the sake of one's family. See her memoir, *Dawn to Dusk: Autobiography of Judith Hubback* (Asheville, NC: Chiron Publications, 2015).

38 Claudia Goldin, "The Quiet Revolution that Transformed Women's Employment, Education, and Family", *American Economic Review*, 26 (May 2006), 1–21 (pp. 20–21), https://doi.org/10.1257/000282806777212350. Pugh, pp. 324, 339–43; McCarthy, *Double*, pp. 331–34.

the United States and Britain.[39] Women now make up almost 40 percent of doctors and lawyers in the US, and more than 40 percent of those fields in Britain.[40] For more than a decade, women have received more than half of the doctorates awarded by American universities.[41]

Women who combine marriage and career are no longer flouting white middle-class conventions; they are part of a trend that is reconfiguring middle-class culture and slowly reshaping workplace practices and domestic life. By 2019, the majority of two-parent households with dependent children in the United States and Britain had two parents who worked.[42]

These changes are gradually transforming men's lives as well as women's. College-educated women, especially GenXers and Millennials, increasingly expect their male spouses and partners to share equally in housekeeping and childrearing. Men's expectations about marriage and their roles in childcare and housekeeping are changing as well. Over the past twenty-five years, college-educated fathers aged 25–34 have increased the amount of time they spend taking care of their children,

---

39   Tom Moberly, "Number of Women Entering Medical School Rises after Decade of Decline", *BMJ*, 27 January 2018, p. 167, https://www.bmj.com/bmj/section-pdf/959692?path=/bmj/360/8138/Careers.full.pdf; Patrick Boyle, "Nation's Physician Workforce Evolves: More Women, a bit older, and toward different specialties", Association of American Medical Colleges, February 2, 2021, https://www.aamc.org/news-insights/nation-s-physician-workforce-evolves-more-women-bit-older-and-toward-different-specialties. Elizabeth Olson, "Women Make Up Majority of US Law Students for the First Time", *The New York Times*, December 16, 2016.

40   Jennifer Cheeseman Day, "Number of Women Lawyers at Record High But Men Still Highest Earners", US Census Bureau (May 8, 2018), https://www.census.gov/library/stories/2018/05/women-lawyers.html; Boyle, "Nation's Physician's Workforce"; Mark Easton, "Which Jobs Have More Women than Men?", *BBC News*, 8 March 2012, https://www.bbc.com/news/uk-17287275.

41   Niall McCarthy, "Women are still earning more doctoral degrees than men in the US", October 5, 2018, https://www.forbes.com/sites/niallmccarthy/2018/10/05/women-are-still-earning-more-doctoral-degrees-than-men-in-the-u-s-infographic/?sh=5cad137345b6.

42   In the US, 62 percent in 2015: Pew Research Center, "Raising Kids and Running a Household: How Working Parents Share the Load" (14 November 2015), 1–23, https://www.pewresearch.org/social-trends/2015/11/04/raising-kids-and-running-a-household-how-working-parents-share-the-load/. In Britain, 73 percent in 2019: Office of National Statistics, "Employment Activity of Mothers and Fathers in a Family" in *Families and the Labour Market, UK 2019* (24 October 2019), https://www.ons.gov.uk/employmentandlabourmarket/peopleinwork/employmentandemployeetypes/articles/familiesandthelabourmarketengland/2019.

and many say they would like to have more time with their offspring. In 2015, two-thirds of college-educated men and four-fifths of college-educated women thought the best marriages were those in which both spouses worked and shared household and childcare responsibilities.[43] In the US, Millennials and GenXers are especially likely to form households in which both parents work full-time.[44] Spouses in such households are more likely to report that they share childcare and home responsibilities equally than spouses in households where the father is employed full-time and the mother works part-time or not all. When both parents have full-time jobs, they are also more likely to say that their careers are given equal priority.[45]

Progress has been made, but much more is needed. The gender gap in domestic roles and expectations has shrunk, but it is still substantial. Middle-class men take more responsibility for childrearing and domestic tasks than they once did, but wives still do the lion's share of this work. Women continue to report that their male partners do less than the men say they do.

The unequal division of labor between working parents became more starkly evident during the Covid-19 pandemic of 2020–2021 — as working mothers took on the brunt of home schooling, childcare, and housework in two-earner families when schools, day care facilities, and offices shut down — but it has a very long history. Even before the ravages of Covid-19, a greater proportion of college-educated wives than husbands said they had trouble balancing family and work life and felt it was harder to advance in a job as a working parent.[46] Balancing

---

43   Claudia Goldin, *Career and Family, Women's Century-Long Journey Toward Equity* (Princeton, NJ: Princeton University Press, 2021), pp. 207–8. College-educated fathers increased the amount of time they spent with their children from 5 hours per week in 1990 to 10 hours per week in 2015. College-educated mothers increased the time they spent with their offspring from 13 hours per week to 21 hours per week over the same years.

44   Genevieve Smith and Ishita Rustagi, "Dual Career Couples are the New Norm. What Business Leaders Need to Know", Berkeley Haas Center for Equity, Gender, and Leadership (January 16, 2020), https://berkeleyequity.medium.com/dual-career-couples-are-the-new-norm-what-business-leaders-need-to-know-8d9e1489726c.

45   Pew Research Center, pp. 3–4.

46   Pew Research Center, pp. 5–7. See also, Claire Cain Miller, "Young Men Embrace Gender Equality, But They Still Don't Vacuum", *The New York Times*, February 11, 2020, and Claire Cain Miller, "Nearly Half of Men Say They Do Most of the Home Schooling. 3 Percent of Women Agree", *The New York Times*, May 6, 2020.

work and family remains especially difficult for working-class women, women of color, and immigrants who are more likely to work in lower-paying jobs with inflexible hours and lack the financial resources available to women in professional jobs.[47]

Home life is changing, but the structure and demands of most professional jobs have been slow to respond to these developments. This adds to the difficulties married women with children experience when they try to balance work and family. Although there have been many legal advances for women, women still earn less than their male counterparts over the course of their careers and are underrepresented at the top pay scales and highest leadership positions — a gap that reflects the time they take off to bring up their children.[48] There is growing flexibility in work hours in some professional jobs, but family-friendly environments are still the exception, and more common in fields that are dominated by women.[49] Paternity leaves are more available, but often underutilized.[50] Most professional work still takes place in a work environment that reflects the career model developed in the nineteenth century, when a

---

47   During the Covid-19 pandemic, 2020–2021, these categories of female workers were disproportionately affected by job losses, compared to men, in part because they did not have jobs they could do remotely. Alisha Haridasani Gupta, "Covid Shuttered Schools Everywhere. So Why was the 'She-cession' Worse in the U.S.?" *The New York Times*, May 28, 2021. See also, Patricia Cohen and Tiffany Hsu, "Pandemic Could Scar a Generation of Working Mothers", *The New York Times*, June 3, 2020; Titan Alon et al., "The Impact of Covid-19 on Gender Equality", National Bureau of Economic Research Working Paper 26947 (April 2020), https://www.nber.org/papers/w26947; and Brigid Francis-Devine, Andrew Powell, and Niamh Foley, "Corona Virus: Impact on the Labour Market", Briefing Paper 8898, House of Commons Library, 25 February 2021, https://dera.ioe.ac.uk/37509/1/CBP-8898%20%281%29%20%28redacted%29.pdf. For the long history of gender inequality in childcare and home management, see Arlie Hochschild with Anne Machung, *The Second Shift, Working Parents and the Revolution at Home* (New York: Viking, 1989), and McCarthy, *Double*.

48   Goldin, *Career*, pp. 5, 151–75.

49   For the US experience, see Goldin, *Career*, pp. 176–220. On the growing flexibility of the medical profession in Britain, see Laura Jefferson, Karen Bloor, and Alan Maynard, "Women in Medicine: Historical Perspectives and Recent Trends", *British Medical Bulletin*, 114 (June 2015), 5–15, https://doi.org/10.1093/bmb/ldv007; Katie Nicholas, "Literature Search: Flexible Working in Healthcare" (UK: Health Education England Knowledge Management Team, 9 September 2020), https://www.hee.nhs.uk/sites/default/files/Flexible%20working%20in%20healthcare.pdf.

50   Seema Jayachandran, "There's a Way to Give Paid Paternity Leave a Push", *The New York Times*, June 27, 2021, p. 6.

man worked very long hours and was supported by a stay-at-home wife who took care of their children and domestic needs.

Without structural adjustments in the workplace, professional advancement will continue to come at a high price for married women with children. Compromise solutions (like "mommy tracks") that restrict a woman's opportunities, reduce her earning power, and underuse her talents not only undermine her position in the workforce but also affect the division of labor within the home. This undercuts what economist Claudia Goldin has dubbed "couple equity": wives who reduce their work hours devote more time to the house and children, while their husbands devote more effort to their jobs.[51] Women rarely make up later in their careers for the time and money they lose if they reduce their work hours while they are raising children — a reality that perpetuates gender inequities in the workforce as well as in the home. It is a vicious cycle.

Nevertheless, the revolutionary changes in the career trajectories of middle-class women that began in the 1970s and 1980s have transformed women's lives and opportunities. The combination of marriage and career — once heroic and extraordinary — is now a necessary aspect of the majority of American and British women's lives, from the hardworking grocery store clerks and health care professionals on whose service everyone depends, to the CEOs and academics that make up the highest echelons of professional life.

The five remarkable women depicted in this book — and the equally remarkable men who married them — helped to pave the way for these changes. Alice, Grace, Elsie, Beatrice, and Lucy would be delighted to know that middle-class women have so fully entered public life and are no longer expected to choose between marriage and a career. They would be thrilled to see that men are taking more responsibility for rearing children and managing the home, although they might lament the loss of live-in servants. And they would undoubtedly applaud the shifting notions of gender — especially standards of masculinity — that are helping to turn modern-day husbands into supportive partners and companionate spouses for accomplished women who find fulfillment in working outside the home.

51   Goldin, *Career*, p. 205.

Selected Bibliography

Archival Sources

American Philosophical Society Library, Elsie Clews Parsons Papers (APS)

Bank Street College Archives, Records of the Bureau of Educational Experiments (BSCA)

Columbia University, Rare Book and Manuscript Library, MS#0884, Lucy Sprague Mitchell Papers (LSM Papers)

Columbia University, Rare Book and Manuscript Library, MSColl\Mitchell, Wesley Clair Mitchell Papers (WCM Papers)

Columbia University, Rare Book and Manuscript Library, Oral History Archives at Columbia, Interviews with Lucy Sprague Mitchell and Lissa Parsons Kennedy

Harvard University, Houghton Library, 50M-199, George Herbert Palmer Correspondence (GHP Papers)

London School of Economics and Political Science, British Library of Political and Economic Science, Passfield Papers [Beatrice Webb Diaries and Correspondence of Beatrice and Sidney Webb], (Passfield Papers)

London School of Economics Digital Library, Beatrice Webb's manuscript and typescript diaries https://digital.library.lse.ac.uk/browse#webb-manuscript

Rye Historical Society, Parsons Family Papers (RHS)

University of Chicago, Hannah Holborn Gray Special Collections Research Center, Robert Herrick Papers (RH Papers)

University of Chicago, Hannah Holborn Gray Special Collections Research Center, Marion Talbot Papers

University of Chicago, Hannah Holborn Gray Special Collections Research Center, William Rainey Harper Papers

University of Chicago, Hannah Holborn Gray Special Collections Research Center, University of Chicago, Office of the President. Harper, Judson,

 https://doi.org/10.11647/OBP.0318.07

and Burton Administrations. https://www.lib.uchicago.edu/ead/pdf/ ofcpreshjb-0066-016.pdf (UC, OPHJB)

University of Liverpool Library, Special Collections and Archives, D.140, Papers of Professor W. H. Young and of his wife Grace Chisholm Young (Young Papers)

University of Liverpool Library, Special Collections and Archives, D.599, Papers of Dr. R.C.H. Tanner, including papers of her parents W. H. Young and Grace C. Young (Tanner Papers)

Wellesley College, Wellesley College Archives, Alice Freeman Palmer Papers (AFP Papers)

Published Sources

Alon, Titan, et al., "The Impact of Covid-19 on Gender Equality", National Bureau of Economic Research Working Paper 26947 (April 2020), https:// www.nber.org/papers/w26947, https://doi.org/0.3386/w26947

Antler, Joyce, *Lucy Sprague Mitchell: The Making of a Modern Woman* (New Haven: Yale University Press, 1987).

Armstrong, Henry E., "Mrs. Hertha Ayrton", *Nature*, 112 (1923), 800–1.

Association of Collegiate Alumnae, *Alice Freeman Palmer: In Memoriam* (Boston: Marymount Press, 1903).

Baatz, Simon, *The Girl on the Velvet Swing: Sex, Murder, and Madness at the Dawn of the 20th Century* (New York: Mulholland Books, 2018).

Banks, Olive, *Becoming a Feminist: The Social Origins of "First Wave" Feminism* (Athens, GA: University of Georgia Press, 1987).

Basch, Norma, *In the Eyes of the Law: Women, Marriage and Property in Nineteenth-Century New York* (Ithaca, NY: Cornell University Press, 1982).

Beddoe, Deirdre, *Back to Home and Duty: Women between the Wars, 1918–1939* (London: Pandora, 1989).

Berg, Maxine, *A Woman in History: Eileen Power, 1889–1940* (Cambridge, UK: Cambridge University Press, 1996).

Blair, Karen, *The Clubwoman as Feminist: True Womanhood Redefined, 1868–1914* (New York: Holmes and Meier, 1980).

Bledstein, Burton J., *The Culture of Professionalism: The Middle-Class and the Development of Higher Education in America* (New York: Norton, 1976).

Bogle, David, "100 Years of the PhD in the UK" (2018), https://discovery.ucl. ac.uk/id/eprint/10068565/

Bonner, Thomas Neville, *Becoming a Physician: Medical Education in Great Britain, France, Germany, and the US, 1750–1945* (New York and Oxford: Oxford University Press, 1995).

____, "Pioneering in Women's Medical Education in the Swiss Universities, 1864–1914", *Gesnerus: Swiss Journal of the History of Medicine and Sciences*, 45 (1988), 461–73.

____, *To the Ends of the Earth: Women's Search for Education in Medicine* (Cambridge, MA and London: Harvard University Press, 1992).

Bordin, Ruth, *Alice Freeman Palmer: The Evolution of a New Woman* (Ann Arbor: University of Michigan Press, 1993), https://doi.org/10.3998/mpub.13480

Boyer, John W., *The University of Chicago: A History* (Chicago: University of Chicago Press, 2015).

Boyle, Patrick, "Nation's Physician Workforce Evolves: More Women, a bit older, and toward different specialties" (Association of American Medical Colleges, February 2, 2021), https://www.aamc.org/news-insights/nation-s-physician-workforce-evolves-more-women-bit-older-and-toward-different-specialties

Boyles, Denis, *Everything Explained that is Explainable: On the Creation of the Encyclopedia Britannica's Celebrated Eleventh Edition, 1910–1911* (New York: Knopf, 2016).

Branca, Patricia, *Silent Sisterhood: Middle Class Women in the Victorian Home* (Pittsburgh: Carnegie Mellon University Press, 1975).

Brandon, Ruth, *The New Women and the Old Men: Love, Sex and the Woman Question* (New York: Norton, 1990).

Briggs, Tracy, "Twenty Years at Greenwich House" (unpublished PhD thesis: The University of Toledo, 2008), https://www.proquest.com/openview/f8c206869eee0373717a42fec748b050/1?pq-origsite=gscholar&cbl=18750

Bruckner, Andrew M. and Brian S. Thomson, "Real Variable Contributions of G. C. Young and W. H. Young", *Expositiones Mathematicae* 19 (2001), 337–58, https://doi.org/10.1016/S0723-0869(01)80019-0

Burrows, E. G., "Alice Freeman Palmer at Michigan", *Michigan Alumnus Quarterly Review*, 61 (Summer 1955), 321–28.

Buzaljko, Grace Wilson, "Theodora Kracaw Kroeber" in Ute Gacs et al., *Women Anthropologists: Selected Biographies* (Urbana: University of Illinois Press, 1988), pp. 187–93.

Byrne, Alyson and Julian Barling, "Does a Woman's High Status Career Hurt her Marriage? Not if her Husband Does the Laundry", *Harvard Business Review* (May 2, 2017), https://hbr.org/2017/05/does-a-womans-high-status-career-hurt-her-marriage-not-if-her-husband-does-the-laundry

Caine, Barbara, *Destined to Be Wives: The Sisters of Beatrice Webb* (Oxford: Clarendon Press, 1986).

Cartwright, M. L., "Grace Chisholm Young", *Girton Review*, 31 (Easter 1944), 17–19.

____, "Grace Chisholm Young", *Journal of London Mathematical Society*, 19:75 (July 1944), 185–92, https://doi.org.10.1112/jlms/19.75_Part3.185

Clark, Linda L., *Women and Achievement in Nineteenth-Century Europe* (Cambridge, UK: Cambridge University Press, 2008).

Cohen, Patricia, "Recession with a Difference: Women Face Special Burden", *The New York Times*, November 17, 2020.

Cohen, Patricia and Tiffany Hsu, "Pandemic Could Scar a Generation of Working Mothers", *The New York Times*, June 3, 2020.

Cole, G. D.H., "Beatrice Webb as an Economist" in *The Webbs and Their Work*, ed. by Margaret Cole (London: Frederick Muller, 1949), pp. 267–82.

Cole, Margaret, *Beatrice Webb* (London: Longmans, Green, 1945).

____, Margaret, ed, *The Webbs and Their Work* (London: Frederick Muller, 1949).

Collier, Virginia MacMakin, *Marriage and Career: A Study of One Hundred Women who are Wives, Mothers, Homemakers and Professional Workers* (New York: Bureau of Vocational Information, 1926).

Collins, Marcus, *Modern Love: Personal Relationships in Twentieth-Century Britain* (Newark: University of Delaware Press, 2003).

Conway, Jill Ker, *True North: A Memoir* (New York: Knopf, 1994).

Coontz, Stephanie, *A Strange Stirring: The Feminine Mystique and American Women at the Dawn of the 1960s* (New York: Basic Books, 2012).

Cott, Nancy F., *The Grounding of Modern Feminism* (New Haven: Yale University Press, 1987).

____, "On Men's History and Women's History" in *Meanings for Manhood: Constructions of Masculinity in Victorian America*, ed. by Mark C. Carnes and Clyde Griffen (Chicago: University of Chicago Press, 1990), pp. 206–8.

Cummings, Mary, *Saving Sin City: William Travers Jerome, Stanford White and the Original Crime of the Century* (New York: Pegasus, 2018).

Davidoff, Leonore, "Class and Gender in Victorian England" in *Sex and Class in Women's History: Essays from Feminist Studies*, ed. by Judith L. Newton, Mary P. Ryan, and Judith R. Walkowitz (London: Routledge, 1983), pp. 16–71.

Davidoff, Leonore and Catherine Hall, *Family Fortunes: Men and Women of the English Middle Class, 1780–1850* (Chicago: University of Chicago Press, 1987).

Day, Jennifer Cheeseman, "Number of Women Lawyers at Record High But Men Still Highest Earners", US Census Bureau (May 8, 2018), https://www.census.gov/library/stories/2018/05/women-lawyers.html

De Hart, Jane Sherron, *Ruth Bader Ginsburg* (New York: Knopf, 2018).

Deacon, Desley, *Elsie Clews Parsons: Inventing Modern* Life (Chicago: University of Chicago Press, 1997), https://doi.org.10.7208/chicago/9780226139098

"Dedication of the Alice Freeman Palmer Chimes", *The University Record of The University of Chicago*, 13:1 (July 1908), 9–17.

Degler, Carl, *At Odds: Women and the Family in America from the Revolution to the Present* (New York: Oxford University Press, 1981).

Delamont, Sara and Lorna Duffin, eds, *The Nineteenth-Century Woman: Her Cultural and Physical World* (New York: Harper and Row, 1978), https://doi.org/10.4324/9780203104118

Demos, John, *The Past, Present, and Personal: The Family and the Life Course in American History* (New York: Oxford, 1986).

Doherty, Maggie, *The Equivalents: A Story of Art, Female Friendship, and Liberation in the 1960s* (New York: Knopf, 2020).

Drachman, Virginia G., *Sisters in Law: Women Lawyers in Modern American History* (Cambridge, MA: Harvard University Press, 1998).

Drake, Barbara and Margaret I. Cole, eds, *Our Partnership* by Beatrice Webb (New York: Longmans, Green, 1948).

Duffin, Lorna, "Prisoners of Progress: Women and Evolution" in *The Nineteenth-Century Woman: Her Cultural and Physical World*, ed. by Sara Delamont and Lorna Duffin (New York: Harper and Row, 1978), pp. 57–91, https://doi.org/10.4324/9780203104118

Dunham, William, *Journey through Genius: The Great Theorems of Mathematics* (New York: John Wiley and Sons, 1990).

Dyhouse, Carol, *Girls Growing Up in Late Victorian and Edwardian England* (London: Routledge and Kegan Paul, 1981).

―――, "Mothers and Daughters in the Middle-class Home, c.1870–1914" in *Love and Labour: Women's Experience of Home and Family, 1850–1940*, ed. by Jane Lewis (Oxford: Blackwell, 1986), pp. 27–47.

Eaton, Mark, "Which Jobs Have More Women than Men?", *BBC News*, 8 March 2012, www.bbc.com/news/UK-17287275.

Eby, Claire Virgina, *Until Choice Do Us Part: Marriage Reform in the Progressive Era* (Chicago and London: University of Chicago Press, 2014), https://doi.org10.7208/chicago/9780226085975.001.0001

Elston, Mary Ann C., "Women Doctors in the British Health Services: A Sociological Study of their Careers and Opportunities" (unpublished

PhD dissertation, University of Leeds, 1986), https://etheses.whiterose. ac.uk/247/1/uk_bl_ethos_375527.pdf

Epstein, Cynthia Fuchs, *Women in Law* (Garden City, NY: Anchor Books, 1983).

Fadiman, Lillian, *To Believe in Women: What Lesbians Have Done for America* (New York: Houghton Mifflin, 1999).

Feaver, George, ed, "Introduction" to Beatrice Webb, *Our Partnership* (Cambridge, UK: University of Cambridge Press, 1975).

____, "Two Minds or One? The Mills, the Webbs, and Liberty in British Social Democracy" in *Lives, Liberties and the Public Good: New Essays on Political Theory*, ed. by George Feaver and Frederick Rosen (Houndmills, UK: Macmillan, 1987), pp. 139–72, https://doi.org.10.1007/978-1-349-08006

Fishbein, Leslie, *Rebels in Bohemia: The Radicals of the Masses, 1911–1917* (Chapel Hill: University of North Carolina Press, 1982).

Francis-Devine, Brigid, Andrew Powell, and Niamh Foley, "Corona Virus: Impact on the Labour Market", Briefing Paper 8898, House of Commons Library, 25 February 2021, https://dera.ioe.ac.uk/37509/1/CBP-8898%20 %281%29%20%28redacted%29.pdf

Frankfort, Roberta, *Collegiate Women* (New York: New York University Press, 1977).

Friedan, Betty, *The Feminine Mystique* (New York: Norton, 2013).

Friedlander, Judith, *A Light in Dark Times: The New School for Social Research and Its University in Exile* (New York: Columbia University Press, 2019), https:// doi.org/10.7312/fried180.18

Gacs, Ute et al., *Women Anthropologists: Selected Biographies* (Urbana: University of Illinois Press, 1989).

Glazer, Penina Migdal and Miriam Slater, *Unequal Colleagues: The Entrance of Women into the Professions, 1890–1940* (New Brunswick, NJ: Rutgers University Press, 1987).

"The Glorified Spinster", *MacMillan's Magazine*, 58 (September 1888), 371–76.

Goldin, Claudia, *Career and Family, Women's Century-Long Journey toward Equity* (Princeton, NJ: Princeton University Press, 2021), https://doi. org/10.1515/9780691226736

____, "Marriage Bars: Discrimination against Married Women Workers, 1920s to 1950s", National Bureau of Economic Research Working Paper 2747 (October 1988), https://doi.org/10.3386/w2747

____, "The Quiet Revolution that Transformed Women's Employment, Education, and Family", *American Economic Review*, 26 (May 2006), 1–21, https://doi.org/10.1257/000282806777212350

Gordon, Lynn D., *Gender and Higher Education in the Progressive Era* (New Haven: Yale University Press, 1990).

Gorham, Deborah, *The Victorian Girl and Feminine Ideal* (Bloomington: Indiana University Press, 1982).

Grattan-Guinness, Ivor, "Mathematical Bibliography for W. H. and G. C. Young", *Historia Mathematica*, 2 (1975), 43–58, https://doi.org/10.1016/0315-0860(75)90036-1

____, "A Mathematical Union: William Henry and Grace Chisholm Young", *Annals of Science*, 29:2 (1972), 105–86, https://doi.org/10.1080/00033797200200431

Griswold, Robert L., *Fatherhood in America: A History* (New York: Basic Books, 1993).

Grose, Jessica, "It's Not your Kids Holding Your Career Back. It's Your Husband", Slate.com, November 18, 2014, https://slate.com/human-interest/2014/11/harvard-business-school-study-it-s-not-kids-but-husbands-that-hold-women-s-careers-back.html

Gupta, Alisha Haridasani, "Covid Shuttered Schools Everywhere. So Why was the 'She-cession' Worse in the U. S.?", *The New York Times*, May 28, 2021.

Hammerton, A. James, *Cruelty and Companionship: Conflict in Nineteenth Century Married Life* (London: Routledge, 1992).

Hardy, G. H., "William Henry Young, 1863–1942", Royal Society of London, *Obituary Notices of Fellows*, 4:12 (November 1943), 307–23, https://royalsocietypublishing.org/doi/10.1098/rsbm.1943.0005

Hare, Peter H., *A Woman's Quest for Science: Portrait of Anthropologist Elsie Clews Parsons* (Buffalo, NY: Prometheus Books, 1985).

Harris, Jose, "The Webbs and Beveridge" in *From the Workhouse to Welfare: What Beatrice Webb's 1909 Minority Report Can Teach Us Today*, ed. by Ed Wallis (London: Fabian Society, 2009), pp. 55–64.

Harris, Marvin, *The Rise of Anthropological Theory: A History of Theories of Culture* (New York: Thomas Crowell, 1968).

Harrison, Royden J., *The Life and Times of Sidney and Beatrice Webb, 1858–1905: The Formative Years* (Houndmills, UK: MacMillan, 2000), https://doi.org/10.1057/9780230598065

Harvard University, Department of Philosophy, *George Herbert Palmer, 1842-1933: Memorial Addresses* (Cambridge, MA: Harvard University Press, 1935).

Hauser, Mary E., *Learning from Children: The Life and Legacy of Caroline Pratt* (New York: Peter Lang, 2006).

Hazard, Caroline, *From College Gates* (Boston: Houghton Mifflin, 1925).

Heilbrun, Carolyn, *Writing a Woman's Life* (New York: Norton, 1988).

Herbert, Charles, "Mrs. Palmer as an Acquaintance", *Boston Evening Transcript*, December 10, 1902.

Herrick, Robert, *Chimes* (New York: Macmillan, 1926).

____, *The End of Desire* (New York: Farrar and Rinehart, 1932).

____, *Wanderings* (New York: Harcourt Brace, 1925).

Hersh, Blanche Glassman, "A Partnership of Equals: Feminist Marriages in Nineteenth-Century America" in *The American Man*, ed. by Elizabeth Pleck and Joseph Pleck (Englewood Cliffs, NJ: Prentice Hall, 1980), pp. 183–214.

Hicks, Paul deForest, *John E. Parsons, An Eminent New Yorker in the Gilded Age* (Westport and New York: Prospecta Press, 2016).

History WestMidlands, "The Mistress of Joseph Chamberlain's Highbury — Mary Endicott Chamberlain" (podcast, November 25, 2019), https://historywm.com/podcasts/mary-endicott.

Hochschild, Arlie with Anne Machung, *The Second Shift, Working Parents and the Revolution at Home* (New York: Viking, 1989).

Holmes, Anna, "The Radical Woman Behind 'Goodnight Moon'", *The New Yorker*, February 7, 2022, 16–22, https://www.newyorker.com/magazine/2022/02/07/the-radical-woman-behind-goodnight-moon

Hubback, Judith, *Dawn to Dusk: Autobiography of Judith Hubback* (Asheville, NC: Chiron Publications, 2015).

____, *Wives Who Went to College* (London: William Heinemann, 1957).

Jacobs, Emma, "Secrets of Successful Dual-career Couples", *Financial Times*, October 13, 2019.

Jalland, Pat, *Women, Marriage and Politics, 1860–1914* (Oxford: Oxford University Press, 1986).

James, Edward T., Janet Wilson James, and Paul Boyer, eds, *Notable American Women: A Biographical Dictionary*, 3 vols. (Cambridge, MA: Belknap Press, 1975–1982).

Jayachandran, Seema, "There's a Way to Give Paid Paternity Leave a Push", *The New York Times*, June 27, 2021.

Jefferson, Laura, Karen Bloor, and Alan Maynard, "Women in Medicine: Historical Perspectives and Recent Trends", *British Medical Bulletin*, 114 (June 2015), 5–15, https://doi.org/10.1093/bmb/ldv007

Johnston, Tiffany L., "Mary Whitall Smith at the Harvard Annex" [n.d], https://berenson.itatti.harvard.edu/berenson/items/show/3030

Jones, Claire G., *Femininity, Mathematics and Science, 1880–1914* (Basingstoke and New York: Palgrave Macmillan, 2009), https://doi.org/10.1057/9780230246652

Jones, Claire, "Grace Chisholm Young: gender and mathematics around 1900", *Women's History Review*, 9:4 (2000), 675–91, https://doi.org/10.1080/09612020000200266

Jones, Margaret C., *Heretics and Hellraisers: Women Contributors to The Masses, 1911–1917* (Austin: University of Texas Press, 1993).

Jorgensen, Elizabeth Walkins and Henry Irvin Jorgensen, *Thorstein Veblen, Victorian Firebrand* (Armonk, NY: Sharpe, 1999).

Kaufholz-Soldat, Eva and Nicola M. R. Oswald, eds, *Against all Odds: Women's Ways to Mathematical Research since 1800* (Cham, Switzerland: Springer, 2020), https://doi.org/10.1007/978-3-030-47610-6

Kelly, Thomas, *For Advancement of Learning: The University of Liverpool, 1881–1981* (Liverpool: Liverpool University Press, 1981).

Kennon, Anne Byrd, "College Wives Who Work", *Journal of the American Association of University Women*, 20 (June 1927), 100–5.

Kenschaft, Lois, *Reinventing Marriage: The Love and Work of Alice Freeman Palmer and George Herbert Palmer* (Urbana: University of Illinois Press, 2005).

Keynes, John Maynard, "Mary Paley Marshall, 1850–1944" in *Cambridge Women: Twelve Portraits*, ed. by Edward Shils and Carmen Blacker (Cambridge, UK: Cambridge University Press, 1996), pp. 73–92.

Klein, Viola, *Britain's Married Women Workers* (London: Routledge & Kegan Paul; New York: Humanities Press, 1965).

Kroeber, Theodora, *Alfred Kroeber: A Personal Configuration* (Berkeley: University of California Press, 1970).

Kuby, William, *Conjugal Misconduct, Defying Marriage Law in the Twentieth-Century United States* (New York: Cambridge University Press, 2018), https://doi.org/10.1017/9781316673096

Lafarge, Oliver, *Behind the Mountains* (Boston: Houghton Mifflin, 1956).

Landry, Bart, *Black Working Wives: Pioneers of the American Family Revolution* (Berkeley: University of California Press, 2000).

Lasch, Christopher, *The New Radicalism in America, 1889–1963: The Intellectual as a Social Type* (New York: Knopf, 1966).

Levine, Philippa, " 'So Few Prizes and So Many Blanks': Marriage and Feminism in Later Nineteenth-Century England", *Journal of British Studies*, 28 (April 1989), 150–74.

____, *Victorian Feminism, 1850–1900* (Tallahassee: Florida State University Press, 1987).

Lewis, Jane, *Women in England, 1870–1950* (Bloomington: Indiana University Press, 1986).

Linenthal, Arthur J., *Two Academic Lives: George Herbert Palmer and Alice Freeman Palmer: A Compilation* (Boston: Privately printed, 1995).

Lyall, Sarah, "At Primary Debates and on Instagram, a Spouse Embraces His Campaign Role", *The New York Times*, August 20, 2020.

Lykknes, Annette, Donald L. Optiz, and Brigitte Van Tiggelen, eds, *For Better or Worse? Collaborative Couples in the Sciences* (Basel: Springer, 2012), https://doi.org/10.1007/978-3-0348-0286-4

Lystra, Karen, *Searching the Heart: Women, Men, and Romantic Love in Nineteenth-Century America* (New York: Oxford University Press, 1989).

MacKenzie, Donald, "Eugenics in Britain", *Social Studies of Science*, 6 (1976), 499–532.

MacKenzie, Jeanne, *A Victorian Courtship: The Story of Beatrice Potter and Sidney Webb* (New York: Oxford University Press, 1979).

MacKenzie, Norman, ed, *The Letters of Sydney and Beatrice Webb*, 3 vols. (Cambridge, UK: Cambridge University Press, 1978).

MacKenzie, Norman and Jeanne MacKenzie, eds, *The Diary of Beatrice Webb*, 4 vols. (Cambridge, MA: Belknap Press, 1982–1985).

McCarthy, Helen, *Double Lives, A History of Working Motherhood* (London: Bloomsbury, 2020).

——, "Social Science and Married Women's Employment in Post-War Britain", *Past and Present* 233 (November, 2016), 269–305, https://doi.org/10.1093/pastj/gtw035

McCarthy, Niall, "Women are still earning more doctoral degrees than men in the US", October 5, 2018, https://www.forbes.com/sites/niallmccarthy/2018/10/05/women-are-still-earning-more-doctoral-degrees-than-men-in-the-u-s-infographic/?sh=5cad137345b6.

McWilliams-Tullberg, Rita, *Women at Cambridge: A Men's University Though of a Mixed Type* (London: Victor Gollanz, 1975).

Marsh, Margaret, *Suburban Lives* (New Brunswick, NJ: Rutgers University Press, 1990).

Martin, Kingsley, "The Webbs in Retirement" in *The Webbs and Their Work*, ed. by Margaret Cole (London: Frederick Muller, 1949), pp. 285–301.

Mason, Joan, "Hertha Ayrton (1854–1923) and the Admission of Women to the Royal Society of London", *Notes and Records of the Royal Society of London*, 45:2 (1991), 201–20.

Mazon, Patricia M., *Gender and the Modern Research University: The Admission of Women to German Higher Education, 1865–1914* (Stanford, CA: Stanford University Press, 2003).

Mead, Margaret, *Blackberry Winter: My Earlier Years* (New York: Washington Square Press, 1972).

Mead, Margaret and Ruth L. Bunzel, *The Golden Age of American Anthropology, 1880–1920* (New York: George Braziller, 1960).

Michalos, Alex C. and Deborah C. Poff, eds, *Selected Correspondence of Bernard Shaw: Bernard Shaw and the Webbs* (Toronto: University of Toronto Press, 2002).

Miller, Claire Cain, "Nearly Half of Men Say They Do Most of the Home Schooling. 3 Percent of Women Agree", *The New York Times*, May 6, 2020.

_____, "Young Men Embrace Gender Equality, but They Still Don't Vacuum", *The New York Times*, February 11, 2020.

Miller, Clair Cain and Alisha Haridasani Gupta, "Why Supermom Gets Star Billing on Resumes for Public Office", *The New York Times*, October 14, 2020.

Mintz, Stephen, *A Prison of Expectations: The Family in Victorian Culture* (New York: New York University Press, 1983).

Mintz, Stephen and Susan Kellogg, *Domestic Revolutions: A Social History of American Family Life* (New York: The Free Press, 1989).

Mitchell, Lucy Sprague, *Here and Now Storybook* (New York: Dutton, 1921).

_____, *Two Lives: The Story of Wesley Clair Mitchell and Myself* (New York: Simon & Schuster, 1953).

Moberly, Tom, "Number of Women Entering Medical School Rises after Decade of Decline", *BMJ*, 27 January 2018, p. 167, https://www.bmj.com/bmj/section-pdf/959692?path=/bmj/360/8138/Careers.full.pdf.

Moore, Wendy, *No Man's Land: The Trailblazing Women Who Ran Britain's Most Extraordinary Military Hospital During World War I* (New York: Basic Books, 2020).

Morantz-Sanchez, Regina M., "The Many Faces of Intimacy" in *Uneasy Careers and Intimate Lives: Women in Science, 1789–1979*, ed. by Pnina G. Abir-am and Dorinda Outram (New Brunswick, NJ: Rutgers University Press, 1987), pp. 45–59.

Morantz-Sanchez, Regina Markell, *Sympathy and Science: Women Physicians in American Medicine* (New York: Oxford University Press, 1985).

Muggeridge, Kitty and Ruth Adam, *Beatrice Webb: A Life 1858–1943* (New York: Knopf, 1968).

Muhlhausen, Elizabeth, "Grace Chisholm Young, William Henry Young, Their Results on the Theory of Sets of Points at the Beginning of the Twentieth Century, and a Controversy with Max Dehn" in *Against all Odds: Women's Ways to Mathematical Research since 1800*, ed. by Eva Kaufholz-Soldat and

Nicola M. R. Oswald (Cham, Switzerland: Springer, 2020), pp. 121–32, https://doi.org/10.1007/978-3-030-47610-6

Murray, Margaret A. M., *Women Becoming Mathematicians: Creating a Professional Identity in Post-World War II America* (Cambridge, MA: MIT Press, 2000).

Musgrove, F. S., "Middle Class Education and Employment in the Nineteenth Century", *Economic History Review*, 12:1 (1959), 99–111, https://doi.org/10.2307/2591084

Nevius, Blake, *Robert Herrick: The Development of a Novelist* (Berkeley: University of California Press, 1962; repr. 2019), https://doi.org/10.1525/9780520337381

Neuman, Johanna, *Gilded Suffragists: The New York Socialites Who Fought for Women's Right to Vote* (New York: New York University Press, 2017), https://doi.org/10.2307/j.ctt1pwt9p2

New York Community Trust, "Lucy Wortham James" [n.d.], https://nycommunitytrust.org/wp-content/uploads/2018/03/Lucy-Wortham-James.pdf.

Nicholas, Katie, "Literature Search: Flexible Working in Healthcare", UK: Health Education England Knowledge Management Team (9 September 2020), https://www.hee.nhs.uk/sites/default/files/Flexible%20working%20in%20healthcare.pdf.

Nord, Deborah Epstein, *The Apprenticeship of Beatrice Webb* (Amherst: University of Massachusetts Press, 1985).

Office of National Statistics, "Employment Activity of Mothers and Fathers in a Family", *Families and the Labour Market, UK 2019* (24 October 2019), https://www.ons.gov.uk/employmentandlabourmarket/peopleinwork/employmentandemployeetypes/articles/familiesandthelabourmarketengland/2019

Oleson, Alexandra and John Voss, eds, *The Organization of Knowledge in Modern America, 1860–1920* (Baltimore: Johns Hopkins University Press, 1979).

Olson, Elizabeth, "Women Make Up Majority of US Law Students for the First Time", *The New York Times*, December 16, 2016.

Osen, Lynn M., *Women in Mathematics* (Cambridge, MA: MIT Press, 1974).

Palay, Claire, "Lea Miller's Protest: Married Women's Jobs at the University of Washington", HSTAA 105 (Winter 2010), https://depts.washington.edu/depress/women_uw_lea_miller.shtml

Palmer, Alice Freeman, *A Marriage Cycle* (Boston: Houghton Mifflin, 1915).

——, "On Women's Duties" (Warren, Ohio: National American Woman Suffrage Association, 1904).

——, "What Women Can Do for the Public Schools", *The Independent* 50 (August 4, 1898), 301–4.

_____, "Women's Education at the World's Fair" in *The Teacher: Essays and Addresses on Education* by George Herbert Palmer and Alice Freeman Palmer (Boston: Houghton Mifflin, 1908), pp. 351–63.

_____, "Why Go To College" in *The Teacher: Essays and Addresses on Education* by George Herbert Palmer and Alice Freeman Palmer (Boston: Houghton Mifflin, 1908), pp. 364–93.

Palmer, Alice Freeman and George Herbert Palmer, *An Academic Courtship: Letters of Alice Freeman and George Herbert Palmer, 1886–1887* (Cambridge, MA: Harvard University Press, 1940), https://doi.org/10.4159/harvard/9780674491830.

Palmer, George Herbert, *The Autobiography of a Philosopher* (Boston: Houghton Mifflin, 1930).

_____, ed, *The English Works of George Herbert Palmer*, 3 vols. (Boston and New York: Houghton Mifflin, 1905).

_____, *The Life of Alice Freeman Palmer* (Boston: Houghton Mifflin, 1908), https://doi.org/10.5479/sil.11703.39088001165349

_____, *A Service in Memory of Alice Freeman Palmer* (Boston: Houghton Mifflin, 1903).

Palmer, George Herbert and Alice Freeman Palmer, *The Teacher: Essays and Addresses on Education* (Boston: Houghton Mifflin, 1908).

Palmieri, Patricia Ann, *In Adamless Eden: The Community of Women Faculty at Wellesley* (New Haven and London: Yale University Press, 1995).

_____, "In Adamless Eden: A Social Portrait of the Academic Community at Wellesley College, 1875–1920" (unpublished PhD thesis: Harvard School of Education, 1981).

Parsons, Elsie Clews, "American Snobbishness in the Philippines", *Independent* 60 (February 8, 1906), 332–33.

_____, *The Family: An Ethnographical and Historical Outline with Descriptive Notes, Planned as a Text-book for the Use of College Lecturers and of Directors of Home-reading Clubs* (New York: Putnam's, 1906).

_____, *Fear and Conventionality* (New York: Putnam's, 1914).

_____, "Feminism and Sex Ethics", *International Journal of Ethics*, 26 (July 1916), 462–65.

_____, "Higher Education of Women and the Family", *American Journal of Sociology* 14 (May 1909), 758–63.

_____, *The Journal of a Feminist* with a New Introduction and Notes by Margaret C. Jones (Bristol: Thoemmes Press, 1994).

_____, "Must We Have Her?", *New Republic*, June 10, 1916, 145–46.

_____, *The Old Fashioned Woman: Primitive Fancies about the Sex* (New York: Putnam's, 1913).

_____, "Penalizing Marriage and Childbearing", *Independent* 60 (January 18, 1906), 146–47.

_____, "Remarks on Education in the Philippines", *Charities and the Commons* 16 (September 1, 1906), 564–65.

_____, *Social Freedom: A Study of the Conflicts between Social Classifications and Personality* (New York: Putnam's, 1915).

_____, *Social Rule: A Study of the Will to Power* (New York: Putnam's, 1916).

_____, "When Mating and Parenthood are Theoretically Distinguished", *International Journal of Ethics*, 26 (January 1916), 207–16.

Parsons, William, Jr., "The Progressive Politics of Herbert Parsons" (unpublished undergraduate thesis: Yale University, April 30, 1965).

Patmore, Coventry, *The Angel in the House* (London: Cassell, 1891), https://www.gutenberg.org/files/4099/4099-h/4099-h.htm

Pearson, Hesketh, *G. B.S.: A Full Length Portrait* (Garden City, NY: Garden City Publishing, 1942).

Pease, Edward R., *The History of the Fabian Society* (New York: Barnes and Noble, 1963).

Perkin, Harold, *The Rise of Professional Society: England since 1880*, 2nd edn. (London: Routledge, 2002), https://doi.org/10.4324/9780203408629

Perkin, Joan, *Women and Marriage in Nineteenth-Century England* (Chicago: Lyceum Books, 1989).

Perl, Teri, *Math Equals: Biographies of Women Mathematicians and Related Activities* (Menlo Park, CA: Addison-Wesley, 1978).

Perrone, Fernanda H., "Women Academics in England, 1870–1930", *History of Universities* 12 (1993), 339–77, https://doi.org/10.7282/T3RB77G6

Peterson, M. Jeanne, *Family, Love, and Work in the Lives of Victorian Gentlewomen* (Bloomington: Indiana University Press, 1989).

Pew Research Center, "Raising Kids and Running a Household: How Working Parents Share the Load" (14 November 2015), 1–23, https://www.pewresearch.org/social-trends/2015/11/04/raising-kids-and-running-a-household-how-working-parents-share-the-load/

Phelps, Elizabeth Stuart, *Doctor Zay* (New York: The Feminist Press, 1993).

Potter, Beatrice, "The Dock Life of East London", *Nineteenth Century*, 22 (October, 1887), 483–99.

Potter, Beatrice, "East London Labour", *Nineteenth Century*, 24 (August, 1888), 161–83.

Potter, Beatrice, "Pages from a Work-girl's Diary", *Nineteenth Century*, 25 (September, 1888), 301–14.

Prescott, Irene M., "Lucy Sprague Mitchell: Pioneering in Education", An Interview Conducted by Irene M. Prescott (Berkeley: University of California, 1962), https://digicoll.lib.berkeley.edu/record/217139?ln=en.

Prochaska, F. K., *Women and Philanthropy in Nineteenth-Century England* (New York: Clarendon Press, 1980).

Pugh, Martin, *Women and the Women's Movement in Britain, 1914–1999*, 2nd edn. (New York: St. Martin's Press, 2000), https://doi.org/10.1007/978-1-349-21850-9

Pycior, Helena M., "Pierre Curie and 'His Eminent Collaborator Mme Curie'" in *Creative Couples in the Sciences*, ed. by Helena M. Pycior, Nancy G. Slack, and Pnina G. Abiram-Am (New Brunswick, NJ: Rutgers University Press, 1996), pp. 39–56.

Pycior, Helena M., Nancy G. Slack, and Pnina G. Abiram-Am, eds, *Creative Couples in the Sciences* (New Brunswick, NJ: Rutgers University Press, 1996).

Radice, Lisanne, *Beatrice and Sidney Webb, Fabian Socialists* (New York: St. Martin's, 1984).

Rauchway, Eric, *The Refuge of Affections: Family and American Reform Politics, 1900–1920* (New York: Columbia University Press, 2001).

Reader, J. W., *Professional Men: The Rise of the Professional Classes in Nineteenth Century England* (New York: Basic Books, 1966).

Richards, Joan L., *Mathematical Visions: The Pursuit of Geometry in Victorian England* (Boston: Academic Press, 1988).

Roberts, David, "The Pater Familias of the Victorian Governing Class" in *The Victorian Family: Structure and Stresses*, ed. by Anthony S. Wohl (London: Croom Helm, 1978), pp. 59–81.

Rose, Phyllis, *Parallel Lives: Five Victorian Marriages* (New York: Vintage, 1984).

Rosenberg, Rosalind, *Beyond Separate Spheres: Intellectual Roots of Modern Feminism* (New Haven: Yale University Press, 1982).

Rossiter, Margaret W., "Doctorates for American Women, 1868–1907", *History of Education Quarterly*, 22 (Summer 1982), 159–83.

____, "The Matthew Matilda Effect in Science", *Social Studies of Science*, 23:2 (May 1993), 325–41, https://doi.org/10.1177/030631293023002004

____, *Women Scientists in America*, 3 vols. (Baltimore: Johns Hopkins University Press, 1982–2012).

Rothman, Ellen K., *Hands and Hearts: A History of Courtship in America* (New York: Basic Books, 1984).

Rothman, Patricia, "Grace Chisholm Young and the Division of Laurels", *Notes and Records of the Royal Society of London*, 50:1 (1996), 89–100, https://doi.org/10.1098/rsnr.1996.0008

Rotundo, E. Anthony, *American Manhood: Transformations in Masculinity from the Revolution to the Modern Era* (New York: Basic Books, 1993).

___, "Patriarchs and Participants: A Historical Perspective on Fatherhood" in *Beyond Patriarchy: Essays by Men on Pleasure, Power, and Change*, ed. by Michael Kaufman (Toronto: Oxford University Press, 1987), pp. 64–80.

Rubinstein, David, *Before the Suffragettes: Women's Emancipation in the 1890s* (New York: St. Martin's, 1986).

Russett, Cynthia Eagle, *Sexual Science: The Victorian Construction of Womanhood* (Cambridge, MA: Harvard University Press, 1989).

Ryan, Mary P., *Cradle of the Middle Class: The Family in Oneida County, New York, 1790–1865* (New York: Cambridge University Press, 1981).

Sachs, Albie and Joan Hoff Wilson, *Sexism and the Law: A Study of Male Beliefs and Legal Bias in Britain and the United States* (New York: Free Press, 1979).

Sanger, Margaret, *Margaret Sanger: An Autobiography* (New York: Norton, 1938).

Scarborough, Elizabeth and Laurel Furumoto, *Untold Lives, The First Generation of American Women Psychologists* (New York: Columbia University Press, 1987).

Scharf, Lois, *To Work and to Wed: Female Employment and the Great Depression* (Westport, CT: Greenwood, 1985).

Schwarz, Judith, *Radical Feminists of Heterodoxy: Greenwich Village, 1912–1940* (Norwich, VT: New Victoria Publishers, 1986).

Scutts, Joanna, *Hotbed: Bohemian Greenwich Village and the Secret Club that Sparked Modern Feminism* (New York: Seal Press, 2022).

Senechal, Marjorie, *I Died for Beauty: Dorothy Wrinch and the Cultures of Science* (Oxford and New York: Oxford University Press, 2013), https://doi.org/10.1093/acprof:osobl/9780199732593.001.0001

Sewell, Mrs. S. A., *Women and the Times We Live In*, 2nd edn. (Manchester: Tubbs and Brook, 1869).

Shanley, Mary Lyndon, *Feminism, Marriage, and the Law in Victorian England* (Princeton: Princeton University Press, 1989).

Shils, Edward, "The Order of Learning in the US: The Ascendancy of the University", in *The Organization of Knowledge in Modern America, 1860–1920*, ed. by Alexandra Oleson and John Voss (Baltimore: Johns Hopkins University Press, 1979), pp. 19–47.

Sicherman, Barbara and Carol Hurd Green, eds, *Notable American Women: The Modern Period* (Cambridge, MA: Belknap Press, 1980).

Simmons, Christina, *Making Marriage Modern: Women's Sexuality from the Progressive Era to World War I* (New York: Oxford University Press, 2011), https://doi.org/10.1093/acprof:oso/9780195064117.001.0001

Slack, Nancy G., "Epilogue: Collaborative Couples: Past, Present, and Future" in *For Better or Worse? Collaborative Couples in the Sciences*, ed. by Annette Lykknes, Donald L. Optiz, and Brigitte Van Tiggelen (Basel: Springer, 2012), pp. 270–94, https://doi.org/10.1007/978-3-0348-0286-4

Smith, Genevieve and Ishita Rustagi, "Dual Career Couples are the New Norm. What Business Leaders Need to Know", Berkeley Haas Center for Equity, Gender, and Leadership (January 16, 2020), https://berkeleyequity.medium.com/dual-career-couples-are-the-new-norm-what-business-leaders-need-to-know-8d9e1489726c

Smith, Logan Pearsall, *Unforgotten Years* (Boston: Little, Brown, 1939).

Solomon, Barbara Miller, *In the Company of Educated Women: A History of Women and Higher Education in America* (New Haven: Yale University Press, 1986).

Spencer, Stephanie, *Gender, Work and Education in Britain in the 1950s* (Houndmills, UK: Palgrave MacMillan, 2005).

Steward, Julian H., *Alfred Kroeber* (New York: Columbia University Press, 1973).

Strachey, Barbara, *Remarkable Relations, the Story of the Pearsall Smith Women* (New York: Universe Books, 1982).

Talbot, Marion, *More than Lore: Reminiscences of Marion Talbot* (Chicago: University of Chicago Press, 1936).

Thomas, Evan, *First: Sandra Day O'Connor* (New York: Random House, 2019).

Tobies, Renate, "Internationality: Women in Felix Klein's Courses at the University of Gottingen (1893–1920)" in *Against all Odds: Women's Ways to Mathematical Research since 1800*, ed. by Eva Kaufholz-Soldat and Nicola M. R. Oswald (Cham, Switzerland: Springer, 2020), pp. 9–38, https://doi.org/10.1007/978-3-030-47610-6

Tosh, John, "Domesticity and Manliness in the Victorian Middle Class: The Family of Edward White Benson" in *Manful Assertions: Masculinities in Britain since 1800*, ed. by Michael Roper and John Tosh (London: Routledge, 1991), pp. 44–73.

____, *A Man's Place: Masculinity and the Middle-Class Home in Victorian England* (New Haven and London: Yale University Press, 1999).

Trimberger, Ellen K., "Feminism, Men and Modern Love" in *Powers of Desire*, by Ann Snitow et al. (New York: Monthly Review Press, 1983), pp. 131–52.

Université de Genève, *Liste des Autorites, Professeurs, Etudiants et Auditeurs. Semestre D'Hiver 1908–1909*, https://www.unige.ch/archives/adm/documents-en-ligne/listes-des-autorites-professeurs-etudiants-auditeurs-et-laboratoires/

_____, *Liste des Autorites, Professeurs, Etudiants et Auditeurs. Semestre D'Hiver 1910–1911*, https://www.unige.ch/archives/adm/documents-en-ligne/listes-des-autorites-professeurs-etudiants-auditeurs-et-laboratoires/

Vicinus, Martha, *Independent Women: Work and Community for Single Women, 1850–1920* (Chicago: University of Chicago Press, 1985).

Walker, Peter J., "Time Traveler: Profile of Harvard Economist Claudia Goldin", *IMF Finance and Development*, December 2018, 40–43, https://scholar.harvard.edu/files/goldin/files/imf_people_in_economics_0.pdf

Walkowitz, Judith R., "Science, Feminism and Romance: The Men and Women's Club, 1885–1889", *History Workshop Journal*, 21 (Spring 1986), 37–59, https://doi.org/10.1093/hwj/21.1.37

Walsh, Mary Roth, *Doctors Wanted: No Women Need Apply* (New Haven: Yale University Press, 1977).

Walvin, James, *A Child's World, A Social History of English Childhood, 1800–1914* (Harmondsworth, UK: Penguin Books, 1982).

Webb, Beatrice, *The Diary of Beatrice Webb*, ed. by Norman MacKenzie and Jeanne MacKenzie, 4 vols. (Cambridge, MA: Belknap Press, 1982–1985).

_____, *My Apprenticeship* (Middlesex, UK: Penguin Books, 1971).

_____, *Our Partnership*, ed. by Barbara Drake and Margaret I. Cole (New York: Longmans, Green, 1948).

Webb, Sydney and Beatrice, *The Letters of Sydney and Beatrice Webb*, ed. by Norman MacKenzie, 3 vols. (Cambridge, UK: Cambridge University Press, 1978).

West, Lauren Claire, "The Uneasy Beginnings of Public Diplomacy: Vira Whitehouse, the Committee on Public Information, and the First World War" (unpublished MA thesis 4718: Louisiana State University, 2018), https://digitalcommons.lsu.edu/gradschool_theses/4718/

Wiegand, Sylvia, "Grace Chisholm Young and Agnes Dunnett." Blog posted February 19, 2013. https://ggstem.wordpress.com/2013/02/19/sylvia-wiegand-grace-chisholm-young-and-agnes-dunnett/

_____, "Grace Chisholm Young and William Henry Young: A Partnership of Itinerant British Mathematicians" in *Creative Couples in the Sciences*, ed. by Helena M. Pycior, Nancy G. Slack, and Pnina G. Abiram-Am (New Brunswick, NJ: Rutgers University Press, 1996), pp. 126–40.

Williams, Joan C., "How Women Escape the Likeability Trap", *The New York Times*, August 16, 2019.

Wilson, F. M. Huntington, *Memoirs of an Ex-diplomat* (Boston: Humphries, 1945), https://babel.hathitrust.org/cgi/pt?id=ucl.$b541385&view=1up&seq=1&skin=2021

Wittenberg-Cox, Avivah, "If You Can't Find a Spouse Who Supports Your Career, Stay Single", *Harvard Business Review Email Newsletter*, October 24, 2017. https://hbr.org/2017/10/if-you-cant-find-a-spouse-who-supports-your-career-stay-single

"Wonder Woman: Alice Freeman Palmer", *Wonder Women of History Comics*, 34 (March-April, 1949).

Yeo, Eileen Janes, "Social Science Couples in Britain at the Turn of the Twentieth Century: Gender Divisions in Work and Marriage" in *For Better or Worse? Collaborative Couples in the Sciences*, ed. by Annette Lykknes, Donald L. Optiz, and Brigitte Van Tiggelen (Basel: Springer, 2012), pp. 220–44, https://doi.org/10.1007/978-3-0348-0286-4

Young, Grace Chisholm, *Bimbo: A Little Real Story for Jill and Mollie by Auntie Will* (London: Dent, 1905).

____, *Bimbo and the Frogs: Another Real Story* (London: Dent, 1907).

Young, Grace Chisholm and W. H. Young, *The First Book of Geometry* (London: Dent, 1905).

Young, L. C., "The Life and Work of WH and GC Young" (2005), (formerly posted at http//w.ww-history.mcs.st-and.ac.uk/Extras/Youngs).

Young, Laurence, *Mathematicians and their Times*, North-Holland Mathematics Studies 48 (Amsterdam and New York: North Holland Publishing, 1981).

Young, W. H. and Grace Chisholm Young, *The Theory of Sets of Points* (Cambridge, UK: Cambridge University Press, 1906; repr. 2009), https://doi.org/10.1017/CBO9780511694240

Zumwalt, Rosemary Levy, *Wealth and Rebellion: Elsie Clews Parsons, Anthropologist and Folklorist* (Urbana and Chicago: University of Illinois Press, 1992).

Index

About the Team

Alessandra Tosi was the managing editor for this book and performed the copy-editing and proofreading.

The index was created by Rosalyn Sword.

Jeevanjot Kaur Nagpal designed the cover. The cover was produced in InDesign using the Fontin font.

Jeremy Bowman typeset the book in InDesign and produced the paperback and hardback editions. The text font is Tex Gyre Pagella; the heading font is Californian FB.

Cameron Craig produced the EPUB, PDF, HTML, and XML editions. The conversion was made with open-source software such as pandoc (https://pandoc.org/), created by John MacFarlane, and other tools freely available on our GitHub page (https://github.com/OpenBookPublishers).

This book has been anonymously peer-reviewed by experts in their field. We thank them for their invaluable help.

This book need not end here...

Share

All our books — including the one you have just read — are free to access
online so that students, researchers and members of the public who can't
afford a printed edition will have access to the same ideas. This title will be
accessed online by hundreds of readers each month across the globe: why
not share the link so that someone you know is one of them?

This book and additional content is available at:
https://doi.org/10.11647/OBP.0318

Donate

Open Book Publishers is an award-winning, scholar-led, not-for-profit press
making knowledge freely available one book at a time. We don't charge
authors to publish with us: instead, our work is supported by our library
members and by donations from people who believe that research shouldn't
be locked behind paywalls.

Why not join them in freeing knowledge by supporting us:
https://www.openbookpublishers.com/support-us

Follow @OpenBookPublish

Read more at the Open Book Publishers BLOG

You may also be interested in:

Margery Spring Rice
Pioneer of Women's Health in the Early Twentieth Century
Lucy Pollard

https://doi.org/10.11647/OBP.0215

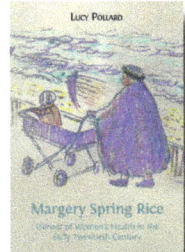

Susan Isaacs
A Life Freeing the Minds of Children
Philip Graham

https://doi.org/10.11647/OBP.0297

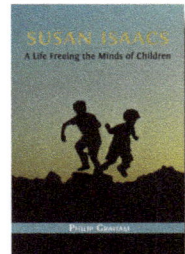

Mary Warnock
Ethics, Education and Public Policy in Post-War Britain
Philip Graham

https://doi.org/10.11647/OBP.0278

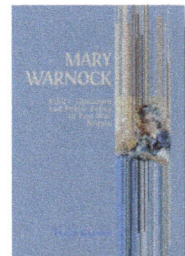

www.ingramcontent.com/pod-product-compliance
Lightning Source LLC
Chambersburg PA
CBHW052009030426
42334CB00029BA/3142